Emancipation

EMANCIPATION

The Abolition and Aftermath of American Slavery and Russian Serfdom

Peter Kolchin

Yale
UNIVERSITY PRESS
New Haven and London

Published with support from the Fund established in memory of Oliver Baty Cunningham, a distinguished graduate of the Class of 1917, Yale College, Captain, 15th United States Field Artillery, born in Chicago September 17, 1894, and killed while on active duty near Thiaucourt, France, September 17, 1918, the twenty-fourth anniversary of his birth.

Published with assistance from the Ronald and Betty Miller Turner Publication Fund.

Copyright © 2024 by Peter Kolchin.
All rights reserved.
This book may not be reproduced, in whole or in part, including illustrations, in any form (beyond that copying permitted by Sections 107 and 108 of the U.S. Copyright Law and except by reviewers for the public press), without written permission from the publishers.

Yale University Press books may be purchased in quantity for educational, business, or promotional use. For information, please e-mail sales.press@yale.edu (U.S. office) or sales@yaleup.co.uk (U.K. office).

Set in Scala type by IDS Infotech Ltd.
Printed in the United States of America.

Library of Congress Control Number: 2023941933
ISBN 978-0-300-27366-3 (hardcover : alk. paper)

A catalogue record for this book is available from the British Library.

This paper meets the requirements of ANSI/NISO Z39.48-1992 (Permanence of Paper).

10 9 8 7 6 5 4 3 2 1

For Anne, with love

Contents

Preface ix

Introduction: Unfree Labor in Crisis 1

Part I • Process

1. Emancipation Launched: Preparation, Process, Terms 33
2. What Kind of Freedom? 73
3. The Struggle Continues: Land, Labor, and Liberty 119
4. The Politics of Freedom 160

Part II • Consequences

5. Free Labor 201
6. Free Labor II: Everyday Life 250
7. Interpreting Emancipation: Change and Continuity, Hope and Disillusionment 307

Epilogue 369

Glossary: Russian and Russian-Language Terms (Russia), English-Language Terms (U.S. South) 379

Notes 383

Bibliographical Note 517

Index 527

Preface

This book is a companion of—and chronological sequel to—*Unfree Labor: American Slavery and Russian Serfdom*. When I published that volume, in 1987, little did I imagine that it would take me so long to complete the sequel, but because it did I should say something about the changes that have occurred in the interim and how they have shaped the current book. During the past thirty-five years, historical interpretations have changed, historical research has been radically revamped, and the Soviet Union—which defined historical approaches to Russian serfdom and its abolition—has ceased to exist. We also live now in a world of personal computers and digital sources, which in some ways make being a historian easier and in some ways harder but most of all make it very different from what it was in the recent past. All this is in addition to "normal" changes that one might expect to be operative, such as new research that reshapes our understanding of the past and the existence of vastly greater quantities of source materials for a somewhat later period of the past. Training a new generation of historians is always a daunting undertaking, but at this particular point it seems likely to require a completely revamped understanding of how we can explain—or at least interpret—our history.

Let me be a little more specific about some of these developments. The collapse of the Soviet Union has had a mixed impact on the writing of Russian history. On the one hand, it has been liberating: historians writing in Russia no longer have to toe the party line. On the other hand, however, that has gone hand in hand with a marked decrease in attention to developments formerly (and I believe properly) at the heart of Russian history, from exploitation of peasants and members of the working class to the struggles of those exploited groups for greater autonomy, economic security, and political power. In part as an effort to control access to the evidence, the Soviet era was marked by a profusion of publications that included not only officially approved historical writing but also an extraordinary variety of primary sources, including sources that at least occasionally went in directions very different from the officially sanctioned interpretations. This is true of material on the "peasant movement," published in a series of massive volumes that remain only partially explored, as well as reports of various government officials, including those from provincial governors, the Ministry of Internal Affairs, the Third Department (political police), and emissaries of the tsar sent to the provinces at the time of emancipation to insure stability. Publication of this material—together with publication of similar kinds of material on emancipation in the Southern United States, such as the ongoing series of volumes called *Freedom: A Documentary History of Emancipation*—has provided historians with an abundance of essential primary sources that make an earlier era of Russian (and Southern) history seem almost inscrutable. Compared to the relative paucity of sources on Russia and the South before the nineteenth century, the sheer abundance of such materials, especially from the middle and late periods of the century, seems striking. Indeed, historians focusing on those regions during the second half of the nineteenth century have so many available sources that they must make difficult choices about which of these numerous sources to use.

In this context, I should note that in this book I pay particular attention to Alabama, attention built on research I conducted many years ago for my first book, *First Freedom: The Responses of Alabama's Blacks to Emancipation and Reconstruction* (1972). Although in the current project I have never relied *solely* on this research, and I have not hesitated to point out occasions when developments in Alabama were atypical (as was the case, for example, with the prominent role of Black "Creoles" descended from early French settlers), I have been willing to use my familiarity with Alabama sources to supplement those on other states, and I continue to believe that in many respects Alabama can serve as a useful proxy for other Deep South states.

When I published *Unfree Labor,* comparing American slavery and Russian serfdom, the volume struck some readers as a peculiar venture, requiring intellectual justification. One hopes that is no longer the case, since the notion that systems of forced labor are comparable—which does not mean identical or the same—is now widely accepted. The comparability of their abolition, an essential ingredient in the making of the modern world, should be equally acceptable, especially since in this particular case—the emancipation of the

American slaves and Russian serfs—that abolition occurred almost simultaneously, in the 1860s, and shaped much of American and Russian history during the last third of the nineteenth century. Actors in each of these two emancipations were vaguely aware of the other's occurrence but not of the details that specified its development; indeed, despite their simultaneity, the two emancipations occurred almost entirely independently of each other, which renders them especially ripe for comparative analysis. In this sense, they differed from the various emancipations from New World slavery (or for that matter Old World serfdom), which were more closely interconnected and therefore subject to the kind of analysis that has recently been termed "transnational."

The structure of this volume is simple. After an introduction setting the two emancipations in broad comparative context, chapters 1–4 cover the *process* of emancipation in Russia and the Southern United States, while chapters 5–7 deal with some of the *consequences* of these emancipation settlements. Chapter 1 focuses on the terms of emancipation in the two countries, one of which was carefully preplanned and other of which became clear only over time. Chapter 2 deals with the immediate responses to emancipation, which in both cases became increasingly disorderly as peasants and African Americans struggled for what they felt was a *real* freedom rather than one that would be in name only. Chapter 3 continues the story, with particular attention to contracts between the freedpeople and their former owners, contracts that were annual in the South but took the form of long-lasting and status-defining statutory charters in Russia. Freedom emerged under very different contexts in the two countries, as is evident in chapter 4, on political developments, which moved in a much more radical—egalitarian—direction in the South than in Russia. Chapter 5 outlines the diverse forms that free labor could take, while chapter 6 focuses on family life, education, and religion, and chapter 7 deals with a variety of historical interpretations of developments in the two countries. Despite the more radical break with the past in the South than in Russia, both saw a growing conservative reaction that was particularly extreme in the South and became especially notable during the last quarter of the nineteenth century. In an epilogue, I once again place developments in broader geographical context, suggesting that the conservative reactions were typical of those that existed elsewhere unfree labor was abolished but were more extreme in Russia and especially in the South, at least in part because of the more radical nature of their emancipation experiences. The epilogue also touches briefly on an issue that has become notable in recent years: the existence of a new—"modern"—form of slavery and abolition.

A few technical matters deserve attention here. I have resisted the current tendency to call slaves "enslaved people" and slave owners "enslavers"; although I find both terms awkward—if we are to avoid the word "slave," "slave trader," "slave ship," "slaveholder," and other terms modified by "slave" should also logically be off-limits—but "enslaver" strikes me as especially problematic, because it implies someone who turned free people into slaves, by "enslaving" them. (Also, calling slaves "enslaved" and slaveholders "enslavers" would seem, in a comparative work, to require me to refer to serfs as "enserfed" and serfholders as "enserfers," which would strike most readers as odd.) Although Russians did not call ex-serfs "freedpeople," I have used this gender-neutral term for former bondspersons in both countries (except when referring to an individual man as a "freedman" and woman as a "freedwoman").

As in *Unfree Labor*, I have used standard Library of Congress guidelines for transliterating Russian words, with a few exceptions. Where English-language equivalents already exist, I have used those equivalents (for example, "Alexander II" rather than "Aleksandr II"). I have also omitted final soft signs from proper nouns ("Riazan" and "Tver" Provinces, for example, rather than "Riazan' " and "Tver' "). More specifically, I have followed three different policies with respect to Russian terms, depending primarily on their frequency of use and ease of translation. In some cases, I have translated such terms: thus, "guberniia" becomes "province," "uezd" is translated as "district," and "predvoditel' dvorianstva" is rendered as "marshal of nobility." Other terms, especially those that have no exact English-language equivalents, remain untranslated; examples include "volnenie" (a peasant disturbance that combined attributes of a small-scale rebellion and a strike), and "desiatina" (a measure of land equal to 2.7 acres). Untranslated terms that appear often in this book (for example, "volnenie" and "starosta") are explained and italicized the first time they are used, but subsequently are not italicized. By contrast, untranslated terms that appear only occasionally (for example, *muzhik* and *baba*) remain italicized throughout. To help the reader make sense of these terms, I have provided a brief glossary, which also includes a small number of English-language terms frequently used in the Southern United States (for example, "Freedmen's Bureau").

Over the years that I worked on this book, I have tried out some of my ideas in a variety of informal talks and more formal papers, at both professional conventions and smaller, more narrowly targeted conferences and meetings. Needless to say, I have greatly benefited from these interactions with other historians and students, in ways that I have not always recognized myself. Innumerable conversations in a variety of settings have helped to shape the interpretations found in this book. Moreover, the need to articulate arguments in a logical manner when challenged on specifics has undoubtedly contributed to whatever persuasiveness those arguments have. In this sense, I am no doubt expressing a kind of collective wisdom, even when developing my own arguments.

I have also tested those ideas in a number of articles and chapters, which it is now my pleasure to acknowledge. These include (in chronological order) "Some Thoughts on Emancipation in Comparative Perspective: Russia and the United States South," *Slavery and Abolition*, 11 (December 1990), 351–67; "The Tragic Era? Interpreting Southern Reconstruction in Comparative Perspective," in *The Meaning of Freedom: Economics, Politics, and Culture after Slavery*, ed. Frank McGlynn and Seymour Drescher (Pittsburgh, PA: University of Pittsburgh Press, 1992), 291–311; "Some Controversial Questions Concerning Nineteenth-Century Emancipation from Slavery and Serfdom," in *Serfdom and Slavery: Studies in Legal Bondage*, ed. M. L. Bush (London: Longman, 1996), 42–67; "Slavery and Freedom in the Civil War South," in *Writing the Civil War: The Quest to Understand*, ed. James M. McPherson and William J. Cooper Jr. (Columbia: University of South Carolina Press, 1998), 241–60, 335–47; "After Serfdom: Russian Emancipation in Comparative Perspective," in *Terms of Labor: Slavery, Serfdom, and Free Labor*, ed. Stanley L. Engerman (Stanford, CA: Stanford University Press, 1999), 87–115, 293–309; "Comparative Perspectives on Emancipation in the U.S. South: Reconstruction, Radicalism, and Russia," *Journal of the Civil War Era*, 89 (June 2012), 203–32; "Reexamining Southern Emancipation in Comparative Perspective," *Journal of Southern History*, 81 (February 2015), 7–40; "Slavery, Commodification, and Capitalism," *Reviews in American History*, 44 (June 2016), 217–26; and "Emancipação na década de 1860: A Rússia e o Sul dos EUA," in *Instituições Nefandas: O fim de escracidão e da servidão no Basil, nos Estados Unidas e na Rússia*, ed. Ivana Stolze Lima, Keila Grinberg, and Daniel Aarão Reis, trans. Tania Reis (e-book, Rio de Janeiro: Fundação casa de Rui Barbosa, 2018), 94–123.

In writing this book, I have received substantial institutional support from the University of Delaware. Aside from helpful interactions with many faculty members, including those who attended my two research presentations at the Department of History's History Workshop as well as my inaugural lecture as a member of the University's Francis Alison Society, this support included a year's fellowship at the University's Center for Advanced Study, as well as expanded sabbatical assistance available to named professors (in my case, the Henry Clay Reed Professorship).

I hesitate to acknowledge the help of particular individuals, for fear that I will forget someone whose help has been essential. (When a project takes this long to reach fruition, there are inevitably many names that deserve to be mentioned.) Nevertheless, there are a few that *must* be mentioned. Joyce Seltzer championed this project from the start and remained supportive of it over the years, as did Aida D. Donald. At a crucial moment, Thomas LeBien offered sage advice. At Yale University Press, Adina Popescu, Eva Skewes, and Joyce Ippolito provided enthusiastic and expert editorial guidance, and Otto Bohlmann edited the manuscript with care. I have also benefited from the comments and suggestions of two anonymous readers for Yale University Press. Among other historians, I should particularly acknowledge Enrico Dal Lago, both for his friendship and for his expertise in comparative history, as well as two scholars who have materially advanced our understanding of the comparison between American and Russian bondage and abolition: Amanda Brickell Bellows, author of the recent volume *American Slavery and Russian Serfdom in the Post-Emancipation Imagination* (Chapel Hill: University of North Carolina Press, 2020), on whose dissertation committee at the University of North Carolina I served as an outside reader, and my former graduate student Sally Stocksdale, whose 2016 dissertation "In the Midst of Liberation: A Comparison of a Russian Estate and a Southern Plantation at the Moment of Emancipation"—which provided a micro-history of emancipation on two estates, one on the Volga River and the other on the Mississippi—has just been published by McFarland under the title *When Emancipation Came: The End of Enslavement on a Southern Plantation and a Russian Estate* (Jefferson, NC, 2022). The influence of other historians on my thinking (and writing), will be evident in the citations found in my work. Finally, my greatest debt is to my wife, Anne M. Boylan, who has read many versions of this manuscript, with the keen eye of a historian and the willingness to be imposed upon of a spouse. Her aid has been invaluable, and this book, like its predecessor, is dedicated to her.

Emancipation

Introduction: Unfree Labor in Crisis

The nineteenth century was a century of emancipation. On both sides of the Atlantic Ocean, as Europeans and Americans came to celebrate "freedom," "republicanism," and "progress," systems of human bondage that for centuries had aroused little opposition (except among their victims) came to seem like barbarous relics of a less civilized age and gave way to various forms of "free" labor. The overthrow of unfree labor in the Western world was a remarkably speedy affair: over the course of a century, beginning with the northern United States during and immediately after the American Revolution and ending with Brazil in 1888, one country after another embraced emancipation. Long prevalent throughout most of the New World and much of Central and Eastern Europe, slavery and serfdom appeared by the end of the nineteenth century as little more than distant memories of institutions whose demise marked the triumph of modernity.[1]

Despite its relative speed, the death of bondage was rarely easy or untroubled. It came in a variety of ways, often decreed by a metropolitan or central government over the protests of local elites, sometimes heralded in wars of national liberation, usually accompanied by unrest and violence from below, and in one case—that of Haiti—set in motion by a massive slave uprising.[2] The birth of the new order was likewise a messy affair, marked by intense fears, hopes, and struggles as former owners nursed bruised egos and sought to preserve as many of their old prerogatives as possible, former slaves and serfs eagerly sought to make real the promised freedom, and government officials grappled with the contours and consequences of "free labor." Despite variations in the specific ways in which these struggles played out, almost everywhere the end result showed one fundamental similarity that belied their different histories: although emancipation produced profound changes in social relations and everyday life, the fruits of "freedom" proved remarkably elusive. Poverty, exploitation, and oppression remained the norm, and over time high hopes increasingly yielded to frustration, disappointment, and bitterness. A generation after emancipation, a sense of profound disillusionment pervaded the lands where servitude had been part of the social fabric, as almost everyone agreed—for very different reasons—that things had gone badly awry.

This book tells that story for Russia and the Southern United States, which by the middle of the nineteenth century contained by far the largest—and seemingly most entrenched—systems of serfdom and slavery in the modern Western world.[3] The story illustrates both the diversity in how freedom came and the broadly similar patterns of post-emancipation developments that ensued. By the middle of the nineteenth century, despite manifold differences in their economies, politics, and cultures, Russia and the Southern United States had become similar symbols of oppression and backwardness, and foreign travelers delighted in skewering both Russia and the South as lands of slothful inefficiency, ignorance, and cruelty. Although emancipation came to both Russia and the South in the 1860s, the process of abolition was very different; indeed, in many ways it is difficult to imagine two settings for the transition from coerced to free labor that differed more than they did in these two cases. These differences render all the more striking the broad similarities in the transition's consequences, for although the struggles that emancipation set in motion played out according to specific local conditions, in the broadest sense post-emancipation developments followed a script that varied more in intonation than in ultimate message. If the inhabitants of Russia and the Southern United States would have seemed very foreign to each other, a perceptive observer might have found the evolution of their post-emancipation social relations eerily familiar.

By the middle of the nineteenth century, unfree labor was so entrenched in Russia and the American South that it seemed to define their very essence.[4] In many ways, Russian serfdom was similar to American slavery. They had similar life spans, emerging in the sixteenth and seventeenth centuries, growing and solidifying over the course of the eighteenth century, reaching maturity in the early nineteenth century, and perishing in the 1860s. Both were preeminently systems of forced agricultural labor, which had originated under conditions of labor shortage in areas of low population density. (In this important sense, Russian serfdom had far more in common with New World slavery than did forms of "slavery" in some other times and places, where slaves could fulfill a variety of noneconomic functions, from filling harems to occupying high governmental offices and serving as victims of ritual sacrifice.)[5] And both were systems in which some people owned others. Although Russian serfdom originated in the late sixteenth and early seventeenth centuries with the tying of peasants to the land, over the eighteenth century it evolved into a system that was in most respects indistinguishable from chattel slavery: serfs could be moved, bought, and sold, and the power of a Russian nobleman over his subjects was virtually the same as that of an American planter over his. (One of the few "rights" that male serfs enjoyed over their slave counterparts was the right to serve in the Russian Army, but this was a dubious privilege at best, since such service was for life until 1793 and for twenty-five years thereafter; peasant recruits could expect never to see their homes or families again.) As a system of labor, Russian serfdom was closer to American slavery—and can best be viewed as a special variant of slavery—than to the kind of serfdom that existed in medieval Western Europe.[6]

Nevertheless, a number of important differences between the Russian and American versions of bondage illustrate the wide diversity of relationships possible under conditions of unfree labor. (The same was also true internally in Russia and the United States, where conditions varied so widely that it is almost more appropriate to use the plural—"serfdoms" and "slaveries"—than the singular in describing supposedly uniform systems of bondage.) Perhaps the most obvious difference was in respect to "race." In the United States, the slaveholders were largely descended from Europeans and the slaves from Africans; in Russia, by contrast, most serfholders and serfs shared a common ethnic, national, and religious background. The apparent centrality of race to American slavery and its absence in Russian serfdom highlight a basic contrast between the historical discontinuity in which American slavery was rooted and the continuity evident in Russia. Africans were outsiders, imported against their will to America, deposited in an alien land and forced to adjust to new ways; Russian peasants were enserfed on their home turf, and their descendants were the lowest beings in a social hierarchy rather than outsiders to the body politic. As late as the Civil War, white Americans continued to talk of sending Blacks—many of whom were fourth- or fifth-generation Americans— "back" to Africa, but no one could imagine Russia without its peasants: they were quintessentially Russian (just as Russia was quintessentially peasant) and constituted more than 80 percent of the population.

This figure points to a second important contrast between American slavery and Russian serfdom: the very different ratios of masters to bondspeople. Put most simply, by American standards, Russian serfholding estates were enormous. Owning fifty slaves in the Southern United States put one in the ranks of very wealthy planters (in 1860, only 2.6 percent of slave owners owned more), but a wealthy Russian nobleman might own thousands or even tens of thousands of serfs. Only a tiny fraction of enslaved Blacks in the United States (2.4 percent) had owners with two hundred or more slaves, but the great majority of bound peasants in Russia (80.8 percent in 1858) had such owners. Unlike Southern slave owners, who constituted about one-third of the white population in 1830 and one-quarter in 1860, serf-owning nobles represented a tiny fraction of the Russian population—well under 2 percent in 1858. Whereas African Americans (slave and free) formed slightly more than one-third of the Southern population, more than four-fifths of Russians were peasants. On the eve of emancipation, the ratio of bondspeople to masters (and their family members) was 2.1 to one in the South and 24.4 to one in Russia. (The contrast between the ratios of Blacks to whites and peasants to nobles was even greater: 0.5 to one versus 51.8 to one.) Unlike most American slaves, most Russian serfs lived in a world of their own, where their owners were remote figures whom they rarely or never saw.[7]

A third contrast is that Russian serfdom lacked the kind of geographically sectional basis that characterized American slavery during its last half century. There was no Russian equivalent to the free states of the American North that increasingly served as bastions of antislavery propaganda directed southward; unlike the United States, Russia was not divided into increasingly antagonistic, democratically ruled sections that eventually would go to war over slavery.

Finally, because serfdom emerged gradually and peasants were not outsiders, the role of tradition in limiting the total control of masters over the lives of their bondspeople was greater in Russia than in the United States, even though juridically the power of nobles over their serfs was as extensive as that of planters over their slaves. Although serfs did not legally own any landed property, most received from their owners allotments that they used to support themselves. Unlike most American slaves, who at least in theory worked for their masters all the time and received sustenance in exchange, most serfs worked only part time for their owners, received little or no support from them, and were expected to maintain themselves. Some serfs worked their "own" land full time, providing their owners quitrent payments (*obrok*) that could be in cash or kind—grain, eggs, butter, meat, and the like—or both. Others owed their masters labor obligations (*barshchina*), cultivating seigneurial land as well as their "own" allotments; by the nineteenth century, custom dictated that such serfs would work three days per week for their owners and three days for themselves, but serfholders were free to set their serfs' workload, as well as to determine whether they would be held on obrok or barshchina (or a combination of both). A dual economy thus undergirded Russian serfdom: the serfs cultivated their owners' land, but they also cultivated their "own" allotted land and were free to use its products as they saw fit.

These differences were important but not always precisely as met the eye. Variations within Russia and the American South often were as great as the contrasts between bondage in the two countries. If on the whole Russian serfs lived on larger estates than American slaves, the size of holdings varied broadly in both countries. In western Kentucky's tobacco counties, for example, one-half of all slaves in 1860 lived on holdings with more than fourteen bondspeople, but in Concordia Parish, Louisiana, the median figure was 117; in Saratov Province, in the southeast of Russia, half of the serfs had owners who possessed more than five hundred male souls in 1858, whereas in Olonets Province, in the north, none did. Because of such variations, some American slaves lived on larger holdings than some Russian serfs. Similarly, if there was no Russian equivalent to the "free North," there were regions of the Russian Empire where serfdom was of minor significance—few serfs could be found in the sparsely populated far north and in the vast expanses of Siberia—and the under-governed borderlands of the south and east attracted fugitives from more settled regions in much the same way that in the United States the North served as a magnet to slaves seeking freedom.

Exceptions in both Russia and the United States also muddied the apparently clear distinction between racial and nonracial systems of bondage. A surprisingly large number of free African Americans owned slaves,[8] Native Americans could be found in the ranks of both slaves and slaveholders, and some slaves had more pronounced European than African ancestry and appeared white to most observers. Meanwhile, on the borders of the Russian Empire ethnic distinctions between serfs and serfholders were common: as Russia expanded eastward, conquered nationalities were absorbed into the serf population, while in the west Orthodox peasants often had Polish Catholic owners.

Although the lack of racial distinction between serfholder and serf may seem strange to those accustomed to the New World norm of "racial" slavery, it was by no means unusual: sociologist Orlando Patterson found that in about a quarter of the numerous slave societies he studied over time and space, some or all slaves and slave owners were of the same "ethnic group" and in about three-quarters they were of the same "mutually perceived racial group."[9] Race was by no means an essential or constituent element of slavery, and its presence in one case and absence in another points to a distinction between specific versions of bondage rather than between slavery and serfdom in general. Nor was the specific contrast as absolute as it appeared to some: as scholars in diverse disciplines now recognize, "race" is a subjective (and shifting) historical construct rather than a fixed biological reality.[10] To many Russians, peasants appeared as different from nobles as Blacks did from whites in the United States; defenders of serfdom, for example, developed arguments that were essentially racial in nature, insisting that peasants were *inherently* incapable of freedom. The comparison of the "nonracial" Russian form of bondage with the "racial" American version is therefore particularly useful in illuminating the constructed—subjective—nature of race.

The contrast between the quasi-economic independence that tradition afforded many Russian serfs and the dependent status of American slaves must also be regarded as considerably less than absolute. Southern slaveholders often provided their slaves with plots of land on which they could grow crops and raise chickens, for example, and historians in recent years have paid increasing attention to the "internal" or "slave" economy in which slaves were able to sell or trade the products they raised and even to inherit property that in theory belonged to their owners. This internal economy rarely provided as much economic autonomy as was common among serfs in Russia (or, for that matter, among slaves in much of the Caribbean), but its very existence makes clear the extent to which the actual condition of slaves could depart from the status that the law imposed on them.[11] In both Russia and the Southern United States, internal variations in the degree of autonomy afforded the bondspeople were substantial. In Russia, nobles were more willing to allow their serfs the relative freedom of obrok cultivation where the climate was harsh and the land relatively unproductive, while fertile soil or proximity to the urban market made direct seigneurial cultivation more attractive. In the South, the internal economy reached its peak of development in the low country of South Carolina and Georgia, where the "task" system and widespread owner absenteeism accentuated the independence available to slave laborers. In both Russia and the South, a small number of bondspeople were able to grasp opportunities beyond the dreams of most—skilled slaves were sometimes allowed to "hire their own time," finding employment on their own and paying their owners a stipulated fee that constituted the American equivalent of obrok—and a tiny number were able to enjoy lives that appeared to defy their unfree status, whether through accumulation of unusual wealth or through exercise of unusual talents. In both countries, however, such privileged lives were not only rare but also tenuous at best, subject to the arbitrary power that could destroy them at any moment. As favored slaves and serfs discovered, even the most benevolent patron could turn overnight into an overbearing tyrant.[12]

As these observations suggest, most of the contrasts I have been discussing are less indicative of fundamental differences between slavery and serfdom than of differences between specific American and Russian versions of slavery and serfdom. In some respects, the conditions under which American slaves lived were as distant from those faced by Jamaican slaves as from Russian serfs—in Jamaica, as in Russia, a tiny master class lived precariously in a world that seemed overwhelmingly foreign (Black or peasant)—and in both Russia and the American South the specific features of bondage exhibited their own widespread variations based on concrete conditions. If American slavery and Russian serfdom were both part of a common system of unfree labor that emerged along much of the periphery of an expanding Europe, they also exhibited the many variations that this system generated, both from one society to another and within each of them. Bondage took a multiplicity of different forms, dictated by a multiplicity of diverse political, economic, social, and demographic conditions. Indeed, partly because of such differences, scholars have been unable to reach a consensus on something so apparently simple as the definition or meaning of slavery.[13]

Nevertheless, taking together the various differences outlined above between American slavery and Russian serfdom, one can suggest a central contrast that shaped fundamentally different interactions both between the bondspeople and their owners and among the bondspeople themselves: despite numerous qualifications, broadly speaking the rural South was a slaveholders' world, in which Blacks were viewed as "outsiders," whereas rural Russia was a peasant world in which nobles felt uncomfortable and were themselves often virtually outsiders on their own estates. With some exceptions, American slaveholders constituted a resident master class, who lived on their farms and plantations and took a personal role in running day-to-day agricultural operations. Russian nobles (like British and French planters in the Caribbean) were more likely to be absentee landlords, but even when they lived on one of their holdings the wealthiest nobles—who owned most of the serfs—were absentee owners to most of their peasants; an owner of fifteen estates scattered across several different provinces would inevitably be a stranger to most of his serfs. Such a nobleman would interact with his peasants through an administrative hierarchy of managers and stewards, some of whom were freely hired and some of whom were serfs themselves. American slave owners impinged more—and more directly—on the daily lives of their slaves than Russians did on the lives of their serfs.

This contrast is central to understanding the way emancipation came to Russia and the American South—and eventually what followed. More directly involved in the day-to-day lives of their bondspeople, American slaveholders displayed a far more persistent and resolute commitment to slavery than the serfholders did to serfdom, a commitment that was evident in (among other things) the extraordinary torrent of proslavery propaganda that they produced during the last years of the slave regime. Although slaveholders and serfholders everywhere clung to their prerogatives, the American proslavery crusade of the 1830s–1850s was unique in the annals of history, both in its volume and in its sophistication. Unique, too, was the slave owners' behavior in time of crisis: rather than allow the inauguration of a president committed to stopping the expansion of slavery, they led a massive rebellion that ultimately brought about what they most feared and what they were acting to prevent: slave emancipation. In Russia, by contrast, although most serfholders were dismayed at the thought of losing their peasants, they did not threaten—or think of threatening—armed resistance. Instead, they showed themselves to be loyal (if at times unhappy) servants of the tsar.

Historians have not had an easy time explaining the rapidity of slavery's demise. Typically focusing on individual countries, they have emphasized the role of specific features peculiar to those countries. Thus, historians of emancipation in Russia have frequently stressed the impact of the Crimean War, which graphically revealed Russia's military backwardness and jolted the country's rulers out of complacency, and have provided detailed accounts of the deliberations of Alexander II and his reforming advisers who drafted the emancipation legislation; similarly, historians of the United States have delineated the "political revolution" of the 1850s that led to the emergence of the Republican Party, the election of Abraham Lincoln as president, the secession of the Southern states, and the Civil War. Scholars seeking to understand the Haitian Revolution led by Toussaint L'Ouverture have found it necessary to take into account the egalitarian ideology and political divisions within the master class produced by the French Revolution, and those addressing the emancipation of Prussia's serfs have had to consider the impact of the Napoleonic Wars. In all of these analyses, the activities of individuals loom large.[14]

But although specific events, produced by specific individuals, triggered specific acts of emancipation, those events and individuals do not help us very much in understanding emancipation as a general phenomenon: unless one assumes that each emancipation occurred entirely independently, for its own unique reasons, and that the almost simultaneous abolition of forced labor throughout Eastern Europe and the Americas was purely coincidental—a position rarely if ever put forth—understanding the coming of emancipation in individual locations also requires analysis on a more general, comparative level. Because emancipation in Russia and the Southern United States occurred as part of a broader transition in the modern Western world from coerced to "free" labor, explaining this emancipation necessitates placing it in a general context and considering why in so many diverse societies slavery and serfdom—which had long been taken for granted—so quickly fell before the abolitionist onslaught.

The most persistent effort to explain this occurrence has been to link it to the development and spread of capitalism. Indeed, one would not go far wrong in suggesting that, aside from the self-serving "whiggish" position put forth by many of the reformers themselves—that abolition was a function of the general moral improvement of human society—this linkage has represented the *only* sustained general explanation of emancipation. Although opposition to the argument that the rise of capitalism doomed (or in some versions eventually would have doomed) bondage has also been strong, its opponents have rarely put forward a general argument in its stead. The debate over the relationship between abolition and capitalism has thus dominated the effort to arrive at a general explanation for the coming of emancipation in the nineteenth century.

The traditional economic interpretation linking abolition and capitalism had two main components that, despite minor variations, showed remarkable commonality and received enunciation in the writings of numerous historians, both at the general level and for the antebellum South and Russia. First, forced labor retarded economic development and was either unprofitable, increasingly unprofitable, or less and less profitable. Second, because slavery and serfdom had reached (or would soon reach) the limits of their economic potential, their abolition served the economic interests of newly dominant groups; bondage fell because it was no longer in the interest of the rich and powerful. "The commercial capitalism of the eighteenth century developed the wealth of Europe by means of slavery and monopoly," wrote Eric Williams in an influential general statement of this thesis, "but in doing so it helped to create the industrial capitalism of the nineteenth century, which turned round and destroyed the power of commercial capitalism, slavery, and all its works." The overthrow of bondage was not the altruistic act that it appeared to be.[15]

Application of this economic interpretation to the South and Russia was widespread. Some historians argued that by the late antebellum period slavery had reached its "natural limits" and was bound if left alone to decline and die on its own; others, from Ulrich B. Phillips to the early Eugene D. Genovese, stressed the decreasing profitability of slavery, a trend that in some versions contributed to a general crisis of the slave system.[16] Similar arguments prevailed among historians of Russia, especially (but by no means exclusively) among Soviet scholars, most of whom followed Lenin in viewing serfdom as an economically retrograde system that kept Russia backward, was increasingly unprofitable, and had entered a crisis stage by the 1850s. In a Soviet version of the "natural limits" thesis, N. M. Shepukova argued that because of increased levels of exploitation serfs were "dying out," but even those who rejected this thesis typically agreed on the existence of a crisis of feudalism that could be overcome only by replacing serfdom with a more progressive and rational system of labor, capitalism.[17]

In recent years, both components of this economic interpretation of abolition have come under withering attack, and much of the traditional version has been effectively refuted. Although the economics of slavery remains a subject of lively debate and controversy, it is now clear that slavery was neither moribund nor unprofitable in the United States and Caribbean in the years preceding its abolition; as Stanley L. Engerman summarized, "A look at the history of slave emancipation in the Americas finds it difficult to find any cases of slavery declining economically prior to the imposition of emancipation."[18] There has been less systematic attention to the economics of Russian serfdom, but a variety of Western, Soviet, and post-Soviet Russian historians have challenged the thesis that serfdom was unprofitable, questioned serfdom's supposed drag on economic productivity, and rejected the notion that on the eve of emancipation the serfs were "dying out."[19] Equally important, on neither side of the Atlantic was opposition to bondage motivated primarily by the narrow economic interests of capitalists. In the United States, most entrepreneurs spurned abolitionists as fanatics bent on disrupting the orderly transaction of the nation's business. In Britain, as in the Northern United States, abolitionism was closely linked to other radical reform movements, and it drew more support from artisans and evangelicals than from "captains of industry." In Russia, and elsewhere in Eastern Europe, capitalism was too embryonic—and capitalists were too politically impotent—to be the driving force behind abolition. As Jerome Blum pointed out, "In none of the servile lands had bourgeois capitalism developed to the extent that its needs could dictate the reshaping of society."[20]

But if traditional economic determinism is dead as an explanation for emancipation, the broader question of the relationship between capitalism and emancipation—and more specifically the idea that the spread of the former was somehow instrumental in the coming of the latter—remains very much alive. Nineteenth-century observers—including travelers—routinely linked forced labor to economic, social, and even political "backwardness," and while their views were often self-serving, they were not entirely inaccurate. Although it is now clear that on the whole owners profited handsomely from bound labor, it is also clear that slave and serf societies grew very differently from those based on free labor and typically continued to exhibit the earmarks associated with "premodern" social organization—rural, agricultural, hierarchical, and committed to tradition. Certainly this was evident in the economies of the antebellum South and pre-reform Russia, both of which continued to expand under slavery and serfdom but neither of which went through the kind of transformation experienced by England and the Northern United States. Indeed, both regions lagged far (and in most respects increasingly) behind the North and the advanced countries of Western Europe in virtually every important index of modernization, from per capita income to industrialization, urbanization, transportation, and literacy. Although historians continue to disagree over both the impact of unfree labor on economic growth and the general compatibility of unfree labor and capitalism, a good case can be made that—as many contemporaries believed—this lag was closely associated with the existence of forced labor.[21]

Much of the debate over the relationship between bondage and capitalism has foundered over competing understandings—indeed, definitions—of capitalism. If the term is understood to denote a system in which individuals strive to make money by buying and selling commodities, then clearly the slave economies of the New World, and to a lesser extent the serf economies of Eastern Europe, were capitalistic; modern slavery and serfdom were rooted in the search for profit (from the labor of slaves and serfs), and there were few societies more commercial or entrepreneurial than that of the slave South. But materialism and markets for agricultural commodities have been present throughout history in societies modern and premodern, agricultural and industrial, free and unfree. What distinguished societies based on coerced labor was the nature of their *productive* relations; relations of exchange may have been market dominated, but those of production were not. As historian James Oakes pithily put it, "A highly developed market economy was a precondition to the emergence of any slave society. Yet master and slave formed what was, at bottom, a nonmarket relationship." Slavery was incompatible with the widespread existence of a capitalism understood as a system of *production* predicated on the free buying and selling of labor power (that is, on wage labor). Significantly, this was precisely the understanding of most contemporary observers (from Karl Marx to mainstream social thinkers), who saw the era's key conflict as one between coerced and free *labor* and referred to capitalism as the "free-labor system."[22] It is this understanding that underlies the recent reassertion of the thesis that emancipation must be understood as a signal event in the transition to a capitalist order, broadly conceived. As David Brion Davis succinctly put it, "Few historians would argue that abolitionism was simply a spontaneous eruption of virtue, wholly unrelated to the rise of modern capitalism and the concomitant redefinition of property, labor, and contractual responsibilities."[23]

The conflict between forced labor and capitalism appeared most starkly at the ideological level. Defenders of slavery and serfdom were instinctively uncomfortable with the ideals that underlay capitalism, because central to those ideals was economic "freedom," including the freedom of laborers to contract for wages. In contrast, from the Northern United States and Great Britain, and increasingly from "enlightened" Russia as well, things looked very different: by substituting the physical coercion of the lash for the economic coercion of the marketplace, slavery and serfdom did violence to a central value implicit in capitalist relations: the freedom to succeed (or fail) through one's own efforts. On both sides of the Atlantic, the mid-nineteenth century saw the rise of "free-labor" thought that celebrated progress, hard work, and economic freedom and condemned slavery and serfdom as backward, degraded, and inefficient, the very antithesis of the free-labor ideal. By mid-century, "enlightened" opinion in the West had come to regard human bondage as both morally reprehensible and socially retrograde.[24]

In short, the abolition of American slavery and Russian serfdom were both part of a more general transition from coerced to free labor that characterized much of the Western world in an era that came to celebrate the centrality of "freedom" to human relations. Although specific factors explain the timing and character of emancipation in various locations, and much of this book focuses on the way concrete conditions shaped the evolution of social relations in post-bondage Russia and the South, it is important to keep in mind that in the two regions this evolution was part of a general process. One virtue of a comparative approach to the emancipation process that is usually studied separately for individual societies is that it simultaneously illustrates both the diverse ways in which this process could play out and the common transition that underlay this diversity.

Two very different crises precipitated the coming of emancipation in Russia and the South. Although neither of these crises reflected an immediate decline in the economic prospects of forced labor, both slavery and serfdom, long taken largely for granted, faced increasing challenges as "backward" anachronisms unsuited for modern times. The Russian crisis, which was largely internal, developed gradually as support for serfdom withered and government officials grappled with how an institution that was at the very heart of the social order could be modified or abolished without unleashing dangerous tensions. The American crisis reflected a very different political dynamic: as slavery came under increasing attack from without, white Southerners rallied to its defense, and it became at once both the earmark of the South itself—the "slave South"—and a threat to the continued survival of the federal republic. By the 1850s, not only were both Russia and the South in crisis, their crises appeared irresolvable.[25]

In both Russia and the United States, unfree labor—which had for centuries seemed unremarkable in the Western world, fully compatible with human progress—came under growing challenge during the century preceding emancipation. The attack on slavery and serfdom embraced a wide variety of arguments, from religious to practical, but the free-labor critique that portrayed bondage as backward, inefficient, and in some versions contrary to the very laws of nature, was increasingly central to the ideological onslaught. Although historians frequently distinguish these free-labor arguments from the "abolitionist" position that rejected slavery and serfdom on *moral* grounds, the difference was essentially one of emphasis (and, of course, of tactics). Free-labor ideologues spoke in a more secular, less apocalyptic language than traditional abolitionists—bondage was harmful rather than sinful—but their argument also rested on a set of moral assumptions. To a free-labor spokesman such as Abraham Lincoln, slavery was wrong not only because of its negative social and economic consequences but also because it degraded both master and slave and was fundamentally illogical and unjust. Because free labor was a "just and generous, and prosperous system" that allowed people to make the most of their God-given abilities, its economic and social superiority constituted a moral superiority as well.[26]

In some respects, the development of free-labor (and abolitionist) arguments followed similar trajectories in the two countries. In both, they first gained substantial currency in the last third of the eighteenth century, as "enlightened" thinkers subjected established ways to new intellectual scrutiny. In both, they received expression in the writings of travelers struck by "backward" conditions, as well as government leaders (from Catherine II to Thomas Jefferson), homegrown intellectuals, exiles, and outside critics. In both, they ran the gamut from purely "practical" arguments that stressed coerced labor's drag on economic development to broader-based critiques that linked deprivation of freedom to social and moral degradation. And in both countries, they generated heated rebuttals from defenders of the social order, rebuttals that also encompassed a wide array of arguments, from those based on religion and social harmony to those asserting that Blacks and peasants were inherently unfit for freedom.

Because they were shaped by opposition to similar institutions and because they were part of a common intellectual climate, the arguments put forth by Russian and American free-labor critics of bondage were in many ways remarkably similar. Take, for example, the writings of two prominent critics of coerced labor, Frederick Law Olmsted, a New York landscape architect who wrote a series of widely read accounts of his travels through the South in the 1850s, and A. P. Zablotskii-Desiatovskii, a prominent government official who in 1841 wrote a private memorandum, "On the Serf Condition in Russia." Describing a South marked by economic backwardness as well as degraded morals and manners, Olmsted blamed slavery for the region's assorted ills—from poverty, ignorance, and laziness to greasy food, absence of enterprise, and lack of punctuality. Admitting that the concentration of wealth in the hands of a few wealthy slaveholders might provide "comfortable houses, good servants, fine wines, food and furniture, tutors and governesses, horses and carriages, for these few men," he noted that it would not produce "good roads and bridges, . . . libraries, churches, museums, gardens, theatres, and assembly rooms, . . . local newspapers, telegraphs, and so on." Zablotskii-Desiatovskii's case against coerced labor was remarkably similar. Arguing that serfdom hindered the development of commerce and industry, he also maintained that it degraded Russian manners and morals, and rendered peasants lazy. Conceding that under particular circumstances landowners might find forced labor more profitable than free, he distinguished between serfdom's utility to the individual owner and its impact on society as a whole and concluded that "it is obvious that serf labor [as an overall system] is less productive than freely hired." Like numerous other free-labor advocates in the 1840s and 1850s, Olmsted and Zablotskii-Desiatovskii maintained that unfree labor was bad for the vast majority of Southerners and Russians, free as well as bound.[27]

But despite these similarities, because they emerged in strikingly different social and political and contexts, the ideological and political struggles over unfree labor evolved very differently in Russia and the United States. To most Southern slaveholders, slavery represented more than a profitable investment; it was a way of life, one that as members of a politically powerful local elite they were determined to defend. It is for this reason that historian C. Vann Woodward observed that "the end of slavery in the South can be described as the death of a society, though elsewhere it could more reasonably be characterized as the liquidation of an investment." By contrast, Russian *pomeshchiki* (aristocratic landowners) lacked either the political independence or the social incentive to develop a sustained defense of serfdom. Certainly most clung to their prerogatives—there is little reason to believe that the majority of noble serfholders had serious qualms about serfdom—but as outsiders in a largely peasant world, they were more interested in serfdom as a source of income than as an all-encompassing social system. As historian Daniel Field succinctly put it, "The provincial pomeshchik appears to have regarded serfdom as nothing more than a matter of land, labor, and money; at least, there was nothing else in serfdom that he cherished—no affective or sentimental element."[28]

Equally important were basic political differences between the two countries. In the United States, the high level of public literacy, the spread of political democracy, and the federal nature of the republic that permitted local elites to wield regionally based (statewide) power made possible an intensifying debate over slavery that by the 1840s and 1850s had become the defining political issue of the day. In Russia, by contrast, autocracy, censorship, and limited educational attainment conspired to contain the debate over serfdom and keep it from assuming a significant public dimension. Until its partial flowering during the actual implementation of emancipation, there was little "public opinion" in Russia; whatever debate existed over what euphemistically came to be known as the "peasant question" was confined to a small number of politically conscious individuals that included high-ranking government bureaucrats, "enlightened" nobles, and an amorphous group of intellectuals that included university students, writers (especially those in exile), and radicals. Indeed, because these groups were distinct if partially overlapping, there was less a common, public debate over the peasant question than a series of separate discussions that in most cases took place in secret.[29]

Under these circumstances, what was most notable about developments in Russia was less the growth of a vigorous anti-serfdom "movement" than the withering of the previously widespread pro-serfdom sentiment among high-ranking officials and educated nobles and the concomitant spread of the notion that serfdom was a retrograde institution—"an embarrassment to educated Russians"—that sooner or later would have to be abolished. "On the eve of the abolition of serfdom in Russia—in contrast to the situation with slavery in the American South—virtually no one defended that institution," wrote historian Nicholas V. Riasanovsky; "the arguments of its proponents were usually limited to pointing out the dangers implicit in such a radical change as emancipation." Because the spread of anti-serfdom opinion occurred largely out of public view, it seemed less threatening and aroused relatively little government suspicion. By contrast, individuals who challenged the established order in public faced drastic consequences, and there was no real equivalent in Russia to the American or British abolitionist *movements*. In 1790, in a highly unusual breach of government censorship, nobleman Aleksandr Radishchev managed to publish a radical abolitionist critique of serfdom that combined free-labor arguments on the harmful social and economic effects of forced labor with an appeal to natural rights and searing denunciations of the cruelty, overwork, and sexual abuse inherent in serfdom. Catherine II had Radishchev banished to Siberia, angrily noting, "The purpose of this book is clear on every page: its author, infected and full of the French madness, is trying in every possible way to break down respect for authority and for the authorities, to stir up in the people indignation against their superiors and against the government."[30]

The challenge to serfdom was multipronged. Foreign travelers noted its stultifying effects, exiles lambasted it as barbaric, and despite heavy censorship, novelists made use of coded language to ridicule it. With the partial exception of the novelists, who like their American counterparts appealed heavily to sentiment and emphasized the serfs' physical and mental suffering as well as the perversion of both serfholder's and bondsperson's character, free-labor arguments stood at the heart of their critique. As Nicholas Turgenev, a former participant in the 1825 Decembrist plot who lived most of his adult life in exile, put it in his book *Russia and the Russians* (1847), "Neither agriculture, industry, nor commerce can prosper in the shadow of arbitrary rule; they need the fresh air and sunlight of liberty." In a typical hyperbolic assertion, Turgenev suggested that although serfdom degraded peasant labor, its effect on the owner was even worse: "How can he respect his own dignity, his own rights," he queried, "who has learned to respect neither the rights nor the dignity of his fellow man?"[31]

Although official censorship and the lack of a large reading population severely limited the development of a public debate over serfdom, free-labor and other anti-serfdom ideas found increasing expression among educated nobles. The most notable quasi-public manifestation of interest in the "peasant question" occurred under the auspices of the Free Economic Society for the Encouragement in Russia of Agriculture and Household Management, an organization founded by a group of noble intellectuals with Catherine II's support in 1765. During the first decades of the nineteenth century, the Free Economic Society continued to sponsor essay contests on controversial questions of political economy, including the organization and condition of labor. In 1814, both the first and the second prize in a competition on whether freely hired or forced labor was more profitable went to contestants who argued on behalf of free labor. Noting that he wrote from personal experience, having actually used hired labor on his small estate in Latvia, runner-up Garlieb Merkel, a German-educated "doctor of philosophy," generalized that, other things being equal, "they will work more who have greater incentives." Such essays posed little threat to the established order, because virtually no one saw them, but they indicate the extent to which Russia's small noble intelligentsia came under the influence of foreign intellectual currents.[32]

Returning to his ancestral estate of four hundred souls (males) in Nizhnii Novgorod Province after the death of his mother in 1813, Prince I. M. Dolgoruki was embarrassed when the serfs, who "work day and night . . . so I can be happy," humbly met him on their knees. "And what am I?" he asked rhetorically in his private journal. "A person, like them." Such egalitarianism did not come easily to owners of human beings, but as the nineteenth century progressed a growing number of wealthy and prominent nobles expressed private reservations over serfdom. Few nobles were wealthier or more aristocratic than Prince M. S. Vorontsov, whose private letters to Count P. D. Kiselev grew increasingly outspoken during the 1830s and 1840s. Responding (as usual, in French) to Kiselev's request for his opinion "sur la grande question des paysans," Vorontsov in 1837 endorsed a legal reform that would have barred nobles from transferring their enserfed peasants to household status, a measure that would, he asserted, bring Russia to "the state at which several countries of Europe were two or three centuries ago." A decade later, he went much further. Declaring "I have always detested personal slavery," he called it "painful to think that more than thirty years ago and well before the emancipation of the Negroes in the English colonies, that unhappy race was better protected by the law than are our peasants in Russia up to the present." Kiselev himself, a high-ranking official who headed a project in the 1840s to reform the condition of the state peasantry, had concluded decades earlier that, as he put it in 1816 in a note to Alexander I, "civil freedom is the basis of national well-being," a judgment that found increasing expression toward mid-century by "liberal" noblemen such as Aleksandr Koshelev and Boris Chicherin, both of whom used a mixture of free-labor and moral arguments to support reforming and ultimately abolishing serfdom.[33]

Increasingly, free-labor assumptions were evident at the highest levels of government as well. In 1767, when a youthful Catherine II told a commission charged with codifying Russia's laws that all cultivators should be allowed to own land because "every man will take more Care of his own Property, than that which belongs to another," her suggestion represented the philosophical musing of a monarch influenced by physiocratic theory and other Enlightenment thought, and had little impact on actual policy. (In fact, during her thirty-four-year reign [1762–96], the empress presided over a significant tightening of already oppressive legislation and oversaw the transfer of hundreds of thousands of state peasants to serf status.) By the 1830s and 1840s, however, Russia's rulers had largely accepted—at least in theory—the notion that serfdom needed to be reformed and eventually abolished; as a report of the Third Department (political police) stated succinctly in 1839, "Everyone is agreed" on the need to begin preparing for an eventual emancipation rather "than wait until it begins from below, from the people." Conservative monarch Nicholas I agreed, telling the State Council in 1842 that "serfdom in its present form is perceptibly and obviously harmful for everyone." During his three-decade reign (1825–55), Nicholas appointed no fewer than ten secret committees designed to grapple with the "peasant question." Although these committees made no progress toward ending serfdom, their very existence indicated the degree to which the need for reform of one sort or another was taken for granted.[34]

Although there is little evidence that the great majority of provincial noble serfholders subscribed to free-labor views or shared the growing conviction among educated Russians, both in and out of government, that serfdom must sooner or later be confronted, at least some of these serfholders were evidently aware of—and alarmed by—the threat to serfdom's future. One of the most striking signs of their concern was the increasing number of pomeshchiki who transferred serfs to the category of house servants (*dvorovye*), in the process taking them away from their villages and appropriating their small plots in order to minimize their own losses in any future landed emancipation. The number of such transfers, which were especially numerous where land was most fertile, far exceeded any possible "need" that nobles may have felt for more domestic help: between 1851 and 1858 the number of male and female house serfs increased by 431,454 (41.6 percent) at a time when the total number of serfs actually decreased slightly, and during those seven years dvorovye increased from 4.79 percent to 6.79 percent of the serf population. In short, although most of these pomeshchiki were not participants in the ongoing dialogue over the "peasant question," many acted as they could to protect their interests in the event of any future reform of the social system. At mid-century in Russia, there was a growing sense that significant change was imminent.[35]

The debate over slavery in the American South evolved very differently. True, the last third of the eighteenth century saw widespread questioning of slavery in the Upper South. Indeed, in the wake of the American Revolution, as Northern states moved toward (in most cases gradual) emancipation, a growing number of Southern slave owners acted on their own to manumit some or all of their human property, and it seemed as if a Jeffersonian form of gradual emancipationism—termed "conditional termination" by historian William W. Freehling—was destined to gain ascendancy throughout the South. Such sentiment, marked by widespread acceptance of the notion that slavery was a temporary evil that would eventually give way to free labor as reason and common sense came to prevail, lingered in parts of the Upper South well into the second quarter of the nineteenth century. One particularly vivid sign of such persistence was the vigorous debate that Virginia's legislature conducted in 1831–32, in the wake of the Nat Turner insurrection, over proposals for gradual emancipation sponsored by delegates from the western counties where slavery was least entrenched, a debate that ended in a decisive victory for the state's proslavery advocates. Equally noteworthy was the publication in 1857 of the booklet *The Impending Crisis of the South,* in which North Carolinian Hinton Rowan Helper lambasted slavery for impoverishing the South and enabling a small, aristocratic minority to profit at the expense of the majority of hardworking white citizens. Terming slavery "a most expensive and unprofitable institution" that kept the South poor, backward, and degraded, he denounced slaveholders as "arrogant demagogues" who had "hoodwinked" and "trifled with" the oppressed white majority, who, he urged, should take action against slavery and thereby "rescue the generous soil of the South from the usurped and desolating control of these political vampires." An indication of just how seriously the South's ruling class took such challenges was the growing effort of proslavery ideologues, in works such as J. D. B. De Bow's *The Interest in Slavery of the Southern Non-Slaveholder*, to stress the benefits that the peculiar institution brought to non-slaveholding whites.[36]

Ultimately, however, despite latent class animosities that continued to percolate, the antebellum white South moved toward ideological unity that at least in public required support for—or at least silence over—slavery. In contrast to Russia, where overt pro-serfdom sentiment gradually withered during the first half of the nineteenth century, in most of the South it was overt *anti*-slavery thought that became increasingly rare. The South remained a slaveholder's world, and in the face of growing criticism from without, politically active Southerners increasingly rallied around slavery, which—both to them and to outsiders—came more and more to represent the South. As early as the 1790s, the Revolution-inspired questioning of slavery, which had never made significant headway in the Deep South, was on the wane, and from the 1830s it became all but invisible. Although prominent border-state politicians such as Henry Clay of Kentucky continued to subscribe to a version of "conditional termination" (Clay was active in the colonization movement designed to send Blacks "back" to Africa), there was no real equivalent among Southern politicians to the "enlightened bureaucrats" in Russia who grappled with how to abolish serfdom, and after the Virginia debate of 1831–32 there was almost no serious public discussion within the South of how or whether to abolish slavery. Thereafter, Southern politics increasingly revolved around who could best protect "Southern" interests and rights—that is, slavery. During the 1830s and 1840s, both Southern Whigs and Democrats presented themselves as the true defenders of the South while portraying the others as crypto-abolitionists who threatened Southern values, and during the second half of the 1850s, as the rise of the Republican Party in the North heralded the sectional triumph of free-labor sentiment, Southern politics became more and more focused on defense of the status quo against the onslaught being launched by those variously termed "red" and "black" Republicans.[37]

In short, a siege mentality gripped the late antebellum South. Although this mentality is sometimes seen as a sign of growing paranoia or irrationality, in fact the slave South was under challenge if not attack from multiple directions. Economically and socially, there was a growing gap between a modernizing, industrializing, urbanizing North and a South that continued to be overwhelmingly rural, agricultural, and committed to a traditional social order; in 1860, for example, only 9.6 percent of Southerners lived in an "urban" area with twenty-five hundred or more residents, while more than one-quarter of all Northerners (and 35.7 percent of Northeasterners) did. The Southern economy was far from stagnant, but its growth was based largely on an impressive expansion in cultivation of staple crops—especially cotton—rather than on the kind of transformation in productive capacity that was sweeping the North between 1840 and 1860; indeed, during those years the South's manufacturing capacity decreased from 18 to 16 percent of the nation's total. Politically conscious Southerners wavered between bemoaning the South's failure to diversify and modernize and celebrating the South's continued adherence to traditional values—during hard times, as in the early 1840s, the former position was especially widespread, whereas during the boom years of the 1850s the latter view was in the ascendant—but none could escape the divergent courses of North and South or the implicit threat that this divergence posed to the South's social order.[38]

Meanwhile, the South seemed increasingly aberrant and isolated internationally: whereas in the early nineteenth century slavery was commonplace in much of the New World and a commitment to order and hierarchy seemed de rigueur in much of the West, by mid-century, in an era that increasingly celebrated democracy and equality, New World slavery survived only in Cuba, Puerto Rico, Brazil, and the Southern United States, and enlightened opinion on both sides of the Atlantic condemned slavery as cruel and degraded. As European travelers increasingly pointed to slavery as the cause of Southern backwardness—"No mismanagement short of employing slaves will account for the deterioration of the agricultural wealth of these states," opined Englishwoman Harriet Martineau—proslavery thinkers showed heightened discomfort and defensiveness. Few illustrated this reaction more graphically than James Henry Hammond, the South Carolina planter-politician who in an influential proslavery letter addressed in 1845 to the English abolitionist Thomas Clarkson responded to antislavery criticism by developing the argument that the "poor and laboring classes" of Britain were "more miserable and degraded morally and physically than our slaves." A few years earlier, during a lengthy grand tour of Europe, Hammond had experienced the perils of egalitarianism firsthand. Showing a typical American ambivalence that combined "an almost mystical admiration" with "arrogant contempt" for European society and culture, he was especially shocked by uppity servants who refused to know their place and took advantage of too much freedom to cheat and talk back to their employers. (Hammond himself spent several hours in a Belgian jail after he "wore out [his] stick" on one such unruly servant.) Returning home feeling more American, Hammond also returned more committed to slavery, convinced of the hypocrisy of critics who condemned Southern slavery even as they paid no attention to the sufferings of their own "free" population.[39]

The Northern ideological assault on slavery—and on the slave South—was relentless. The 1830s saw a sharpening of the antislavery onslaught, with the spread of a new, militant form of abolitionism that departed from most earlier critiques of slavery both in the intensity of language used and in the insistence that slavery was a nonnegotiable evil (or sin) that had to be abolished immediately. In 1831, renouncing the "pernicious doctrine of *gradual* abolition," William Lloyd Garrison used the inaugural issue of his journal the *Liberator* to announce that he would be "as harsh as truth, and as uncompromising as justice" and would no longer "think, or speak, or write, with moderation." "Tell a man whose house is on fire, to give a moderate alarm," he continued; "tell him to moderately rescue his wife from the hands of the ravisher; tell the mother to gradually extricate her babe from the fire into which it has fallen;—but urge me not to use moderation in a cause like the present." Both because of their radicalized language and because they came almost entirely from outside the South, the new abolitionist attacks provoked among slaveholders an intensely defensive reaction, at the heart of which was an equally militant proslavery movement predicated on the previously rarely articulated idea that slavery was a "positive good" rather than a temporarily necessary evil.[40]

Radical abolitionism seemed threatening enough to defenders of slavery, but at least they could take comfort in the knowledge that it represented a fringe movement; in the North as well as in the South, most whites in the 1830s and 1840s considered abolitionists to be dangerous fanatics who threatened the stability of the social order. Far more dangerous (because it won far more adherents in the North) was the combined assault of free-labor arguments and their political manifestation in a surging "free-soil" movement to contain slavery within its current borders and reserve new western lands for hardy, free (usually white) settlers. Republicans like New York Senator William Seward and Massachusetts Senator Charles Sumner neatly captured the essence of both free-labor and free-soil principles when they ridiculed the slave South as backward and degraded. "It was necessary that I should travel to Virginia to have an idea of a slave state," Seward declared. "An exhausted soil, old and decaying towns, wretchedly neglected roads, and in every respect an absence of enterprise and improvement, distinguish the region. . . . Such has been the effect of slavery." Even more telling was the implied threat evident in Abraham Lincoln's famous "House Divided" speech of 1858, which suggested that slavery's demise was near: "I believe this government cannot endure, permanently half *slave* and half *free*. . . . It will become *all* one thing or *all* the other," he proclaimed, before proceeding to explain which half he thought would—and should—triumph. "The result is not doubtful," he concluded. "We shall not fail—if we stand firm, we shall not fail. *Wise councils* may *accelerate* or *mistakes delay* it, but, sooner or later the victory is *sure* to come."[41]

Although it seemed to many as if American slavery and Russian serfdom were living on borrowed time, abolishing them proved to be unusually difficult. In the South, the coexistence of a powerful resident slave-owning class, a decentralized American political system, and an aggressive ideological assault from without combined to generate an exceptionally militant and far-reaching defense of the peculiar institution that by the 1850s found expression in an apparently unified political opposition to any kind of antislavery action. In Russia, censorship and autocracy prevented the emergence of a real antiserfdom movement, while fear of peasant disorder in a vast, thinly governed empire prevented the government from risking anything that might destabilize the social order. In both countries, governmental paralysis indicated the extent of the emerging crises.

By the 1850s, efforts to reform serfdom had a history of more than half a century. Whereas the thrust of legislation on serfdom until the late eighteenth century had aimed at protecting the rights of serfholders and assuring the subordination of serfs, increasing attention thereafter was directed—as in the United States—at "softening" bondage and protecting its victims from the worst abuses of arbitrary rule. The resulting legislation ranged from the frivolous and symbolic (such as a 1792 measure forbidding auctioneers from using a hammer when selling serfs apart from land) to the serious and substantive. Several acts set restrictions on excessive punishment of serfs and provided for placing the estates of pomeshchiki who abused their powers under the temporary control of guardians. Others facilitated the freeing or partial freeing of individuals or groups of serfs: these included a law on "free agriculturalists" (1803) that allowed nobles to free serfs (who henceforth became state peasants) in exchange for collective self-purchase, a law on "obligated peasants" (1842) that allowed serf owners to reach voluntary agreements with their serfs defining their obligations and duties, and a law of 1847 that allowed serfs the right to buy their freedom if they were sold at public auction to pay off their owners' debts. These measures were not entirely insignificant. Not only did they indicate a new governmental concern to limit the most flagrant mistreatment of serfs, they also provided real benefits to some people; between 1803 and 1855, 114,000 male souls were able to become free agriculturalists. But with the exception of a unique set of reforms in the early nineteenth century that applied to the empire's newly acquired Baltic provinces (see below in this section), the legislation was largely aimed at protecting those who lived under serfdom or *allowing* individual nobles to free their serfs, not at bringing an end to serfdom as a whole. Indeed, despite the consensus evident by the second quarter of the nineteenth century that serfdom could not last, there was virtually no progress made toward a general emancipation, and the reasons for this lack of progress point to the crisis that Russia's rulers faced.[42]

The basic problem, one that to decades of policy makers approximated squaring the circle, was how to produce what amounted to a revolutionary change in the social order without destabilizing social relations in Russia's undergoverned countryside, or—as Vorontsov urged Kiselev—how to "direct the movement and not let it direct itself." Concern over this dilemma, pervasive among both individual nobles sympathetic to reform and government bureaucrats, dictated restraint when it came to meaningful action, and time after time "reformers" coupled their calls to action with even more strenuous expressions of caution. In 1835, when the head of a secret committee debating the peasant question reported to the tsar that the commission members recognized the necessity of transforming the status of the peasants, he added the important qualification that they also agreed that "haste, rash action, and even one mention of freedom pronounced [too] early could have disastrous consequences"; above all, it was important to establish beyond doubt that land was the inalienable property of the nobility. In his 1845 memo to Nicholas "On the Abolition of Serfdom in Russia," Minister of Internal Affairs I. A. Perovskii warned that although he supported the general concept of emancipation as "humane and Christian," erroneous peasant ideas of freedom would result in "complete anarchy and insubordination." Perovskii noted an additional dilemma: although freeing the peasants without providing them land to support themselves was undesirable, giving them land was also impossible, since this would require confiscating noble property; the only way out for the time being, he concluded, was an intermediate step leaving all land—and police powers—in the hands of the pomeshchiki, while carefully defining the terms under which the peasants would cultivate this land and allowing them the right to own personal property. It is hardly surprising that his plan came to nothing.[43]

The land issue proved to be especially vexing. Virtually all participants in the debate over the peasant question insisted on the importance of avoiding the emergence of a landless proletariat and the accompanying social turmoil that Russian officials associated with Western Europe. It became a stock argument that whatever course Russia followed, it was essential not to replicate the experience of the three Baltic provinces of Estland, Lifland, and Kurland, where the landless emancipation of some eight hundred thousand serfs between 1816 and 1819, undertaken at the request of noble representatives upset by previous reform measures regulating and defining relations between landowners and serfs, had left the peasants in a deplorable condition by separating them from what was most essential for the maintenance of true peasant status—land. Similar if less influential in shaping the thought of Russian officials as they grappled with how to end serfdom was awareness of emancipation settlements in Prussia (1807) and Austria (1848) that had left "free" peasants with sharply reduced access to land and largely dependent on their former owners. Warning that Russia should not follow such policies, Prince S. V. Volkonskii urged that "in setting about to change our peasants' way of life"—a common euphemism in the late 1850s for emancipation—"we must not imitate, but create something new and distinctive."[44]

But if a landless emancipation seemed imprudent, providing land to emancipated peasants was even more problematical. After all, the land belonged to the noble serf owners, and beyond revolutionary circles there was little or no willingness to consider a confiscatory policy. The dilemma became more acute after 1848, when revolutionary violence in Western Europe confirmed the worst fears among Russia's rulers concerning the destabilizing potential of a landless emancipation; indeed, after 1848 what limited progress Nicholas I's government had made in the direction of reform largely ground to a halt. While reformers worried about how to "keep the peasants peasants"—that is, to keep them from being turned into landless wage laborers—those concerned with noble prerogatives fretted that transferring land to the peasants threatened disaster because "without supervision and incentive, the majority of peasants ... are so lazy that to sustain themselves they prefer beggarliness to work."[45]

The concern that government officials expressed over the potentially destabilizing effect of emancipation was far from misplaced. Even under "normal" conditions, peasant unrest was common (and increasingly frequent over time), and authorities legitimately feared that any precipitous loosening of controls in the overwhelmingly peasant countryside risked unleashing major disorder. The peasant world was one in which rumors—whether founded, partially founded, or totally unfounded—spread with amazing speed. Although few serfs took advantage of the 1847 *ukaz* allowing them collectively to buy their freedom if the estate on which they labored was sold at auction—from December 1847 to March 1849, such purchases occurred on only seven of 266 auctioned estates—the ukaz led to widespread misunderstandings and disorders among serfs who became convinced that they had the right to redeem themselves even if their estate was not auctioned off. Other "outside" events, from the Napoleonic invasion to the accession to the throne of Nicholas I in 1825 and of Alexander II in 1856, set off widespread disorders, but the events of 1848 provided perhaps the most striking confirmation—until the Crimean War—of how susceptible peasants were to rumor, how they interpreted these events in ways favoring their own interests, and how change had the potential to destabilize the social order. Outbreaks were especially widespread in the western provinces, where the impact of revolutions in Central and Western Europe and of inventory reforms in Russia's southwestern provinces was most keenly felt. During the last years of serfdom, as many peasants became convinced that serfdom was on its last legs, almost anything could set off rumors of freedom's arrival; the phenomenon reached especially massive proportions during the Crimean War of 1854–55, when many serfs became convinced that they and their families would be freed if they volunteered for military service and tens of thousands left their estates to take advantage of this opportunity.[46]

Small wonder, then, that so many government officials and other noblemen were panicked that any public hint of a move toward emancipation risked chaos and disaster. Even Aleksandr Nikitenko, a highly unusual former serf who became a university professor and then a government censor after securing his freedom in 1824, expressed fear of an uncontrolled emancipation: raising the question in his diary of whether the general emancipation for which he longed "would come when the people themselves cast off their bonds" or when they "receive freedom from the government," he pronounced: "God save us from the former!" Russia's ruling class lived in mortal fear of violence from below.[47]

In short, Russia was stuck. On the one hand, enthusiasm for serfdom had all but vanished, and enlightened voices agreed that its days were numbered; the question was less whether to abolish it than how and when. On the other hand, government officials worried that changing things too rapidly risked plunging Russia into chaos and class warfare. Nicholas I graphically captured the gist of the problem in his 1842 speech to the State Council on the "harmful" nature of serfdom. Conceding that "the present situation cannot continue *forever*," the monarch countered that "to touch [serfdom] now would be even more disastrous" than to do nothing. At mid-century, the government exhibited little inclination to defend serfdom but little will to risk abolishing it.[48]

Although arrived at very differently, a similar deadlock prevented meaningful action against slavery in the United States. By the late 1850s, Southern politicians seemed united on the need to defend slavery, if not on precisely how. While a growing perception of Southern distinctiveness combined with the accelerating ideological assault from without to convince virtually everyone in the South's ruling class that slavery faced an ominous threat that required a firm response, a series of highly visible incidents—from the Compromise of 1850 to the Kansas-Nebraska Act, the Dred Scott decision, and John Brown's raid on Harpers Ferry—drove home to politically conscious Southern whites the heightened seriousness of the situation. The final culmination of this process was the accession to the presidency of Abraham Lincoln, an "anti-Southern" Republican elected on the basis of an entirely sectional vote. Some Southern politicians responded to the challenge by proposing to reopen the African slave trade, some favored working with compliant Northerners—"doughfaces" in the colorful language of the day—to secure a political compromise that would guarantee forever slavery's continued existence, and others still concluded that the hour for such compromise had passed and the only solution was the creation of a separate Southern republic. Virtually all agreed, however, on the need to defend slavery as the basis for the Southern social order. The response to the publication of Hinton Helper's *Impending Crisis* in 1857 was telling: like earlier critics of slavery such as Sarah and Angelina Grimké, Helper was forced to flee the South for his very safety, a victim of the intellectual conformity that now gripped the section. Warning Northerners not to "agitate the question of slavery," South Carolina Senator James Henry Hammond boldly declared in 1858 that the Southern social order was invincible: "You dare not make war on cotton," he taunted. "No power on earth dares make war on it. Cotton *is* King."[49]

Southern slavery at mid-century seemed both flourishing and in crisis. Economically, the crisis was barely evident. The almost tenfold increase of cotton cultivation between 1820 and 1860 underlay a surge in slave-generated profits, and—except in some border-state areas such as Delaware and Maryland—there was little evidence that slavery had reached or would soon reach the limits of its productive capacity and begin to decline, as many of its critics suggested was inevitable. Indeed, the 1850s witnessed an increasing demand for slave labor that fueled a sharp rise in slave prices and provided an economic rationale for politically motivated calls to reopen the African slave trade. But the siege mentality and increasingly closed nature of Southern society, with public challenge to slavery virtually impossible, pointed to the reality of a broadly *political* crisis, as slavery—and the Southern social order that it supported—came under withering attack from without. The juxtaposition of the slave South and the free-labor North in one federal republic meant that the crisis of slavery was also a crisis of the Union.[50]

As in Russia, there appeared no easy way out. Although abolitionists called for the immediate overthrow of slavery, they remained politically marginalized as the newly ascendant Republicans, who put forth various free-labor and free-soil versions of antislavery, closed ranks in calling for the *containment*, not the immediate abolition, of slavery. Once again, Lincoln expressed the mainstream sentiment: even as he reiterated his hatred of slavery as fundamentally wrong because it denied slaves access to the most basic American right—self-government—he also insisted that the Constitution did not grant the federal government the power to interfere with slavery in states where it already existed and that preserving the federal Union was paramount. Lincoln expressed this fundamental dilemma clearly in (among other places) his first debate with Senator Stephen Douglas, in 1858. On the one hand, he proclaimed the fundamental injustice of slavery, insisting "there is no reason in the world why the negro is not entitled to all the natural rights enumerated in the Declaration of Independence, the right to life, liberty and the pursuit of happiness." On the other hand, he made clear that despite his hatred of slavery, he had "no purpose directly or indirectly to interfere with slavery in the States where it exists," adding, "I believe I have no lawful right to do so, and I have no inclination to do so." Lincoln reiterated this position as late as 4 March 1861, in his inaugural address, quoting from and reaffirming his earlier promises not to interfere with slavery where it already existed. Here was the crux of the problem: despite the spread of antislavery sentiment throughout the North, it was unclear how or even whether slavery could be brought to an end in the foreseeable future. If there was little public opposition to it within the South, there was little will from without to push for its immediate end, even among the free-soilers, who assumed national power with Lincoln's election as president in 1860.[51]

Both Russia and the United States faced political paralysis. The Russian government, overcome by fear and inertia, was unwilling to act; the American government, facing constitutional limitations and sectional breakdown, was unable to act. In both countries, only some shock from without could produce a new political dynamic that would bring resolution of the crises.

In both countries war provided that shock, and new governments seized the moment to overcome the seemingly intractable paralysis that had gripped their predecessors, but specific conditions dictated major differences in the way emancipation arrived. Russia's defeat in the Crimean War convinced high officials—including the highest—of the need for major reforms and gave them the resolve to do what they had wanted to do (and had talked about doing) for a long time: end serfdom. In the United States, the prolonged Civil War led to the disintegration of slavery within the South and at the same time gave federal leaders—including the highest—the opportunity to act against an entrenched system that they hated but had been unable to confront. Russia's serf emancipation, which came in the aftermath of war, was gradual and complex, set forth in advance in elaborate detail in documents cobbled together in protracted meetings of secret governmental committees. America's slave emancipation, which proceeded apace in the midst of war, was sudden and conceptually simple, but the ultimate shape of the new order emerged only *after* emancipation, as Congress (and Americans in general) engaged in a very public postwar debate over the place of former slaves in an egalitarian society. The ensuing terms of emancipation were in most respects more radical in the United States than in Russia, and the new balance of forces following defeat of the Confederacy suggested the potential for a more fundamental restructuring of the South as well. In both Russia and the South, however, emancipation unleashed new forces—and new hopes and fears—that would continue to play out for many years to come.

1 • Process

1 • Emancipation Launched
Preparation, Process, Terms

In both Russia and the United States, war provided the jolt that new governments needed to overcome political paralysis and initiate emancipation. Elsewhere, war had often proved troubling for slaveholding regimes, as military conflict enabled bondspeople to take advantage of unsettled conditions to secure their freedom. During the American Revolution (and to a lesser extent the War of 1812), for example, tens of thousands of slaves (including some who joined the British) ran away from their owners; although the fugitives met mixed fates ranging from death, recapture, and re-enslavement to successful entry into the rapidly growing ranks of free Blacks, slavery appeared seriously threatened for a time, especially in areas of the United States suffering most from war-induced disruption. Sometimes, war set in motion the eventual abolition of slavery, as in the Northern United States, Cuba, and much of the Spanish-American mainland. The Napoleonic invasion was instrumental in bringing serfdom to an end in Prussia (although in the French Caribbean Napoleon appeared as a re-enslaver rather than a liberator), as was the Revolution of 1848 in Austria. Usually, however, wars led to freedom for *some* slaves or paved the way for the *future* ending of bondage rather than bringing about an immediate *general* emancipation. Indeed, despite the enhanced opportunities for freedom provided by the American War of Independence, there were about twice as many slaves in the United States at the conclusion of the Revolutionary era (in 1800) as there had been at its onset (in 1770); similarly, although the rebels in Cuba's Ten Years' War (1868–78) increasingly championed abolition as well as independence, slavery survived until 1886. With the exception of the always exceptional Haitian Revolution, the war-triggered transformations of the social order in Russia and especially in the Southern United States were unusually sweeping. Few other countries experienced the equivalent of Reconstruction or the Great Reforms.[1]

Despite this common characteristic, the way war precipitated and shaped the Russian and American versions of emancipation differed substantially. Russia's unexpected defeat in the Crimean War shocked members of the governing elite out of their complacency and convinced them that fundamental changes were needed to modernize the country and make it competitive. Along with the opportune accession of Alexander II to the throne in 1855 upon the death of Nicholas I, a man of conservative temperament who had become increasingly preoccupied with maintaining order, military defeat changed the political climate and enabled Russia's new ruler to initiate action that his predecessors had discussed—and put off—for decades. In the United States, a much longer and more wrenching Civil War led both to the partial unraveling of slavery under the pressure of war and to a new determination among Republican leaders—and a radicalized Northern public—to seize the moment and take more decisive action against slavery than anyone but the most committed abolitionists had previously contemplated. Although war triggered the decision to abolish bondage in both countries, emancipation's wartime origins ultimately shaped its character far more in the United States than in Russia, both because of the unusually destructive and all-encompassing nature of the American Civil War and because it was waged against a slaveholding power. It was a small step from fighting against slaveholders to fighting against slavery—and *for* a new, more egalitarian South.

In both countries, deciding on the terms of the new order proved a drawn-out process that required years of deliberation and debate. Here, too, a number of important contrasts belied the common essence of emancipation itself—the shift from coerced to "free" labor. Perhaps most obvious were differences in the timing of and participants in the deliberations. In Russia, these deliberations occurred largely *before* the implementation of emancipation, and they occurred mostly in private, among men concerned above all with making sure that the changes they were instituting did not get out of hand. In the United States, by contrast, they took place largely *after* emancipation was already a fait accompli, as a democratic society engaged in an extended—and very public—debate over the proper shape of both the postwar South and the country as a whole. It is not entirely surprising that the results of these very different decision-making processes were also very different.

Indeed, although emancipation constituted a major break or discontinuity in the history of both Russia and the United States, the new alignment of forces resulting from the Civil War made possible much more radical political initiatives in the democratic United States than in hierarchical, autocratically ruled Russia. At the end of the war, most Northerners considered Southern planters traitors who had been the driving force behind the Confederate Rebellion; as Vice President (and future President) Andrew Johnson proclaimed in 1864, "Treason must be made odious, and traitors must be punished and impoverished. Their great plantations must be seized, and divided into small farms, and sold to honest, industrious men."[2] Certainly, such traitors could hardly expect to play a leading role in determining the fate of their former slaves, "loyal" Southerners whose interests now appeared to be synonymous with those of the republic itself. Russian nobles, by contrast, remained the bulwark of the autocracy. Their interests required careful consideration, and they would be key players in overseeing implementation of the new order.

The Russian emancipation decree of 19 February 1861 and the accompanying statutes were the product of more than four years of complex wrangling that at first appeared unlikely to yield positive results but under the prodding of Tsar Alexander II provided a consensus for reform that took on an increasingly far-reaching character. As often before, the accession to the throne of a new emperor produced widespread rumors among the peasantry that something big was about to happen, that the "good" tsar would overcome the stubborn opposition of conniving officials and greedy nobles and finally liberate the long-suffering people. At first, such a result seemed as unlikely as it had been in the past. This time, however, although the new monarch lacked most of the qualities of a popular redeemer, the rumors turned out to contain more than a grain of truth. The cautious new ruler set in motion a process that would revolutionize Russian society, and at key moments when the process seemed likely to grind to a halt he provided the support necessary to keep it alive.[3]

A short outline of the byzantine twists and turns that preceded the 1861 reform reveals both the evolving nature of the emerging consensus and the sharply confined ideological parameters within which the planners operated. The first opaque sign of the tsar's intent to pursue reform came on 30 March 1856, when, in an address ostensibly designed to reassure the Moscow Province marshals of nobility that rumors of emancipation were "unfounded," he told them that any talk of abolition was premature, but added cryptically that "of course . . . the present order of owning souls cannot remain unchanged." In a revised version of the address intended for broader distribution, he warned that "it is better to start to abolish serfdom from above, than to wait for that time when it starts to abolish itself from below," asked the assembled marshals to "think about the best way to carry this out," and suggested that they convey his thoughts "to the nobles for consideration." A few months later, Alexander appointed a Secret Committee on the Peasant Question.[4]

So far, none of these measures seemed especially startling. Alexander's father, Nicholas I, had appointed ten similar committees (one of which Alexander had in fact chaired) and had also mused from time to time about the eventual need to abolish serfdom. Like most of its predecessors, the new committee was dominated by conservatives, and like them it concluded (in August 1857) that despite the theoretical desirability of emancipation, it was not currently feasible, because the serfs were "not at all prepared to receive liberty suddenly and abruptly." Warning that an immediate emancipation would disrupt "the age-old relations" between serfs and pomeshchiki and threaten the "peace and order of the State," the committee proposed looking into the possibility of gradual measures modeled on earlier decrees of 1803 and 1842. As historian Daniel Field succinctly put it, "Like the late tsar Nicholas and his counsellors, they perceived that it was desirable to abolish serfdom but they conceived that it was impracticable to do so."[5]

Faced with the usual procrastination, Alexander proved unusually insistent. To convince the Secret Committee that he expected more than empty verbiage, he added as a new member his brother Grand Duke Constantine, already known as a proponent of reform. More noteworthy still was the "rescript" he sent to Governor-General V. A. Nazimov inviting nobles in the three Lithuanian provinces of Vilno, Kovno, and Grodno to elect provincial committees that would draft proposals to reform relations between pomeshchiki and serfs. Referring specifically to "organization and improvement in the way of life of the serfs"—which soon became a euphemism for emancipation—the monarch set forth a series of cautious guidelines that included the right of pomeshchiki to "ownership of all the land," stated that the proposals should be implemented "gradually, so as not to disturb the existing agricultural organization on seigneurial estates," and warned authorities to make sure that the peasants remained "in full obedience to the[ir] pomeshchiki" and did not pay attention to "any ill-intentioned suggestions or lying rumors." Hardly a ringing endorsement of freedom, the rescript, which was soon published and circulated to governors and marshals of nobility throughout the empire, indicated nevertheless that the emperor was determined to proceed toward emancipation. Although some nobles continued to insist that "improving the condition" of the peasants did not necessarily mean freeing them, in effect the decision to abolish serfdom was now public. Early in 1858, the Secret Committee, whose existence was no longer secret, was renamed the Main Committee on the Peasant Question.[6]

Over the next two years, preparation for emancipation proceeded along two fronts. At the provincial level, committees of noblemen—each consisting of two members elected by district, two appointed by the governor, and the provincial marshal of nobility who served as committee chair—debated and drafted proposals to submit to the Main Committee in St. Petersburg. Although differences existed among committee members (see below), these differences were largely over the *terms* of the emancipation settlement; the tsar himself had already settled the question of whether emancipation would occur. Whatever their differences, members of the provincial committees were largely united in defending noble prerogatives as they understood them, both in terms of the results of the emancipation legislation and in terms of their role in bringing about this legislation. Carefully praising the tsar for having invited the nobility to participate in drafting the emancipation provisions, a group of noble deputies representing many of the provincial committees petitioned Alexander, complaining that government "bureaucrats" were ignoring them. "Our sorrow, Sire, cannot be expressed," they lamented.[7] Their complaint was largely accurate. Although Alexander and his advisers maintained the fiction that the provincial nobility was playing a major role in drafting the reforms, and invited representatives of the provincial committees to St. Petersburg to present their suggestions in two successive "summonses," their influence was relatively minor. The government was willing to listen to their views and adopt some of their recommendations, and in a general sense the emancipation legislation reflected their interests, but that legislation was largely the product of work by high government officials—bureaucrats—with crucial support from the tsar.

During the course of 1858 and 1859, those officials put together a complicated plan for emancipation that, within the conservative context in which they operated, seemed increasingly radical. At the heart of this plan, which was in continual evolution until its final implementation, were three central principles: emancipation would be introduced gradually, the former serfs would receive—and pay for—land, and communal self-government among peasants would partially replace the authority formerly wielded by noble pomeshchiki. Instrumental in putting together this plan, and in beating back opposition from the "aristocratic opposition," was a group of "enlightened bureaucrats" such as Nikolai Miliutin and Andrei Zablotskii-Desiatovskii who had long favored "liberal" reforms, and who at crucial times were able to win the grudging support of powerful conservative figures, including General Ia. I. Rostovstev and eventually Alexander himself. In February 1859, in order to spur on the reforms, Alexander created four Editing Commissions, which in effect operated as one large commission chaired by Rostovstev, to go over the proposals of the provincial committees and draft emancipation statutes that would be submitted to the Main Committee; although the commissions' thirty-eight members included some prominent conservatives, the majority were reformers, many selected by Rostovstev himself. "In addition to individual freedom, the peasants must have the chance to obtain sufficient land as property for their subsistence," stressed Rostovstev in addressing the newly established commissions in March 1859, "for otherwise [their] lives would improve only in word and not in reality."[8]

Despite continued efforts of conservatives to weaken the emerging draft legislation—they were particularly concerned with maintaining as much land and political authority as possible in the hands of pomeshchiki—the commissions pressed on with their work. With the tsar's support, not even the elderly Rostovstev's failing health and eventual death in February 1860 could derail the process. Rostovstev's replacement, the conservative minister of justice Viktor Panin, was more sympathetic than his predecessor to appeals for relief from aggrieved representatives of the provincial committees, but as a loyal servant of the tsar he guided the emancipation plan to completion with only minor changes. In October, the Editing Commissions submitted the statutes to the Main Committee on the Peasant Question, now headed by Grand Duke Constantine, which in turn passed them along to the State Council for approval. On 28 January 1861 Alexander addressed the council, terming emancipation "vital" for "the development of [Russia's] strength and might." Asserting his conviction that the assembled dignitaries were no doubt "as convinced" as he was "of this measure's utility and necessity" and paying lip service to the fiction that the reform came in response to "a call from the nobility itself," the monarch assured the council that "all that could be done to protect the interest of the pomeshchiki was done," warned that after four years "any further procrastination could be ruinous for the state," and asserted his determination to proceed as quickly as possible. While inviting suggestions for change from the council, Alexander reminded its members that "the basis of this whole affair must be the improvement in the way of life of the peasants and improvement not only in words and on paper but in reality." In short, Alexander left the council little choice, and after asserting their authority by tinkering with the draft before them, the councilors gave their consent.⁹

On 19 February 1861, Alexander signed the emancipation statutes (*Polozheniia:* sometimes translated as "Regulations"), which came to more than 360 pages of text, and issued an accompanying manifesto. The wordy document was hardly a ringing endorsement of freedom. In it, Alexander dryly summarized the highlights of the complicated emancipation provisions and took special pains to set the new departure within the context of high-minded action on the part of both the nobility and his own predecessors on the throne. Pointing to the ideal of "patriarchal relations of sincere solicitude and benevolence on the part of the estate owners and good natured submission from the peasants," the monarch noted that a "decline in morals" had undercut "paternal relations" and led to an "arbitrariness that had been burdensome for the peasants and not conducive to their welfare." Citing the commitment of Alexander I and Nicholas I to "improving the condition of the serfs," he heaped praise on the nobility for "voluntarily renounc[ing] any rights to the persons of the serfs," and warned the peasants not to misunderstand freedom, because "prosperity is acquired and increased only by hard work . . . and, overall, by an honest, God-fearing life." The manifesto set a grudging tone to the onset of a momentous change in Russia's social order.¹⁰

A number of observations about this arcane preparatory process seem in order. First, in understanding Alexander II's decision to undertake emancipation, it is useful to keep in mind the underlying political environment. Because intellectual support for serfdom had largely evaporated by the 1840s, the question was not so much whether serfdom should be abolished but when and how. The combination of a new tsar and the shock of military defeat in the Crimean War provided the opportunity for decisive action that Russia's rulers had long considered but had been unable to embrace. Historian Alfred A. Rieber has argued that Alexander II's principal concern was modernization of Russia's armed forces, a goal that the Crimean debacle convinced him required freeing the serfs as a prerequisite to reforming the antiquated system of military recruitment. As Rieber noted, "To Alexander the army represented the mightiest bulwark of the autocracy, a fund of energetic and reliable advisers, a constant source of pride and pleasure." Although not all historians agree that upgrading the military was the driving force in abolishing serfdom, in a broader sense there was a growing conviction among Russia's governing class that serfdom was keeping the nation backward and weak—militarily as well as economically and politically—and that modernizing Russia required emancipation. Certainly, in the words of historian Larissa Zakharova, the tsar was by temperament "not a man of liberal beliefs." He did, however, have a good deal of "common sense" and the "capacity to size up a situation quickly and to grasp it as a whole," and given the free-labor consensus that Russia's progress was dependent on abolishing serfdom, his decision to seize the moment could be seen as representing less a decisive break with the past than an essential new step toward fulfilling the traditional goal of making Russia great and strong.[11]

As officials inched toward devising an emancipation plan, they were acutely aware of pressure from below. Liberal and radical exiles bombarded the government from abroad with the kind of ringing demands for freedom—and more—that could not be uttered publicly within Russia. The most influential of these appeals appeared in Alexander Herzen's London-based journal *Kolokol* (*The Bell*), which published not only Herzen's own writings (under the pseudonym "Iskander") but also those of allied dissidents, including Nikolai Ogarev, and was read by many at the highest levels of government, including Alexander himself. At first lamenting that the new tsar seemed no more inclined to move toward emancipation than his predecessors and warning that "soon it will be [too] late to solve the question of freeing the serfs peacefully" because "the *muzhiki* will solve it by themselves" and "rivers of blood will flow," Herzen grew increasingly excited as he became convinced of Alexander's reforming proclivity. In January 1858, *Kolokol*'s lead article, headed "THE FREEING OF THE PEASANTS," noted the tsar's rescript to the Lithuanian nobles and, while expressing some concern about the term "improvement in the peasant way of life," concluded that "the matter is in the deed, and not the name." A month later, Herzen threw caution to the wind: "The name Alexander II from now on belongs to history," he gushed, adding that "even if his reign were to end tomorrow" he had initiated the serfs' liberation and "future generations will not forget this!" In subsequent issues, Herzen alternated between such giddy exultation and a more sober-minded concern over the slow pace of progress and the possibility that the terms of emancipation would be less than generous to the peasants; urging the government on, he noted widespread reports of "local peasant uprisings" and warned that "one cannot serve two masters, one cannot at the same time free the peasants and whip them!"[12]

Within Russia as well, preparation for emancipation took place in an atmosphere of unprecedented—and growing—intellectual ferment, as excitement over the impending changes created a new mood of self-generating public debate and expectations among the small circle of educated Russians. As talk of major changes proliferated and rumors swirled, the government—as if helplessly propelled by events—partially lifted its rigid controls on public expression and movement; between 1856 and 1860 the number of Russian periodicals surged from 110 to 230, and the number of passports issued for travel abroad more than quadrupled, from six thousand to twenty-six thousand. Englishman Charles Henry Pearson, who traveled in Russia in 1858, was amazed to find "almost perfect liberty of discussion and thought. On the railway and in the steamer men discuss political questions as freely as if in their own houses, and with closed doors," he observed. "New journals are everywhere swarming into life." Former serf Aleksandr Nikitenko, himself a government censor, noted in his diary the "endless talk about emancipation" and mused that "the force of the torrent into which we have hurled ourselves will carry us to whither we cannot yet foresee." In St. Petersburg, at least, a sense of high excitement prevailed.[13]

The pressure from further below seemed considerably more threatening. Despite warnings from figures as different as Alexander II and Aleksandr Herzen that if serfdom was not abolished soon the serfs would take matters in their own hands and emancipate themselves, there was no massive peasant uprising such as the Pugachev Rebellion of 1773–74 that continued to terrify nobles almost a century later. Rather, as rumors of impending changes swirled, peasants watched and waited in edgy anticipation. Although changed conditions in the past had often provoked peasant *volneniia* (collective disorders that bore characteristics of both strikes and small-scale uprisings), now it seemed as if almost anything could set them off. In 1854 and 1855, tens of thousands of serfs left home to volunteer for military action in the Crimean War, under the widespread but mistaken belief that the tsar had invited their service and promised freedom to those heeding his call; detained and sent home by distressed authorities, often after receiving physical punishment, these volunteers (and many of their fellow serfs) typically became convinced that they were being cheated out of the freedom they had been promised. In 1856, tens of thousands more, acting on rumors of a government call for them to settle on ruined lands, set out for the Crimea; like those of 1854–55, these migrants, who were especially numerous in the empire's southern provinces, were arrested and sent home, although some chose to return "voluntarily" rather than face punitive action. And in 1859, in what the Third Department (political police) termed a "totally unexpected" development, peasants objecting to high liquor taxes not only began to abstain from alcoholic beverages but also physically attacked taverns, pillaging 220 drinking establishments in twelve provinces.[14]

As government committees worked on the emancipation legislation, serfs displayed increasing signs of restiveness and anticipation. S. T. Slovutinskii, an official who helped put down volneniia in Riazan Province in the 1840s and 1850s, later observed with puzzlement that for some reason during the last years of serfdom "there began to develop in the serf population a general unwillingness to endure serf dependence any longer, even though it had become much lighter than before." Although some conservative nobles drew the opposite conclusion, Slovutinskii, like some other "liberal" observers, suggested that the serfs' "readiness to remove themselves" from serfdom "demonstrated the necessity to end serfdom as quickly and decisively as possible." Quantifying the number of volneniia is fraught with difficulty, and historians attempting to do so have come up with strikingly different totals, but the upward trend during the last years of serfdom seems clear. According to V. A. Fedorov's study of the "peasant movement" in seven central-industrial provinces, the number of estates participating in volneniia increased from ninety-seven in 1846–50 and eighty-four in 1851–55 to 385 in 1856–60, while the number of participating villages increased during the same years from 144 and 153 to 651. B. G. Litvak has calculated an increasing level of disturbances in six provinces in the black-earth center *during* the four years preceding emancipation, with seven volneniia in 1857, twenty-two in 1858, and forty-three in 1859–60, as well as an increase in the proportion of conflicts that involved access to land. It is important not to exaggerate: the countryside was not exploding in violence, many of the disputes between peasants and pomeshchiki were similar to those that had long been a staple feature of serfdom, and some historians have been more impressed by the relative calm that prevailed than by breaches in that calm. It was not so much violence as fear of violence that weighed on the minds of government officials and other noblemen as they debated the terms of emancipation. As the Third Department's report for 1857 observed, even though "disorders have occurred rather rarely," the "majority of noblemen" were convinced that with emancipation "volneniia, pillage, and murder will be inevitable."[15]

The Third Department itself was hardly immune to concern over peasant intentions. The report for 1858, noting that many serfs were refusing to perform their obligations and that "some think that the land belongs to them as much as to the pomeshchiki," urged that local administration be strengthened and extreme care taken in selecting provincial governors. But rather than violence, jockeying and waiting seemed most characteristic of peasant behavior as emancipation neared. Some struggled with pomeshchki over the size of their land allotments, as both sides calculated (correctly) that the post-emancipation settlement would be based at least in part on current holdings; others dragged their feet in performing seigneurial labor. But mostly they watched and waited. Reporting from Voronezh Province in December 1860 on the widespread expectation that emancipation was imminent, a staff officer of the Corps of Gendarmes told the head of the Third Department that the governor was "seriously worried" at not having received "any preliminary instructions" on how to handle the event; pomeshchiki expected favorable terms but "[felt] an instinctive fear of the consequences," while the peasants, although peaceful, were so convinced of the coming "distribution to them of all seigneurial land ... that it [was] impossible not to foresee a dangerous disappointment" in the future.[16]

If serfs waited with keen anticipation, their owners typically exhibited sullen resignation. Lacking a strong tradition of independent political expression, nobles offered little resistance to the tsar's decision to end serfdom. They dragged their feet but did not dare to offer public opposition to the will of the tsar, once that will was clear. Although at first it was possible to argue that Alexander was talking quite literally about "improving the condition" of the serfs, not freeing them, his public endorsement of emancipation soon rendered this fiction untenable, and in their provincial committees (and elsewhere) noblemen focused not on whether the serfs should be emancipated but on what the terms of that emancipation should be. In the short-lived (1858–59) semimonthly *Zhurnal zemlevladel'tsev (Landowners' Journal)*, almost all the articles took for granted that the serfs would be freed, and concentrated on what the new order would and should be like. One contributor, for example, raised the question of whether hired labor or rental arrangements would be "most advantageous to landowners." Another began by proclaiming that "in compiling the rules for the improvement in the way of life of the serfs" it was essential to "maintain a beneficial tie and good relations between pomeshchiki and peasants, based on mutual advantages" without "interference from bureaucrats," but then abruptly shifted tack and asserted that the nobles had to maintain land and supervisory authority because most of the peasants were "so lazy" that they would prefer "beggarliness" to work. Still another landowner stressed the importance of introducing reforms gradually, "so as not to disrupt the existing economic structure of seigneurial estates." In general, the correspondents displayed a hardheaded concern with the economic interests of pomeshchiki, writing far more about practical matters such as the size of peasant allotments and payments than about paternalistic ties between masters and serfs.[17]

As this hardheadedness suggests, noble serfholders *did* defend their interests, as they understood them. In doing so, they showed considerable divergence of opinion—within a narrow ideological framework. In explaining these differences some historians have stressed regional interest, while others have been more impressed by individual proclivity. Clearly both existed. In the fertile black-earth region, it was in the interest of pomeshchiki to keep as much land as possible in their own hands and minimize the amount available to peasants, but where land was less productive and most peasants were on obrok, pomeshchiki were more willing to accept substantial peasant allotments in exchange for hefty compensation; as historian Michael Confino summarized the situation, each of the proposals put forth in the provincial noble committees "clearly reflected the influence of material conditions (economic and climatic) of its author's region of origin." Differences also existed within as well as among provincial committees, however, with at least a few "liberal" voices heard even in the committees dominated (as most were) by those determined to keep change to a minimum. Such liberal views were unusually prevalent in the committee from Tver Province, where the majority supported the program put forth by two reformist members, A. M. Unkovskii and A. A. Golovachev, a program that in the words of historian Terence Emmons did not so much reflect personal economic interests as "liberal abolitionist sympathies of a younger and better-educated group of gentry." Arguing that serfdom was immoral as well as a barrier to the progress of Russian agriculture, Unkovskii and Golovachev called for not only a rapid transition to the new order but also an end to labor obligations and (more provocatively) full civil liberties for the emancipated peasants. Such liberal views were not only unusual among the nobility but also anathema to authorities committed to defending hierarchy and order, and the government showed its displeasure by removing Unkovskii from his position as Tver marshal of nobility and sending him into temporary internal exile in Viatka.[18]

Although nobles disagreed over the details of how to proceed with emancipation, their disagreements should not be exaggerated. Once it was clear that Alexander was serious in his intent to abolish serfdom, outright opposition was off the table; at the same time, virtually no nobles subscribed to the peasant notion that the land belonged (or should belong) to those who worked it and that a true emancipation would end the nobility's privileged position. Indeed, central to the basic consensus produced by four years of deliberations was the understanding that if the peasants were to receive land, they had to pay for it. Liberals as well as conservatives accepted the premise that the land belonged to the nobility and that pomeshchiki would have to receive full compensation for any allotment of land to the peasants—even land that they had already been cultivating as their own. As the Tver Province liberals put it in making their case for a landed emancipation, it was essential that pomeshchiki receive compensation "both for the land removed from their ownership, *and for the emancipated peasants themselves.*" In short, liberals and conservatives were not as far apart as they appeared on the broad outlines of emancipation: whatever changes occurred, Russia would remain an autocratic, stratified society in which the interests of the nobility were protected.[19]

The gap between the government in St. Petersburg and the provincial committees was also less gaping than it seemed: although the committees sought a larger role than they were allotted in preparing the emancipation legislation, as Daniel Field has noted, "while the pomeshchiki were excluded ... from the legislative process, the pomeshchik mentality exerted a powerful inertial force." After all, the government bureaucrats were—like the provincial pomeshchiki—noblemen themselves, with the same set of associations and assumptions, and most of them were serfholders as well, with the same set of interests. Lacking any tradition of independent political power, corporate consciousness, or paternalistic regard for their "people," noble landowners were most of all concerned with protecting their economic interests and receiving the respect that they believed they were due. Given an emancipation policy that in fact protected their interests, together with a little flattery from the tsar, they showed little disposition—and had no real ability—to challenge the reform. Under the circumstances, maybe emancipation wouldn't be so bad after all.[20]

In the United States, emancipation evolved according to a very different scenario, the product of very different power relations. As in Russia, war upset the existing political deadlock and enabled a new administration to take decisive action against a well-entrenched system of labor. The wartime destruction of slavery proceeded along two parallel fronts, as changing conditions and new military imperatives permitted an antislavery government to move against the peculiar institution even as it was partially unraveling from below. But in the United States, unlike Russia, the destruction of slavery preceded rather than followed discussion of what would come next, and when that discussion occurred it was largely without the participation of the slaveholders and their representatives. As a result, the eventual terms of emancipation were—compared to those in Russia—tilted more in favor of the former bondspeople and less of the former owners.

In considering the destruction of slavery, it is appropriate to begin with the war-generated erosion of existing slave-master relations that occurred within much of the South, both because of its intrinsic importance and because it helped set the stage for the government action that ensued. Despite fears among slave owners and Confederate authorities, the war did not produce a general slave uprising on the order of the Haitian Revolution, and after the war defenders of the old regime created an elaborate mythology—for decades embraced by many historians as well—centered on the idea of "loyal darkies" who stood by their beloved owners in their hour of greatest need. The reality was different (although there were in fact slaves who protected and cared for their owners when federal troops arrived): throughout the South, slaves took advantage of wartime disruption to test opportunities provided by weakened authority, chip away at the normal routine of master-slave relations, and when possible escape from those relations altogether. Their responses were diverse, reflecting variations in both geographic conditions and relations between individual masters and slaves, but in general, as one historian has put it, "slaves moved cautiously but deliberately to seize their freedom." As in Russia, watchful waiting characterized the behavior of many bondspeople even as the slave grapevine spread rumors of imminent change, and some acted to nudge that change along, but the massive confusion and disruption occasioned by the increasingly desperate Confederate struggle for survival provided the slaves with opportunities to advance the cause of freedom that were unprecedented in the South and far greater than those available to the Russian serfs. Recent historians have not always agreed on the character of slave behavior during the Civil War, but—unlike most historians who wrote during the first half of the twentieth century—the vast majority have been impressed by the slaves' "agency" in advancing their own freedom.[21]

At the heart of this process were two interrelated developments that struck devastating blows to the slave regime. The first was massive flight (which Steven Hahn has called rebellion). On an unprecedented scale, slaves took advantage of the war to strike out for freedom. The proximity of federal troops—increasingly common as the Confederate defense perimeter shrank—proved especially conducive to flight, as first hundreds, then thousands, and ultimately hundreds of thousands of slaves sought freedom behind Union lines; as General Ambrose E. Burnside reported to Secretary of War Stanton from Newbern, North Carolina, on the surge of fugitives, "It would be utterly impossible if we were so disposed to keep them outside of our lines as they find their way to us through woods and swamps from every side." At first fugitives faced an uncertain and varied reception from federal commanders and soldiers, depending in part on the proclivity of individuals and in part on military and political considerations. In November 1861, Major General John A. Dix reassured "the People of Accomac and Northampton Counties, Va.," that "special directions have been given not to interfere with the conditions of any persons held to domestic service," with commanders "instructed not to permit any such persons to come within their lines." After Congress passed the Second Confiscation Act, on 17 July 1862, however, it became federal policy to welcome escaped slaves as "contrabands of war" and when possible put them to use in support of the war effort. Although there were significant geographic variations to patterns of wartime flight—it was most pervasive in and near areas of early occupation by federal forces and least widespread in remote areas such as Texas, where the reduced level of fighting also reduced the war's impact on social relations—its sheer volume was enormous. By war's end, hundreds of thousands of former slaves were laboring on fortifications, serving as laundresses and cooks, fighting as soldiers in the Union Army, and crowding into the "contraband camps" that the military established to handle the swelling population of runaway men, women, and children. When and where enslaved Blacks had a chance, they "voted with their feet" for freedom.[22]

As significant as its size was the fugitive population's composition. Before the war slaves had typically fled alone (less often in pairs or very small groups), and the overwhelming majority of runaways had been young men, but wartime conditions made possible *collective* flight by large groups, including families and at times the entire labor force of farms and plantations. Equally noteworthy was the presence among the defectors of special slaveholders' favorites, including trusted house servants. The flight of privileged body servants, drivers, and house slaves was particularly shocking to slave owners, and led to a widespread sense of betrayal, tinged with both resignation and resentment. Noting that "in too numerous instances those we esteemed the most have been the first to desert us," Georgia rice planter Louis Manigault concluded that such desertions revealed the "ingratitude evinced in the African character." Mrs. W. D. Chadick, of Huntsville, Alabama, lamented, "Our servants have all left us with the exception of Uncle Tom"; "he will doubtless go next—old as he is"; "there is a powerful charm in the word 'Freedom.' " To slaveholders who prided themselves on their benevolent paternalism and spoke endlessly of their "love" for their "people," the discovery that they did not know their slaves as well as they thought was painful. This discovery would be repeated often in the future.[23]

Of course, most slaves did not escape to Union forces, but on countless farms and plantations behind Confederate lines slavery came under pressure and showed growing signs of disintegrating; as historian James Roark put it, "Slavery eroded, plantation by plantation, often slave by slave, like slabs of earth slipping into a Southern stream." Once again, the process was uneven, and it was most pronounced where Union forces were near, but even in more remote areas the war had a corrosive effect on slavery as masters—and mistresses—struggled to maintain their authority in a rapidly changing world. Although the Confederate Congress passed a law in October 1862 granting exemption from military conscription to one white man on every plantation of twenty or more slaves, the military service of most able-bodied young white men changed power relationships on farms and plantations, created fears among whites left behind, and encouraged slaves to test the limits of weakened authority. Aside from running away, they dragged their feet, seemed less subservient than in the past, and increasingly refused to act like slaves. "The negroes are worse than free—they say they are free," wrote Susanna Clay, the wife and mother of influential Democratic politicians, from the family estate in northern Alabama. "We cannot exert any authority." Plantation mistresses—unused to wielding firm authority or engaging in "masculine" activities such as punishing slaves—found it especially difficult to maintain order and complained of heightened "impertinence" and "insubordination." "All think I am a kind of usurper & have no authority over them," observed one mistress of the slaves she managed; another found, in a typical complaint, that her "orders [were] disregarded more & more every day"; still another pronounced that she was "sick of trying to do a man's business."[24]

Equally destructive of normal master-slave relations was the increasing intrusion of the Confederate government on the authority of slaveholders, telling them what to grow, imposing new taxes, conscripting their sons for military service, and commandeering their slaves for military labor. While independent-minded slave owners chafed under such government intervention and frequently showed more interest in defending their prerogatives than in defending the Confederacy—in the words of James Roark, "Planters usually chose the household over the homeland"—slaves marveled at the vulnerability of those who had once appeared all-powerful and drew the appropriate conclusion. Meanwhile, slaveholders faced another potential challenge from reformers who proposed to "humanize" slavery through measures such as providing legal recognition of slave marriages. Although these measures were not directed at abolishing slavery—and in some ways represented a continuation of antebellum efforts to strengthen slavery by making it more paternalistic—they did pose a potential challenge to owners used to unlimited power over their "people." Even more threatening was the proposal to save the faltering Confederacy by using hundreds of thousands of Black soldiers, who would be rewarded with their freedom. Although most slaveholders considered this idea inconceivable—what sense did it make to free slaves in order to further a slaveholders' rebellion?—shortly before the war's end, in a desperate effort to avert the inevitable, the Confederate Congress authorized the enlistment of up to three hundred thousand Black troops. The war was over a month later, before the unlikely plan could be executed, but its adoption underscored the extent to which slavery had become a casualty of the war begun for its preservation.[25]

More disruptive of actual master-slave relations than this unfulfilled plan to enlist slave soldiers was the mushrooming effort of frightened slaveholders, as federal forces neared, to evacuate many or all of their slaves to safer ground—a procedure known as "refugeeing"—in the process exposing them to new relationships and new opportunities for flight, and further revealing the owners' loss of control. In the short term, evacuated slaves often suffered severe hardship, but as historian Clarence Mohr noted, "refugeeing struck an important psychological blow at the myth of planter invincibility" and constituted one more corrosive element eating away at slavery; "refugee planters ceased to be masters in the full sense." Growing Confederate gloom and slave owner anxiety were accompanied by barely concealed slave elation, as the "slave grapevine" spread news of Union advances and of the Yankees' antislavery intentions. Slave rumors were not always accurate in detail, but the slaves were correct in their general understanding that the war had become a contest over slavery and that their fate hung in the balance. After learning of the Emancipation Proclamation, Henry, the driver on Charles Pettigrew's Magnolia plantation in Washington County, North Carolina, announced to the overseer that he was now the plantation's owner. (Soon thereafter, he moved off it.) As the Yankees neared her Montevideo plantation in Georgia, Mary Jones, widow of Presbyterian minister and planter Charles C. Jones, reported in January 1865 that "the people are all idle on the plantations, most of them seeking their own pleasure." Two weeks later, she lamented that "their condition is one of perfect anarchy and rebellion. They have placed themselves in perfect antagonism to their owners and to all government and control."[26]

Heightened attention to the slaves' role in bringing about the wartime disintegration of slavery has recently led to a historical debate over "who freed the slaves." Stressing the way the slaves' wartime resistance forced the hand of the federal government, some historians have argued that rather than being the recipients of freedom handed down from on high, the slaves in effect freed themselves. "Once the evolution of emancipation replaces the absolutism of the Emancipation Proclamation and the Thirteenth Amendment as the focus of study," proclaimed the editors of the *Freedom* documentary history of emancipation, "the story of slavery's demise shifts from the presidential mansion and the halls of Congress to the farms and plantations that became wartime battlefields." With that perspective, they added, "slaves . . . become the prime movers in securing their own liberty." Arguing that the slaves themselves forced a reluctant President Lincoln to embrace emancipation, historian Barbara J. Fields (herself one of the *Freedom* editors) insisted that "by the time Lincoln issued his Emancipation Proclamation, no human being alive could have held back the tide that swept toward freedom." Steven Hahn (also a *Freedom* editor) put forth a slightly different chronology, suggesting that "by the middle of 1864 if not before, the status quo antebellum was probably beyond resurrection no matter what the outcome of the Civil War." Other scholars, however, while recognizing slave agency, have concluded that the thesis of "self-liberation" goes too far. James M. McPherson, for example, disputed the notion that slave resistance doomed slavery whatever the war's outcome, insisting that the "slaves did not liberate themselves; they were liberated by the Union army." Rejecting "the new and currently more fashionable answer" to the question "Who Freed the Slaves?" he defended the "traditional answer" that "Abraham Lincoln freed the slaves."[27]

Although advocates of the "self-liberation thesis" have performed a valuable service in showing the complex ways in which slaves took advantage of the Civil War to advance their own freedom, their contribution is most effective when it is viewed not as a *replacement* of the "traditional" interpretation so much as a modification of it. In a sense, the "self-liberation" argument is the American equivalent of the Russian "revolutionary situation" interpretation that stressed the importance of peasant unrest in compelling the tsar and his advisers to opt for emancipation. The American version is more compelling, because Civil War conditions made possible more powerful and diverse actions against slavery than those that could be mounted in Russia (or could have been mounted earlier in the antebellum South), but it is once again important not to exaggerate: slaves' wartime behavior was highly diverse, but overall it seems best characterized not by outright rebelliousness so much as by a cautious—and increasing—willingness to take advantage of opportunities for freedom when the risks did not appear too overwhelming. "Whenever possible, black people avoided the deadly prospects of massive, sustained confrontations," noted historian Vincent Harding, "for their ultimate objective was freedom, not martyrdom." Equally important, their actions could not—in themselves—have brought an end to slavery (although, like the actions of slaves during the American Revolution, they did lead to freedom for many individuals), and it is unlikely that, in the absence of a Union victory, slavery would have perished in the foreseeable future in the South. In short, "Who freed the slaves?" may be the wrong question. Rather than asking *who* deserves credit for emancipation, it makes more sense to ask *what* made emancipation possible, and the answer to this question must include the antislavery actions of both the slaves and the federal government, under radically changed, wartime conditions. Absent the war, neither resistance by slaves nor the free-labor commitment of Republicans was powerful enough to topple the slave regime; as a result of the war, together they were. Indeed, as historian Stephanie McCurry observed, "the Confederacy . . . sealed the destruction of slavery and of slaveholders as a viable political force in Western history."[28]

Although the wartime erosion of slave relations set the stage for the federal abolition of slavery through the Emancipation Proclamation and the Thirteenth Amendment to the Constitution, it was by no means initially clear that this would be the case. Whereas most Confederates recognized the preservation of slavery as one of the central war aims of their Rebellion—as Confederate Vice President Alexander H. Stephens put it, the "cornerstone" of the Confederacy rested on the "great truth that the negro is not equal to the white man; that slavery . . . is his natural and moral condition"—the avowed goal of the federal government in 1861 and 1862 was not the destruction of slavery but preservation of the Union. When overeager commanders exceeded their authority and took action against slavery in areas under their control, President Lincoln repudiated and revoked that action, and as late as August 1862 he disingenuously lectured Republican editor Horace Greeley on the irrelevance of slavery as a major concern. "My paramount object in this struggle *is* to save the Union, and is *not* either to save or destroy slavery," he declared. "If I could save the Union without freeing *any* slave I would do it, and if I could save it by freeing *all* the slaves I would do it; and if I could save it by freeing some and leaving others alone I would also do that. What I do about slavery, and the colored race, I do because I believe it helps to save the Union."[29]

Lincoln's initial caution stemmed not from any proslavery proclivities—he had on numerous occasions made clear his hatred of the peculiar institution—

but from practical military considerations. These included concern for the loyalty of the four slave states (Maryland, Delaware, Missouri, and Kentucky) that remained in the Union; desire to maximize support for the war among Northern Democrats, most of whom were adamantly opposed to turning what they considered a legitimate effort to preserve the Union into an illegitimate— revolutionary—attack on slavery; and fear that moving against slavery at a time when the war did not appear to be going well would be seen as an act of desperation aimed at securing victory by fomenting slave rebellion. These were serious concerns, but because they involved practical considerations rather than principle, they could easily be overcome should conditions change. After all, Lincoln and the Republicans in general had come to power on the basis of their antislavery convictions, convictions that drew reinforcement from the war against the "slave power." And because after the secession of the Southern states few proslavery politicians remained in the federal government, opportunities for antislavery action were greatly enhanced. Indeed, from the very beginning of the war, most Republicans were determined to take advantage of changed conditions in a way that was impossible in time of peace; as historian James Oakes put it, everyone at the time knew "that the Republicans hated slavery, that they intended to undermine it in a variety of ways, [and] that they assumed slaves would claim their freedom by taking advantage of the opportunities war and policy had created."[30]

As the war progressed, practical considerations dictating a move against slavery increasingly outweighed those suggesting caution. To those engaged in foreign diplomacy, it seemed evident that so long as the Confederates could portray the war as one for self-determination their effort would find considerable support among Europeans, whereas redefining the war as one over slavery was likely to undercut such support and prevent European powers (especially Great Britain) from recognizing—and providing aid to—the Confederacy. Such a redefinition could also help alleviate the growing manpower shortage faced by Union military forces as the initial enthusiasm of volunteers expecting a quick victory faded and the reality of a long, bloody conflict set in. One did not have to be an ardent egalitarian to favor the use of Black troops; as Iowa Senator James W. Grimes put it, he would prefer to "see a negro shot down in battle rather than the son of a Dubuquer." But the most powerful force pushing the Union war effort in an antislavery direction was the growing radicalization of both Northern public opinion and the Republican Party (which increasingly represented Northern public opinion). As the war dragged on without a foreseeable end, an expanding contingent of radical Republicans sought to give the

Union cause meaning by transforming the war into a struggle for freedom. Reviled by their politically impotent Democratic opponents as dangerous revolutionaries and "nigger lovers," radicals saw themselves as the vanguard of the future who would help transform the United States—including the South— into a new, more democratic society. "The radical men are the men of principle . . . ," declared Ohio's Senator Benjamin F. Wade. "They are not your slippery politicians who can jigger this way or that, or construe a thing any way to suit the present occasion."[31]

Given that Lincoln shared most of the radicals' goals—although not always their temperament—it is hardly surprising that he took advantage of the changed political landscape to move against slavery; because of his passionate commitment to free-labor ideals, explaining his decision to emancipate is considerably easier than explaining Alexander II's. Indeed, by the time he wrote the famous letter to Greeley, Lincoln had already made his decision. Working closely with Republicans of all stripes, he skillfully maneuvered to outflank those who counseled continued caution, warning the Rebels on 22 September 1862 that unless they laid down their arms he would issue an Emancipation Proclamation at the start of the new year, and then making good on his warning. Later, Lincoln continued to work for passage of a new constitutional amendment, an amendment that (unlike his Proclamation) would abolish slavery throughout the United States, in loyal as well as Rebel territory.[32]

Like Alexander II's 1861 edict, Lincoln's Emancipation Proclamation appears as considerably less than a clarion call to freedom; indeed, historian Richard Hofstadter quipped that it "had all the moral grandeur of a bill of lading." Declaring free all slaves in the "States and parts of States" currently in rebellion, Lincoln urged them to "labor faithfully for reasonable wages" and "abstain from all violence, unless in necessary self-defence," and announced that they would henceforth be "received into the armed service of the United States." Although terming the Proclamation "an act of justice," the president justified it on the ground of military necessity, as a measure taken by the "Commander-in-Chief . . . in time of actual armed rebellion against the authority and government of the United States." As historian Laura F. Edwards pointed out, the Emancipation Proclamation applied to *some* slaves but did not abolish slavery; there was "no universal offer of freedom." In fact, because it applied only to slaves in areas controlled by the Confederacy, the Proclamation did not immediately free anyone held in actual bondage.[33]

Nevertheless, it would be hard to overstate the Proclamation's significance. It marked both a symbolic and an actual turning point in the war, the transformation of a war to preserve the Union into a war to remake the Union. Henceforth, there could be no doubt that a Union military victory would bring with it the end of slavery. The Proclamation provided hope to proponents of freedom, from slaves in the South to abolitionists and radicals in the North, and it began the process of enshrining Lincoln in the minds of Black and white Americans as the Great Emancipator and Father Abraham. It opened the way to military service for more than a hundred and eighty thousand African Americans, the majority former slaves from the South, who played an increasingly important role in securing Union victory and whose service further radicalized Northern public opinion by demonstrating to often skeptical whites the ability of Blacks to be more than Sambos. The presence of Black troops among the advancing Yankees had a particularly galvanizing impact on Southern African Americans (and proved correspondingly horrifying to many Southern whites). Meanwhile, with the federal government now firmly committed to the eradication of slavery, Union military commanders increased their experimentation with various forms of free and semi-free labor in the ever-expanding areas liberated from Confederate control, from the sea islands off the coast of South Carolina and Georgia, to the lower Mississippi Valley; missionaries and teachers flocked to these areas as well. Already practically dead at the war's end, slavery expired legally in December 1865, when three-quarters of the states had ratified the Thirteenth Amendment to the Constitution, passed by Congress almost a year earlier. The forty-three-word amendment barred slavery and "involuntary servitude" from "the United States, or any place subject to their jurisdiction," and gave Congress power to enforce the measure "by appropriate legislation."[34]

The Thirteenth Amendment said nothing about the status of the former slaves or the terms of the emancipation settlement. Although these questions received some attention during the war, the decision of what to do with the South—and with the four million newly freed African Americans—came only *after* the defeat of the Confederacy, when Americans engaged in an intense three-year debate over the proper course of what came to be known as "Reconstruction." In settling on the terms of the new order only after emancipation was already a fait accompli, the American process of reform differed strikingly from the Russian. Equally significant was the contrast between the largely secret planning that preceded emancipation in Russia and the very public—democratic—debate over Reconstruction in the United States, where three years of Congressional deliberations occurred in full public spotlight, and indeed with widespread public participation. Throughout the country Americans debated the proper course of action, bombarded newspaper editors and

Congressmen with letters, and voted for political candidates on the basis of their views on how to remake the South.[35]

Not only did the public play a much larger role, the former owners were far less involved in the American than in the Russian deliberations: unlike Russian nobles, whom Alexander carefully cultivated as pillars of the autocracy, Southern planters found themselves pilloried as traitors who deserved severe punishment—even death. "I would hang liberally . . . ," declared Indiana's fiery radical Congressman George W. Julian in 1865. "I would dispose of a score or two of the most conspicuous of the rebel leaders, not for vengeance, but to satisfy public justice, and make expensive the enterprise of treason for all time to come." Julian's views were extreme, but most Northerners agreed that leading Confederates deserved some sort of punishment for having rebelled against the United States; certainly they should not be allowed to help decide the fate of their former slaves. On a practical level, Northern Democrats, who appeared as backward-looking obstructionists intent on sabotaging Republican efforts on behalf of progress and freedom, were almost as marginalized politically. In the Thirty-Ninth Congress, which sat from 1865 to 1867, Democrats could command only forty-six of 191 votes in the House of Representatives and ten of fifty-two in the Senate. The debate over Reconstruction took place largely within the Republican Party, whose members differed sharply on particulars but shared a broad commitment to free labor and equal rights.[36]

That shared commitment helps explain the far-reaching character of the Republicans' emancipation policy compared to the policy followed in Russia—and for that matter most other countries that abolished slavery and serfdom in the nineteenth century. At the end of the war, Republicans had already agreed on two unusually radical principles: emancipation would be immediate, and it would be uncompensated. Over the next two years they moved far beyond these two principles, putting together a Reconstruction program that centered on providing equal civil rights to all citizens and equal political rights to all male citizens. There were several sources propelling this leftward trend, which peaked in 1867 but continued to find expression thereafter in such measures as the impeachment of President Andrew Johnson in 1868, the passage and ratification of the Fifteenth Amendment to the Constitution in 1869 and 1870, and a more powerful civil rights act in 1875. These sources included a war-generated enthusiasm for remaking the South; a new recognition of African American capabilities—from military valor to a demonstrated passion for learning—that at least for a while helped turn racists into egalitarians; and growing anger at reports that many Southern whites, encouraged by President

Johnson's lenient "restoration" plan, were showing increasing unwillingness to accept the results of the war. Whereas former Confederates seemed compliant immediately after the surrender, a spate of reports by Northern travelers—from politicians to journalists—warned by the fall of 1865 that Southern whites were increasingly defiant and atrocities against freedpeople (and white Unionists) increasingly common. Describing a region characterized by resentment and an "absence of that national spirit which forms the basis of true loyalty and patriotism," General Carl Schurz reported in December that hostility to free African Americans was so widespread in the South that "unadulterated free labor cannot be had at present, unless the national government holds its protective and controlling hand over it." "For the future of the republic," Schurz concluded, "it is far less important that this business of reconstruction be done quickly than that it be well done."[37]

Other Republicans agreed, and when Congress assembled in December 1865, it refused to accept President Johnson's restoration plan (whose principal requirements of the ex-Confederate states were that they ratify the Thirteenth Amendment and disavow the right to secession) or to seat the congressmen elected under it, and instead created a Joint Congressional Committee to consider the best course of Reconstruction. Over the next two years, the South remained in political limbo, with state governments elected by whites under the Johnson plan jockeying for power with military occupation forces, which routinely countermanded state laws, including those passed to keep African Americans in a state of subservience. Collectively known as "black codes," these laws varied from state to state but typically restricted Blacks' property ownership and occupations, and often restricted their geographic mobility through provisions allowing officials to impose forced labor on "vagrants" and children without adequate parental support. Meanwhile, the Joint Congressional Committee on Reconstruction held hearings and drafted legislation, which Congress debated, revised, and eventually passed, often over President Johnson's veto. Based on the constitutional requirement that Congress ensure the states a "republican form of government," this legislation culminated in four "Reconstruction Acts" of 1867, which set the ground rules for the South's new political order, and the Fourteenth and Fifteenth Amendments to the Constitution, which completed the revolutionary expansion in civil and political rights begun by the Thirteenth Amendment. The increasingly radical nature of congressional sentiment is indicated by measures that did not pass as well as those that did. Whereas in Russia virtually no one (except the peasants) could conceive of confiscating landed estates and distributing them to the former bondspeople, Pennsylvania congressman Thaddeus Stevens's proposal to root the creation of a more democratic South in precisely such a policy received serious consideration—and the support of about one-third of the Republican representatives—in early 1866. (Later that year, Congress *did* pass a Southern Homestead Act designed to provide free federal land to "loyal" citizens—principally Black Americans—in five Deep South states.)[38]

Although it was not yet apparent, the defeat of Stevens's proposal for land confiscation, which was predicated on the dual goals of stripping a bloated aristocracy of its economic base and providing for the freedpeople "until they [could] take care of themselves," presaged a serious limitation in the evolving Republican consensus. Based on "republican" and "free labor" principles that rejected the legitimacy of legally recognized special privileges for the rich and powerful, this consensus also precluded providing what appeared to be special rights for the downtrodden; most Republicans did not agree with Stevens that it was the duty of the federal government to "take care of" the freedpeople. Reconstruction did see some deviation from the dominant laissez-faire understanding of "free labor," most notably in the Freedmen's Bureau, but this government agency was seen by most of its advocates as a temporary, transitional body, not a permanent feature of the new order. Although there was continuing tension between the idea of helping former slaves overcome the results of previous deprivation and allowing them to manage without interference, most Northerners believed that the freedpeople deserved *equal* rights, not *special* consideration; once the constraints of slavery and legal discrimination had been removed, they were to be free to sink or swim on their own. Such an understanding is evident even in the writing of Frederick Douglass, one of the era's most passionate defenders of equal rights. Asking on the eve of emancipation "What shall be done with [the former slaves]?" he replied: "Do nothing with them; mind your business, and let them mind theirs. . . . Just . . . let them alone." This prescription sounded good, but under changed conditions such neglect could be anything but benign.[39]

Given the differences in the way emancipation came to Russia and the Southern United States, it is not surprising that there were also significant differences in the terms of the two emancipation settlements: in most respects these were more favorable to the freedpeople in the South than in Russia, more solicitous of the former owners' interests in Russia than in the South. The broad nature of these differences was indicated by the gradual and compensated emancipation in the one versus the immediate and uncompensated emancipation in the other. More generally, these differences reflected divergent understandings of the new order that belied the common transition from forced to free labor. Despite the pervasive white racism that to some extent worked at cross-purposes with the favorable climate faced by Southern Blacks, in the United States freed slaves were to become citizens of a country whose polity was defined by republican principles of legal equality and democratic principles of equal political rights (for all men). In Russia, by contrast, freed serfs would remain peasants in a country whose order was predicated on political autocracy, social hierarchy, and privileges and obligations that differed according to one's legally defined status.[40]

The Russian legislation of 1861—hundreds of pages long, divided into seventeen separate statutes and two annexes—set in motion a bafflingly complicated process of emancipation. "I have the manifesto and legislation on the peasants," wrote an estate steward in Nizhnii Novgorod Province to his employer several weeks after official promulgation of the emancipation measures, "but so far it is hard for me to understand them clearly." Indeed, as historian G. T. Robinson noted, the provisions were "so verbose, so full of variables, so loaded down with qualifications and exceptions, and in general so astonishingly involved and complicated, that it is difficult to understand how any serf could ever by any possibility have known what rights might be hidden in this legislative haystack." The point is a good one, although of course even if the legislation had been less arcane there would have been plenty of opportunity for confusion among peasants, since few of them were able to read it. Perhaps more noteworthy is the observation that getting a handle on the terms of emancipation posed (and poses) a daunting challenge to *anyone,* including the historian.[41]

A summary overview can help by way of introduction. Although serfs received their "personal freedom" immediately, they remained under the partially circumscribed authority of their former owners as "temporarily obligated" peasants. The actual status of these temporarily obligated peasants was defined separately on each landed estate in "statutory charters" composed by their owners (or those owners' agents), under the watchful eye of "peace mediators," a new group of government officials charged with supervising the peasants' transition to freedom. After a two-year transition period, most temporarily obligated peasants could begin the process of becoming "peasant proprietors" through a complex and drawn-out process known as "redemption," whereby they collectively paid for their land allotments—and in effect for their freedom—with interest, over a forty-nine-year period. House servants, who did not have landed allotments under serfdom and were therefore excluded from the redemption process, were free to leave their former owners after the two-year transition period was over.[42]

If that summary seems complicated enough, the full complexity of Russia's emancipation process becomes evident only in the myriad provisions spelled out in excruciating detail in the 1861 legislation. To oversee the transition from serfdom to freedom, this legislation created an elaborate new governmental bureaucracy. The key figures in this new machinery were the peace mediators, whose task was to supervise peasant affairs and peasant-landlord relations at the local level. Typically numbering some thirty to fifty per province and charged with handling "controversies, complaints, and misunderstandings" between pomeshchiki and temporarily obligated peasants, the peace mediators in some ways constituted the Russian equivalent of American Freedmen's Bureau officials; notably, however, all the mediators were noblemen, and the great majority were serfholders. In each provincial district, the mediators collectively constituted the District Conference of Peace Mediators, above which was the Provincial Office for Peasant Affairs, which in turn was subordinate at the national level to the Main Committee for the Organization of Village Conditions. All the members of these supervisory agencies, as well as the various government officials who interacted with them—the district police chief (*ispravnik*), the district marshal of nobility, the provincial marshal of nobility, and the provincial governor—were noblemen.[43]

At a lower level, the newly freed peasants had their own administrative organizations, also defined in the 1861 legislation. Building on the traditional village commune (*obshchina* or *mir*), which now received official governmental recognition, the third section of the General Regulation established two new peasant bodies—the village *obshchestvo* (or community) and above it the *volost'* (or township), which consisted of several *obshchestva*—each with its own assemblies and elected peasant leaders; each *volost'* also had a peasant court with four to twelve elected peasant judges. These new bodies were designed to regularize peasant self-government, act as intermediaries between village and government, and partially replace the authority of former owners. As under serfdom, peasants would continue to be subject to local communal authority as well as the higher authority of pomeshchiki and the state, but with the reduced powers of noble landlords, the role of peasant communal organizations would be substantially enhanced; they would now decide, for example, whether and when peasants could leave their home villages. Peasant life would continue to be highly collective, and on a day-to-day basis higher authorities—whether pomeshchiki, noble officials, or the state—would continue to seem remote. As historian Alfred J. Rieber put it, "The state had virtually no effect on peasant culture.... It was a kind of absentee government." The "personal freedom" that peasants received with emancipation was in many respects collective rather than individual.[44]

It was also at first severely limited. Although they could no longer be sold, and they had the right to marry at will and own both personal and real property, "temporarily obligated" peasants remained under the "estate and police guardianship" of their former owners. Equally important, although the obligation to provide those former owners with payments in kind (such as butter, eggs, milk, and chickens) ceased "immediately and everywhere," for the time being the peasants still had to pay essentially the same cash obrok dues that they had as serfs and perform up to three days of barshchina per week for men and two for women. Skeptical peasants might very well be justified in wondering whether they really were "free."[45]

Indeed, the next step in the gradual transition to freedom regularized rather than abolished the freedpeople's obligations to their former owners. Statutory charters that pomeshchiki were charged with drafting within one year of the 19 February 1861 emancipation decree were to stipulate the obligations and land allotments of their temporarily obligated peasants, according to detailed guidelines that varied according to local conditions. The twenty-seven provinces of Russia, New Russia, and Belorussia were divided into three zones (non-black-earth, black-earth, and steppe), which in turn were subdivided into nine, eight, and twelve "localities." For each of these localities, the legislation set out the maximum and minimum permissible size of peasants' average landholdings on an estate, with adjustments required if their existing allotments were too small or too large. In the non-black-earth zone the maximum size of allotments ranged from three to seven desiatiny per soul, while in the more fertile black-earth zone the range was 2.75 to six desiatiny; in both zones, the minimum size was fixed at one-third the maximum. (In the steppe zone, by contrast, rather than having minima and maxima, there were fixed allotment sizes ranging from three to twelve desiatiny per soul, according to local conditions.) Meanwhile, the charters were also to stipulate the labor and quitrent obligations that peasants owed their pomeshchiki, with barshchina henceforth limited to no more than forty days per year for men and thirty for women; labor obligations that had previously exceeded these limits would be commuted into obrok payments, which now constituted the peasants' principal obligation to their former owners. For peasants holding the maximum allotments, annual obrok payments were set at eight to twelve rubles per soul, while those with smaller holdings would pay proportionally less.[46]

Once it was drafted, the statutory charter would be submitted to the local peace mediator for verification, although if a pomeshchik (or his agents) failed to compose a charter within the one-year limit, the mediator was to draft it for him. Following the verification process—attended by the landowner or his agent, peasant representatives, and "three conscientious outside witnesses" (who were usually neighboring peasants)—the charter would be read to all the peasants on the estate and signed by representatives of all the parties. Although the peasants had the right to withhold their approval, they did not have the ability to prevent a charter's implementation, which could go into effect with or without their consent: if the peasants objected to the terms of a charter, the peace mediator would attach an explanation of their objections, and in extreme cases get approval from the Provincial Office for Peasant Affairs, but the mediator was not obliged to pay any heed to those objections. Indeed, it would eventually turn out that a majority of peasants had charters imposed on them without their consent.[47]

All statutory charters were to be in force by 19 February 1863, bringing to an end the initial two-year transition period and setting in motion the next stage in the drawn-out sequel to serfdom, known as "redemption," in which the peasants began paying for their landed allotments and thereby left temporarily obligated status to become "peasant proprietors." Although redemption of the peasants' "farmsteads" (*usad'by*)—the small plots of land attached to their huts—was mandatory immediately on implementation of the statutory charters, the redemption of their much more extensive field land was a more complicated—and costly—affair. It could begin immediately if peasants and pomeshchiki were able to work out redemption agreements or if pomeshchiki chose (as was their right) to impose such agreements on their peasants unilaterally, but it could also be delayed for years or even decades. Once begun, the redemption payments would stretch out over forty-nine years.

The peasants' redemption bill (paid collectively, by all the peasants on an estate and usually calculated per male soul) was directly based on the level of their annual obrok payments as defined in the statutory charters, by capitalizing that obrok at 6 percent; an annual six-ruble obrok would yield a total redemption price of a hundred rubles. But there was another option: peasants who were unable or unwilling to take on the normal level of redemption debt could choose to accept smaller land allotments, equal to one-quarter the maximum size (and therefore smaller than the minimum size prescribed in the charters) without owing any redemption payments at all. (Eventually, fewer than 10 percent of the former serfs opted to receive these small "gratuitous" holdings.) The actual redemption transaction, except for peasants who accepted gratuitous holdings, involved a complex three-sided arrangement under which the government would advance pomeshchiki most of the money they were to receive from their peasants—80 percent if the peasants received maximum allotments, 75 percent otherwise—partly in 5 percent government bonds and partly in certificates that would gradually be converted into such bonds. Pomeshchiki who had unilaterally imposed redemption on their serfs would receive only this 75 to 80 percent (which provided a disincentive to such unilateral imposition). Pomeshchiki who had entered into voluntary redemption agreements with their former serfs would receive the remaining 20 to 25 percent directly from the peasants under terms mutually agreed upon, such as payment in money or labor services over several years. The main—and more onerous—redemption obligation shouldered by the freedpeople was repaying the government, with interest, the money it had advanced to pomeshchiki on their behalf. With each annual installment amounting to 6 percent of their redemption loan (and thus the equivalent of their old obrok), the peasants' eventual redemption payment (including interest), stretched out over forty-nine years, would equal 2.94 times the value of their loan (0.06×49).[48]

Subsequent legislation modified but did not fundamentally change this redemption process. In 1863, concerned over the potentially destabilizing impact of the Polish Revolution on peasants in the western provinces, the government transferred all peasants in eight Belorussian and western Ukrainian provinces from temporarily obligated status to peasant proprietorship, abolished their remaining barshchina obligations, and reduced their obrok fees (as defined in the statutory charters) by 20 percent. Two imperial decrees issued in 1881 transferred all remaining temporarily obligated peasants (about one-fifth of those covered by the 1861 emancipation) to redemption status as of 1883, and slightly reduced the redemption payments that both they and existing peasant proprietors would henceforth owe. Finally, in 1905, under mounting revolutionary pressure, the government cut redemption obligations in half for 1906 and canceled them entirely beginning in 1907—some forty-six years after the initiation of emancipation. Few of the adult serfs freed in 1861 lived to see this culmination of the emancipation process.[49]

Although the terms of the American emancipation settlement—as defined in the Reconstruction legislation—were the product of lengthy debate and political compromise, they were conceptually far simpler than their Russian equivalents and are easier to summarize. The underlying principle on which the evolving American legislation rested, and from which it occasionally deviated, was the extension to the former slaves of equal civil and political rights. Some proponents of a radical restructuring of the social order favored going considerably further, providing compensatory benefits (such as free land) to the freedpeople and imposing punitive restrictions (such as long-term military rule) on the defeated Confederates. Some opponents of the eventual compromise were leery of giving equal rights to African Americans and warned against going too far in revolutionizing the South. In the end, however, the opponents of Reconstruction proved too politically marginal to have much influence in determining the nature of the new order, while the supporters of more radical change, although a significant force in the Republican Party, were able to secure only limited steps beyond establishing equal rights. At the heart of the Reconstruction compromise was the decision to turn slaves into republican citizens.[50]

It proved easier to agree on civil than on political rights. By March 1866, when Congress passed the country's first civil rights act, the Republican Party—despite being divided into diverse factions and subfactions—gave the measure almost unanimous support: no Republican senators and only six Republican representatives voted against it, and the following month Congress overrode President Johnson's veto, enacting a bill over a presidential veto for only the seventh time in American history. The 1866 act provided the first clear definition of United States citizenship, which belonged to "all persons born in the United States and not subject to any foreign power, excluding Indians not taxed," and declared that citizens "of every race and color" had equal civil rights "in every State and Territory of the United States." These rights included "the right to make and enforce contracts, to sue, be parties, and give evidence, to inherit, purchase, lease sell, hold, and convey real and personal property, and to full and equal benefit of all laws and proceedings for the security of person and property." The Fourteenth Amendment, passed by Congress in 1866 and ratified by the states in 1868, enshrined the Civil Rights Act's definition of citizenship in the Constitution and replaced its somewhat cumbersome listing of citizens' rights with a simpler and more elegant declaration that extended basic rights to noncitizens as well as citizens: "No State shall make or enforce any law which shall abridge the privileges or immunities of citizens of the United States," the measure declared; "nor shall any State deprive any person of life, liberty, or property, without due process of law, nor deny to any person within its jurisdiction the equal protection of the laws."[51]

Securing political rights to African Americans was more complicated, in part because doing so at the federal level involved a major breach of the traditional understanding that suffrage was a matter controlled by the individual states and in part because the abstract question of who should have the right to vote was closely tied to the practical question of how to go about reconstructing the Southern states. Nevertheless, by the summer of 1866 there was little doubt that Black suffrage would lie at the heart of this reconstruction effort. The Fourteenth Amendment, without quite requiring such suffrage, provided a strong incentive for it (especially to states with large Black populations) by mandating that if a state withheld the franchise from any of its adult male citizens, "except for participation in rebellion or other crime," that state's representation in Congress would be proportionally reduced; if South Carolina did not allow Black males to vote, it would lose more than half its congressional representation. The Fifteenth Amendment, passed in 1869 and ratified in 1870, succinctly removed any ambiguity, declaring that "the right of citizens of the United States to vote shall not be denied or abridged by the United States or by any State on account of race, color, or previous condition of servitude."[52]

If equal civil and political rights constituted the central principles of the new order, their method of implementation was set forth in the Reconstruction Act that Congress passed over President Johnson's veto in March 1867, clarified and strengthened by three supplemental Reconstruction Acts, also enacted over presidential vetoes. Declaring that "no legal State governments or adequate protection for life or property now exists in the rebel States," this measure divided the former Confederacy (except for Tennessee) into five military districts, each under the command of a Union general who, supported by a "sufficient military force," would "protect all persons in their rights of person and property" and supervise the construction of new, loyal governments. The process required each state to call a constitutional convention whose delegates were "elected by the male citizens . . . of whatever race, color, or previous condition," which in turn would draft a "republican" constitution that provided for full manhood suffrage, submit that constitution to popular statewide ratification, and then forward the ratified measure to Congress "for examination and approval." Once the constitution was approved and the new state legislature elected under it had ratified the Fourteenth Amendment to the Constitution, the state would regain both its representation in Congress and its right to self-government, and military rule would come to an end. In short, the Reconstruction Acts provided for a rapid restoration of self-rule to the ex-Confederate states rather than the prolonged military government that some radicals favored, and based the remaking of the Southern order on the newly democratized states themselves, bolstered by Black suffrage, rather than federal supervision.[53]

There were at least two significant exceptions to this quintessentially American consensus against relying on an expanded federal bureaucracy or on what would now be termed "affirmative action" to help Southern African Americans in their transition to freedom. The first and most important was the Bureau of Refugees, Freedmen, and Abandoned Lands, popularly known as the "Freedmen's Bureau." Established by Congress in March 1865, and staffed largely by Union army officers, it performed a variety of functions, from supervising the establishment of the free-labor system and helping set up schools for former slaves, to distributing food to destitute whites and Blacks and mediating disputes between planters and plantation laborers. Indeed, the Freedmen's Bureau constituted the first major "welfare" agency undertaken by the federal government, in some ways a precursor to New Deal agencies created some seven decades later. Also a noteworthy departure from the laissez-faire principles that guided the federal government's approach to the freedpeople was the Southern Homestead Act, passed by Congress in 1866 to enable residents of five Deep South states to acquire land previously held by the federal government. Homesteading on public land would (the measure's sponsors hoped) enable tens of thousands of former slaves to become independent farmers and serve as a partial if less sweeping substitute for the defeated plan to confiscate and redistribute Rebel plantations.[54]

But despite their significance, the history of the Freedmen's Bureau and the Southern Homestead Act in many ways demonstrates the limits rather than the extent of efforts to move beyond the equal rights consensus. Understaffed and underfunded, the Freedmen's Bureau was always seen as a temporary agency rather than a long-term establishment, and for this reason its creation drew support from virtually all congressional Republicans, including moderates opposed to basing Reconstruction on a significant expansion of federal power; although not officially abolished until 1872, the bureau sharply cut back most of its functions once normal state governments were functioning in 1868. The Southern Homestead Act also fell squarely within the equal rights paradigm. Modeled on the national Homestead Act of 1862, it was available to white as well as Black Southerners (although during its first six months of operation it gave preference to those who had been loyal during the war), and by relying exclusively on public land, it avoided the taint of radical agrarianism associated with failed proposals for land redistribution. Although any effort to provide former slaves with land represented a new departure in what had been a slaveholding republic, the modest scope of the effort belied the enormity of the challenge: for a variety of reasons (given in chapter 2), only about four thousand Black Southerners—most of whom resided in the still sparsely settled state of Florida—filed homestead claims between 1866 and 1869.[55]

In short, despite the desire of some radicals for far-reaching federal programs that would redress the wrongs suffered under slavery and provide a long-term guardianship over the ex-Confederate states, equal legal rights and competition in the marketplace constituted the guiding principles of the American emancipation settlement. Although Frederick Douglass became a strong proponent of a far-reaching Reconstruction policy, his 1862 statement (see earlier in this chapter and note 39) that "nothing" should be done with—or by implication for—the freedpeople except to "let them alone" captured the thinking behind the American emancipation settlement. The former slaves would receive equal rights but no special compensatory favors.

In the broadest sense, the world's two great emancipations of the 1860s had much in common. In both Russia and the United States, governments that for decades had struggled unsuccessfully with how to end entrenched systems of human bondage took advantage of new conditions to take the plunge. Slaves and serfs received their personal freedom, and societies predicated on unfree labor underwent massive transformation centered on the construction of new, free-labor relations. In both countries, this transition to free labor was a process fraught with uncertainty, one that aroused great hopes, fears, and confusion among the freedpeople, their former owners, and a variety of observers in the two countries and beyond. In both Russia and the South the announcement of emancipation marked not only the end of unfree labor but also the beginning of an intense struggle over precisely what would succeed it.

But juxtaposing the terms of the emancipation settlement in the two countries also makes clear some fundamental differences both in those terms and in the prospects for successful restructuring of the social order. In Russia, emancipation was to be gradual, former serfholders would receive compensation, most former serfs would receive—and pay dearly for—land allotments, and the peasants would continue to have a distinctive legal status in a hierarchical and autocratic society in which different groups had different rights and obligations. In the South, emancipation was immediate, the former slaveholders received no compensation for their losses, and the former slaves became the beneficiaries of legislation that made them full citizens in a republican society that—at least in theory—provided equal legal rights to all. The American settlement was conceptually simple: the freedpeople were now citizens, but (with some temporary exceptions) they would have to fend for themselves as individuals in a competitive environment. The Russian version was far more complicated, in terms of both how the new order would be implemented and what it would actually mean for peasants in a society that treated different social groups differently.

Underlying these differences was a contrast in the way the balance of power operated in the two countries. Because most slave owners were supporters of the Confederate Rebellion, they lost the right to help determine—and in most respects to supervise the creation of—the new order. Despite the widespread racism that still existed throughout America, African Americans were at least briefly the beneficiaries of a considerable amount of good will among Northerners who had come to see the Civil War as a war against slavery. There was no equivalent discrediting of Russian nobles, who retained both their high social standing and their dominant power in the countryside, and who played a key role in implementing the new order. A clear indication of this contrast emerges from comparing Freedmen's Bureau officials and peace mediators, who in some ways performed similar tasks in supervising at the ground level the creation of "free" societies. As becomes evident in future chapters, both groups ran the gamut from enthusiastic supporters to determined opponents of the freedpeople's interests, and both can be seen as subscribing to intermediate ideals that did not conform entirely to the wishes of either the freedpeople or their former masters. That said, the composition of the two groups was strikingly different, and presaged different results from their efforts as well. The vast majority of Freedmen's Bureau agents were Union Army officers, conditioned by four years of war to view Southern planters as the enemy, traitors to the nation and oppressors of African Americans. Virtually all the peace mediators were local noblemen who, despite the benevolent intentions of many, were conditioned by a lifetime of experience to see other noblemen as honorable men (with whom they were often acquainted) and to see peasants as distant and mysterious beings. It is hard to avoid the conclusion that the mediators were in a notably poor position to provide even-handed judgments when supervising pomeshchik-peasant relations; indeed, asking them to protect the interests of the former serfs resembles nothing so much as asking the fox to guard the chickens.

The juxtaposition of these two versions of emancipation casts new light on developments in both countries, by placing them in broader context, and can contribute to reevaluation of historical interpretations for each. Because historians focusing on one country are prone to consider its history as "normal," considering it in the context of alternative versions of similar historical processes can be salutary.

Take, for example, a recent debate over the severity of Russia's terms of emancipation. Although most historians have considered those terms highly unfavorable to the peasants, some recent scholars have questioned whether the economic condition of the post-emancipation peasantry was in fact as dire as often assumed; in the most detailed and technically impressive of these challenges to the conventional wisdom, historian Steven L. Hoch went beyond questioning the impoverishment of Russian peasants in the late nineteenth century to insist that "the land legislation of 1861 was tilted more favorably toward the serfs than has been appreciated." Pointing to serious flaws in the many statistical studies of land prices, redemption costs, and allotment sizes, he countered that when these flaws are corrected peasants actually paid "a fair, if not below, market price for a viable subsistence plot." Noting that "the vast majority of serfs upon being freed either kept their existing allotment or had their allotment reduced to the prereform modal (most common) size," he suggested that "this was neither an unreasonable state policy nor an undesirable social and economic outcome" and concluded that "unlike slaves in the American South, serfs in Russia got a whole lot more than freedom."[56]

Despite its technical proficiency, Hoch's analysis was limited by a set of unquestioned assumptions about what is "fair," "reasonable," and "desirable," as well as by a limited understanding of how Russian emancipation fit into the broader context—in this case particularly that provided by the emancipation of American slaves. Posing the question of whether peasants paid "too much" for "too little" land implies a particular understanding of what was the *right* ("fair") price for land and how much land peasants *should* have received that unselfconsciously reflects the values of Russia's governing class: a fair price would be the prevailing price, under existing conditions. From the peasants' point of view, however, such a judgment was beside the point because there was no such thing as a fair price: they regarded the land as theirs and believed that under a true emancipation they would not have to pay *anything* for it. They were, in any case, quite unaware of whether they were paying slightly more or slightly less than the land was worth—as, Hoch demonstrated, was almost everyone else.

In short, despite Hoch's dazzling analysis demonstrating the statistical ignorance of virtually everyone who came before him, this analysis is significant only within a very narrow conceptual framework. Hoch addressed the land question almost totally in isolation, as if selling peasants the "right" amount of land for the "right" price defined a just emancipation; indeed, he maintained that the peasants got such a good deal that "the landed nobility may not have possessed the economic hegemony to ensure the manor or estate even in a much attenuated form." But economic hegemony cannot be addressed in isolation from political hegemony: post-emancipation Russia was hardly a democracy in which peasants confronted nobles on an even playing field. More important, an observer with a broader contextual framework might very well suggest that there was a good deal of sense in the peasants' judgment that an emancipation settlement forcing them to *pay* for land that they had been using all along, while maintaining for the foreseeable future the obrok obligations that they owed their former owners, was a fraudulent emancipation—whether or not the cost of the land and the size of the obrok obligations were set "fairly." As one group of peasants told a local official in Orenburg Province, "We do not recognize the manifesto of February 19, because the tsar promised us liberty, but now they force us to pay or work for land, and there can be no liberty without land."[57]

But it is Hoch's casual use of the American terms of emancipation to argue that the Russian serfs got a good deal that seems especially blinkered. True, some contemporary Americans made the same argument; as Hoch noted, Thaddeus Stevens, eager to promote land distribution to Southern freedpeople, pointed to the Russian model as a precedent, praised Alexander II as a "wise man" for "compell[ing] the serfs'] masters to give them homesteads upon the very soil which they had tilled," and declared that "the experiment has been a perfect success." But both Stevens and Hoch were misinformed—the former about what happened in Russia and the latter about what happened in the Southern United States. The peasants were not *given* land but forced to buy it, and the former slaves received considerably more than "freedom"; they also received (in law and for a while in fact) equal civil and political rights.[58]

As this example suggests, a comparative framework is also useful in clarifying the nature of the *American* emancipation settlement, which historians have usually studied in isolation. Although for many years most historians condemned Reconstruction as a radical folly that raised the former slaves above their owners, more recently most have questioned (or denied) this radicalism and argued that Reconstruction did not go nearly far enough. Some have stressed the failure of the federal government to protect Black Southerners, others have lamented the failure to distribute land to the freedpeople or provide them with integrated schools, and others still have pointed to the lack of a Republican commitment to break the "class rule" of Southern planters and the consequent "missing revolution" that characterized the post-emancipation South. In overturning the notion of Reconstruction as a vindictive assault on the Southern (white) people, historians typically kept the notion of

Reconstruction as a "tragic era," rooting the tragedy in insufficient rather than excessive radicalism.[59]

If it is easy to detect racism in the traditional view of Reconstruction as *too* radical and more recent liberal or progressive values as underlying the opinion that Reconstruction was not radical *enough*, it is apparent that both judgments reflect a focus that lacks context and is therefore too narrow. The need for broader context is both chronological and spatial. As Howard N. Rabinowitz pointed out, condemning Reconstruction governments for not providing African Americans with integrated schools seems to make sense, until one realizes that the alternative to the segregated schools that mushroomed during Reconstruction consisted not of integrated schools but of no schools at all; in his elegant formulation, the alternative to segregation was not integration but "exclusion." When judged from the vantage point of one hundred and fifty years later, the American emancipation settlement may appear excessively timid, but to most contemporaries such a judgment would not have made much sense. In 1860, anyone suggesting that in ten years not only would slavery be abolished in the South but the former slaves would even be sitting on juries and representing their states in Congress would have been regarded as hopelessly deluded. Context counts.[60]

But it is through comparison over space that the unusually radical nature of the American emancipation settlement—made possible by the unusual way in which American slavery came to an end—becomes most clear. If the very different terms of Russia's emancipation legislation make the American version of emancipation seem notably far reaching, it is worth observing that in most respects it was the United States rather than Russia that proved unusual. Only in Haiti, where slavery was overthrown by violent revolution, did the balance of power seem to favor the freedpeople more than in the American South. Elsewhere, as in Russia, emancipation was often a gradual process, the former bondspeople became apprentices or at best suffered benign neglect, and the former owners received compensation for their losses. Today, advocates of racial justice sometimes propose that the descendants of slaves should receive "reparations" for the atrocities committed against their ancestors; at the time of emancipation, however, the debate was typically over whether and how the former *slave owners* should be compensated for the loss of their human property. Usually they were.[61]

In both Russia and the United States, the freedpeople faced daunting obstacles as they struggled to make the most of their newfound freedom. The obstacles were most apparent in Russia, where a convoluted and drawn-out emancipation process to be conducted under a balance of power that heavily favored pomeshchiki over peasants defined a less-than-promising environment for the birth of freedom. But in the United States, where the Civil War–induced destruction of planter power and enthusiasm for making citizens of former slaves created an environment that in the short term was unusually favorable for the freedpeople, at least two potential roadblocks suggested likely problems over the longer run. The first of these was an ingrained white racism that, although most virulently expressed in the South, was also widespread in the North and lurked just beneath the surface even among many proponents of a far-reaching Reconstruction policy. The second was the laissez-faire proclivity—accentuated by institutional characteristics that included especially a decentralized (federal) system of government—that underlay the Reconstruction policy and implied an unwillingness to intervene on behalf of the freedpeople except in extraordinary circumstances. The particular extraordinary circumstance that generated this intervention was the coincidence of Reconstruction as a sequel to slavery and Reconstruction as a sequel to the Civil War, but a perceptive observer might have wondered how long the favorable climate for the freedpeople would last, as wartime passions cooled and war-generated sympathy for African Americans waned.

For the time being, however, such worries were remote. To those who saw themselves as friends of liberty—abolitionists, free-labor advocates, and of course the freedpeople themselves—events in Russia and the United States seemed to presage the dawning of a bright new era. Herzen praised Alexander II as a "liberator" and published an enthusiastic letter from the Italian revolutionary Giuseppe Garibaldi proclaiming that in freeing the serfs the tsar had "placed himself in the ranks of the greatest benefactors of humanity." Herzen's colleague Nikolai Ogarev gushed, "The Manifesto of 19 February has initiated the freedom of the Russian nation [*narod*]." English missionary J. Lang lauded both "the present Emperor and the Russian liberals for this noble act of serf emancipation" and predicted that it would serve as a positive example to other countries—including the United States—to "go and do likewise." American proponents of abolition also saw a positive lesson in Russian emancipation. Writing in the *Atlantic Monthly* in 1862, A. D. White hailed Alexander's triumph over reactionary nobles and predicted a bright future for Russia, while Thaddeus Stevens eagerly asked where he could "find in English a correct history of the emancipation of the Russian serfs, and the terms of their liberation."[62]

The overthrow of American slavery produced equally rapturous responses. After ratification of the Thirteenth Amendment in December 1865, William Lloyd Garrison, who for more than three decades had promoted not only abolition but also other radical causes from women's rights to pacifism and who had always scorned halfway measures, announced suspension of the *Liberator,* noting that its main objective, "the extermination of chattel slavery," had been "gloriously consummated." Georges Clemenceau, as a young (and still idealistic) Washington correspondent for the Paris newspaper *Le Temps,* heaped praise on the radical Republicans for leading a "far-reaching revolution" and was especially impressed by Thaddeus Stevens, who "devoted heart and soul to the service of one ideal, the immediate abolition of slavery." Among the radicals, perhaps no one expressed better than George W. Julian the extraordinary excitement with which they looked to the transformation of the South from a debauched land of slavery to a model republican society. "Instead of large estates, widely scattered settlements, wasteful agriculture, popular ignorance, social degradation, the decline of manufactures, contempt for honest labor, and a pampered oligarchy," Julian's vision of a new South encompassed "small farms, thrifty tillage, free schools, social independence, flourishing manufactures and the arts, respect for honest labor, and equality of political rights." A tall order, perhaps, but in the United States in 1865, as in Russia in 1861, virtually anything seemed possible.[63]

2 • What Kind of Freedom?

The launching of emancipation settled one question—that slavery and serfdom would be abolished—and raised a host of new ones that centered on what would replace them. If it was clear that the former slaves and serfs would now be "free," the precise meaning of that freedom remained to be determined. Even as Americans and Russians felt and expressed a complex combination of hopes, fears, excitement, and despair, they faced uncertainty over what lay ahead. With the nature of the new order up for grabs, emancipation set off an intense class struggle between the freedpeople and their former owners, while government agents sought to impose on an often-confused population their own varied and sometimes murky versions of "freedom." Time, and the playing out of the class struggle, dispelled some of the uncertainty in the two countries but did not resolve the very different understandings of what "freedom" was—or should be—about.

Even before emancipation, Americans and Russians had displayed diverse understandings of "freedom," based in part on diverse interests and in part on diverse experiences. As historian Eric Foner has shown, the pervasive American commitment to "freedom" (and its close twin, "liberty") has masked highly varied ideas about the term's meaning. Not only has the understanding of "freedom" changed over time, it has carried multiple meanings at any given time; for a graphic illustration of this elastic characteristic, one need only note that both abolitionists and proslavery ideologues saw themselves as brave defenders of freedom. Although "freedom" did not fulfill the same unifying function for Russians that it did for Americans, Russians, too, had varied understandings of the term. "Between freedom and freedom, and between slavery and slavery, there is a difference," wrote conservative playwright and poet Ivan Boltin in 1788, in a comment that echoed the sentiments of many proslavery ideologues in the United States; "there is freedom that is worse, more intolerable, than slavery."[1]

Of course, it was a particular kind of freedom that was at issue with emancipation: that of slaves who were Black and serfs who were peasants. Here, too, wildly different understandings competed. Defenders of bondage ridiculed the notion that Blacks and peasants were ready (if they ever would be) for freedom, and they warned ominously that loose talk of freedom could unleash violence, anarchy, a race war, or a new "peasant war" such as the massive Pugachev Rebellion of 1773–74. Some ideologues distinguished between freedom for Blacks or peasants, which was clearly inconceivable because they would confuse freedom with license, and freedom in general; especially in the South, even as they defended the enslavement of African Americans, proslavery propagandists celebrated the freedom of America and its white citizens. But to many defenders of the traditional order, "freedom" itself seemed a dangerously slippery concept, especially since by the middle of the nineteenth century it was increasingly linked with "equality" and revolution. Although he did not intend it to apply to actions by slaves, Thomas Jefferson's declaration that "the tree of liberty must be refreshed from time to time with the blood of patriots and tyrants" could hardly be reassuring to owners of human property.[2]

Just as defenders of bondage used a wide variety of arguments to support their core belief that freeing Blacks and peasants would lead to catastrophe, abolitionists and free-labor advocates shared a core belief in the virtues of freedom even as they had sharply varying notions of what that freedom would—and should—entail. Beginning with the premise that Blacks and peasants were people (a premise that most *defenders* of bondage accepted), opponents of slavery and serfdom insisted that it was wrong for some people to own others. Even those who stopped well short of full-blown abolitionism were troubled by the commodification of human beings. But if Prince I. M. Dolgoruki expressed discomfort at owning "400 persons like me" (see above, Introduction, note 33), to abolitionists and free-labor advocates the ownership of humans represented a burning contradiction. Terming slave owners "manstealers," William Lloyd Garrison based his abolitionism on the fundamental belief that "every man has a right to his own body." The right to what opponents of bondage termed "self-ownership" was central to their evolving understanding of freedom.[3]

Precisely what they meant by "freedom" and "self-ownership," however, was anything but clear. Indeed, often they did not bother to explain their vision for "free" Blacks and peasants, and when they did they expressed a range of views that defy easy categorization. Certainly "freedom" did not necessarily imply "equality." After all, there were already hundreds of thousands of Blacks and millions of peasants—free Blacks and state peasants—who enjoyed some variant of freedom without any pretense to economic or social equality let alone equal political rights, and one could easily imagine the newly "freed" Blacks and peasants simply joining their ranks. At the other extreme, some radical abolitionists (including some white abolitionists) in the United States were racial egalitarians who believed that after the overthrow of slavery there should be no distinction between white and Black, and some Russian radicals—especially those in exile—believed that the overthrow of serfdom should lead to the emergence of a society without legal distinctions among hereditary estates. The relationship between "freedom" and "equality" was an especially pressing problem in the United States, where democratic principles seemed to leave little place for a large group of people who were free without being citizens. Because Russia was a highly stratified society in which different groups had different rights and obligations, it was much easier to contemplate a position for former serfs that stopped well short of legal equality.[4]

Despite the myriad possible positions between these extremes, two basic if overlapping understandings of "freedom" and "self-ownership" for Blacks and peasants characterized the thinking—often, more precisely, the assumptions—of those who opposed bondage. According to the first understanding, the essence of freedom was the right to be compensated for work, and the central feature of self-ownership was the right to sell one's labor power on the open market. Under this formulation, most Blacks and peasants would constitute a free but subservient laboring class. According to the second understanding, freedom meant the right to control one's own life without interference from above, and self-ownership therefore implied the concomitant right to "self-government." Free Blacks and free peasants would no longer be directed by others. Although the first vision of freedom was most common among free-labor advocates, who tended to think most of how overthrowing slavery and serfdom would benefit society at large, and the second among abolitionists, who concentrated more on alleviating the hardships of the slaves and serfs themselves, the two were by no means mutually exclusive; opponents of bondage fit along a continuum stretching between the two outlooks rather than always falling neatly in one category or the other. Indeed, an especially striking expression of the "self-government" ideal is evident in the prewar speeches of Abraham Lincoln (even as he refrained from pressing for the *immediate* abolition of slavery).

Propounding one of the most radical versions of the free-labor doctrine—"that labor is prior to, and independent of capital; indeed, that, in fact, capital is the fruit of labor"—he asked, "If the negro *is* a man, is it not to that extent, a total destruction of self-government, to say that he too shall not govern *himself*?" Lincoln's democratic insistence that "the doctrine of self-government is right— absolutely and eternally right," implied an unusually far-reaching (if yet ill-defined) vision of a post-emancipation world.[5]

Indeed, "self-ownership" and "self-government" were also at the heart of the way slaves and serfs conceived of "freedom." Their implications were somewhat different, if complementary. The bondspeople's understanding of freedom as self-ownership was directly tied to their sense of exploitation— their belief that their owners reaped all or most of the rewards of their labor. Displaying an elemental, intuitive grasp of the labor theory of value, they adhered to what Frederick Law Olmsted referred to as the "agrarian notion . . . that the result of labour belongs of right to the labourer." Both slaves and serfs regarded appropriating goods from their owners as "taking" rather than stealing, and considered as theirs property—land, goods, and money—that legally belonged to their owners. This understanding was especially strong in Russia, where noble estates were typically divided between seigneurial land and allotment land that peasants held communally—"We are yours but the land is ours," the peasants tell their masters in a widely known proverb—but slaves in the Southern United States as well possessed what they considered "their" property. After the Civil War, when the Southern Claims Commission was set up to hear complaints of wartime property loss by "loyal" Southerners, many of the claims were filed by former slaves. Unresolved, and usually unasked, was the question of whether slaves and serfs regarded as rightfully theirs *all* the land they cultivated or only a significant share of it, but implicit in their understanding of self-ownership was the belief that freedom had to end the exploitative relationship in which their owners grew rich off their labor. Needless to say, this was an understanding of "self-ownership" that differed significantly from that of all but the most radical of the abolitionist and free-labor reformers.[6]

Even more important than "self-ownership" in their understanding of freedom was the bondspeople's longing for "self-government." Central to this longing was the desire to get as far as possible from the servile dependence imposed by slavery and serfdom, to secure as much independence as possible. There were many different manifestations of this striving for self-government, as slaves and serfs struggled to carve autonomous spheres in which they could live at least partially away from the supervision of owners and their subordinates. Although these efforts were on the whole more successful in Russia than in the South, because American slavery was in general more intrusive than Russian serfdom in the lives of the bondspeople, in neither country were owners able to establish total control over their human property. Still, the control was galling enough that to slaves and serfs escaping it became a defining feature of "freedom." Under this understanding, "freedom" meant not being ordered around or constantly told what to do, and not facing punishment for displeasing authority in ways too numerous to count. Frederick Douglass's admonition to "just to let them alone" perfectly captured this understanding of what freedom should entail: to be free would be to manage one's own affairs, without outside interference.[7]

Still, such an understanding left lots of questions unanswered, many of which can be subsumed under the question "Self-government by whom?" Lincoln's version—which was also implicit in the understanding of the bondspeople—focused on the right of the individual to control his or her body, but there were other possibilities as well. Russian serfs were already familiar with self-government at the local level, through the peasant commune, and research by Anthony Kaye and others suggests that many American slaves also had a proto-peasant form of local consciousness, seeing themselves as members of "neighborhoods." Such consciousness stood in tension, however, with a sense of being slaves and serfs in general, which in turn overlapped with African American and peasant identities, and raised the question of some sort of broader—popular—self-government. But who constituted a people? The prospect of emancipation seemed likely to make "blackness" and "peasantness" more salient than servile (and then former-servile) status, but at the same time recollection of the shared experience of bondage could hardly be expected to vanish quickly. Finally, what would be the relationship between self-government—whether conceived in individual, communal, or collective terms—and the existing Russian and American governments? To what extent would freedpeople participate in governing Russia and the United States, or particular regions or localities of Russia and the United States? What—if any—political rights would they enjoy?[8]

The onset of emancipation indicated that resolving these questions would not be easy. As freedpeople and government officials acted on diverse understandings of what freedom was all about, the former masters vacillated wildly between wishful assertions that any changes would be cosmetic and fearful lamentations about a world turned upside down. "The landowners thought that everything would remain the same, and that only names would change," recalled one peace mediator. "Thus ... *barshchina* would be called work obligations, *obrok* money obligations, serfs temporarily obligated persons, and the authority of the landowner would be enforced not by the *ispravnik* or the *stanovoi* but by the peace arbitrator." A letter in the *Huntsville* (Alabama) *Advocate* expressed almost precisely the same view: "The negro ... bears the *same relation* to us *now, de facto,* as *before*. We controlled his labor in the *past*, (at our expense) and *will* control it in the *future* (at his). His condition *before* the war and *since* are almost identical." Reassurances that "things go on, as before," coexisted with sour-grapes expressions of good riddance to slavery. Explaining that his slaves had "never been of use" to him, an Alabama planter declared gamely that he was "ready to let them go," adding, "I have been the slave myself."9

But these assertions alternated with expressions of alarm at the revolutionary changes that were about to ensue. Such expressions were especially pointed and numerous in the South, where planters suffered not only the loss of their slaves but also the loss of their war, and hatred of Yankee conquerors combined with fear of an unknown future to create intense anxiety, bitterness, and humiliation. "If I ever have children," wrote one Georgia planter, "the first ingredient of the first principle of their education shall be uncompromising hatred & contempt of the Yankee." In the words of historian James Roark, planters faced what seemed to them to be "nothing less than a world turned upside down." But many Russian pomeshchiki showed similar alarm over their prospects under the new dispensation, an alarm heightened by their realization that without the controls provided by serfdom, maintaining their authority over a vast peasant majority would be a daunting task. Deploring the "unsatisfactory" effects of the emancipation legislation, a petition of Tula Province noblemen warned Alexander II that the nobility faced "complete ruin," while a similar resolution from noblemen in Voronezh Province complained of their "powerlessness" and moaned that "the significance of the Gentry as a class wanes with every day that passes." To many former owners in both Russia and the Southern United States, the future seemed not only uncertain but also terrifying.10

As emancipation unfolded, the confusing multiplicity of expectations over what would and should ensue in the aftermath of slavery and serfdom coalesced into three broadly differing (if at times overlapping) sets of competing goals, espoused by three different groups of protagonists. The freedpeople sought most of all to maximize their autonomy, to get as far as possible from the servile dependence that had previously characterized their status. Their former owners sought to preserve as many of their prerogatives as possible, including both their economic well-being and their authority over their former bondspeople. Government representatives—at varying levels but most evident in peace mediators and Freedmen's Bureau officials—fully supported the position of neither the freedpeople nor their former owners, favoring instead a broad range of "in-between" policies centered on an understanding of "free labor" that at the same time rejected the "agrarian" notion that the fruits of their labor belonged by right to the freedpeople and insisted that freedom implied certain basic rights, including the right to be compensated for one's work. Because each of these goals represented clusters of often unarticulated hopes, desires, and fears, it could be manifested in a bewildering variety of ways, with differing implications. Although in general, for reasons put forth in chapter 1, for example, most Freedmen's Bureau officials were more sympathetic to the desires of their African American charges than the peace mediators were to those of the peasants, both American and Russian authorities took a variety of positions that reflected the diverse views of individuals with very different personal experiences and very different understandings of what should be done. The tripartite struggle among freedpeople, their former owners, and government officials evolved on the ground, in thousands of local confrontations that collectively gave shape to the new order.

The announcement of freedom and establishment of the institutional structures designed to supervise transition to the new order followed different trajectories in Russia and the Southern United States. In the former, these were carefully worked out (at least in theory) in advance, and detailed in the emancipation statutes of February 1861. In the latter, they evolved piecemeal, at first during the war as the federal government and military commanders were forced to decide what to do with former slaves who came under their control and then during the postwar Reconstruction debates. The way these structures operated on the ground bore some notable similarities with each other, however, even as they differed from the way they were originally conceived and varied over space as well. The most carefully prepared script could not anticipate the actual behavior of the protagonists in the drama of emancipation.

The Russian government took elaborate precautions to secure an orderly introduction of the new regime. Concerned about the possibility of peasant violence, the government delayed releasing the emancipation manifesto until after the pre-Lenten Carnival Week and directed church officials to warn local priests who might be too sympathetic with their parishioners not to "spread any kind of false rumors" but rather to explain the statutes "according to the letter of the law." To prevent such "false rumors," the Ministry of Internal Affairs undertook to blanket the country with a massive distribution of official information about what could be expected, including 220,000 copies of the emancipation decree, 190,000 copies of the General Regulations on emancipation, and 140,000 copies of the regulation setting specific ground rules for the transition in Russia, New Russia, and Belorussia. The tsar also sent a special imperial aide-de-camp to each province, whose charge was to ensure an orderly initiation of the emancipation process, supervise developments until the peace mediators and provincial offices for peasant affairs were in place, and report problems direct to officials in St. Petersburg.[11]

Careful preparation could go only so far, however, and the actual promulgation of the emancipation decree and establishment of the supervisory institutions proceeded more erratically than the paper plan envisioned. The decree was first made public in Moscow and St. Petersburg on 5 March, but it took almost a month for word of the new dispensation to spread throughout the empire, as the imperial aides-de-camp arrived in their appointed provinces with copies of the emancipation documents and gathered residents together in churches and town squares to hear readings of the tsar's manifesto. Typically, such readings occurred first in provincial capitals and then over the following two or three weeks elsewhere. In some cases, the tsar's emissaries brought copies of the emancipation legislation with them, but usually they had only a few copies until more arrived over the next few weeks for distribution to estates and officials; some of the aides also had extra copies printed. Meanwhile, they took what action they could to maintain order, explaining to the peasants that despite their "new rights" they still owed "obedience to [their] pomeshchiki," and sending regular reports back to the tsar. The aides' length of service in the field varied, but typically they remained on the job about three months, until June or July.[12]

One reason for staying until then was that setting up the new administrative agencies designed to supervise the emancipation process on the ground took longer than expected. The initial—and easiest—step consisted of creating the provincial offices for peasant affairs, which were composed of ex-officio as well as selected members, all of whom were noblemen. (Each provincial committee was headed by the governor and included the provincial marshal of nobility, the head of the provincial board of state property, the provincial prosecutor [*prokurator*], two members chosen by the provincial noble assembly, and two appointed by the Ministry of Internal Affairs in St. Petersburg.) Choosing the peace mediators was a more complicated process. First the district noble assembly had to define the borders of the each mediator's precinct (*uchastok*); then the district marshal of nobility made up a list of noblemen eligible to serve (the main qualification consisted of being a hereditary nobleman with at least five hundred desiatiny of land, or 250 desiatiny if he had received a higher education); the noble assembly then verified this list and sent it to the governor, who in turn appointed the peace mediators (and sometimes alternate candidates) from the list submitted to him—which typically contained ten to fifteen possible names for each position—and forwarded their names to the Senate in St. Petersburg for what was usually routine confirmation. The cumbersome nature of the selection process and the accompanying wrangling over appointments guaranteed that most of the 1,714 mediators would not be in place until several weeks (typically two to four months) after the announcement of emancipation.[13]

Because American emancipation was not the result of the kind of careful and deliberate planning that occurred in Russia, both the arrival of freedom and creation of the administrative structure designed to supervise its introduction were messier and more contested than their Russian equivalents. Indeed, rather than one moment of freedom, there were at least four. The first of these, the Emancipation Proclamation of 1 January 1863, marked the transformation of a war for union into a war for freedom but did not immediately liberate anyone, since it applied only to areas in rebellion, where the federal government had no practical power.[14] The fourth and last, the Thirteenth Amendment to the Constitution, banned slavery throughout the United States, but by the time it was ratified and went into effect in December 1865 it seemed almost an afterthought. Indeed, if the Emancipation Proclamation presaged a future freedom, the Thirteenth Amendment ratified a freedom that already existed. Both had tremendous symbolic importance, but neither actually freed many slaves.

For many Southern African Americans the moment of freedom came at various times during the war, when hundreds of thousands of them fled to Union lines and hundreds of thousands more—from the Sea Islands off the coast of South Carolina and Georgia to northern Virginia, southern Louisiana, western Tennessee, and other areas within the ever-shrinking perimeter of the Confederacy—lived in regions occupied by Union forces. Federal officials in those areas introduced diverse measures designed to explore various forms of freedom, but these measures, which often contained coercive elements that rendered them closer to semi-freedom than freedom, were widely recognized as experimental; the ultimate terms of freedom remained to be determined.

What is more, because federal troops came and went, the gains they brought to the enslaved population appeared fragile and even reversible. "The negroes' freedom was brought to a close today," recorded one South Carolina plantation mistress in her diary near the war's end, before telling how local whites had gathered "the negroes" and explained that "they were not free, but slaves, and would be until they died.... Poor deluded creatures!" she exclaimed in mock sympathy. "Their friends the Yankees have done them more harm than good."[15]

But in most of the South, the moment of freedom with the greatest immediate impact came with the defeat of the Confederacy, an event commemorated in Black folklore as "the surrender." (In one version, Presidents Lincoln and Davis "met under de ole apple tree. Lincoln stuck a shot-gun in Jeff Davis' face an' yelled, 'Better surrender, else I shoot you an' hang you.' Davis told him, 'Yessir, Marse Lincoln, I surrender.'") General Robert E. Lee's surrender to General Ulysses S. Grant on 9 April 1865 not only marked the end of the war but also established with certainty the end of slavery and brought to center stage the debate over what would happen next in the defeated South. Although news of the surrender—and emancipation—did not reach African Americans in most of Texas until federal troops landed at Galveston on the nineteenth of June, a date subsequently celebrated as "Juneteenth," elation and despair swept over the South in the spring of 1865 as Blacks and whites anticipated the new order.[16]

That spring also saw the proliferation across the South of new federal institutions designed to supervise the transition to freedom, the most notable of which was the Bureau of Freedmen, Refugees and Abandoned Lands, more commonly known as the Freedmen's Bureau. The brainchild of the three-man American Freedmen's Inquiry Commission, a wartime body designed to consider what to do with emancipated slaves once the war was over, the bureau was created by Congress in March 1865 as a temporary body that would expire in one year. (Congress later extended its life.) Housed in the War Department, it was staffed largely by Union military officers and organized in military fashion. At the top, in Washington, was Commissioner O. O. Howard, a general with strong antislavery credentials. Under him were assistant commissioners, virtually all high-ranking Union officers, many initially men who had served under Howard's command in the Army of the Tennessee; in most cases, each assistant commissioner had jurisdiction over one state. Assistant commissioners, in turn, appointed their immediate subordinates, sub-assistant commissioners (several in each state), who supervised the work of lower-ranking agents. Although occasionally civilians received commissions as Freedmen's Bureau agents, the vast majority were military officers, and the bureau operated according to a military chain of command. Not only was the composition of bureau officials strikingly different from that of Russia's peace mediators, so too was their process of selection and to some extent their very mission. Like the peace mediators, Freedmen's Bureau officials were to maintain order, mediate disputes between freedpeople and their former owners, and generally supervise the transition to free labor. They also were to promote educational work among the freedpeople, however, distribute food and other supplies to the destitute (Black and white), and—in the initial understanding—help freedpeople gain access to abandoned and confiscated lands.[17]

As with the peace mediators, getting bureau officials in place was not always easy. As the late arrival of news of emancipation in Texas indicates, military control over remote areas of the South remained tenuous at war's end. Even elsewhere in the South the military was stretched thin, securing the loyalty of former Confederates took top priority, and finding the appropriate personnel for the bureau—from assistant commissioners at the top to local agents in the field—often took months. It was not until 3 June, for example, that Thomas W. Conway, the bureau's New Orleans–based general superintendent for the Department of the Gulf, could report to authorities in Washington that he had begun establishing the Freedmen's Bureau in Alabama, by opening offices in Montgomery, Selma, and Baldwin County; setting up other offices in Alabama took months longer. In Georgia, as late as August there was no bureau presence beyond Augusta and Savannah. In most of the South, as in Russia, the supervisory scaffolding for transition to the new order emerged only gradually.[18]

Even then, bureau officials faced serious challenges to their authority. If "for newly freed blacks, it was 'the government,' " the Freedmen's Bureau was hardly the only government. Until the winter of 1867–68, each Southern state had a rival governmental structure set up under President Andrew Johnson's contested restoration policy, from governor and state legislature down to probate judges, which was only marginally loyal to the United States and usually less than marginally interested in securing the rights of the freedpeople. That lack of interest was contagious. "When we came here," reported Captain D. W. Whittle to Commissioner Howard from Union Springs, Alabama, "the general impression seemed to prevail among the planters, that the ceasing of hostilities had made void the Emancipation Proclamation, and that they could retain the same hold upon their negroes as formerly, until *their state* had passed laws freeing them; they have consequently told the negroes they were not free." In short, rival governmental authorities—one represented by the Union Army and the Freedmen's Bureau and the other by the newly restored if not universally recognized state governments—vied for control of the Southern countryside.[19]

Once in place, despite their very different composition, Freedmen's Bureau agents and peace mediators faced similar challenges. Both appeared, at least on paper, to represent formidable organizations backed by the full force of governments committed to unprecedented reforms. In Russia, some 1,714 peace mediators—about one for every thirteen thousand freed serfs—represented the tip of the iceberg of a bureaucratic hierarchy that stretched from the Ministry of Internal Affairs at the top to the governor and provincial marshal of nobility at the province level, to the *ispravnik* (police chief) and district marshal of nobility at the district (*uezd*) level. Below these noble officials, at the local level, was a peasant administrative structure that was in part a creation of the emancipation legislation and in part a holdover from peasant communal organization already in place, and on call in case of trouble was the vast if unwieldy Russian Army. In the Southern United States there were fewer Freedmen's Bureau officials (nine hundred at the bureau's peak in late 1866 and early 1867, fewer most of the time), but because the freed population was much smaller, each Bureau official was in charge of fewer freedpeople than was the typical peace mediator—an average of four thousand or so when the bureau was at peak strength, although significantly more most of the time. (The ratio of bureau agents to freedpeople also varied from state to state and even within states.) In support of these bureau agents was a large (although gradually diminishing) occupation army; because most Freedmen's Bureau officials were themselves army officers, their relations with the occupation forces were especially close.

Both Freedmen's Bureau officials and peace mediators faced daunting challenges as they strove to guide the transition to freedom. In part, these challenges reflected the confusion inherent in the very process of abolishing entrenched systems of forced labor and establishing new, contested replacements predicated on some version of freedom. But particular complexities exacerbated both the confusion and the challenges. In Russia, these stemmed primarily from the arcane terms and process of emancipation, and the gulf that separated the vast peasant population from the tiny class of nobles seeking to maintain control of what threatened to be an explosive situation. In the Southern United States, they stemmed from divided—and competing—governmental authority, continued struggle in Washington over the shape of the new order, and a decentralized federal system that permitted significant variation of policy from state to state. Beyond these particular complexities lay the tension between two interrelated but divergent missions of Freedmen's

Bureau officials and peace mediators. On the one hand, they were supposed to protect the freedpeople and guide their journey to freedom. On the other, they were to maintain order, the principal threat to which seemed to come primarily from the freedpeople themselves. Although this threat from below seemed most one-sided in Russia (in the United States, former Confederates posed an additional threat to security), in both countries bureau agents, peace mediators, and other government officials saw it as an essential part of their mission to impress upon the freedpeople the difference between "freedom" and "license" and to make sure that they remained peaceful and orderly.

Indeed, in both countries as officials prepared to embark on uncharted waters, they went to great lengths to dispel what they considered extravagant expectations on the part of the freedpeople. "Be industrious, be charitable and kind in your feelings; be peaceable, forbearing, sober; cherish no spite," Brigadier General C. C. Andrews told former slaves in Selma, Alabama. Urging them to show that they were "worthy of freedom," he explained that "liberty alone is not happiness. Self-control and self-support are required to make it pleasant." Captain Charles C. Soule warned freedpeople in Orangeburg District, South Carolina, not to believe wild rumors, urged them to stay on their plantations and wait until the end of the growing season before seeking to be reunited with their spouses, and explained that for the time being the only benefit of freedom was that they could not be sold. "You are talking too much; waiting too much; asking for too much," he lectured. Alexander II's aide-de-camp in Vitebsk Province was also concerned about "lying rumors" spread by "various swindlers and scoundrels"; explaining to peasants that "the Sovereign Emperor demands from you obedience and respect for your pomeshchiki," he warned that at the first sign of trouble he would summon "a significant number of soldiers," noting that although the tsar's "mercy is great, ... his anger is frightful." The monarch himself took the message to a group of peasant elders in Moscow Province (and elsewhere as well), explaining that he had given them "lawful freedom, not a license to do what you want." Throughout the countryside, with varying degrees of severity, officials lectured Blacks and peasants on the need to work hard, remain obedient, reject unfounded rumors, avoid making excessive demands, and refrain from violence. As one Union general succinctly put it, "Those who work shall be paid; those who are dependent on their labor and do not work must starve."[20]

The freedpeople had other ideas. Resisting a limited freedom that recognized the right to be paid for their labor but otherwise left them subservient to their former owners, Blacks and peasants strove for what they regarded as *real* freedom, predicated on their understanding of the right to self-ownership and self-government. Indeed, both in the rural South and in Russia, emancipation initiated intense class struggles over land, labor, and the meaning of freedom itself. Marked by rumor, misunderstanding, pretended misunderstanding, compromise, and at times violence, these struggles evolved in two overlapping waves. The first occurred largely during the initial months of the emancipation process and centered on defining the general nature and terms of the new dispensation; the second, which was ongoing, involved contests over specific conditions during and after the implementation of emancipation—especially relations of labor and access to land. The first is the subject of the remainder of this chapter, the second of chapter 3 and subsequent chapters.

Former serfs and slaves reacted to news of their freedom in diverse ways that appeared to defy easy categorization. Conflicting reports from the South and Russia indicated the prevalence of varying conditions and a bewildering combination of responses that included joy, jubilation, defiance, sullen indifference, confusion, gratefulness, hope, mistrust, and bitterness. Although to some extent magnified by the difficulty of construing the behavior of the freedpeople, the variations were real. They were not, however, as random or contradictory as they seemed—either to contemporaries or to some subsequent historians. Although manifested in a multiplicity of ways, the unifying theme that underlay the responses of Blacks and peasants was their desire to secure and maximize *real* freedom, as they understood it.

As peasants gathered in churches and village centers to hear readings of the emancipation manifesto, authorities were unsure what to expect. Hoping for joy, gratitude, and above all calm, they feared anger, recriminations, and above all violence. They received all of these, and more.

Many officials reported positive peasant responses. Although these reports to some extent reflected the fawning, formulaic tone of those eager to curry favor with higher authority, their diverse origins indicate that they caught (if exaggerated) one element of complex peasant reactions. In Vologda Province, assembled peasants received the news "as one might expect from Orthodox and true subjects of your throne," reported aide-de-camp Prince K. L. Dadiani to the tsar: with joy and shouts of "hurrah." His counterpart in Ekaterinoslavl Province, noting that the peasants reacted "completely peacefully," added that not only were they obedient, they "in many cases turned with complete trust to their former owners for explanation of the new rights most graciously given to them." Peasants in Orenburg Province also displayed "overwhelming joy" and shouted "hurrah," while in Samara Province they heard the manifesto with "deep reverence." On many estates in Tambov Province, according to the tsar's aide-de camp, pomeshchiki treated their peasants to liquor and together toasted the emperor's health, after which the peasants "unanimously" blessed his name and thanked the pomeshchiki for their generosity. Summarizing the numerous reports that he had received from around Russia, Minister of Internal Affairs Sergei Lanskoi remarked with satisfaction on the "peacefulness and calm" that the peasants had shown, noted that in many places they had held grateful prayers for the tsar's health, and marveled over the flood of donations "from all sides" for the "construction in Moscow of a temple in the name of Aleksandr Nevskii." Lanskoi added that despite fears that peasants would engage in drunken celebrations, widespread and "unexpected" reports indicated that peasants' "use of alcohol [had] markedly diminished."[21]

At the same time, however, other evidence suggested very different peasant emotions. A steward reported from Nizhnii Novgorod Province that after the emancipation manifesto was read in churches the peasants were behaving "extremely rudely." The tsar's aide-de-camp in Simbirsk Province noted that although the manifesto elicited little response, as soon as the emancipation legislation was distributed "acts of disobedience" began to appear "on many estates." In Kostroma Province, soon after the manifesto was promulgated peasant "walkers" began arriving in the capital city from throughout the province with petitions complaining about their treatment, and "acts of disobedience" broke out "in almost all [the province's] districts." After the manifesto was read to 350 peasants on one estate in Grodno Province, they told the aide-de-camp, "in one voice, and rudely," that the document was "counterfeit" and that the *real* manifesto provided full freedom with an immediate end of all servile obligations; he attributed the misinformation to "false interpretations" spread by illiterate peasants and Jews (two of whom were arrested). In Kaluga Province, a peasant woman who could not restrain herself after hearing of her freedom "unceremoniously gave the finger (a greasy finger) in the direction of the manor house." Such reports of rudeness, hostility, and wild rumors not only alarmed authorities but also gave a hint of what was soon in store for them.[22]

Still, overtly hostile behavior did not characterize the behavior of most peasants upon their hearing of emancipation. Rather, their most prevalent response was silent impassivity. From the point of view of authorities, this was not necessarily troubling, since their greatest fear was disorder; indeed, many of the early reports from officials and pomeshchiki stressed—and welcomed— the peaceful way in which peasants responded to news of emancipation. At times, however, it seemed a little too peaceful. After welcoming the calm that prevailed throughout Penza Province upon promulgation of the manifesto, a staff officer of the Corps of Gendarmes noted that in fact "it nowhere produced any particular impression on the populace"—except for the nobility, which "in general [was] pleased by the new legislation." From Kiev Province a correspondent supposed that the peasants who heard the manifesto read "must not have understood it," because he "did not detect any joy on even one face." (He too added that "the pomeshchiki were very pleased with the legislation.") In Nizhnii Novgorod Province, a group of peasants heard news of emancipation "with unusual indifference," a reaction that "severely pained" the provincial governor, who had expected the peasants to show "wild enthusiasm"; even when officials waded into the crowd and tried to elicit shouts of "hurrah," they were unmoved. The aide-de-camp in Tambov Province noted that, as elsewhere after reading of the manifesto, "complete order and quiet [prevailed] throughout the province," but he detected "apprehension" among pomeshchiki that at the start of spring field work peasants would display a "spirit of insubordination." It was hard to avoid suspicion that the quiet response to emancipation represented a calm before the storm.[23]

Authorities (and other observers) had a ready explanation for the peasants' indifferent response to the news of emancipation: they just did not understand what it meant. As the aide-de-camp for Moscow Province explained to the tsar after noting the "rather indifferent" peasant response to a reading of the manifesto, "the peasant population did not understand" what they heard, and "did not comprehend your Majesty's good intention." At least, he added, reading of the manifesto did not produce any disorders. From Podolia Province, the aide-de-camp explained that peasants who heard the reading of the manifesto "poorly understood its content," and he noted that the spread of "incorrect rumors" had already created a "false understanding of freedom" among them. (He added that pomeshchiki generally reacted to the manifesto "with joy," not because they favored emancipation but because they now realized that they would not suffer as much "material damage as they had feared.") Over and over, officials and pomeshchiki stressed the peasants' incomprehension and confusion, linking them to their lack of visible enthusiasm or gratitude.[24]

There is no doubt that peasants *did* have trouble understanding what they heard; after all, the emancipation provisions were extraordinarily confusing, even to those familiar with the stilted language in which they were written. To most peasants they seemed incomprehensible, in need of the proper "reading" or interpretation. Lack of understanding could easily turn into misunderstanding. When Aleksandr Nikitenko—an unlikely example of a former serf who had not only won his freedom but become a government official—visited his dacha outside St. Petersburg in August 1861, the peasant *starosta* "listened to [him] with head bowed and kept repeating that everything had been fine for them until now, and that now only God knew what would become of them." A few days later, Nikitenko gave a party for the peasants, and many of them expressed the same bewilderment. "Their understanding of freedom . . . ," he concluded, "is very hazy."[25]

But if the details were obscure, in some ways the peasants understood the general gist of the provisions all too well. As they listened to officials read the emancipation manifesto and summarize the accompanying legislation, as they heard authorities explain that they still owed labor and monetary obligations to their former owners and would soon have to pay hefty sums to receive land allotments that they considered already theirs, and as they received admonitions to be obedient to pomeshchiki and saw signs of the impending intrusion in their lives of a bewildering new body of government agents, it was hard for them to avoid the suspicion that something was being put over on them, that this was not the real freedom for which they had waited. The rapid circulation among peasants of rumors—evident almost immediately upon promulgation of the manifesto—that greedy landowners and dishonest officials were engaged in a massive effort to substitute a fake, exploitative emancipation for the one intended by the tsar suggested that the peasants' cautious initial response to news of their liberation did not so much reflect satisfaction as mask an underlying sense of unease, suspicion, and resentment that threatened to get out of hand at any moment. Indeed, the initial self-congratulatory official reports of a peaceful if not joyful peasant response to emancipation would soon give way to reports with a very different message.

The arrival of freedom presented similar challenges, manifested differently, to African Americans in the Southern United States. Because they did not have to decipher the arcane details of emancipation legislation—as yet, there were virtually none—they did not express the same doubts about the specific terms of the new order. But as in Russia, in the South freedpeople reacted to news of their liberation in diverse ways that belied a common desire to reap the fruit of the tree of liberty, and as in Russia, they displayed a particular understanding of freedom that to many Southern whites indicated confusion and misunderstanding.

Given that there was no one moment of emancipation throughout the entire South, generalizing about the immediate reaction to news of freedom there requires more qualification than in Russia. During the war, military conditions shaped—and sometimes constrained—Black behavior. As noted in chapter 1, African Americans displayed varied responses to changing circumstances, from biding their time to fleeing to Union lines, from cautiously welcoming Union troops to enthusiastically volunteering for military service, from standing loyally by endangered slave owners to ransacking cotton gins after their owners had fled. The presence of Yankee soldiers, even when temporary, almost always upset existing relationships. "Their visit here has to a great extent demoralized the negroes," wrote one northern Alabama planter of federal soldiers; complaining that "they made the ignorant blacks beliefe they had come to free them" and noting that "the negroes were delighted with them," he concluded that "since they left enough can be seen to convince one that the Federal army[,] the negroes and white Southern people cannot inhabit the same country." But because of wartime uncertainties, the growing determination of African Americans to seize the moment and strike out for freedom reflected not so much responses to a promulgated emancipation as efforts to take advantage of new opportunities to escape an increasingly crippled slavery. In most of the South, real freedom—and the chance to react to it—came with the surrender and the shift in power that accompanied it. Ratification of the Thirteenth Amendment may still have been eight months away, but this seemed a technicality: in the spring of 1865 the reality of emancipation was palpable.[26]

Many African Americans greeted the defeat of the Confederacy—and their ensuing liberation—with joyful celebration. One former slave woman from Virginia described how, on the first Sunday of freedom, "ole Sister Carrie" suddenly burst out

> Tain't no mo' sellin' today,
> Tain't no mo' hirin' today,
> Tain't no more pullin' off shirts today,
> Its stomp down freedom today.
> Stomp it down!

The other freedpeople joined in and continued the celebration all day. "Dat was one glorious time!" the woman recollected. If the most ecstatic versions of such celebrations typically occurred in the quarters, out of the sight of whites, the defeat of the Confederacy and protective presence of Yankee troops enabled many former slaves to drop the curtain of impassivity with which they had typically masked their emotions when addressing unknown whites, and to display more overt delight at emancipation than was common among

Russian peasants. When a Northern correspondent asked an old Black woman in Georgia why she had left her former master, the response was pointed: "What fur?" she puzzled. " 'Joy my freedom!'" Throughout much of the rural South, African Americans "enjoyed" their first days of freedom with a giant, collective "jubilee" celebration.[27]

One component of this jubilee was leaving their homes, something that before emancipation had been impermissible without a pass. In some cases, such departures represented a continuation (and final installment) of the widespread flight that had occurred as slaves took advantage of wartime disruption to escape from their owners—and from slavery itself. Such flight was especially noteworthy—and galling to slave owners—among trusted house servants, who as before often revealed themselves to be less (or more) than the faithful servants their owners had imagined. Lamenting that her supposedly devoted maid had taken off one night "without provocation or warning," one North Carolina mistress added in shock that "she actually left . . . without bidding me good bye."[28]

But the defeat of the Confederacy made possible a more general—and more open—movement of former slaves that represented not so much an escape from particular slaveholders as the beginning of a massive reordering of social relations throughout the South. If some Blacks took the opportunity to visit friends or loved ones, or simply to escape from the normal work routine, others took to the road to test their freedom and establish the reality of changed conditions. "When the first announcement was made that the negroes were free, they exhibited a strong tendency to leave their homes and wander about the country," reported the Freedmen's Bureau assistant commissioner for Florida, adding that "this migratory spirit lasted from four to eight weeks." Other freedpeople crowded into urban areas, long destinations of potential refuge for fugitives and now doubly attractive because of the security frequently provided by federal soldiers and Freedmen's Bureau offices. A letter to the *Montgomery Advertiser* complained that the city was "crowded, crammed, packed with multitudes of lazy, worthless negroes," and the Selma *Times* complained of "impudent and noisy" freedpeople; the paper noted that Black women were "talking and laughing unbecomingly and annoyingly loud" while the men were "sporting oaths, vulgar laughs, and using indecent language."[29]

As in Russia, former slave owners complained that the freedpeople did not understand what freedom was all about, confused liberty with "license," and assumed that emancipation meant they would no longer have to work. In a typical diary entry mocking the supposed confusion of the gullible freedpeople, a small planter in Alabama observed that local Blacks, convinced that a "great dinner" would be "given them by the Yankees," were crowding every road to Talladega; the next day, he recorded their inevitable disillusionment, "returning in dust and heat" after they "got no dinner & [were in] other ways disappointed." To whites used to Black subservience and circumspection, the unauthorized movement, loud talk, and visible delight in changed relationships not only indicated impudence but also seemed to confirm their previous conviction that Blacks desperately needed proper control and supervision.[30]

As their frequent lectures to freedpeople on the need to work and be orderly indicated, many federal officials and other Northern observers shared at least some of white Southerners' perceptions and fears. Complaining that "well-meaning but thoughtless public speakers" had "given the freed people unreal and mistaken ideas of freedom, equality, and the rights secured to them," General Tillson Davis, the Freedmen's Bureau's assistant commissioner for Georgia, reported to Commissioner Howard that he was spending much of his time trying to disabuse Blacks of their extravagant expectations. Army officers and Freedmen's Bureau officials were frequently struck by the "perfect reign of idleness on the part of negroes" as well as what one referred to as "the hegira of negroes from plantations." Noting the massive wandering of rural African Americans following the war, Charles Stearns, a Yankee (and abolitionist) who purchased a plantation near Augusta, Georgia, with the goal of showing "the practicability of the co-operative principle, in carrying on a large farm," recalled his dismay at discovering on his arrival that "the hands utterly refused to work." Declaring that "we's free now," the maid announced that "us ant gwine to get down to *ye,* any more than to them as rebs." To such observers, idleness, disorderliness, and wanderlust not only indicated the freedpeople's faulty understanding of freedom but also seemed to threaten the prospects of creating a viable free-labor society in the South. Reporting from Eastport, Mississippi, that his subordinate in nearby Okalona had found that "demoralized" Blacks were increasingly becoming "vagrants," deserting their homes "in whole gangs, always leaving at night," General Edward Hatch expressed an unusually extreme version of this negative judgment. "I fear that the freedmen of these interior regions *are not able* to be free," he opined. "For them to be free is for them first to beg, then to steal and then to starve."[31]

This view did not, however, reflect the sentiment of most federal officials. Indeed, Hatch's report received a quick rebuttal from Mississippi's Bureau head Samuel Thomas, who denounced what he termed the general's "extraordinary" comments and suggested that Hatch was sympathetic to slavery. Reporting to Commissioner Howard a week later, Thomas countered that after visiting eastern Mississippi he was convinced that "the negroes are at home working quietly." Other officials agreed with Thomas that rural freedpeople were hardworking and orderly—"when the planters acknowledge[d] their freedom and agree[d] to recompense them for their labor"; as Brigadier General Andrews, who had previously issued a stern warning to Blacks in the Selma area on the responsibilities that came with freedom, put it, "Where the masters have been candid, kind, and truthful men, the blacks continue on in their duties quietly as a general thing." Some former slaveholders also questioned the idea of widespread Black misbehavior. "Families still have plenty of servants," wrote Baptist minister Basil Manly from Tuscaloosa in June, adding, "The servants that remain are even more docile and obedient than before." "None of mine . . . have left, or showed any wish to do so." Observing that the freedpeople were "in a state of excitement and jubilee," former Confederate general Josiah Gorgas quickly noted that although "idle," they were "not insubordinate nor disrespectful."[32] In short, as in Russia observers offered divergent interpretations of the freedpeople's immediate responses to emancipation.

Although Black migration would continue to be an important feature of life in the post-emancipation South, much of the initial "jubilee" movement proved to be a temporary phenomenon designed to break previous subservient relationships. As one Black man told journalist Whitelaw Reid, "I's want to be free man, cum when I please, and nobody say nuffin to me, nor order me round.' " Amid all the talk of whether or not Black people "understood" the meaning of freedom, one of the few white observers to grasp the significance of the apparently senseless "wandering" was the abolitionist general Carl Schurz, who at the request of President Johnson toured the defeated Confederate states during the summer of 1865 and then reported on his findings. Schurz suggested that Blacks "left the plantations" both "to obtain the certainty of their freedom" and "for the purpose of leaving the places on which they had been held in slavery," which for the first time they could now do "with impunity." (He also noted that many freedpeople "remained with their former masters and continued their work on the field, but under new and unsettled conditions, and under the agitating influence of a feeling of restlessness.") Along with the "refusal" to work and the "insolent" behavior, leaving home constituted a calculated effort on the part of freedpeople to establish their new status both to themselves and to others even as it also presaged a variety of future acts, from the relatively rare attempts to seize the land they worked to the widespread refusal to work under the direction of overseers, that would be central to the class struggle during coming years. As such, these celebratory acts indicated not a misunderstanding so much as a *different* understanding of what freedom was all about, as well as a recognition of the need to seize the moment to fight for a *real* freedom before it was too late.[33]

Although almost any Black behavior short of slave-like obsequiousness seemed insolent and uppity to most Southern whites, and some federal officials shared their fears that African Americans would take advantage of the new order to be indolent and disorderly, the freedpeople pursued their version of freedom in a decidedly cautious manner during the weeks immediately following the surrender. Defeat of the Confederacy and the formal abolition of slavery enabled former slaves to do a variety of things that were previously forbidden, but the balance of power remained tenuous and militated against rash behavior. The substantial white presence in most of the South, the existence of competing governmental authorities, the uncertainty of federal policy—not to mention the proclivities of individual federal officials—and the very newness of their freedom combined to produce a cautious, tentative tone as the freedpeople pursued their goals, feeling their way and making sense of both new opportunities and new hurdles.

This caution was especially evident at the public level, when during the immediate postwar months African Americans articulated their goals in a number of statewide (and local) "colored conventions." Although the conventions displayed some variation, their delegates—among whom ministers, urban Blacks, and those who had been free before the war were especially prominent—typically adopted what historian Eric Foner termed a "conciliatory approach," seeking legal equality but at the same time striving to allay the fears of anxious whites. The fifty-six delegates to the Alabama Colored Convention that met in Mobile in November 1865, for example, adopted a series of moderate resolutions designed to show that no one had anything to fear from free African Americans. "It will be our purpose to work industriously and honestly," they proclaimed, urging a policy of "peace, friendship, and good will toward all men—especially toward our white fellow-citizens among whom our lot is cast." Editorials in white Southern newspapers often expressed relief at this evident moderation; the conservative *Daily Selma Times* noted with satisfaction that the Mobile resolutions "inculcate[d] morality, the duty of labor, and the obligation to render conscientious obedience to the civil law."[34]

Relief at the freedpeople's circumspect behavior, however, went only so far. What seemed prudent to newly freed Blacks and cautious to subsequent analysts could appear ominous to whites unused to any sign of Black self-assertion. "Unauthorized" migration and assembly were troubling enough, but, as in Russia, it was hard to avoid the suspicion that worse was in store. With the postwar peace fragile and the social order up for grabs, both Blacks and whites were edgy and on guard.

Indeed, both in the South and in Russia the initial restraint that characterized the freedpeople's behavior increasingly gave way to more muscular efforts to make sure that the freedom they had won was more than a freedom in name only. Although Blacks and peasants used different tactics in pursuing this goal, their central objective in both cases was securing a *real* freedom that provided a maximum degree of "self-government" and met their expectations about specific conditions, particularly with respect to land and labor. Within a few weeks of the Russian emancipation manifesto and the Confederate surrender, self-satisfied reports of orderly behavior on the part of the freed population were typically tinged with expressions of concern, and then often outright alarm, over real and imagined threats to rural tranquillity. As conflicting rumors of imminent change spread through the Russian and Southern countrysides, it would become clear that the abolition of bondage signaled not an end to the struggle over the social order but rather the inauguration of a new stage of that struggle.

The initial Russian reports of a quiet peasant response to emancipation proved remarkably short lived. Indeed, by the spring of 1861, almost every official who had at first rejoiced over the peaceful inauguration of the new dispensation was singing a different song. Peasant impassivity now appeared less an indicator of obedience and loyalty than a precursor of trouble. Over and over again, officials—including the same ones who had stressed the peasants' gratitude and orderly behavior—now described scenes of disorder and insubordination, as observations about the peasants' "misunderstanding" mutated into a growing alarm over behavior that seemed to threaten the security of the countryside and, at the most extreme level, the very stability of the government.

A typical example of this pattern can be seen in nine reports of Major General N. G. Kaznakov, the tsar's aide-de-camp for Kaluga Province, reports that spanned the two-month period from 18 March to 23 May. In his first report, Kaznakov stressed the "favorable impression" that the emancipation manifesto made on the peasants as they listened attentively to news of the new dispensation, in some places standing together with their former owners "as if still constituting one family." Noting peasant reactions that ranged from respectful silence to "undisguised joy and sometimes even ecstasy," he remarked with satisfaction that "nowhere were order or decorum breached." Three weeks later, Kaznakov reported that the arrival and explanation of the emancipation regulations had also gone smoothly, with peasants rejoicing over their new personal freedom, although in a somewhat discordant—and portentous—note he added that there were a few places where peasants, confusing freedom with "complete liberty and the free distribution of land," were "dissatisfied."[35]

Beginning a few days later, Kaznakov's reports manifested a distinctly less sanguine tone. On 16 April he noted the existence of "many cases" of peasant "disobedience" and refusal to fulfill traditional obligations, adding reassuringly that so far, with two exceptions, local authorities had been able to reestablish order without resort to force. Thereafter, conditions continued to deteriorate. On the one hand, Kaznakov strove to reassure anxious nobles convinced that the provincial governor was too sympathetic with the peasants; acting "with extreme circumspection," he managed to alleviate their worst fears and proudly reported that they reacted to his efforts "with particular courtesy and even joy." On the other hand, and far more serious, peasants were taking advantage of the situation to shirk their duties. Calling pomeshchik complaints that one-quarter of the spring crop remained unsown exaggerated, Kaznakov reminded the tsar that in recent years, in anticipation of emancipation, the peasants had already begun to work badly, and he suggested that they were unlikely to work well without the serfdom-induced fear of "personal and immediate punishment." Concluding that the decline in cultivation had progressed "from the sphere of conjecture and supposition to the level of ... accomplished fact," he warned ominously of a dangerous increase in the price of grain that threatened to become "a lasting and widespread source of poverty, sickness and disorders."[36]

Kaznakov's fears were extreme, but his observations were no aberration. Time after time, reports from aides-de-camp, other officials, and pomeshchiki showed the same progression during the spring of 1861 from satisfaction to concern to alarm, as early reassurances that everything was going smoothly yielded to accounts of trouble. The trend is perhaps most clearly evident in the weekly reports to the tsar issued by Minister of Internal Affairs Lanskoi and, beginning on 4 May 1861, by his successor, Petr Valuev, reports that in turn summarized information gleaned from officials in the various provinces. Lanskoi's early reports, while varying over whether peasants were joyful or impassive and noting considerable peasant "misunderstanding" of the new dispensation, almost uniformly stressed the positive, mentioning especially the absence of major disorders. Before long, however, his reports manifested an increasing tone of anxiety, accompanied by descriptions of misunderstandings, rumors, disobedience, and unrest, descriptions that were even more prevalent in Valuev's terse, unreflective accounts, many of which during the late spring and early summer were almost entirely devoted to peasant disorders. In a rare generalization on the causes of the unrest, Valuev placed principal blame on the peasants' "lack of understanding" of their new temporarily obligated status and "lying rumors," sometimes spread "under the influence of ill-intentioned people," although he noted that in "some cases" the burdensome nature of continued barshchina and obrok obligations was an exacerbating factor. Usually, however, he simply listed with brief descriptions the most significant peasant outbreaks, along with the means used to suppress them. In a typical statement, he cited the assertion of the governor of Samara Province that "the usual police measures" were sufficient in dealing with most peasants, who were credulous and easily misled, but that such lenient treatment was "insufficient" for those deliberately misinterpreting the emancipation legislation, who needed to be exiled to "places not populated by seigneurial peasants" (that is, former serfs).[37]

Such reports reflected considerable alarm on the part of officials and pomeshchiki, but they were far from alarmist. Indeed, during the spring of 1861 a wave of peasant unrest swept over much of the countryside, unrest that at least briefly seemed to threaten the very stability of the social order. The rapid emergence of these outbreaks of disorder indicates the extent to which the peasants' initial response to news of emancipation represented a momentary calm before the storm. If the tsar's manifesto aroused a combination of enormous hopes and puzzled incomprehension, circulation of the actual emancipation legislation over the succeeding weeks stoked the peasants' fears that the benefits to them of the new order would be considerably less than they had hoped or expected. Although many of the details of the complicated emancipation process were almost impossible to understand, the more the peasants heard of these details the more it seemed to them that their promised deliverance was about to be snatched away. Many of them determined to resist this theft.

Although the occasion and goals of these protests were new, in form they followed a long-established pattern of peasant resistance that had been worked out over generations of serfdom. The most important—and archetypal—form of action was the *volnenie* (plural: *volneniia*), a word with no precise English equivalent that includes dictionary translations of "commotion," "agitation," and "disturbance" and in practice constituted a collective action that combined elements of a strike and a mini-rebellion. Volneniia could be small and easily suppressed or they could be large—encompassing many estates—and drag on for months. Typically, however, their participants included all or most of the peasants on an estate, and they were characterized by considerable organization as well as negotiations between peasant leaders and a progression of antagonists that would usually begin with a variety of estate stewards and administrators before moving on to local noble officials (including the district *ispravnik* and, in the emancipation era, the peace mediator) and when necessary higher officials up to the provincial governor. In most cases, these negotiations would resolve the conflict, but sometimes—especially in the 1861 protests—only military force would restore order. Once peace was restored, those peasants identified as "instigators" would typically receive harsh physical reprisals—whippings, beatings with birch switches, subjection to the feared knout, and in extreme cases exile and penal servitude—often administered in public before the assembled peasants for maximum effect. The mass of peasants, however, frequently escaped direct punishment. The resolution of volneniia was highly unpredictable: sometimes they ended in total defeat for the peasants, but at times the protesters managed to achieve what amounted to a compromise through which at least some of their demands were met.[38]

A few examples of volneniia during the months immediately following the announcement of emancipation reveal, on the one hand, the diversity of these disturbances and, on the other, the ways in which peasants who had a strong sense of their "rights" used timeworn tactics to pursue long-desired goals that had previously been out of reach. The first, a relatively minor incident whose ultimate resolution remains unknown, occurred in June when the peasants on an estate encompassing three villages in Iaroslavl Province refused to perform any more seigneurial field work, under the belief that the tsar had commuted previous barshchina obligations to no more than thirty rubles obrok; as peace mediator Nikolai Sabaneev reported to the province's vice-governor, when he went to investigate the peasants told him that they were "ready" to pay the stipulated obrok, but "would not go to work" for the pomeshchik. The peasants refused to believe Sabaneev's explanation that the thirty-ruble limit applied only to house serfs and that they still owed their previous owner the same labor obligations as before, and when the mediator offered to give them a day to think things over before he reported on their misbehavior to the governor, they responded that "even if you wait a week and write to the Tsar himself, we will not go to work." Blaming the peasants' stubborn behavior "in part on ignorance, in part on [their] false understanding of the new laws," Sabaneev urged the vice-governor to take immediate action to restore order, as "the slightest indulgence of such disobedience can have an extremely harmful influence on neighboring villages," and he noted that the case was especially troubling because the estate manager, who had originally brought the complaint to his attention, "was always indulgent and fair to the peasants," who in fact "live very well."[39]

As this incident suggests, one of the major causes of unrest was the peasants' conviction that they were being cheated out of their real, promised, freedom. Many found it hard to believe that they still had to work for their owner. According to the steward of an estate encompassing two villages in Voronezh Province, women were refusing to perform seigneurial labor. When the district ispravnik arrived, he was able to restore order in one of the villages, but in the other the peasants engaged in "fits of willfulness and disobedience," leading him to call in a company of Ukrainian foot soldiers; eight men and one woman were punished with birch switches. From the same province, a staff officer of the Corps of Gendarmes noted of house servants (*dvorovye liudi*), "[They] resolutely do not want to believe that they must receive freedom without land." In many places, when informed of this, they gave "almost the same answer," insisting that things would change in two years, when they too would receive land. On the basis of this erroneous belief, he observed: "Many of them reject the freedom that pomeshchiki readily offer them without demanding from them any kind of compensation."[40]

Some volneniia could involve stubborn, protracted confrontations. On an estate in Tula Province, the peasants refused an order from the steward (*prikazchik*) to plow in preparation for the sowing of spring rye, insisting that this work should be performed the following year rather than in September; at a communal meeting, the starosta Fedor Nikitin, together with another peasant, "aroused the others to disobedience." Since the local peace mediator turned out to be the very steward whose orders the peasants were flouting and so was unlikely to appear a neutral figure to those peasants, he turned for help to the mediator from the adjoining precinct, who promptly arrested Nikitin and appointed a new starosta. This violation of the widely accepted right of peasants to choose their own leaders had a predictable result: in a communal meeting the peasants "resolutely refused to submit to the orders of the mediator," and when he tried to detain one of the "rudest" peasants, they all left the meeting and gathered in the street outside, where they "began boisterously to demand the return of the arrested starosta and . . . shouted that they did not recognize the new starosta." When they surrounded the building where Nikitin was being held, the frightened mediator left the scene. After several days of unsuccessful negotiation, during which the peasants refused to yield Nikitin and other "instigators," the governor decided to send in the district marshal of nobility, backed by a military command. The peasants' continuing recalcitrance led the marshal to order the "main instigators" to undergo corporal punishment, whereupon the assembled peasants rallied to their leaders' defense, crying out, "Whip us all." After twenty-one more peasants underwent punishment and six of the "instigators" were arrested and held for future trial, reported the Tula governor to Minister of Internal Affairs Valuev, the protestors finally admitted defeat and agreed to perform the plowing that they had resisted.[41]

Or so it seemed. In fact, although the aggrieved peasants appeared beaten into submission, they remained far from compliant. After receiving no reply in response to a petition to the governor, they turned to the highest authority—the tsar himself. A first petition, which may have gone astray, was followed by a second in May 1862, eight months after the original confrontation. Narrating the events of September 1861, the peasants explained that their pomeshchik not only improperly required them to plow for the spring crop in the fall but also continued to impose a burdensome workload, forcing them to toil "beyond the stipulated days," including holidays, and allowing them insufficient time to provide "for the subsistence of [their] children." Once again, they implored the "August monarch," we "beseech and beg you for protection." As was usually the case, however, there is no evidence of any response from the "August monarch."[42]

Examination of two larger volneniia reveals the scope of peasant expectations as well as the problems faced by authorities. On 7 April, a staff officer of the Corps of Gendarmes for Voronezh Province reported that peasants on several adjacent estates of Bobrovskii district were in "revolt," and that both the ispravnik and the district marshal of nobility were convinced that only military force could restore order. In response, the governor sent in a battalion of the Azovskii foot regiment, and together with the tsar's aide-de-camp for the province personally went to the scene to direct operations. Arriving in the village of Tishanka, they approached a crowd of some thousand assembled peasants "who were shouting loudly among themselves." When the governor asked what was the matter, they responded that as a result of the tsar's "gracious charter" they were now free and did not need to perform seigneurial labor or pay obrok dues. Informed by the governor that they needed to be peaceful and at least for the time being continue performing their previous obligations, they threw their hats in the air and shouted, "We do not want a master, down with the master. . . . It's time for freedom!" Fearing that the two companies of 160 soldiers were no match for Tishanka's 2,500 determined souls, the governor and the imperial emissary retreated to the nearby village of Kurlak.

Although the arrival of four more companies of the Azovskii regiment helped authorities restore order in several of the rebellious villages, the 254 souls in Khleborodnaia "stubbornly" refused to submit, insisting that an ukaz of the Holy Synod they had obtained from a local priest confirmed their claim to immediate freedom. Eventually, however, under threat of military action, the peasants "expressed repentance and begged for forgiveness," whereupon the governor imposed widespread corporal punishment on the spot and sent eight ringleaders to the city of Bobrov for trial. The agitated inhabitants of Tashanka proved more troublesome—although orderly, they continued to insist that they did not need to obey their pomeshchik—but eventually they too were subdued, the "rudest" of them subjected to "severe" punishment, and the "instigators" arrested and held for trial. Although the volnenie lasted only a few weeks, by the time order was restored in the village of Novaia Chigla it had embraced some ten thousand souls spread over neighboring estates owned by several pomeshchiki.[43]

An even larger volnenie, which led to an intense confrontation between peasants and government authorities, rocked the Spassk district of Kazan Province in April. Centered at the village of Bezdna, on an estate of some 831 souls, the unrest came to encompass "as many as 90 villages of Spassk District," where thousands of former serfs rallied behind peasant Anton Petrov, who claimed that the *real* emancipation was being suppressed. Like many other "readers" whom peasants sought out, Petrov proclaimed that the true edict and legislation awarded the serfs not just immediate freedom—with a cessation of all monetary and work obligations—but the nobles' land as well. Despite the contrary assertions of government officials who included the ispravnik, the district marshal of nobility, and even the provincial governor, P. F. Kozlialinov, the peasants showed "complete insubordination to the authorities." Massing by thousands in ever-larger numbers, the peasants announced that they would never surrender Petrov to soldiers who came to arrest him and maintained that they were "united for the tsar" and therefore in any military attack, they told the officials, "You will be shooting at the Sovereign Alexander Nikolaevich himself." Eventually, however, the soldiers did capture Petrov—holding what he insisted was the true emancipation legislation on his head—in the process killing at least fifty-one peasants and wounding seventy-seven more. As Adjutant General Apraksin, who commanded the troops, explained, the military action "was necessary in order to restore tranquillity not only in this village, but among the whole population of several districts of Kazan province"; he warned the tsar that although conditions were improving after Petrov's arrest, "subversive persons [were] still circulating rumors." Petrov was shortly thereafter tried by court-martial, found guilty of inciting peasants to rebellion, and executed on 18 April, but the suspicions he expressed about the suppression of the real freedom continued to circulate among the peasantry—and evidently among others as well: "a number students at Kazan University and the Kazan Theological Academy held a requiem service in Kazan for the peasants killed at Bezdna," and a professor who had delivered a eulogy for the deceased was briefly jailed and then "fired from his post and forbidden to teach elsewhere."[44]

A final example illustrates how a relatively small, unthreatening volnenie could end in something of a compromise, with a concession to peasant demands even as peasant leaders underwent punishment for challenging order and authority. Like many volneniia in the spring and summer of 1861, this one reflected the desire of peasants to defend what they understood as their new rights. In January 1861, in an effort to lock in advantageous labor service from her peasants before the anticipated emancipation decree, a small landowner in the Pskov district of Pskov Province—"the widow of an insignificant official"—transferred her thirty souls from obrok status to barshchina. After promulgation of the manifesto, the peasants informed her that although they would continue to pay their obrok, as they had for the previous eighteen years, now that they were free they would not perform seigneurial labor; they also sent petitions to the district and provincial marshals of nobility and to the governor explaining their position. The case soon landed with the newly established Provincial Office of Peasant Affairs, which decided that "although it is difficult for them to go over to barshchina, having been on obrok for 18 years, the pomeshchitsa had the right to do this." Nevertheless, the office *advised* her to respect the wishes of the peasants rather than force them to labor for her.[45]

When pomeshchitsa Iordan rejected this advice, however, the peasants refused to submit to what they regarded as an illegal demand. Even after the peace mediator arrived with twenty-five invalid soldiers and imposed corporal punishment on some of the peasants, they remained recalcitrant and continued to insist that as they were free they did not have to perform compulsory labor. Having failed to resolve the dispute by coercive means, the mediator abruptly changed tacks; working on the pomeshchitsa instead of the peasants, he finally persuaded her to relent and allow the peasants to remain on obrok. "The insubordination has ended and the punitive expedition has been removed," reported a relieved staff officer of the Corps of Gendarmes. "The peasants agreed to all the conditions, so long as they do not have to go onto barshchina." In effect, they had "won" the confrontation.[46]

These and hundreds of other volneniia differed from one another in many ways. Some were modest in size, confined to one small estate, whereas others were large, encompassing several neighboring estates that in turn contained multiple villages with thousands of inhabitants. Some were resolved quickly, whereas others dragged on for weeks and even months. In some cases government officials engaged in protracted negotiations with peasants, whereas in others they made little effort to probe what lay behind peasant concerns. Volneniia varied in terms of what triggered their outbreak, whether the discontented peasants received any redress of their grievances, how many peasants were punished and what the nature of the punishment was, and whether military force was used to restore order. In most respects, such variations were similar to those that had characterized pre-emancipation-era volneniia, and they indicate a considerable degree of continuity over time in peasant consciousness and behavior.

The same was true of the common patterns that gave unity to this apparently amorphous form of peasant protest. As before emancipation, the peasants showed a high degree of collective consciousness, a strong sense of what they regarded as their rights, an unwillingness to be pushed around by "outsiders," and a concomitant desire to run their own affairs. As before, rumor often played a major role both in spurring the peasants on and in guiding the responses of the frightened authorities, who were often as much in the dark about the peasants' intentions as were the peasants about theirs. And as before, the outcome of any volnenie was highly unpredictable. Indeed, in a sense this characteristic not only underlay but made possible the survival of the volnenie as a major form of peasant protest; if volneniia had always ended in abject failure and brutal suppression, it is hard to imagine peasants continuing to resort to them as often as they did. Suppression may have been the most common consequence of volneniia, but hope for some redress of grievances—a hope nurtured by the peasants' pervasive "naïve monarchism"—was essential to their endurance.[47]

But despite this basic continuity in form that linked the disturbances that broke out in the spring and summer of 1861 with those that had been endemic in the era of serfdom, the new volneniia departed from the earlier ones in significant ways. Perhaps most central—and in turn responsible for other important differences—they were associated with a real rather than an imagined change in conditions. As a result, the rumors that swirled around and fueled these volneniia, although based in part on "misunderstandings" of specific provisions of the emancipation legislation, were grounded in a broad general reality. The combination of the reality of emancipation with the murky and arcane details that defined its terms and implementation proved fertile soil for the growth of peasants' conviction that they were the objects of a massive campaign to substitute a fraudulent seigneurial settlement for the freedom they had been promised by the tsar. In a sense, they were right, for noble landowners did everything in their power to preserve their prerogatives and minimize the effects of the reforms.

These changed conditions gave rise to peasant unrest that dwarfed the disturbances that had characterized the decades leading up to emancipation. Soviet historians (and some post-Soviet and Western ones as well) devoted considerable time and effort to measuring and categorizing the elements of the "peasant movement," both during the immediate aftermath of the emancipation edict and in general. Such efforts inevitably suffer from incomplete records—large volneniia were more likely than small to generate paperwork, and even when paperwork was abundant it was not always preserved—and from difficulties in agreeing on methods of categorization. (For example, because volneniia sometimes encompassed more than one estate, counting the number of estates involved in unrest yields larger figures than counting the number of individual volneniia, and because some were much larger than others, looking at numbers of peasants involved can suggest still different trends.) Nevertheless, the unprecedented nature of the emancipation-generated unrest is clear: the compilers of the massive *Krest'ianskoe dvizhenie* series, noting that additional evidence from local archives would substantially add to their totals, identified 1,889 volneniia that occurred during the calendar year 1861, with the highest concentration between April and June. By contrast, according to figures provided by those same scholars, the average annual number of estates involved in volneniia during the period 1796–1855 was 37.7, and during that period by far the largest annual number, 161, came in 1848, when unrest in Russia's western provinces was stoked by the revolutionary movements that erupted in central Europe. By conservative standards, the disorders of 1861 were fifty times as numerous as in the average pre-emancipation-era year, and more volneniia occurred in 1861 than in the entire forty-five-year period 1811–1855.[48] Indeed, although the term aroused a good deal of skepticism among post-Soviet and Western historians, many Soviet scholars argued that as Russia grappled with peasant emancipation the country was gripped by a "revolutionary situation" that threatened the very basis of the existing social order.[49]

As they struggled for their rights, peasants faced conditions that were in some ways considerably more favorable than those they had faced in the past. With emancipation, their struggle took on a new aura of legitimacy, one that was recognized by the state itself if not by most pomeshchiki. Although peasants faced formidable odds when challenging authority, those odds seemed a little less formidable than they had in the past, and outside forces seemed a little less uniformly hostile. The government's official position for the first time had endorsed a substantial expansion of peasant rights and recognized that expansion in detailed legislation, and a new group of officials—the peace mediators—were in theory neutral figures whose task was to supervise transition to the new order, not to maintain the supremacy of the old. Although peasants were largely unaware of outside sentiment, there was a significant amount of sympathy for their cause among progressive reformers—the "enlightened bureaucrats"—and even more from the small radical intelligentsia that burst into public view as censorship in St. Petersburg was relaxed and reform became the watchword of the day. And, of course, peasants were convinced that they had an ally where it counted the most, in the tsar.

At the same time, however, the peasants' aspirations faced a major obstacle in the government's unwavering commitment to maintain order at all costs. An early hint of that commitment and a harbinger of future developments came in April, with the replacement of the "liberal" minister of internal affairs S. S. Lanskoi by the law-and-order bureaucrat Petr Valuev. Determined to prevent "lying rumors," "misunderstandings," and dangerous radicals from taking advantage of a precarious situation, the government engaged in a massive effort to put down the mushrooming disorders. Although not all officials took an uncompromising position in dealing with peasant demands—some peace mediators took their roles seriously—many did, and even officials most sympathetic to peasant aspirations were unwilling to tolerate what they saw as rowdy challenges to legitimate authority. Indeed, if the unrest that followed the onset of emancipation was unprecedented, so too was the severity of the government response. Whereas in the past authorities had resolved the great majority of volneniia through a combination of negotiations, promises, trickery, and exemplary punishment of ringleaders, during what increasingly seemed like a crisis in the post-emancipation months panicky officials turned to the military to restore order in about half the peasant outbreaks. Noting that "Whip!" had become the "motto and cry of the district nobility," one nobleman in Vladimir Province observed that local authorities were in fact "whip[ping] indiscriminately and without mercy." "Never in the most terrible times of known law," he added, "has there been so much extra-judicial punishment as now."[50]

There was a lot of whipping in the American South as well. The balance of power and the particular conditions that prevailed in the defeated Confederate states guaranteed that even more than in Russia, despite some officials' fears of the freedpeople's "extravagant" expectations, violence and potential violence came primarily from the former slave owners. Lacking the numerical majority in most of the South that peasants enjoyed in Russia and concerned that any hint of unruly behavior could provoke massive retribution from embittered whites, African Americans were usually careful to appear nonthreatening even as they cautiously strove to test the limits of their new freedom. Many white Southerners, however, seething at the loss of not just their slaves but also their war, showed less caution. Although the presence of federal soldiers and Freedmen's Bureau officials served to set limits to anti-Black violence, these Yankee occupiers were spread too thinly to provide more than the most tenuous protection to "loyal" Southerners, white or Black.[51]

Indeed, violence against African Americans was pervasive in the postemancipation South. During the spring, summer, and fall of 1865, military officers, Freedmen's Bureau officials, Northern travelers and journalists, and Southern Blacks themselves told of a surge of anti-Black atrocities that in some areas constituted nothing short of calculated terrorism. Writing from Meridian, Mississippi, in July, Lieutenant C. W. Clarke reported "many complaints" from neighboring counties in Alabama of "great cruelties"—including "whipping and the most severe modes of punishment"—"practiced upon freedmen by their former masters." A bureau official in Fernandina, Florida, wrote Commissioner Howard of widespread "force and violence" used by planters to "induce the freedmen to remain and labor as usual." A story in the Huntsville *Advocate* told of planters offering labor contracts to freedpeople that specifically allowed them "to be whipped when they need[ed] it," with the planters reassuring them, "You know none but bad negroes are whipped, and you are good negroes." Lieutenant Colonel C. S. Brown, after describing brutal atrocities against Blacks and Union soldiers in South Carolina, suggested that the former slaves there were in fact "not Freedmen and women"; although "nominally such," he declared, "their condition *indeed* is worse than bondage itself." After touring the Southern states and hearing harrowing accounts of physical abuse, President Johnson's emissary General Carl Schurz agreed that the use of force against African Americans was so extensive that their freedom remained in question. Observing that "although the freedman is no longer considered the property of the individual master, he is considered the slave of society," Schurz concluded that the only practical way to provide protection to the freedpeople was to give them "a certain measure of political power."[52]

As Schurz's recommendation suggests, the steady stream of reports on atrocities against the freedpeople—together with accompanying reports on the continued disloyalty of many Southern whites—provided a major impetus toward Congress's adoption of an increasingly radical Reconstruction policy. In early 1866, the Joint Congressional Committee on Reconstruction held extensive hearings that provided additional evidence confirming the widespread reports of violence against, and in some cases rape and murder of, former slaves, hearings that both led to new civil rights legislation and presaged on a smaller scale similar hearings that would be held five years later in response to a new wave of terror engineered by the Ku Klux Klan. If the very existence of these hearings points to serious governmental efforts to confront anti-Black violence, it also indicates the scope of the problem that former slaves faced as they sought to build new lives for themselves as free citizens. Even when apparently contained, violence and the threat of violence defined the parameters of the class struggle in the postwar South.[53]

As in Russia, the former slaves sought a *real* freedom, one that conformed to their notions of self-government as well as self-ownership. In areas where Black people formed an overwhelming majority of the population, this effort could produce tactics that—at least to many whites—invoked long-harbored fears of Black insurrection. After his appointment by Assistant Commissioner Rufus Saxton as the Freedmen's Bureau superintendent for Georgia's Sea Islands in April 1865, the Northern-born African American Tunis Campbell spearheaded an ambitious plan to turn the area into a separate, all-Black enclave with its own government headquartered on St. Catherine's Island. Barring whites from the islands (which slaveholders had fled when federal troops arrived early in the war), Campbell encouraged new Black settlers, raised a militia, and "steadily nudged the colony toward black self-determination." Although the scheme soon met with defeat—Saxton's successor, Davis Tillson, fired Campbell from his bureau position in early 1866—it indicated one extreme of what might be possible under the fluid conditions that prevailed in 1865. Tillson, who supported a far more conservative version of "free labor" than did Saxton (let alone Campbell), encouraged whites to return to their former plantations and issued Special Order 130 barring Campbell, whom he labeled "guilty of dishonest practices," from Sapelo Island. The fiery leader would continue to be active in Reconstruction politics, however, testing the limits of Black assertion, inspiring hope among South Carolina's Lowcountry freedpeople, fear among former slave owners, and disapproval among most white Republicans.[54]

In most of the South, however, the freedpeople pursued their goals during the immediate postwar months in a decidedly more cautious, less threatening manner. Unlike the Russian peasants, they did not focus on rejecting what they considered false readings of emancipation, because the terms were still to be determined; like the peasants, however, they sought to shape those terms for the better, based on their understanding of the right to control their own lives. In so doing, they embarked on a long-term struggle that encompassed numerous areas of life, from defending (and renegotiating) the integrity of their families to running their own churches (discussed in chapter 6). As in Russia, the freedpeople's quest for *true* freedom was a general one, with diverse manifestations whose unifying feature was the effort to maximize independence, to establish relationships that were as far removed as possible from slave-like subservience. Central to that effort was establishing new, "free," forms of labor relations.

One particularly revealing manifestation of this struggle to shape the new terms of labor was the freedpeople's widespread refusal to work under the supervision of overseers, a refusal that was instrumental in restructuring the post-emancipation plantation in much of the South (discussed in chapter 5). In June 1865, the freedpeople on Henry Watson's large plantation in Greene County, Alabama, took advantage of their owner's absence in Germany to engage in a protest that looked very much like a Russian volnenie. Refusing to acknowledge the overseer's authority, they engaged in negotiations with a succession of figures that began with Watson's friend J. A. Wemyss and brother-in-law John Parrish and quickly escalated to include federal authorities. Noting that "their complaints were universal, very ugly," Parrish turned for support to a newly appointed Freedmen's Bureau agent, while seventeen of the freedpeople left to seek help from Union soldiers in nearby Uniontown. The agent, however, disappointed Parrish by "modif[ying] . . . in the negroes['] fav[or]" a "compromise" arrangement that Wemyss had earlier reached with the plantation hands. Coming home from Germany later in the year, Watson returned to a radically changed environment: the freedpeople "claim of their masters full and complete compliance on their part," he complained, "but forget that they agreed to do anything on theirs." "They are all idle," he added, "doing nothing, insisting that they shall be fed off their masters."[55]

The struggle that Watson's former slaves waged, together with the reaction of the planter and his agents, are revealing in a number of ways. They show a planter class that still took for granted a slave owner's worldview.[56] In writing to Watson about events on his plantation, Parrish referred to the freedpeople as "your negroes" and indicated that they had "rebelled" against the overseer; Watson still called himself and his neighboring planters "masters" and expected slave-like subservience from the freedpeople. Those freedpeople, by contrast, were already living in a post-slavery world, in which their goal was to maximize their autonomy, to get as far as possible from the servile dependence that planters still expected of them. Any "compromise" between these two positions had to be highly unstable, a temporary measure that each side would seek to modify as soon as possible. As significant as the contrasting goals were the changed forms of struggle that emancipation had made possible. The kind of collective action that Watson's former slaves displayed represented a rapid adjustment on their part to the new environment in which they found themselves. If the freedpeople quickly embraced and gradually fine-tuned new forms of struggle, planters found the adjustment a wrenching one. Nevertheless, they too would develop new methods of promoting their interests, methods that were compatible with the new, free-labor world in which they now lived.

Although the freedpeople's desire to control their own lives was inevitably manifested in the pursuit of specific goals and the effort to overcome specific forms of exploitation, of overriding importance immediately after the war was the question of who would control the freedpeople's labor, and how. That question, which precipitated the dispute on the Watson plantation over subservience to the overseer's authority, more generally underlay the effort of freedpeople to influence how—and how much—they worked, and the widespread complaints of white Southerners that Blacks were refusing to work. Such complaints were in part products of a lingering slave owner mentality, and the conviction of former masters that without compulsion African Americans would inevitably exhibit their natural tendencies toward laziness and irresponsibility, but they also reflected the very real alarm of landowners who faced an uncertain future and who were determined to maintain a semblance of what they understood as normality in tumultuous and frightening times. The autonomy that the former slaves saw as the essence of their new freedom appeared to planters as an assault on civilization itself, an assault destined to produce, in the words of one Louisiana planter, "the end of what has been the most splendid [of] agricultural countries in the world."[57]

It is in this context that the widespread white fear that freed Blacks would not work must be understood. Determined to prevent the triumph of a fake emancipation, freedpeople did, in fact, find controlling—and at times withholding— their labor not only an earmark of their freedom but also an invaluable tactic in their struggle to guarantee the reality of that freedom. Aside from their refusing to work under the supervision of overseers, a variety of features would characterize this struggle over the coming months, and in some cases were already evident in 1865. These included an effort to acquire land or, barring that, to find work that provided maximum independence; continued migration, in order to secure such employment; and the partial withdrawal from field labor of women and children, who were now able to allocate their time in ways previously forbidden, from engaging in homemaking to attending school. But the most striking manifestation of the freedpeople's effort to gain control over their own labor in the summer and fall of 1865 was their reluctance to enter into labor arrangements for the coming year. If the new labor contracts that the Freedmen's Bureau promoted as central to the free-labor system seemed suspect to many freedpeople—how could they be sure that in signing such contracts they were not in fact signing away their freedom?—they quickly learned that their maximum leverage in shaping the terms of labor came *before* they entered into any agreement. Dragging their feet, sometimes to the extent of refusing or apparently refusing to sign new contracts, proved a potent weapon in the struggle to improve their conditions of labor. It also proved infuriating to planters who already felt deeply humiliated by the need to negotiate with their former slaves.[58]

As in Russia, rumor and pretended rumor at multiple levels accompanied the birth of free labor in the post-emancipation South.[59] Beginning innocuously enough with habitual complaints that Blacks, displaying both their innate laziness and their mistaken understandings of freedom, would not work without compulsion, white Southerners soon began warning that the freedpeople expected a general land redistribution or, in a more ominous version, were planning a massive insurrection on Christmas Day 1865 or New Year's Day 1866. These rumors were already widely circulating by summer of 1865. In August, for example, former Confederate major Josiah Gorgas observed from Alabama, "The negroes still seem to expect a division of lands and hope for some undefined good on the 1st of January," while North Carolina's Freedmen's Bureau head E. Whittlesey reported that "many freedmen" were refusing to work "because they believe[d] that farms [would] be given them by the United States government."[60]

As summer gave way to fall, complaints of the freedmen's refusal to work, expectations of land, and planned insurrection became more persistent and more urgent. "It is very certain that the negroes are expecting a distribution of property this winter," wrote Mississippi's provisional governor W. L. Sharkey to bureau chief Howard, "and it is also certain that we have many reasons to believe that a general revolt is contemplated in case the property is not distributed." A white Alabamian, noting "considerable excitement," wrote her brother: "Some think there will be a rising of the negroes here on Saturday or Monday night." This observation was unusual only in warning of an immediate revolt rather than one at the end of the year or beginning of 1866. A low-level bureau official, reporting on the creation of "Black Patrols" in the Tuskegee, Alabama, vicinity, noted this widespread "impression" among freedpeople: "Something will transpire about the close of the current year by which they are going to be greatly benefited," while a white militia commander wrote Alabama's governor Lewis Parsons from Shelby County that Blacks were "arming themselves" and "becoming very impudent"; he added, "Unless something is done very soon I fear the consequences." Referring to fears of insurrection, Georgia's bureau assistant commissioner Davis Tillson placed part of the blame on proverbial outside agitators: "Throughout the State great harm has been done by well-meaning but thoughtless public speakers who have given the freed people unreal and mistaken ideas of freedom, equality, and the rights secured to them."[61]

As the reports by Tillson and Whittlesey indicate, Freedmen's Bureau officials sometimes not only reported on but also at least partially subscribed to the fears of Black insurrection. Even agents who saw themselves as friends of the freedpeople and were skeptical of planters' motives worried that there might be some grounds for their fears. South Carolina's assistant commissioner Rufus Saxton, a strong supporter of greater rights for African Americans, observed that freedpeople did not trust the promises of planters to pay them after the completion of work instead of in advance, and were therefore refusing to enter into labor contracts for the following year. "The impression is universal among the freedmen," he added, "that they are to have the abandoned and confiscated lands in homesteads of forty acres in January next." Florida's assistant commissioner T. W. Osborn, far from a mouthpiece of the state's planters, agreed with them that the rumor of land redistribution was "quite prevalent all through the State" and noted that freedpeople were therefore refusing to enter into contracts "until after Christmas[,] when they say the lands are to be distributed." Throughout the South, federal authorities, unsure of African Americans' intentions, strove to disabuse them of excessive expectations. Alabama's assistant commissioner Wager Swayne, noting the widespread belief among Blacks in a general land redistribution "about the close of this year," deplored this expectation as "fruitful of idleness, disappointment and mischief, and of no good whatever" and urged them to continue working faithfully for their current employers. Swayne's subordinate, Assistant Superintendent S. S. Gardner, published a set of "Facts for Freedmen" explaining that there would be no land distribution and advising Blacks to stay in the countryside and enter into labor contracts; at the same time, he advised them to reject contracts that allowed corporal punishment and to seek reasonable compensation for their labor—he suggested $10 per month.[62]

Even as they sought to refute what they considered exaggerated expectations, however, Freedmen's Bureau officials typically expressed considerable skepticism over reports of impending Black insurrection. After noting Florida's freedpeople's expectations of land, Assistant Commissioner T. W. Osborn added that he considered fears of Black insurrection "groundless." Other federal officials went much further, seeing those fears as not simply groundless but deliberately provocative. Four days after Mississippi's governor Sharkey wrote Howard warning of a planned insurrection, Samuel Thomas, the state's assistant commissioner, ridiculed the idea as "absurd." Two weeks later, Thomas sharply criticized Sharkey, suggesting, "People who talk so much of insurrections, and idleness, and vagrancy among the freedmen have an ulterior motive." In their reports from the field, Thomas's agents typically denounced rumors "circulated by designing men" of an impending Black revolt while at the same time *crediting* reports that freedpeople expected a year-end land redistribution. In other words, freedpeople held unrealistic expectations of land distribution, but white fears of Black insurrection were equally farfetched.[63]

The widespread belief among freedpeople that a general land division was imminent, widespread fears among white landowners that Blacks were planning a massive uprising, and widespread uncertainty among Freedmen's Bureau officials over what to believe indicate the overall state of confusion under which the emancipation settlement unfolded in the immediate postwar period. As in Russia, the freedpeople and the former owners had very different notions of what freedom was about and jockeyed to defend their particular versions of it. But who really believed what was unclear in this fluid situation. Many federal officials were convinced that white Southerners were inventing—or at least manipulating—fears of a Black insurrection for self-serving reasons; as Carl Schurz reported to President Johnson, "Rumors are spread about impending negro insurrections evidently for no other purpose than to serve as a pretext for annoying police regulations concerning the colored people." But other officials suspected that these fears were not entirely groundless, and their frequent admonitions to African Americans to be orderly and deferential indicate the extent to which they shared at least some of the planters' concern about possible Black disorder. Meanwhile, throughout the South freedpeople showed concern over attempts to trick them out of their promised freedom; in the words of one report, African Americans believed "that if they hire themselves for the next year, they will be [compelled] to remain with the same employer for five years." In their determination not to be cheated, supposedly gullible freedpeople could show a healthy suspicion when dealing with unknown whites. When Freedmen's Bureau officials told Blacks in the South Carolina Lowcountry that they would not receive the land that they had been promised by General Sherman, Captain Charles C. Soule reported to Howard, they were convinced "that these envoys were not United States officers, but planters in disguise 'hired' to cajole them into 'signing away their freedom.' " Why else would those unknown whites be urging them to sign contracts that committed them to work for their former owners?[64]

A comparison of the former serfs' and slaves' responses to emancipation, and to the new conditions they faced in the immediate post-emancipation months, suggests varied behavior in support of similar goals. In some ways, the differences appear most striking. In general, the American freedpeople displayed more open enthusiasm than the Russian, who often masked their emotions with inscrutable impassivity. Building on their long history of organized confrontations with those who had authority over them, the peasants engaged in widespread collective actions—*volneniia*—in defense of what they regarded as their just rights. Lacking the same kind of numerical majority and the same tradition of collective resistance, African Americans took advantage of new opportunities to act in common, as in their refusal to recognize the authority of Henry Watson's overseer or to accept coercive labor contracts, but overall they behaved cautiously, aware that they were in a sense on trial; the presence of Yankee allies—both in Washington and on the ground in the South—encouraged this effort to prove their responsibility and trustworthiness as "loyal" Southerners who deserved the thanks of the nation. And within each country as well, freedpeople reacted in diverse ways to news of their freedom and in their subsequent struggles to make the most of a changed world; these internal variations receive more attention in chapters 3 and 4.

Despite such contrasts and variations, the freedpeople pursued a common goal centered on securing what they regarded as *real* freedom, grounded in self-ownership and self-government. Precisely what that meant was not always clear, or perhaps more accurately came in different versions. More clear was what it did *not* mean. In both countries, even as they looked forward expectantly to their new status, freedpeople harbored deep suspicions that they faced a massive effort to cheat them out of the liberty they were "supposed" to receive. This suspicion was especially pervasive in Russia, where peasants found it hard to credit the good intentions of nobles, whether they appeared in the form of estate owners or government officials; in the United States, the presence of Yankee allies counteracted to some extent the suspicion that no white person could be fully trusted. But confidence in Yankee protection could go only so far. Not only were Union forces spread too thin to provide full security and federal intentions too uncertain to reassure anxious freedpeople, interaction with Northerners yielded at best mixed messages. Constant exhortations to be orderly and responsible seemed eerily similar to the sermons slaves had heard from white ministers, and at least some freedpeople found white Northerners to be little different from white Southerners. The Federal Writers Project collection of interviews with former slaves contains numerous accounts of mistreatment at the hands of Union soldiers, especially theft and destruction of property—including that of slaves; when one Black woman reprimanded a soldier for stealing from the slaves for whose freedom they professed to be fighting, he responded bluntly, "You're a G—D—liar, I'm fightin' for $14 a month and the Union."[65]

The freedpeople's fear that they were about to lose their freedom before they had fully received it was to some extent founded (as outside observers suggested) in ignorance: far removed from seats of power, peasants and African Americans found it easy to credit a wide variety of conflicting versions of what was going on, from the "naïve monarchism" that had long been a staple of Russian peasant culture and had a number of American equivalents, including belief in the imminent arrival of "forty acres and a mule," to (at the opposite extreme) the conviction that by giving written consent to labor contracts or statutory charters they risked legitimizing whatever inequities might follow. To largely illiterate peasants and African Americans the written word could assume almost mystical powers, as evident in such fear of signing away their freedom, the proliferation (especially but not exclusively in Russia) of "readers" who claimed the ability to interpret the arcane emancipation provisions "correctly," and the freedpeople's fervent desire to promote literacy (and more generally education itself). That desire would be a continuing characteristic of the post-emancipation era.

But if the freedpeople were unfamiliar with the details of legislation and could exhibit a credulous readiness to accept the reality of what more educated and informed observers considered ridiculous (or "extravagant"), in a broader sense peasants and African Americans were remarkably prescient in their understanding of the obstacles they faced, an understanding born of experience. To those who had endured the multiple burdens of a lifetime in bondage, it did not seem unreasonable to be leery of oppressors who now professed to be friends, or to be concerned about being cheated out of their freedom. In fact, those fears were far from groundless: the freedpeople did in fact face a concerted effort on the part of their former owners and their political allies to set such severe limits on the new freedom that it would be more in name than in fact. In short, the freedpeople understood all too well the intensity of the ongoing class struggle.

Making sense of the multiple, overlapping rumors, suspicions, and beliefs that circulated in the immediate post-emancipation period in Russia and the American South is a herculean task. If many contemporary observers and some subsequent historians were most impressed by the freedpeople's gullibility and lack of understanding, some more recent scholars have recognized in this "gullibility" a set of beliefs and behavior that indicated far more than lack of understanding—in other words, these scholars have begun to take the worldview and aspirations of the freedpeople seriously. Central to this understanding is the insight that "foolish" or "outlandish" beliefs could be useful to those who held them and that "irrational" behavior could have a logic of its own. Indeed, rumor could serve as a "weapon," one that simultaneously reflected the sometimes "naïve" hopes and aspirations of the freedpeople and helped them promote those hopes and aspirations.

Among the historians who have begun to explore the freedpeople's consciousness, Daniel Field and Steven Hahn have offered particularly valuable and nuanced analyses of the way they used rumor to pursue their interests. Noting the difficulty of fathoming peasant thought— "Peasants were intractable to their contemporaries and, a century or more later, they are intractable to us"—Field set the peasants' post-emancipation behavior in the context of their long-standing "naïve monarchism," which he reformulated as simultaneously an ingrained element of peasant culture and a clever, consciously crafted strategy that "provided a ready-made and acceptable excuse for insubordination." "The myth of the tsar was useful to peasants in conflict with the authorities," he explained. Arguing that "there is . . . no necessary contradiction between sincere belief and manipulation, defensive or otherwise," Field refused to choose between whether peasants truly adhered to the many beliefs that contemporaries considered outlandish or espoused them for opportunistic reasons; sincerity and manipulation were inexorably intertwined. Still,

Field's analysis suggested the centrality of self-interest in explaining peasant behavior: "Naïve or not, the peasants professed their faith in the tsar in forms, and only in those forms, that corresponded to their interests."[66]

Hahn's analysis, in some ways very similar to Field's, pushed the argument a step further to embrace the use of rumor by the ex-owners as well as the ex-slaves. Like Field, Hahn set the freedpeoples' post-emancipation behavior in historical context, noting the widespread circulation among slaves of rumors of an impending emancipation and placing the freedpeople's behavior "in the tradition of involving the just and good ruler betrayed by unfaithful subordinates." Like Field, Hahn denied that the freedpeople's many beliefs that contemporaries considered outlandish should be "dismissed as mere 'illusions' entertained by ex-slaves," instead seeing them as a "weapon" that the freedpeople consciously used to pursue their goals. But Hahn suggested that rumor served as a weapon of planters seeking to resist change as well as of freedpeople seeking to promote it: both sides embraced, for their own purposes, "mutually reinforcing rumors of a world turned wholly upside down either by federal government fiat or armed Black insurrection." Sincerely held hopes and fears served at the same time as carefully constructed instruments to advance specific goals: "Just as white landowners turned rumors of land distribution into harbingers of insurrection so as to reassert their local prerogatives, the freedpeople used the rumors of land redistribution to bolster their own bargaining positions."[67]

One reason so many overlapping and conflicting rumors flourished in the immediate wake of emancipation is that what lay ahead appeared unusually murky: because precisely what would replace slavery and serfdom was not yet clear, almost anything was conceivable. Before emancipation, the naïve monarchism of the serfs—and to a lesser extent of the slaves—was unsupported by actual evidence that a benevolent ruler intended to act on their behalf; after emancipation, that evidence was abundant, if poorly defined. In short, the freedpeople's expectations of something better, delivered from on high, was for the first time to some degree based on reality. So, too, were the fears of the former owners, who now faced an unpredictable future in an uncertain world. An environment in which uncertainty coexisted with rapid change, where virtually anything seemed possible but at the same time nothing could be taken for granted, was ready-made for the proliferation of competing rumors, which required competing action. If everything was up for grabs, making sure that the "correct" version of the future in fact ensued was of utmost importance. For the freedpeople, it made sense to expect the best—in the process helping to bring it about—while being prepared to resist the worst. For the former owners, it made sense to prepare for—and if possible resist—the worst, in the process preventing its implementation.

In both Russia and the South, the initial phase of the emancipation-induced crises, which seemed to some to threaten the survival of civilization itself, passed quickly. Although order remained precarious in the Russian countryside, officials breathed a sigh of relief as the new instruments of rural government—provincial and district offices of peasant affairs, peace mediators, and at the lowest level the peasant "communities" that expanded local self-government—took shape and managed to restore a measure of stability. By midsummer, the tsar's aides-de-camp and provincial governors were sending reassuring messages to St. Petersburg, crediting the establishment of the new administrative bodies with bringing about more harmonious relations in the countryside. Frequently, the aides noted—often in their final report—that their presence was no longer needed because "complete calm" had been restored. If some officials attributed these improved conditions to the arrival of the peace mediators, others pointed to the positive influence of the newly elected peasant officials. Typical was Minister of Internal Affairs Valuev's September 1 report that the governors of several provinces were praising the newly elected peasant leaders for dispelling "false interpretations of the [emancipation] legislation." In his final report from Simbirsk Province, the imperial aide noted that there had been no peasant complaints since the arrival of the peace mediators, but he also praised the "most beneficial influence" of peasant self-government, noting that having chosen their own leaders, the peasants "[saw] them as defenders of their rights." By July, the new rural administrative agencies were largely in place, most of the imperial aides had been withdrawn, and a shaky calm had been restored.[68]

Fears of a general Christmas or New Year's Day uprising that Southern—and some Northern—whites harbored proved equally transitory, and at the start of the new year observers noted a sharp change in mood. "Since my last report," wrote an army officer in January 1866 from Georgetown, South Carolina, "the Freedmen have apparently given up the idea that they will have lands given them or divided among them." From Bennettsville, South Carolina, a planter remarked with surprise that "the negroes are not only working, but working better than when they were slaves." The situation was similar elsewhere. Mississippi's assistant commissioner Thomas reported to Howard, "The Freedmen have all gone to work," adding that white sentiment toward

African Americans was markedly improved. "Everywhere the negroes were praised for their readiness to work and their general good conduct . . . ," he noted. "The foolish stories that seemed to distract the state so long, are no longer heard." "One thing is obvious," observed a planter in Alabama, "the negroes, who are hired are farming and working much better than anyone predicted they would work." Rather than complaining of their refusal to enter into contracts, Freedmen's Bureau officials, army officers, and even some Southern whites praised the freedpeople for being orderly and hard working.[69]

As officials in the South and Russia congratulated themselves on the restoration of order, the freedpeople's quest for *true* freedom entered a new phase of what would be a protracted struggle, a struggle that evolved within political environments that were increasingly different in the two countries. In Russia, the unprecedented liberalism that had flourished in the months leading up to issuance of the emancipation manifesto was already on the wane by the spring of 1861, as was evident in the replacement of Lanskoi by Valuev as minister of internal affairs and the harsh suppression of anything that smacked of peasant insubordination, which officials almost always interpreted as representing disorder. During subsequent years the government's move to the right would accelerate, as the tsar acted to stifle intellectual dissent, appease anxious nobles, suppress a Polish insurrection, and make sure that no one misunderstood "reform" as legitimizing a challenge to autocracy. In the United States, a Congress frustrated with President Johnson's obstruction of its Reconstruction policies moved sharply to the left, passing a broad array of measures that earlier had seemed unlikely and that aroused growing hopes among the freedpeople and their radical allies. As peasants grew increasingly fearful that their promised freedom was in danger of being snatched away, African Americans grew increasingly hopeful that their promised freedom was at hand. In both countries, a protracted fight for that freedom lay ahead.

3 • The Struggle Continues
Land, Labor, and Liberty

The weathering of what had appeared to be a general threat to the social order in the months immediately following emancipation ushered in a protracted struggle over the details of that order in both Russia and the American South. As they sought to shape the nature of their new status, freedpeople in Russia and the South faced conditions—and obstacles—that were in many ways similar. In both countries, the determination to secure a *real* freedom and disappointment over its elusive quality were palpable. Although this disappointment remained more tentative in the South because the precise terms of the emancipation settlement there remained to be finalized, innumerable signs—from the federal government's return of confiscated lands to their original owners to repressive measures taken by "restored" state governments—provided cause for concern. In both countries, the freedpeople quickly learned that transforming "freedom" into something more than a legal technicality would require continuing struggle.

Despite these shared goals and concerns of the former slaves and serfs, their struggles evolved within political contexts that were increasingly different. In Russia, virtually no one in power contemplated uncompensated land redistribution, whereas in the United States a significant proportion of the dominant Republican Party, including some of its most influential leaders, did. Although a land redistribution bill failed to pass Congress (and would have faced a certain veto by President Johnson if it had), the substantial support that it garnered indicated the growing potential for a far-reaching policy to remake the South along more democratic lines; in June 1866 Congress passed a Southern Homestead Act that featured the right to claim eighty acres of public land in five Deep South states, a right that for the first six months was restricted to "loyal" Southerners (most of whom were former slaves).[1] More generally, as political reaction intensified in Russia, political Reconstruction in the United States grew increasingly radical, providing new hopes to those who favored a sweeping effort to remake the Southern social order.

Still, the extent to which—and how—these differing contexts actually shaped conditions on the ground remained to be determined. Governments in St. Petersburg and Washington had only so much direct influence on local relations between the former owners and the former bondspeople, and these relations evolved in the context of an uncertain and untested balance of power. Even as the freedpeople sought to grasp the moment, their former owners waged a determined effort to maintain as many of their prerogatives as possible, in the process gaining considerable support from local governments, while new officials—Freedmen's Bureau agents and peace mediators—wrestled with issues that seemed both intractable and unpredictable. The end result of this combustible mix appeared up for grabs.

As the freedpeople struggled to secure a *real* freedom, they encountered two agencies—the Freedmen's Bureau and the Office of Peace Mediators—that embodied the governments' efforts to shape the new order. In many ways, these two agencies were similar. Both were temporary bodies designed to facilitate and guide the transition from bondage to freedom; although the Russian version remained in place longer than the American, both were substantially reduced in strength within a few years and abolished soon thereafter—the Freedmen's Bureau gradually, between 1869 and 1872, and the Office of Peace Mediators suddenly, in 1874. The mandate of the American organization was broader than the Russian, including such diverse functions as feeding the hungry (Black and white) and providing logistical support for the establishment of freedpeople's schools, but both focused their attention in the immediate post-emancipation period on supervising the transition to a free-labor system. In doing so, each had to walk a narrow path, protecting the rights of the freedpeople while making sure that they did not "abuse" those rights by being lazy or disorderly.[2]

In both countries, the uncertain nature of the new labor relations was central to this transition, and despite guidelines from on high that were especially precise and detailed in Russia, Freedmen's Bureau officials and peace mediators had to work out on the ground, in hundreds of separate actions and decisions, how these guidelines would be put into practice. As they did this, they faced potential opposition from the former slave owners and serf owners and the former bondspeople, even while receiving impassioned appeals and complaints from both as well. The mediating officials were spread thin: at their peak strength of 1,714 peace mediators and nine hundred Freedmen's Bureau agents, each official supervised an average of about thirteen thousand and four thousand freedpeople, respectively, although, especially in the United States, such average figures hid wide disparities. When necessary, the officials could call on military support, although (again, especially in the Southern United States) the military itself was spread too thin to provide more than temporary, sporadic intervention.[3]

Both at the time and among subsequent historians, evaluating the character of the two agencies has generated considerable disagreement. Even as Blacks and peasants turned to Freedmen's Bureau agents and peace mediators for help in securing what they considered real freedom, many of them complained that those officials were less than fully supportive, and—especially in Russia—the freedpeople saw them as outsiders, representatives of a hostile government bureaucracy who sought to maintain more than to challenge the status quo. Many former owners—especially in the South—even as they looked to the new officials to maintain order and disabuse freedpeople of extravagant expectations, considered these officials interlopers who were at best misguided and at worst part of a revolutionary effort to turn naturally submissive Black people and peasants against their masters. Facing "hostility from all parties involved," peace mediators and Freedmen's Bureau officials had to engage in the almost impossible task of balancing the conflicting hopes, expectations, and fears of former bondspeople who sought to maximize their new freedom and former owners who sought to limit it.[4]

In the broadest sense, the historiography of the Freedmen's Bureau and that of the peace mediators have evolved along similar lines over the past half century. The "revisionist" interpretation of the Freedmen's Bureau that prevailed from the late 1960s into the 1980s bore striking similarities to the standard Soviet-era portrait of the peace mediators: both groups appeared—together with most government officials in general—as instruments of class oppression, more interested in preserving order and turning the freedpeople into hardworking, subservient laborers than in securing their newfound freedom. Since the 1980s, however, post-Soviet and post-revisionist historians have typically offered more nuanced—and usually more positive—assessments of the bureau agents' and mediators' varied character, goals, and abilities. Challenging the notion that the mediators "serve[d] primarily to defend the interests of the pomeshchiki, as is so often asserted in Soviet historiography," N. F. Ust'iantseva described most of the early mediators as "liberals" who "resisted the encroachments of the nobility." Similarly, Barry Crouch rejected the "generational chauvinism" underlying negative judgments of the Freedmen's Bureau, concluding that the bureau's "agents, at least in Texas, acquitted themselves rather remarkably." Although this broad historiographical evolution has by no means obliterated conflicting portraits of peace mediators and Freedmen's Bureau agents—some scholars continue to be more impressed by the class- and race-based limitations of the officials than by their fair-minded neutrality (let alone their interest in uplifting the oppressed)—recent historical research and reevaluation have somewhat narrowed the interpretive differences.[5]

Central to this reevaluation is a recognition of the extraordinary diversity that characterized both Freedmen's Bureau officials and peace mediators. Army officers who worked for the Freedmen's Bureau ranged from racists determined to promote Black subservience and free-labor advocates who saw their role as supervising the inauguration of an efficient wage-labor system to ardent egalitarians committed to advancing equal rights and protecting the freedpeople against continued oppression and exploitation. Agent Jno C. Moore considered Blacks in Fayette County, Alabama, careless and lazy; they were, he opined, "inclined to be roguish" and engage in petty theft, would work only under careful supervision, abused livestock, and had "but little respect for each other." But other agents were less concerned about misbehavior among Black people than among whites: in Tuskegee, Alabama, Assistant Superintendent A. Geddis, who found the freedpeople "very well disposed . . ., desirous to do right," bitterly denounced the brutal treatment of them by both local planters and Union soldiers who "worked with a view to please the white citizens, at the expense of, and injustice to, the Freedmen." Captain C. B. Wilder, bureau superintendent in Virginia's Ninth District, ordered his subordinate "to seize ½ of the crop of every planter who has failed to make contract with their Laborers," with the confiscated crop "to be used in paying the Colored people who have worked it." By contrast, Georgia's assistant commissioner Davis Tillson instructed his agents to follow a laissez-faire policy that "leaves labor, like any other commodity to sell itself, in the open market, to the highest bidder." The Freedmen's Bureau employed a tiny number of African American agents, including Tunis Campbell (see chapter 2) and John Mercer Langston, an Oberlin College graduate, abolitionist, and future United States representative from Virginia, who served as the bureau's inspector general of schools.[6]

Diversity also characterized the peace mediators, who—"neither uniformly progressive 'heralds of liberty' nor entirely greedy landlords in disguise"—

spanned the spectrum from idealists committed to transforming Russia into a "liberal" modern state with equal citizenship rights for all to self-seeking careerists and "cruel petty tyrants" unwilling or unable to take peasant aspirations seriously. Mediators included men from distinguished families, including Leo Tolstoy, M. S. Lanksoi (the son of the minister of internal affairs), and Nikolai Bakunin (brother of the radical Mikhail Bakunin). They also included men such as Nikolai Obolenskii, who felt nothing but hostility and contempt toward his peasant charges and complained that with only "moral force" he lacked the ability to combat their "striking insubordination." Although always a minority among the mediators, the liberals and idealists were most in evidence at the very onset of emancipation, when enthusiasm for the new reforms was widespread among educated Russians, from "enlightened bureaucrats" to intellectuals; over time, they increasingly yielded in numbers to "careerists" who were more interested in the perquisites of government service than in the well-being of the freedpeople and showed little inclination to challenge the interests of their fellow nobles. Even at the onset of emancipation, however, such careerists were far from absent among the mediators.[7]

Freedmen's Bureau agents and peace mediators not only varied considerably in approaching their new duties, they also sometimes disagreed with one another—both privately and in public—and elicited reprimands from higher authority. In November 1865, for example, conservative Brigadier General Joseph S. Fullerton, serving as temporary bureau assistant commissioner in Louisiana, telegraphed Commissioner Howard, sharply criticizing his predecessor, Thomas W. Conway, for being too solicitous of the freedpeople and too critical of Southern whites: "Do not give Conway any place . . . ," Fullerton urged. "Do not notice his letters." A few days later, in an official report to Howard, Fullerton broadened his target, complaining of other bureau agents who were hostile to Southern whites and encouraging freedpeople to subscribe to "exaggerated" hopes. Denying reports of widespread mistreatment of freedpeople, he noted "a growing disposition on the part of the planters to act justly and fairly toward the freedmen" and suggested that Blacks had little need of new government intervention because, in his words, "there is not amongst them an able-bodied man who cannot get employement and good wages." Soon thereafter, anticipating the report he would receive, President Johnson, increasingly distressed by what he considered excessively radical policies pursued by bureau agents, sent Fullerton, together with Major General James B. Steedman, on a tour to investigate bureau operations. Taking their cue from the president, Steedman and Fullerton reported that the bureau was encouraging laziness among African Americans and that whatever services it provided could be more effectively handled by regular army officers.⁸

Similar administrative discord was evident in Russia, where central government officials increasingly concerned with maintaining order had to cope with a minority of "liberal" peace mediators (and other officials in the provinces) who seemed excessively pro-peasant. Nikolai Tsilorovskii, a mediator in Orenberg Province, was arrested, jailed, and charged with the "criminal intention of raising rebellion among the peasants" after he went too far in expressing sympathy for their plight, telling them, "We will be brothers! I am demanding these concessions for you; if we don't get them, I am for arms!" In Tver Province, where liberal sentiment among nobles was unusually widespread, eight mediators and several other government officials were arrested and committed to a mental hospital for two years after they issued a statement in February 1862 calling the emancipation legislation a "failure" and advocating democratic political action "without respect to estates." Minister of Internal Affairs Petr Valuev was not always successful, however, in his efforts to muzzle liberal mediators; a special Senate investigation into supposed insubordination of such officials in Kaluga Province found no basis for complaint and suggested that in Vladimir Province authorities had—far from showing a pro-peasant bias—"colluded with the illegal activity of the landowners." There as elsewhere, in dealing with disputes between peasants and pomeshchiki, mediators were more likely to follow the path of those who, as noted by the governor of Riazan Province, "ben[t] their decisions in favor of the pomeshchiki" than of liberals who challenged abuse by noble landowners.⁹

Although diversity renders generalization difficult, and abundant evidence can be found supporting group portraits of Freedmen's Bureau officials and peace mediators that range from friends of the oppressed to agents of the oppressors, most of the officials tried to pursue some version of a middle course, reflecting the goal of establishing a "free labor" system that both the Russian and the American governments sought. Although they typically sympathized with the aspirations of the freedpeople, the mediating officials often shared the landowners' conviction that those freedpeople had unrealistic expectations and needed guidance in their transition to freedom. Concerns over the potential for disorder were pervasive among officials in both countries, and although many Freedmen's Bureau officials saw the threat as coming from former Confederates even more than from freedpeople, they also shared the peace mediators' understanding that one of their central tasks was convincing the freedpeople that freedom was not to be confused with license. Even Commissioner Howard, who was widely (and correctly) perceived as a supporter of African American rights, stressed the bureau's role in ensuring that order rather than chaos characterize the new freedom. Noting that immediately after the war planters "generally were without faith in the new order of things," Howard explained that bureau officials "succeeded to a considerable extent in arresting [the freedpeople's] tendencies to leave the plantations and flock to the cities, in inducing them to contract with the planters[,] in developing among them an increased sense of moral obligations, and in making them reliable laborers under the free system."[10]

Still, although most of the new officials fully shared the perspective of neither the former owners nor the former bondspeople, the Americans tilted more toward the freedpeople than did the Russians—or perhaps it would be more accurate to say that the Russians tilted more toward the landowners than did the Americans. Although Freedmen's Bureau officials displayed a wide range of temperaments and ideological proclivities, and many of them shared at least some of the racial views that prevailed among Southern whites, they were overall very much a centrist force, mediating between the former slaves and former owners and committed to the idea of free labor. Their racial prejudice was tempered by the war-generated sympathy for African Americans, and as Union army officers they were usually cool at best—and often downright hostile—toward former Confederates. In Russia, by contrast, the peace mediators, despite the existence of a minority of trophy liberals and humanitarians among them, found it difficult to take a middle position between peasants and pomeshchiki. Not only were almost all of the mediators noblemen and former serfholders themselves, most had local ties in the precincts where they were supposed to mediate, including ties of friendship and sometimes blood with the local nobility. When Vasilii Yazykov, a large landowner in Simbirsk Province, turned to the local peace mediator to help settle relations with his peasants, that peace mediator turned out to be his cousin. When peasants in Tula Province objected to the labor demands of their owner, that owner was not only a high-ranking nobleman (*statskii sovetnik*) but also the local peace mediator himself. There were peace mediators of good will toward the peasants, but everything in their upbringing, interests, and associations predisposed them to see matters through the eyes of nobles.[11]

In both countries, the struggle over the implementation and specific terms of the new order centered on land and labor relations but also encompassed resistance to a variety of other forms of treatment and mistreatment. Above all, the former bondspeople sought to avoid being pushed around or treated as servile dependents. Efforts to improve their specific economic conditions, therefore, were intertwined with the desire to maximize their autonomy or "self-government" and with their broad rejection of what they saw as a bogus freedom under which their former owners continued to behave like "masters." In Russia, the most immediate phase of the struggle—what historian Allan Wildman has termed "the defining moment"—occurred with implementation of the statutory charters that according to the emancipation legislation were to prescribe relations between pomeshchiki and "temporarily obligated" peasants on each landed estate.[12] In the Southern United States, a similar although less clearly stipulated process occurred as freedpeople and planters entered into annual contracts that defined the terms of labor and often the general conditions surrounding them. The charters and the labor contracts constituted innovations that both landlords and freedpeople approached with a mixture of hope, trepidation, and resignation. If to former owners putting the laborers' rights and obligations in writing removed some of the uncertainty that surrounded the introduction of the new order, the very act of having to secure the assent of former slaves and serfs—"bargaining" with them—seemed degrading, a violation of the respect and deference that superior social standing had always commanded. To the former bondspeople, charters and contracts held out the hope of codifying their new freedom but also threatened to subvert it. Subscribing to documents they could not read and often could not understand was a risky undertaking at best, and the freedpeople approached doing so with caution—and sometimes, especially in Russia, outright refusal.

According to the emancipation legislation, the statutory charters constituted a preliminary step on the winding road to freedom, one that would introduce new relations between peasants and pomeshchiki until they were superseded by redemption agreements under which peasants would begin paying for their landed allotments and would move from "temporarily obligated" to "peasant proprietor" status. Excruciatingly detailed guidelines set the maximum and minimum size of peasant allotments according to varying regional and local conditions, and prescribed what the charters would contain. Charters were supposed to be drafted—by pomeshchiki or their subordinates—within one year of the emancipation manifesto and approved within two years, but if a pomeshchik failed to meet this schedule the local peace mediator was to compose the charter himself. The approval process involved submitting the charter to the peace mediator for verification (in front of the landowner or his agent, peasant representatives, and three to six outside "witnesses" who were typically peasants from a neighboring estate), followed by reading the charter to the assembled peasants. The last stage of this complex process was for representatives of the various parties to sign the charter; according to the bizarre provisions of the emancipation legislation, the peasants had the explicit right to reject a charter (by withholding their signature), but they lacked the power to prevent its implementation, which could occur with or without their approval.[13]

The statutory charters set forth the new pomeshchik-peasant relations in four sections according to a prescribed, formulaic style. The first section listed the (male) peasant population of an estate, according to the tenth (1858) census, distinguishing house serfs from landed peasants and noting any changes in status that had occurred since 1858. The second section covered land, listing peasant allotments before emancipation; noting the specific guidelines (according to the region, locality, and quality of land) that the emancipation legislation provided for allotments per soul; and stipulating the charter's application of these guidelines to the designated estate, the result of which could increase or decrease the size of already existing peasant holdings. The third section addressed subsidiary land arrangements, including such items as common pastures, fisheries, and any moving of peasant farmsteads (*usad'by*)—the little plots of land surrounding their cottages—to new locations. The fourth section listed the peasants' obrok and barshchina obligations before emancipation, stipulated the new obligations that they would owe their former owners, and provided for the mandatory communal redemption (purchase) of their farmsteads in two payments over a one-year period. (Redemption of their much larger field allotments were usually covered later, in redemption agreements the terms of which would take forty-nine years to fulfill.) The second and fourth sections of a charter were the most important: the former defined peasants' landholdings and latter set their post-emancipation obligations.[14]

Two examples can render this complex process more concrete. A charter dated 25 October 1862 defined relations for the peasants formerly owned by Prince Nikolai Borisovich Iusupov in the village of Krasnen'kaia, in the Biriuchenskii district of Voronezh Province. Section I listed the male population: 588 peasants, all of whom except seven house servants (*dvorovye*) were to receive landed allotments. Section II established the dimensions of these allotments. Before emancipation, these peasants had been allotted 4,215 desiatiny, 1,098 sazheni of land, of which 239 desiatiny, 2,208 sazheni consisted of peasant farmsteads and common pastureland. Since this figure substantially exceeded the 1,743 desiatiny that the peasants could receive under the three desiatiny per soul that the emancipation legislation stipulated as the maximum for this locality, the remaining land that had been in peasant use—2,472 desiatiny, 1098 sazheni "in fields remote from the village"—were detached "for the immediate disposal of the landowner." The peasants thus lost more than half the land they had previously regarded as their own. Section III stated that the peasants had the right to use the watering ponds and wells, but it gave the pomeshchik possession of the windmill. Section IV provided that for receipt of their three desiatiny per soul allotments, the peasants would owe Iusupov an annual obrok of ten rubles per soul, or 5,229 rubles for the whole village, payable in semiannual installments in August and December. For use of their farmsteads they owed an additional obrok of 871 rubles, fifty kopecks (one ruble, fifty kopecks per soul), until they redeemed these farmsteads for 14,525 rubles, a redemption expense derived by capitalizing the obrok at 6 percent (871 rubles, fifty kopecks = 6 percent of 14,525). The charter was signed for Iusupov by his head manager, Ivan Aleksandrovich Belykh (himself a nobleman), and for the illiterate peasants by the volost' clerk (pisar'), Nikopor Luklianov. Peace mediator Cherepanov certified that the charter was in compliance with the relevant emancipation legislation, and the conference of district peace mediators certified that the "cutoffs" from the peasant allotments were "legal."[15]

The "cutoffs" suffered by the peasants at Krasnen'kaia were unusually large; as the following charter—which covered the sixteen (male) landed peasants and eight (male) house servants in the village of Chervishchi, owned by Nadezhda Pavlovna Brant in the Luzhskii district of St. Petersburg Province—indicates, peasants did not always lose land under the new order, nor did they always accept the charter they were presented. Before emancipation, the sixteen peasants held allotments that totaled seventy-three desiatiny, slightly more than four and a half per soul. Since this size was smaller than the maximum five desiatiny, twelve hundred sazheni per soul allowed for the locality, their post-emancipation allotments remained unchanged. The obligations they owed, however, changed significantly. Under serfdom, twelve of the peasants had performed three days of barshchina per week, while the remaining four had paid an obrok of thirty rubles each per year. Now, the barshchina obligations were sharply reduced (as required by the emancipation legislation): males would perform thirty-five days of seigneurial labor per year (twenty-one in the summer, fourteen in the winter), and females would perform twenty-six days (sixteen in the summer and ten in the winter), with the rest of their obligations commuted into obrok. The peasants would owe four hundred rubles to cover the mandatory immediate redemption of their farmsteads, payable within a year in two installments. An unusual feature of this charter, which departed from the normal mutual or communal responsibility of the peasants, was the provision that "for the punctual fulfillment of obligations *each head of household* is responsible *individually.*" Less unusual was the peasants' refusal to approve the charter. As the peace mediator noted, after he had verified the charter in the presence of three witnesses from neighboring villages and read it to three peasant representatives, "they did not attach their signature to this charter," to which they raised a variety of objections, most of which centered on the quantity, use, and convenience of land. Nevertheless, he proceeded to register the document.[16]

As these two cases suggest, the statutory charters showed widespread variation—over the size of estates covered; whether the size of peasant allotments would be increased, decreased, or stay the same; the nature and extent of peasant obligations; the handling of common lands, pastures, and water access; provisions concerning house servants; the speed with which the charters were drafted and implemented; whether they were composed by pomeshchiki, stewards, or peace mediators; how peasants reacted to them and ultimately whether they agreed to have their representatives sign them; and how authorities handled disputes over them. There were also some regional and temporal variations. In the great majority of cases, the charters, although providing for the mandatory one-year redemption of peasant farmsteads, did not cover the more onerous redemption of allotment land, which was deferred until the completion of future agreements between peasants and pomeshchiki over the terms of payment (or, barring such agreements, implementation of redemption provisions without the peasants' consent, as the legislation permitted). Occasionally, however, the charters included simultaneous agreements for the immediate beginning of allotment redemption.[17]

Despite such variations, collectively the charters initiated a new stage in the ongoing struggle between peasants and pomeshchiki over the nature of the new order. On one level, the struggle involved the specific terms of land and labor that would characterize their new relationship, but more generally it reflected differing understandings of the very meaning of freedom. Although they did not always understand all the details that were "explained" to them, many peasants found it difficult to believe that the charters they were being asked to accept represented the true freedom for which they had yearned or indeed the freedom that the tsar intended them to have. Convinced that soon—in a common version two years after promulgation of the tsar's 1861 emancipation manifesto—they were to receive the *real* freedom (*volia*), most peasants refused to accept the charters' legitimacy.[18]

From the beginning, drafting and implementing the charters were fraught with difficulties and proceeded more slowly than authorities had expected. Part of the problem stemmed from the cumbersome nature of the process itself. Requiring pomeshchiki or their subordinates to compose the charters proved a double burden: not only did each of them have to walk an impossibly thin line in reconciling his own personal interests with the appearance of fairness, he (or occasionally she) had to engage in a good deal of research in the process, determining the relevant pre-emancipation (1858) data on his estate—the number and categories of serfs, the size (per soul) of allotments, the nature and extent of barshchina and obrok obligations—as well as the pertinent guidelines that the emancipation legislation set forth for the new dispensation in the estate's particular locality. If an estate steward or manager composed the charter (as was the norm on large holdings), he would have to check with his typically absentee employer before submitting it to the peace mediator, who would then engage in *his* phase of the process, verifying the document's "legality" (which in some cases involved checking with the conference of district peace mediators), lining up witnesses, and finally arranging to read and explain the charter to the assembled peasants. Since a mediator had to perform these tasks on multiple estates in his precinct—and had to compose charters himself in the event of the landowners' failure to do so—lengthy delays were frequent. But the biggest sticking point was persuading peasants to accept charters that often seemed unfair in their specific features and more broadly illegitimate in representing a false (pro-pomeshchik) version of freedom rather than the true *volia*.

As provincial governors reported to St. Petersburg on the progress of adopting charters in their respective provinces, the dimension of the problem quickly became clear. As early as 19 October 1861, in his weekly report summarizing dispatches from provincial governors, Minister of Internal Affairs Valuev noted the widespread "unwillingness of peasants to sign statutory charters, based on their expectation of a 'full freedom' in two years." The usually taciturn Valuev repeated and elaborated on this observation often in subsequent reports. Commenting on "mistrust" among the peasants and the "circulation among them of false expectations of a new *volia*," he blamed "various ill-intentioned people" seeking "personal gain." Governors from Tambov, Riazan, and Orenburg Provinces reported that the peasants were resisting the charters "despite all the concessions and most advantageous proposals" put forth by pomeshchiki. The same problem existed in Podolia Province, where—prompted by the "false expectations ... of a new *volia*"—peasants continued to regard "all proposals presented to them with mistrust," even though the proposals were "obviously advantageous to them." Even after the Ministry of Internal Affairs circulated a speech by Tsar Alexander debunking peasant hopes for a new *volia*, governors in most provinces reported that the speech "did not have the expected effect in reducing false rumors," although the governor of Kazan Province dissented, noting that the tsar's words had produced positive results and the peasants were "becom[ing] less gullible every day." When the governor of Podolia Province prepared a circular designed to convince peasant officials of the necessity of accepting the charters and backed it up with a personal tour of the province, some peasants, "after the governor's departure, expressed the suspicion that he was not the governor but a dummy figure 'bribed by the pomeshchiki to fool the people.' " Some seventeen months after the emancipation manifesto, only 21.24 percent of the former serfs lived on estates where charters had been put into effect.[19]

Land and labor were also at the center of the former slaves' struggle for *real* freedom. Although they lacked the Russian peasants' tradition of communal *volneniia*, Southern Blacks increasingly embraced collective action as they sought to improve their condition and achieve as much independence as possible in the wake of emancipation. Like the peasants, they struggled both over the specific terms of their new status and for what they considered the general rights that were embedded in it. They also shared the peasants' suspicion that they were being cheated out of the full freedom they were supposed to receive, and the expectation that if they refused to submit to efforts to enforce their subservience and dependence, something better—an American version of *volia*—would soon arrive. Although planters and some federal officials derided these expectations as unfounded and extravagant, they were—unlike those of their Russian counterparts—at least partially grounded in reality, because the still only partially defined terms of emancipation in fact became more favorable to the freedpeople as they evolved.

Although the Thirteenth Amendment said nothing about landownership, acquisition of land loomed large in the former slaves' understanding of the new order. When Secretary of War Stanton and General Sherman met with twenty Black clergymen in Savannah, Georgia, as the war drew to an end, the group's spokesman, Garrison Frazier, put the matter succinctly: "The way we can best take care of ourselves is to have land, and turn it and till it by our own labor." Where possible—especially where former owners had abandoned land as they retreated before advancing Union forces—Blacks took matters into their own hands. "During the present year the laborers have subdivided the lands among themselves," wrote Lieutenant Colonel A. J. Willard from Georgetown, South Carolina, in November 1865, "and great difficulties have arisen from their unwillingness to do anything except cultivate and harvest their own little lots." To those who had spent much of their lives forced to work the land of others without pay, owning one's own land seemed a clear marker of freedom itself.[20]

Acquiring it was another matter. Unlike Russian serfs, American slaves did not have their "own" land, except for the tiny garden plots that many slaveholders allowed them, and continued access even to these was now in question. Congress's failure to pass a land redistribution bill meant that if African Americans were to become landowners, most would have to acquire it on their own. Those freedpeople who had been the beneficiaries of General Sherman's Special Field Order No. 15 awarding ex-slaves exclusive right to Lowcountry and Sea Island lands in South Carolina and Georgia, as well as to others who had either appropriated abandoned lands or been given them by the Freedmen's Bureau, got an early lesson in freedom's contingency when President Johnson revoked Sherman's action and restored abandoned lands to pardoned ex-Confederates. Complaining that Blacks who had received Sea Island lands "were spending their time in fishing, hunting and destroying the cattle," Davis Tillson, the unusually hardline assistant commissioner of the Freedmen's Bureau in Georgia, noted with satisfaction that once former owners were allowed to reclaim their plantations conditions quickly improved because freedpeople did better working for others than on their own.[21]

The process of dispossessing Black "squatters" could drag on for years, especially when authorities disagreed over it. In February 1867, Assistant Inspector General F. D. Sewell ordered the bureau's superintendent for Virginia's Fifth District to expel hundreds of African Americans from, as he put it, "Camps and Colonies . . . where the premises which they now occupy have been returned to former owners," adding, "It is believed that this can be effected by you without the use of force." Five days later, Sewell reported to Commissioner Howard that there were thousands more still to be resettled from lands in the vicinity of Norfolk, Fortress Monroe, and Yorktown, but this was easier said than done. "For nearly five years you have had possession of land which belongs to others, the possession of which the owners now probably have a right to ask," Howard told the six hundred inhabitants of Taylor Farm in 1869. (Taylor Farm was one of the locations Sewell had mentioned two years earlier.) Warning them that there was nothing he could do "if the Courts shall determine that you have no longer the right to hold this land," the aggrieved commissioner lamented: "I have no longer the means of helping you." Still, he tried. The same day that Howard told the freedpeople on Taylor Farm that they would probably have to move, he wrote Major General Canby, commander of the First Military District, asking him to "protect the interests of those who remain" by securing them legal counsel who could "attempt to make some compromise with Mr. Taylor providing either for their remaining on the farm at reasonable rent or for their removal without much suffering."[22]

Despite these setbacks, former slaves continued to hope and strive for land. Some—at first a relatively small number—would be able to acquire it on their own (discussed in chapter 5). Many more shared the belief of Russian peasants that before long they would receive land from on high. As in Russia, the initial failure of this land distribution to materialize—in the American case on Christmas Day 1865 or New Year's Day 1866—did not so much dispel such expectations as produce a readjustment in the expected timing. Sentiment indicating continued belief in an imminent land redistribution was evident in reports by Freedmen's Bureau agents and Southern whites in 1866 and especially in 1867, as Congress debated and then passed increasingly radical legislation providing for the political Reconstruction of the Southern states. A letter to the *Montgomery Advertiser* from an alarmed "Autauga *Citizen*" offered this warning: "Some of the negroes have taken up the idea that something is sure to 'turn up' in their favor," while a paper in nearby Greensboro warned that political agitation was creating "an unusual amount of insubordination"; Blacks were, it stated, "impressed with the belief that they are soon to be placed in possession of the lands now owned by their employers." In a speech in Autauga County, Alabama, a "negro man by the name of Gilbert" predicted that Congress or the Loyal League would soon give former slaves land, and then asserted that if that did not occur "they had the power to take it" themselves, "by force." As earlier, reports that African Americans were hoping for, expecting, or in some cases acting to effect land distribution were often spread by hostile whites for political purposes, but such opportunistic behavior did not negate African Americans' very real longing for land, or their awareness that Congress was, in fact, drafting new Reconstruction legislation that would profoundly affect their lives. Uninformed attention to national politics could also produce rumors of a very different sort, however, as in Northumberland County, Virginia, where an idea "to some extent believed by both Whites and

Freedmen" spread that President Johnson's veto of the Freedmen's Bureau bill (a veto soon overridden by Congress) not only presaged "the immediate abolition of the business of the Bureau in the State" but also indicated "that slavery was to be reestablished."[23]

The most concrete evidence supporting the expectation of an impending distribution of land came in the Southern Homestead Act, whose passage in mid-1866 set off a flurry of interest among freedpeople in the five Deep South states to which it applied—Alabama, Arkansas, Florida, Louisiana, and Mississippi. (South Carolina later established a state program of its own, with a special Land Commission, to facilitate the acquisition of land by African Americans.) Restricted until 1867 to "loyal" Southerners, the great majority of whom were Black, the new act had the biggest impact in Florida, a frontier state with abundant, high-quality federal land. By contrast, in the other four states much of the land that remained in the public domain was of marginal quality, and—despite the initial enthusiasm that the act aroused—homesteading proved both less rewarding and more difficult than anticipated.[24]

A comparison between two of these states, Florida and Alabama, illustrates the unusual opportunities that homesteading offered in the former, as well as the hopes and ultimately the difficulties associated with it in the rest of the Deep South. Passage of the Homestead Act set off a "rush on the part of the Freedmen for Government lands" in Florida, which in the words of one bureau agent "frightened the planters so that they are rather 'currying favor' with their laborers." By October 1866, only two months after the opening of the first land office in the state, Assistant Commissioner Foster reported to Howard that Blacks had already claimed some thirty-two thousand acres "and their interest in the subject seem[ed] to be on the increase"; by 1868 more than three thousand claims for homesteads had been filed by African Americans in Florida, a number that equaled perhaps one-fifth the Black families in the state. Blacks in other states also showed interest in Florida lands, especially after John A. Sprague, Foster's successor as assistant commissioner, urged Howard to facilitate the migration of unemployed Black people to southern Florida, where they could homestead. Ralph Ely, a self-styled "civil agent for emigration," excitedly proclaimed that he was preparing to bring "125 families of Freedpeople" from South Carolina to New Smyrna, Florida, with "twice as many" to follow soon thereafter.[25]

Although Alabama freedpeople also showed an intense interest in the possibility of homesteading—as a bureau agent in Tuscaloosa put it, "Freedmen are constantly applying for information relative to lands"—taking advantage of the opportunity proved unexpectedly difficult. The paucity and distance of land offices (there were only three in the state), the inferior quality of much of the available land, complications and expenses related to filing claims and hiring surveyors, fraudulent action by swindlers offering to "help" Blacks secure land, and beginning in 1867 (once the six-month exclusion of ex-Confederates had expired) competition from white settlers made homesteading almost impossible for most African Americans; in April and May 1867, of 545 land claims in northern Alabama, only eight were filed by Blacks. Noting that "a great many" freedpeople "[were] entering or desiring to enter Government lands," a bureau agent in Mobile who listed "expenses varying from 12 to 37 dollars for entering forty or eighty acre tracts" pointed out that given the depressed price of land, freedpeople could *purchase* "similar farms ... for the same money and secure titles at once." Suggesting that "the intention of the Homestead Act [was] practically defeated," he concluded that it was not "judicious to advise [Blacks] to enter land at [the time]."[26]

Even in Florida homesteading did not live up to the optimistic expectations of some enthusiasts—an aide to Assistant Commissioner Foster estimated that there were nineteen million acres of public land in the state available for homesteading, enough for two hundred thousand settlers—and Black land seekers proved easily susceptible to fraud. Ely's New Smyrna venture, for example, "proved an entire failure, owing to the incompetence of the project." When the twelve hundred would-be homesteaders arrived in the Florida "wilderness," they found that no homesteads were waiting for them—none had even been surveyed—and most of the migrants, who "suffered considerably until relieved by the Bureau," took jobs working for neighboring planters. "Major General Howard directs me to say that he did not intend to employ you as an Agent of the Bureau in your late operations in Florida," an angry Acting Assistant Adjutant General F. D. Sewell wrote Ely—who had received $10 from the head of each migrating family—"and does not understand by what authority you so assumed to act." Other homesteaders had trouble as well. Noting the "exorbitant" and "unlawful charges" imposed on homesteaders by the Land Office in Tallahassee, whose practices required "ventilating," a bureau agent reported: "The freedmen are coming to me crying at all hours of the day and even of the night begging that their little homestead ... be not taken away from them."[27]

Homesteading in Florida continued to attract great interest—in 1868, Assistant Commissioner Sprague predicted, "The freedmen in Florida will hereafter be independent," wildly exaggerated the scope of homesteading, and asserted, "The larger number of them now have from ten to forty acres of land"—but most of the African Americans who took preliminary steps toward acquiring homesteads either did not follow through with the process or quickly lost their land: the 1870 census counted 1,063 Black landowners in the state—a significant number, but only about one-third the number who had filed claims by 1868. Elsewhere, the number of homesteaders was far smaller; indeed, more Blacks were able to take advantage of the Southern Homestead Act in sparsely populated Florida than in the combined other four states to which the act applied. African Americans continued to hope for—and expect—land distribution, and some were able to acquire land on their own (discussed in chapter 5), but the inadequacies of the homesteading process, combined with the failure of Congress to pass a land redistribution bill, guaranteed that at least in the near term the vast majority of freedpeople would work on land owned by whites (and usually by former slave owners).[28]

Under what conditions they would work this land, however, remained to be determined. Most free-labor advocates assumed that with the abolition of slavery Black people would now work for wages—indeed, that working for wages lay at the heart of the free-labor system. To many freedpeople, however, wage labor seemed insufficiently "free," in that it maintained a relationship in which dependent laborers would take direction from employers and often overseers. African Americans struggling to escape slave-like subservience showed a strong preference for working for themselves, ideally on their own land but barring that on land that could be rented or cultivated under a variety of relationships that came to be called "sharecropping." Labor relations evolved unevenly, and showed considerable geographic variation (discussed in chapter 5), but underlying this uneven evolution was the freedpeople's struggle to make freedom real, to secure as much independence as possible. They also strove, whether as wage workers or sharecroppers, to maximize their share of the income their labor produced.

The specific terms of labor in the post-emancipation years were typically defined in contracts between former slaves and their employers, contracts that in some ways served as the American equivalent of the Russian statutory charters. As Amy Dru Stanley has shown, to advocates of "free labor," "contract became a dominant metaphor for social relations and the very symbol of freedom." Voluntary contracts—whether between laborers and employers, business associates, or husbands and wives—distinguished the relationships of free people from those of slaves. "The antislavery claim of the nineteenth century was that abstract rights of freedom found concrete embodiment in the contracts of wage labor and marriage," Stanley explained, "—that the negation of chattel status lay in owning oneself, in selling one's labor as a free market commodity, and in marrying and maintaining a home." That understanding underlay government efforts to introduce free labor to the South and in the process to transform a backward and despotic region into a flourishing—and republican—society.[29]

Use of contracts to define terms of labor between employers and freedpeople, which had begun during the war when federal officials introduced systems of free and semi-free labor as Union armies gained control of ever-expanding areas of Confederate territory, became pervasive after emancipation. Contracts were a central tool of the Freedmen's Bureau as it sought to guide the transition from forced to free labor, but unlike the drafting of statutory charters in Russia, there was little standardization in how they were composed or what they covered. In November 1865, Florida's Assistant Commissioner T. W. Osborne issued a circular directing that contracts should be issued in triplicate and should provide freedpeople with basic rations of cornmeal and bacon; he also suggested that on large plantations "freedmen should be advised to provide in the contracts ... for the education of the children in reading and writing." Georgia's Assistant Commissioner Tillson, by contrast, required that contracts had to be in duplicate, and approved by a bureau agent, but proclaimed that free-market principles did not allow the bureau "to fix a price for labor or allow it to be done by any community or combination of people." In Arkansas, the bureau kept a "Register of Contracts" in a bound volume, but when Freedmen's Bureau officials began operations in Alabama they were shocked to find that many contracts were simply "verbal agreements" and others were "merely a paper drawn up by [the freedpeople's] late owners, in which the negro promises to work for an indefinite time for nothing but his board and clothes, and the white man agrees to do nothing." In response to such practices, Alabama's Assistant Commissioner Wager Swayne drew up guidelines for labor contracts stipulating that laborers had to receive compensation, adding, "Part of the compensation is required to be in food and medical attendance." Half a year later, in Madison, Florida, a bureau agent found that contracts were being drawn up by justices of the peace, who were "ill-disposed towards the freedpeople" and "clever enough to draw up contracts suitable to the employer." Contracts varied not only over space but also within particular localities; as one bureau agent noted, "The form of contracting with Freedmen is different in almost every case."[30]

As these examples indicate, despite free-labor theory the labor contracts were hardly documents reflecting voluntary agreements between equal parties.

Whether composed by Freedmen's Bureau agents, former owners, or other white authorities, and whether or not they conformed to guidelines set forth by bureau officials, the contracts were typically presented to largely illiterate freedpeople for collective "signing," with each laborer affixing his or her mark in the form of a large X. Under these circumstances, it is not surprising that, like the Russian statutory charters, the contracts produced considerable "misunderstanding" among freedpeople. A bureau agent in South Carolina requested instructions on how to handle freedpeople who unknowingly signed contracts permitting their employer to dismiss them and then objected that the specific details of the contract were "never explained to them." A bureau sub-assistant commissioner in Florida came to the conclusion that because it was so easy for planters to trick illiterate laborers, "the contract system" was a "pernicious institution . . . rather calculated to oppress the freedpeople." Despite official policy, some high-ranking bureau officials agreed: "The contract system does not work well for the negro," Florida's Assistant Commissioner J. G. Foster wrote to Howard, explaining that it gave planters an "opportunity . . . to take an unfair advantage of the ignorant laborer, either in the framing of its conditions or in its application."[31]

Nevertheless, for a least three reasons the labor contracts were less one-sided than the Russian statutory charters. First, Freedmen's Bureau officials and other Union army officers tended to be more sympathetic to the plight of the freedpeople than were peace mediators and other noble bureaucrats, and more willing to intervene on their behalf. Second, despite intense pressure on Black workers to sign them, the contracts were in fact voluntary in the sense that—unlike the charters—they could not be implemented without the consent of both parties; refusal to sign the contracts represented more than a symbolic act. Third and perhaps most important, the contracts were not one-shot affairs: unlike the charters, they lasted only one year, after which employers and laborers had to sign contracts again—and then again—for another year. Given that freedpeople had maximum negotiating leverage before agreeing to contracts, their temporary nature created the opportunity for the continued renegotiation of relations between planters and freedpeople, and enabled the latter to learn from previous mistakes. In short, annual contracts provided flashpoints for continued class struggle in the post-emancipation South.

On the ground in Russia, the abstraction of "false expectations" took on concrete dimensions in the struggle over statutory charters, dimensions that reflected both the peasants' specific interests and their general concerns. When the peasants of Sukulak village, in Orenburg Province, refused to recognize the emancipation manifesto, explaining that although "the Tsar promised us liberty ... there is no liberty without land," they explicitly used the word *volia*—with its radical connotation of peasant self-rule—for "liberty." Learning that similar sentiment was spreading to neighboring villages and that on one estate the peasants were refusing to pay their obrok and demanding "to go on some sort of special tsar's allotment," the governor decided to call for troops. A few days later he reported with satisfaction that after seven peasants in Sukulak and one in Troitskaia had received corporal punishment, the remaining peasants agreed to accept their charters, and the soldiers were withdrawn.[32]

In standing up for what they considered their rights, peasants frequently resorted to the venerable tradition of sending petitions to various authorities, including the tsar.[33] In July 1862, Stepan Ivanov Malyshev, a peasant representative from the village of Poliany, in the Varnavinskii district of Kostroma Province, presented a lengthy petition to the tsar. Written for the illiterate peasant by a soldier from the Stavropol' infantry regiment, it put forth a litany of complaints that underlay a prolonged volnenie. The trouble began almost a year earlier, in August 1861, when pomeshchik Prince Petr Nikitich Trubetskoi presented the peasants with a statutory charter under which—according to Malyshev—they would have had to pay their old obrok and work their old land allotments for twenty years. Upon their rejection of the charter, the angry pomeshchik departed, leaving the peasants at the mercy of an abusive estate manager, Rozenberg, who accused them of "rebelling," after which the situation quickly deteriorated. A series of interactions with various officials—including the clerk of the volost' administration, the district ispravnik, the district attorney (*striapchii*), the peace mediator, and later the provincial vice-governor—at first appeared to hold some promise, but events reached an impasse when the peasants continued to reject their charter. The officials brought in "batmen" (*denshchiki*) who threatened to apply physical punishment to a sixty-year-old man—he was spared when "all the peasants, falling on their knees, begged for mercy"—and did punish twenty other villagers so severely that "starosta Laptev died" and an elderly peasant "lost his eyesight." The petition concluded by detailing previous unanswered appeals to various local and provincial officials, one of which had elicited a threat by Rozenberg to kill Malyshev, and it begged the tsar to send someone he trusted "to put an end to our agonizing situation."[34]

A report by Kostroma governor N. A. Rudzevich to Valuev confirmed and elaborated on the details in Malyshev's petition—from a very different perspective.

Describing Malyshev as a longtime troublemaker who had eluded arrest at a communal gathering when 250 rowdy peasants shouting "impudent threats" protected him, Rudzevich detailed how he continued to spread "false rumors" that were "extremely harmful to tranquility"; showing a document supposedly given to him from "one of the members of the imperial family," he convinced the peasants that "those who adhered to it would enjoy extraordinary privileges, while the others would remain in eternal slavery." After the "mild measures" of the mediator and ispravnik proved unsuccessful, various district and provincial figures tried to no avail to reason with the peasants. At first it appeared they might succeed, but when peasant Zametaev, who had been in St. Petersburg with Malyshev, returned with word that Malyshev had presented a second petition to the tsar, the peasants "totally changed their manner" and became recalcitrant, and Rudzevich sent for more troops. At a communal meeting in Poliany that was also attended by peasants from sixteen additional villages making up Trubetskoi's estate, the governor informed the gathered peasants that they would have statutory charters with or without their approval, to which they responded "firmly and unanimously that they wanted to remain in their previous position." After repeating Alexander's insistence that "there will be no new *volia*," Rudzevich became convinced that the peasants' faith in Malyshev was "so blind and limitless" that reasoning with them was futile.[35]

The next day, a frightened peasant elder brought Governor Rudzevich news that the peasants were gathering in a field to take an oath on a cross that they would not agree to anything until Malyshev returned from St. Petersburg. When the governor personally confronted them and tried to reason with three of the most influential peasants, one of the protestors shouted that "the whole mir is as one," whereupon Rudzevich ordered him seized and punished in front of the crowd. "Hardly had he been given 12 strokes with birch switches," the governor reported with satisfaction, "when the whole crowd fell on their knees and begged for mercy," promising "unconditionally to submit to the law and all authorities." The governor then chose a few representatives to sign statements affirming their obedience, after which—he asserted with considerable exaggeration—the charter was implemented "by voluntary agreement." Concluding his report, he boasted that "complete tranquility and obedience [had been] brought to the estate of more than 3,000 souls without any extreme measures," adding that in order to calm the spirit of the peasants "not just on this estate, but on others," Malyshev should be exiled.[36]

Not all petitions led to such drawn-out confrontations, but, like Malyshev's, most combined specific grievances—including specific terms of the charters—with general challenges to the legitimacy of the emancipation process and an unwillingness to be pushed around in violation of what peasants considered their rights. A petition to Alexander from the peasants of Podosinovka, in the Novokhoperskii district of Voronezh Province, for example, complained about the allotments provided the village's six hundred male souls—four desiatiny each of sandy, hilly land—and noted that the pomeshchitsa, Anna Mikhailovna Raevskaia, reserved for herself three hundred desiatiny of the best land. The petitioners also complained that after they rejected the deficient charter, some two hundred of them were subjected on orders of the governor to "cruel and merciless" punishment with birch switches; the victims included "innocent women" and men who were "former soldiers for faith, tsar, and fatherland." In addition to these specific grievances, however, it was the illegitimacy of their treatment that drew the peasants' attention. In complaining of their insufficient allotments, they pointed to "some" pomeshchiki—including Raevskaia—who were allocating peasants land "not according to the law," in violation of the limits set forth in the local guidelines. Complaining that the governor had ordered their punishment without asking them a single question, they entreated the tsar to make sure they received allotments "according to the local polozhenie . . . as required by law."[37]

Similar peasant views, and interactions with authorities, were evident throughout Russia, indicating a combination of skepticism about the general validity of the emancipation being offered and specific grievances about its terms. The peace mediator of the fourth precinct of the Valuiskii district in Voronezh Province found that when he tried to read the charter to three hundred assembled peasants on the 1,116-soul estate of Countess S. V. Apraksina, they "rudely asserted that they did not want any allotment from the pomeshchitsa, but would wait for the allotment they were promised by the Tsar." The next day, the crowd swelled to some one thousand peasants, with reinforcements from a neighboring village, leading the ispravnik to summon three companies of an Odessa infantry regiment. The peasants turned to their local priest, Aleksandr Bedin, who surprised the officials by siding with the villagers, assuring them that they were "not obligated to accept the landed allotment and statutory charter" and explaining that the charter was "illegal" because it was imposed unilaterally by the mediator without the participation of pomeshchitsa Apraksina and without the signature of local authorities. The confrontation continued to escalate, with the governor calling in additional military forces and ordering the priest detained, while the assembled peasant mob continued to grow, reaching three thousand. "Only after the instigators were arrested and physically punished" reported the exasperated governor, "did a significant number of them confess, promising to adhere to the demands of the law." The governor added an ominous warning, noting that other priests shared Bedin's sympathy for the peasant cause and that he had "repeatedly heard from peace mediators and pomeshchiki that the clergy, currying favor with the peasants, secretly support[ed] their distrust of the law and government authorities."[38]

Although authorities had good reason to be concerned about the close ties between peasants and parish priests, whose style of life, material standing, and worldview were often closer to those of their parishioners than of the conservative church hierarchy, the behavior of priests during the emancipation struggles was unpredictable, heavily influenced by the varied relationships between individual priests and the peasants they served. Some priests unequivocally sided with peasants and even egged them on: when the peasants in numerous villages in the Ushitskii district of Podolia Province resisted the charters they were presented, a local priest assured them that because two years had elapsed since the emancipation manifesto they did not have to work or pay obrok. Noting that the priest had "gained the most harmful influence over the peasants, who sent him deputations from the surrounding villages for similar exhortations," the governor consulted with the archbishop of Podolia and then had the priest arrested and sent to a monastery. But when the peasants of Podosinovka complained to the tsar of the cruel punishment they received from authorities, they pointedly noted that their priest, "Father Petr," had "fawningly" sided with their oppressors rather than acting to avert the bloodshed of innocent humanity.[39]

As peasants resisted the statutory charters and defended what they considered their rights, they manifested a strong sense of communal identity, a central element of which was their right to choose their own leaders and not be pushed around from without. When a peace mediator in the Kashirskii district of Tula Province removed and arrested a starosta whom he considered the "main culprit of disorder" in the village of Rostovtsy, and then on his own appointed a replacement, the villagers "wildly demanded the return of the arrested starosta and . . . shouted that they did not recognize the new starosta." The petition from peasant representative Semen Ivanov Ziukin on behalf of the inhabitants of a large estate in Kursk Province who engaged in a prolonged volnenie whose suppression required some two hundred infantrymen and forty mounted warriors made clear that much of the trouble stemmed from the authorities' attempt to flout the will of the community and bypass the peasants' elected leaders. When the peasants replaced their existing starosta and starshina, whom they saw as too compliant, and the new starshina, Efim Feshchenko, refused the peace mediator's order to accept a statutory charter that they regarded as illegal because it had been "composed without the participation of the whole community," the mediator arrested Feshchenkov and ordered everyone to obey the deposed starshina, Demid Korobov. Despite the entreaties of the mediator and the ispravnik, however, followed by beatings and "bloody" punishment with birch switches, the peasants refused to recognize Korobov's authority, and a communal gathering determined that "because of his vile deeds [they would] not obey him."[40]

Of course, not all peasants resisted the imposition of statutory charters, and because such resistance generated more paperwork than did cheerful compliance, the surviving documentary evidence may paint an exaggerated picture of universal peasant discontent. Still, there can be no doubt that such discontent was widespread, and that physical resistance to the charters represented only the tip of the proverbial iceberg. The discontent is evident in the pervasive reports from government officials—ranging from Minister of Internal Affairs Valuev to provincial governors and district and local figures—officials whose interest usually lay more in minimizing than in exaggerating the extent of peasant disorders. It is also evident in the behavior of the peasants themselves, who dragged their feet and expressed frequent outrage over and disbelief in the terms of the charters they were presented. The outrage and disbelief were rooted in, and in some ways tempered by, the widespread peasant conviction that the charters represented a fake—landlords'—dispensation that would be superseded by the real—tsar's—emancipation (*volia*) at the end of the two-year transition period, on 19 February 1863. Indeed, historian Allan K. Wildman has suggested that because so many peasants were convinced that the coming *volia* would soon award them the land that was rightfully theirs, they were less concerned by the size of the land allotments that charters provided than by the monetary obligations they imposed. The peasants' widespread belief that by signing charters they would also be signing away their promised freedom lay at the heart of many of the volneniia that erupted throughout Russia in 1862 and early 1863, volneniia that were surpassed in number and severity only by the outbreaks that greeted emancipation in the spring and summer of 1861 and that far exceeded the "normal" peasant disturbances of preceding decades.[41]

But the most striking evidence of the peasants' rejection of the statutory charters lies in their refusal to sign them. Beginning on 11 August 1861, the weekly reports issued by Minister of Internal Affairs Valuev provided running totals of the number of charters drafted, the number implemented, and the number signed by the peasants. Early progress was slow; as Valuev reported, "The pomeshchiki want to compose the charters with the consent of the peasants, but the latter shun signing them." Some fifteen months after the emancipation manifesto, the chairman of the Bogurcharskii district conference of peace mediators in Voronezh Province, noting that one of the mediators had recounted that in his precinct the peasants had not accepted a single one of the fifty charters presented to them by pomeshchiki, reported that the conference had reached the "sad conclusion that on some estates the statutory charters cannot be put into effect without the use of physical force." Under pressure to implement charters within the allotted two-year period, officials reported an increased rate of completion in the summer and fall of 1862: as of 2 May, 24,918 charters had been composed, of which 10,751 (covering estates with 1,048,000 souls, or about one-tenth of the emancipated male population) were already in effect; two months later, those figures had approximately doubled, with 2,158,380 souls covered. The pace of charter implementation continued to quicken as the two-year deadline approached: by 1 November charters covered 5,073,208 souls—almost exactly one-half of the former serfs—and in January 1863, on the eve of the two-year anniversary, 95,300 charters had been composed, of which 73,195 were in effect, covering 6,747,894 souls, some 68.6 percent of emancipated male peasants living on holdings of twenty or more souls.[42]

The January 1863 figures provide compelling evidence of the former serf population's dissatisfaction with the statutory charters two years after emancipation. To begin, they indicate the continued foot-dragging that had characterized the entire process of composing, approving, and implementing the charters: as the end of the two-year transition period approached, only about two-thirds of former serfs lived on estates where charters were fully in effect. (See table 3.1.)

Progress was less marked still on small estates with fewer than twenty souls (which contained only about 3 percent of the former serf population). On these small estates, where inventories rather than statutory charters were prescribed, completed inventories covered about one-fifth of the eligible peasant population. (See table 3.2.)

The most telling figures, however, were those indicating that a majority of peasants had refused to sign the charters: a slight majority of the charters were unsigned, but because those estates were in general larger than those that received peasant signatures, they contained a substantial majority (58 percent) of the peasants. Given the extraordinary—and often violent—pressure that

Table 3.1. Charters on estates with at least twenty male peasants

Number of charters composed	95,300
Number of charters implemented	73,195
Number of charters signed by peasants	36,413
Number of charters rejected by peasants	36,782
Number of male peasants on estates with charters implemented	6,747,894 (68.6%)
Number of peasants signing charters	2,834,716 (42%)
Number of peasants rejecting charters	3,913,178 (58%)
Number of male peasants per estate with charters implemented	92.19
Number of male peasants per estate with peasants signing charters	77.85
Number of male peasants per estate with peasants rejecting charters	106.39

Source: Report of 3 January 1863, *Otmena krepostnogo prava: Doklady Ministrov vnutrennikh del o provedenii krest'ianskoi reformy, 1861–1862* (Moscow: Izdatel'stvo Akademii nauk SSSR, 1950), 282–83.

Table 3.2. Charters on estates with fewer than twenty male peasants

Male peasants	337,940
Inventories compiled	7,415
Male peasants on estates with inventories implemented	67,000 (20.03%)
Male peasants per estate with inventories compiled	9.04

Source: Report of 3 January 1863, *Otmena krepostnogo prava: Doklady Ministrov vnutrennikh del o provedenii krest'ianskoi reformy, 1861–1862* (Moscow: Izdatel'stvo Akademii nauk SSSR, 1950), 282–83.

was brought to bear on peasants to sign the charters, this majority rejection indicates the massive resistance that the government faced in imposing its version of the new order on peasants convinced that they deserved—and would soon receive—something better.[43]

The two-year anniversary of the original emancipation manifesto came and went without the much-awaited *volia,* and over the following years overt peasant unrest gradually subsided. Figures compiled by editors of the *Krest'anskoe dvizhenie* series—partial estimates that did not take full account of obscure data in local archives and therefore counted only the most documented (and presumably most noticed) outbreaks—show a marked decrease in the incidence of volneniia from the exceptionally high levels that had prevailed from the spring of 1861 to the spring of 1863, with an even sharper decrease in the number of outbreaks whose suppression required military force. (See table 3.3.) Measured purely in terms of the frequency and severity of peasant disturbances, the crisis initiated by the onset of emancipation appeared to be over.[44]

Peasant belief in a soon-to-come *volia* did not die, however, nor did the unrest and the potential for violent confrontation that such belief generated. In the Konstantinogradskii district of Poltava Province peasants abruptly stopped performing their obligations in February 1863, explaining that the promised hour ("sluchnyi chas") had come and that they were eagerly awaiting the arrival of the new Polozhenie; a local priest encouraged their insubordination, urging them to "demand the Tsar's redemption." The following year, peasants from several villages in the Mozyrskii district of Volhynia Province refused to verify charters or make the stipulated payments, insisting that "all the officials, including the governor himself, are bribed by the noble landowners

Table 3.3. *Volneniia,* 1861–69

Year	Volneniia	Suppressed by military force
1861	1,859	937
1862	844	450
1863	509	185
1864	156	70
1865	135	61
1866	91	35
1867	68	24
1868	60	14
1869	65	7

Source: L. M. Ivanov, ed., *Krest'ianskoe dvizhenie v Rossii v 1861–1869 gg.: Sbornik dokumentov* (Moscow: Izdatel'stvo sotsial'no-ekonomicheskoi literatury, 1964), 18.

[*pany*] and hide the real sovereign ukaz on the granting of freedom." In two of the villages, women drove away the witnesses who had arrived for the charter verification and the men assembled and agreed that they would "stand their own to the death"; meanwhile, convinced by an influential peasant that they were not required to make any payment for six years, they awaited a resolution from the tsar.[45]

The non-arrival of the *real* freedom did not so much shatter peasant expectations as force their recalibration: the true *volia* was still to come, even if it had not arrived in 1863, and expectations of the imminent arrival of the new dispensation would surface repeatedly in the future. More immediately, however, beginning in 1863 a new issue increasingly replaced the statutory charters as the primary source of rural discontent and catalyst of class struggle: agreeing on terms for the redemption of land allotments that would complete the former serfs' transition from temporarily obligated status to full-fledged peasant proprietors. Completing those agreements would turn out to be a process equally as contentious as—and far more protracted than—implementing the charters.

The introduction of labor contracts in the post-emancipation American South amounted to a crash course in collective bargaining, and the freedpeople proved to be apt pupils as they strove to secure both better material conditions and maximum social autonomy. Early contracts were often highly restrictive, including not only minimal (or no) pay but also harsh disciplinary provisions. A June 1865 contract between Henry Watson and the more than fifty former adult freedpeople on his plantation in Greene County, Alabama, provided compensation in the form of one-eighth of the crop, in addition to food, clothing, housing, and medical care; the contract required "said negroes" to work "in accordance with such rules as may be prescribed by said Watson[,] his agents or manager," forbade the freedpeople from leaving the plantation "without a written permission from the manager," and stipulated that if they moved off the plantation before the end of the year they would forfeit their entire share of the crop. Some other contracts were harsher still. Although few if any contracts after 1865 allowed freedpeople "to be whipped when they need[ed] it," as was common in the area around Montgomery, Alabama, immediately after the war (see above, chapter 2), even in 1866 and 1867 restrictive and punitive provisions were far from absent. In February 1867, the "freed men and women" on Bill Gourdin's South Carolina plantation committed themselves to cultivate two and a half acres of cotton each and one of corn in exchange for the right to till "what land they chose . . . for themselves," from which they would provide their own rations. The contract also provided that the hands could be "turned off the place" if they refused to work "when requested" and indicated that "no person [would] be al[l]owed to come on the plantation" without Gourdin's approval.[46]

But freedpeople who agreed to oppressive terms of labor in 1865 usually learned the appropriate lesson and rarely made the same mistake again. The freedpeople's struggle to make sure that they were free in fact as well as in name, which had been at the heart of the insurrection scare of December 1865 (see chapter 2), continued in subsequent years, and laborers made increasingly sophisticated use of the contracting process to better their condition. In doing so, they employed a variety of tactics designed to take advantage of—and exacerbate— the shortage of labor that rendered planters increasingly concerned about their ability to secure a cheap and docile workforce. The former slaveholders vigorously resisted these tactics, but the presence of the Freedmen's Bureau and Union Army limited their ability to exercise the kind of unchallenged control of dependent laborers that they took for granted, and their experience as slaveholders—together with the labor shortage—left them poorly prepared for bargaining with free workers. Former slaves did not get everything they sought, but they were able to force changes that dramatically increased their social and economic autonomy.

The annual nature of the Southern contracts, which necessitated continued renegotiation of the terms of labor, provided freedpeople with a potent tool in their effort to secure a *real* freedom, a tool that they readily embraced: the threat to withhold labor. Indeed, although it was not universal, a seasonal pattern similar to that in evidence during the insurrection scare of late 1865 reappeared widely in subsequent years, especially in the Deep South, where the demand for labor was most intense. At first laborers dragged their feet when it came to signing new contracts, and planters complained vociferously of Black laziness and insubordination while pronouncing free Black labor a dismal failure. Then, by spring of the new year, Freedmen's Bureau agents and Southern whites alike noted with relief that the freedpeople were hard at work after all, and they commented on the improved racial and labor relations that had miraculously materialized. The more perceptive of these observers also noted the improved terms of labor that the new contracts provided. Of course, such a generalization to some extent obscures a far messier reality that included geographical variation, divergent judgments at any given moment, and an evolving context that—especially with the onset of Black suffrage in

1867—accentuated conflicting evaluations of conditions and prospects. Nevertheless, underneath the apparent diversity if not randomness of social relations across the rural South lay a persistent cyclical pattern of a struggle shaped by the seasonal economy and annual contracts.

Normally tense labor relations typically frayed further during the fall harvest, and then appeared to reach a breaking point as it came time to negotiate contracts for the new year. Throughout the South, freedpeople complained of being discharged on technicalities by planters who sought to steal the fruits of their labor, and numerous reports by Freedmen's Bureau agents confirmed the extent of the practice. Those who worked for a share of the crop, and were not paid until after the harvest was complete and the crop divided, were especially likely to fall victim to such treatment. In a typical summary of the practice in Florida, a Freedmen's Bureau agent reported that "for small offences" planters would "frequently discharge such as they want[ed] to get rid of, without remuneration for any part of their labor during the year"; noting that "the stipulations of the contract" often permitted discharges, he added that he intended to advise freedpeople to avoid entering into such contracts in the future.[47]

Similar reports were common in other states. Noting "a desire to swindle the Freedmen out of their portion of the crops," a bureau agent in South Carolina estimated that four-fifths of the planters had violated their contracts, although he suggested that three-quarters of the laborers had committed infractions as well. In late 1866, Mississippi's assistant commissioner Gillem received "very numerous" complaints from freedpeople "that it was impossible for them to obtain any compensation for their entire year's labor," while in Alabama "many unprincipled men" in the area around Tuscaloosa were "discharging [freedmen] upon the most trivial offenses" and then hiring "women an[d] children . . . to gather the crop at very low wages." The problem recurred in 1867, as an additional impetus to fire Black laborers appeared when for the first time they sought to vote; in December, Virginia's assistant commissioner O. Brown sent Howard a fourteen-page list of 280 Blacks who were discharged for voting contrary to the wishes of their employers. When Alabama planter George S. Houston attempted to fire sharecropper Bernard Houston for his political activities, the freedman not only complained to the Freedmen's Bureau but also wrote an indignant letter to his employer: "When I can attend political meetings, without injury to my interest and yours in the crop, I shall do so, of which I shall be the judge." But as before, planters also discharged African Americans in order to appropriate their earnings, as in Mississippi, where "the planters in many cases [were] anxious to diminish their expenses by discharging their laborers before the expiration of their contract."⁴⁸

As the end of the year approached, African Americans exhibited considerable caution—and sometimes more than caution—in signing new contracts, and alarmed planters (together with newspapers that shared their viewpoint) denounced Blacks' laziness and refusal to work, pronounced free labor a failure, and speculated on the disappearance of the Black race. From Butler Island, Georgia, Frances Butler—daughter of wealthy planter Pierce Butler and his ex-wife, the English actress and author Frances Ann Kemble—lamented the freedpeople's "sullen unwillingness to work," adding, "All round us people are discussing how to get other labourers in the place of negroes." In the Alabama Black Belt, the Selma *Daily Messenger* complained: "Up to this time," because of the freedpeople's refusal to contract, "we have not heard of a single planter who has made arrangements for another year's work," and a planter's agent added this confirmation: "The negroes are nearly all idle." South Carolina's assistant commissioner reported that in the Charleston area Blacks were refusing to sign contracts because they wanted their own land, and in Rockbridge County, Virginia, a bureau agent noted that despite the good wages they offered to laborers, planters were complaining of those laborers' refusal to accept contracts. Planters put forth a confusing gamut of sometimes contradictory complaints, from Black idleness to shortage of labor. Some were convinced that the Black race was dying out—after asking, "What has become of the Freedmen?" an Alabama newspaper suggested "death, immigration, or some other cause is rapidly thinning their ranks"—while others toyed with the idea of hiring sturdy white immigrants to replace "demoralized" African Americans. "The negro will soon have to be disposed of in some way, perhaps as the indians were," opined one white Alabamian in a telling if not entirely typical statement. "They will soon become quite as savage, useless, and *more troublesome.*"⁴⁹

By springtime and early summer, however, such apocalyptic comments had frequently turned into observations of a very different sort: Blacks who a few weeks earlier had seemed lazy, impertinent, and disinclined to enter into contracts were now hard at work, and conditions appeared generally promising. In April 1867, Mississippi's assistant commissioner Gillem reported to Howard that Blacks were working better than ever, white prejudice against them was declining, and overall conditions were improving. A year later, the story was similar: although at the start of the year prospects had appeared "gloomy and unpromising," by February planters and freedmen were signing new contracts, and by March the "signs of the times" appeared "flattering to both classes." The assistant commissioner rejoiced, "Notwithstanding the almost hopeless prospect to the freedmen at the opening of the season, . . . they have risen superior to all obstacles and . . . have gone to work more vigorously this year than at any other time since the war."⁵⁰

There were exceptions. In February 1868 a planter complained that in Morgan County, Georgia, many ex-slaves were refusing to work or even sign contracts despite the ready availability of employment at "fair wages" because of continuing rumors that the government was "about to divide the land." Two months later an Alabama planter lamented, "Most of our hands have broken their contracts and day laborers taken offense and left"; he added that they were "thoroughly deceptive and unreliable."⁵¹

But throughout the South, many Freedmen's Bureau agents issued positive reports during the late winter and spring of 1867 and 1868, and Southern whites praised the surprising responsibility of Black laborers. In March 1867, Florida's assistant commissioner Sprague reported that Blacks were working well under contract, and he expressed satisfaction at "the good order that prevail[ed]" as well as "the industry" of the freedpeople. A year later he proclaimed that conditions were better than expected: "A mutual confidence prevails between the whites and the freedmen far beyond that which existed a year ago." The situation was similar in Georgia, where Assistant Commissioner C. C. Sibley found improved labor relations in both 1867 and 1868: "The freedmen are working more to the satisfaction of their employers," he proclaimed in June 1868, "than any time since their emancipation." In Virginia, Assistant Commissioner Brown also reported improved conditions, which he attributed partly to passage of the Reconstruction Acts of 1867; noting that Blacks were appropriately industrious, he rejoiced, "Complaints of their indolence and shiftlessness are becoming rare," and "employers are paying better wages and more promptly than last year." A letter published (in identical form) in two Alabama newspapers in May 1867, reported from Newbern: "The freedmen, according to universal testimony, are working better than they did last year," a judgment echoed by a bureau agent in Greene County, who reported, "Freedmen are working much better this year than last," and "crops are in much better condition." The following year generated similar reports. In June the (Alabama) *Independent Monitor* proclaimed with satisfaction, "The negroes have worked better than they did last year," and crops were good; planter Henry Watson's former overseer, who despite his previous difficulties with free laborers had rented Watson's plantation and now had to deal with them on his own behalf, reported to Watson: "We are getting along very well," and "the negroes are working very well this year." The (Alabama) *State Sentinel* conceded the existence in cities of "a few worthless negroes . . . who are idle and too lazy and indolent to work" but pronounced "the freedmen . . . are very generally at work with an earnestness certainly creditable to them."[52]

Although the apparently schizophrenic responses of planters (and many other Southern whites) to the changed conditions they faced in part reflected the tenuousness of their position and the uncertainty of their future, as they alternately bemoaned the passing of the old order and grasped at straws suggesting that all was not lost, the seasonal rhythm of their comments and the extent to which Freedmen's Bureau officials provided similar descriptions of (although not usually similar normative judgments about) prevailing labor relations indicate that more was at work than simply sour-grapes desperation of the defeated and humiliated. Former slaves *were* in fact reluctant to sign contracts, but this reluctance reflected not so much opposition to contracts themselves—much less a generalized "laziness" or misunderstanding of what freedom was about—as a desire to use the process of contracting to their own advantage and make sure that contracts provided terms consistent with their understanding of a *true* freedom. After all, contracts provided laborers with specific advantages, distinguishing them from slaves by spelling out the conditions under which they would labor, and freedpeople realized that exploitative as many of the contracts were, working without contracts was likely to tip the balance of power much further in the planters' direction.

Planters recognized the same thing and continued to try, when possible, to secure labor that was unencumbered by annoying written restrictions. Although strenuously opposed to the practice of relying on "verbal contracts," the Freedmen's Bureau was unable to stamp it out, and such contracts continued to surface. "Planters desire to enter into verbal contracts with their hands for the sole purpose of swindling them," wrote Louisiana's assistant commissioner in July 1867; two months later, he estimated—probably in exaggeration—that the "large majority of laborers" in Louisiana had been working "under none other than verbal contract," many "without any remuneration whatever for their services." As South Carolina's assistant commissioner Scott recognized, the freedpeople did not object to contracts themselves—there was "little difficulty in inducing freedmen to make contracts . . . with those planters who had made a reputation for fair dealing"—but they showed "a great disposition . . . not to contract upon such terms as would give the entire control of their time to the landlord." That disposition underlay much of their behavior as they sought to use the contracting process to secure greater independence.[53]

A specific manifestation of the freedpeople's determination to maximize control over their own labor was evident in their widespread rejection of the free-labor hierarchy of values that placed wage labor at the pinnacle of the ideal social order. Most—but not all—bureau agents and other federal officials took it for granted that wage labor was preferable to sharecropping, not only because it represented the essence of the "free labor" system but also because "shares in the crop g[a]ve too much chance for swindling." Although cropping did in fact provide planters abundant opportunity to cheat laborers by expelling them from plantations before paying them their share of the crop at the end of the season, Blacks usually considered cropping a step up from wage labor because it provided them a greater degree of autonomy. Whereas wage work seemed a form of dependent labor in some respects not far removed from slavery, sharecroppers were (at least in theory) partners of landowners, able to exercise greater control over their conditions of labor without the direct supervision of a master or overseer. (In this sense, sharecropping was reminiscent of the slaves' labor on their "own" garden plots, which had provided them with a modicum of autonomy and facilitated the development of an "internal" slave economy partially independent from that of their owners.) When Bernard Houston resisted the effort of his former owner George Houston to expel him from Leonard Place, the freedman proudly noted that he was working—by contract—for one-third of the crop and would insist on his contractual rights. "I am not working for wages," he explained, "but am part owner of the crop and as I have all the rights that you or any other man has I shall not suffer them abridged."[54]

Sharecropping, which could assume many forms, some of which were more advantageous than others (discussed in chapter 5), was less a goal in and of itself than a means toward securing greater independence, and when the means seemed deficient—as, for example, when planters took advantage of it to discharge laborers before the crop was divided—it could quickly lose its appeal. A Freedmen's Bureau agent in Mississippi noted what he considered a "strange fact," remarking, "Those freedmen who worked on shares during the past year insist upon stipulated wages, while those who worked for wages are anxious to work for shares"; this was in fact not as strange as it appeared to him. Nor was a preference for negotiating contracts that provided laborers control of their own labor rather than working under the kind of supervision that some bureau officials considered desirable, because they associated it with wage labor. When Bureau Assistant Commissioner Scott noted the "great disposition" of South

Carolina freedpeople not to work under arrangements that gave planters "the entire control of their time," he expressed disapproval of—and termed "injurious"—the "many contracts being made by which the freedmen agreed to work part of the time for the planter and the remainder for themselves." Southern whites were typically less restrained in their judgments: complaining "We have no freedmen under our control" because "they wish to be free from restraint" and "are mostly setting up for themselves," a planter in Talladega County, Alabama, declared glumly, "Their wishes will not work," adding, "They must be poor so long as the men only half work & keep so many idle consumers about them."[55]

As these comments indicate, although African Americans did not fully realize their goal of securing economic and social autonomy, planters were not successful in reimposing a system of dependent labor that amounted to slavery in all but name. Indeed, despite widespread variations that reflected geography, diverse political contexts, specific routines needed to cultivate different crops, and personal idiosyncrasies, over the second half of the 1860s there was a trend toward what Mississippi's assistant commissioner Gillem termed "better contracts." Throughout the South, after 1866, contracts provided greater remuneration and less often contained restrictive provisions such as those limiting who could leave or visit plantations. The trend was most marked in the Deep South, where the shortage of labor put Blacks in a better bargaining position, but even in Virginia Assistant Commissioner Brown reported in 1867 that "employers are paying better wages and more promptly than last year," although he added that freedpeople did not receive "a full compensation for labor performed."[56]

After 1866, contracts often provided less direct supervision of Black labor. Reports from Florida indicated a pervasive move from wages to shares in 1867—in one district, 304 of 314 contracts were for shares, and in another "almost all" were—a trend that was widespread in much of the South, especially where cotton production prevailed. Equally important was a notable shift from a system that some economic historians have termed "share wages," under which laborers collectively contracted to work for a landowner in exchange for a share of the crop (and usually also for food and other supplies), to one of "share renting," under which individual croppers contracted to pay a landowner a stipulated portion of the crop in exchange for plots of land that they could cultivate on their own. Although both forms of sharecropping were based on dividing the crop between landowner and laborer, the newer form made possible a much more fundamental change in labor relations (detailed in chapter 5), reducing the direct control of the cropper's labor in a way that could lead to increased *social* autonomy as well. "Last year employers worked large numbers of hands on shares . . . under their own superintendence and who were entirely dependent on them for subsistence," explained Mississippi's assistant commissioner Gillem in 1868, "while this year planters work only a limited number of laborers themselves[,] renting portions of their plantations to freedmen independent of their control." The beginnings of a similar shift were already in evidence in 1867 in Alabama, where a bureau agent noted the decision of "a few farmers" to "divide their plantations into small farms," which they would "rent or lease to industrious freedmen for several years." That same year, the *Montgomery Daily Advertiser* reported: "Several large land owners have broken up their old 'quarters' and have rebuilt the houses at selected points, scattered over the plantation."[57]

Needless to say, the improved conditions of labor were hardly gifts from on high; although Freedmen's Bureau agents and evolving federal (and then state) legislation provided a more favorable context for their struggle, it was the freedpeople themselves who seized the opportunity to wring concessions from reluctant—and often outraged—planters. As they sought to get as far as possible from a condition of slave-like dependence, they resisted working in gangs under overseers, accelerating the shift from wage labor to sharecropping. They also withheld female and child labor, both of which had been essential under the old regime, thereby accentuating the shortage of labor. One newspaper article complained in 1867, "The men among our colored laborers are working very well," but it would soon be necessary to rely on white laborers because "women, girls and boys are gradually quitting the cotton and corn fields." (As an added insult, the paper noted: "It is difficult to get suitable cooks and house servants.")[58]

But perhaps most alarming to planters was the increasing evidence of collective action among their laborers. Two reports on the same day from Georgetown, South Carolina, one complaining of "an extensive coalition among the blacks" and the other rejoicing, "It is wonderful how unanimous they are," hint from opposite perspectives at what in many cases seem like miniature versions of peasant volneniia as the ex-slaves resisted signing unfavorable contracts. Of course, there was a long history, dating to slavery days and manifested more recently in the insurrection scare of Christmas 1865, of panicked Southern whites seeing signs of Black conspiracies everywhere, but there can be little doubt that considerable organization underlay the freedpeople's negotiating tactics as a free-labor economy evolved. (Such organization would be even more in evidence as African Americans mobilized in earnest for political activities in 1867 and 1868.) Occasionally, collective action took a more formal shape: at a "meeting of Freedmen" in Cherokee County,

Alabama, the participants "bound themselves together, under a penalty of fifty lashes, to be laid on the naked back, not to contract to work for any white man during the present harvest for less than two dollars per day."[59]

Planters responded with a vengeance. To former slaveholders and other whites who took dependent Black labor for granted, this kind of assertiveness came close to insurrection and demanded concerted action. Occasionally, like Black workers, they organized to defend their interests; in Sumterville, Alabama, a meeting of "citizens" unanimously adopted a set of resolutions advocating "concert of action . . . among those hiring laborers," pledging not to hire those previously "discharged for violation of contracts" and recommending limits on compensation for both sharecroppers and wage laborers. Such guidelines proved impossible to enforce, however, and more often employers acted on their own, discharging—and engaging in violence against—laborers they considered troublemakers, bemoaning the passing of the good old days, complaining (sometimes to Freedmen's Bureau agents) about the unreliability of free Black labor, and toying with (but usually not acting upon) the idea of securing white workers, who would somehow be more docile and dependable than former slaves. Admitting that her hands had "humbugged" her "by their expressions of affection & desire to work," Georgia's Frances Butler complained in 1868: "Everywhere sullen unwillingness to work is visible," adding, "All around us people are discussing how to get other labourers in the place of negroes." (Five years later, she in fact experimented with British workers but found them "rowdy" and lacking in diligence, and sent them home.)[60]

In short, the struggle remained unresolved between former slaves eager to establish new, more independent, relationships and former owners intent on salvaging as much as possible from the old. Although former slaveholders insisted that "the *labor,* upon which the planter has to rely, *must be subject to his control,*" enforcing this kind of subservience proved increasingly difficult given the shortage of labor, the increasingly radical political climate, and the growing willingness of African Americans to stand up for what they saw as their rights. Complaining that they had "failed in many instances to get justice at the hands of" the local Freedmen's Bureau agent and two justices of the peace, forty-one Blacks from Tuscumbia, Alabama, wrote Assistant Commissioner Swayne begging him to "depose them from their office" and replace them with other, specified, individuals who would enable them to "obtain [their] just Dues." Even under the best of circumstances, the Freedmen's Bureau lacked sufficient manpower to provide the kind of support the petitioners sought—in neighboring Mississippi, the assistant commissioner estimated that he would need twenty more agents to keep Black laborers from being discharged from plantations on trumped-up charges—but the growing assertiveness of freedpeople prevented planters from riding roughshod over them and sustained an uneasy, continually contested, compromise (or perhaps better, stalemate) between the two sides. Black participation in local and state politics would soon add a new dimension to the ongoing class struggle.[61]

Freedpeople in Russia and the Southern United States entered the world of free labor with broadly shared goals. The details differed, of course, reflecting specific circumstances and histories, but at the most basic level, both the former serfs and the former slaves sought to build relationships that would secure them the fruits of their labor and, more generally, enable them to escape the servile dependence that had characterized much of their previous lives. The desire for independence or autonomy—which was evident in and helped reshape diverse areas of the freedpeople's lives that receive attention in part II—underlay the struggle for a "true" freedom that peasants and African Americans believed was their right, rather than any of the various versions of "free labor" that would leave them free in name but largely subservient to their former owners. In short, at the heart of post-emancipation history lay the struggle to define what freedom was all about.

Tactically, too, much united the former slaves and the former serfs in their struggle for a true freedom. Although the balance of forces did not permit Southern Blacks to engage in the kind of large-scale volneniia that were common in Russia, they showed impressive collective resistance to restrictive contracts, resistance that was in many ways similar to that of peasants who refused to sign statutory charters that disappointed them. In both cases, their reluctance to accept documents that they did not fully understand but that clearly did not provide the kind of freedom they expected alarmed landowners and authorities, and—especially in the South— forced former slave owners to engage in the kind of bargaining with laborers that they found deeply humiliating. In both, the former bondspeople used rumor, and real or pretended belief that they had the support of the highest authorities, to further their cause. African Americans and peasants quickly realized that their moment(s) of maximum leverage occurred when their consent to legal documents was on the line. Although peasants did not enjoy the multiple opportunities for negotiation and renegotiation that annual contracts provided, they were soon to receive a second chance when it came time to reach agreements on the terms of redeeming their landed allotments. The use to which largely illiterate populations put legal documents provides impressive testimony to their ingenuity and determination.

Despite these shared goals and tactics, the contexts within which their struggles evolved displayed significant—and growing—differences. As before emancipation, the demographic balance meant that outsiders impinged far less on the day-to-day lives of the peasants than of the African Americans. Rural Russia was a peasant world in a way that the rural South was not a Black world, and for better or worse peasants in Russia were in general far more on their own than were African Americans in the South. This isolation could prove both advantageous and disadvantageous to the peasants, who enjoyed a kind of benign neglect that most African Americans would have welcomed but did not receive the kind of protection that Southern freedpeople often did from Freedmen's Bureau agents, Union soldiers, and government officials.[62]

As noted at the end of chapter 2, emancipation in the South and in Russia evolved in increasingly different political environments. Those environments already differed substantially at the moment of emancipation, as evidenced by the following contrasts: democracy versus autocracy, a violent overthrow of slavery versus a relatively uncontested end to serfdom, a planter class that most federal officials considered traitorous versus a loyal and subservient (if at times resentful) nobility, a former slave population that through loyalty to the Union and military service had won the right to citizenship versus a peasant population that most elite Russians considered foreign beings deserving uplift but hardly ready to participate as equals in governing the country. The differences between Freedmen's Bureau officials and peace mediators were symptomatic of many of the contrasts: at the onset of emancipation, members of the governing class in the United States were far more likely than those in Russia to favor policies that could be termed "pro-freedpeople," policies designed to produce fundamental changes in the existing social order.

Over the course of the immediate post-emancipation period, this contrast grew increasingly sharp, as the Russian government embraced a law-and-order conservatism that belied the hopes of liberal reformers while the federal government embarked on a far-reaching program to reconstruct the South along more democratic lines. In Russia a heightened emphasis on "order" under the direction of Minister of Internal Affairs Petr Valuev, the crushing of a liberal Polish uprising in 1863, and a crackdown on intellectual dissent marked the end of the country's first era of "glasnost." In the United States, by contrast, a series of increasingly radical legislative measures—most notably the Civil Rights Act of 1866, the Reconstruction Acts of 1867, and the Fourteenth and Fifteenth Amendments to the Constitution—initiated a remarkable and unprecedented effort to make full citizens of former slaves. As former serfs sought to "redeem" their landholdings and former slaves sought to secure conditions of labor that would maximize their economic and social autonomy, governmental reforms enabled both to enter the political arena. In Russia, however, the impact of these reforms was severely limited, and peasants were most politically active at the local level, running their own village communes; in the United States, Reconstruction legislation introduced new democratic state and local governments throughout the South that depended on Black votes for their very existence. At the most basic level, the freedpeople's struggle for a better life was intensely political, but in Russia their political realm was largely confined to families, estates, villages, and local administrative units, whereas in the South it reached all the way up to the highest levels of government.

4 • The Politics of Freedom

Emancipation unleashed a new stage in the struggle of peasants and African Americans for "self-government." Politics infused this struggle in both the narrow and the broad meanings of the term: politics as formal government, whether electoral or not, and politics as the wielding of power, in virtually all relationships. At the individual level, emancipation enabled former slaves and serfs to exercise more control over their daily lives, from property ownership to family life, work routine, and freedom from arbitrary rules imposed by masters and their subordinates; this is the form of self-rule that Abraham Lincoln promoted when he attacked slavery as a violation of the fundamental American principle of self-government. At the local level—estates and plantations, peasant communes and African American communities or "neighborhoods"— freedpeople received new rights, built on previous customary privileges, and struggled to maximize their collective autonomy. At a higher level, free Blacks and peasants were able for the first time to become part of the larger body politic—albeit in different ways, within very different political systems—from the district/county to the provincial/state (and in the United States national) levels. Underlying all of this activity was the tension between efforts of peasants and Blacks to define themselves as a "people" and competing forms of political identification.

Although both groups of freedpeople embraced the struggle for self-government, the extent and character of their political activities differed significantly. In Russia, emancipation made possible an expansion of the communal self-rule that had already held customary standing under serfdom, whereas in the South, where such self-rule had never received formal recognition under slavery, Black leaders achieved new visibility and influence, whether as community spokesmen, teachers, or religious figures. If at the local, proto-political level Blacks were playing catch-up to an already established form of peasant self-government, at a higher level political involvement of the former slaves catapulted forward in a manner unmatched by that of the former serfs: Russia saw nothing like the American effort to turn former bondspeople—at least bonds*men*—almost instantaneously into full-fledged citizens, able to play an active role in state and even national government. The ability of former slaves to take part in running not just their own lives but also those of Southerners (and Americans) in general gave "self-government" a dual meaning that was largely absent among Russian peasants, and accentuated the ambiguity of political attachments that were present in both countries.

As freedpeople confronted their new future in a "free" society, they built upon a long tradition of proto-political activities in which they had engaged as slaves and serfs. Such activities were most clearly evident in Russia, where serfs had often exercised a considerable degree of self-rule through the peasant commune, whose officials simultaneously constituted the lowest level of their owners' administrative apparatus and peasant representatives who oversaw internal village relations, from supervising periodic reallocation of peasant landholdings to mediating familial disputes, and represented peasants' interests in negotiating with (and sometimes resisting) their owners. Because such activities lacked institutional legitimacy among Southern slaves—there was no equivalent of the peasant commune—the process of harmonizing disputes among slaves and the existence of particular slaves who wielded unusual influence over others was less obvious to outsiders, and the emergence of "new" Black leaders after the war seemed particularly sudden. In both countries, the freedpeople and their leaders faced new dynamics as they struggled to adjust to changed conditions and take advantage of new opportunities.[1]

The emancipation legislation both legitimized and strengthened the customary proto-political peasant institutions that had existed under serfdom. Following the imperial government's proclivity for order, regularity, and symmetry, the legislation systematized the lower levels of peasant (self-)administration by creating two new institutions: the *sel'skoe obshchestvo* (village society, community) and the *volost'* (canton, township). The obshchestvo represented a regularized modification of the peasant commune (*obshchina, mir*), and the terms were often used interchangeably; "composed of the peasants *settled on the land of one pomeshchik*," an obshchestvo could consist of an entire village, part of a village belonging to more than one pomeshchik, or several small adjacent settlements belonging to a single pomeshchik. The volost', a new, larger geographic unit whose radius was not to exceed twelve *versty* (almost thirteen kilometers), was made up of several contiguous obshchestva; each volost' contained between three hundred and two thousand (male) souls, often living on estates owned by several pomeshchiki.[2]

Although the sel'skoe obshschevto in many respects represented a continuation of the peasant commune that had existed under serfdom, the emancipation legislation defined its structure and duties in new detail and expanded its powers to handle some functions that had previously been the responsibility of the peasants' owners. At the center of the obshchestvo was the village assembly (*skhod*), a gathering normally composed of all peasant heads of households and headed by an elected *starosta* (elder). The assembly performed myriad functions, from electing peasant officials (who in addition to the starosta could include such figures as tax collectors, supervisors of grain supplies and schools, forest and field watchmen, and clerks) to supervising peasant land use and the division of landed allotments, apportioning obrok and taxes, presenting petitions to various authorities, selecting military recruits, allowing (or not allowing) family divisions, and determining who could join and leave the obshchestvo. The starosta called and presided over meetings of the assembly, supervised village affairs, and acted as the peasants' representative in dealing with the outside world. At the same time, it was his responsibility to "promptly fulfill the legal demands of the pomeshchik," "detain vagrants, fugitives, and military deserters," and generally cooperate with higher authorities in enforcing laws and maintaining order. As under the serf regime, peasants themselves performed the lowest level of policing the countryside, electing one member from every ten households as a *desiatskii* (tenth or tenner) and one from every hundred as a *sotskii* (hundredth) who helped maintain order and reported to the higher chain of police command.[3]

Creation of the volost' and the volost' administration, by contrast, represented a significant departure, establishing a new, higher level of local peasant government. As with the obshchestvo, the governing body of the volost' was also an assembly, but rather than including all heads of households it was composed of one representative from every ten peasant families. The assembly members elected a variety of officials, the most important of whom was the *starshina*, a super-elder who stood to the volost' as the starosta did to the obshchestvo; most of the other officials assisted the starshina, performing chores similar to those encountered at the obshchestvo level (clerk, tax collector, and so on), but important exceptions were the four to twelve judges elected annually for the new volost' court established to deal with low-level peasant offenses, including "disputes and lawsuits among peasants, as well as their minor misdemeanors." With a jurisdiction limited to internal peasant affairs, the court could impose light sentences that included no more than six days of communal labor, three-ruble fines, seven-day detentions, or—more ominously—twenty blows with birch switches.[4]

Although the systematization and explicit legal recognition of peasant self-government were new, in many ways its basic functioning represented a carryover from the pre-emancipation era. This was also true of the peasant leaders who staffed the various communal positions. As before, officials were usually drawn from the ranks of the "best" peasants—"prosperous men who were orderly and good"—men considered responsible by their fellow villagers and often by higher authorities. Still, although older than the average peasant—typically starosty were between forty and sixty years old—they were not far removed from the villagers they represented. The great majority of starosty were illiterate (as were most of the judges in the volost' courts)—that is why it was so important for each obshchestvo to have a literate peasant who could serve as a clerk—and because turnover was high and starosty rarely served more than one or two three-year terms, they did not constitute a permanent governing stratum within the peasantry. Often aided by informal advisers known as "stariki" (literally, "old men," whose age and experience presumably conferred wisdom), they continued to play a mediating role between the village and the outside world, even as they also served as the face of the village to that outside world. The volost' added a new level of bureaucracy to the complex hierarchy of rural administration, but overall the post-emancipation system of village self-government provided considerable continuity with the primitive form of peasant "democracy" that had partially mitigated the oppressiveness of the serf regime. At the same time, the abolition of serfdom provided peasants the opportunity to expand and regularize their self-rule, and it partially reduced the arbitrary nature of their treatment by higher authorities.[5]

The newly regularized obshchestvo and volost' administrations represented a democratic form of local peasant self-government—with significant limitations—that differed significantly both from Abraham Lincoln's understanding of self-government as stemming from the right of a "man" to control his own life and from nineteenth-century understandings of republicanism based on the participation of an informed citizenry in governing the nation-state. Peasant life continued to be highly communal, and peasant rights continued to be understood largely as belonging to the group rather than to individuals. Under the statutory charters (and, subsequently, under the redemption agreements), peasant obligations continued to be defined collectively, based on average landed allotments and monetary dues per male soul, and except for a small number of revolutionaries and liberal dreamers, few contemplated including peasants in a general, trans-estate body politic. This understanding was broadly shared as well by peasants, who, as historian G. A. Kavtaradze argued, saw emancipation as permitting a "return to an initial point" that had prevailed before serfdom, one characterized by an idealized form of peasant democracy in which the mir would regulate peasant life free from outside interference.[6]

It is hardly surprising, then, that peasant self-government reflected this continued communal consciousness. The basic deliberative body of local politics, the village assembly, operated on the principle of unanimity rather than majority rule, and the formulaic records that clerks kept of assembly deliberations and resolutions (*prigovory*) present a picture of a united peasantry rather than revealing internal disagreements that sometimes existed among them. This mode of deliberation in fact constituted a system based on the decisions of what might best be termed "supermajorities"—after extensive discussion, assembly members typically reached a broad consensus in which occasional dissenters would acquiesce—and there is abundant evidence that villagers shared a common understanding of their values and interests, which they expected their officials to share as well. "This was not Western liberal democracy," explained historian Boris Mironov, "but patriarchal egalitarian democracy." Although peasant leaders had to walk a thin line representing the views of their "constituents" without antagonizing authorities, it is clear that the once-common argument of some Soviet historians that peasant leaders served principally as agents of the noble regime was off the mark.[7]

Indeed, as was evident in chapter 3, peasant officials often took the lead when villagers confronted outside forces, and peasants typically rallied around such officials, especially when authorities tried to replace them with more compliant figures. When a peace mediator, convinced that starosta Fedor Nikitin was the "main perpetrator of disorder" among peasants in Rostovtsy village in Tula Province, arrested him and appointed a new starosta, the assembled peasants "turbulently" demanded the release of Nikitin and "cried out that they did not recognize the new starosta." Leaders who did not promote peasant interests could suffer the consequences: when starshina Demid Korobov made the mistake of accepting a statutory charter on behalf of the peasants of Bogoshcha village in Kursk Province without consulting them, they replaced him with Efim Feshchenkov, who better represented their wishes: "I will not take the statutory charter," he explained to authorities, "because the entire obshchestvo does not authorize it."[8]

Although emancipation accentuated peasant autonomy, both by systematizing communal institutions and by reducing the extent to which pomeshchiki interfered in the peasants' lives, the limitations on communal self-rule remained considerable, and peasant self-government always operated under the constraints of real or potential interference from above. Indeed, the emancipation legislation specifically granted the pomeshchik police powers over his temporarily obligated peasants and defined him as the "guardian" of the obshchestvo with the right to replace peasant officials "in case of abuse or general improper fulfillment of their duties." If a pomeshchik discovered an assembly decision that was "harmful for the wellbeing of the sel'skoe obshchestvo or infringing on pomeshchik rights," he was required to suspend the decision and report it to the peace mediator, who in turn was "obligated to quickly fulfill the legal demands of the pomeshchik." Peasant democracy was always conditional. Equally important, the peasants' engagement in politics was confined to internal (peasant) affairs; even after the creation in 1864 of new district and provincial bodies (*zemstva*) in which peasant representatives rubbed shoulders with those of other estates (see below), they had virtually no role in governing non-peasants, or Russia as a whole.[9]

Because the terms of emancipation in the Southern United States emerged only gradually, during two years of contentious congressional debate, the extent to which freed African Americans would become part of the broad body politic was at first unclear. But even more than in Russia, American emancipation made possible a sharp expansion of proto-political activity among the freedpeople. Despite the lack of a formal institutional basis for Black self-government under slavery, with the end of the war Black "leaders" appeared as if out of thin air. Their manifestation represented both the coming out into the open of previously clandestine activity—as the "invisible" church became visible, for example, so too did the prominent community role of Black preachers—and new opportunities stemming from the overthrow of slavery.

Although antebellum slaves shared much in terms of experience and consciousness, they had never been an undifferentiated mass of downtrodden laborers. The "vast mechanical skill" that Freedmen's Bureau official Charles W. Buckley noted among African Americans on his arrival in Alabama in August 1865 reflected the occupational diversity of a slave population that had not only performed field labor but had also provided most of the South's carpenters, blacksmiths, coopers, seamstresses, weavers, and other skilled artisans that made the slave economy work. Even as most Blacks toiled in the fields, others served—either full-time or part-time—as ministers, dockworkers, house servants, gardeners, grooms, nurses, coachmen, drivers, and shoemakers; sometimes the same people engaged in both field work and more specialized endeavors, either at a given point or over a life cycle of work. The minority of Blacks who were free before the war had additional opportunities, in terms not only of occupation but also of such realms as property ownership and education, but recent research has revealed the extent to which slaves as well could be de facto property owners, cultivating their "own" plots of land that legally belonged to their owners, accumulating movable property that by custom could be inherited, selling goods in local markets, and employing the labor of other slaves, who included but were not confined to their family members. Such differentiation ensured that some slaves had more influence and power than others, influence and power that could be used for individual as well as community purposes and therefore had the potential to create tension between individual and collective interests. "Few slaves could earn much by working alone," noted historian Dylan C. Penningroth. "When enslaved people accumulated property, they usually did it by finding someone else to work for them." But such differentiation also provided the preconditions—on a less institutionalized and less recognized basis—for a kind of self-government that was not altogether different from that of Russian peasants.[10]

Throughout the South, the end of the war saw the appearance of Black leaders—men who professed to speak for the African American population at large. They came from diverse backgrounds. Some had played similar if clandestine leadership roles under slavery, whereas others assumed leadership positions because of new opportunities—especially educational and economic—that emerged with emancipation. In some cases, such opportunities had already emerged during the war, in Union-occupied areas. When federal troops liberated the slaves on Joseph Davis's two adjoining plantations at Davis Bend, on the Mississippi River, and established a "home colony" intended to be a "negro paradise," the Black driver Benjamin Montgomery organized the workforce and turned the plantations into what amounted to a self-governing community; later he would acquire them as his own and become Mississippi's first Black justice of the peace. In New Orleans, free African Americans began publishing a newspaper, the *New Orleans Tribune*, in 1864, in both English and French; although at first it served as a mouthpiece of elite, light-skinned "mulattoes" who carefully distinguished themselves from the mass of Black slaves, by the end of the war it was promoting the interests of freedpeople in an increasingly radical manner.[11]

The rapidity with which Black spokesmen emerged after the war, and the nature of their advocacy, indicated the potential for a consciousness that embraced far more than local or particularistic concerns. As noted in chapter 2, at the same time that freedpeople were engaging in a host of proto-political activities—from contracting over conditions of labor to refusing to work under overseers—Black leaders were coming together in "colored conventions" to articulate common interests. These gatherings built on a long history of such conventions in the antebellum North, as prominent African Americans sought to promote the interests of not only free Blacks but also their enslaved brethren. The postwar conventions, however, operated in a strikingly changed political environment, in which new opportunities seemed practically limitless. Meeting in the South, sometimes locally and sometimes on a statewide basis, they focused on problems faced by newly freed slaves and reflected a rapidly evolving understanding of what was possible—and desirable—in a post-slavery era. Although at first attendees were typically cautious in enunciating goals—historian August Meier noted the "moderate, if not sycophantic tone" evident in 1865 and 1866—they soon displayed a growing confidence and took advantage of the increasingly radical Congressional Reconstruction policy to press for equal citizenship in a manner that rendered them, in the words of historian Steven Hahn, "Americas's true Jacobins." This evolution is evident in the contrast between Alabama's first two statewide colored conventions, the first held in Mobile in November 1865 and the second in the same city in May 1867. At the first convention, the delegates adopted a set of resolutions designed to reassure anxious whites of their good intentions: urging the promotion of "peace, friendship, and good will toward all men—especially toward our white fellow-citizens among whom our lot is cast," they promised that freed Blacks would "work industriously and honestly." At the second colored convention, the delegates allied themselves with Alabama's nascent Republican Party and boldly asserted their "undeniable right to hold office, sit on juries, to ride on all public conveyances, to sit at public tables, and in public places of amusement."[12]

If emancipation unleashed new kinds of proto-political action, from negotiating over labor contracts (which in their original form were—like their Russian counterparts—usually collective) to engaging in occasional strikes and petitioning for federal protection, it was Reconstruction that made possible the emergence of full-fledged electoral politics among the freed population. The Reconstruction Acts of 1867, which provided for reorganized "republican" (and Republican) governments that would rely heavily on the votes of former slaves, set in motion a wave of new political activity that swept across—and transformed—the South. Although the character and extent of this transformation was not fully evident until these Reconstruction governments were firmly ensconced, the period immediately preceding their establishment was a heady time of ferment, excitement, and "millennial hopes" among Southern Blacks, who embarked on a crash course in political democracy, including "a groundswell of black grassroots mobilization," as states prepared for and held constitutional conventions that drafted new constitutions providing full manhood suffrage and then submitted these constitutions to newly enlarged electorates for ratification.[13]

A central role in the political education of African Americans fell to the Union League (also sometimes called the Loyal League), an organization that originated in the North during the war to promote support for the Union cause and after the war became instrumental in forming and campaigning for Republican parties throughout the South. Although local chapters consisting primarily of white Unionists were evident as early as mid-1866, from the spring of 1867 league organizers focused on mobilizing the newly enfranchised Black voters who would form the shock troops of the Reconstruction governments. Freedmen's Bureau officials and other Union Army officers played a leading role in spreading the leagues, which in turn helped enroll Black voters in a process supervised in each electoral district by three-member registration boards made up of "loyal" citizens (including African Americans). "I am doing well about making voters of the Blacks," one league organizer in Talledega, Alabama, wrote to the state's superintendent of registration in April, 1867. "I have taken about 500 in the *League* and am taking them in about one hundred a week." By fall 1867, virtually all Black men—over 90 percent everywhere except Mississippi, where the figure was 83 percent—had registered to vote.[14]

This registration was accompanied by an extraordinary outburst of Black enthusiasm, as well as by expressions of alarm and ridicule from former slaveholders. Throughout the South—especially in plantation districts with substantial African American majorities—freedpeople attended barbecues and rallies, marched and drilled, listened to and increasingly delivered speeches, and enthusiastically embraced their new status as full-fledged citizens. The process of sudden political immersion was a heady—if at times confusing—one for former slaves, and it aroused a sense of impending change in some ways reminiscent of earlier expectations of land distribution; indeed, such expectations, never entirely dispelled, once again flourished. To many white Southerners, however, the new order seemed virtually unimaginable, a stunning manifestation of a world turned upside down. Blaming "Yankee traveling agents, the meanest looking men you ever saw," for riling up naturally docile Blacks, a typical complainant observed with alarm: "You never saw a people more excited on the subject of politics than are the negroes of the South. They are perfectly wild." Despite the hostile tone, this statement captured the state of palpable excitement that gripped Black (and some white) Southerners in what seemed, much like emancipation itself, to herald the dawning of a new age. Building on the kind of collective behavior already evident in the freedpeople's efforts to secure more equitable labor contracts—behavior that historian Steven Hahn has described as rooted in "kinship and shared experience"—African Americans prepared to engage in a broadened version of self-government that entailed running not only their own lives but also those of other Southerners. Although this new version of self-government was one that—like the American version in general—presupposed politics as a male preserve, the extent to which women at times threw themselves into the fray indicates the depth of the collective, kinship-based effort undertaken by an entire people. "A considerable number of colored female beauties have organized themselves into a union League under the title the 'Loyal Association of Colored Ladies,'" smirked the *Montgomery Advertiser*. "They hold meetings every week, and are addressed by each other on the political issues of the day." In fact, there is considerable evidence that many African Americans held the kind of family-based and collective political consciousness that encouraged political participation among women as well as men. "On 1 August [1867], the day the Republican state convention opened in Richmond," narrated historian Elsa Barkley Brown, "thousands of African American men, women, and children absented themselves from their employment and joined the delegates at the convention site." As was also true elsewhere in the South, women as well as men "participated from the gallery, loudly engaging in the debates."[15]

Freedpeople grasped the essentials of their new citizenship with remarkable rapidity. At first, most Black participants at Union League meetings and political rallies were content to listen to their white instructors, absorbing the details of what was to come and basking in the excitement of the moment. Indeed, conservative white newspapers, which typically blamed Yankee meddlers for the new state of affairs, often reassured their readers that Black attendees were docile and well behaved, and that when they did speak they abjured radical views. One paper noted, for example, that at a "Radical" (that is, Republican) meeting in Selma, "almost all the colored men who spoke made Conservative speeches," while another praised the "practical wisdom" of a Black speaker at a Republican meeting in Hayneville, Alabama, noting, "He exhorted his people to be honest, industrious, and frugal." In a typical remark, the *Montgomery Advertiser* heaped praise on a Black Baptist minister for penning a letter asserting that [white] Southerners were the freedpeople's "best friends" and urging Northerners to help build schools rather than meddle in politics. But such reassurances, which inevitably smacked of wishful thinking, soon alternated with and then largely gave way to denunciations and ridicule of Black radicalism. Conservative white "cooperationists" such as South Carolina's (Confederate) general Wade Hampton, who had assumed that they would be able to co-opt the votes of a docile people who knew that their former masters were their "best friends," joined recalcitrants who had from the beginning seen manhood suffrage as an affront to civilization, in denouncing Black perfidy and mocking the very notion that African Americans were fit for political participation. Suggesting that Hale County, Alabama, activist James K. Green (whom it referred to as "Jim Green") "appears to consider himself a second *Moses*," the Alabama *Beacon* lambasted him for "making one of the most incendiary speeches ever delivered to an infuriated crowd," and proclaimed that he had *"rendered himself exceedingly obnoxious to the community."* In a more restrained expression of this sentiment, a Talladega County, Alabama, planter lamented archly in his diary, "The negro element have mostly taken up bad men to be their candidates."[16]

In fact, just as the colored conventions had become increasingly radical in tone, so too did the newly aroused Black electorate—only this time over a period of months rather than years. The political process itself proved invigorating, and as realization of the extent of the impending changes sank in, African Americans took a more active role in political agitation and more readily expressed radical ideas; as historian Julie Saville noted, the drilling and marching of "quasi-military 'companies' " in South Carolina not only aroused fears among whites of Black insurrection but helped "to forge a disciplined solidarity across plantation boundaries"; largely rejecting the appeals of their would-be conservative friends, Black spokesmen sought to forge a "social movement." After addressing a political meeting in Wetumpka, Alabama, the nascent Black politician William V. Turner observed, "One thing I noticed: the more Radical the speeches, the better the colored people liked them."[17]

The political mobilization that was in full swing by the summer of 1867 hastened an evolution—or better, transformation—in the nature of the emerging Black leadership, an evolution that paralleled its growing radicalization. African American leaders who emerged immediately after the war were disproportionately urban, literate, light skinned, and—especially where there had been significant numbers of free Blacks, such as Charleston, New Orleans, and Mobile—previously free rather than enslaved; many members of the early colored conventions were ministers, figures of authority who were experienced at speaking in public. By 1867, however, as political Reconstruction unleashed a massive effort to mobilize Black voters, rural freedmen—often artisans—were playing an increasingly prominent role, joining although not entirely replacing the previous cadre of Black leaders. The differences between the makeup of Alabama's 1865 and 1867 colored conventions are indicative of the rapidly changing character of postwar leaders. Whereas most of the delegates to the former were preachers and the president E. S. Winn was a Methodist elder, the second convention saw increased representation from the Black Belt counties, and the delegates chose as their president Holland Thompson, a former plantation slave who by 1866 had established himself as owner of a grocery store in Montgomery and would later serve in various political offices, including in the state legislature.[18]

In the spring of 1867, Orlando Brown, the Freedmen's Bureau assistant commissioner for Virginia, directed agents to identify "six of the most intelligent of the freedmen" in each county, "in whom both races have confidence and who have the most influence over their own people." The 621 names he received—from some counties, more than six—provide a good portrait of this transitional group of Black leaders, at least as identified by the Freedmen's Bureau, on the eve of a new political era that would bring Republican Reconstruction regimes to power throughout the South. As revealed in historian Richard Lowe's analysis, they were disproportionately light skinned (34.6 percent), literate (62.2 percent), and formerly free (35.4 percent) compared to the state's overall Black population. At the same time, unlike their counterparts in the highly atypical city of New Orleans, where more than 90 percent of the identified leaders were of mixed race and had been free before the war, they were in many ways not far removed from the broader African American population: only a small minority (14.2 percent) were clergymen, almost half (45 percent) were either farmers, farm laborers, or tenants, and more than two-thirds owned no landed property. They represented a transitional and ultimately ephemeral group between the privileged urban spokesmen who emerged during and immediately after the war and an evolving Black leadership that would be much more centered in the plantation countryside: indeed, only a few of them—twenty of the 621—"were among the 350 or so black Virginians known to have held . . . public office during and after Reconstruction."[19]

The frenzy of political activity that swept over the South in 1867 accentuated the ongoing changes in Black leadership. Hundreds of African Americans served on the three-man Boards of Registrars that in each district registered voters for the election of delegates to the constitutional conventions and hundreds more ran as convention candidates, while at the local level Blacks began serving in a variety of positions, from sheriff to city councilman. The numbers of these new officials were staggering: in the South as a whole, African Americans composed 268 of the 1,018 convention delegates, ranging from about one-tenth of those elected in Arkansas, North Carolina, and Texas to a majority in South Carolina and Louisiana. Black political activists were especially common in plantation areas where African Americans formed a large majority of the population, such as the "Natchez District" that encompassed four counties in Mississippi and two in neighboring Louisiana; historian Justin Behrend recently "identified over four hundred black men who held political office or party leadership position in these six counties," where Blacks constituted about 82 percent of the population. Meanwhile, thousands of additional African Americans throughout the South were assuming quasi-political roles in their communities as teachers, ministers, and small-scale businessmen, roles that would make them ready targets of conservative white hostility (see below, especially chapter 7).[20]

Indeed, even at this early stage, it was clear that Black leaders faced daunting challenges. Black registrars received not only ridicule but also violence at the hands of conservative whites determined to thwart the looming participation of African Americans in the political process. Although the Ku Klux Klan, a white terrorist organization formed in Tennessee in 1866, did not become active in most of the South until 1868, threats and denunciations occasionally turned deadly during the 1867 campaign: in June, Alex Webb, the Black registrar in Alabama's Hale and Greene Counties, was murdered. Even when overt violence was absent, serving as registrar could be an intimidating experience for African Americans, especially when they served in an area they considered remote and insecure. "The colored men are few and far apart and ought to have the light sent to them in this dark part of the country," wrote black registrar George W. Cox from Tuscaloosa, Alabama. "I want to get through and get back to Montgomery so bad I don't know what to do," he lamented; "this place is too far in the woods for me now—it can never be my home any more." Nevertheless, even in areas where African Americans were "few and far apart," they threw themselves into electoral politics with extraordinary enthusiasm. In Montgomery County, Virginia, for example, where Blacks made up slightly more than one-fifth the population, 566 men—virtually the entire male population over twenty-one—registered to vote in 1867, 506 actually voted, and "504 voted Republican."[21]

The composition of the convention delegates illustrates the continuing rapid evolution of Black political leadership, as well as the extent to which the new leaders—even as they exhibited unusual abilities and qualifications—were not far removed from their Black constituents. Almost half of the delegates were freeborn, but most of these were from Louisiana and South Carolina, both of which had unusually large and educated free Black populations under the slave regime; elsewhere, the great majority of delegates had been slaves. Minister, teacher, artisan, and farmer were the most prevalent occupations, with a small number of field laborers. At least forty of the 268 had served in the Union Army—a common route to Black advancement—but most lacked formal education, and few owned enough property to pay taxes. They constituted a group that was both distinct from the mass of African Americans but close enough to them to understand (if not always share all) their hopes and aspirations; not surprisingly, they usually represented districts with Black majorities. They also represented a leadership cadre with remarkable staying power: 147 of them would later serve as state legislators, and nine would be U.S. congressmen.[22]

As the delegates prepared to take part in constitutional conventions that would spearhead an unprecedented experiment in political democracy, an unresolved—and usually unspoken—tension existed over precisely whom they represented. Unlike Russia's peasant leaders, who were chosen only by other peasants and who headed purely peasant institutions, the Black convention delegates, and later the Black state legislators, were chosen by electoral districts that contained Blacks and whites, former slaves but also former slave owners—and others in between, from African Americans who had been free to whites who had not owned slaves and in some cases had nothing to do with slavery. No one suggested that peasant officials represented all Russians, but the introduction of full manhood suffrage meant that Black officials represented—and made laws for—the whole body politic, even as they also represented a newly enfranchised population that some saw as a "people," or in the words of historian Steven Hahn a "nation."[23] There was, in short, a dual character to the "self-government" that emerged as former slaves became republican citizens, and two kinds of representation that rested in uneasy equilibrium.

Also unresolved, both in Russia and in the South, was the potential divergence between the interests of Black and peasant leaders and the masses they represented. In both countries, there was a tension between the aspirations of newly chosen leaders to further their own interests and their role as spokesmen for "their" people. This tension was to some degree unavoidable because those leaders had to work with (and be careful not to alienate) powerful outsiders. If this need was most obvious in the South, where Black politicians represented white as well as Black voters, it existed as well in Russia, where peasant leaders also in effect had multiple "constituencies" to whom they had to answer; aside from the mass of peasants, these included noble landowners and government officials—both of whom still had legally defined powers over rural society—and unusually prosperous peasants who despite lack of official status wielded disproportionate influence among their fellow villagers. In short, there were potential conflicts between the interests of the freedpeople as a whole and those of particular Black and peasant individuals who acted as their spokesmen. If this conflict was often held in check by the limited degree of stratification that existed among the freedpeople, it was likely to increase along with the stratification that would inevitably emerge in a post-emancipation era.

The new and accentuated political roles of African Americans and peasants, and the new political environment they faced, profoundly influenced the playing out of social relations on the ground. As freedpeople sought to assert and defend their independence, their most immediate task was to promote nonservile conditions of labor, even as planters and pomeshchiki sought to perpetuate as much as possible of the old order. The central question that gripped post-emancipation society was who would work for whom, under what terms. For the freedpeople this meant how could they support themselves without entering into subservient relations with their former owners, while for those former owners it meant how could they secure the labor that had previously been performed by slaves and serfs? In both the South and Russia, this question was resolved through a continuous process of negotiation and struggle, which gave birth to a patchwork of new labor relations that defied easy categorization. "Free labor" came in many forms.

In Russia, the redemption process was at the center of these negotiations and struggles. Although mandatory redemption of the peasants' farmsteads (*usad'by*)—the small plots of land that immediately surrounded their huts—was included in the statutory charters that pomeshchiki or their agents had drafted and that local authorities had then ratified and supervised (see chapter 3), redemption of their much larger field land allotments usually remained to be initiated. This process could occur either through voluntary agreements between peasants and their former owners or through unilateral decisions of those owners; as with the statutory charters, peasants could voice their objection to redemption but could not stop its implementation. In theory, the terms flowed directly and automatically from the allotments and payments stipulated in the statutory charters already in place, with the state advancing pomeshchiki 75 or 80 percent of the redemption loans in 5 percent bonds and the peasants repaying the state, with 6 percent annual interest, over forty-nine years. When redemption occurred through mutual agreement, the peasants would then need to arrange separate ("supplementary") payments of the remaining 20 or 25 percent directly with their former owners; these payments could be made immediately or could stretch out over many years, and they could be in cash or its labor equivalent, or a combination of the two. When pomeshchiki imposed redemption on peasants unilaterally, however, those peasants were spared the necessity of making supplementary payments and the landowners received only the 75 or 80 percent advanced by the state.[24]

Peasants had a lot to consider as they decided how to approach the redemption operation, including especially whether they would enter into voluntary agreements with their former owners—and if so what the terms of their supplementary payments should be—or wait for those owners to impose redemption on them. Another option still was to accept very small "gratuitous" allotments equal to one-quarter the size of the maximum holdings, without having to make any redemption payments at all. Given that peasants who reached agreements with their former owners would face higher redemption fees than those who had redemption imposed on them, it is hardly surprising that "the redemption operation ... gave rise to massive peasant protest" and that peasants were generally reluctant to enter into voluntary agreements; indeed, just as most statutory charters had been implemented over peasant opposition, so too of 41,627 redemption operations begun by 1 January 1870 a slight majority were imposed unilaterally. Nor is it surprising that many pomeshchiki were in no hurry to impose redemption without securing peasant consent and thereby receive reduced compensation. In short, there was plenty of opportunity for confusion, misunderstanding, and disagreement over detail. Both peasants and pomeshchiki had incentives to move slowly: if peasants could reduce their expenses by refusing to enter into voluntary agreements, pomeshchiki could increase their potential income by refraining from acting unilaterally in the hopes of eventually convincing peasants to enter into such agreements.[25]

An example of a mutual redemption agreement illustrates how the process could work when all went according to plan. In November 1863, representatives of the peasants on an estate in the Biriuchenskii district of Voronezh Province concluded such an agreement with the agent of their former owner, Agrafena Ivanovna Korostovtsova. The agreement committed the eighty (male) souls to redeem all the land that they had been allotted in a previously implemented statutory charter, which amounted to two hundred and three and two-thirds desiatiny, for which as temporarily obligated peasants they had been paying an annual obrok of 632 rubles and sixteen kopecks. Based on the stipulated formula of capitalizing that obrok figure at 6 percent, the peasants owed 10,536 rubles for the land (632.16 = 6 percent of 10,536). As indicated in the redemption legislation, the government advanced 80 percent of this sum—8,428 rubles and eighty kopecks—to pomeshchitsa Korostovtsova, with the peasants to repay the state over forty-nine years. The peasants agreed to pay the remaining 20 percent of the redemption loan—2,107 rubles and twenty kopecks—directly to Korostovtsova over six years, in semiannual installments of 175 rubles and six kopecks (175.6 × 12 = 2,107.20). The agreement, which also described the location of the land, was signed for Korostovtsova by agent Mikhail Mikhailovich Grevs, but since the fourteen peasant representatives were illiterate, "at their personal request" the volost' clerk Iakov Kurdiukov, a state peasant, signed for them. Finally, the area's peace mediator, V. Shidlovskii, certified that the agreement was written by Grevs and witnessed by three neighboring peasants, who were themselves illiterate and therefore secured the signature of a merchant, Vasilii Volozhkin, on their behalf. Noting that the agreement had been voluntarily reached by Grevs and the peasants, who were fully aware of its provisions, Shidlovskii affixed his signature to the document on 24 December 1863, some five weeks after the two sides had given their assent.[26]

As this straightforward example suggests, the redemption process was cumbersome under the best of circumstances, and fraught with potential complications. Although peasants had little incentive to reach voluntary agreements, under which they would have to commit to making significant supplementary payments directly to their former owners, they were often unhappy with the terms of the obligatory redemption that landowners imposed on them. Even though there was little opportunity to contest the size of the forty-nine-year redemption debt they owed the state—which flowed automatically from capitalizing their statutory charter-imposed obrok at 6 percent—there were plenty of other points of potential contention.

One of the most notable was the quality of the land allotments the peasants would be redeeming. During the summer of 1865, peasants on multiple adjoining estates in Uhkotskaia volost' of Olonets Province began a prolonged, large-scale volnenie, complaining that they were receiving inferior land in the obligatory redemption settlements being imposed on them. Those who had belonged to a local peace mediator named Gerol'd made complaints that were "especially persistent and sharp," describing the bulk of their allotment land as consisting of "mossy swamp." The volnenie contained many familiar features, including "impudent and persistent" demands, refusal to pay obrok obligations, negotiations with progressively higher officials from peace mediators and district ispravnik to the provincial governor, peasant solidarity manifested in "shouts and noise [that] intensified daily," and exemplary arrests and punishment. Less typical was Governor Iu. K. Arsen'ev's growing suspicion that despite the landowners' insistence—confirmed by the peace mediators— "that the allotments were done correctly and that the peasant complaints did not deserve any attention," the complaints might in fact have some validity. "It is hard to say who is right," he wrote to Minister of Internal Affairs Valuev in February 1866, "but I cannot imagine that the whole crowd [of peasants] were telling falsehoods . . . so long and stubbornly."[27]

Further investigation strengthened Aresen'ev's doubts. After concluding that in fact "the allotment was done unscrupulously badly," he raised the possibility with Valuev of dismissing two peace mediators (including Gerol'd) but evidently thought better of the idea, perhaps after instructions from Valuev. Ultimately, despite recognizing the validity of the peasants' basic complaint, the governor displayed a characteristic unwillingness to side with peasants against authorities. Asserting that "the police have conducted themselves in this whole affair carefully and with tact," he noted: "The population of Ukhotskaia volost' has consistently displayed insubordination and an extremely quarrelsome character" and confided that the inhabitants of one of the most insubordinate villages were rumored to be descended from three Polish families that had arrived in the seventeenth century. "They have a certain type of personality," he continued; "they are obstinate and hate any authority." Two years later the unrest still simmered, and Aresen'ev had two particularly troublesome peasants exiled from the province for "inciting disobedience to authority and nonfulfillment of state obligations."[28]

Other peasants, too, were unhappy with the land they were forced to redeem. In some cases, peasants found themselves resettled against their will on new land, a process that predictably led to peasant resistance. When the peasants of Nizhgosttsy, in St. Petersburg Province, refused such resettlement with "unprecedented obstinacy" and insisted on returning to their old homes, the peace mediator confessed his inability to handle them with the limited force at his disposal—"Moral force no longer works on the Nizhgosttsy peasants"—and begged the province's vice-governor for help. Six weeks later, noting that the disorder was having a demoralizing effect throughout not just the volost' but the whole district, he warned that the situation "demand[ed] quick and practical measures" and suggested that temporarily stationing cavalrymen in the village would produce a "beneficial" impression on the unruly residents. The situation was similar in the village of Bruska, in Tula Province, where an ispravnik resorted to bringing in outside peasants to destroy the houses of those who refused to resettle, thereby removing "any possibility of their living in their former places." When even that did not quell the peasant disorder, the provincial governor sent troops to the village, with the desired effect; after some exemplary punishments, "the peasants begged permission to move to their new settlement without compulsion by armed force." Finally, the governor was able to report, "They have begun to move their buildings, although under military supervision." If some peasants resisted resettlement, others actively sought it. Unhappy with their land allotments and redemption payments, the peasants of Gorodskoi Umet, in Tambov Province, gathered to petition for resettlement "on free lands." Urged on by the village miller, they spurned the advice of various local officials—including their starosta and the volost' starshina—and engaged in violent tussles with these officials and the district ispravnik that ended only when the governor sent in soldiers, who arrested eight of the peasant agitators and subjected five of them, "at the order of the peace mediator," to punishment with birch switches.[29]

More generally, many peasants were convinced that forced redemption, without the consent of the mir, was illegitimate. Sometimes, their resistance to such obligatory redemption constituted a continuation of similar resistance to statutory charters that had been imposed without their consent. In April 1864 the peasants on Count Tolstoi's estate, centered at Begoshcha village in Kursk Province, would not accept the certificate of landownership (*dannaia*) they were presented as part of the redemption process and refused to make the stipulated redemption payments. When the governor dispatched two hundred infantrymen and forty mounted soldiers to restore order, the peasants sent a petition to Alexander II linking their action to their earlier rejection of the charter imposed on them. Complaining that the charter had been "composed without participation of the whole obshchestvo" and was accepted by the volost' starshina (whom they then replaced) on his own, without their agreement, they narrated a string of abuses they had suffered at the hands of the Putivl'skii district authorities, including punishments with birch switches and the jailing of seven of their leaders, and begged the monarch for relief. Similarly, when the peasants on Countess Ekaterina Dmitrievna Kusheleva's large estate in Voronezh Province resisted obligatory redemption and refused to accept the certificate of landownership, it turned out that they had earlier rejected the statutory charter imposed on them unilaterally, a charter that reduced their previous allotments of more than eight desiatiny per soul to three and a half desiatiny. Despite entreaties of officials ranging from the district ispravnik to the governor, the peasants refused to yield, tussling with authorities over the certificate, refusing (after holding two special communal meetings) to make redemption payments, and demanding the right provided in the emancipation legislation to receive small "gratuitous" allotments, prompting the governor to "personally" supervise the punishment of the "most stubborn" peasants and thereby secure the submission of the rest. "Severe measures" had been necessary, the Kursk provincial governor explained to Minister of Internal Affairs Valuev, because peasants were withholding payments "in other locations" as well, "awaiting the outcome of this affair."[30]

As these examples indicate, although dissatisfaction with specific redemption terms, from the amount and quality of land to the size of redemption payments, was widespread among peasants, a more general assumption that the redemption operation represented an "illegal" effort to put something over on them underlay most of their specific objections. Over and over, peasants drove home their conviction that no redemption was legitimate without their participation and consent, and that the effort to impose redemption unilaterally was part of a fake—"noble" rather than "tsar's"—emancipation. When the peasants of Tokmovo village, in Penza Province, objected to the terms of the redemption imposed on them by their former owner, who even earlier had brought them to "extreme ruin" and was now taking the best land for himself, they held what the governor later termed an "unauthorized" ("samovol'no") communal gathering in which they changed the village leadership, "stubbornly refused" the redemption payments they owed, and selected walkers to take a petition to the tsar. Complaining that they had no idea who had composed the redemption settlement, which was "totally without our consent," they begged authorities to annul it and allow another to be composed in their presence, "according to the Polozehnie sent by his imperial majesty the sovereign Emperor."[31]

Elsewhere, too, peasants insisted that redemption without their consent was illegitimate. When Baroness Maria Dmitrievna Sheping imposed obligatory redemption on her large estate at Khar'kovka, in Voronezh Province, the peasants held a communal gathering at which they "loudly proclaimed that all the officials had been bribed by the pomeshchik" and denounced the redemption settlement as a "noble" rather than "tsar's" version. Refusing to make the stipulated payments or recognize their shift to peasant proprietor status, they proclaimed that because "the redemption was made without their consent, ... they remained in their previous [temporarily obligated] position." When the aggravated provincial governor pressed communal elders on their understanding of a tsar's versus a noble's redemption, they replied that "they had heard there are two kinds of redemption, and that they did not want the noble [kind] but would pay the tsar's." A group of hired hands (*batraki*) in Vitebsk Province were also convinced that officials—including the peace mediator—were suppressing the tsar's orders, in this case by hiding an imperial ukaz giving them land; when the peace mediator explained the nonexistence of such an ukaz, a crowd "attacked and beat the volost' starshina, tearing the badge from his chest," requiring a company of soldiers to restore order by arresting the "main instigators of the violence."[32]

Although peasants dissatisfied with the terms of their redemption settlement and convinced that they were being cheated out of what was rightfully theirs ultimately had few alternatives to accepting what they were presented as a fait accompli, they did have one unappealing option that some nevertheless embraced: the so-called gratuitous or beggars' allotment—equal to one-quarter the maximum allotment size as defined in the emancipation legislation—that they could receive free of any redemption expenses. Although such allotments were almost never large enough to permit self-sufficient agriculture—indeed, conservative Prince Pavel Gagarin had succeeded in having the gratuitous option added to the emancipation legislation at the last moment so that peasants would find it necessary to cultivate noble lands as well as their own—the possibility of avoiding redemption payments was attractive enough to lure about 5 percent of the former serfs into choosing to accept the minuscule allotments. Several considerations could motivate peasants to make such a choice. Some calculated that they would be better off if they could avoid redemption payments and use the saved funds to rent or buy additional land. Such calculation was especially common in the relatively less populated black-earth provinces of the south and east, where land was less expensive than in the more densely settled central and western regions; in 1879, almost half the peasants who had received beggars' allotments in the twenty-seven provinces of European Russia were located in two such provinces—Perm and Saratov. Others, believing that the tsar would soon order—or had already ordered—a general land distribution, were willing to accept tiny allotments on a short-term basis; indeed, historian Allan K. Wildman has suggested that for this reason, when jockeying over statutory charters, peasants had typically been more concerned with minimizing payments than with maximizing the size of their landholdings.[33]

Choosing to accept holdings that were far too small to provide sustenance represented a desperate gamble that usually had unsatisfactory consequences. Expectations of a land distribution were unfulfilled, and as land prices rose, purchasing or renting additional land appeared increasingly burdensome. In 1883, peasant representatives from two villages in Voronezh Province petitioned the governor, detailing their hardships. In 1863 they had chosen to receive gratuitous allotments that amounted to a minuscule 2,080 sazheni (86.7 percent of one desiatina) per soul; since then, however, population growth had reduced their allotment size by more than one-half, to eight hundred sazheni per soul. The petitioners, hungry for land, explained, "We fell into full dependence [on] neighboring landholders," who took advantage of them to charge exorbitant rent. Imploring the governor to deliver them from "final ruin and misery," the peasants begged him to facilitate a loan from the Peasant Land Bank so they could purchase 3,222 desiatiny of land from a local merchant for the hefty sum of 273,870 rubles (85 rubles per desiatina). The 2,458 male souls would receive a measly average of 1.31 desiatiny each, for which (not counting interest) they would owe 111.42 rubles per soul. A petition from peasants in a neighboring village was more succinct if more far-fetched: noting that since emancipation they had held "only an insignificant amount of gratuitous land," they begged the governor to take heed of their "straitened and desperate position" and allot them three and one-half desiatiny per soul.[34]

Both peasants and pomeshchiki faced competing pressures in the redemption process. Peasants who refused to enter into agreements with landlords and waited for those landlords to impose redemption unilaterally gained reduced payments but lost the ability to influence the terms of the settlement and postponed their transition to peasant proprietor status. Those who opted for gratuitous allotments escaped redemption payments altogether but could not support themselves on the tiny plots they received. Those who entered into redemption agreements had more say in determining the parameters of their lives as peasant proprietors but had to endure larger redemption payments. From the landlords' perspective, imposing mandatory redemption on peasants offered the advantage of being able to shape the settlement without pesky peasant interference and enabled them to receive their redemption money immediately without engaging in potentially lengthy negotiations, but this came at the cost of redemption payments reduced by 20 to 25 percent and potential resistance from aggrieved peasants. Under the circumstances, it is not surprising that a good deal of jockeying occurred on both sides, with many peasants preferring not to enter into hasty agreements—especially given their widespread expectation of an imminent new dispensation that would *give* them some or all of the noble-held land—and many pomeshchiki reluctant to suffer the consequences of acting on their own.

Indeed, the pace of initiating redemption was slow, and just as the majority of peasants had refused to approve the statutory charters they were presented, so too a majority refused to enter into voluntary redemption agreements. At the beginning of 1864, almost a year after the period for establishing statutory charters had expired, more than 90 percent of former serfs remained under temporarily obligated status. Thereafter, the rate of redemptions picked up, at least for a while: by early 1870, about two-thirds of the former bondspeople had become peasant proprietors and begun repaying their redemption loans. Both the pace of redemption and the proportion reached by mutual agreement varied considerably among (and even within) provinces, as peasants and pomeshchiki adjusted their tactics according to local conditions—including the fertility of the soil, size of landholdings, prevalence of obrok or barshchina obligations under serfdom, and sometimes idiosyncratic preferences. In Moscow Province, for example, where proximity to the largest urban center provided nonagricultural opportunities for many peasants, 81 percent of the redemptions initiated by 1870 were at the insistence of pomeshchiki and only 19 percent by mutual agreement, whereas in Kursk Province, where the land was fertile and the great majority of serfs had worked under barshchina, 65 percent of the redemptions were voluntary and only 35 percent imposed.[35]

During the 1870s the transition process slowed and peasant resistance to it increased, and at the end of the decade about 15 percent of the former serfs remained temporarily obligated. What is more, whereas earlier a slight majority of redemptions had been the result of unilateral action on the part of pomeshchiki rather than agreements between pomeshchiki and peasants, more than two-thirds of the redemptions initiated during the 1870s were imposed on peasants without their consent. The increasing proportion of redemptions imposed over the objections of peasants reflected both the growing impatience of pomeshchiki eager to receive the government-advanced redemption loan (which the peasants would repay) and the persistent unwillingness of many peasants to agree on redemption terms because they remained convinced that if they held out something better would soon materialize. A mini-spike in rumors of a new dispensation occurred in 1869, with the spread of the notion that nine years after the issuance of the emancipation manifesto peasants would gain the right to renounce their allotments, together with the dues that accompanied them. Temporarily obligated peasants on three adjacent estates in Samara Province insisted that they no longer had to use the land assigned to them in the statutory charter under which they still labored, or sow winter wheat, while an official in Saratov Province reported: "Among the peasant proprietors there exists the belief that they have the right to renounce [their] land"—and the concomitant redemption payments with which they were burdened.[36]

Rumors of impending change became more widespread toward the end of the 1870s, as the twentieth anniversary of the emancipation decree approached. In Nizhnii Novgorod Province, an official reported on "stubborn" rumors that on 1 January 1880 "land [would] be taken from the pomeshchiki and divided equally among the cultivators," who would acquire title to the land on 19 February; "for this reason," he added, "in many places obrok and rental payments [were] not being received on time." A landowner in Tambov Province complained about the spread of "socialist propaganda" among the peasants, including the suggestion that "nobles want[ed] to murder the tsar" because he wanted to confiscate their land, and pointed to talk in one district of the need to "wring the necks of all pomeshchiki [and] distribute their property and land." From Tula Province, an officer of the Corps of Gendarmes warned that "as before," peasants were expecting an imminent "augmentation of their allotments from noble lands." At a meeting of the Committee of Ministers, Minister of Internal Affairs L. S. Makov warned that similar rumors of an impending land redistribution were rampant in at least fifteen provinces.[37]

In fact, although such expectations went unfulfilled, 1881 did bring significant change to the redemption process. Under the combined pressure of peasant dissatisfaction with burdensome redemption payments, the continued refusal of about 15 percent of former serfs to enter into redemption agreements, and the crisis mentality that gripped the Russian government in the wake of Alexander II's assassination by members of the revolutionary-terrorist organization People's Will (*Narodnaia Volia*) on 1 March 1881, his successor (and son), Alexander III, issued two decrees on 28 December. The first initiated the mandatory transfer to peasant proprietor status, as of 1 January 1883, of all remaining temporarily obligated peasants, who—because of the mandatory nature of this transfer—would be spared the additional 20 or 25 percent of redemption dues that peasants who entered into voluntary redemption agreements paid direct to their landlords. The second decree substantially reduced—according to one historian's estimate by 27.3 percent—the level of redemption payments for all former serfs throughout the thirty Russian and Ukrainian provinces. It also held out the hope for additional relief by directing the collection of "detailed information on those villages of former serfs which, as a result of unfavorable conditions, [were] in an especially ruinous economic position," so that their inhabitants could receive special consideration. Although Alexander III would earn a reputation as a reactionary monarch, his reign began with measures that reduced the redemption obligations with which the great majority of former serfs were saddled, measures that marked the end of the protracted transition stage of "temporary obligation" that had been at the heart of Russia's gradual process of emancipation.[38]

They did not mark, however, the end of the class struggle between former serfs and pomeshchiki, or of government perception that peasants were out of control. "Peasant proprietors" continued to owe redemption payments until 1907, when, as stipulated in an ukaz issued by Tsar Nicholas II in 1905, all remaining redemption debt was canceled. They also continued to fall into ever-increasing arrears on these payments, and to show sporadic resistance to what they regarded as the inequitable emancipation settlement. Noting the "uncertainty" of agricultural relations, either "in reality or in the eyes of the peasants," a report compiled by the Department of Police at the instruction of Minister of Internal Affairs Dmitrii Tolstoi in 1889 concluded that peasants always gave preference to "their personal interests, real or imagined, paying no attention to either the demands or the indisputable rights" of outsiders. Lamenting the peasantry's isolation, the report complained: "[Peasants] have faith only in that which seems immediately advantageous" to them, "without paying any attention to the instructions and demands of the authorities." The obvious conclusion, on which the government would soon act, was that peasants needed closer supervision by "wise leader[s]."[39]

In the American South, the freedpeople's struggle for a "real" freedom played out in a very different context, one that at least for a while seemed to offer former slaves remarkable opportunities to help shape the new order but was met by a massive campaign of violence on the part of those determined to limit change and preserve "white supremacy." Even as African Americans took an increasingly active part in Reconstruction governments, and as those governments acted in varying degrees to promote a more egalitarian society, opponents of the new order mobilized legal and illegal forces in opposition. Revolutionary changes were met with no-holds-barred counterrevolutionary terrorism that would eventually produce an American version of "redemption" very different from that in Russia, a version that rolled back the most visible features of Black power but could not fully undo the changes set in motion by emancipation. While Russian peasants challenged the central components of what they considered a false emancipation settlement, and used new and existing peasant institutions to run their own affairs (but not those of other Russians), African Americans embraced the increasingly radical, Reconstruction-defined terms of emancipation to take part in self-government not only as a people shaping their own lives but also as republican citizens in the larger body politic. As historian Steven Hahn has suggested, the experience "proved to be a turbulent and telling experiment in the meaning of democracy."[40]

The constitutional conventions that the Reconstruction Acts of 1867 mandated for the ex-Confederate states (aside from Tennessee) initiated this decade-long experiment. Held at varying times from November 1867 to May 1868 (except in Texas, where delegates did not complete their work until 6 November 1869), the conventions reflected the fluidity and uncertainty of the evolving political climate. Overall, a majority of the delegates (56.4 percent) were Southern whites, while Northern whites—reviled by many ex-Confederates as "carpetbaggers"—formed the smallest contingent (16.1 percent) and African Americans placed in between, with a little more than a quarter of the delegates (26.3 percent). There were sharp variations, however, from state to state: Black representation ranged from 10.9 percent in Texas to 59.9 percent in South Carolina. Black delegates usually represented districts with African Americans majorities, and most came from states with high concentrations of Black residents as well, but only in South Carolina and Louisiana did the proportion of African Americans in the conventions equal or surpass their proportion of the population.[41]

The Black delegates spanned a broad range of backgrounds and occupations, from men formerly free (and in a few cases highly privileged) to those newly emancipated. A few were already famous, such as South Carolinian Robert Smalls, who had gained notoriety in 1862 by commandeering a Confederate ship in Charleston harbor and delivering it to nearby Union forces, an accomplishment that earned him a commission as second lieutenant in the Union Navy. A few were relatively wealthy, such as Louisiana's Emile Bonnefoi, a free, light-skinned planter before the war with assets in 1860 worth $7,000. The great majority, however, were men of fairly modest means: the median property holding of Black delegates was $700, and the average (skewed higher by a small number of wealthy individuals) was $1,637—far less than the wealth of white delegates (whether Southern or Northern). These new Black politicians had already managed to distinguish themselves in a variety of ways—usually literacy, occupation, and leadership—from the mass of freedpeople, but in many respects they shared much with their constituents in background, association, and outlook, and they were well positioned to represent their interests.[42]

The conventions served as political schools for the Black delegates, most of whom would later serve in elective office. New to the political game, they usually wielded less power than (and sometimes deferred to) their white allies, and although about one-quarter of the delegates were Black, only 6.5 percent of committees were chaired by African Americans. (By contrast, Northern white delegates typically were more influential than their limited numbers might suggest.) The Black delegates were by no means silent, however, nor were they the pawns of troublemaking carpetbaggers mockingly depicted by conservative whites. Indeed, although Black delegates were especially persistent in advocating "radical" measures—including equal rights provisions, the establishment of common public schools for children regardless of race, and in some cases measures that would protect agricultural workers from abuse by planters—they did not always follow the lead of white radicals: as enthusiastic supporters of full "manhood" suffrage, for example, they were less likely than white radicals to favor continued voting restrictions on former Confederates. Nor did the Black delegates always agree among themselves. As strong proponents of equal rights, most of them opposed any discrimination on the basis of race, but some joined conservative delegates in favoring measures prohibiting marriage between whites and Blacks; light-skinned "mulattoes," who in other respects usually took positions favoring "social equality," could find interracial marriage a particularly sensitive subject. In Alabama, for example, seven of seventeen African American delegates voted in favor of banning "the intermarriage of white persons with persons of color, to the fourth generation," and Mobile's John Carraway, himself the son of a white planter and a Black slave, offered an amendment—that along with the measure as a whole was soon tabled—providing that "any white man intermarrying or cohabiting with colored women, shall be imprisoned for life."[43]

Despite some differences among them, almost all the Black delegates—and most of their white Republican allies—subscribed to a radical vision of creating a new republican society centered on equal rights. Although some recent historians—perhaps in part in reaction to those of an earlier generation who depicted the emerging Black politicians as ignorant field hands not far removed from African savagery—have suggested that African American leaders were too distant from the mass of freedpeople to share their radical aspirations, the Black delegates shared more in background with their constituents than most political leaders, either at the time or in American history overall. Although most Black convention delegates were not field laborers at the time of their election, many had been, and most had been slaves. It is not surprising, then, that many of them championed measures—not always successfully—that went well beyond establishing political equality for all men. As Steven Hahn has suggested, "Although black delegates sometimes had a difficult time getting proposals of interest to rural laborers a general hearing, . . . almost everywhere, they brought such proposals into the proceedings."[44]

Among the most notable of these proposals were "lien laws" designed "to protect the wages of rural and urban workers" from confiscation by employers, and measures that would facilitate Black homesteading. In Alabama's convention, John Carraway sponsored a resolution—adopted without roll call—to petition Congress for relief from the "serious difficulties" would-be homesteaders were encountering as a result of "abuses in the land office," abuses that included "incorrect surveys" for which applicants were charged "the enormous sum of thirty dollars." A few days later, Alfred Strother, a propertyless farm laborer representing overwhelmingly Black plantation-rich Dallas County, introduced a resolution that passed 53–31 instructing the convention's Committee on Ordinances to consider "an ordinance empowering the colored people of this State to collect a fair equivalent for their services from those persons who held them in slavery from the 1st day of January, 1863, to the 20th day of May, 1865." Thomas Bayne, a fugitive slave who became a dentist in Boston before returning to represent Norfolk in Virginia's convention, urged the enfranchisement of women, as did William J. Whipper, a free-born mulatto from Pennsylvania who had served in the Union Army and represented Beaufort County in South Carolina's convention. "The time will come," he proclaimed, "when every man and woman in this country will have the right to vote."[45]

At the heart of the proposals espoused by the Black delegates and their white allies was the creation of a republican society with equal civil rights for all and equal political rights for all men. This goal was not so much in opposition to the radical aspirations of the mass of freedpeople as complementary to them; indeed, establishing equal citizenship and a democratic political system would make possible the pursuit of a variety of social reforms in the future. Nothing testifies to the revolutionary nature of this republican departure—and of the participation of Black delegates in its pursuit—more than the vitriolic opposition that it aroused among conservatives (who formed the majority of the white population). These conservatives would devise a variety of sometimes contradictory tactics to combat the Reconstruction experiment, but from the beginning the very participation of former slaves as architects of the new order seemed ludicrous to proponents of the old regime, who typically mocked the Black delegates for engaging in "violent and highly inflammatory harangues [and] demanding entire social equality with the whites" or, alternately, dismissed these delegates as childlike pawns of nefarious Yankee meddlers. Indeed, even allowing Blacks to vote—let alone serve in elective office—struck many white Southerners as a dreadful perversion of democracy. Objecting that "intelligence, virtue, and patriotism are to give place, in all elections, to ignorance, stupidity, and vice," a committee of white South Carolinians denounced the new state constitution as "the work of Northern adventurers, Southern renegades, and ignorant negroes" and opined that "not two percent of the negroes who voted for its adoption understand what the act of voting implied." The committee warned that "the white people of our State will never quietly submit to negro rule."[46]

The conventions varied in a number of ways, from the length of their deliberations to the composition of their delegates. South Carolina and Louisiana were the only two states where African Americans formed a majority of the delegates. Conventions in Texas and Georgia were the only two without radical majorities—except for Florida, where two rival conventions, one dominated by radicals and the other by moderates, struggled for recognition before Congress finally decided to allow the constitution drafted by the moderate convention to be submitted for ratification. Alabama's convention, the first to assemble, was also the first to complete its work, whereas that of Texas, which labored for 127 days during two tumultuous sessions, was the last. (Texas also had not only the fewest African American delegates but also the fewest radicals.) North Carolina's convention had the largest number of Southern white delegates, as well as the largest number of Southern white delegates who were radicals. When the constitution of Alabama was submitted to the public for ratification, white voter abstention initially caused the document to be rejected, whereupon Congress modified the ratification process to require a majority of those voting instead of a majority of those eligible to vote. Congress also provided for a second ratification vote in Mississippi, after determining that the initial election, in which the constitution was narrowly defeated, had been marred by voter intimidation; conservatives boycotted the second ballot, and the constitution won overwhelming approval.[47]

But despite these variations, all the constitutions provided for the creation of new, republican state governments predicated on the revolutionary principle of equal citizenship for all, including former slaves, typically enunciated in bills of rights that "made it abundantly clear that a 'mighty revolution' had occurred." In conformity with the Reconstruction Act, they mandated universal manhood suffrage, and in conformity with the understanding of most Republicans that an educated public was an essential ingredient of republican society, they provided for the establishment of new public school systems. Although some went further—in the words of historians Richard Hume and Jerry Gough, giving "special attention to working men"—for the most part they left such legislative details to the new state governments that would follow. These were "modern democratic documents" that laid the foundation for a new social order in the South that would itself be modern and democratic. The erection of that new order, however, would prove more difficult than its architects imagined.[48]

The adoption of new, forward-looking constitutions initiated a period of Reconstruction government in the Southern states that provided what was in many ways an unusually positive context for the evolution of free society and the concomitant ongoing struggle of African Americans to control their own lives, both of which are a focus of this book's part II. At the same time, however, the context was also a perilous one for African Americans because they faced continued—indeed, growing—opposition from planters and other ex-Confederates willing to use all means, including deadly violence, to defend their interests and combat what they regarded as tyrannical rule by those determined to foist "social equality" on the already suffering (white) South. A brief outline of this Reconstruction context highlights its contradictory, Janus-faced, nature.

Republican Reconstruction governments varied considerably in terms of longevity and overall character. In general, they survived the longest and showed the most radical proclivities in the Deep South, where African Americans formed the largest share of the population (and, therefore, of voters): the four states where the overthrow of Reconstruction governments (dubbed "Redemption" by their conservative opponents and often by subsequent historians) came last—Florida (1877), Louisiana (1877), South Carolina (1876), and Mississippi (1875)— were also the four with the highest proportion of African Americans. By contrast, in states with substantial white majorities, Reconstruction governments were less viable: in North Carolina, where African Americans constituted 37 percent of the population, Republicans lost statewide control in 1870, and in Tennessee (26 percent Black, and a special case because the state was deemed already reconstructed and therefore exempt from the 1867 Reconstruction legislation), Republican rule ended in 1869. Even after early "Redemption," however, significant numbers of white and Black Republicans continued to serve in elective office in areas with Black majorities; the decentralized structure of American politics permitted the continuation of *local* Republican power even after the party lost control of state governments.[49]

Despite these variations, Reconstruction governments throughout the South were alike—at least for a while—in their effort to remake the social order, turn what had been a slave society into one based on free labor, and make citizens of former slaves. The effort was not just unprecedented but also unmatched elsewhere. At the heart of this Reconstruction enterprise was a redefinition of "republicanism" and the "republican form of government" guaranteed by the United States Constitution to include equal rights regardless of "race, color, or previous condition of servitude." In embarking on this venture, Republicans consciously embraced the war-generated opportunity to reshape the Southern states along more democratic lines: if the war's outbreak enabled them to push for the immediate abolition of slavery, the war's successful conclusion—and, as Gregory P. Downs has recently emphasized, the Union Army's military occupation of the South—created the preconditions for a more radical social and political transformation. The unusual Reconstruction experiment was a direct consequence of the unusual way in which American slavery was abolished—through civil war.[50]

Throughout the South, state governments adopted measures—both in their new constitutions and in subsequent legislation—promoting free labor and civil rights, creating statewide public school systems for Blacks and (usually for the first time) whites, and (in conformity with the Fourteenth and Fifteenth Amendments to the Constitution) guaranteeing universal manhood suffrage. Some went further. Several states passed legislation similar to Alabama's act of 1868 giving laborers a "lien" on the crop they produced, an act that prevented planters from driving laborers off plantations and appropriating the fruits of their labor and therefore, as Freedmen's Bureau Assistant Commissioner Edward Beecher noted, had "a most beneficial effect among the farming population." South Carolina supplemented the Southern Homestead Act that Congress had passed in 1866 by creating its own Land Commission that helped about fourteen thousand Black families acquire land at discounted prices. Unlike most Southern states, which established separate schools for white and Black children, Louisiana and South Carolina provided in their constitutions for equal access to schooling "without distinction as to race," and for several years Louisiana experimented actively with integrated schools, especially in New Orleans.[51]

Despite their many achievements, however, the Reconstruction governments were not able to put an end to the violence from which freed African Americans had suffered in the immediate aftermath of the Civil War. Although this violence was by no means ubiquitous—at times and in places it appeared that peace and stability were taking hold—it became increasingly clear that those committed to the old order would use whatever means were available to thwart the revolutionary changes sweeping the South. As Blacks strove for self-government in its various manifestations, they and their white Republican allies faced the determined opposition of former slaveholders reluctant to accept the loss of their slaves, former Confederates seething at the loss of their war, and whites determined to maintain as much of "white supremacy" as they could. "The fact is patent to all that the negro is utterly unfitted to exercise the highest functions of the citizen," declared a convention of white South Carolinians in September 1867. Asserting that "military power" could not "lawfully reestablish civil government in South Carolina," the delegates asserted that they could never "acquiesce in negro equality" or see "an ignorant and depraved race . . . placed in power and influence above the virtuous, the educated and the refined." The federal government (and to the extent that they could, state governments) strove to maintain order: after a joint congressional committee held extensive hearings in 1871 that detailed atrocities committed by the Ku Klux Klan, the group was effectively dismantled. But the rapidly dwindling federal military presence in the South was too small—and spread too thinly—to protect more than "pockets of control surrounded by chaos," and a host of new terrorist organizations (such as the Red Shirts and the Knights of the White Camelia) continued the Klan's work.[52]

The violence was directed especially at symbols of the new order: freedpeople seen as too independent and "uppity," Black political leaders, and Republicans in general. Black schools and churches were notable targets, but so too were Blacks and whites who voted for Republicans (who were easy to identify in an era before the adoption of the secret ballot). Atrocities—which included a full range, from beatings, murders, and rapes to warnings, intimidation, and the torching of property—were widespread on an individual level, but many were products of careful organization by the Ku Klux Klan and its successors. If to freedpeople these seemed eerily reminiscent of the feared slave patrols of an earlier era, the organized violence they perpetrated can also be regarded as low-level guerrilla warfare by ex-Confederates who conceded their formal defeat—and indeed insisted that they were after all United States citizens who had all the rights of other Americans—but on a practical level refused to accept the consequences of that defeat. As historian Anne Sarah Rubin has suggested, "being a postwar [white] Southerner meant dividing oneself into a political American and a sentimental Southerner."[53]

If the scope of this rampant terrorism indicates the enormous headwinds that freedpeople faced as they sought to forge normal lives as *free* people, it also testifies to the revolutionary nature of the changes sweeping the South, changes that generated fear, loathing, and counterrevolutionary determination among many white Southerners. Particularly jarring to those Southerners was the transformation of former slaves into republican citizens who exercised not only their right to personal freedom but also their right to equal membership in the body politic. Just as during the Civil War the presence of Black men in the Union Army had seemed a particularly potent provocation to Confederates, so after the war did the participation of Black men in politics and government. Indeed, this development was so shocking to many Southern whites that it seemed to them that African Americans were now ruling the South—hence a host of phrases to describe the new state of affairs, from "Black Reconstruction" to "the bottom rail is on the top." Noting "the revolting spectacle of excited negroes riding through our streets and on the public roads with guns on their shoulders, revolvers and dirks hanging at their sides, matches in their hands, yelling, cursing, and threatening to shoot down and cut the throats of the whites," the Grand Commander of the Knights of the White Camelia in Louisiana denounced "negro supremacy" and demanded—"not as a favor . . . but as a right"—" that ten proud and intelligent States be not converted into ten African provinces."[54]

In fact, the South did not experience anything close to Black rule. Although African American political participation was impressive, only in the context of its previous absence—and of ex-Confederates' persistent hopes (often merged with expectations) that postwar changes in the social order would be largely cosmetic—did newly enfranchised Black citizens appear to be riding roughshod over their former owners. Only in South Carolina did Black representatives ever constitute a majority in the state legislature, and in every state African Americans formed a smaller proportion of officeholders than of the population. Black officeholders were exceedingly rare at the highest levels; during Reconstruction there were no Black governors (except for Pinckney B. S. Pinchback, who as president pro tem of the Louisiana Senate inherited the position of lieutenant governor on the death of that official and then served five weeks as acting governor—9 December 1872 to 13 January 1873—during unsuccessful impeachment proceedings against Governor Henry C. Warmoth); there were only two Black senators (both from Mississippi) and fourteen Black representatives in Congress (eight of whom came from South Carolina).[55]

At the state and local level, by contrast, hundreds of African Americans served in a wide variety of governmental positions. Especially in areas of heavy Black concentration, African Americans held such positions as "mayor, alderman, postmaster, county-supervisor, police juror, coroner, justice of the peace, constable, county treasurer, tax collector, assessor, school board member, and clerk of the court," and also served in various nongovernmental political positions such as "delegate to a party convention, member of the Republican executive committee, officer in a local political club, and candidate for office." Although their numbers were proportionately lower in office than in the overall population, their very existence testified to the dramatic changes that were sweeping the South. What is more, not only the election of Black officials but also the Reconstruction governments themselves rested largely on Black votes; in this sense, there *was* a "Black Reconstruction." Although not part of the formal political process, Black women pressed their husbands to vote—and vote Republican—to the extent of urging women (in the words of one freedman) to "quit their husbands" who voted for Democratic candidates. Noting that "all across the South . . . black women acted as party agents, using intimidation and coercion to assist in Republican voter mobilization campaigns," historian Justin Behrend has suggested that in Concordia Parish, Louisiana, where Black women "jeered" at men who voted Democratic and threatened them with castration, "the actions of unenfranchised black women" may have been decisive in preventing a Democratic victory in 1876.[56]

There was a strong correlation between the proportion of Blacks in a state's population and the number of African Americans elected to governmental office. Indeed, more than half the Black officeholders during Reconstruction were from the four "Blackest" states: 810 (53.6 percent) of the Reconstruction South's 1,510 Black officeholders served in (or from) South Carolina, Florida, Louisiana, and Mississippi. Although only fifty-eight of these came from Florida, when adjusted for Florida's small population the state had the second-highest proportion of African American officeholders, behind only South Carolina. (See table 4.1.)[57]

If Black state legislators were conscious of speaking for their own "people," with their own particular interests that stemmed from their distinctive

Table 4.1. Black officeholders as percentage of population, 1870

State	Black officeholders	1870 population (/1,000)	Officeholders per capita (× 1,000)
SC	316	706	0.448
FL	58	188	0.309
LA	210	727	0.289
MS	226	828	0.273
NC	187	1,071	0.175
AL	173	997	0.174
GA	135	1,184	0.114
AR	46	484	0.095
DC	11	132	0.083
VA	85	1,225	0.076
TX	49	819	0.060
TN	20	1,259	0.016
MO	1	1,721	0.006

Sources: Eric Foner, *Freedom's Lawmakers: A Directory of Black Officeholders during Reconstruction*, rev. ed. (Baton Rouge: Louisiana State University Press, 1996), xiv; *The Statistical History of the United States from Colonial Times to the Present* (New York: Basic Books, 1976), 24–36.

historical experiences in slavery, they also represented all the citizens in their districts and legislated for all residents in their states. Although the tension between these two forms of representation was to some extent inherent in American democracy, it was accentuated in the post-emancipation South by the breathtaking rapidity with which slaves were transformed into republican citizens. Black leaders' dual understanding of their political role both reflected and partially resolved this tension: even as they sought to express the particular aspirations of African Americans, they were also conscious of being participants in a broader radical movement to create a democratic government that would serve the interests of all its citizens.[58]

Certainly, nothing similar occurred in Russia, where no one in a position of power contemplated the immediate creation of a republican—let alone a democratic—political system. With emancipation, peasants who had long played a major role in governing their communities gained increased (although still limited) authority at both the village and the volost' levels, and the creation of new peasant courts constituted a significant expansion of local "self-rule" (as indicated earlier in this chapter). But their self-rule was always as peasants, not as members of the broader body politic. The idea of peasants—or for that matter *most* non-peasants—governing Russia was inconceivable except to small groups of radicals and revolutionaries; freed peasants were subjects of the tsar, not republican citizens.

The one partial exception to this generalization illustrates the particularistic nature of peasant self-government and underlines the very different contexts within which the freed population built their new lives in the two countries. Although reform-era Russia remained both autocratic and bureaucratic, legislation of 1 January 1864 initiated a limited experiment in cross-estate government at the local level by creating new provincial and district assembles known as *zemstva* (singular: *zemstvo*). The assemblies were hardly exercises in political democracy: each estate chose its deputies separately, under arcane rules that provided massive overrepresentation to noblemen. (Peasant deputies to the district zemstva—one for every three thousand male peasants—were elected in volost' assemblies.) Although peasants constituted the vast majority and noblemen formed only about 1.6 percent of the population, the first district zemstva, chosen in nineteen provinces in 1865–66, had more noble deputies than peasant (42 percent to 38 percent), and in the provincial assemblies peasants held a minuscule 10.6 percent of the seats. Still, although noblemen dominated the assemblies—one historian observed that "the zemstva became nests of gentry"—for the first time government bodies contained peasant deputies who rubbed shoulders and debated with nobles and urban property holders.[59]

The zemstvo assemblies at first aroused a good deal of enthusiasm, and historian Catherine Evtuhov recently argued that "by about 1870" they "had succeeded in winning the trust of the population." Aside from the election by district assemblies of justices of the peace—the lowest level of judges in the new judicial system created by the reform legislation enacted in 1864 (a system totally separate from the already existing all-peasant volost' courts)—the most important function of the zemstva was their sponsorship of schooling and public health care. But as government bodies the zemstvo assemblies had relatively little power: they met only briefly, once a year, and did little in the way of actual governing. Of more lasting significance than the assemblies were the permanent zemstvo boards that the reform legislation created, boards that hired a growing number of technical experts—"doctors, medical assistants (feldshers), and teachers, and later agronomists, veterinarians, insurance agents, and other professionals." The boards also supervised the collection and publication of statistical information, ranging from birth and death rates to property holding. (Peasants were even less conspicuous on the boards than in the district assemblies: in the first batch, established in 1865–66, peasants and Cossacks formed 19 percent of the board membership.)[60]

In contrast to the boards, the zemstvo assemblies failed to live up to whatever potential some may have seen in them, and peasants (who were unpaid for their service) quickly lost interest in serving as deputies in the noble-dominated bodies; as historian Dorothy Atkinson put it, by the 1870s peasant "curiosity" in the zemstva quickly waned, and "disappointed reformers began to complain of the 'apathy' and 'indifference' of the peasants toward the zemstvo." This disappointment was a harbinger of a more massive disillusionment among government officials and nobles, to whom it would soon seem increasingly clear that peasants were too childish and lazy to participate responsibly in government, not only in trans-estate bodies but even in their own villages. In short, American-style republican citizenship—for peasants or anyone else—was not a viable option under Russian autocracy.[61]

The politics of freedom—struggles over shifting power relations both between freedpeople and employers/authorities and among freedpeople themselves—continued to evolve over the post-emancipation years (and, indeed, decades). Although the context of these struggles differed significantly between the emerging republican society in the South and the continued bureaucratic autocracy in Russia, at the heart of both was the shift from forced to free labor. In both countries, a diverse variety of labor relations reflected both the preponderance of power on the part of the former owners (a preponderance that was especially pronounced in Russia) and the determination of the freedpeople to make freedom *real*. Although most African Americans and peasants continued to work at least part of the time for their former owners (or other employers), they were also able to secure for themselves a greater degree of independence through strategies that included land rental, land purchase, the promotion of several kinds of sharecropping, and migration—both temporary and permanent—to nearby cities and landholdings as well as those farther afield. Meanwhile, planters and pomeshchiki, who alternated between expressing the expectation that despite the nominal freedom of their former bondspeople not that much would change in practice and bemoaning the horrors of a world turned upside down, increasingly withdrew from directing the labor of those whom they saw as ungrateful and difficult to control and left the management of day-to-day agricultural operations to the freedpeople themselves.

In both countries, the evolving faces of free labor went hand in hand with continued striving by freedpeople for "self-government"—control of their own lives—that was central to the new politics of freedom in areas as diverse as families, churches, schools, and communities, striving that in turn generated massive pushback from planters, pomeshchiki, and eventually government officials, who became increasingly "disillusioned" with what they considered the irresponsible behavior of freedpeople unprepared to cope with the complexities of life under freedom. Contradictory trends were everywhere, as freedpeople grasped at new opportunities that inevitably led to greater socioeconomic stratification and experiential differentiation even as differences between former slaves and free Blacks and between former serfs and peasants owned by the state or the Crown gradually receded, and being African American and being peasant increasingly eclipsed status differences *among* African Americans and peasants: in terms of both self-identification and the perception of others, the end of unfree labor accentuated the salience of race and estate. The resulting picture, sketched in part II, was a complex mixture of change and continuity, hope and disappointment, unity and diversity, as the politics of freedom reshaped relations between the freedpeople and their former owners as well as among the freedpeople themselves, and as societies predicated on rank and hierarchy lurched unevenly toward modernity.

II · Consequences

5 • Free Labor

During the decades after emancipation, new patterns of life emerged among the former slaves and serfs—and their former owners—in both Russia and the Southern United States. These new patterns exhibited change, continuity, and above all, diversity as freedpeople struggled to remake their lives as *free* people while their often-bewildered former owners strove to defend their interests in a new world, with new ground rules. The freedpeople sought not so much change per se—indeed, in some cases they clung to familiar ways—as specific kinds of change that would give them more autonomy, more control over their own lives, and more economic security. Planters and pomeshchiki sought to maintain as many of their old prerogatives as possible, but they also promoted new ways of defending their interests. As the two classes struggled to find their places in a changed environment, both underwent significant transformations that heralded the halting but ineluctable creation of societies predicated upon free labor.

Underlying this transformation was the continuing struggle over the very meaning of "free labor," a term that had potentially divergent implications even as it came to represent the essence of what in a new age would inevitably replace the bondage of the old. Blacks and peasants were now "free" and would no longer toil under compulsion for the benefit of their owners, but the precise nature of what would replace the coerced labor of the past remained to be defined. In fact, within very different political and economic contexts, Russia and the South saw the emergence of patchworks of overlapping and sometimes competing systems of labor that defied easy categorization, patchworks that were neither as similar as the term "free labor" implied nor as different as one might expect given the contrasting contexts. All this played out within national and international contexts that were largely beyond the freedpeople's control.

At the heart of these diverse variants of free labor that emerged in both Russia and the South lay the central question of who would work for whom, and under what conditions. The freedpeople, of course, hoped to work for themselves (although even that occurrence did not preclude the possibility of some freedpeople exploiting the labor of others). This hope was not entirely chimerical; indeed, a major byproduct of emancipation was the emergence of greater economic autonomy for the former slaves and serfs. In both countries, however, there were significant limitations to this autonomy, limitations stemming from unequal power relations and—especially in the South but also in Russia—from the land poverty of most freedpeople, who were usually unable to support themselves entirely through self-sufficient agriculture and consequently found it necessary to work at least some of the time for others. This work could be found in cities and in the countryside, and it entailed a variety of occupations that ranged from barge haulers and factory hands to skilled craft workers, cooks, laundresses, and nannies. Because Russia and the South remained overwhelmingly agricultural societies, however, dependent labor most often involved working for—and on land owned by—planters and pomeshchiki, almost all of whom were former slaveholders and serfholders.

As the freedpeople struggled for autonomy and economic security, they operated within very different contexts that facilitated and limited their opportunities in divergent ways. Among the most important of these contextual differences were access to land, geographic mobility, and political environment. Relatively few African Americans acquired land of their own during the decade after emancipation, whereas the redemption process provided most former serfs with land allotments, albeit allotments that were usually slightly smaller than those they had been assigned under serfdom and were increasingly insufficient to provide the income needed to support peasant families and pay the hefty redemption expenses they continued to owe. The ability of former slaves to move partially offset their land poverty both by allowing them to take advantage of the shortage of labor that was especially intense in the Deep South so as to negotiate favorable terms of labor and by allowing them to seek new opportunities elsewhere. Peasants were increasingly mobile as well, but unlike their American counterparts they lacked the ability to move at will: those who wished to do so required the permission of their commune, in the form of short-term passes ("passports") to engage in seasonal work away from home, longer-term passes to live and work elsewhere while remaining members of a commune, or authorization to withdraw from it altogether and move away permanently. Meanwhile, at least for a few years, African Americans in much of the South could count on governments at the state and local levels that were at least theoretically committed to protecting equal rights, a concept that was beyond the imagination of virtually anyone in Russia.

The right to move was both an earmark and a guarantee of freedom to the former slaves, and they took advantage of this new right on a massive scale. Although the "hegira of negroes from plantations" that alarmed many white observers during the "Great Jubilee" immediately following emancipation proved to be a temporary eruption, substantial Black migration continued to characterize the South in the post-emancipation decades. In increasing numbers African Americans moved to cities, which had long been places of refuge for fugitive slaves, both to seek security and to take advantage of new occupational opportunities. Responding to the intense demand for labor, they moved from the Upper South to the Southwest (and to a lesser extent to Florida), continuing—now voluntarily—a process whereby surplus slave workers had been shipped to toil on the cotton and sugar plantations of Mississippi and Louisiana. In 1879–80, in a post-Reconstruction era of increasing suppression throughout the South, they engaged in a brief but notable trek of "Exodusters" to Kansas, and in the early years of the twentieth century they began a more massive movement—one that would continue for some half century—to Northern cities such as Chicago, Detroit, and New York. Meanwhile, as the high hopes of Reconstruction were dashed in a new era of Jim Crow segregation and terrorist violence, many contemplated—although few actually went through with—emigrating abroad, most notably to Africa.[1]

But most of all, African Americans continued to exercise their freedom to do what had been forbidden under slavery, moving locally within the rural South, both to resist any effort to turn them into semi-bound peons and to take advantage of opportunities to improve their condition. This persistent local movement was evident immediately upon emancipation, and it continued even in the face of the escalating political suppression of the late nineteenth and early twentieth centuries. As historian William Cohen concluded, in a careful study that repudiated his earlier belief in widespread debt peonage, "throughout the period up to World War I, blacks in most parts of the South appear to have moved with relatively little interference when jobs were available." If forced migration had pervasively shaped the lives of African Americans under slavery, voluntary movement, beginning with the massive flight of Blacks from Southern farms and plantations during the Civil War and continuing in diverse forms over subsequent decades, was central to the efforts of African Americans to make better lives for themselves under freedom.[2]

In Russia, it was harder for former serfs to move at will. Not only did their possession of landed allotments render them more rooted than the largely landless African Americans, as members of peasant communes they also lacked the individual freedom of movement that Southern freedpeople enjoyed. After emancipation, peasants still needed permission to leave their villages to seek outside employment, whether on a temporary or permanent basis, now from the peasant commune rather than their owners. The emancipation statutes provided some detail on the process of temporary outmigration (*otkhodnichestvo*, from the Russian word for departure, *otkhod*) as well as the more extreme step of permanently moving away and thereby leaving the commune. The latter step required—among other measures—renouncing one's share of communal land, paying reimbursement for a share of the redemption fees and taxes owed on it, and in some cases gaining parental consent. Engaging in *temporary* outmigration, which—because *otkhodniki* (departers) were still members of the commune, to which they paid redemption expenses, and often brought in extra money earned from outside work—could be advantageous rather than burdensome to the commune, was far easier to arrange. Nevertheless, otkhodniki still had to secure formal approval from communal officials in the form of short-term or long-term passports—approval that was commonly given but was not automatic, and to overcome the assumption that they *belonged* in their villages. As one essayist noted in a "memorandum book" published by the Kaluga Province Statistical Committee in 1863, the long-term "desertion" of young male peasants threatened to produce villages filled mainly with "old people, young children, and women," a development that he deemed harmful to agricultural cultivation, manners, and morals.[3]

Still, post-emancipation peasants left home in increasing numbers. Although at first relatively few took the drastic and difficult step of permanently renouncing membership in their communes, an increasing number during the last third of the nineteenth century (and after) moved eastward to take advantage of sparsely settled land; the movement was especially marked after 1889, when a new law enabled peasants to move to Siberia with governmental rather than communal permission and—in a Russian version of homesteading—provided for the allotment of state lands to would-be peasant settlers. (Later, restrictions on migration were loosened further, culminating in a 1906 decree containing this provision: "Every Russian subject has the right freely to choose [his or her] place of residence and occupation.") Although precise statistics are lacking, historian Donald Treadgold estimated that between 1861 and 1900 more than 1.5 million peasants migrated voluntarily to Asiatic Russia—others arrived as exiles and prisoners—the great majority in the 1880s and 1890s, and N. A. Iakimenko suggested that between 1871 and 1916 some 3.7 million peasants moved to Siberia and the far east of Russia, with millions more going to the borderland areas of central Asia, New Russia, the Caucasus, Transcaucasia, and the Southern Urals. Although the population of the Russian Empire as a whole grew at an annual rate of 1.54 percent between 1857 and 1897, Siberia's annual rate of growth was 4.86 percent, while growth rates in the Northern Caucasus and New Russia were 3.25 percent and 2.40 percent, respectively.[4]

Far more peasants engaged in temporary migration, as otkhodniki, while remaining members of their village communes. "Temporary" was a technical concept and could indicate movement that ranged from very short-term to virtually permanent (without officially embracing abandonment of one's communal attachments). Both because emancipation made it easier for peasants to move and because the land allotments it provided them were usually too small to support self-sufficiency—let alone the payment of hefty redemption fees—increasing numbers of peasants sought work away from home. "The land was so parsimoniously apportioned that the enfranchised peasants were utterly unable to provide themselves with the first necessities of life," wrote "Stepniak," the pen name of the revolutionary populist Sergei Kravchinskii, from exile in 1888. "With few exceptions, the bulk of our peasantry are compelled to look to wage labor, mostly agricultural, on their former masters' estates and elsewhere, as an essential, and often the chief, source of their livelihood." As several respondents from Vladimir Province to an ethnographic survey taken in the 1890s noted, peasants supplemented their work on relatively unproductive land with outside employment that ranged from carpentry to factory work, trade, and railroad construction. Although in parts of the province most peasants continued to work the land, the respondent from the Viaznikovskii district noted that there was little agricultural activity in his region and everyone obtained provisions "on the side," importing bread by river from a German colony in Saratov Province; "the main occupation" in the district, he reported "is trade."[5]

Peasants supplemented the income they earned from working their own allotments, and the land of their former owners, in a variety of ways. Tens of thousands of migrant laborers made an annual trek from central Russia and northern Ukraine to the southeastern steppes, where they found employment at giant hiring fairs, contracting to engage in seasonal agricultural labor on large, commercially oriented estates. Others found work nearer to home, in a wide variety of jobs, from river transport to factory labor, while others still flocked to nearby cities, where they sometimes found long-term employment. Such outwork increased markedly in the decades after emancipation: the average number of passports issued annually to peasants increased from 1.2 million in the 1860s to 3.6 million in the 1870s, 4.7 million in the 1880s, and 6.2 million in the 1890s. By the last decade of the nineteenth century, 15 to 20 percent of the adult population of European Russia were receiving passports each year to seek work away from home. Variations were widespread in terms of geography, sex, and length of term. Otkhodnichestvo was especially prevalent in the less fertile central industrial region, where most peasants found it necessary to supplement cultivation of their allotments with outside work; men formed a substantial majority of otkhodniki, outnumbering women by about six to one in the 1890s, despite an increase in the proportion of women migrants (especially to cities) in the late nineteenth century, and the trend was increasingly toward short-term passports of one to three months, although here too geographical variations were evident, with longer-term outwork more common in the less fertile areas of the north and northwest.[6]

Because much of the post-emancipation movement of freedpeople was designed to take advantage of new occupational opportunities, geographic mobility among Black Americans and Russian peasants was closely linked to—and contributed to—occupational mobility. Even under bondage, of course, African Americans and peasants had not constituted an undifferentiated mass: aside from the "default" occupation—field labor—slaves and serfs had served as skilled craft workers, gardeners, drivers and stewards, coachmen, preachers, boat hands, dock workers, factory laborers, and (especially among women and children) house servants. Most serfs had more opportunities to engage in their own economic activities than most slaves, and real—although limited—economic stratification characterized peasant villages; a few serfs became quite wealthy, occasionally even purchasing (in their masters' names) their "own" serfs. In the South, there was considerable occupational differentiation among the small number of free Blacks; this was especially true in cities, but in the countryside as well some African Americans became landowners and even slave owners.[7]

But slavery and serfdom, together with the overwhelmingly agricultural economies of the South and Russia, sharply restricted the occupations available to the vast majority of bondspeople, most of whom lived in the country and cultivated staple crops for those who owned or hired them. Far fewer Southerners than Northerners lived in cities in the antebellum period, but that was especially true of *Black* Southerners. Slaves were increasingly confined to the region's farms and plantations, both because of the insatiable demand for agricultural labor (particularly in the Deep South) and because it was easier to control a dependent population on isolated rural holdings than in towns and cities, where illicit pleasures such as gambling, alcohol, and fraternizing with other slaves—and free Blacks—were more readily accessible. As Frederick Douglass noted, "A city slave is almost a freeman, compared with a slave on the plantation." Slave owners commonly complained that cities offered too many temptations to irresponsible Blacks—as one Georgia slave owner put it, "Savannah is the last place in the world for servants inclined to evil"—and strove successfully to prevent the unchecked growth of a potentially troublesome urban slave population. During the late antebellum years, slaves declined from 18.1 percent to 7.3 percent of the population in the South's eight largest cities, and in 1860 no more than about 5 percent of the enslaved population lived in an "urban" area with at least 2,500 inhabitants. (By contrast, 9.6 percent of all Southerners—including slaves—and more than one-quarter of all Northerners resided in urban areas).[8]

The situation in Russia, where in 1851 the urban population stood at 7.8 percent of all Russians, was similar. Cities were small—in 1856 the average number of residents per city was 8,400, and 64 percent of the urban population lived in towns with fewer than twenty thousand people—and as with slaves in the Southern United States, serfs made up a declining proportion of Russia's urban population in the first half of the nineteenth century. Although small numbers of (usually male) serfs were allowed by their owners to find urban employment as otkhodniki (the Russian equivalent of slaves being allowed to hire themselves out), most serfs who resided in cities were house servants of nobles who had abandoned their isolated estates for the comforts of urban life. In 1838, for example, Tula Province's twelve cities contained 95,039 people (more than half in the provincial capital), of whom 3,667 were domestics and 796 were other serfs; similarly, Riazan Province's twelve cities had a population of 67,374, of whom 5,753 were domestics and 1,346 other serfs. (Cities in both provinces also had small numbers of state peasants.) Except for house servants, urban serfs were something of an anomaly: tying serfs to the land had been central to the establishment of serfdom in the sixteenth and seventeenth centuries, and although nobles gradually gained the right to move their human property at will, serfs clearly "belonged," along with state peasants as well, in the countryside. On the eve of emancipation, only 2.5 percent of the peasant population lived in one of Russia's 669 cities (compared to 14 percent of all non-peasants).[9]

All this changed dramatically with emancipation. In both Russia and the South, the post-emancipation era saw urban growth in societies that continued to be predominantly rural and agricultural, growth that was especially notable among African Americans and peasants. During the last third of the nineteenth century, lured by the promise of both greater safety and greater economic opportunity, increasing numbers of African Americans moved to the South's cities. By the end of the nineteenth century, almost one-third (31.0 percent) of the South's urban population was Black, and African Americans were almost as likely to live in a town or city as were whites: the 1900 census indicated that 18.5 percent of the South's whites were urban, versus 17.1 percent of "Negroes and other" races (almost all of whom were African Americans). In five major Southern cities (Nashville, Atlanta, Richmond, Montgomery, and Raleigh), the Black population surged 308.1 percent between 1860 and 1890—the white population grew by a smaller although still hefty 191.5 percent—and as a percentage of the cities' overall population African Americans increased from 34.3 percent to 42.0 percent.[10] Meanwhile, as Russia's urban population almost doubled between 1867 and 1897 and the number of cities with more than fifty thousand inhabitants increased from eight in 1856 to forty-five in 1897, peasants—pressed by insufficient land allotments and attracted by the lure of new opportunities—took advantage of eased restrictions on movement to settle either permanently or temporarily in nearby cities. The urban growth was most notable in Moscow and St. Petersburg, both of which saw their populations surge to more than a million by the end of the nineteenth century, but peasants also sought work in smaller provincial towns, especially in the less fertile north of the country, including the central industrial region and the northwest. Overall, urbanization was less pronounced among Russian peasants than among southern Blacks, in part because of their attachments (both legal and emotional) to land allotments and village communes, but between 1856 and 1897 the proportion of peasants living in towns increased from 2.5 percent to 6.7 percent. (The proportion of nobles whose primary residence was urban increased from 32.9 percent to 57.6 percent.) Even though the vast majority of peasants remained in the countryside, by 1897 peasants made up more than 40 percent of the urban population.[11]

Although the growing urban presence of Blacks and peasants reflected both the general urbanization of the southern United States and Russia and the specific attraction to freedpeople of cities that had previously been off-limits, there were significant differences in the way the process played out in the two countries. Much of the peasant migration, unlike Black migration, was conditional and (at least in theory) temporary, with urban residents still considering their "home" to be a village, where their families, to whom they typically sent much of the income they earned at work, remained. Indeed, unlike African American migrants, otkhodniki most often came to cities alone—usually married men but with increasing frequency single young women—with far-reaching consequences for family and gender relations (discussed in chapter 6). In 1874, male peasants living in St. Petersburg, for example, outnumbered female by more than two to one even as all other (non-peasant) residents were evenly divided between males and females. Regional variations in urbanization among freedpeople existed in the South, but they were especially pronounced in Russia, where otkhodnichestvo was substantially more common in the less fertile north than in the agricultural south and where Moscow and St. Petersburg, which far exceeded the size of other cities, drew heavily on laborers from nearby villages—not only from Moscow and St. Petersburg Provinces but also from other provinces within striking distance. The relatively poor, densely settled Tver Province, for example, saw massive outmigration, much of it to nearby St. Petersburg: in 1879 the province had 108,877 male and 27,528 female otkhodniki, equivalent to 14.6 percent of the adult male and 3.3 percent of the adult female peasant population; by 1896, these numbers had swelled to 258,221 (30.4 percent) and 82,521 (8.9 percent), respectively.[12]

In most post-emancipation cities in the American South, by contrast, Black women were more numerous than Black men. As under slavery, the demand for agricultural labor in the countryside—especially in the Deep South—together with the plethora of service jobs in cities resulted in an urban Black population that was disproportionately female (although not so disproportionately as the urban peasant population in Russia was male). In Atlanta, for example, the proportion of African American residents who were female fluctuated between 55 and 59 percent between 1870 and 1900. (Whites in Atlanta were evenly divided by sex.) Far more than peasants in Russian cities, where otkhodniki typically arrived alone and maintained strong familial and communal ties with their home villages, African American urban residents usually lived in families, with the significant exception of domestic servants—most often women—who typically lived with their employers.[13]

Urban Blacks engaged in a wide variety of endeavors, some of which were familiar to them as slaves but now provided compensation and others of which were largely or entirely new. The vast majority continued to occupy what historian Howard N. Rabinowitz aptly termed "low-status positions that came to be known as 'negro jobs.' " Although often described as "unskilled," most of these jobs in fact required very specific skills and would not have appeared easy for the uninitiated to perform; they were, however, jobs characterized by heavy physical labor, menial status, and often a lack of security. Such work included day labor on streets, at docks, and in railroad yards; industrial employment (as in Richmond's tobacco factories); and low-level service work in hotels, restaurants, and—especially for women—private homes. A much smaller number of urban Black men—rarely women—secured "skilled" positions as carpenters, masons, cobblers, and other artisan occupations that put them in growing competition with white rivals, as did barbering, long considered work particularly appropriate for African Americans. Such skilled work was especially prevalent among Blacks who had been free before the war, in cities like New Orleans and Mobile.[14]

But new occupational diversity in post-emancipation Southern cities was most evident in the emergence of a class of elite African Americans who engaged in endeavors that for them had been impossible, or severely restricted, under slavery. These included professionals—especially teachers and ministers (discussed in chapter 6)—and businessmen, among whom owners of groceries and barbershops were most numerous. These members of the "rising black middle class" were relatively few in number, and most of the businessmen were far from wealthy. In Atlanta, for example, 4.5 percent of Black men in 1890 had professional or "proprietary" occupations, compared to 26.4 percent of native-born whites, and throughout the last third of the nineteenth century "the typical black businessman either failed or barely made a living." Compared to that of white Southerners, the "middle class" of Blacks appeared insignificant. Compared to what had existed under slavery, however, the rapid emergence of black professionals and property holders seemed nothing short of revolutionary. As James K. Green, a successful self-employed carpenter and contractor in Montgomery, told a Senate investigating committee in 1883, like other freedpeople he had been "entirely ignorant" at the time of emancipation and "knew nothing more than to obey [his] master." But when "the tocsin of freedom sounded . . . we walked out like free men," he continued, "and met the exigencies as they grew up, and shouldered the responsibilities." An index of urban property accumulation can be seen in the rapid growth of home ownership among urban

Blacks, who typically invested much of their wealth in real estate: between 1870 and 1890, the number of Black nonfarm homeowners in the South surged from 4,842 (5.3 percent of Black nonfarm families) to 116,526 (16.0 percent).[15]

Few urban peasants owned their own homes, or even lived in families. Most arrived alone, many as married men who had families in their home villages, others as unmarried young women who sought employment as domestic servants, and still others as unmarried young men who sought to supplement the meager income that their parents (and other family members) earned from agricultural cultivation by working in a wide variety of mostly low-level urban jobs requiring heavy physical labor, though occasionally in more "skilled" work as artisans or petty traders. Prostitution, ranging from casual exchange of favors to full-time sex work, was widespread, especially in the largest cities. Domestic servants typically lived with their employers, while other peasant workers scrounged for affordable housing, but few lived with husbands, wives, or children: in 1897, only 3.7 percent of male workers in Moscow and 5.2 percent of those in St. Petersburg were "heads of households residing with their families."[16]

As part of the broader pattern of post-emancipation peasant otkhodnichestvo, migration to the city represented—as it did for African Americans in the Southern United States—a particular manifestation of the effort to take advantage of expanded opportunities made possible by the end of bondage. To many, the lure of the city—with its economic abundance and sophisticated lifestyle—was new, exciting, and irresistible, as was the hope for quickly accumulated riches. And, in fact, migrants *were* able to send back substantial sums of money to bolster the well-being of their home villagers. Although these migrants remained peasants, with strong ties to their villages, they also gradually embraced many of the trappings of modernity that they came into contact with in urban settings, from belief in economic rationality to consumer culture and manufactured clothing. Long-term peasant residents of cities increasingly merged with the lower stratum of urban dwellers (*meshchane*), and "a unified subculture of unprivileged urbanites and peasants developed in the towns." Meanwhile, others kept their village connections (and families), returned home often, and became conduits for the spread of new ideas and values—including "rationalism, pragmatism, economic calculation, and individualism"—ideas and values that some critics feared would undermine traditional peasant ways.[17]

Despite movement to the cities, most African Americans and peasants continued to live in the countryside during the initial post-emancipation decades, and most continued to work the land. Whose land they would work, however, remained to be determined. In both the South and Russia, freedpeople sought above all to work for themselves, on their own land, with a minimum of outside supervision. In both, they were partially—but only partially—successful in this endeavor. Because of the particular—landed—nature of the Russian emancipation settlement, peasants found it easier than Blacks to support themselves through self-sufficient cultivation: most former serfs received landed allotments, for which they owed hefty fees spelled out in the redemption agreements they worked out with their former owners (discussed in chapter 4), whereas freedom at first left almost all former slaves landless. Over time, however, this distinction became less pronounced. An increasing number of African Americans managed to purchase land, while others were able to rent land under terms that gave them considerable agricultural independence. Meanwhile, as their population grew, freed peasants increasingly found that their land allotments were too small to support their families. In both countries, therefore, freedpeople engaged in independent agricultural production while also working in various dependent capacities for landowners who were usually former slaveholders and serfholders. At the same time, although there were fewer new occupations available in the countryside than in cities, some rural freedpeople found nonagricultural employment in work that in most respects had also existed under bondage—notable exceptions were Black teachers—but that now came with new terms (including monetary compensation).

Only gradually did a significant number of African Americans in the postemancipation South acquire land of their own. The limitations of the Southern Homestead Act (considered in chapter 3) meant that with the partial exception of Florida the main route to landownership for freedpeople was through purchase rather than homesteading, and at first few ex-slaves had the resources to make such purchases. Indeed, although the phenomenon has been little studied and the details are murky, with emancipation many freedpeople suffered the loss of landed allotments that had become widespread during the antebellum period and that slaves had often come to regard as in effect their own (even though legally these allotments belonged to the slave owners). As historian Dylan Penningroth has shown, a significant share of claims for lost property filed by "loyal" Southerners with the Southern Claims Commission were those of ex-slaves, and in some cases those claims resulted in compensation being paid, but because the commission focused on loss of "movable" property rather than land, "ex-slaves did not list land among their possessions" even though they "felt entitled to the land they lived on." Freedom for enslaved African Americans also freed them from "their" land. Such expropriation—and the resulting absence among Black Southerners of the kind of stake in land common among Russian peasants—underlay not only continuing hopes among African Americans for land distribution but also their widespread willingness to migrate in the post-emancipation decades.[18]

As slaves became freedpeople, they harbored two overlapping but distinct understandings of their right to land—neither of which was sustained. The first was general—the widespread "agrarian" notion that land belonged by right to those who worked on it; the second was specific—belief that particular parcels of land belonged by right to those who had received them as allotments under slavery, or who had been given them during the Civil War by the U.S. Army and the Freedmen's Bureau. The failure of Congress to enact land redistribution measures, the failure of the Southern Claims Commission (and other authorities) to recognize as property the landed allotments possessed by many slaves, and the decision of President Johnson to restore the rights and possessions of Rebel landholders meant that most former slaves began their lives as free citizens with—in the words of historian Eric Foner—"nothing but freedom." Although emancipation led to a significant renegotiation of property rights both between freedpeople and planters and among freedpeople themselves, acquisition of land would be almost entirely through purchase.[19]

Almost immediately some freedpeople did begin making such purchases. Land was relatively cheap in the postwar South, and African Americans who had managed to accumulate small amounts of money eagerly used much of it to purchase land of their own. Such purchasers included those who already were in relatively favorable positions, such as light-skinned free Blacks along the Gulf Coast in southern Louisiana and Alabama, and freedpeople who could command good wages because of their particular skills, whether as artisans, barbers, or cooks. Noting the "vast amount of mechanical skill" among Blacks in Alabama—including "Shoemakers, Carpenters, Masons, Blacksmiths, Weavers, Spinners, and Seamstresses, Cooks &c as well as negroes familiar with agricultural pursuits"—a newly arrived Freedmen's Bureau official reported from Montgomery in 1865 that some were "ready to purchase land." Testifying before the Joint Committee on Reconstruction a few months later, Major General Clinton B. Fisk agreed: asked "Are there any negroes who have any means of buying property at present?" he replied that indeed there were "many" in north Alabama. Still, given the impoverished condition of most newly emancipated Blacks, acquisition of land was at first out of reach of all but a tiny fraction of the rural population. Nowhere was this more true than in

Alabama, where in 1870 only about 1.3 percent of Blacks who were engaged in agriculture owned their own farms, but progress in other states was not much faster: in 1870, about 2 percent of Blacks who worked the land were landowners in the Deep South, and about 2.2 percent were in the Upper South.[20]

As personal wealth increased in subsequent decades, however, landownership among African Americans became increasingly widespread, and by the end of the nineteenth century about one-quarter of Black "farmers" owned their own farms (as did more than three-fifths of white "farmers"). The growth of landownership was especially impressive in the Upper South, reaching one-third of the Black farming population by 1890 (and higher still over the subsequent two decades). As Daniel B. Thorp has shown in his study of African Americans in Montgomery County, Virginia, the number of Black landowners there increased more than twentyfold between 1870 and 1890—from eighteen to 374—and "by the end of the nineteenth century, approximately 40 percent of African American families . . . owned at least some land." Even in eight Deep South states, however, almost one-fifth of Black farmers owned land. (See table 5.1.) Most of these farms were very small, and of modest value: in the Lower South in 1870, for example, many of the holdings were valued at no more than $200, and the average Black-owned farm was worth $544. What was especially impressive about the growth of these small-scale Black holdings, however, was that their accumulation continued *after* the overthrow of Reconstruction governments, in an era of increasing anti-Black racism. In short, this landownership was less a product of support from sympathetic whites—although that helped—than of the determination and sacrifices of struggling freedpeople themselves, even under increasingly under adverse conditions.[21]

The problem for Russian peasants was not so much access to land as access to *enough* land, on the right terms. The emancipation provisions provided that

Table 5.1. Black farm owners, 1870 and 1890

	1870	1890
Lower South	10,926 (2%)	73,721 (18%)
Upper South	6,859 (2.2%)	39,859 (33%)

Source: Computed from Loren Schweninger, *Black Property Owners in the South, 1790–1915* (Urbana: University of Illinois Press, 1997), 164, 174.

most former serfs would receive land allotments, the precise nature of which was defined in a complicated two-step process, involving first pomeshchik-imposed statutory charters and then negotiated or pomeshchik-imposed redemption settlements. This process allowed for considerable variation, with landholdings in some cases imposed from above through different guidelines for different geographic zones and in others resulting from decisions by pomeshchiki and peasants themselves, as they sought to make sense of the arcane regulations and achieve the most advantageous possible terms. As was evident in chapters 3 and 4, many of the struggles unleashed by emancipation revolved around the charters and land redemption, and indicated the centrality of land to the evolution of social relations under the new order.

Russian serfs, like American slaves, had widely subscribed to the notion that the land belonged by right to those who cultivated it, and, as they faced a new era of "freedom," the freedpeople in Russia also held two complementary versions of this notion. One of these suggested that the peasants deserved to own—and would soon receive—*all* (or almost all) the noble land, and the other focused more specifically on their right to the land that they had been allotted for self-support under serfdom. As in the United States, however, neither of these understandings received confirmation. Despite continuing peasant expectations, until the Bolshevik Revolution of 1917 there was never a serious possibility of a massive land redistribution that would confiscate noble estates and divide them among the laboring population. Nor was there any consideration among the architects of emancipation of the more limited idea that the former serfs had a legal right to the allotments they had long considered theirs. A central component of the emancipation settlement was the decision to *sell* some approximation of these allotments to the peasants. Requiring freedpeople to pay for land they already held made sense to government planners and the pomeshchiki they represented, but to peasants it seemed like a monumental injustice—indeed, a massive theft that threatened to make freedom a total sham.

What the peasants actually received in this process of forced purchase has elicited disagreement among historians. Most—especially Soviet but also Western scholars—have seen a rapacious emancipation settlement that left the peasants daunting prospects when it came to making ends meet under conditions of supposed freedom. As N. M. Druzhinin put it, "There can be no doubt that the procedure of introducing the statutory charters deprived the peasants of the Russian provinces of a huge expanse of land and did not enable them to conduct self-sufficient agricultural labor and pay the established dues to the state and pomeshchiki." P. I. Lyashchenko put it more bluntly, in declaring that "the landowners with great success expropriated a substantial part of the peasant lands, . . . eventually retaining a form of semifeudal economic dependency through the peasants' 'obligatory' services, labor dues, and so forth." More recently, however, some historians have questioned the severity of the emancipation settlement and argued that former serfs fared reasonably well in the last third of the nineteenth century. Foremost among these historians has been Steven L. Hoch, who concluded that "the land legislation of 1861 was tilted more favorably toward the serfs than has been appreciated."[22]

There are at least three distinct components to this debate. The first, whether the emancipated peasants were actually as badly off as is commonly assumed, is addressed in chapter 7. The second, whether the peasants paid "too much" for their allotments, reflects, as I suggested in chapter 1, a peculiarly one-sided set of assumptions about what would have been a "fair" price to make peasants pay for land that they already considered their own. When peasants objected to a statutory charter on the grounds that "the Tsar promised us *volia*, but now they make us pay or work for land, and there is no *volia* without land," they expressed a widely shared belief that requiring them to pay *any* price for their land—and thus in effect for their freedom—was illegitimate. Whether peasants paid "too much" for their land is not a fruitful subject for historical investigation, because the answer depends less on historical evidence than on one's understanding of what "should have" happened or what was "fair."[23] By contrast, the third component, how much land the peasants received and to what extent it allowed them to support themselves without engaging in outside work, deserves attention here.

This third issue is more complicated than it first appears, not only because of sometimes conflicting evidence, but also because of significant variations in terms of how much land peasants actually received and how much land was needed for self-sufficiency. As we have seen, the statutory charter guidelines for the size of peasant allotments varied significantly according to type and quality of soil—in Great Russia, Belorussia, and New Russia there were three geographic zones (non-black-earth, black-earth, and steppe), each subdivided into numerous "localities"—but they also differed in much of Ukraine, where peasant land was less often held communally, and in western provinces, where larger allotments were designed to undercut potential peasant support for Polish revolutionaries. The size of allotments also varied depending upon the extent to which pomeshchiki were able to impose "cutoffs" (or less often, when required by the guideline's minimum requirements, to provide "add-ons"). Some peasants, expecting a general redistribution of land, chose to accept the tiny "beggars' allotments" that enabled them to avoid redemption payments. And although most peasant allotment land was held communally and measured in number of desiatiny per (male) soul, some families received more land than others—based at least in part on number of workers—and their holdings could be increased or decreased in the occasional redistributions carried out by most communes. Because the charter guidelines established maximum and minimum sizes for allotments, at least in some provinces there occurred what Hoch termed a "massive levelling" of peasant holdings, with fewer very small and very large allotments.[24]

Overall, however, there is little doubt that most peasants received allotments that were rarely bigger and usually smaller than those they had held as serfs. Historian Carol Leonard's conclusion that "former serfs generally acquired less land than they had held before emancipation" is in line with the judgment of almost all other historians; even Hoch agreed that "the vast majority of serfs ... either kept their existing allotment or had their allotment reduced to the pre-reform modal (most common) size." David Moon's suggestion of an average 20 percent reduction in overall allotment size is consistent with the conclusion of many more local studies, although regional variations render such broad generalization in need of qualification, and other estimates yield a smaller average contraction, of about 4 percent. In the fertile black-earth region, where pomeshchiki sought to keep as much land as possible in their own hands, allotments tended to be less generous than in the non-black-earth region or the central industrial region and the northwest, where pomeshchiki were more willing to part with unproductive land that—even when allotments were substantial—was unlikely to support peasants in self-sufficient agriculture. According to B. G. Litvak's detailed study of six black-earth provinces, the charters deprived ex-serfs of 16.2 percent of their pre-emancipation allotment land, but this contraction varied from an average of 12.6 percent in Tula Province to 26.7 percent in Voronezh Province. (Variations within each province were even greater.) In Novgorod Province, although peasants who had previously held very small allotments usually received larger holdings, far more peasants suffered cutoffs, yielding some "leveling" together with an average reduction of 28.5 percent of peasant-held land. The situation was similar in St. Petersburg Province, where far more peasants endured cutoffs than received add-ons and the average reduction was 34.1 percent; additional leveling occurred *within* the province, with reductions smallest near St. Petersburg city, where dense settlement had limited the size of pre-emancipation peasant holdings, and largest in the peripheral districts.[25]

As the peasant population grew during the half century after emancipation, the size of allotments—measured in desiatiny per soul—decreased substantially, and peasants found it ever more difficult to support themselves without outside work. Although methodological differences have produced varying figures—some focused on former serfs, whereas others also included former state peasants (whose allotments were somewhat larger), some covered all of the Russian empire, while others focused on Russia proper or specific regions, some counted only allotment land, whereas others included additional land purchased by peasants—all historians have agreed on the decreasing per capita size of peasant holdings. According to Leonard, the average size of all peasant allotments decreased from 4.8 desiatiny per soul in 1860 to 2.6 by 1900, "far less than their guaranteed subsistence allotment of six desiatiny," while A. M. Anfimov and P. N. Zyrianov, looking at former serfs in the fifty provinces of European Russia, pointed to a decrease from 3.5 to 2.6 desiatiny per soul during those years. Between 1858 and 1878, the average size of allotments in thirty Russian provinces decreased from 3.38 to 2.91 per soul. Allotments were largest where land was least valuable and smallest in the fertile Central Agricultural Region; in Tambov Province, which remained overwhelmingly agricultural, with peasants making up 94 percent of the population in 1897, allotment land per capita (both sexes) decreased from 1.74 to 1.19 desiatiny between 1858 and 1897. According to historian Boris Mironov, "Between the 1860s and 1890s . . . per capita land allotment holdings (for males) declined virtually everywhere in European Russia, from 5.3 to 2.8 hectares, at the same time as the local rural population . . . increased from 53.8 to 83.4 million." Mironov noted that "various estimates put the proportion of surplus hands at 22, 27 to 35, or even 52 percent of the able-bodied male population." In short, peasant allotments that at the time of emancipation were already smaller than those held under serfdom shrank steadily over the following decades, even as the peasants were burdened with redemption payments that would continue throughout their lives and in most cases the lives of their children. In order to survive, as the drafters of the emancipation legislation had intended, most former serfs would have to supplement work on their own land with outside work, often for their previous owners or nearby pomeshchiki.[26]

Over the decades following emancipation, peasants sought to supplement the allotments they had redeemed. As I discuss below, they rented additional land from nobles on a variety of terms that in some ways resembled the range of sharecropping to cash rental seen in the Southern United States. They also purchased additional land from nobles reluctant to supervise the labor of free peasants and eager to take advantage of rising land prices. From 1863 to 1882, peasants in twenty-eight provinces of European Russia made 110,197 purchases of land, totaling 4,844,236 desiatiny, at an average price of 18.8 rubles per desiatina. Such purchases were more common in the non-black-earth than in the black-earth provinces, where land was most expensive and nobles continued to show interest in engaging in their own agricultural production. Peasants bought additional land both communally and in private transactions by individuals or groups of individuals acting on their own, usually in small lots of under ten desiatiny each. Peasant access to additional land (both through purchase and rental) accelerated in the late nineteenth century: from 1877 to 1905, the amount of land under direct peasant and Cossack cultivation increased from 123.3 million to 163.4 million desiatiny, with almost half the increase the result of private transactions.[27]

The increase was significant but ultimately insufficient. Because of the surging population (most of whom were peasants), the amount of peasant-owned land per capita or per soul continued to decline, even counting the new communal and individual purchases. Most peasants simply could not afford to buy additional land—whether individually or communally. Indeed, they often could not—some have suggested *would* not—afford the payments on their existing allotments that they were obligated to make for forty-nine years, and they fell into rapidly increasing arrears on these payments.[28]

In short, both in the Southern United States and in Russia the freedpeople strove but failed to achieve agricultural self-sufficiency. In the South, despite land purchases by a growing minority of African Americans (especially in the Upper South), the great majority had to work for others, often on land owned by nearby planters. In Russia, the land allotments that most ex-serfs were forced to buy were too small to provide self-support and income for redemption payments, and peasants also found it necessary to seek outside work or to cultivate land owned by pomeshchiki. In both countries, freedom had multiple meanings and gradations, and to most freedpeople it offered major contrasts to the bondage from which they had emerged. For most Black Americans and Russian peasants, however, "free labor" meant dependent labor, even if the form of dependence was far removed from the abject servility of slavery and serfdom.

Because both the South and Russia remained overwhelmingly rural societies during the post-emancipation decades, dependent labor for most freedpeople was dependent *agricultural* labor. The nature and degree of this dependence, and the terms under which freed African Americans and peasants toiled, were hardly constant: labor arrangements differed both within and between the two societies, and continued to evolve over time as well. During the first generation of freedom, the majority of Blacks—in the Deep South the vast majority—continued to work on farms and plantations owned by white landowners, almost all of whom had been former slave owners. Although they possessed landed allotments of their own, many Russian peasants—in some areas the great majority—found it necessary to supplement work on these allotments with outside work for noble landowners, almost all of whom had been serfholders. In both the South and Russia, free-labor relations took a bewildering variety of forms that defied easy categorization, both because of their diversity and because of their evolution, as freedpeople and their former owners struggled to define the shape and meaning of free labor.

Although most post-emancipation African Americans performed the same kind of agricultural operations they had as slaves, they did so under radically changed conditions, as free men and women. Some contracted annually, whereas others worked under short-term agreements or without contracts altogether. Some received food and lodging as part of their compensation, whereas others secured their own (especially food). Some received wages; some rented land; some worked under a confusing variety of sharecropping arrangements that at opposite extremes have been termed "share wages" (because they received a share of the crop as compensation for their labors) and "share renting" (because they *paid* a share of the crop in exchange for the land they worked). Contracts could be collective, with a farm or plantation's entire labor force signing—or more often affirming with their "mark"—or individual, with a single freedperson or a single family. Arrangements varied over space and by crop but could also be diverse within any given locality and for cultivators of a specific crop. Arrangements also reflected the proclivities of individual landowners. There had been a great deal of variety—diverse "slaveries"—before emancipation, but free labor brought with it a significant expansion of this variety as former slave owners and former slaves struggled to defend their often-conflicting interests in an environment with ground rules that seemed poorly defined.

Despite this multiplicity of relationships that seemed to suggest "free labor" could take an almost infinite variety of forms, certain patterns emerged that permit broad generalizations. In most of the South—in areas where cotton and tobacco cultivation prevailed—sharecropping quickly came to prevail over wage labor, and the most prevalent form of cropping evolved from a variant of collective share *wages* to share *renting* on an individual or family basis. The beginnings of this transformation were already evident in the late 1860s (see chapter 3), as freedpeople struggling to achieve as much autonomy as possible and landowners who were strapped for cash and often recoiled at the idea of micromanaging free workers reached uneasy compromises that offered advantages to both sides but fully satisfied neither. As early as 1867 Freedmen's Bureau agents began noticing the inclination of landowners to "divide their plantations into small farms" that they would then "rent, or lease to industrious freedmen." "Negroes are engaged upon almost every conceivable plan, and everything appears experimental," a correspondent of the Mobile *Daily Register* reported two years later from Hale County, Alabama. "Many planters have turned their stock, teams, and every facility for farming, over to the negroes, and only require an amount of toll for the use of their land, refusing to superintend, direct, or even, in some cases, to suggest as to their management." Whereas in 1865 most Blacks in Montgomery County, Virginia, had "continued to work for the men and women who had held them as slaves," receiving no wages except for "board & clothes," by 1867 "most of the freedmen in the county had left their former owners' employ," they received compensation, and "nearly a third were sharecroppers or farming independently on leased land." A planter in Florida noted the "tendency on the part of hands . . . to break up in very small squads, as for instance a man with his wife and children," and in the interior of Georgia, Freedmen's Bureau Superintendent of Education John W. Alvord reported succinctly, "Freedmen are buying or renting, and raising their own crops." The transformation accelerated in the 1870s, and as economic historians Roger L. Ransom and Richard Sutch have demonstrated, although plantations endured as units of ownership, by 1880 plantation agriculture—in terms of "tenure arrangements, size, and form of labor organization"—had largely disappeared in much of the cotton South. Tenant farmers who either rented for cash or more often engaged in a variety of sharecropping coexisted with small farm owners (most of whom were white), and "almost 80 percent of the farms reported 50 acres or less in crops."[29]

What was perhaps most striking was the diversity and "experimental" nature of work arrangements. Consider developments on the Davis Bend of the Mississippi River, not far from Vicksburg. At Palmyra, which Northern-born Joseph Lovell inherited from his "fire-eater" father-in-law John A. Quitman in 1858, a bewildering mixture of labor arrangements was in evidence. Although the plantation was temporarily confiscated by federal forces and turned into part of a model "home colony" during the war, in 1866 Lovell—like many other former

Confederate planters—was the beneficiary of President Johnson's lenient amnesty program and regained control of his property, which he proceeded to turn into a lucrative cotton-producing enterprise. Employing large "squads" of Black laborers, each of which was headed by a "leader" and subdivided into "teams," Lovell relied heavily on employees whom he secured on trips to New Orleans and Selma, but other workers—including migrants from the Upper South—arrived at Palmyra on their own, and still others were recruited by agents who served as "head hunters." Sometimes, too, he contracted separately with individuals. Often he engaged workers on a temporary—seasonal—basis, "pay[ing] them in either wage or crop shares at the season's end"; some of the workers came with families, but many were single men. Throughout the postwar years Lovell seems to have shown considerable flexibility in labor relations, engaging in continued "adjustments and calibrations."[30]

Things proceeded differently on two neighboring Davis Bend plantations, Hurricane and Brierfield, originally owned by Joseph E. Davis, the Confederate president's older brother. Unlike Lovell, who worked hard at making postemancipation Palmyra a profitable enterprise, Davis showed little entrepreneurial spirit. Indeed, after regaining legal control of his plantations in late 1866, he sold them to Benjamin T. Montgomery, who while still a slave had managed the holdings for Davis, not only supervising the enslaved laborers but also overseeing the unusual, paternalistic system that Davis had encouraged. (This system included a degree of self-government in some ways reminiscent of a Russian peasant commune, including—among other features—slave courts.) The sale price—$300,000 to be paid at the end of ten years, preceded by annual interest payments of $18,000—indicated the extraordinary value of the two plantations and the extraordinary ambition of Montgomery, who, although already the wealthiest freedman in Mississippi, could not come close to paying the annual interest installments, let alone the eventual principal.

For a while, Montgomery and his sons ran a flourishing Black colony, leasing much of the land to sharecroppers in units of ten to thirty acres while also employing wage laborers on the "home" plantation of Brierfield, where Jefferson Davis had once lived. In 1871, Montgomery, who had already branched out into diverse commercial ventures in addition to running a plantation store, expanded his operation by purchasing the neighboring Ursino plantation for an additional $100,000. He was never able to make his annual interest payments, however, and beginning in 1874, with the twin blows of political redemption and economic depression, Montgomery's fortune (and that of his tenants) took a turn for the worse. Low cotton prices exacerbated his "condescending paternalistic attitude toward the freedmen at Davis Bend"—he repeatedly complained about their "slothfulness" and "lack of industry and frugality"—and in 1874 Jefferson Davis brought suit, claiming that Brierfield was legally his, a suit that was at first dismissed but in 1878, under a more conservative court, proved successful.

Montgomery did not live to see this loss—he died in 1876—but his sons Thornton and Isaiah strove to maintain the family business, diversifying from what now seemed an overreliance on cotton and reducing the number of sharecroppers in favor of wage laborers, who were presumably easier to manage. In 1879, hundreds of disaffected tenants from Davis Bend joined the trek to Kansas—seventy left in March alone—and two years later, unable to pay the remaining debt for the purchase of Brierfield and Hurricane, a debt that had ballooned to $392,000, the Montgomerys lost the plantations, which when auctioned off brought the Davis family only $75,288. By then, almost all the original sharecroppers and hired hands had abandoned the once-promising colony; "no more than 10 percent of the families resident on the Montgomery plantations in 1870 were still there in 1880." Refusing to concede defeat, however, Montgomery's son Isaiah initiated a sequel to the Davis Bend "dream" in 1887, establishing a new, self-governing colony—this time composed of Black landowners—at Mound Bayou, Mississippi. The village flourished for a while, especially in the early twentieth century; by 1907, it "had become the center of a thriving agricultural colony of some 800 families." By the time its founder died in 1924, however, it had gone into a steep decline and by 1940 appeared "as a dilapidated, depopulated town with little to excite race pride."[31]

Neither developments at Palmyra nor those at Brierfield and Hurricane were entirely typical of those in the post-emancipation South, or even in post-emancipation Mississippi. Indeed, because of the diversity and continued evolution of labor arrangements, which varied not only among the South's regions but also within them, it is impossible to pinpoint *one* typical labor system. As historian Laura F. Edwards aptly noted in describing conditions among freedpeople in Granville County, North Carolina, at the southern edge of the tobacco belt that included much of Virginia as well, "an uneven patchwork of tenancy, waged labor, and small-scale landownership emerged" by the 1870s, but the differences among these system of labor organization were sometimes less pronounced in practice than in theory, "since waged labor and rental agreements could be more alike than they were different." Blacks who engaged in various forms of sharecropping and renting "spanned the range from abject poverty to opulent prosperity," and although they "tended a specific piece of land," poor croppers "were otherwise indistinguishable from wage laborers." Sometimes, Blacks who were able to acquire land of their own sublet some of this land to other African Americans or hired Black farmhands.[32]

Consider the Mississippi River Delta, the subject of a fine study by historian John C. Willis. Stretching from the Tennessee border in the north to the Louisiana border in the south, the Delta region at the time of emancipation was characterized by an intense shortage of labor and "heavily capitalized plantations" along the banks of the Mississippi and Yazoo Rivers, but it was still largely "an untamed wilderness in the backcountry." On the riverfront, post-emancipation labor quickly evolved from gangs of freedpeople to small squads "comprised of three to a dozen ex-slaves" and then, by the 1870s, to individual family farmers who rented small plots of land, usually for a share of the crop. Meanwhile, away from the river, the late 1860s to the 1880s constituted a kind of golden age when "a generation of ex-slaves found and grasped prosperity in the Delta's interior." Many African Americans—including the Mound Bayou colonists led by Isaiah Montgomery—were able to purchase largely unsettled land at bargain prices, and by the turn of the twentieth century "two-thirds of the region's farm owners were black, not white." More Blacks still *rented* land, paying for its use in a staggering variety of ways, including "crops, cash, fencing, industrial labor, and by clearing wilderness areas." Beginning in the 1890s and accelerating in the early twentieth century, however, the filling up of the "wilderness," economic depression, and ever-increasing political suppression brought this golden age to an end, and thereafter "few black farmers . . . held realistic expectations of buying good Delta land. Instead, they struggled to escape peonage." Even as in much of the South the rate of Black landholding continued to increase, the once-welcoming Delta had become "more a place to be escaped than a promised land of agrarian opportunity."[33]

Although in most of the cotton and tobacco-producing regions of the South the trend was toward one of several variants of sharecropping, elsewhere wage-labor proved more in evidence. Nowhere was this more the case than on the large sugar estates of southern Louisiana, which after emancipation never fully regained their prewar position of aristocratic preeminence. The "patchwork of waged and semi-waged relations" that emerged after emancipation was in some respects a continuation of the system that had prevailed under slavery, when many planters had hired extra hands—especially during the cane-cutting season—a system that Generals Benjamin Butler and Nathaniel Banks built upon when they formally established free labor on the sugar plantations during wartime occupation by federal forces. After emancipation, however, the persistence of gang labor in a time of pervasive labor shortage enabled sugar workers to negotiate improved terms, both with respect to monetary compensation and conditions of life, even as planters successfully resisted their efforts to acquire land, either as owners or as sharecroppers. Far more than sharecroppers in the cotton and tobacco South, sugar hands represented a "proletarianized labor force" with a collective, working-class consciousness, and labor relations took on a semi-industrial character. Only at the turn of the twentieth century did "cash strapped landlords" concede defeat and embrace the replacement of gang labor by the kind of tenant-operated farming that prevailed in most of the South. By that time, even as foreign competition had decimated Louisiana's once-flourishing sugar industry, the increasingly oppressive political climate guaranteed that "the fall of the plantation order" was accompanied by something sugar growers had long sought: a cheap and subservient labor force.[34]

In the Lowcountry of South Carolina and Georgia, free labor also emerged in the midst of, and exacerbated, a long-term decline of once-flourishing plantations—this time rice—that struggled in the face of foreign (and to a lesser extent domestic) competition, a decline that by the end of the nineteenth century rendered "a region that was once so rich ... the poorest part of the poorest census region in the United States." South Carolina's share of American rice production declined from 75 percent in 1839 to 23.6 percent in 1889, before collapsing to 2.5 percent in 1909. After emancipation, rice-country laborers, many of whom had enjoyed an unusual degree of autonomy (although not material well-being) as slaves working under the "task" system for often-absentee owners, struggled to build on that autonomy, with mixed results, under rapidly evolving conditions. Early prospects of widespread landownership were dashed following President Johnson's reversal of General William T. Sherman's Field Order Number 15 in September 1865 (see chapter 3), but during the Reconstruction years freedpeople took advantage of the shortage of labor and their huge numerical majority to win significant concessions from pardoned Confederate planters. Although some of these planters tried to introduce wage labor, African Americans used to the relative independence they had enjoyed under the task system typically rejected (often but not always successfully) the direct supervision that waged labor implied—"We want to work just as we have always worked," one explained—in favor of arrangements that would allow them to engage in their own cultivation. Such arrangements included purchase of land; various forms of sharecropping that ranged from share renting to the "two-day" system, a partial replication of tasking under which workers spent two days per week working for planters in exchange for being free to work the rest of the time on their "own" allotments; and in some cases squatting on planter-owned land that they had previously been allotted. Ultimately, after years of uncertainty, turmoil, strikes, and increasing political repression, a massive shift from plantation-based production to small-scale, subsistence agriculture came to characterize Lowcountry rice cultivation. As Eric Foner noted, by 1890 between 71 and 81 percent of the farms in three Lowcountry South Carolina counties "were cultivated by their owners, the vast majority of them blacks."[35]

As they began their lives as free people, former slaves faced major obstacles even as they enjoyed unusual and unexpected opportunities. The obstacles, which were entirely predictable (although not always predicted), seemed overwhelming: poverty, illiteracy, racism, and the resentment of former slave owners bitter at the loss both of their war and of their slaves. The opportunities stemmed from emancipation itself, and from the unusual way Southern slavery died—through civil war—which produced an unusually radical Reconstruction policy. As African Americans pursued these opportunities, the possibilities seemed almost limitless—various forms of compensated labor, property accumulation, new occupations, not to mention more intangible but equally important features such as citizenship and equal rights—even as there was considerable evidence of their contingency. If emancipation itself was irreversible, the radical Reconstruction program was not, and there were numerous early signs of trouble in the rampant terrorist violence directed at Blacks and their allies. Over time, the anti-Reconstruction backlash would prove unexpectedly virulent and usher in an era of reaction that reversed many of the most visible earmarks of the new order, especially in the political sphere. Despite the ensuing terror and disappointment, however, the backlash could not undo the changes that had resulted from emancipation itself or stop the continuing evolution and growing complexity of social relations under free labor.

Like African Americans in the post-emancipation South, most peasants in post-emancipation Russia performed the same kind of rural labor they had in bondage, under changed conditions. Arguably, the basic framework was less radically changed than in the South, since free peasants continued to cultivate both their own allotments and in many cases the estates of noble landowners, as they had when serfs. Still, free labor in Russia, like that in the Southern United States, assumed a multiplicity of forms. Peasants worked their own allotments, purchased additional land, and rented more land still. They paid nobles for rented land in cash, but they also engaged in a variety of sharecropping arrangements that included paying half the crop as well as a system known as *otrabotka* (working off) whereby they paid for debts incurred, whether from buying or renting land to falling into arrears on previous obligations, by working on noble land. Peasants also sometimes worked for wages, both for nearby pomeshchiki and as seasonal migrant laborers in the steppes of the southeast, and they engaged in industrial work, not only in urban areas, but also in rural factories attached to noble estates. Others received short-term passports to perform a wide variety of services, from barge hauling to construction. Peasants who had opted for the tiny "beggars' allotments" were especially likely to work most of the time in dependent relationships, since they could not come close to supporting themselves on their minuscule holdings. Meanwhile, those who were still "temporarily obligated" continued to negotiate over—and sometimes resist coming to—redemption agreements to purchase land allotments from their former owners, until the imperial decree of 1881 making redemption mandatory and transferring all remaining temporarily obligated peasants to peasant proprietor status as of 1883. As in the American South, these diverse arrangements reflected both regional variations and particular preferences, and evolved over the post-emancipation decades.[36]

As in the post-emancipation South, so too in Russia a pervasive decline in planter or pomeshchik-directed agriculture accompanied—and helped define—the emergence of free labor among the former bondspeople. Former serf owners were no more comfortable supervising the labor of freedpeople than were former slave owners—as one official reported succinctly from Pskov Province, "In the opinion of the pomeshchiki, in general work is going much worse than before"—and many pomeshchiki wasted little time distancing themselves from the day-to-day annoyances of directing the labor of freed peasants, in the process providing peasants with new opportunities for self-directed production despite their continued dependence on and subservience to former masters and other outsiders. As peasants sought to supplement income from their inadequate allotments, they acquired new obligations. Peasants who purchased more land incurred new debt on top of the redemption payments they already owed. Those who rented additional land also had to pay for it, which they did in a variety of ways. The variety is indicated in the diverse answers of nine respondents from Vladimir Province to a question focusing on peasant occupations in the ethnographic survey headed by Prince V. N. Tenishev in the 1890s. Although some of the respondents stressed the prevalence of agricultural work, most indicated that because the soil was unproductive many peasants had to scrape by in other ways, from breeding cattle to engaging in small-scale trade, working as carpenters in Moscow, boatmen on the Oka River, and factory hands in a nearby city or at a local brickworks; whole families—"but most of all widows with children"—resorted to nearby factory work. Other peasants still found their way to temporary work in more distant cities—Odessa, Baku, and Sevastopol—and "many of the peasants took part in construction of the railroad in Siberia."[37]

Working for pomeshchiki, however—in many cases their former owners—remained the most common way peasants paid for land, paid off debts, and supplemented the meager earnings their allotments provided. Although some peasants received wages for such work—especially if they ventured far from home, as migrant laborers—in the early post-emancipation years most peasants, like African Americans in the American South, traded work for access to land through sharecropping, the most common version of which was *otrabotka*. Reviled by Soviet scholars (including, most notably, Vladimir Lenin) as a remnant of a backward social order and an impediment to the development of more progressive, capitalist, agriculture, *otrabotka* allowed peasants in need of land—or sometimes other items, including money—to receive it from pomeshchiki and pay off what amounted to their loan by cultivating the land of those pomeshchiki. Typically, peasants working under *otrabotka*, unlike wage workers, provided their own agricultural implements, which they also used to cultivate their allotments, but agricultural relations covered a span of arrangements that belied the supposedly neat distinction between wages and "working out." Peasants who cultivated the land of noble pomeshchiki could engage in such labor full-time or part-time, and they could be paid with money, produce (as in half the crop), land, or some combination of these. According to nobleman Aleksandr Nikolaevich Engelgardt, who took up residence on his family estate in Smolensk Province in 1872, peasants would sometimes work for nobles "out of respect," "just in case," without any compensation except for "refreshments, and vodka above all else, of course." In some ways, as critics charged, *otrabotka* resembled a continuation of "the old barshchina system" under which many serfs had labored, but (as with sharecropping in the Southern United States) the peasants were less directly under the control of their employers than they had been of their owners. Unlike serfs, peasants who worked the post-emancipation land of pomeshchiki did so by choice—or at least under economic rather than legal compulsion. They also had other options.[38]

Increasing numbers of peasants—mostly men—engaged in otkhod to work not in cities but in the countryside. Hundreds of thousands of migrant laborers, most but not all from the central black-earth provinces and northern Ukraine, undertook seasonal work as wage laborers on large, commercially oriented noble estates in the newly settled steppes of the southeast. Responding to a strong demand for labor, these hired hands (*batraki*) contracted to work for periods of one to six months at hiring fairs or markets that could attract thousands of job seekers: during the 1870s, the largest such fair, held in May at Kakhova, in Tauride Province, drew some fifty thousand workers, who saw their very negotiations with potential employers—sometimes conducted in part by elected "artel" (or union) leaders—as festive occasions that reflected their newly acquired status as free men. Contracts were "often consummated by the employer standing the workers to a ruble advance and a drink at the local tavern," after which the "newly hired harvesters handed over their passports, sickle, or an article of clothing as a visible pledge of good faith." Workers took advantage of the shortage of labor to press for very short-term contracts—sometimes as short as one week—that maximized their bargaining power and allowed them to renegotiate provisions that proved troublesome. As in much of the American Deep South, the intense demand for labor in the newly settled steppes of "New Russia" put workers in a relatively good bargaining position, especially when their willingness to contract was in doubt. As historian Timothy Mixter suggested, to "migrant workers[, who] knew that they had some power inside the hiring market and little outside of it," the threat of refusing to conclude a contract proved a powerful weapon.[39]

Throughout Russia, increasing numbers of peasants sought and received passports to engage in work away from their villages. Sometimes, this work was agricultural: in Smolensk Province, for example, Engelgardt noted the existence of peasants known as "diggers" who "joined together in small artels of five to ten men" and "look[ed] for work nearby on the estates of neighboring landowners." Led by a foreman who contracted with a pomeshchik for spring and summer work, members of each artel pooled their income (typically thirty-five rubles each for the season) and expenses (principally food) and were considered industrious workers, Engelgardt wrote, "among the prosperous peasants in our region." But often, especially in less fertile areas where the demand for agricultural labor was limited, peasants supplemented their income with various nonagricultural pursuits that ranged from artisanal work to employment in local factories. One of the Vladimir Province respondents to the Tenishev ethnographic survey stated that although agriculture was still the main peasant occupation, "in some places it [was] beginning to lose its exclusive significance," while from a different district another respondent reported that the inhabitants no longer cultivated the land, securing grain by river "from colonies of Germans in Saratov Province." Elsewhere in the province, because the land was not fertile, many young men sought employment as factory hands in a nearby city, and others, traveling farther afield, worked as miners in the Urals. And "[a] surprisingly large segment of [Russia's] industrial labor force" consisted of children, especially (but by no means exclusively) in the cotton textile mills of Moscow Province and St. Petersburg Province.[40]

Not all peasants who worked in factories were otkhodniki. Under serfdom, some nobles had owned factories attached to their rural estates, and this practice continued—albeit with significant changes—after emancipation. A good example is provided by Vasilii Yazykov's woolen factory that was part of his Yazykovo Selo holding in Simbirsk Province. Established in 1853 as one of several factories in the province that manufactured (and sold to the government) military uniforms for soldiers in the Crimean War, Yazykov's factory soon employed some three hundred peasant laborers, although the end of the war and emancipation reduced this number to 160 in 1862 (as indicated in the estate's statutory charter) and 144 (seventy men, four women, and seventy children) in 1870. Before emancipation, all of these workers were unpaid serfs owned by Yazykov, but emancipation brought significant new developments. Yazykov withdrew from direct supervision of the factory, renting it to a series of merchants who paid the workers wages that in 1870 amounted to six hundred rubles (or, on average, almost four rubles each) per month. Equally notable, the factory evidently began employing new peasants, who had not formerly been owned by Yazykov: in 1876, the factory's merchant-manager "placed an ad in a local newspaper for 'teenage children' to come to work at the factory [at Yazykovo Selo] 'for wages.' "[41]

As Russia's regional division became increasingly pronounced during the post-emancipation decades, more and more peasants who lived in the less fertile areas of the central industrial heartland, the northwest, and the far north abandoned the quintessential peasant occupation—cultivation of the land—in favor of outside employment. According to historian Carol S. Leonard's recent estimate, by 1913 only 14 percent of the arable land in the "consumer" north was under cultivation, compared to 60–73 percent in the "producer" south. Otkhodnichestvo increased markedly throughout Russia—the average number of passports issued to peasants surged from 1.2 million in the 1860s to 3.6 million in the 1870s, 4.7 million in the 1880s, and 6.2 million in the 1890s—but the increase was most notable where the land was least productive (and near the major cities of Moscow and St. Petersburg). As early as the 1870s, well over 10 percent of adult peasants (of both sexes) in most of the central industrial provinces as well as those of the far north and northwest were receiving passports to engage in outwork, and by the 1890s the proportion had increased to 15–20 percent; by the latter date, 29.9 percent of the adult peasants in Moscow Province and 28.9 percent of those in St. Petersburg Province were receiving passports. By contrast, otkhodnichestvo increased at a much slower pace in the agricultural provinces of the central black-earth region and Ukraine: from the 1870s to the 1890s the proportion of peasants receiving passports increased from 4.2 percent to 5.9 percent in Tambov Province, 1.6 percent to 1.9 percent in Samara Province, and 2.5 percent to 8.5 percent in Kiev Province.[42]

The massive increase in what was theoretically temporary peasant out-migration, and the proliferating occupational diversity that accompanied it, had major repercussions for peasant life, economy, and culture, some of which are treated more fully in chapter 6, but it is worth noting here one of the most striking consequences: the growing sexual disparity in many villages. Women did engage in outwork, both in cities and "in textile mills in or near peasant villages," and they also increasingly engaged in small-scale handicraft production; near Moscow, many knit woolen gloves and stockings for the urban market, while in the northwest some sold "agricultural and dairy products" to feed residents of St. Petersburg. But overall, outwork was dominated by men: in Tver Province, for example, 14.6 percent of adult male peasants and 3.3 percent of adult females were otkhodniki in 1879, numbers that surged to 30.4 percent and 8.9 percent, respectively, by 1896.[43] As a result, especially in the less fertile areas, the number of female village residents often substantially exceeded that of male. The disparity was especially great among the young, since male otkhodniki often returned to live in their home villages at middle age: in the villages of rural Iaroslavl Province in 1890, for example, there were 1,760 women aged twenty to twenty-nine for every thousand men. Even as "uniform and growing economic distress forced most men into wage labor" in the central industrial region, "women stayed on the land as long as something could be scratched from it." As early as 1863, an observer in Kaluga Province complained that with "the absence of the young male population," villages were largely composed of "old people, young children, and women." Just as in the American South enslaved women had often been more central than men to slave plantation communities, so too under very different conditions greater male mobility left women as anchors of peasant villages—and even sometimes of communal organization. "Some assumed their husbands' places at the village assembly," noted historian Barbara Engel, "and fulfilled the offices of representative and elder."[44]

As in the Southern United States, in Russia the basic continuity provided by what was still an overwhelmingly rural and agricultural society belied fundamental changes in the lives and social relations of the freedpeople. In both countries, these changes were a result of the shift from coerced to free labor, reinforced by the beginnings of a long-term economic transformation, the most notable features of which were industrialization and urbanization. Free labor meant compensated labor, and in both countries the compensation varied widely in form and degree. Free labor also meant labor that was far more mobile than that under slavery and serfdom, and this geographic mobility served as a fundamental underpinning of the freedpeople's aspirations. Free labor, freer movement, and especially in the South supportive legislation also underlay the proliferation of occupations available to the freedpeople, and contributed to ensuing changes (examined in chapter 6) in family and communal life as well as in the freedpeople's consciousness and sense of identity. At the heart of all these developments lay an intense class struggle, as former owners and former bondspeople sought to advance their own interests under new ground rules that were not always clearly defined, that shifted over time, and that differed considerably between the two countries. If at first the political environment was far more supportive of the freedpeople's aspirations in the Southern United States than in Russia, the fierce racist reaction that Reconstruction provoked soon indicated the full extent of the resistance that those aspirations would face.

As African Americans and peasants sought to build new lives as free people, it did not take them long to realize that they faced massive opposition from their former owners. The problem was not so much ill will (although that existed) as conflicting interests: the freedpeople's desire for independence and economic security was incompatible with the effort of planters and pomeshchiki to secure cheap, dependent labor and to preserve as many of their former prerogatives as possible. Similarly incompatible were ideas of equal rights with assumptions of hereditary privilege and inherent inferiority of Blacks and peasants, and of belief that the land belonged by right to those who labored upon it with defense of the private property rights of landed elites. The class struggles that enveloped the post-emancipation South and Russia were defined by very different understandings of the freedpeople and their former owners of what constituted a just moral order.

The conflict of interest and the intensity of the class struggle were exacerbated by specific features of the way emancipation occurred. In the Southern United States, the former slaveholders' resentment at what seemed the injustice of forced emancipation was magnified by bitterness at their defeat in the Civil War, their hatred of Yankee invaders, and their pervasive racism. In both countries, the new ground rules were uncertain and poorly understood. Planters, pomeshchiki, and freedpeople had to interact with a proliferation of new officials—especially Freedmen's Bureau agents and peace mediators—and in the South with dual and at times antagonistic authorities represented by state governments and the Union Army. In both countries rumor competed with reality as former owners warned of incipient rebellions, while former bondspeople hoped for land redistribution but feared that the *real* freedom promised from on high was being subverted by officials on the ground whose goals were very different from those in Washington and St. Petersburg.

In the face of these confusing counterforces, freedpeople enjoyed to varying degrees three contextual advantages that partially mitigated the far greater power of their former owners. In much of the South and parts of Russia, shortage of labor strengthened the bargaining hand of laborers vis-à-vis employers. The very existence of formalized bargaining—whether over contracts in the South and to a lesser extent in Russia or over terms of Russian redemption agreements—seemed both to the freedpeople and to their former masters an indication of just how much things had changed: however much slaves and serfs may have engaged in implicit negotiations under bondage, they did not receive recognition as parties with the right to take part in contractual agreements, and the ability to do so after emancipation was a major marker of their changed—free—status. And as they sought better terms, their ability to move constituted their ultimate bargaining weapon—their most potent way of withholding labor—one that they exercised on a massive scale in both Russia and the South. Especially under conditions of labor scarcity, geographic mobility was central to the freedpeople's pursuit not just of economic security but of freedom itself.

The struggle between freedpeople and former owners was ongoing, with dozens of manifestations. As Blacks and peasants sought independence and economic well-being, they employed tactics that ranged from withholding labor to insisting on their newfound rights. They dragged their feet when it was time to contract, they rejected statutory charters drafted by landowners, they moved, they resisted the apprenticing of their children, they sought to buy land of their own or barring that to rent under favorable terms, they engaged in political activities that in Russia were mostly at the communal and volost' levels but in the South ranged from local to statewide, they appealed for support to peace mediators and Freedmen's Bureau agents, and—especially but not exclusively in Russia—they clung to the notion that the land they worked was by right theirs and would soon be theirs in fact as well.

Although under slavery Southern African Americans had lacked the tradition of intensely communal lives evident among Russian peasants, emancipation facilitated new kinds of collective organization and action in much of the rural South, from occasionally pooling resources to purchase land and forming model "colonies" such as that in Mound Bayou, to forming labor unions and engaging in strikes. Aside from large-scale actions among hired workers on the sugar estates of southern Louisiana and the rice plantations of the Georgia and South Carolina Lowcountry, smaller collective efforts were evident in both rural and urban areas. Complaining that "the laborer recieves [sic] a very little recompense for his labor," for example, rural freedpeople in Frederick County, Virginia, banded together in March 1871 to form a "labor union under the jurisdictions [sic] of the National Labor Union"; "we are indeavoring [sic] to work a plan to better our condition," they wrote Freedmen's Bureau Commissioner Howard, "and petition you for your advice and assistance." Organizing workers was easier, and strikes were more common, in cities. In Mobile, hundreds of dockworkers went on strike "for higher wages" in March 1867, declaring that "no one should work for less than fifty cents an hour." In Atlanta, when Black laundresses—dubbed "Washing Amazons" by hostile whites—took advantage of preparations for the International Cotton Exposition of 1881 to form a Washing Society, within three weeks "their ranks swelled from twenty to three thousand strikers and sympathizers," and before long their "actions had inspired cooks, maids, and nurses to demand higher wages" as well. Although these efforts were rarely successful in the short run, the widespread withholding of labor, whether agricultural or urban, and the tough bargaining over contracts that accompanied it, clearly took considerable if unheralded organization and *did* yield positive results in terms of both compensation and conditions of work. In both the South and Russia, specific strikes could easily be crushed, but the general, apparently spontaneous labor action of hundreds of thousands of freedpeople was another matter.[45]

Planters and pomeshchiki responded in kind, seeking to maintain as many of their former prerogatives as possible, to make freedom more nominal than real. They did everything in their power to minimize compensation, retain the proper respect of their former property, and make sure that "free labor" remained subordinate labor. One tactic that they tried in the South was to counter labor organization with their own collective endeavors. A flurry of such efforts occurred in the Alabama Black Belt—and in much of the Deep South—in the fall of 1867, when African Americans were becoming more visibly active politically and were increasingly taking advantage of labor shortages to press for improved conditions. In October 1867, a "meeting of citizens" in Sumterville, Alabama, agreed that "concert of action is indispensable among those hiring laborers" in order to overcome "the present disorganized and inefficient System of Labor." The "citizens" adopted a series of resolutions promising to discharge laborers who violated their contracts, pledging not to hire discharged workers "without a certificate of recommendation from the person last employing them," setting limits to the compensation of both sharecroppers and wage laborers, and defining "a day's labor" as ten hours in the summer and nine in the winter. Two months later, when a planters' convention in Selma passed similar recommendations designed to limit compensation, "[a] large number of the colored men present voted against the adoption of the report, but the[ir] votes were not counted." In reporting on still another planters' gathering that fall, a local newspaper succinctly summarized the heart of the employers' understanding of free labor: "The *labor*, upon which the planter has to rely, *must be subject to his control*" the paper proclaimed, adding, "No laborers should be employed who will not bind themselves to do any and all kinds of farm-work that may be required of them."[46]

The tactics that former owners employed sometimes differed between the South and Russia, because so too did the demographic and political contexts in which free labor emerged. Russian pomeshchiki did not try to create employers' organizations, as Southern planters did, because they lacked the American tradition of forming civic associations, did not suffer from an intense shortage of labor in most of the country, and did not face the same kind of political opposition that conservative white Southerners did during Reconstruction. Instead, they turned to the government, which put forth detailed guidelines for statutory charters and redemption agreements, and provided military support when peasants appeared to get out of hand. If in Russia soldiers helped put down volneniia and imposed ritualized public punishment on peasant leaders, in the South—at least for a while—the military was more likely to protect African Americans from abuse by hostile whites (although even during Reconstruction beleaguered Blacks could never be sure whose side soldiers would take). In both Russia and the South, however, military force was far too thinly spread to provide more than selective intervention; as historian Gregory P. Downs has suggested, the rapid withdrawal of federal forces left the Black and

Unionist white Southerners with only "pockets of peace and stability" in an increasingly chaotic, terror-ridden region. In the South as well as in Russia a period of sustained counterrevolutionary conservatism would set in during the last two decades of the nineteenth century—a period that in the South was presaged by massive anti-Black and anti-Reconstruction violence—but well before this reaction was evident, planters and pomeshchiki were struggling with how to defend their interests and limit the radical potential of "free labor."[47]

The ideal of a docile labor force—an ideal that conformed to the general goal of Russian authorities and even in the United States received support from some (although not all) free-labor ideologues—was central to the goals of planters and pomeshchiki. As working for pomeshchiki with minimal compensation, "out of respect," indicated, peasants understood the advantages of showing proper deference when dealing with nobles. Georg Brandes, a Danish literary agent who spent three months in Russia in 1887, was amazed at the continued peasant groveling when seeking favors from noblemen—and especially noblewomen—including "falling flat on the face at [their] feet. . . . No remonstrances," he concluded, "can make them give up this custom." Historian Dylan Penningroth has noted the American equivalent of working "out of respect," describing Northern teacher Laura Towne's account of "cunning" African Americans who sought to ingratiate themselves with Northern benevolent workers in Lowcountry South Carolina, just as they had with former slaveholders, with small gifts "such as poultry, sweet potatoes, and, above all, eggs" for which "they refused to take anything in return." As Penningroth observed, "Black men and women had been nursing along useful acquaintances with whites since the days of slavery, painting a soft veneer of flattery and gifts over tough bargaining."[48]

Increasingly, however, planters and pomeshchiki became convinced that docile and respectful behavior was a lost cause. From the very beginning, they complained of Blacks and peasants who worked poorly, talked too loudly, and were ignorant, lazy, and in need of direction; as former overseer Wilson Oberry noted of Black laborers on Paul C. Cameron's absentee-owned plantation in Hale County, Alabama, it was "a tuff business" to farm the land "with free Negroes." Freedom itself seemed virtually incompatible with Blacks and peasants behaving in an orderly manner and showing proper deference to their superiors (see chapters 1–3). Over time, former slave owners came, of necessity, to accept free labor, but they did not come to accept the aspirations of the free laborers, whom they continued to see as childlike creatures lacking in maturity and self-control. As one white witness after another in 1883 told a U.S. Senate committee hearing on labor relations, freedom—compounded by the folly of Reconstruction—had transformed African Americans from hardworking, well-behaved laborers into restless, self-absorbed louts. In a typical comment, one witness complained of Blacks "running about night and day," no longer, in his words, "willing to be controlled or guided by their employers, because they have an idea that that is submitting to slavery again." Another succinctly opined, "Young negroes here are growing up very worthless," adding, "You can't get them to work." The views of educated Russians toward peasants were more complex—not driven by the rampant racism of Southern whites, some Russians (at least in theory) came to see peasants as virtuous, simple folk who represented the essence of the Russian nation (addressed in chapter 7)—but most pomeshchiki also found dealing with free peasants troublesome and bemoaned the ignorance, drunkenness, laziness, and corruption that flourished without the guiding hand of (supposedly) paternalistic masters. As historian James I. Mandel noted, by the late 1870s there was a widespread perception among the "governing classes" that peasant self-government had degenerated into "dissolute chaos," and, more generally, that emancipation was a failure because the peasant was "a backward and unruly child, who required patient guidance and control."[49]

Convinced that emancipation had rendered previously hardworking Blacks unfit and unwilling to be obedient laborers, some former slave owners sought to recruit compliant replacements from abroad. In doing so, they followed a strategy already in place in parts of the Caribbean—such as Trinidad and Tobago—where planters recruited indentured East Indian laborers to replace Blacks who withdrew from the labor force to practice self-sufficient agriculture, and soon to be pursued by planters in southern Brazil, who would increasingly rely on Italian immigrant labor. "All around us people are discussing how to get other labourers in the place of negroes," wrote Frances Butler in 1868, explaining that freed Blacks had "lost their old habit of work, . . . and everywhere sullen unwillingness to work [was] visible." Increasingly distraught by the "demoralised and disorganised condition" of her workforce, Butler returned to her Butler's Island, Georgia, estate in 1873 after two years in England with not only a new husband (after which she became Frances Butler Leigh) but also eight young Englishmen—all but one single—who would supplement the labor of her more than eighty Black hands as well as the seven Irishmen whom she had already hired "to do the banking and ditching on the island."[50]

The experiment was not a success. Although at first the Englishmen "seemed in good spirits and well satisfied," they soon proved utterly incompetent, "like so many troublesome children"; they fought with the Irish ditchers and, Leigh complained, "shirked their work so abominably, that our negro foreman Sey begged that they might not be allowed to work in the same fields with the negroes, to whom they set so bad an example." Admitting that she had not known "what poor stuff the English agricultural labourer is made of as a general rule," Leigh recalled that "when the end of their second year came we were most thankful to pay their way back to England and get rid of them." Although she rehired the Irishmen, whom she had discharged in favor of the English laborers, she soon decided that the Black workers were not so bad after all—or perhaps more accurately were the best of a bad lot. True, they were childlike as well as "unreasoning and easily influenced," but so long as they were managed by paternalistic "gentlemen" they were willing to work well and were preferable to unruly whites: "To a gentleman's rule they will submit," she observed, "but to no other." When she returned to Butler's Island in 1882 after an absence of six years, she was pleased to find that local Blacks were still grateful to their former masters, to whom they said, "We your people massa." Meanwhile, those ex-slaveholders were better off than they had been formerly, "relieved of the terrible load of responsibility which slavery entailed."[51]

Leigh's experience was not atypical. Elsewhere as well, planters flirted with the idea of replacing "demoralized" African American laborers with—or at least supplementing them by—non-Black immigrants who presumably would be more orderly, hardworking, and subservient. After Leigh "leased a neighboring island to an energetic young planter," he "brought down thirty Chinamen to work it. It remains to be seen whether they will do the work better than the negroes," she mused, adding that "they could not do it much worse." The most substantial experiment with Chinese labor, however, occurred on the sugar plantations of southern Louisiana, where labor-hungry employers hired hundreds of Chinese immigrants—often termed "coolies" by white Americans—recruited at first mostly from Cuba but then increasingly from California and direct from China. Denounced by Republicans—and some white Southerners who could not afford the hefty recruitment and transportation fees that wealthy planters paid labor agents—as virtual slaves who were threats to the free-labor system rather than voluntary immigrants, "coolies" seemed to many Southern whites to offer a welcome solution to the existing labor shortage while serving as an object lesson to turbulent freedpeople that they could easily be replaced by more compliant workers. As Northern journalist Whitelaw Reid described the "prevailing sentiment" among whites in the "interior of Mississippi" in 1866, "We can drive the niggers out and import coolies that will work better, at less expense, and relieve us from this cursed nigger impudence." Initial reports of Chinese laborers were highly favorable, and "planters at first roundly praised them" for their diligence and docility. "The Chinaman is naturally industrious and obedient," gushed one enthusiastic planter, adding, "He is also usually honest, inclined to fulfill to the letter his contract, and is not disposed to shirk or slight any labor responsibility." As late as 1870 the New Orleans *Times* proclaimed succinctly, "The Chinese are industrious, mild and easily governed."[52]

Before long, however, planters were singing a different tune. Pointing to their "low, cunning, ignoble countenances," Leigh concluded that the Chinese workers on the neighboring estate were "far more repulsive than the negroes." In Louisiana, they proved equally unsatisfactory, unwilling to submit to draconian discipline and resistant to reduced wages. From the very beginning there were signs of trouble, and even as some planters touted the "coolies" as the region's salvation, others experienced bitter disappointment. In 1867, the *Semi-Weekly Natchitoches Times* described Chinese recently arrived from Cuba as "lazy, mutinous, obstinate and thievish," and judged them "a sorry substitute for our former negro slaves." Two years later, in Assumption Parish, the plantation manager at Elm Hall reached a similar conclusion, deriding the Chinese hands as "stubborn, treacherous, and lazy" and declaring that he would rather have "one negro on the place than five Chinese." The Chinese laborers coming from California and China in the early 1870s proved equally troublesome. Often arriving under three-year contracts that promised wages of $14 to $16 per month—somewhat less than the prevailing wages paid to Black and European workers—the Chinese were typically dismayed by conditions that differed substantially from what they had expected, including harsh treatment, the withholding of pay for insufficient work, and efforts by planters to coordinate cuts in wages. Many responded by fleeing to New Orleans or smaller cities, while others remained in the countryside but rejected their long-term contracts in favor of offering themselves—like migrant peasant laborers in Russia's southeastern steppes—for short-term work at specific tasks, in the process gaining more bargaining power and securing higher wages. Small, itinerant labor gangs sprang up, much to the displeasure of prospective employers (and other whites). "The pig-tail celestials seem to be of a wandering disposition," complained the *Donaldsonville* (Louisiana) *Chief* in 1874, "and unable to stay for any length of time in the same place." With the panic of 1873 (and the ensuing depression), flight, collective resistance, and strikes became increasingly common, and "planters' dreams of replacing freedmen with Chinese workers ... lay in shambles." Louisiana's planters continued to flirt with the idea of replacing troublesome freedpeople with other laborers who would supposedly be less demanding and more responsible—the Louisiana Immigration Company formed in 1871 promoted the use of sturdy European workers, including especially Germans and Italians but also other nationalities—but they too proved disappointing.[53]

Elsewhere in the Deep South, the story was similar. Planters, editors, agricultural societies, and conservative politicians continued to talk about the desirability of attracting new laborers—whether Northern, European, or Asian—to replace unruly freedpeople, but such efforts bore little fruit. Almost always, those new laborers who *were* recruited disappointed their employers, because they were unwilling to submit to conditions that Blacks had found intolerable. Employers typically blamed specific racial or ethnic traits for their troubles: as an official of the Alabama and Chattanooga Railroad opined in 1871 after numerous Chinese laborers the company had hired abruptly quit—with many of them making their way south to Mobile and then Louisiana—"Until Chinamen become less clannish, less stubborn, *less Chinese* . . . it is labor by no means desired." The gist of the problem, however, in the view of the British consul in New Orleans in 1872, was that, from the point of view of planters, "a labourer is a labourer . . . whether he be French or German, Italian or Norwegian, British or Chinese, he is to be housed, fed, and treated just as the black race used to be." Immigrants were no more willing to submit to slave-like subservience than were former slaves: those who signed up to work on plantations proved— in the words of one Georgia planter—"more expensive to feed and keep" than the freedpeople, and they rarely stayed long. Indeed, although talk of replacing African Americans with migrants who would be more tractable, disciplined, and hardworking persisted for decades, it soon became clear that the hope was chimerical, and that planters would have to come to grips with the reality of free Black labor.[54]

Still, for those accustomed to *slave* labor this reality proved hard to swallow, and planters increasingly withdrew from direct supervision of free workers. Some withdrew from the South altogether. Thousands of white Southerners— mostly former slave owners—who were outraged by the loss of their slaves, humiliated by the defeat of the Confederacy, and alarmed by the increasingly radical course of Reconstruction, sought to remake their lives outside the United States, preferably in countries with conservative governments that would welcome their aspirations. The goal of everyone who "could possibly get away," one distraught South Carolinian explained, was to avoid the "revolting" prospect of "liv[ing] in a Land where Free Negroes make the majority of the population"—where "every mulattoe is your equal & every 'Nigger' is your superior & you haven't even a country." Initially some emigrants sought refuge in Mexico, where Emperor Maximilian welcomed disgruntled Confederates, but the absence of slavery there proved a serious deterrent, one compounded by the emperor's overthrow and execution by republicans in 1867.[55] The country of choice for would-be emigrants quickly became Brazil, which remained not only a monarchy but also (until 1888) a slave society. During the decade after the Civil War, "disappointed and sore over the 'lost cause' and fully resolved never to submit to nigger rulers appointed by the Yanks," several thousand white Southerners sought to replicate the Old South in Brazil, with at best mixed results. If the opportunity to resettle in a slave society was appealing, the hardship of adjusting to life in a strange country, where people spoke Portuguese, customs seemed bizarre, and the numerous free Blacks were accorded rights that violated the Southerners' notions of white supremacy, proved daunting. A few settlers remained in Brazil despite these obstacles—the largest surviving settlement of "Confederados" was in the south, near São Paulo, where some of their descendants remain to this day—but before long most became disillusioned; some died, and others, either homesick or unable to adjust to what seemed an alien culture, returned to the United States.[56]

A few disgruntled white Southerners sought refuge in Cuba—like Brazil a country where slavery still existed, albeit on its last legs, and like Brazil a country that proved unsatisfactory to those trying to recreate the Old South abroad—or in Europe (especially France and England), where despite the absence of slavery Yankees and experiments with racial equality seemed far removed.[57] Others, who had been prone to flee their estates during the sickly summer months, extended their absences. Seasonal absenteeism was especially prevalent among a small number of aristocratic planters in the subtropical Lowcountry of South Carolina and Georgia, as well the sugar country of southern Louisiana, and some of these grandees maintained secondary homes (which could change into primary homes) in nearby cities such as Charleston, Savannah, and New Orleans—or even in more distant cities such as Philadelphia and New York. Georgia planter Charles C. Jones Jr., the son of a prominent Presbyterian minister noted for his effort to evangelize the slaves (and for his paternalistic defense of slavery), decided to put his three holdings in Liberty County up for sale as early as November 1865, but he evidently did not find any buyers willing to take his hefty asking price; two months later, after noting of the "Arcadia" tract that "as landed property there is none more valuable in Liberty County," his mother, Mary, living in Savannah, complained, "The place has been running down very fast" because "the Negroes have ruled entirely there this year." Charles Jr., who was already spending most of his time practicing law in New York, where he was "pretty well fixed in [a] new home," urged Mary to join him there—"Your room is all ready"—and mused on the difficult "transition in the status of the Negro," who, he wrote, "has always been a child in intellect" and "without the most distant conception of the duties of life and labor now devolved upon him." As late as 1882, Charles Jr. was still making an "annual visit" to his plantation headquarters, Montevideo, but he found the place "sadly marred by the disintegrating influences of time" and, indeed, the "entire region . . . strangely changed, . . . peopled only with the phantoms of things that were." When he returned to Georgia in 1877, it was not to live at Montevideo (which remained in the family's possession until its sale in the early twentieth century) but to practice law in Augusta, where he died in 1893.[58]

Jones was hardly alone in putting distance between himself and freed Blacks. Like a small number of other wealthy Lowcountry families, generations of Butlers had commuted among their Georgia properties (headquartered on Butler's Island) and their homes elsewhere—in this case Philadelphia and England. After Frances Butler inherited the properties from her father in 1867, she spent parts of the next decade coming to grips with free labor, but she thought nothing of absenting herself for months—and in one case two years—at a time, and she moved away permanently in 1877. Elsewhere as well, planters who were able chose to cope from afar with changed conditions that they found distressing. In 1865, Alabama planter Henry Watson escaped for several months to Germany, leaving his large Greene County estate in the hands of his overseer, George Hagin, who in turn was loosely supervised by Watson's brother-in-law. Upon returning from Germany several months later, a disgusted Watson found the freedpeople "all idle, doing nothing," and "eating off their masters." Still considering himself by right a "master," Watson was unable to accept his loss of mastery and vowed to "have nothing to do with the hiring of hands or the care of the plantation." The following year, Hagin, to whom Watson had ceded control of the plantation, himself tired of coping with free labor and broke up the plantation, renting individual lots to Black families, who were then essentially on their own. Watson himself moved to Massachusetts, and although he made annual visits to his Alabama plantation, he "maintained no direct, continuous involvement in the lives of his workers."[59]

Although most former slave owners did not move to Brazil, travel extensively in Europe, or retreat to homes in Philadelphia or New York, many followed the less extreme course of distancing themselves from their former slaves while remaining at home. Indeed, the new sharecropping arrangements that increasingly enabled rural Blacks to operate as independent proprietors even though most did not actually own the land they farmed also enabled dissatisfied white landowners to escape the humiliating task of supervising free Black labor. Beginning in 1866 and accelerating thereafter, widespread reports noted that as freedpeople pursued independent operations through renting, sharecropping, and less often buying land, planters were "refusing to superintend, direct, or even, in some cases, to suggest" anything concerning agricultural labor, insisting—often with more than a hint of a sour grapes mentality—that they were better off freed from the obligation of caring for their ungrateful laborers. The rapidity with which men and women who had once prided themselves on paternalistically looking after—and, indeed, loving—their "people" came to celebrate their own emancipation from slavery was remarkable. Frances Leigh's conclusion that the "masters" were "far better off . . . relieved from the terrible load of responsibility which slavery entailed" echoed the sentiment of Tuscumbia, Alabama, planter J. B. Moore (and countless other former slaveholders) that the end of slavery had freed him of a terrible burden. "I have been the slave myself," he proclaimed, "to keep them fed and clothed." "Free Negroes frets me so much," declared another planter in perhaps the most succinct statement of the rationale behind the desire to abandon plantation management, "that I very seldom go among them."[60]

Most Russian pomeshchiki, although they were distressed at the freeing of their serfs, did not seek alternatives to peasant labor or—except for a tiny number of political radicals—seriously consider fleeing the country. Given that the vast majority of Russians—83 percent on the eve of emancipation—were peasants, most of Russia did not suffer from a labor shortage similar to that in the Southern United States, and that hostility to peasants did not assume the vitriolic racist form of white American hostility to Blacks, finding non-peasant laborers was not a serious goal of former serfholders. Nor, given that most pomeshchiki lacked any real equivalent to the despair generated in white Southerners by defeat in the Civil War, was leaving the country. Almost by definition, agricultural labor meant peasant labor.[61]

Nevertheless, *free* peasant labor seemed as problematical to many pomeshchiki as free Black labor did to planters, and post-emancipation Russian noble landholders displayed the same tendency as that of Southern white farmers and planters to distance themselves from their former human property. Many noble landholders became convinced that the less contact they had with their former serfs the better, given the struggles over statutory charters and redemption agreements, the continued belief by peasants that noble lands were rightfully theirs and would soon be divided among them, and more generally nobles having to recognize—and deal with peasants who were at least vaguely aware of—a variety of new rights pertaining to such matters as bargaining, compensation, landholding, communal authority, and freedom from physical punishment. Even under serfdom, pomeshchiki had typically held fewer paternalistic pretensions and shown greater absenteeist tendencies than their American counterparts. In part, this reflected the physical impossibility of maintaining close contact with a vast peasant population: wealthy nobles, who often had multiple estates and who owned most of the serfs, were of necessity absentee owners for the great bulk of their serfs. But even when owners were physically present, they often showed little concern for or knowledge of the lives of most of their peasants and seemed correspondingly remote to those peasants. In the words of historian Daniel Field, to the typical "provincial pomeshchik" there was "no affective or sentimental element" in serfdom. That remoteness became more pronounced with emancipation.[62]

Nobles who were used to enserfed labor harbored deep fears about what *free* labor would bring. Almost immediately upon emancipation, pomeshchiki began complaining that peasants were working less diligently than before. Although reports varied, many of the tsar's special emissaries concluded that former serfs were becoming troublesome, recalcitrant, and lazy under the new regime. As one wrote succinctly from Kaluga Province, it was a given that "[temporarily] obligated labor" could not be as productive as "serf labor," conducted "under the fear of personal and quick reprisal from the owner." From Pskov Province, a staff officer of the Corps of Gendarmes reported: "In the view of pomeshchiki, work is in general going much worse than formerly." British ambassador Sir John Crampton predicted that emancipation would bring about an immediate decline in agricultural production, noting widespread fears that "the peasant having been so long accustomed to connect the idea of serfdom with work, will for a long period connect the idea of freedom with idleness and inaction"; his successor, Francis Napier, agreed: "The people will only work with good will on their own plots for their own interests." Responses of pomeshchiki to the new order varied. The governor of Voronezh Province noted that most landowners were reducing the area under cultivation, while in Chernigov Province the governor observed that pomeshchiki were dragging their feet when it came to drafting statutory charters, "with the aim of preserving, if only for a short period, the former order." From Kazan Province, the governor told of pomeshchiki refusing to come to redemption agreements with peasants out of fear that they would lose their laborers.[63]

But in the long run, the most pervasive response was to have less to do with peasants. Post-emancipation nobles distanced themselves from peasants in a variety of ways, and to a variety of degrees. The simplest way was to live in a provincial city—or even in Moscow or St. Petersburg—rather than on an estate (or for wealthy nobles one of their estates). Almost half (47.8 percent) of the 3,087 (male and female) hereditary nobles living in Iaroslavl Province in 1865, for example, resided in one of the province's cities rather than on a country estate, and because rich pomeshchki were likely to have more than one estate and were more likely than their less prosperous fellows to have urban homes, far more than half of the province's peasants had absentee landlords. Although statistics from the 1897 census appear to show a similar, relatively unchanged residential pattern for Russian nobility as a whole, with 47.2 percent of hereditary nobles in European Russia living in cities, these statistics are skewed by the lopsided rural character of the nobility in the nine western provinces acquired from Poland in the late eighteenth century, where the noble population was unusually large and unusually (77.7 percent) rural: excluding these provinces, more than two-thirds of the nobility (68.7 percent) was urban at the end of the nineteenth century. As A. P. Korelin has shown in his careful study of the post-emancipation nobility, despite a minor (although highly touted) "back-to-the-land" movement in the 1880s, during the last third of the nineteenth century Russian nobles—who had always shown strong absenteeist tendencies—increasingly left the countryside for the cities.[64]

Even when they did not totally abandon their country estates, pomeshchiki increasingly abandoned—directly or indirectly—the supervision of peasant labor. Many sold some or even all of their land; as historian G. M. Hamburg put it, "The response of many pomeshchiki, faced for the first time with the necessity to run estates without serf labor, was to sell their lands."[65] Of course, even without such sales their landholdings were substantially reduced by the emancipation settlement, whereby they sold to their former serfs much of the allotment land those serfs had cultivated as their own, in the process receiving generous compensation. In addition to such redemption sales, however, noble landholders increasingly disposed of the land that remained in their hands, selling (or in some cases renting) it to non-nobles who had previously had little or no access to landownership. These buyers and renters included merchants, who had been barred from owning serfs but were able to employ free peasant laborers, and most of all land-hungry peasants eager to add to their increasingly undersized allotments. In separating themselves from the land, pomeshchiki not only pushed to a logical conclusion their already existing absenteeist proclivities but also contributed to ongoing transformations of both the nobility as a privileged estate (considered more fully in chapter 7) and the political economy of the Russian countryside.

An interesting if not entirely typical example of this growing separation from the land is evident in nobleman Vasilii Yazykov's disengagement from his home estate of Yazykovo Selo in Simbirsk Province, which he had inherited from his father—along with multiple other properties—in 1851. Even as Yazykov continued to be a prominent provincial figure, serving in a variety of governmental and philanthropic positions—including marshal of the nobility for Simbirsk District from 1862 through 1873—he increasingly abandoned his role as a pomeshchik and almost totally avoided dealing with his pesky ex-serfs, who (like many peasants in Simbirsk Province) resisted the terms of the statutory charter imposed upon them and refused to come to a redemption agreement until mandatory redemption was enacted in 1881. Cutting ties with the estate's woolen factory came first, beginning in 1860, as Yazykov hired a series of merchants, who soon essentially leased the factory (under two-year contracts) and ran it as their own, paying wages to the peasant workers. Meanwhile, beginning in 1873, Yazykov began selling the landed estate (home to some 393 male souls) to the merchant who was renting his factory, a process that was completed in 1881 with the transfer in ownership of the entire estate, including the factory and the estate mansion. More unusual was Yazykov's decision also to abandon his urban mansion—in Simbirsk City—renting it from the late 1860s and selling it in 1875 to another merchant, named Kartashov, who turned it into a hotel (at first called Yazykov Suites and then Kartashov Suites). The peripatetic Yazykov reserved a room in the hotel for when he was in town.[66]

More common than selling land to merchants was selling or renting it to peasants. Unlike Yazykov's sale of his land and factory, sales to peasants were rarely of entire estates. Rather, pomeshchiki took advantage of peasants' eagerness to supplement their shrinking allotments through purchase and rental of additional land, to cut back both on seigneurial production and on the necessity of grappling with free agricultural labor. If the willingness of peasants to take on new debt in addition to their already burdensome redemption obligations was a sign of their desperate hunger for land, the willingness of nobles to part with seigneurial land, on top of land they had already lost in the redemption process, was an equally potent sign of *their* dissatisfaction with the post-emancipation social order and their grudging acceptance of a reduced role in the free-labor agricultural economy. As nobleman A. N. Engelgardt lamented in 1872, after returning to his ancestral estate in Smolensk Province for the first time in fifteen years, "The gentry let their estates go after Emancipation, neglected the fields and meadows, and ran off into [government] service.... The gentry do not farm," he added glumly; "they have abandoned the land, they don't live on their estates."[67]

Despite the exaggeration, Engelgardt was right about the trend. During the half century after emancipation, there occurred a massive "peasantization" of Russian agriculture, as nobles continued to sell off their land, mostly to the peasants who actually worked it. The trend was least pronounced in the fertile steppes of the southeast, where nobles continued to engage in—and indeed expanded—large-scale commercial agriculture based on hired peasant labor: in Saratov Province, for example, the amount of noble-owned land decreased by a modest 13.4 percent between 1867 and 1883 (and, because there were fewer noble landowners, the size of the average noble holding actually increased by 14.2 percent, from 921.5 to 1,052 desiatiny). In the country as a whole, however, the shift from noble-based to peasant-based agriculture was striking. Although individual nobles bought and sold land, during the half century after emancipation nobles as a whole sold about twice as much land as they bought, and the proportion of nobles who were landless surged from about one-fifth to about three-fifths. Between 1861 and 1905, the amount of land owned by nobles decreased—on top of the loss brought about through redemption—by more than 40 percent; by 1905, nobles, who before emancipation had held a virtual monopoly on private landowning, owned only 22.1 percent of Russia's agricultural land. Peasants owned 67.9 percent, while merchants and members of other intermediate groups owned the remaining 10 percent.[68]

Even these figures, however, understate the decline of noble-run agriculture, because peasants *rented* and farmed additional noble-owned land, so that the peasantization of agriculture was significantly greater than the peasantization of landownership. A survey by the Noble Land Bank revealed that by the late 1880s about one-third of large noble estates (those of five hundred or more desiatiny) were leased to peasants, another third were under direct noble cultivation, and still another third had mixed arrangements. After the 1880s, peasantization became more pronounced, in part because of continued noble land sales to peasants and in part because of increased rentals. If nobles owned only 22.1 percent of land under cultivation (excluding state land) in 1905, the rental of about half this remaining noble land to peasants meant that "direct farming" by nobles fell to "about 10 percent of the arable land." By 1917, historian Carol Leonard recently estimated, the noble share of all cultivated fields in thirty-four provinces of European Russia stood at only 7.7 percent. "The picture is mainly that of a mass of family farms," wrote Teodor Shanin, "in which nine-tenths of the rural population lived and produced."[69]

Although the term was not used in the United States, a similar process of peasantization occurred in the post-emancipation South as former slave owners distanced themselves from the management of free labor. More than in Russia, where peasant landholding was ubiquitous, this American version of peasantization was based on the rapid proliferation of various rental arrangements. Unlike Russian pomeshchiki, Southern planters did not engage in the massive selling off of their land during the post-emancipation decades, but as Roger Ransom and Richard Sutch have shown, they did engage in the same kind of flight from the management of agricultural labor: plantations in the Deep South persisted as units of landownership, but not in most cases as units of production. By 1880, the vast majority of agricultural operations in the cotton-producing states of the Deep South consisted of small farms—some rented (usually but not always by Blacks) and some owned (usually but not always by whites)—and only 0.9 percent were run as plantations; those plantations contained 8.9 percent of the agricultural acreage, a figure remarkably similar to the share operated directly by pomeshchiki in Russia in the late nineteenth century. Historian Gavin Wright made a similar point about the economic revolution that accompanied emancipation when he proclaimed the transformation of Southern planters from "laborlords" into "landlords."[70]

In short, as bondage was replaced by free labor, both the South and Russia saw the widespread proliferation of family farming among the freedpeople. Needless to say, family farming did not imply economic democracy, an egalitarian social order, or an absence of exploitation. Most rural freedpeople remained poor, living on the margins, and most remained economically dependent even as they were able to take more control of their everyday lives. Blacks and peasants continued to supplement their "own" agricultural production with a wide variety of outside work, and equally important, their family farming was itself based on dependent economic relations with planters and pomeshchiki, whether in terms of sharecropping and other rental arrangements or—in the Russian case—the need to pay off the long-term redemption debt they owed on their own land. Peasants and Blacks remained politically subservient as well, despite the brief and sporadic—if remarkable—Reconstruction experiment with political democracy. In the South, planters continued to own most of the land, and in Russia, where nobles were well compensated for the emancipation of their serfs and then for the land they often sold to them, noble holdings on a per capita or per soul basis continued to dwarf those of peasants even as most of the land came under peasant control.

Still, in terms of the actual management of agricultural labor, the transformation of former bondspeople into independent proprietors was striking. This was especially so in the South, where many slaves had worked in gangs under the supervision of overseers and drivers and where most slaves had toiled under close supervision of slave owners or their representatives; by American standards, even as serfs Russian peasants had enjoyed a substantial degree of communal autonomy. After emancipation, this autonomy was greatly enhanced, and in both countries the former owners increasingly abandoned the direct, day-to-day control of agricultural labor that they had once exercised. Free labor did not produce economic equality, but it did lead to a significant increase in the autonomy of those who toiled on the land.

The free-labor transformation took place in an environment of intense class struggle as Black Americans and Russian peasants organized to defend their interests while planters and pomeshchiki responded in kind. Meanwhile, day in and day out, freedpeople strove to build new, more independent, lives for themselves. The ensuing changes were especially profound in the South, because slave owners had intervened more pervasively in the everyday lives of Blacks than pomeshchiki had in those of peasants, but in both Russia and the South, despite the increasingly unfavorable political climate, more independent labor relations were accompanied by—and facilitated the spread of—a host of changes that reshaped families, enabled Blacks to forge new kinds of collective endeavors, accentuated the authority of peasant communes, and provided educational opportunities that in turn made possible increased occupational diversity. In short, the introduction of free labor was a central element of a far-reaching revolution in the lives of African Americans and peasants as they underwent the transition from bondage to freedom. These changes in everyday patterns of life are the subject of chapter 6.

6 • Free Labor II
Everyday Life

The proliferation of variants of free labor in the post-emancipation years was accompanied by—and contributed to—multiple changes in patterns of life among the freedpeople. There was also much that did not change, in some cases because the changes that freedpeople sought were unfulfilled and in others because the freedpeople actively resisted such changes. This complex interplay of change and continuity created a world that in some ways seemed turned upside down and in others seemed entirely familiar, so it is perhaps not surprising that historians have differed over the extent to which emancipation "revolutionized" everyday life. They have also differed over the nature and significance of systemic changes—how fundamentally different the world of free labor was from that of unfree labor, and how one should characterize the changes that occurred. This chapter focuses on evolving patterns of life among the freedpeople as they struggled to cope with a new playing field even as the players themselves were mostly the same as before; chapter 7 returns to historical interpretation of the post-emancipation order, an order in which—as with the freedpeople's patterns of life—fundamental change coexisted with societal inertia.

It is appropriate to begin with the most immediate arena of the freedpeople's lives: their families. In both Russia and the Southern United States, emancipation brought substantial—albeit very different—changes to freed families. These changes were greater—and more obvious—among the former slaves than among the former serfs, because slavery had impinged more intrusively than serfdom on family life. Although house serfs lived apart from the village world of most peasants, and nobles did not hesitate to interfere in the family lives of their human property, most peasants did not face the constant threat—and frequent reality—endured by enslaved African Americans of being torn forever from their spouses and children. Nevertheless, emancipation fundamentally reshaped peasant families, as it did African American families, in terms both of relationships and of structures.[1]

Emancipation bolstered freed African American families in several important ways. Although historians have persuasively rebutted the once-prevalent view of slave families as weak, nonexistent, or dysfunctional, those families did face enormous obstacles, both legal and practical. Legally, no slave state recognized the existence of marriage between enslaved men and women, and ultimate authority over enslaved children rested not with their parents but with their owners. Practically, slave owners—and other whites—interfered with slave families on a massive and varied basis, from sales that ripped families apart to sexual exploitation of women (and sometimes men) to, on a more prosaic level, prescribing rules and regulations for everyday lives. The resilience of slave families under such conditions was impressive, but it could not entirely overcome the pervasive assault those families suffered. With the abolition of slavery, freedpeople were able to defend—and sometimes to reconstruct—their families in ways that had previously been impossible.[2]

After the abolition of slavery, freedpeople had the right—and in some cases the obligation—to marry. A good deal of confusion surrounded this issue. Shortly after the war's end, the Freedmen's Bureau assistant adjutant general for South Carolina, Georgia, and Florida issued General Orders No. 8, stating, "The marriages of all parties living together as husband and wife at the time of obtaining their freedom, or solemnized since obtaining it, will be acknowledged as legal & binding." Most states, under the conservative "restoration" regimes set up by President Johnson or the more radical Reconstruction governments that soon followed—or both—also passed laws legitimizing retroactively the marriages of freed couples who had lived together as slaves. In 1865, for example, the South Carolina legislature passed a measure declaring that although in the future Blacks wanting to marry would have to undergo official weddings, those previously living together as husband and wife would be regarded as such, and in Alabama both the conservative constitutional convention of 1865 and the radical convention of 1867 passed ordinances with similar provisions. The precise terms of these laws varied, however, and many Freedmen's Bureau officials took the position that official weddings were needed to sanctify existing relations. The same General Orders No. 8 that seemed to recognize de facto slave marriages also provided that "all parties whose marriage was only a mutual agreement between themselves, with no public form or ceremony, are required to have their marriages confirmed by a minister, & obtain a certificate of the same," and Alabama Bureau's chief, Assistant Commissioner Wager Swayne, contradicted the constitutional convention's recognition of slave marriages in an 1865 circular directing that a "general re-marriage (for the sake of the record) of all persons married without license, or living together without marriage, should be insisted upon by employers and urged by all who have any connection with or knowledge of such persons." Swayne went on ominously to threaten that those refusing to conform to "this necessity of social life" would be "prosecuted and punished."[3]

Freedmen's Bureau officials—like other free-labor reformers and some Southern whites as well—were obsessively concerned with the freedpeople's marital relations. As historian Amy Dru Stanley has emphasized, in an era when "contract was above all a metaphor of freedom," marriage—and the marriage contract—assumed contradictory significance, denoting both "freedom" and "constraint." Convinced that the slave South had been a region of sexual depravity, bureau agents typically expressed distress at what they regarded as the lax moral standards that freedpeople continued to display. Noting that he was "pained, daily, at the connubial relations of the colored people," Alabama's assistant commissioner Swayne declared that the widespread sexual infidelity that he considered an unfortunate legacy of slavery "cannot be looked upon in any light than a huge system of prostitution, by sane persons. It ought to be stopped." Many bureau officials in other states agreed. Although John Mercer Langston, a rare African American agent, wrote Commissioner Howard praising the family morality of North Carolina freedpeople, calling attention to their opposition to "the unholy and adulterous relation, in many cases, existing between white men and colored women, bred by slavery," more common was Mississippi assistant commissioner Alvan C. Gillem's report deploring the lack of understanding that "the more ignorant class of freedpeople" showed to their "marriage relations." Noting that freedpeople in rural Mississippi tended to "marry and afterwards abandon one another without the least cause," he suggested that only in urban Vicksburg did Blacks understand and adhere to "the laws relative to marriage." An agent in South Carolina agreed that many freedpeople had "no regard for the marriage relation" and "separate[d] for slight reasons."[4]

If their Northern allies were eager to enforce the benefits of bourgeois morality on supposedly backward freedpeople, African Americans were equally eager to escape the constraints that slavery had imposed on their connubial relationships. Many couples rushed to legitimize their marriages with formal weddings, in some cases to comply with pressure from Freedmen's Bureau officials and missionaries—given the legal ambiguity, remarriage could hardly hurt—but more generally to assert their new status as free people. One of the most striking manifestations of this effort was the widespread proliferation of group ceremonies, which could range from relatively perfunctory events in which couples legally confirmed their married status to formal weddings conducted by clergymen. When twenty-six couples sought official marriage at a church in rural Alabama, "the minister told them that the State Constitution [of 1865] had legalized their former marriages," but they insisted upon—and received—a formal marriage ceremony. In South Carolina as well, despite a December 1865 act of the state legislature that recognized couples living together under slavery as legally married, Chaplain M. French, Freedmen's Bureau supervisor of missions and marriage relations, reported nearly a year later, "Parties numbering from five to nearly forty . . . have come before me, and in the presence of large congregations, and before God, solemnly promised to live in love and fidelity to each other until death should part them." Elsewhere as well, despite minor differences from state to state in legislation and Freedmen's Bureau procedures, freedpeople rushed to legitimize existing—often long-standing—relationships. In Florida, where in 1866 the state legislature passed a law requiring freedpeople living together as man and wife to be officially married within nine months, "hundreds" of them "legalized their relations by again being married by proper authority," although "a few" refused to do so. A year later, the state's assistant commissioner boasted to Commissioner Howard, "There are now few, if any freedpeople in the State, living openly as man and wife, who cannot show their marriage certificate."[5]

In several states, Freedmen's Bureau officials composed forms—which ranged from simple "registers" to elaborate "certificates"—to record marriages and remarriages of freedpeople. A fairly complicated certificate of marriage for nine couples in Arkadelphia, Arkansas, in September 1865, listed—for both men and women—names, residence, age, color, color of father and mother, previous spouses and cause of separation from them (usually sale or death), number of children with previous spouses, and the name and signature of the officiating minister. In Mississippi, before the state legislature passed an act legitimizing the marriages of freedpeople living together, the bureau assistant commissioner drew up a simple printed form to be signed by a clergyman indicating that he had "this day joined in lawful matrimony" two freedpersons, and reported with satisfaction, "The Freedmen are being married, in accordance with the circular issued from this office, & the registers kept by officers of this Bureau." After the Virginia state legislature passed legislation retroactively legitimizing slave marriages but made no provision for their certification, Freedmen's Bureau officials began issuing certificates and recording the marriages in countywide registers, which according to a new act passed by the Reconstruction legislature in April 1867 were to be accepted by county court clerks. Describing these developments, the state's bureau head declared that it was "gratifying to report a marked improvement in the morals" of the freedpeople.[6]

The introduction of legal marriage for former slaves was accompanied by efforts at strengthening their families that went well beyond ritual commitment to marriage vows. One widespread but usually frustrating feature of these efforts was the search for loved ones who had been sold apart as slaves. (Others were separated during chaotic wartime conditions, as slaves were moved to safer ground or took advantage of lax controls to run away, men enlisted in the Union Army, women and children flooded into contraband camps, and thousands died from epidemics that ravaged the wartorn population.) Freedmen and women desperate to locate family members tried diverse means, from turning to Union Army officers and Freedmen's Bureau agents for help to publishing advertisements in publications that ranged from short-lived Black newspapers to missionary society organs such as the Philadelphia-based *Christian Recorder*. Often under the heading "Information Wanted," these advertisements listed particulars such as name, relationship, age, former owner, place of ownership, and any known subsequent details such as later ownership or residence. "INFORMATION WANTED Of my father Jerry Hodges, of Norfolk county, Va.," read a typical notice in the *Christian Recorder* in 1870. "I was sold from him when a small girl about 30 years ago. My mother's name was Phoebe, and she belonged to a man named Ashcroth. Should any of the family be living in the vicinity of Norfolk, they will please address EMELINE HODGE Leavenworth, Kan. N.B."; the notice concluded: "Ministers please read in church." The listings were usually short and clinical, although occasional references, such as those to children being "stolen" or " 'owned' " and " 'property' " in quotation marks, indicate the raw emotion that underlay the notices.[7]

Although occasionally freedpeople were able to locate long-lost spouses, children, and parents—the superintendent of freedmen in Hilton Head, South Carolina, reported enthusiastically on "[b]roken families coming together after years, painful years, of separation"—in the majority of cases their searches were doomed to failure. Hopeful former slaves continued for decades to search—and advertise—for loved ones, but their efforts were more significant as markers of their determination than of their ability to restore family ties. "Most people never found their relatives," explained historian Heather Andrea Williams in her detailed study of the subject. "Too many miles and too many years lay between them." Observers related stories of unexpected reunions, some of which were evidently apocryphal. In Mississippi, according to one such story, "in talking over their history," two freedpeople who planned to marry "found to their great astonishment and joy that they were mother and son." The prospective groom, who "had been sold from his mother[']s arms when an infant child thirty years before," proceeded to purchase "a little house by his industry and," reported an admiring Freedmen's Bureau official, "supports his mother." Less felicitous if no doubt more common was a reunion that illustrated the problems that could ensue when separated spouses entered into new relationships, problems that conservative newspapers delighted in mocking. Upon returning to New Orleans, Erastus Letour, "a very 'patriotic' darkey" who had "left his wife and all that was dear to him at home to enlist in the 19th U. S. Colored regiment," returned to find "his wife living in a very respectable family with her 'second husband' "; when she chose the new husband over Letour, he ransacked the house, for which he was fined $25. Such stories served to titillate readers and drove home conflicting didactic messages, but in fact "the desires of former slaves to find family members were rarely fulfilled," and accurate "stories of reunification [were] scarce." More successful than the efforts of former slaves to restore previous family relations by finding missing loved ones would be those to strengthen existing family ties and assert their families' autonomy, while renegotiating what family members owed each other.[8]

Although the impact of emancipation on the families of former Russian serfs was also substantial, it was very different from that on those of the former slaves in the Southern United States. Indeed, in some ways freedom produced opposite results in the two countries. If freed African Americans gained new recognition—and new rights—as husbands, wives, and parents, and sought to bolster family cohesion and independence, Russian peasants found that increased freedom often led to a new fragmentation of traditional, patriarchal families. New conditions of life led to new tensions, as peasants sought work outside their villages, young adults seceded from multigenerational households, and—like African Americans—peasants engaged in basic renegotiations of relationships.

A surge in the number of peasants who sought work away from their home villages was a major cause of this fragmentation. Such outwork was especially—and increasingly—widespread in the central industrial region, where the peasants' small plots of mediocre land were insufficient to provide full support and work in various nonagricultural endeavors. This practice had long been common, but even in the fertile agricultural or black-earth region peasant plots were (deliberately) too small to support freed families, whose members supplemented work on their own land with work for others (in most cases, pomeshchiki). Permission to engage in otkhod, which under serfdom had rested with serfholders, now was a prerogative of the peasant commune, which usually welcomed the possibility of earning outside income and rarely rejected applications for various permits ("passports"), ranging from the very short-term to renewable annual passes that could become essentially permanent. The post-emancipation years therefore saw an enormous growth of temporary labor migration, as former serfs with allotments that were too small and often too unproductive sought to support themselves and their families. Because otkhodniki were usually individual men and women rather than couples or families, and because men engaged in outwork far more often than women, the proliferation of otkhod had profound implications for peasant families.[9]

Almost immediately after emancipation, local authorities and pomeshchiki began complaining about the deleterious effects of the surge in outwork. An article in a "memorandum book" put out by the Kaluga Province Statistical Committee for 1862 set the tone for these complaints. Noting that young peasant men were traveling to "distant parts of Russia" in search of work, the author lamented that they typically lost their attachment to home and agriculture, while cultivation of land fell increasingly on the shoulders of "old men, young children, and women." Three years later, a similar publication from Iaroslavl Province, with a population of just under one million persons (the great majority peasants), listed 130,761 provincial residents—most but not all of whom were peasants—as away on either long-term passports good for six months to three years or short-term "tickets" lasting one to three months. (Well over half of them held long-term passports.) In other words, about 13 percent of the population (and substantially more than 13 percent of the adult population) was engaged in outwork. Otkhodnichestvo was already a massive enterprise.[10]

Over the following decades, it became more massive still (see chapter 5). The rate of otkhodnichestvo varied considerably by region and province, with the practice far more common in the north and the central industrial region than in the more fertile Ukraine, Volga, and southern agricultural regions: in the 1870s, for example, an average of 17 percent of the adult (male and female) peasant population in Iaroslavl Province received passports, compared to 3.8 percent in Saratov Province and 5.3 percent in Kursk Province, but the number grew almost everywhere. By the 1890s, in the forty-three provinces, an average of 15 to 20 percent of adult peasants were receiving passports, and in nonagricultural provinces near Russia's major cities, Moscow and St. Petersburg, the proportion of otkhodniki was substantially higher. (The figures for Moscow and St. Petersburg Provinces in the 1890s were 30 percent and 29 percent of the adult peasant population, respectively.) Male otkhodniki outnumbered female in 1897 by about six to one, but although the impact of male outwork differed from that of female (see below), both contributed to substantial strains on peasant families: a significant and increasing proportion of peasants lived apart from their spouses and families for months and sometimes years at a time.[11]

A related—and in some ways more fundamental—change in peasant family relations involved the increasingly frequent breakup of large, extended family structures through a process known as *razdel,* or "division," whereby traditional multigenerational families were subdivided into smaller nuclear units consisting most often of father, mother, and children. Under serfdom, extended families had occasionally split, but the practice was relatively rare and required the permission of serfholders, who had reasons to favor large families, which were widely considered more economically viable and which— through their patriarchal structure—replicated the authoritarian character of serfdom itself. After 1861, when the peasant commune replaced the serfholder as arbiter of families' right to divide, and when peasant families experienced new centrifugal tendencies associated with otkhod, traditional families came under increasing pressure. As the exiled Populist activist "Stepniak" (Sergei Mikhailovich Kravchinskii) put it in emphasizing the new individualism that shook patriarchal authority, "The children, as soon as they are grown up and have married, will no longer submit to the bolshak's whimsical rule. They rebel, and if imposed upon separate and find new households, where they become masters of their own actions."[12]

The number of such separations did in fact soar during the post-emancipation decades, much to the displeasure of diverse observers and "experts" convinced that divisions indicated—variously—selfish individualism, youthful disrespect, and female jealousy, and typically led to peasant impoverishment. According to incomplete data, there was an annual average of 82,705 divisions among peasant families in all of Russia between 1861 and 1873, and 140,335 from 1874 to 1884. These divisions took several different forms, with differing causes and consequences as well. Some occurred after the death of the family patriarch (*bol'shak* or *khoziain*), others when a son (with his wife and children) set up on his own with the father's permission, and others still as a result of generational conflict between son and father (in which case a departing son lost any share in the equal inheritance rights that male heirs typically enjoyed). Opportunities for off-estate work could figure prominently as well, as did the reduced length of military service from twenty-five to fifteen years in 1859 and then to six years (followed by nine years in the reserves) in 1874, resulting in new tensions as soldiers who previously were effectively gone from their families forever now returned to the fold. Although in theory family divisions required permission of the communal assembly, most in fact occurred informally, without such permission: in Voronezh Province, there were 490 family divisions among former serfs authorized by village assemblies during the decade 1874–84 versus 14,552 that occurred "willfully." If educated observers and government officials tended to blame excessive individualism—especially among peasant women (*baby*, singular: *baba*)—for divisions and took it for granted that *razdely* were "the main source of peasant ruin," peasants typically had a very different perception. As historian Christine Worobec explained, "Peasants attributed the splintering of households to large family size or, in slightly different terms, cramped living quarters, as well as family tensions" springing from "objectionable" behavior, arguments, generational conflicts, and women's grievances.[13]

Throughout the Southern United States, emancipation was accompanied and followed by a massive readjustment in family relations, as human beings were almost overnight transformed from property to citizens—with the attendant rights and obligations—and as family farming became the dominant form of labor among former slaves. Even as men and women acquired legal status as husbands and wives, parents gained new control over their children, and family members faced interacting with each other largely (although not entirely) free of the outside interference to which they had previously been subject. Although most slaves—with important exceptions, including especially house slaves—had lived in family units, in slave cabins, they had also been members of their owners' extended households; most freedpeople, by contrast, had their own households, which were often at the center of independent economic activity (usually farming) conducted not only by landowners but also by various forms of renters, including especially sharecroppers. The transformation of (largely female and child) house servants into members of independent Black households—carefully documented by historian Thavolia Glymph in her book *Out of the House of Bondage*—was perhaps the most striking manifestation of this readjustment. Equally significant (and affecting more freedpeople), however, was the family-based organization of life and labor among the majority of agricultural workers, as plantations were divided into small farms and supervised gang labor gave way to independent, family-oriented cultivation. Just as the abolition of slavery unleashed a massive renegotiation of the terms of labor, so too it made possible—indeed, made necessary—a similar renegotiation of African American family relationships, of how free Black men and women, parents and children, should interact absent the controlling influence of white masters.[14]

This renegotiation took place within the dual and sometimes conflicting contexts of efforts by the freedpeople's putative friends—Yankee reformers from Republican politicians to Union Army officers, Freedmen's Bureau officials, and missionaries—and former owners to impose new standards to replace those now gone with the wind. The reformers offered mixed messages, to varying degrees insisting on the eternal verity of what they regarded as traditional patriarchal values but sometimes making exceptions for the sake of practicality and blaming the corrosive legacy of slavery for the freedpeople's failure to adhere to these values. Although paying lip service to similar if not exactly the same patriarchal values, former owners were usually far more concerned with maintaining Black subservience and labor than they were with cultivating the building blocks of good citizenship among the freedpeople. Meanwhile, most ex-slaves sought to defend their families' independence, even as they also struggled to understand what often appeared to be arcane if not totally unfathomable expectations for their behavior. Explaining that "my object . . . in writing is to ask what I must do," freedman William Bird begged Alabama bureau chief Wager Swayne for advice about how to handle problems stemming from his wife's infidelity, problems that included not only how he could, he wrote, "compel her to obey me" but also who had ultimate authority over their children. Declaring that he did "not want to do anything wrong," Bird beseeched the general, "Answer my letter plainly, so that she and I can understand it fully." Freedman Bill Wyrosdick, who was arrested for living with a white female employee of his, made a similar request in a letter to Swayne, explaining, "[I] proposed to mary hir" so their relationship would be legal "but the Judge woodent suffer me." Imploring Swayne for help—"I shall loose my crop if you don't do something for me"—he concluded deferentially,

"I am igno[r]ant of the laws of the Country. I will try to do write in the future." As Wyrosdick's letter indicated, the rigid sexual separation of the races that whites typically sought to enforce in the post-emancipation years could seem confusing to African Americans, especially in light of the widespread sexual contact that had existed under slavery, most often (but not exclusively) forced, between white men and Black women.[15]

How to avoid doing anything "wrong"—let alone how to "do write"—must have seemed a tall order to many freedpeople, given the eagerness of white observers and authorities to lecture them on their wayward behavior. Although there were numerous manifestations of the determination of African Americans to uphold the integrity of their families while at the same time conforming to societal expectations of correct behavior and resisting efforts to treat their freedom as nominal rather than actual, two issues assumed particular importance during the early post-emancipation years: control over Black children and the work roles of Black women. In both cases, the determined action of freedmen and women was instrumental in securing the autonomy of Black families under precarious conditions.

Gaining control over their children was an essential concern of post-emancipation Black parents. Although legally the abolition of slavery meant that slaveholders lost whatever claim they had over African American children, in practice emancipation unleashed an intense struggle over the extent to which freed children would in fact be free, as many former slaveholders sought to continue in loco parentis. There were several significant elements of this effort, but the most contentious was the widespread movement throughout the South to have Black children apprenticed to their former owners, who claimed that they had the children's best interests at heart. Freedmen's Bureau officials and other observers did not usually buy the argument that planters seeking to apprentice Black children were acting in a disinterested manner, but they often agreed that these children were out of control and needed supervision. "There are many little black children, (say of fourteen Years and under) roving about through the Country," one complainant detailed in a typical report from Auburn, Alabama, "some of them without Fathers, some without mothers and some without either, . . . and there are many black women who have more Children than they can support and no one to help them do it. . . . Worse than all," he concluded ominously, "many of these Children have no one to control them hence they are learning bad Habits."[16]

From the perspective of freedpeople the situation looked very different: slave owners were trying to steal back their children. There was abundant evidence to support such a conclusion, especially since those seeking to apprentice Black children often conflated having no parents with having no parents able to provide suitable support, and apprenticing laws typically provided that a child's prior owner should have first claim to his or her labor. Indeed, in state after state, the conservative "restoration" governments established by President Johnson passed legislation establishing what amounted to a system of forced labor that they hoped would be seen as consistent with the Thirteenth Amendment to the Constitution. In Alabama, for example, the December 1865 apprenticing law, which applied specifically, in its words, to "freedmen, free negroes and mulattoes under the age of eighteen years . . . who are orphans, or whose parents have not the means, or who refuse to provide for and support said minors," directed probate court judges "to apprentice said minors to some competent and suitable person," with the added provision that "the former owner of said minor shall have the preference when proof shall be made that he or she shall be a suitable person for the purpose." For his trouble the apprenticing judge, the law stated, "shall be entitled to a compensation of one dollar to be paid by the master or mistress."[17]

The resulting struggle for control of African American children was intense but short lived, and despite minor variations from state to state eventually ended in victory for those resisting the attempted apprenticing. Developments in two very different states—Alabama and North Carolina—illustrate both the variations and the overall victory. Freedpeople flooded Freedmen's Bureau offices with complaints about efforts by former slave owners to steal their children, aided by judges who clearly interpreted inability or unwillingness to provide support as loosely as possible, both by forcefully taking children away from desperate parents and by ignoring the care provided to children by extended families. Occasionally, literate African Americans wrote to officials—one petitioned President Johnson directly, begging for help in securing the release of his children held in DeKalb County, Alabama, explaining, "The man that have my Childrond says that if I come after them he will kill me"—but most freedpeople complained in person, in an avalanche that threatened to overwhelm bureau agents, some of whom were initially surprised by the volume and intensity of the complaints and unsure how to respond, but most of whom became increasingly willing to intervene on behalf of the bound children. Probate judges, too, were evidently caught off guard by the freedpeople's hostility to apprenticing: one, who inquired of Alabama bureau chief Wager Swayne whether he could "apprentice children without the consent of a mother," noted with some surprise, "Freedwomen . . . have a great antipathy to their children being apprenticed," an aversion that he suspected was "the result of ignorance of the contract and a want of confidence in the faithful performance of the guardian."[18]

North Carolina Freedmen's Bureau officials quickly found themselves at loggerheads with state officials over apprenticing. Responding to Governor Jonathan North's complaint that bureau agents were interfering with the lawful apprenticing of children—"You claim for yourself and subordinates the right to disregard our laws and cancel their decision on *exparte* evidence"—Assistant Commissioner Robinson replied that there had to be no "distinction between the whites and blacks in the apprenticing of children," adding, "No child whose parents are able and willing to support it can be bound without the consent of the parents." Although Robinson's initial position was that the bureau would stop interfering with the apprenticing process as soon as the laws were applied equally to Black and to white children, authorities in Washington soon instructed Robinson's successor, Colonel J. Bomford, to take a tougher stand on the issue. Calling his attention to a decision of the North Carolina Supreme Court invalidating the indenture of children without prior notification of their parents, Acting Assistant Adjutant General A. P. Ketchum declared, "This decision will operate to annul all cases of apprenticeship in the State where the children have been bound out against the will of their parents, and in the future to protect the freedpeople from injustice and oppression in this respect. In cases already reported," Ketchum directed Bomford, "you will instruct your Officers and Agents to take the necessary steps to secure the cancellation of all indentures thus decided to be illegal." Bureau agents quickly complied with the new directive: the superintendent in charge of Warren, Franklin, and Granville Counties "canceled seventy-seven indentures in the first eight months of 1867 alone," and as historian Laura F. Edwards observed, with North Carolina's new Republican regime that came to power in 1868, "African-American households now occupied the same legal position as white households," most judges were elected rather than appointed, Black men served on juries, and, "not coincidentally, apprenticeship cases all but disappeared."[19]

The struggle over apprenticing in Alabama proceeded along similar lines, although the practice was more widespread—especially in the state's plantation-dominated Black Belt region, where the shortage of labor was severe—and the resistance correspondingly more intense. Beginning in December 1865, almost immediately after passage of the state's apprenticing law, and accelerating through 1866, freedpeople and sympathetic whites bombarded Freedmen's Bureau offices with complaints protesting the forced apprenticing of Black children. Such complaints were especially numerous about Probate Judge J. F. Waddell, in Russell County, who as early as 27 December 1865 received an inquiry from a bureau agent stating, based on reports, "that you are binding Color[e]d minor Children and making No distinction between those who have Parrents [sic] and those who have none." In a plaintive deposition, freedwoman Laura Taylor, whose two children were bound without her knowledge or consent to a planter in Russell County, told how she "stole her children, but the Sheriff of the County pursued her and took the children back." When she begged Waddell "to have the children restored to her, he would not listen to her, saying the children were bound, no matter with or without her consent. He threatened to put her in Jail if she would come again." Elsewhere in the state as well, distressed African Americans implored Freedmen's Bureau officials for help in securing their children. A "humble freedwoman" named Lucy Abney explained how her thirteen-year-old granddaughter, whose parents were both dead, had "cried at the thought of separating from her grandma" when she was bound out to a man who claimed to be a bureau agent, adding that "her father was hardly cold" and "there was to[o] much hurry to get her." "General, I don[']t know the way to apply to you in because I don[']t know your rules," she explained to Assistant Commissioner Swayne; "I have got a white friend to write this for me." In another appeal to Swayne, a correspondent wrote that three children who "were 'bound' last December in a few hours after their mother's death" were living "now in worse slavery than they ever were," even though their uncle and aunt were "doing well as freedmen" and wanted to care for the children. Like judges elsewhere, those in Alabama appeared to be surprised by the number and intensity of complaints about apprenticing coming from African Americans: "These people have a great hor[r]or to being apprenticed," generalized one judge who himself had bound out children, adding that even though the apprentices were "well treated[,] yet not one of them would suffer their children for any amount, to stand in the relation an apprentice does to the master."[20]

At first, Alabama's Freedmen's Bureau officials were unsure how to handle the apprenticing issue, to which they responded in diverse ways. If some agents assumed from the beginning that apprenticing children without their parents' permission was inappropriate and perhaps illegal, others were unsure. Assistant Superintendent Spencer Smith, who had complained about Judge Waddell's eagerness to separate children from their parents and "sent some of the minors so apprenticed [back] to their Parrents," sought clarification from higher authorities: "Please inform me whether I am correct in the course I am pursuing or not," he begged. "It is causing an immense amount of trouble to the Freedmen." Swayne himself at first took a cautious stand, accepting the legitimacy of apprenticing so long as it was applied in a race-neutral manner: "Nothing in the tenor of these laws or their present channel of administration forbids application to colored orphans, or other children," he declared in a circular, "where humanity plainly requires such interposition, the same as if they were white persons."[21]

Before long, however, the sheer volume of complaints rendered such complacency untenable—not only to bureau agents but also to some judges. As early as January 1866, one probate judge decided that he would stop binding out children without first consulting with their parents about the appropriateness of their apprenticeship, and if he decided to proceed, determining "their wishes as to whom they desire them bound to." Significantly, the main reason for his change of heart was the inconvenience—to him—caused by Black parents seeking to have indentures revoked. "Cases of this sort will be constantly occurring and it is occupying too much of my time," he explained to Swayne. "There are very few if any cases where parents will be willing to bind their children whether they can support them or not or whether their children can support them[selves]." In short, his modified policy, the judge wrote, was necessary to "avoid having every freedman in the County annoying me by explanations, applications, &c." Similar inconvenience, growing doubts about both the feasibility and the desirability of forcibly assigning Black children to the care of their previous owners, and the changing political climate eventually led the bureau to take decisive action. Stating, "Complaints of hardship in the needless apprenticing of minors ... have been almost incessant," Swayne's General Orders No. 3, issued in April 1867, instructed "Probate Judges, upon application, to revise the action taken in such cases, and as a rule to revoke indentures made within the past two years, of minors who were capable of self support." Later, in explaining his action to Commissioner Howard, Swayne denounced "the corrupt exercise of a discretionary power" whereby "every former slaveholder might have the children of his former slaves apprenticed to him until they were twenty one."[22]

The combination of massive Black protests, the Freedmen's Bureau's toughened stand, and the accession to power of the (Republican) Reconstruction regime in 1867 brought to an end the post-emancipation effort of Alabama planters and conservative politicians to institutionalize the forced apprenticeship of young African Americans. A spate of reports from bureau officials in June 1867 indicated that new apprenticing had largely ceased and judges were revoking existing indentures in conformity with General Order No. 3, "upon all applications by the parents of apprenticed children. The number of these applications," reported one bureau agent, "is large." In other states as well, the story was similar: the determined resistance of the freed population was instrumental in defending the integrity of Black families and preventing the effective perpetuation of slavery through the co-optation of child labor. At the same time, the effort to combat the involuntary apprenticing of Black children revealed the important role not only of immediate parents but also of extended family members and the broader African American community as freedpeople strove to develop lives independent of their former owners.[23]

The effort to appropriate Black *women's* labor met with a similar response from freedpeople, who once again combined to defend family integrity and resist a hated remnant of slavery. Under the slave regime, as members of both the slaveholders' extended households and their own family households, most enslaved women had toiled involuntarily for their owners—whether in the big house or, more often, in the field—even as they also performed the bulk of domestic labor for their own families. Emancipation freed them from this double obligation and allowed them to devote more of their time to their newly independent Black households. In their doing so, they not only struck a blow for the autonomy of those households but also put to the test the commitment of white Americans—from their Republican allies to their former masters and would-be employers—to various versions of patriarchy centered on the ideal of "separate spheres," an ideal that prescribed rigid gender roles confining women largely to the domestic sphere rather than that of paid labor. In theory, most proponents of "free labor" were also committed to separate spheres; as General Clinton Fisk, the Freedmen's Bureau's assistant commissioner for Kentucky and Tennessee, lectured the freedpeople, a true woman was "man's strength, the charm of the household," whereas "a foolish, vain, cross, idle, slovenly woman is the meanest creature that ever clotted the fair creation of God." But for many proponents of this ideal, including some bureau officials and Republican politicians, domesticity somehow seemed a condition less appropriate for freedwomen than for bourgeois ladies; indeed, the risk that Black women would not work without physical compulsion—often equated with laziness—appeared a greater threat to free-labor morality than the breaching of separate gender spheres.[24]

Throughout the South, a central component of the freedpeople's struggle to defend their interests as free workers was the determination of freed *women* to reduce the time they spent doing field work for planters. Observers gave different explanations of this phenomenon—and of the motive behind it. Some, like the head of the Freedmen's Bureau in Florida, placed the primary blame on

Black *men,* describing them as "averse to their women and children going into the field as common laborers," wanting them instead "to attend to *the house work,* as they express it, *like white folks.*" Planters—and other defenders of the old regime—typically accused freedwomen of wanting to "play the lady and be supported by their husbands 'like the white folks do.' " The Selma *Daily Messenger* complained, "Most of the field labor is now generally performed by men, the women regarding it as the duty of their husbands to support them in idleness," a view echoed by a probate judge in the Alabama Black Belt who lamented that although Blacks had large families, "none of them [would] work except the man, the head of the family." He added, "Many of the women and children have ceased to work and lead an idle life." Some bureau agents agreed that free Black women seemed disinclined to work: John W. De Forest denounced the "evil of female loaferism" in up-country South Carolina, noting, "[Freedwomen] have aspirations to be like white ladies and, instead of using the hoe, pass the days in dawdling over their trivial housework, or gossiping among their neighbors." A Black man in Georgia put still a different spin on work and laziness, accusing his sister, who, he said, "abscondit from Savannah two months ago," of joining a group of prostitutes at Hilton Head. "Dear General," he wrote to Commissioner Howard, "my sister and the other Women will tell [you] that they make Dresses," but in fact "they spent the night sinfull and sleep to 10 o'clock every morning," adding, "The Colored Wom[e]n on Hilton Head are a disgrace to our race."[25]

In fact, the much-noted withdrawal of female laborers from field work reflected both shared assumptions about proper gender relations among free people and a desire of many women to work more for their families and less for their former owners. These women did not necessarily *abandon* agricultural labor—over time, economic exigency led many to return to plantation labor, and others continued to cultivate their own crops even as they spurned being engaged as hired workers—but they did *reduce* their participation in the paid workforce: even as peasant women in much of Russia were assuming a greater share of agricultural labor as their husbands sought work away from home, freedwomen in much of the South were performing a smaller share of traditional cultivation. In some cases, as on many Lowcountry rice estates, they opted for part-time rather than full-time field work: in South Carolina's Georgetown District, the proportion of women contracting as "full" hands fell between 1866 and 1868 from 69 percent to 34 percent, while others "worked according to their own preferences, frequently disregarding the terms set forth in written contracts." More often, in the cotton South, some freedwomen continued to engage in plantation field labor even as others cut back or turned entirely to household engagement. The 1870 manuscript census returns for Alabama showed a patchwork of seemingly conflicting trends that together added up to a significant shift in women's work patterns: in some sample districts, most Black women were listed as working (usually as agricultural laborers), while in others most were "keeping house" or "at home"; the contrast seemed to cut across geographic regions such as Black Belt and hill country and may in part have reflected the idiosyncratic reporting of individual census takers, but it is clear that throughout the South emancipation made it possible for many women to pay more time and attention to their own families. The same was true of women who had worked as domestic servants—who, as historian Thavolia Glymph has shown, often moved from the "big house" to their own households and who engaged in intensive bargaining with plantation mistresses to limit the kinds of domestic work they would now perform as well as the number of hours they would be expected to put in—and indeed the hours of many freed*men* as well. Historians Roger L. Ransom and Richard Sutch estimated that in the 1870s, rural Blacks in the cotton South reduced the number of hours they worked per year for their employers by an average of between 28 and 37 percent compared to the hours they had logged as slaves in the 1850s, with the reductions greatest for women (41–55 percent) and children (39–54 percent), but still a hefty 16–22 percent for men. Despite the widespread charges of Black laziness, freedpeople continued to work hard, but they were now working somewhat less for their former owners and considerably more for themselves. As historian Sharon Ann Holt put it, independent household production was "the crucial 'escape clause' in the freedpeople's agreement to till the white man's land."[26]

In contrast to the former slaves, who sought to bolster families that had been battered under the slave regime and faced continued threats to their independence even after emancipation, former serfs in Russia often sought to escape the confining features of traditional peasant families, in the process initiating a substantial transformation of both the size and the structure of those families. Despite significant variations based on region, status, and individual proclivities (of both pomeshchiki and serfs), traditional peasant families before emancipation had been both large and authoritarian. Often consisting of three or four generations rather than the small nuclear units typically found in slave households of the Southern United States, and sometimes extended laterally (with two or more brothers and their families living under one roof) as well as vertically, serf families were dominated by the family patriarch—the *bol'shak* or *khoziain*—whose despotic rule replicated the hierarchy and authoritarianism of serfdom itself. Both serf owners and communal officials believed that large families were economically more viable than small, and they acted to encourage early marriage and prevent family divisions; in a typical instruction to his stewards, one eighteenth-century serf owner ordered them to promote large households so as to avoid "squalor." Before emancipation, the average serf household contained more than eight persons, a figure substantially higher than did the pre-serfdom peasant household—about five.[27]

That changed dramatically during the post-emancipation years. As families divided and millions of peasants sought work away from their villages, the number of residents per household contracted, the proportion of families that conformed to the traditional patriarchal structure decreased, and new tensions emerged with families struggling to take advantage of changed conditions and "modern" norms challenging time-honored customs. Because large peasant households inevitably produced enmity and tension, wrote Englishman Sir Donald Mackenzie Wallace, who traveled extensively through Russia in the 1870s, "when the authority of the landed proprietors was abolished by the Emancipation Edict of 1861, the large peasant families almost all crumbled to pieces. The arbitrary rule of the Khoz[i]aïn was based on, and maintained by, the arbitrary rule of the proprietor, and both naturally fell together." Wallace added, "[Although] this change has unquestionably had a prejudicial influence on the material welfare of the peasantry, . . . it must have added considerably to their domestic comfort, and may perhaps produce good moral results." It would be an exaggeration to say that village life was totally "revolutionized," and some historians have been at pains to stress the basic continuity of traditional ways, but peasant families underwent significant changes, some of which became evident fairly quickly, while others were less obvious and evolved over decades.[28]

Easiest to document is the decreased size of peasant households. At the local level, this decrease is clearly evident in population statistics for the Saratov district of Saratov Province, in the agricultural heartland, where the fall in household size was especially marked. On the eve of emancipation, in 1858, the district had 14,893 peasant households with 118,888 residents (58,430 males and 60,458 females), for an average of 7.98 persons per household. Twenty-five years later, the census of 1882–83 listed 27,957 peasant households with 150,435 residents (74,378 males and 76,062 females), for an average of 5.38 persons per household. In one generation, the average household had decreased in size by almost one-third (32.6 percent). Not all regions of Russia saw equally great declines in household size. In the central non-black-earth region the average number of peasants per household fell 23.5 percent between 1850 and 1897 and in the northwestern provinces the decrease was 17.6 percent, whereas in the more fertile agricultural areas—even as peasant families remained larger than those where land was unproductive and otkhod was greatest—the contraction of households was greater still: 38.2 percent in the central black-earth provinces and 34.1 percent in the Volga region. Still, throughout Russia as a whole the trend was clear: in 1850 there was an average of 8.4 peasants per household, whereas in 1897 the average was only 5.8—a decrease of 31 percent.[29]

Just as significant as the decrease in the *size* of peasant households was the beginning of an accelerating change in their *structure*, especially in nonagricultural regions. Although the process was uneven (and in some areas in little evidence), the large, multigenerational family dominated by a powerful patriarch increasingly gave way to a smaller, nuclear family—husband, wife, and children—sometimes with an additional relative or nonrelative as well. This trend was most prevalent—almost by definition—among young couples who left the extended family for life on their own, but it was also common more generally. In eight sample agricultural villages in Riazan and Tambov Provinces, for example, where "undivided" (usually multigenerational) families had prevailed under serfdom, by the 1890s such families remained only slightly more common than those with a nuclear structure—187 to 120. Answering questions contained in the wide-ranging Ethnographic Bureau survey conducted in the 1890s under the direction of Prince V. N. Tenishev, respondents in Vladimir Province indicated the prevalence among peasants of "small," nuclear families. "Families now are small," reported one respondent from the province's Vladimir district. "Married sons rarely live with their father." In the Shuiskii district, wrote another, "large families are few, and each year they are becoming fewer." In the Melenkovskii district as well, nuclear families, consisting "only of a husband, a wife, and their children," were most common.[30]

Vladimir Province, in the central industrial region and not far from Moscow, was not entirely typical of all Russia. Still, in a careful study, historian Boris Mironov has found that by the national census of 1897, "the nuclear family dominated in all regions except the central black-earth region and Byelorussia," although because extended families were significantly larger, more peasants continued to live in extended than in nuclear families. The trend, however, was clear: everywhere, "the younger generation preferred nuclear families." One result, which partially explained the economic concerns that family divisions precipitated, was a decrease in the number of working hands per family. Even in the overwhelmingly agricultural Voronezh Province, smaller families resulted in fewer members to work the land: in 1874, 30.9 percent of 72,108 families of former serfs had three or more workers, whereas a decade later the corresponding figure had shrunk to 24 percent of 84,127 families. During the same period, the proportion of families with only one worker increased from 36.6 percent to 44.7 percent.[31]

As the sharp increase in family divisions suggests, changed conditions inevitably produced tensions within peasant families. Some of these tensions were new, created by the need to renegotiate relations both among peasants themselves and between peasants and outsiders, whether former owners or government authorities. Others represented exacerbations of existing frictions in lives that were already far from harmonious. This dual character can be seen as lending support both to scholars emphasizing changes in postemancipation family relations among peasants and to those stressing the basic continuity of peasant family life, or, to put it differently, as rendering apparently conflicting interpretations—sometimes put forth by the same historian—more compatible than they first appear. To take one example, Mironov, who described the traditional patriarchal family as "an absolutist state in microcosm," argued that "in the last third of the nineteenth century, the weakening of the family's old patriarchal system accelerated" and "relations within the peasant family gradually became more humane." He also suggested, however, that, especially in agricultural provinces, "by relying on traditional institutions such as the commune, the peasantry was able to resist these changes," and estimated that "the authoritarian family was democratized among [only] 15 percent of the peasant population and underwent a slow decline among the remaining 85 percent."[32]

Before exploring the growing tensions among peasant families, it is instructive to revisit the Southern United States, where internal tensions also accompanied the transformation of freed families as freedpeople renegotiated relationships under radically changed conditions. The transfer of power over Black families from slaveholders to the family members themselves raised significant questions relating to what these family members owed—and could expect from—each other, questions that pertained to relations between husbands and wives as well as between parents and children. The freedpeople's requests (noted above) for explanation of the "rules"—what was and was not permissible under the new dispensation—indicated the extent to which relationships among free men, women, and children required both renegotiation and clarification. Historians have recently begun to pay more attention to disputes and violence among slaves, and the idea of a harmonious slave community now seems a quaint artifact of a particular moment in historical interpretation rather than an essential feature of slave life. But although discord within African American families was not entirely new, there is considerable evidence that the overthrow of slavery led to heightened struggles over authority and control within Black families. As historian Wilma King sensibly suggested, "Just as freedom offered a chance to exchange nuptial vows and legalize marriages, it also provided the opportunity to terminate undesirable unions." More generally, if slave owners no longer owned Black families, who was in charge? And with what authority?[33]

Four quotations together hint at the nature and scope of the problem. A Freedmen's Bureau official in South Carolina observed—in a typical statement—that freedpeople "seem to have no regard for the marriage relation," noting, "They separate for slight reasons, and if compelled to live together again, do so for a short time only" and adding, "Many freedmen seem to think they have a perfect right to whip their wives." As if to respond directly to the charge of neglecting the sanctity of marriage, Dink Watkins, a Black woman in North Carolina who had left her husband for another man, announced, "I am my own woman and I will do as I please." Alabama freedman William Bird, who had very different ideas about women's independence and husbands' marital rights, wrote the state's bureau chief Wager Swayne asking how he could keep his wife in line: "Can I not by *moderate* chastisement compel her to obey me?" he inquired. And one of the bluntest assertions of male authority came from freedman Silas Green, in Washington County, Mississippi, who described his wife Mary Jane as "owned by me as a wife" and noted, "She has always been called by my name."[34]

As these (and other similar) comments suggest, the abolition of slavery raised serious questions about the relations not only between former slaves and former owners but also between freedmen and freedwomen. There was a thin line between women having the right to shun field work so they could pay more attention to their families and women having the right to choose new families; there was an equally thin line between men expecting their wives to devote themselves to domestic duties and men expecting women to be subordinate and obedient at home. During the immediate post-emancipation period, even as some freedmen complained about insubordinate or inattentive wives, freedwomen flooded Freedmen's Bureau offices with complaints about abusive husbands. As historian Dylan Penningroth has pointed out, the break-up of the slave quarters and women's increased focus on household labor meant that women were now working more than before "under the watchful eyes of their husbands and relatives," who came to take unpaid women's work for granted. Bureau agents were often sympathetic with the plight of such women, and the bureau did set up Freedmen's Courts in several states to handle minor disputes (in other states bureau officials acted on their own, without Freedmen's Courts), but as historian Mary Farmer-Kaiser has argued, barring particularly egregious cases the agents were usually more interested in securing "racial rather than gender equality," and they typically assumed "female dependency," including the right of "black men to control and contract the labor of family members."[35]

The increased parental authority that came with emancipation often resulted in new tensions between parents (especially fathers) and children as well. Even under slavery, child labor had been an essential ingredient of work on the garden plots that many enslaved families were able to work as their "own," and—as with Russian peasants—the size of slave families contributed directly to their accumulation of property. As formerly enslaved men became "masters" of their own households, the opportunities for their exploitation of children increased dramatically, whether through the appropriation of their labor or the exercise of physical compulsion on their bodies. As Penningroth has noted, "Many black people assumed that freedom would entitle them to claim their younger relatives' working hours" and "years later, some former slaves had searing memories of the work their parents demanded from them in the 1860s and 1870s." Some parents also welcomed the right to physically punish their children that had previously belonged to slave owners. "By the 1870s, white landowners still stood at the top of the South's economic order," suggested Penningroth, "but few of them bossed black children in the fields any more. Black grown-ups did." As historian Catherine A. Jones pointed out, occasionally "children who felt ill-treated by their parents" challenged those parents' authority over them, and "evidence of parental abuse or neglect . . . occasionally convinced the Freedmen's Bureau to intercede" on their behalf, "over parental objections." The question of who had the right to punish whom underlay the struggle over mastery itself, a struggle perceptively framed by historian Nancy Bercaw: "Blacks protested when whites beat them, women protested when their husbands beat them, and black men and women protested when whites beat them for beating each other. . . . The complex web of abuse reflected the struggle on the part of blacks and whites to assert independence and control by commanding others by force."[36]

As an old man, Ned Cobb (known as Nate Shaw in his remarkable autobiography recorded by Theodore Rosengarten) still had harrowing memories of being exploited by his father in late nineteenth-century Alabama. "My daddy was a free man but in his acts he was a slave," Cobb related, describing a loveless relationship in which his father ordered him around—"do so-and-so-and-so"—and valued him solely for the work he could perform. "That's what he wanted me for," Cobb recalled. "He didn't know nothin but to work me." Self-centered and impulsive, the senior Cobb beat his wife and severely whipped Ned, who "never did forget none of his treatments" and followed through with his determination to obey his father until he turned twenty-one—and not a day longer. "A child aint got no business buckin his parents," Ned explained, but "parents aint got no business beatin a child."[37]

Ned Cobb was an exceptional person—in many ways the opposite of the father he depicted in his autobiography—remarkable for his near-photographic memory, his industriousness, and his sense of decency. Certainly, the physical punishment of children that he condemned was widely accepted among white and Black Americans. The generational tension that he described, however, was evident to other observers as well, even if they did not always reach the same conclusions about its causes or significance. Indeed, even as they complained about Black men playing the master by punishing children (and women), many white Southerners were convinced that the chief problem faced by free Black children was too little discipline, not too much. This was certainly true of several witnesses who testified before a U.S. Senate committee investigating labor relations throughout the United States that held hearings in Alabama in 1883; at these hearings, one white witness after another described Blacks growing up in the post-slavery era as turbulent and out of control. Former governor Robert Patton complained, "[Whereas] in slavery times, the young negroes were raised under discipline and government, . . . now they are running about night and day" because "their parents have not the capacity or the intelligence to control them." A carriage manufacturer in Opelika was more succinct. "The young negroes are growing up here very worthless," he declared. "You can't get them to work. They seem to want to make a living without work."[38]

Despite these comments, in many ways Black families, freed from the constraints of slavery, came to resemble white families. This was most notably true with respect to their size and structure, especially in the countryside, where the vast majority of Black and white Southerners lived. In nine sample districts of Alabama (five rural and four urban), the manuscript census returns of 1870 revealed Black and white households that were about the same average size (between four and five residents per household), had similar marital rates for adult residents, and contained about the same number of children (between two and three) per married couple. (Racial differences were greater in the relatively small number of "mixed" households, containing both Blacks—usually house servants—and whites.) Variations among the districts were typically greater than variations between white and Black families within individual districts. Although cities tended to have more unmarried adults than rural areas, only in Mobile's sample Second Ward were about half the adults (both Black and white) unmarried; elsewhere, the proportion of unmarried adults typically ranged from one-fifth to one-third for both whites and Blacks, and the great majority of both white and Black families with children were headed by husband-and-wife couples. Historian Vernon Burton found similar results in Edgefield County, South Carolina: in 1870 and 1880, about two-thirds of both the white and the Black households consisted of nuclear families, about three-quarters of these households contained children, and the vast majority—83.7 percent for Black and 82 percent for white households—had adult males present. Only in the county's "small towns and villages"—it contained no real city—did Black families show evidence, after the end of Reconstruction, of "the first signs of the disruption that became characteristic of their counterparts in the great cities of industrial America."[39]

The point is not that Black families were exactly the same as white families (which differed among themselves as well). Indeed, recently historians increasingly began stressing the diversity and variability of Black families, after emancipation as well as before. Nancy Bercaw, for example, has noted the "flexible households" that continued to exist in the Mississippi Delta, with informal relationships developed under slavery, including "taking up" and "sweethearting," coexisting with formal marriage, "which many freedpeople fit into a broader understanding of household." Noralee Frankel has suggested that, unlike white families, Black families in post-emancipation Mississippi "were male-headed but not patriarchal": although "African American men exercised more power in relation to African American women than during slavery, . . . they held much less power than white men did over white women." And some distinctive traits of slave families—including a heightened role of extended family members and in some cases the broader community—continued to buttress the more narrowly focused nuclear family in much of the South.[40]

Post-emancipation Black families faced the dual tasks of defending their interests in a hostile environment even as they also contended with renegotiating internal relations among family members. Although these renegotiations produced tensions that to some extent cut across their parallel efforts to build free autonomous families, the freedpeople successfully resisted efforts of former slave owners to intervene in their family lives, insisted that they controlled their own children, and—in the countryside, where most of them lived and worked—rooted independent families in independent productive households. In the process, they both built on kinship ties that had existed under slavery and created new, transformed families as they grappled with the uncertainties of a precarious freedom.

Despite the significant differences in the way emancipation affected the families of the former slaves and serfs, emancipation in Russia, as in the United States, accentuated both generational and gender conflict. The former was central to the growing number of young married couples who insisted on leaving their extended families to set up on their own, in the process challenging both the authority of and respect for the family patriarch, or *bol'shak*. "Humane" treatment of peasant children, which had been rare under serfdom, remained less than common under the new dispensation. Many children died before reaching adulthood, and those who didn't seemed valued principally for their ability to work and, as the number of otkhodniki surged, to send money back to relatives remaining in their villages. Respondents to the Tenishev Ethnographic Bureau survey painted a grim picture of childhood in Vladimir Province, with parents having "complete authority" over their children, including hiring them out and arranging their marriages (although "in recent times"—the 1890s—the number of forced marriages was "diminished"). If children were treated "gently"—at least by being left to themselves—until the age of six or seven, when they typically began to work, thereafter they were handled "more strictly and exactingly"; for "pranks," one respondent explained, adults "beat them, swore at them (using such epithets as 'dogs,' 'damned,' and 'base'), and punished them with whips"; from an early age, they frightened children with diverse "horrors," from various evil spirits to "doctors and priests." Peasants used to being ordered around easily applied similar standards to their own children—as one scholar, in noting "no especial closeness or affection . . . between parents and children," generalized, "children were brought up strictly," with "complete obedience . . . demanded of them." Yet outside observers often concluded that (as in the Southern United States) the post-emancipation generation was "less deferential and more threatening" or in the words of one nobleman "wild, lazy, thievish, obstinate, afraid to be alone, impudent and frenzied, like a beast in a crowd." Olga Tian-Shanskaia, a young noblewoman who carefully observed the peasants near her family's estate in the Dankov district of Riazan Province a generation after emancipation, not only stressed the harsh treatment that peasants meted out to their children but also commented on what she considered the declining morality of the young: "In the past, there were quite a few [sexually] inexperienced boys and girls," she wrote, "but nowadays 'innocent' boys are not to be found and even girls without experience are rather few." She noted, however, that whereas parents punished girls for engaging in premarital sex, they did not apply similar sanctions to boys.[41]

This differential treatment of sexual experimentation by boys and girls represented only the tip of the iceberg of what amounted to pervasive misogyny among the peasants that not only led to increased tensions between men and women after emancipation but also distinguished the experiences of Russian from American freedpeople. Both the patriarchal family itself and widely accepted communal values conspired to shape the unhappy lot of female peasants, who were typically objects of derision and violent abuse at all stages of life, from before birth—when couples hoped for the arrival of a boy rather than a girl—to adulthood, when women were commonly objects of suspicion, hostility, and beatings. In response to the Tenishev survey, a respondent from Vladimir Province's Melenkovskii district noted that peasants regarded the birth of a boy as a "blessing," whereas the arrival of a girl seemed a "burden." As historian Rose Glickman generalized, although women's subordination was hardly unique to Russia, there "the peasant woman was subordinate not only to one father or one husband but to the entire male community."[42]

Emancipation put to the test the patriarchal structure of peasant families, created new opportunities for—as well as tensions between—men and women, and in some cases led to challenges to women's extreme subordination. The increasing prevalence of outwork made possible by emancipation meant that many men and women were living apart from each other more often, and for longer stretches; such separation—which most often resulted from otkhod of married men—had numerous repercussions, which, depending on one's outlook, had both positive and negative implications. The prevalence of male otkhod near major cities and more generally in the less fertile provinces meant that women were disproportionately central not only to family interaction but also to agricultural labor. If the extra agricultural burden on women with absent husbands was most obvious, there could be significant advantages to such women as well. Absent husbands did not substantially increase the wives' share of childcare, because most peasant men ordinarily spent relatively little time with their children, and lengthy male absence also reduced this burden, by reducing the number of children women bore. (In two districts of Kostroma Province where male otkhod was especially prevalent, even though "the rate of marriage ... was higher than the average for rural Kostroma, the birthrate per thousand inhabitants was considerably lower.") Meanwhile, because village women often received money and goods from absent husbands, and were spared the frequent beatings and abuse that was the lot of many wives, some women saw real advantages in being married to otkhodniki. One of the most pronounced of these advantages was greater independence: as historian Barbara Engel put it, "In men's absence, women worked harder but breathed more freely." In some cases, such women not only became, in effect, household heads but even "assumed their husbands' places at the village assembly and fulfilled the offices of representative and elder."[43]

The outwork of peasant women had less impact on rural families, both because female otkhod was so much rarer than male and because, unlike most male otkhodniki, women who sought outside work were typically unmarried. Of course, for the women themselves, many of whom engaged in domestic work in cities and others of whom worked in textile factories or engaged in "backbreaking, dirty, poorly paid labor in other people's fields," the impact was all-encompassing and often long-term: in the 1890s, women from Iaroslavl Province remained away from home—often in Moscow—for an average of more than nine years. For most peasant women in cities, life was precarious: they were poorly paid, usually lived alone, faced difficulty finding husbands, experienced sexual exploitation, and often bore illegitimate children. (In both Moscow and St. Petersburg, more than one-quarter of births were to unmarried women in the late nineteenth century, compared to under 2 percent in villages.) Urban prostitution was widespread, and although otkhodniki hardly had a monopoly on the practice—they constituted about half of St. Petersburg's prostitutes in the late nineteenth century with another 7–13 percent consisting of *soldatki* (wives and daughters of soldiers)—they often suffered from reputations for having "loose" sexual morals. At the other extreme were small numbers of peasant women who either "live[d] a life of prayer and celibacy," living on their own and supporting themselves through "spinning, weaving, knitting, or day labor," or joined "unofficial women's religious communities" (*zhenskie obshchiny*) that were essentially nunneries.[44]

The extent to which emancipation weakened the patriarchal peasant family— a subject that has generated considerable disagreement among historians— depends on what one means by the term. In addition to the decreased size of many families, new opportunities provided by otkhod decreased the ability of the *bol'shak*—whom one historian described as "a weakened figure by the end of the [nineteenth] century"—to wield absolute authority over family members (and for that matter the ability of his wife, the *bol'shukha*, to control the family's domestic life and to tyrannize daughters-in-law), as did the growing independence of women in villages where male outwork was widespread as well as of women otkhodniki on their own in urban areas. One sign of this growing independence was the frequency with which women "refused to play by the rules of peasant patriarchy" by resisting mistreatment, complaining to local authorities, and—rarely—seeking divorce from abusive husbands. Just as Black women often complained of domestic violence to Freedmen's Bureau officials, so too peasant women took advantage of the newly established volost' courts to bring charges against abusive family members—usually in-laws but also husbands. On the basis of 2,108 sample court cases from forty-four townships in four provinces (Moscow, Kostroma, Iaroslavl, and Tambov) during the period 1866–72, historian Beatrice Farnsworth found that women were involved in about one-third of the cases, and that at least some of the time the courts found in their favor, imposing punishments that most often involved floggings and in eight of twelve cases allowing women to separate from their husbands. Noting that "peasant women . . . asserted and exercised rights, and instigated family and community change to a degree not hitherto recognized," Farnsworth suggested that these cases "represent[ed] the tip of the iceberg of discontent."[45]

The weakening of patriarchal authority—as Barbara Engel put it, "Rural patriarchy was modified, but it nevertheless remained intact"—went hand in hand with the partial (and increasing) subversion of traditional values by new ways introduced in part by otkhodniki returning to or visiting their home villages and boosted by emerging "market relations" among the post-emancipation peasantry. New luxuries appeared in villages—especially in the central industrial region—from more elaborate peasant cottages to kerosene lamps, fancy furniture, clocks, cosmetics, manufactured clothing, and "urban" food such as white bread, while parish priests (and others) fretted that otkhodniki were losing their faith and failing to fulfill requisite orthodox rituals. Despite these tentative signs—and fears—of newly emerging "modern" values among the peasantry, however, most historians have been more impressed by the persistence than by the erosion of traditional peasant ways. Arranged marriage remained the norm and—unlike in Western Europe—marriage was at an early age and almost universal, courting and marriage rituals were often largely unchanged, and the strengthened role of the village commune undergirded continued respect for traditional relationships. Engel's assertion of the continuation of a modified peasant patriarchy is consistent with the judgment of many other scholars, such as Laura Engelstein's that even after emancipation "patriarchy had barely been touched by the winds of change" and Boris Mironov's that despite the beginnings of "democratization," among the vast majority of the peasant population—85 percent—"the authoritarian family" saw only "a slow decline."[46]

The most persistent and distinctive feature of continued patriarchy in the peasant family was in the subordinate—indeed, degraded—position of women. As in the Southern United States, the postscript to bondage involved a good deal of uncertainty, and sometimes a peasant would—in the words of noblewoman Olga Tian-Shanskaia—treat his wife "as his personal property." But the level of mistreatment and frequency of physical violence in Russia were exceptional, and commented on by numerous observers, both at the time and later. "A young husband who finds out that his bride has not been chaste sometimes beats her cruelly on his wedding night," wrote Tian-Shanskaia from Riazan Province, "and this may serve as only a prelude to beatings that stretch out over the course of several months." Noting the widespread violence meted out to peasant women and children in the 1890s, land captain Aleksandr Novikov concluded that peasants should not be blamed for their "roughness," because they knew no better and thought of family members only in terms of their utility and value. Describing a case in which a peasant who was carrying on an affair with a neighbor's wife beat her severely when he found out that she was also sleeping with a peasant from a nearby village, pomeshchik Aleksandr Nikolaevich Engelgardt noted, shortly after returning for the first time in years to his family estate in Smolensk Province in 1872, "The muzhiks watch out for the babas of their village, so they don't amuse themselves with outsiders; it's no big deal if they go with men of their own village, that's the husband's affair, but with outsiders—they had better not." Noting that most (male) peasants accepted wifebeating—although not *excessive* wifebeating—as normal, historian Christine Worobec observed that women who complained of mistreatment to volost' courts rarely found justice at the hands of "[m]ale peasant judges [who] supported the patriarchal system." Instead, "*volost'* court judges arrested women for stubbornness, rudeness, coarseness of language, and disobedience toward their husbands in the courtroom." Historian Sally West, who studied advertising in post-emancipation Russia, noted the "strong vein of misogyny" in "Russian peasant and urban lower class popular culture," including "denigration of wives, stereotypes of old hags, and lewd innuendo about loose women." Advertisements directed at men emphasized "strength and sexual virility," whereas for women "smooth skin was important ... but more essential still [was] a large bosom, [which] combined beauty and womanhood." Historian Laura Engelstein put it more simply: "If the peasants were a foreign country, women were a foreign race." But perhaps nothing indicates the contrast between the position of freed girls and women in Russia with that in the Southern United States so much as their different experiences with schooling and literacy during the decades after emancipation.[47]

For both freed African Americans and freed peasants, educational opportunities loomed large. In both cases, populations that were largely (but not totally) illiterate now had the ability to receive rudimentary—and sometimes more than rudimentary—education. In both cases, freedpeople responded to this opportunity with considerable enthusiasm, associating knowledge, and especially literacy, with power, economic advancement, and freedom itself. Also, in both cases observers were impressed by their passionate interest in book learning, as well as by what was, at least to some of these observers, the Blacks' and peasants' unexpected ability to excel in their studies. Ultimately, however, there were significant differences in the educational experiences of these two freed populations, differences that included the level of outside support that they received, the rapidity with which the unlettered became literate, and the extent to which their educational exposure and progress were shaped by ingrained attitudes not only about identity and race but also about gender.

Before emancipation, the vast majority of slaves and serfs were illiterate. There were significant exceptions. Although the Southern states enacted legislation during the antebellum years making it illegal to teach slaves to read and write, these laws were inconsistent, frequently changed, and poorly enforced, and small numbers of slaves learned to read (and less often to write), either from their owners or through their own ingenuity; as a child, for example, Harriet Jacobs learned to read from her mistress, and Frederick Douglass deliberately made friends with "white boys," whom he "converted into teachers." There was no law against teaching serfs to read, but there was little likelihood of literacy making much headway in rural Russia. Although a tiny number of elite peasants became wealthy and even received formal instruction, and a basic literacy was essential for some communal officials—especially clerks who kept estate records and stewards who ran the estates and corresponded with their owners—these literate bondsmen, however notable, were rare exceptions. Depending on one's standards for judging someone "literate," on the eve of emancipation perhaps 5 to 10 percent of adult slaves and even fewer serfs could read and write at a rudimentary level.[48]

From the very beginning emancipation promised big educational changes. The process began first, although not by much, in Russia. "The cause of education is identified with emancipation," wrote English missionary J. Lang, who spent five months in Russia during the summer of 1863. "Already within two years, more than 8,000 new schools have sprung into existence.... These 8,000 schools have arisen spontaneously from the wishes of the peasants, aided by the clergy and gentry," he observed. "The government has spent nothing on them." Noting that "American slavery has lasted a long time," Lang predicted that the successful Russian "revolution" would induce "other countries... to 'go and do likewise.' " Lang was right on several counts. The months immediately following Russia's emancipation edict were marked by a surge of educational interest and activity. Information gathered by the Kaluga Province Statistical Committee indicated that by 1863 there were already 270 schools in villages inhabited by former serfs in that province alone, most but not all run by the church. Lang's prediction that a similar process would soon begin in the Southern United States was equally prescient. Indeed, well before the Thirteenth Amendment formally abolished slavery, Northern missionary teachers began arriving in areas of the South liberated by Union troops, and by the Civil War's end the flow became a flood, as newly formed freedmen's aid societies, most under the control of diverse Protestant denominations such as the (Congregational) American Missionary Association and many with their own monthly journals, entered the fray. Meanwhile, former slaves flocked not only to these missionary-run schools but also to those taught by African Americans themselves, and the Freedmen's Bureau undertook a substantial program to provide financial and logistical support for the freedpeople's education.[49]

In some ways, the educational experiences of American and Russian freedpeople followed a similar trajectory, although not always with the same intensity. In both countries, schooling for freedpeople evolved from informal private or semiprivate enterprises to formal government-sponsored institutions. Teachers in these schools were surprisingly diverse: in addition to missionaries sent by Northern benevolent societies in the South and by Orthodox priests (and other church figures) in Russia, they included Southern whites, Russian landowners and intellectuals, and significant numbers of African Americans and peasants. Beside teaching elementary skills and knowledge—reading, writing, arithmetic, basic geography, and history—teachers conveyed values deemed necessary to live successfully as free persons: religion, morality, and (especially in the United States) such "bourgeois" values as cleanliness, orderliness, honesty, and punctuality. Praising the "decided improvement" in her pupils' deportment, a teacher employed by the National Freedman's Relief Association reported from Norfolk, Virginia, in 1865, "Now they come and go in a quiet, orderly manner," in contrast to their earlier rowdy behavior; with new attention to "their dress and neatness of person," she added, "they take more pains to have their hair combed, and their hands and faces clean, than formerly." Freedpeople in both countries showed considerable enthusiasm for book learning, impressing sometimes-dubious observers with their ability to learn. During the immediate post-emancipation years, hundreds of thousands of Blacks and peasants received elementary educations, and before long much smaller numbers were entering newly established institutions of higher learning—high schools, normal schools, and gymnasia.[50]

Intertwined with these basic similarities, differences in degree and tone—and in some instances of fundamental substance—distinguished the introduction of schooling to the two newly freed populations. The differences can be seen in the responses of the freedpeople to new educational opportunities, as well as in their role in promoting these opportunities. Both peasants and Blacks showed an impressive early enthusiasm for schools, and a willingness to undergo considerable sacrifice to support them, but these traits were especially evident among the ex-slaves in the South. Even during the war, in Union-occupied areas, the educational interest and achievements of African Americans had made a marked impression on many Northerners and—together with Black military prowess on behalf of the Union cause—helped spread abolitionist and then radical sentiment among those who had previously been unsure of whether Blacks were truly capable of being transformed into republican citizens. As the American Freedmen's Inquiry Commission noted in its "preliminary report" after touring Union-occupied areas of the Confederacy in early 1863, the freedpeople, "eager to obtain for themselves, but especially for their children, those privileges of education which have hitherto been jealously withheld from them," were already enthusiastically "support[ing], in part, both teachers and pastors." A Presbyterian missionary in Louisiana was more evocative: remarking that African Americans were "pleading to be taught, willing to do anything for learning," he added, "Their cry is for 'Books! Books!' and 'when will school begin?' "[51]

After the war, the freedpeople's eagerness for schooling became an unmistakable tidal wave, reshaping Southern life. As the second annual report of the New England Freedmen's Aid Society, which by early 1865 employed some fifty-four teachers in the South, observed of the freedpeople, "Their belief that reading and writing are to bring with them inestimable advantages, seems, in its universality and intensity, like a mysterious instinct." Throughout the South, African Americans demonstrated what historian Eric Foner termed a "seemingly unquenchable thirst for education," flocking to a wide variety of educational institutions, from those run by Northern benevolent associations to small, barely noticed operations conducted by Blacks themselves, Sunday schools (which focused much of their attention on basic literacy and arithmetic, albeit in a broadly religious context), and normal schools, which turned out a growing supply of Black teachers. Meanwhile, exhausted but determined adults attended special "night schools," after putting in a full day's work in the fields. The freedpeople's enthusiasm was contagious, as Northern missionaries, Freedmen's Bureau officials, and even some white Southerners commented with delight on the freedpeople's passion—and ability—to learn. "The colored people seem to understand, as by intuition, that knowledge is power, that mental improvement is synonymous with their education," declared the head of a large-scale missionary effort that began with four teachers in Newbern, North Carolina, in 1863 and had mushroomed to employ seventy-three teachers two years later; "nothing has surprised me more than their aptness to learn. . . . Colored children, *even now,* with equal facilities, will learn as fast as the average of white children in our Northern districts." An emissary of the American Missionary Association went further, reporting from Alabama, "[Blacks have] made the same progress in a few months that we should expect at the north in several years"; in the association's schools "an influence for good is exerted on the minds of these people such as no race of men ever had an opportunity to exert since the world began."[52]

Especially noteworthy was the role of African Americans themselves in promoting the South's educational transformation. Aside from enthusiastically flocking to schools, freedpeople bore much of the financial burden of their children's education (and that of adults who went to night schools), especially before the state Reconstruction governments established public school systems between 1868 and 1871. Although the Freedmen's Bureau sometimes paid the transportation expenses of Northern teachers, as well as supplying textbooks, and benevolent societies helped pay the salaries of the teachers they sponsored, African Americans often raised money for the construction or purchase of school buildings, and a significant minority of Black parents paid monthly tuition fees that ranged from fifty cents to $1.50—substantial sums for the largely impecunious freedpeople. In April 1867, for example, Freedmen's Bureau records indicate that 451 schools throughout the South were "sustained" by the freedpeople and an additional 426 schools were "sustained in part" by the freedpeople, who paid tuition for almost one-quarter of the pupils who attended school. As Alabama's Freedmen's Bureau chief Wager

Swayne noted, although the truly destitute were admitted free of charge, "the principle has been enforced that while all should be made welcome, those who could must pay."[53]

African Americans also provided a growing proportion of those who taught in the freedpeople's schools. Freedmen's Bureau General Superintendent of Education John W. Alvord noted the trend as early as December 1866, reporting to Commissioner Howard, "It is evident that the Freedmen are to have teachers of their own color" and adding, "Rural districts and plantations give them preference, though inferior in their qualifications." Alvord was right about the preference, although one could argue that Black teachers had other qualifications—including familiarity with the customs and culture of their students—that offset their lack of formal education. Noting "a rather peculiar feeling among the colored citizens here, in regard to the management of the schools," a representative of the New-England Freedmen's Aid Society reported from Savannah in 1865: "They have a natural and praiseworthy pride in keeping their educational institutions in their own hands. There is a jealousy of the superintendency of the white man in this matter. What they desire is assistance without control."[54]

White teachers sent by the Northern benevolent societies delighted in boasting not only of their pupils' aptitude but of their gratitude as well, accounts of which appeared regularly in the societies' monthly journals. "I cannot tell you how very thankful I am to the dear friends of the North who have done so much for our education," wrote a nine-year-old girl from Charlottesville, Virginia, in 1868, praising her "kind and dear teacher who does all she can to make us learn as fast as possible." In fact, there is a good deal of evidence that freedpeople were indeed grateful for the "assistance" (if not the control) they received from benevolent societies and the Freedmen's Bureau and often welcomed the missionary teachers with open arms. But freedpeople were especially proud of, and looked up to, the African American teachers who—like Black ministers—quickly established themselves as leaders within Black communities and frequently went on to be active in politics as well; indeed, at least 176 Black teachers subsequently held political office (former teachers constituted about 11 percent of the 1,510 Black men who held elective or appointed positions during Reconstruction), and others participated in Union League and Republican Party organizations. Throughout the South, such teachers materialized as if out of nowhere, first among literate Blacks (sometimes but by no means always free before the war) and then among early beneficiaries of schooling who—often after only a few months of study—turned from students to teachers. A Freedmen's Bureau official in South Carolina described how "classes were formed in negro huts, where the most intelligent [i.e., informed] freedmen, who, while slaves, had acquired some knowledge of the alphabet & syllables[,] commenced the work of teaching." A white teacher in Virginia, explaining that *her* school had "only about twenty pupils" because, in her words, "about thirty of our scholars are [themselves] teaching at night," lamented, "Some of the colored people, who have always felt *too proud* to let us see how ignorant they are, will go to teachers of their own race." As historian Heather Williams noted, "As soon as they mastered the rudiments of reading and writing, adult and younger students began teaching others."[55]

Early Black teachers, who were especially prevalent in plantation areas and in small, out-of-the-way communities beyond the reach of Northern missionaries, were more numerous than was readily apparent because they frequently taught in what white observers termed "private" schools, which often were not included in official Freedmen's Bureau statistics (and were sometimes listed as "non-reporting"). After listing relatively meager statistics on the number of schools and pupils in Alabama in his January 1866 report, General Superintendent of Education Alvord noted, "From my personal observation, much more is being done than finds its way into the above statistics," adding that night schools and Sunday schools—among others—"[were] not usually included in the regular returns." Non-reporting schools, which were especially prevalent among small schools with mostly Black teachers, in rural areas far from Freedmen's Bureau offices, became more numerous over time: in his January 1870 report, Alvord, observing that many teachers were no longer reporting to the bureau, noted, "[In] one County ... I found twelve colored schools in operation that I knew nothing of before." The same thing occurred in other states as well. Complaining to Commissioner Howard that it was difficult to get information on them, the Virginia bureau's superintendent of education observed in 1867: "The number of small private schools, mostly taught by freedmen, is rapidly increasing, particularly in the rural districts—many of them in obscure localities." Historian Christopher Span found that in Mississippi, by 1865, ex-slaves had already established "a network of virtually independent schools," and in 1870, fifty-six of seventy-two schools were "sustained" by the freedpeople.[56]

Historian Ronald E. Butchart recently compiled a database that provides a rough portrait of 11,672 known teachers who served in Black schools between 1861 and 1876, who he estimates constituted more than two-thirds of all the teachers in these schools. Slightly more than half (53.2 percent) of those whose race could be determined were white, while slightly less than half (46.8 percent) were Black. (Almost one-quarter of the total were of undetermined race.) Among the known whites, twice as many were Northerners as Southerners (although Butchart suggested that the number of Southern white teachers was far larger than indicated by these statistics), whereas among the known Blacks the great majority (82.3 percent) were Southerners. Northern white teachers were twice as likely to be female as male, whereas more Southern white and Black teachers were male (1.5 times as many and twice as many, respectively). If the motives of the Black teachers and white Northerners were easily understood as idealistic, Butchart noted that for most of the white Southerners "teaching was a task of convenience or a work of necessity," dictated by poverty—"they were poor to the point of desperation"—rather than by a belief in the desirability of uplifting former slaves; as a result, many of the Southern whites taught only briefly. The number of documented Southern white teachers peaked at 739 in 1870–71 and then decreased sharply, although Butchart suggested that the actual number was greater. (Presumably, the discrepancy resulted at least in part from the teachers' embarrassment at having to resort to what seemed to them a degrading way of making a living.) African American teachers, by contrast, became much more numerous over time; Butchart estimated that their numbers increased from seven hundred in 1865–66 to twenty-eight hundred in 1869–70 and sixty-seven hundred by 1874–75. They were passionately committed to their work, which they saw as a cause rather than just a job.[57]

Missionary teachers and Freedmen's Bureau officials sometimes derided Black teachers as "unqualified." The bureau's superintendent of education for Tennessee, for example, remarked on how "amusing" it was to see schools run by "colored teachers" where "not one word in five was pronounced correctly," Similarly, a white Northern teacher in Virginia ridiculed African Americans who he said "felt *too proud* to let us see how ignorant they are," mockingly adding, "[They] go to teachers of their own race until they get so as to 'know right smart' in reading, spelling and arithmetic." But African American teachers were qualified enough to provide the kind of rudimentary knowledge that the first generation of freedpeople needed and typically received—basic literacy, arithmetic, religious and moral precepts, simple civics—and they were often able to relate to their pupils in a way that the outsiders (however well motivated) could not. Especially pertinent in this regard was the passionate commitment many of them held for educating other African Americans. "More than I desire my own life," proclaimed one Black teacher, "I desire to elevate these, my people." The same Tennessee superintendent of education who made fun of the pronunciation of Black teachers was also struck by the freedpeople's determination to learn, and he reported with pleasure that 140 Black pupils were planning soon to become teachers. Noting the existence of what he termed "wayside schools," with unorganized efforts at learning, he explained: "A negro riding on a loaded wagon, or sitting on a hack waiting for a train, or by the cabin door, is often seen, book in hand delving after the rudiments of knowledge. A group on the platform, after carefully conning an old spelling book, resolves itself into a class." It was hard not to be impressed by this determination.[58]

More formally "qualified" teachers followed soon enough, as graduates of newly established normal schools and other more specialized advanced institutions proliferated. If white observers perceived a need for the training of "qualified" Black teachers, African Americans sought such training as well. "[I am] very anxious to be useful to my Country and my people," a young Black teacher in Columbus, Mississippi, with "a little bit of Education" wrote in a letter to a Freedmen's Bureau official begging to be told "how a young man who is a faithful member of the Union League of America can get into a high School where he Can remain for a year or So improving himself for the good of his race," adding, "I am willing to go to any place that I may be sent to obtain Knowledge." Over the next few years, thousands of ambitious African Americans in fact attended such institutions of higher learning. Although the vast majority of day and night schools were "ungraded" and focused on simple reading, writing, arithmetic, and geography, as more African Americans acquired these basic skills "graded" schools became more common, and beginning in 1867 both high schools and normal (teacher training) schools mushroomed, the latter often founded with the help of Northern benevolent societies. The proportion of African Americans who attended such institutions of higher learning—"variously called universities, colleges, academies, high schools, institutes, and normal schools"—was relatively small: at the turn of the twentieth century, only 2,331 African Americans (equivalent to 0.027 percent of the Black population) "had earned the degree of A.B. or B.S.," and as late as 1916, when 1,175,000 Black pupils were in elementary schools, only 24,189 (equivalent to less than 2 percent of those aged fifteen to nineteen) were receiving higher education. Still, in the words of historian Adam Fairclough, the normal schools and colleges "became dynamos of educational advance," training the Black instructors who by the late 1860s already constituted more than half the teachers in the "freedmen's schools" and came to constitute the great majority of teachers in the Black public schools established throughout the South in the 1870s; by the late nineteenth century, whites "constituted only a tiny fraction of the [schools'] teaching force."[59]

Freedmen's Bureau statistics indicate that the number of high and normal schools increased from eight in February 1867 to forty-seven in February 1870, with the number of attending students increasing from 435 to 3,966, but these figures are incomplete, and Ronald Butchart estimated that there were "nearly ninety high schools, normal schools, and higher education institutions" by the beginning of 1870 and 125 by the end of that year, with additional "normal classes" in local schools. Enrollment in Talladega Normal School (which later became Talladega College), founded by the American Missionary Association in Talladega, Alabama, in 1867, soared from an initial eight students to 130 by 1869, taught by eight teachers. Before long, its graduates—whose admission had required passing a test in "Reading, Writing, Spelling, Elements of English Grammar, General Geography, [and] Arithmetic through fractions"—were teaching in numerous local schools in Talladega and adjoining counties, where, in the words of the Freedmen's Bureau superintendent of education for Talladega County, "the good results are astonishing to all." By the start of the 1870s, there was a rapidly growing supply of formally trained African American teachers available for the new public schools that were established by the Reconstruction governments.[60]

These public schools, which were phased in between 1869 and 1871, represented an ambitious effort to found a republican social order on an educated citizenry, and they quickly reached far more students than the semiprivate freedpeople's schools that they largely replaced. In Alabama, which held the first Reconstruction constitutional convention among the ex-Confederate states and therefore had a head start when it came to appropriating money for public education, the school system was up and running by the fall of 1870, with enrollments of 41,308 Black and 75,760 white children, figures that increased to 54,336 Blacks and 86,976 whites the following year. Other Southern states were not far behind, in most cases enrolling about half the school-age population at any given time and substantially more than half over a several-year stretch. With the exception of New Orleans and some surrounding areas, white and Black children were instructed separately, in all-white and all-Black schools; even in South Carolina, whose constitution, like that of Louisiana, had laid the groundwork for integrated schooling, authorities quickly yielded to the evident unwillingness of white parents to send their children to mixed schools, with the resulting dual school systems that would last into the 1950s and would become potent symbols of racial discrimination. It is worth noting, however, that in the 1870s these segregated schools seemed to hold out the prospect of enormous opportunities to the freed population. Not only was the most rampant discrimination still well in the future—in 1871, teachers in Alabama's Black schools actually received an average monthly salary that exceeded that of teachers in white schools by 91 cents ($43.06 to $42.15)—but, as historian Howard N. Rabinowitz pointed out, the most likely alternative to segregated schooling for African Americans was not integrated schooling but no schooling at all. Providing widespread schooling to former slaves was at once a symbol of the commitment to grant them full and immediate citizenship and a source of enormous hope and excitement to the freed population.[61]

Russian peasants also displayed enthusiasm for education, although on a somewhat more limited and conditional basis. The weekly reports of Minister of Internal Affairs Petr Valuev, which summarized reports that he received from provincial governors, contained frequent references—especially in 1862—to such enthusiasm. From Podolia Province the governor noted the peasants' "yearning for teaching their children to read" and boasted that in less than a year 1,115 village schools had been established, with enrollments of 25,958 peasant children. In Smolensk Province, there were already 612 schools under the control of parish churches, and "schools [were] being opened everywhere." The governor of Vologda Province noted that "at the suggestion of peace mediators" the peasants were agreeing to pay ten kopecks per soul to build and maintain village schools, while in Perm Province a temporarily obligated peasant who had achieved a degree of prosperity as a tradesman donated six hundred rubles to establish a primary school for boys. Peasants showed a strong preference for learning from other peasants, and in the immediate post-emancipation years, before local (zemstvo) governments and the Orthodox Church began the widespread organizing and funding of rural schools in the 1880s and 1890s, the "peasants themselves" were the "driving force" in the construction of semiprivate schools that proliferated in villages throughout the country.[62]

But compared to the enthusiastic embrace of education by former slaves in the South, the responses of the Russian peasants—who unlike the former slaves had never been legally barred from being taught to read and therefore did not come to identify literacy with freedom in the same way—seemed muted if not ambivalent, and the enthusiasm seemed more ephemeral. "Right after the Emancipation, the peasants applied themselves seriously to the schools, so that even now among the twenty to twenty-five-year-olds there are rather many who are literate . . . ," wrote pomeshchik Aleksandr Nikolaevich

Engelgardt from Smolensk Province in 1874. "But then things eased up with the schools and there are already very few literate boys in the village." Providing a telling example of peasant ambivalence concerning the benefits of education, Engelgardt told of a peasant who came to him for help because his son was being taken to school "out of turn. My son served his time in school last winter," the peasant complained, but "they're making him go again this year." Other observers were struck with the schools' failure to bring about the expected transformation of the peasants' backward mentality. While land captain Aleksandr Novikov continued to believe that education would provide the peasants' salvation, he reported sadly that in Tambov Province schools were few and far between thirty years after emancipation, and even when they existed peasant children rarely attended them because their parents wanted them home working. Olga Tian-Shanskaia told a similar story from Riazan Province a decade later: although peasants were increasingly sending their children to school, at least for a while, the impact seemed surprisingly slight. "For some reason, school fails to change the peasants' view of the life around them," she mused. "There is school and then there is life, and in the minds of the peasants a line always divides the two." Historian Ben Eklof was more succinct. Noting that peasants did at times show real enthusiasm for education during the half century after emancipation, he generalized that although they were "learning to read," they were "not yet learning from reading."[63]

Unlike African Americans in the Southern United States, who eagerly embraced the opportunities provided them by the Reconstruction experiment and who welcomed the Northern educational missionaries despite their sometimes paternalistic views, Russian peasants, whose communal world and worldview rendered them far more suspicious of outsiders, did not benefit from anything like the Reconstruction effort to provide them with full citizenship and equal rights, let alone universal access to education. As in the Southern United States, freedpeople in Russia were the "driving force" behind much of the early educational endeavors, from sending their children to private "free" (*vol'nye*) schools and "literacy" schools (*shkoly gramoty*, or *gramotnosti*) that operated independently of government control (and lacked legal status until 1882) to bearing a significant share of the related financial burden. As Engelgardt noted, peasants, wanting to have their children learn "in 'their own,' not in compulsory schools," would sometimes get together and "hire some kind of soldier for the winter, and he [would] teach," and they continued to raise money to pay for a major share of their educational expenses through the last third of the nineteenth century. Peasants, who initially took most of the initiative to seek schooling for their children, might turn to "a literate villager [to] teach his neighbors' children in his own cottage," but they also hired outsiders, including itinerant teachers who offered themselves for hire, and they banded together to finance the construction of special buildings that would serve as "commune schools."[64]

But unlike the Southern United States, where Northern benevolent societies launched a major campaign to educate and uplift the freedpeople and the Reconstruction governments then established public school systems that in the 1870s reached the majority of Black and white school-age children, Russia saw more talk than action when it came to schooling in the immediate post-emancipation years. The Orthodox Church in some ways played a role similar to that of Northern benevolent societies in the United States, but "priests and other clerical employees" generally lacked the ideological passion displayed by benevolent society missionaries, and after an early flurry of activity immediately upon emancipation, as historian Jeffrey Brooks put it, they "discovered that they had neither time nor inclination to supplement regular parish duties with voluntary teaching"; in the 1870s "the makeshift and haphazard Church schools of the 1860s disappeared rapidly." Only in the 1880s and especially the 1890s did the church launch a major educational campaign, employing priests, members of clerical families, deacons, and laypersons; in 1891, the government officially placed the peasant-backed "literacy schools" under church control. A similar pattern was evident in the district and provincial zemstvo assemblies that were established in much but not all of Russia during the second half of the 1860s, assemblies that had some peasant representatives but were heavily dominated by nobles (especially at the provincial level): there was considerable discussion within the zemstvo assemblies of the importance of educating the peasantry, but only in the 1880s and 1890s was this talk backed up by much action. In the early years of the twentieth century, the Ministry of Education in turn increasingly assumed control of the zemstvo schools.[65]

In short, if during the 1860s and 1870s peasants sponsored their own "free," "literacy," and commune schools, during the 1880s and 1890s these peasant-backed schools increasingly yielded to—and in some cases were taken over by—schools under the direct control of zemstva and the Orthodox Church. Then, in the early years of the twentieth century, the Ministry of Education became increasingly active in running schools—especially at first in provinces without zemstva—although zemstvo and church schools continued to flourish as well. As late as 1894, almost half (44 percent) of the existing peasant schools were literacy or commune schools, but by 1914 these made up only 6.5 percent of the total. During the same period, the proportion of church, zemstvo, and Ministry of Education schools increased from 48.7 percent to 93 percent (21 percent to 32 percent, 26 percent to 41 percent, and 1.7 percent to 20 percent, respectively). As in the Southern United States, the schools accommodated the work schedules of children who also engaged in seasonal agricultural labor, and the emphasis was on providing very rudimentary training to pupils who typically—especially in the early years after emancipation—could be expected to stay only a year or two: reading, writing, and arithmetic were standard, supplemented by heavy attention to religion (including, especially but not exclusively in church schools, instruction in Church Slavonic). As was the case with Blacks in the Southern United States, however, a tiny number of peasants managed to continue their educations in gymnasia and universities (although, unlike Southern Blacks, they did not attend segregated—"peasant"—institutions). In 1880, peasants, who constituted the overwhelming majority of Russia's population, made up 6.9 percent of its gymnasium and 3.3 percent of its university students; almost all of them were males.[66]

Throughout this process, peasants showed both a continued interest in gaining literacy and an enduring suspicion of outsiders bent on subverting traditional peasant ways. If education could be a valuable tool, too much education, and the wrong kind of education, were dangerous. As one peasant put it, "Why literacy? You don't need it to make cabbage soup." Even as the number of rural teachers surged from twenty-four thousand in 1880 to 126,501 in 1911, peasants continued to view most of them as outsiders, whether they were hired by the church, the zemstva, the state, or the peasants themselves. This was even true of teachers who were peasants, who in fact increasingly were not from, or known in, the villages where they taught. During the three decades 1880–1911, the proportion of teachers who were peasants rose from 30 percent to 40.8 percent, while the proportion with clerical backgrounds decreased from 37.8 percent to 22 percent and the proportion of nobles fell from 10.9 percent to 6.7 percent. Peasants were especially prevalent among male teachers; even as the teaching profession as a whole was "feminized"—in 1911, 55 percent of the rural teachers were women, whereas earlier men had been in the majority—peasants increased from 36.1 percent to 61.9 percent of the male teachers. By contrast, among female teachers, daughters of priests formed the largest contingent, although one that decreased from 43.6 percent to 32.6 percent of the total, while peasants increased from 6.5 percent to 20.7 percent. Poorly paid and lacking in prestige, teachers were, in Ben Eklof's words, " 'ousiders,' newcomers, not to be trusted but also not to be feared. . . .

[They] had no way to impose their will—on the contrary they could be abused *at will.*"⁶⁷

Despite the surge in schools and teachers after 1880, Russian peasant children were considerably less likely to receive schooling than were African American children, especially if they were girls. As the statement about not needing literacy in order to make cabbage soup indicated, the subordination of females that characterized Russian society in general was as evident in peasant education as in any other sphere of life. Statistics on school attendance by sex indicates that, in contrast to former slaves in the Southern United States, former serfs in Russia rarely sent their daughters to school during the 1860s and 1870s, regarding it as a waste of time that would fill their heads with needless knowledge and make them less fit for their feminine duties. The evidence is consistent and overwhelming. Among African Americans in the Southern United States, girls were at least as likely as boys to attend school: the Freedmen's Bureau Consolidated Monthly School Report for June 1867, for example, listed 45,855 male and 52,981 female pupils in the schools that it monitored throughout the South; in almost every state, female pupils outnumbered male, although in Louisiana there were slightly more males than females. The decennial census returns showed a similar pattern between 1870 and 1910: school enrollment rates in the United States for Black children aged five to nineteen (the great majority of whom lived in the South) were fairly evenly balanced between the sexes, with female rates slightly higher than male in four of the five census years. (The male rate was slightly higher than the female in 1880.)⁶⁸

Among Russian peasants, by contrast, boy pupils vastly outnumbered girls. In Kaluga Province in 1862, 7,478 peasants were in school, of whom 6,855 were male and 623 female. Three years later, in Iaroslavl Province, there were 3,484 male pupils and 521 females. In Saratov Province's Saratov district, 4,478 boys attended school in 1883 versus 1,190 girls; in the province's more rural Tsaritsynskii and Petrovskii districts, the gap was much greater—1,198 boys versus 106 girls and 2,684 boys versus 310 girls, respectively. The first school in the village of Viriatino, in Tambov Province, which opened in 1872, had seventy-eight boys and three girls in 1875, but the number decreased thereafter; in 1881, school attendance stood at thirty-three boys, while "no girls attended." A respondent to the Tenishev survey in the late 1890s noted that thirty-three boys and seven girls went to the local school in the Shuiskii district of Vladimir Province. He explained that although both boys and girls living within two to three *versty* (or kilometers) of the school were likely to attend it, the boys, for whom illiteracy would be a disadvantage during military service, stayed in school much longer; girls typically dropped out after "a year or two" to help their mothers, as a result of which they rarely used their "received knowledge" in everyday life, and everything—"even writing"—was "forgotten." The daughter of a landowner in Tambov Province had a similar recollection: remembering "how difficult it was to persuade the villagers to send their children to school," she noted that "they were more willing to send boys" than girls, because beginning in 1874 the government gave "special privileges . . . in military service to literate young men," whereas "parents maintained that their daughters were needed at home for various duties." Overall, statistics provided by the Ministry of Education and the Holy Synod indicated that females constituted 17.7 percent of the primary school population in 1878 and 21.3 percent in 1896, but these figures overstate the proportion of girls from ex-serf families because they include non-peasants as well as peasants and exclude pupils in literacy schools.[69]

Given this gender gap in school attendance, it is not surprising that a similar gap existed between male and female peasant literacy—something that did not exist among African Americans in the American South and further differentiated the two freed populations. The gap was evident in early reports that came from diverse provinces, some of which were the same reports as those indicating the gender differential in school attendance. The Saratov Province report noted above, for example, listed 14.1 percent of male peasants and 4.2 percent of female peasants as literate in Saratov district, with much greater gaps—11.2 percent versus 0.25 percent and 7.2 percent versus 0.4 percent—in the more rural Tsaritsynskii and Petrovskii districts. In Moscow Province's Moscow district (which did not include the city of Moscow) 6,685 of 47,954 males (13.9 percent) and 1,168 of 52,895 females (2.2 percent) were literate according to an 1869 census. In Viriatino, forty-six of 922 adult peasants were literate in 1881, but "not one of these was a woman." The literacy rate for rural men in Russia, which historian Boris Mironov estimated at between 17.4 and 19.1 percent in 1857 and between 22.2 and 22.8 percent in 1867, stood at 39.3 percent by the time of the census of 1897, while the rate for rural women, estimated at between 7.3 and 9.5 percent in 1857 and between 9.4 and 10.3 percent in 1867, increased only slightly, to 13.4 percent, by 1897. Especially noteworthy was the overwhelming illiteracy of all but the youngest women: in 1897, as a result of (admittedly limited) school attendance, 13.6 percent of rural girls aged ten to nineteen were literate, as were 10.1 percent of young women aged twenty to twenty-nine, but among older women the literacy rate quickly fell to levels that seemed barely changed from those before emancipation, ranging from 7.1 percent for women in their thirties to 3.5 percent for women in their seventies.[70]

Within a few years of emancipation African Americans were in general more educated and more literate than Russian peasants, male or female. Although the early freedpeople's schools—and especially Black teachers in them—were objects of vicious terror attacks, particularly during periods of heightened political tension, and the Black public schools established during Reconstruction faced sharp cutbacks in funding by the "Redeemer" governments that came to power in the post-Reconstruction years, African Americans continued to show enthusiasm for education and continued to make impressive educational progress as well. This progress can be seen in the number of children who attended school—attendance at the freedpeople's schools of the late 1860s was soon dwarfed by that at the new public schools, which were attended at least briefly by a majority of Black school-age children—but the simplest index of educational achievement lies in the dramatic increase in the Black literacy rate, which surged in the United States as a whole from 20.1 percent in 1870 to 69.5 percent in 1910. Over a period of two generations, Southern African Americans were transformed from an overwhelmingly illiterate to a broadly literate population.[71]

This transformation looks especially noteworthy in light of what happened among Russian peasants. The half century after the abolition of serfdom did see a significant growth in peasant literacy, growth that studied in isolation appears impressive—and has struck some scholars, including Mironov and Eklof, as such—but that growth seems less remarkable when placed in the context of what happened in the Southern United States. According to Mironov's estimates, the literacy rate for rural men in Russia increased from a range of 17.4 to 19.1 percent in 1857, on the verge of emancipation, to 39.3 percent in 1897 and 53.2 percent in 1917, and for rural women it increased during the same years from 8.2–9.8 percent to 13.4 percent to 22.6 percent; taking the midpoint in the 1857 ranges and assuming approximately equal numbers of men and women, Mironov's figures yield an increase in the combined literacy rate of all rural Russians during the four decades 1857–97 from 13.6 percent to 26.3 percent, with an additional increase to 37.9 percent on the eve of the 1917 Revolution. Since this rate for rural Russians included non-peasants as well as peasants, the literacy rate for peasants alone would have been somewhat lower in all of those years. These figures are born out in a series of zemstvo studies in the 1880s that suggested a literacy rate among *peasants* over nine years old of 12.3–14.1 percent (although Mironov has suggested that this figure is probably too low, and should have been closer to 18 percent). Other statistics, while varying slightly, confirm these very low literacy rates: Ministry of War figures for new army recruits, for example, indicated literacy rates of 8.7 percent in 1867, 12.2 percent in 1873, and 21 percent in 1876. (The sharp increase after 1873 resulted in great measure from the drop in age of new recruits, who until 1874 were in their twenties but thereafter "came almost exclusively from twenty-one year olds.") Even the vast majority of village elders, according to Ministry of Internal Affairs data on the thirty-four provinces with zemstva, were illiterate: in 1880, only 19 percent of these elders could read.[72]

In its rapid spread of literacy among the freed population, it was clearly the United States, not Russia, that was the outlier. In Brazil, for example, 34.7 percent of people over the age of fifteen were literate in 1900—a figure more in line with the situation in Russia than in the Southern United States—and the literacy rate among former Brazilian *slaves* was almost certainly much lower. In literacy—in part because "the eagerness to learn among American Negroes was exceptional in the case of a poor and recently emancipated folk"—wrote W. E. B. Du Bois in 1935, "the American Negro today ... surpasses Spain and Italy, the Balkans and South America." Similarly, stressing the atypicality of the "amazing rise in African American literacy," historian Edward J. Blum noted that in the West Indies Black literacy grew much more slowly than in the United States, and he pointed out that by the turn of the twentieth century, despite the legacy of slavery, African Americans were considerably more literate than Spaniards and Italians.[73]

It is important not to exaggerate the educational achievements of postemancipation African Americans. Recently, Adam Fairclough pointed out some of the limitations of Black schools and Black teachers. He noted that, unlike Black ministers, Black public school teachers were appointed and paid by largely white bodies (school superintendents and school boards) and that unlike ministers, who spoke the language of the Black masses, teachers "sought to *change* the way blacks spoke, thought, and behaved." Pointing to "tensions between teachers, children, and parents," he observed that—like white children—many Black children disliked going to school and attended irregularly, and suggested that in some cases African Americans resented middle-class Black teachers for speaking like whites. In short, African Americans may have at least occasionally shown the same kind of distrust of teachers (whether Blacks or Northern whites) as outsiders trying to impose alien values that was evident among Russian peasants. Fairclough also stressed the low quality of many of the public schools—especially those in the countryside, where one-room schoolhouses and ungraded schools were the norm, teachers typically lacked advanced training, and corporal punishment remained widespread. Suggesting that "urban public schools were, virtually by definition, better than rural schools," he emphasized the superiority of "mission" schools founded by Northern aid societies, schools that he defended against critics who saw them as emphasizing bourgeois values and assimilationist thought. Suggesting that their "most salient characteristic ... was, in fact, their vast superiority over the public schools," he argued that "the mission schools kept alive the ideal of racial equality and trained another generation of teachers."[74]

Although a useful corrective to starry-eyed interpretations (including, perhaps, my own), these observations do not vitiate the basic transformation that occurred in Black education and consciousness so much as add nuance and context to it. In both Russia and the Southern United States, emancipation made possible far-reaching changes as former serfs and slaves struggled to adjust to new conditions, and in both, the freedpeople actively embraced new educational opportunities, which in turn affected other areas of life. For reasons detailed above, however, the ensuing changes were greater for the ex-slaves than for the ex-serfs: although the freedpeople in both countries showed enthusiasm for schooling, and made effective use of the new opportunities that it opened to them, whether measured in terms of school attendance, changed consciousness, or—especially—growing literacy, the changes were particularly notable among African Americans in the Southern United States.

As the former slaves and serfs struggled to adjust to—and take advantage of—their new status, they were subject to contradictory centrifugal and centripetal forces. In Russia, even as the peasant commune emerged in a strengthened position after emancipation, inheriting functions previously performed by noble serfholders and gaining in relative power as a result of the diminished authority of those pomeshchiki, peasants increasingly acted independently of the commune, working away from home, often for lengthy periods, and breaking away from extended families, in the process sometimes leaving their native villages altogether but even when remaining weakening the commune-bolstered authority of the family patriarch. In the Southern United States, where slave life had generally lacked the communal structure that existed in peasant villages, emancipation further accentuated African American individualism with the breakup of the slave quarters, the end of gang labor on most plantations, and the widespread growth of family farming. At the same time, however, freed African Americans were able to display a greater sense of communality as collective endeavors that had been barred under slavery—including especially independent Black churches and Black schooling—flourished and Blacks were able to join political organizations, attend rallies, and engage in electoral politics, as well as form more mundane community institutions such as clubs and self-help organizations. In short, in both countries developments in some ways bolstered and in others weakened communality and collective life.[75]

The new communal identification and expression among African Americans were especially evident in the Black churches that seemed to emerge from thin air throughout the South. The religious attachments of Black Southerners briefly appeared fluid—if many under slavery had been lesser members of white churches, where they sat in segregated "slave galleries" even as they worshipped with whites, others had secretly held their own services, led by African American preachers, in what came to be known as the "invisible church"—and the immediate postwar months saw a vigorous denominational struggle for membership of freedpeople whose loyalty appeared up for grabs. At first, the white leadership of established Southern churches often strove to keep their Black parishioners, while (especially among Methodists and Congregationalists) Northern missionaries sought to win what they assumed would be easy converts among former slaves, and the freedpeople themselves showed a clear preference for Black over white ministers.

Before long, however, white Southerners were routinely complaining of Black "savagery" and "superstition" and encouraging rather than resisting the departure of the former slaves, especially where African American parishioners were in the majority and control over existing churches was in question. In 1868, a committee of (white) Alabama Baptists reported on the moral deterioration of the "colored people": "Naturally superstitious and credulous," the committee members asserted, African Americans had "surrendered themselves to the guidance of 'prophets' and 'prophetesses,' who are leading them into every abominable and revolting excess of idolatry." Under the circumstances, it now made sense to encourage rather than resist the desire of Blacks to leave the white churches. As a committee report of a local Baptist association concluded of its Black members in 1869, "Owing to their excessive ignorance, and want of confidence in the white people, produced by the evil influence of designing men, we would suggest that the churches advise and bring about a separation or withdrawal of the colored portion of the churches." In lamenting their evident failure to attract more than a tiny number of converts, Northern missionaries voiced similar if more moderately phrased concerns: describing "the religious types of the freedmen" that he found "every where the same," one Congregationalist clergyman generalized that Blacks showed "an excessive effervescence of emotional feeling, with very little intelligent understanding of even the first elementary principles of the gospel." Complaining that they saw Jesus as "a second Moses," he asserted that they lacked "an *intelligent* notion of the atonement." As historian Joe M. Richardson concluded in his careful study *Christian Reconstruction,* freedpeople welcomed the educational assistance provided by the Congregationalists' American Missionary Association, but "thirty years of AMA prayers, work, and money made only a feeble impression on black religion."[76]

Independent Black churches proliferated with startling suddenness after emancipation, most notably among Baptists and Methodists (the largest denominations among Southern whites as well). If the cold rationalism of the Congregationalists held little appeal for most African Americans, the condescension of Southern (white) Methodists and Baptists, whose evangelical fervor they shared, appeared even more troublesome as it became clear that these white Southerners expected their African American coreligionists to retain their slave-like subservience even when they constituted the great majority of parishioners. As a result, Blacks in the South wasted little time in seceding from the Methodist and Baptist Churches. In doing so, Black Methodists received considerable help from religious denominations already established in the North—the African Methodist Episcopal and African Methodist Episcopal Zion Churches and to a lesser extent the white Northern Methodist Episcopal Church—whereas Black Baptist secession, like Baptism in general, was a more spontaneous, less hierarchical, and less centralized affair. The end result, however, was the same: the rapid emergence of independent, Black-controlled churches, with African American ministers who catered to African American parishioners. As early as 1866, only 78,742 African Americans remained in the white Methodist Episcopal Church, South, compared to the previously reported 207,766, and within a couple of years most of those would be gone as well. "A few years ago, nearly all the blacks worshiped with the whites," noted the Republican Mobile *Nationalist* in July 1866, "but now they are everywhere establishing separate churches, so as to be able to worship by themselves."[77]

Because churches became the most prominent independent African American institutions—Black owned, Black managed, and catering to a Black clientele—it is not surprising that they served Black communities in a multitude of ways, including educational and political, and that Black ministers quickly established themselves as community leaders. Before emancipation, in 1856, the Wall Street Baptist Church, in Natchez, Mississippi, had 499 Black and sixteen white members, but when it became clear after the war that whites would maintain control of the church and would expect the former slave members to remain in a subservient position, the African American parishioners walked out and under the leadership of preacher Henry P. Jacobs built a new church in 1866—the Pine Street Baptist—the first fully independent Black church in Mississippi. Jacobs, who had escaped to Canada a decade earlier with his wife and children, was soon active in a variety of other community ventures, serving two terms in the Mississippi House of Representatives and creating the Jacobs Benevolent Society, which—like other Black mutual aid societies—promoted educational endeavors and enabled members to purchase insurance that would care for the ill and pay funeral expenses. Jacobs was an unusually enterprising leader, but he was typical of many other African Americans in combining a career in the Black church with political, educational, and mutual aid activities. The independence of Black churches rendered ministers ideally positioned to lead African Americans in other capacities as well. Black preachers were especially active in politics during the early years of Reconstruction; as historian Edmund L. Drago put it, "The church . . . produced most of Georgia's political leaders during Reconstruction."[78]

There was no Russian equivalent of the Black church: after emancipation, as before, the Orthodox clergy continued to constitute a largely separate estate, although its caste-like character was partially reduced by a series of reforms undertaken in the 1860s and early 1870s that abolished clerical endogamy, whereby clergymen could marry only members of the clerical estate (that is, children of other churchmen), and in theory—although relatively rarely in practice—allowed new recruits to enter the ranks of the clergy. Also as before, priests continued to have contradictory and unpredictable relations with their peasant parishioners—on the one hand, sometimes close to them in worldview and supportive of their aspirations but on the other the lowest cogs in an organization that buttressed the power and authority of the autocracy and the nobility. British traveler Sir Donald MacKenzie Wallace observed, "The parish priest rarely enjoys the respect of his parishioners," a comment echoed in some of the responses to the Tenishev survey. As one respondent put it, the peasants were afraid of the clergy and treated them "without respect," while another asserted that peasants were "superstitiously" afraid of meetings with the clergy, especially priests. Other respondents disagreed, however, describing "respectful" and "deferential" relations with the clergy, with one noting the peasants' appreciation of their "simple manners" and another stating that peasants "like[d] to receive them in their homes."[79]

Although the government regarded the church as an important source of stability and order, the emperor and many of his advisers worried that under the wrong conditions it could threaten rather than encourage those values, and could easily promote instability and disorder. As K. P. Pobedonostsev wrote shortly after being named the chief procurator of the Holy Synod in 1880, "There are terrible priests—priests who are nihilists and propagandists of revolutionary teachings." More pertinent here, unlike the African American ministers who assumed leadership positions within the new Black churches that sprang up throughout the South after emancipation, Russian Orthodox priests (and the supporting cast of deacons and readers who held lesser ranks within the clerical hierarchy) were outsiders as far as the peasants were concerned; there were no peasant priests, and rural villagers did not form their own churches that represented their interests and outlook. Unlike the emotional religion of the heart practiced by African Americans, the religion of Russian peasants was often formalistic and ritualistic. Wallace's observation that Russians were in general "profoundly ignorant of religious doctrine" was consistent with many of the responses to the Tenishev survey that indicated a widespread lack of interest among peasants in church attendance. As one respondent reported from Vladimir Province, "Peasants rarely go to church, especially the men," adding that they approached church "without zeal, more with carelessness." Other respondents agreed that peasants were less than enthusiastic about going to church, in one case explaining that they preferred to devote their free time to "trade."[80]

If peasants lacked a church—or churches—of their own, they continued to practice a lively folk religion based largely on pre-Christian beliefs and practices that the Orthodox Church in some cases accommodated and in others sharply resisted as superstitious threats to true religion. Peasants continued to live in a magical world populated—at least in their imagination—by a diverse multitude of spirits to be feared, respected, appeased, controlled, or avoided, depending on their specific characteristics. Despite increasing peasant exposure to the outside world—through otkhod (departure), education, and the growing use of commercial products—historians have been impressed by the extent to which traditional beliefs and customs persevered, especially in villages that were remote from major urban centers. As Christine D. Worobec put it in stressing her "largely static" picture of peasant life, "Culture generally changes at a much slower pace than economic and political relations"; despite significant economic changes following the end of serfdom, "peasant mores, worldview, social relations, and institutions were not immediately transformed." Whether or not this was true of institutions and social relations, scholars have generally agreed that a traditional worldview persisted among many peasants well after emancipation, and that at the heart of this worldview—in the words of historian Chris J. Chulos—was "direct contact with the supernatural" in much of everyday life.[81]

Much of this contact involved navigating relations with evil-minded spirits that threatened to inflict major harm on those who were insufficiently careful. Indeed, aside from the *domovoi*, or house spirit, a friendly if sometimes mischievous being who when properly respected looked after a home's inhabitants, most of the supernatural spirits with which peasants had to contend were potentially hostile beings who reflected the many dangers inherent in everyday life. These spirits lurked practically everywhere, taking their names from the features of nature where they resided—forest spirits, hill spirits, water spirits, bath spirits—and could cause trouble at virtually any time. There were also devils, who could assume human form (or, alternately, turn themselves into black cats or frogs) and put the evil eye on their targeted victims; werewolves, who could take the form of wild beasts; witches, "raging women" possessed by evil forces that needed to be exorcised; and a variety of sorcerers, magicians, and people who claimed to be healers but could also commit harmful acts against the unsuspecting. Responses to the Tenishev survey in Vladimir Province indicated both the widespread peasant belief in these forces of darkness and diverse understandings of what one could expect from them. A respondent from the Viazemskii district indicated that water spirits married drowned women, while one from the Melenkovskii district reported that peasants considered it dangerous to swim at midday, after dark, and without a neck cross. From the Viazemskii district, a respondent wrote, "Peasants believe in the bath spirit [*bannik*]," and also believed that to keep devils from using the bania, or steam bath, it was important not to leave water in it. From the Vladimir district, a respondent explained that the bath spirit originated as "the most frightful house spirit," who "live[d] in the bania" and threatened those who washed themselves without praying; using the bania was acceptable for married women but "sinful" for widows and single girls (although forgiven if accompanied by a prayer). But from the Muromskii district came a totally different explanation of the bath spirit's origin, as a "forest spirit [*leshii*] living in a bania," and to avoid him "one should not go to the bania at night."[82]

Peasants developed detailed recipes for how to handle spirits, either by propitiating or confronting them. According to a respondent to the Tenishev survey, peasants believed that "to be saved from a werewolf, one must run to a cross-roads and pronounce 40 times the word 'amen,' and read a special prayer." To deprive sorcerers or witches of "their magical power," one could use a violent blow, knock out a tooth, or curse the offender as a "heretic." Sorcerers and witches caused various ill effects, from illnesses to crop failures, and they could use their magical powers to determine whether a girl was a virgin. One effective way of determining whether someone was a witch was to make her run through a fire: "Whoever refuses to pass through this fire is considered a witch." Sorcerers were often invited to "merrymaking and weddings" to prevent them from causing harm, and complaints against them were not filed in court.[83]

As these examples suggest, numerous prescriptions and proscriptions defined the peasants' magical world and circumscribed their everyday actions. "The Russian peasantry are still wallowing in superstitions," wrote "Stepniak" (populist Sergei Mikhailovich Kravchinskii) in his 1888 study, *The Russian Peasantry*. "With the advent of Christianity the heathen gods and goddesses were not annihilated, but only driven from heaven into hell." Certainly, examples of such "superstitions" were pervasive. One should not destroy a black beetle, because it is a sign of coming wealth. One should avoid spinning on Fridays. To encourage success in river fishing, one should first bathe in and drink the river water. At any agreement consummating a purchase, sale, or rental, a gift was "obligatory," and one should not regret selling one's cattle or they would take a long time to get used to their new owner. A thin line separated the useful magic performed by healers (*znakhari* [literally, "knowers"]) from the magic of sorcerers and witches, but although both used herbs and incantations, the former used prayers as well, and their power came from God, whereas the latter used "unclean" or "impure" power, had tails, and never looked one in the eye. Although healers acted "without the help of unclean power," they sometimes borrowed the knowledge of forest spirits.[84]

Given the misogyny prevalent in nineteenth-century Russia, it is not surprising that restrictive views of women were evident in Russian folk religion as well. An especially striking example appears in the treatment of menstruation. "They treat a woman in the period of monthly cleansing as impure," a respondent to the Tenishev survey reported of peasants in the Melenkovskii district; "she is prohibited from attending church and washing with her family in the bania." A girl's first period received considerable prescriptive attention.

In the Melenkovskii district, her friends would take her out into the snow for a ritual cleansing, pouring water on her and setting her shirt on fire. In the Viazemskii district, a girl was supposed to be quiet about the onset of her first period "or else it might start on her wedding day." In the Shuiskii district, a mother would wash the linens of a girl having her first period in order to limit its length. There, as elsewhere, a woman's period occasioned a variety of "interdictions," from cutting bread to engaging in religious activities: she "does not approach a priest for benediction, does not light an icon lamp, does not go to church, and does not kiss a cross or icon."[85]

Although both church and governmental officials looked down on the peasants' folk religion as backward, and in theory tried to suppress what they considered its most heretical features as "crimes against the faith" and threats to clerical authority, in practice these officials often tolerated beliefs that were too widespread to combat effectively, so long as the peasants also accepted official church doctrine. And, indeed, as historian Chris Chulos has argued, the peasants themselves often viewed practices that to critics seemed distinctly unchristian as fully consistent with Orthodox religion: "Thinking themselves to be Orthodox in every way," he suggested, "peasants did not consider their enchanted view of the world anything less than Christian." In effect, the two worldviews were not that difficult to reconcile: both were based on the same kind of faith in supernatural powers, and both relied heavily on a mechanistic use of magic to achieve desired effects or ward off threats posed by evil forces. Even as most peasants continued to adhere to a multitude of pre-Christian beliefs and practices, they also "remained ... strongly attached to the religious belief and practice that operated within the framework of parish life," and easily assimilated Orthodox Christianity into their folk religion. As one respondent to the Tenishev survey noted, peasants, whose homes were filled with holy icons, "pray[ed] at home morning and evening" and observed requisite fasts so strictly that it was "difficult to convince the sick to drink milk." They considered all non-Russians to be "unchristian," he added, and treated them "with "contempt."[86]

African Americans in the Southern United States also had little trouble reconciling their Christianity with a largely pre-Christian folk religion. Partly based on remnants of African traditions and partly developed on Southern slaveholdings, this folk religion bore both similarities to and differences from that of Russian peasants. African Americans, like Russian peasants, lived in a magical world in which—with the right rituals, potions, and experts—one could bring about desired goals, from curing disease to harming an enemy. Especially under slavery, many African Americans trusted the power of conjurors and Black doctors more than that of officially sanctioned (white) ministers and doctors; as former slave George White, whose father had been owned by a doctor, told an interviewer many years later, "Papa was a kinda doctor too like his master, an' papa knowed all de roots. . . . I know all de roots too," he added, boasting, "I can cure most anything, but you have got to talk wid God an' ask him to help out." Belief in lucky charms, love potions, and magic spells was widespread enough to cause serious embarrassment to ex-slave autobiographers and educated Blacks. H. C. Bruce, for example, who published his autobiography in 1895, described slave conjurors as "a shrewd set of fellows" who succeeded in "fool[ing] the less informed."[87]

For at least three reasons, however, African American folk religion was less all encompassing than that of Russian peasants, and especially by the postemancipation period less apparently threatening to Christian theology. First, there was no real equivalent among Black Americans to the spirits that represented forces of nature—water, mountains, forests, and so on—to the peasants, or for that matter to the wide variety of sorcerers, witches, werewolves, and evil magicians who populated the peasant imagination. Slavery itself, rather than a hostile natural environment, was the principal target that African Americans strove to overcome. Equally important, whereas Russian peasants lived in their ancestral villages, which were largely isolated from the outside world and therefore hospitable to the persistence of traditional values, the cultural discontinuity that the transatlantic slave trade imposed on African Americans, together with the widespread contact with whites under slavery, weakened the persistence of African customs in most of the South, as did the slaves' widespread adoption of Christianity. Finally, the rapid emergence of independent Black Christian churches that accompanied emancipation provided a powerful counterweight that weakened continuing adherence to alternative versions of relating to the supernatural in a way that was largely absent in Russia. In both countries the freedpeople were able to adhere simultaneously to Christianity and elements of their folk religion, but the independent Black churches provided African Americans with an alternative of their own that was largely lacking to Russian peasants. Whereas most Black Southerners enthusiastically embraced their churches, which came to embody their spiritual existence, for Russian peasants the power of traditional folk religion continued to touch almost every aspect of everyday life.[88]

The freedpeople in Russia and the Southern United States experienced both change and continuity as they strove to adjust to their new status in life.

Standing back from the complex and often confusing interplay of these developments, one might suggest that emancipation produced broadly similar outcomes in the two countries that were often experienced differently because of contextual variations. In both countries, emancipation resulted in more freedom for the former slaves and serfs, freedom that had to be continually tested and rewon in struggle and that even then remained circumscribed. In both countries, emancipation made it possible for freedpeople to exercise a greater degree of choice, whether that choice ultimately meant acting in the pursuit of individual and family interests or as members of larger, more general bodies—or both. And in both cases, choice meant the ability to adhere to familiar ways as well as the ability to pursue new opportunities. Ultimately, however, despite the complex interplay of change and continuity that affected freedpeople in both countries, the transformation in the lives of the former slaves was more sweeping than that in the lives of the former serfs, both because slavery had impinged on African Americans in the Southern United States more thoroughly than serfdom had on peasants in Russia and because the post-emancipation regime—at least for a while—was more radical in its goals and policies in the United States than in Russia. As chapter 7 indicates, a similar contrast was evident in the systemic character of what followed slavery and serfdom in the two regions. In both the South and Russia, the post-emancipation social order contained a baffling mix of the new and the old, but changes seemed more revolutionary in the former, more piecemeal and gradual in the latter.

7 • Interpreting Emancipation
Change and Continuity, Hope and Disillusionment

Emancipation brought major changes to the well-being—and perceived well-being—of the population in Russia and the American South. It also reshaped the economic systems of these two societies and led to significant changes in the way people related to each other. At the same time, even as these often-wrenching readjustments were ongoing, there was much that did not change. Emancipation represented an initial step rather than a final determination of the new order: the post-emancipation years saw a continuing struggle over the shape of that order, and freedpeople quickly found that they had to be vigilant in defending what they considered a viable freedom. Historians and other observers have had difficulty agreeing on what changed and what did not, as well as on the nature of relationships that often defied easy characterization; both contemporaries and subsequent analysts disagreed over what standards should be used in evaluating these conditions. If the various protagonists were prone to give preference to subjective impressions over objective measurement, historians often lurched to the other extreme, paying insufficient attention to the context of new (and old) relationships and privileging what could be counted over what was felt. Making sense of this complex stew of change and continuity requires careful consideration both of how people at the time felt and of what they could not recognize—in other words, of two apparently conflicting bases for making historical judgments, one by seeing through the eyes of contemporaries and the other by applying historical hindsight.

As the new order evolved, almost everyone expressed an increasing level of frustration and disappointment—in some cases measured against past conditions, in others by hopes. Such sentiment, which was in part a function of disillusionment driven by dashed expectations and was greatest precisely where those expectations had been most sweeping, was especially evident in comparative context. Because in both the South and Russia emancipation was part of more general efforts to reorient the social order—efforts that went by the name of "Reconstruction" in the former and the "Great Reforms" in the latter—the disillusionment there was more pronounced than in most other post-emancipation societies. This was especially true in the Southern United States, where the collapse of Republican regimes was followed by a massive assault on the ideal of equal citizenship that had been central to the Reconstruction experiment, but in both Russia and the South the last third of the nineteenth century saw the balance of power tip decisively and with increasing virulence against the freedpeople. It is important to note, however, that even as this reaction intensified, the freedpeople managed to hold on to some of the gains they had won, and indeed to make additional, often unheralded, advances: their defeat was a partial one, belied by countless—often ignored—achievements that differentiated their condition from what had prevailed under slavery and under serfdom.

The interplay of change and continuity that characterized the post-emancipation era in Russia and the Southern United States has made it difficult for historians to generalize—and agree—about what was going on. Although it might seem obvious that it was better to be free than to be held in bondage, some historians have challenged the idea that emancipation significantly improved the condition of those who were freed. Recently, several historians of the South have paid increased attention to the immediate hardships resulting from the disruption caused by war and emancipation. After years of neglect, a number of scholars have been exploring the brutality and suffering of life in the contraband (refugee) camps—suffering that led, in the words of historian Thavolia Glymph, to a "growing humanitarian crisis"—while Jim Downs has presented a harrowing picture of Black misery in his recent study *Sick from Freedom*. Noting that "tens of thousands of freed slaves became sick and died due to the unexpected problems caused by the exigencies of war and the massive dislocation triggered by emancipation," he asked, "What does freedom mean if many people failed to survive the war and emancipation? If freedom cannot adequately articulate the ending of slavery, what can?" Although most Southern whites were convinced that "blacks rarely committed suicide," historian Diane Miller Sommerville has argued that "many black Southerners did engage in suicidal activity after the war." Pointing to "a new set of conditions that caused considerable suffering"—conditions that included "untold physical and material hardships that temper the familiar jubilee story"—Sommerville suggested that "many African Americans experienced psychological disorders that at times" led them to kill themselves. Generalizing on the recent "unwriting" of the "freedom narrative"—a narrative that posited a "Whiggish march toward greater and more perfect freedom"—historian Carole Emberton suggested the need for "a twenty-first-century reboot" and concluded that it is time to turn our attention not just to the hardships associated with the end of slavery but also to the racism, violence, exploitation, and "more devious tyrannies" that "long outlived slavery."[1]

A similar challenge to the idea that emancipation improved the status of Russian peasants is evident in the writings of some historians of Russia—especially (although not exclusively) Soviet scholars, who faced the tricky task of reconciling emancipation's revolutionary character with the continued hardship among and exploitation of the freed peasantry. While social revolution and continued hardship were not intrinsically contradictory, many Soviet historians had a hard time emphasizing both at the same time, and when forced to choose they often took the position that whatever freedom and economic amelioration emancipation provided were essentially illusory. "By the Reform the landowners with great success expropriated a substantial part of the peasant lands," concluded Peter I. Lyashchenko, who stressed the peasants' continued "semifeudal economic dependency" and growing economic distress. The editor of a set of documents on the responses to freeing the serfs in Voronezh Province agreed that emancipation constituted a "serfholder's reform" that led to the "progressive impoverishment of the village, [and] a massive impoverishment and dying off of peasants." The result was not freedom but continued "semi-serf exploitation." The emphasis by these historians on the inadequate character of emancipation was similar to that of some American historians, although there was usually a greater stress on the long-term immiseration of the peasantry as a result of growing population pressure on the land than on the disruptive effects of emancipation itself. Usually, but not always: for an assertion of emancipation's negative short-term impact, see the argument of post-Soviet historian B. N. Mironov that "in the first decade after Emancipation, peasants were worse off than they had been under serfdom."[2]

Other scholars have challenged these assertions of emancipation's negative impact. Among historians of the South, some—especially those with an affinity for Marxist analysis—have grappled, like their Soviet counterparts, with the contradictory nature of emancipation, as both revolutionary and exploitative, simultaneously productive of major changes and undercut by holdovers from the old order. Thavolia Glymph, for example, even while stressing the "revolutionary impact of emancipation," concluded that "in the end, the consequences were catastrophic for all southerners, but particularly for blacks." Similarly, Eric Foner described emancipation and Reconstruction as constituting an "unfinished revolution" but ultimately came down on the side of what was *not* accomplished: "Whether measured by the dreams inspired by emancipation or the more limited goals of securing blacks' rights as citizens and free laborers ... ," he concluded, "Reconstruction can only be judged a failure." Along the same lines, Edward L. Ayers asserted that "Reconstruction truly was radical" but then explained that although "the Republicans constructed a remarkable machine at every level of government and society, they ran out of electoral fuel to run that machine." The end result was therefore "complete legal segregation, disfranchisement, and subjugation of black Southerners." And Lee-Anna Keith, who praised the "Radical Republicans" as true revolutionaries, "culture warriors, committed to a nearly mystical vision of representative government based on free labor," conceded that "their aims were not pure, and even during the Civil War the Radicals manifested a venality and love of power that coexisted uneasily with their humanitarian goals." Still other historians, however, even while admitting their limitations, emphasized the positive changes brought by emancipation and Reconstruction. James L. Roark, for example, acknowledged the "image of continuity" but dubbed it "as much illusory as real"; suggesting that "slavery had been a kind of log jam behind which the forces of social and cultural change had stacked up," he concluded that "with emancipation, the South moved toward the mainstream of American development." And when it came to change and progress versus continuity and stagnation among Blacks in North Carolina, Robert Kenzer came down squarely on the side of the former. Noting their "slow but steady progress in acquiring real estate" during the fifty years after emancipation, he emphasized the "economic opportunities" open to what he termed "enterprising southerners."[3]

Historians of Russia have also disputed assertions of the growing hardship among the freed population. If some Soviet historians stressed the cruelly exploitative nature of the emancipation settlement, others, like P. A. Zaionchkovskii, gave equal weight to the impact of "personal freedom," which he noted had "a huge positive significance." Still others combined the two arguments by suggesting that relatively little changed *immediately* for the peasants but a far-reaching capitalist transformation became pervasive from the 1880s.

Meanwhile, many scholars in the United States and Britain have questioned the supposed immiseration of Russia's post-emancipation peasantry. Summarizing this scholarship, Carol S. Leonard recently concluded that during the last third of the nineteenth century "peasants were not as impoverished as once thought," a conclusion echoed in David Moon's observation that "in recent decades historians have seriously challenged the whole idea that there was a 'crisis' in peasant living standards after 1861," as well as in David Saunders's assertion that "despite appearances, the reforms of the 1860s can be said to have improved the prospects of the peasantry," and in Boris Mironov and Brian A'Hearn's suggestion that recent scholarship on Russian peasants' standard of living in the post-emancipation era "is moving the consensus . . . away from agrarian crisis interpretations and toward a cautiously optimistic assessment."[4]

Making sense of these divergent judgments is not easy, but one can begin by distinguishing between emancipation's short-term and long-term consequences. There is considerable evidence that as an immediate result of the disruption caused by emancipation—which in the Southern United States was closely linked to the much greater disruption caused by the Civil War—many freedpeople experienced a decline in measurable living standards. Black wartime flight was compounded by Black removal, as slave owners sought to relocate their bondspeople in "safer" areas, far from advancing Union troops, and was then compounded anew after the war as African Americans tested their freedom by leaving their homes and continuing to migrate to find better jobs. Movement spread disease, not only to contraband camps, which in the words of historian Chandra Manning were "places where absolutely everybody was up against more than he or she could manage," but also throughout the entire South; as historian Jim Downs put it, "The most significant factor that led to the widespread outbreak of disease was the massive dislocation that the war and emancipation caused." If movement was an important weapon for Blacks as they sought better wages, it was also a source of disruption, hardship, and death, as "the Civil War precipitated a health crisis unprecedented in the nation's history." Pointing to "a worsening of health" after the Civil War, economist Edward Meekar suggested a temporary sharp decline in life expectancy at birth among Southern Blacks, with figures of twenty-eight for males and twenty-nine for females in 1880, before rebounding by 1910 to thirty-one for males and thirty-four for females.[5]

Although Russian peasants did not experience anything like the chaos and destruction that accompanied the American Civil War, the Crimean War of

1853–55 and more generally the emancipation that began in 1861 also led to substantial disruption and a concomitant decline in peasant well-being. Historian B. N. Mironov, who pointed to a temporary deterioration in "the diet of the poorer and middle strata of the peasantry as well as that of the urban poor," has calculated that the "mean height of military recruits" born in the late 1850s and 1860s decreased significantly, before rebounding for those born thereafter. Russian mortality rates remained exceptionally high in the years following emancipation—especially for children, with almost one-third dying before the age of one and almost one-half before the age of five.[6]

Of course, short-term effects—including the stunted height of Russian recruits and the depressed life expectancy of African Americans—were just that: short-term. Even as the inevitable disruption caused by war and emancipation created real suffering, the groundwork was being laid for fundamental changes that would evolve over subsequent decades. As Daniel B. Thorp suggested in his recent study of African Americans in Montgomery County, Virginia, it is important to consider the "Long Reconstruction" that brought significant changes to the lives of former slaves. "Indeed," he pointed out, "extensive economic changes were just beginning when [official] Reconstruction ended in the commonwealth [1870], and they continued in the decades that followed. Similarly, by 1870 black churches and [public] schools were just beginning to emerge in Virginia, and they continued to grow and develop in important ways over the next thirty years." What is more, even in the short term, hardship and suffering were accompanied by joy occasioned by the end of bondage, and by observations of positive changes (such as the surge in new schools for former slaves and serfs, together with their passionate desire for education). In *Troubled Refuge,* historian Chandra Manning tellingly warned against two opposite interpretive mistakes—on the one hand "sanitizing suffering with an 'all for the best' outlook" and on the other "getting stuck in the violence and pain, unable to see any meaning at all in it beyond utterly senseless, gratuitous suffering." Noting that "the death of slavery was violent," she countered that "slavery, not the act of exiting it, was the killer." Her point is an important one: painful as it was for its victims, the suffering brought on by social revolution should not be allowed to become that revolution's only—or principal—story.[7]

Over time, even as freedpeople continued to struggle for what they considered a real freedom, they experienced significant changes, from increased literacy rates to increased mobility and increased property ownership. Although many of these changes have been treated in previous chapters, it is worth revisiting them here in summary fashion—together with what did not change—as we seek to come to grips with the interplay of change and continuity in the post-emancipation lives of peasants and African Americans. Variations over space complicate the picture, as do variations resulting from personal characteristics of freedpeople, landowners, and officials, and considering developments in the comparative context of what happened elsewhere where emancipation occurred adds still a different basis for judging developments in Russia and the Southern United States.[8]

It is worthwhile to begin with two important characteristics that did *not* change for most peasants and African Americans: the kind of labor in which they engaged and their continued relative poverty. Despite modest industrialization and urbanization, both Russia and the South remained overwhelmingly rural, and although increasing numbers of freedpeople took advantage of opportunities in diverse fields of endeavor, most continued to perform some form of agricultural labor, as they had under bondage. Equally important, despite their legal freedom—and in the United States their legal equality—former slaves and serfs remained on the whole far poorer than other Southerners and Russians, especially their former owners. Most former serfs received very small landholdings—holdings that were smaller than those they already considered their own and that became substantially smaller over time as the peasant population increased and with it the pressure on land—for which they owed hefty redemption payments for the rest of their lives; peasants were mired in debt. Most former slaves began their lives as freedpeople with even less property than former serfs: census records of 1870 and 1880 indicate that the great majority owned no real or personal property at all, while those few who had managed to accumulate any personal possessions typically owned very little. As the title of one of Eric Foner's books indicated, emancipation provided them "nothing but freedom."[9]

But to say that Black Southerners and Russian peasants were poor and exploited, and continued to engage in the same kind agricultural work they had performed as slaves and serfs, hardly means that nothing changed; throughout history, most people have been poor and exploited—in a variety of different ways, under a variety of different conditions. As historian Joseph P. Reidy has argued, the question of "whether the Civil War destroyed slavery" deserves "a qualified yes," despite the persistence of "exploitation" and "discrimination based on race." The existence of legal freedom—and in the United States at least in theory equal legal rights—meant that when old ways persisted, they did so within a fundamentally changed context. In Russia, for example, peasant life continued to be heavily communal, but the commune acquired important new functions—such as deciding whether peasants could leave their villages or split their families—to replace functions that had previously been the prerogative of serfholders. In the Southern United States, the breakup of the slave quarters and (in most places) the end of gang labor reinforced the individualism that had already been a pervasive feature of slave life, even as countervailing trends facilitated widespread organizational activity and collective endeavor.[10]

In both countries, emancipation led to important new departures that made possible significant changes in the lives of the freedpeople. In Russia, otkhod surged as peasants increasingly sought employment away from their villages, and household divisions multiplied as young couples sought to set up their own families free from the control of family patriarchs, in the process challenging both patriarchal and communal authority—and often that of pomeshchiki as well. Meanwhile, although peasants did not have access to the kind of political activities that mushroomed among freed African Americans, traditional communal "justice"—*samosud*—was supplemented by new peasant courts, and peasants elected representatives to zemstvo assemblies at both the district and the provincial levels. In the South, the shortage of labor and the ability to move facilitated a new kind of collective bargaining between African Americans and white landowners, even as the proliferation of diverse forms of labor relations, together with the growth of family farming, fundamentally reoriented the lives of rural freedpeople. Meanwhile, Blacks eagerly embraced new opportunities for collective action, in churches, schools, group land purchases, and political activity. And both Russia and the South saw a groping toward new relationships not only between freedpeople and their former owners but also among the freedpeople themselves—especially in their families, as relations between both men and women and parents and children underwent renegotiation and redefinition.

If the changes were more sweeping in the American South than in Russia—and I think they were, both because slavery had impinged more on the lives of its victims than serfdom had on those of its victims and because the way freedom came to the American slaves, through Civil War, made possible more of a break with the past than occurred in Russia—emancipation brought fundamental changes to both societies. In dozens of big and small ways, "personal freedom" transformed the lives of the former slaves and serfs, from the ability to move and marry without the consent of former owners to the ability to be compensated for their labor. In the broadest sense, freedom meant a significant reduction in the power that planters and pomeshchiki exercised over their former bondspeople, and an opening of new opportunities for the freedpeople. Slaves and serfs had never constituted homogeneous bodies, but emancipation made possible a significant and accelerating increase in their diversity—whether measured by occupation, mobility, economic well-being, family and other relationships, or educational level.

Underlying these developments were fundamental changes that—despite differences between their precise nature in Russia and the South—can be characterized by the term "peasantization." In Russia, emancipation and the attendant land redemption initiated a vast transfer of productive agricultural resources from the nobility to the peasantry, a transfer that gained momentum over time as peasants bought and rented additional parcels of noble land not included in the redemption agreements. Although African Americans did not acquire most of the land that had formerly been held by slave owners, they too underwent a process of peasantization, based on the spread among them of family farming, whether by farm owners or farm renters (including various types of sharecropping). Unlike many slaves, who lived in the "quarters" and worked in gangs under the control of white owners or overseers, an increasing proportion of rural African Americans ran their own farms. In both countries, some freedpeople worked for and took directions from (white or noble) landowners, but they constituted a shrinking minority of the Black and peasant populations.

The existence of this peasantization raises tricky questions about the "transition to capitalism" that many historians have seen as central to emancipation in both Russia and the Southern United States, and a growing number of scholars have either rejected the "transition to capitalism" model altogether or proposed major modifications of it. Among historians of Russia, the most prominent critic of the capitalism thesis was Teodor Shanin, who in a 1985 book, *Russia as a "Developing Society,"* stressed the peasant-based character of post-emancipation agriculture and rejected the notion of a linear progression from feudalism to capitalism as based on a flawed understanding of the Russian economy, which he saw as neither feudal nor capitalist. "At the turn of the [twentieth] century," he wrote, "Russia was a 'developing society,' arguably the first of its kind." Many other historians have followed Shanin in stressing the extent to which Russia's agricultural economy was based on peasant production, without necessarily adopting the "developing society" model. Rather than laboring for "capitalist" landowners, for wages, most peasants were farmers working their own land (or in some cases land they rented); as historian Robert Bidelux observed, "Hired agricultural labourers made up only about

5 percent of the agrarian workforce in European Russia in 1900," and as Carol S. Leonard pointed out, by the eve of the Bolshevik Revolution nobles controlled only 7.7 percent of Russia's agricultural land. Historians of the Southern United States have also rebutted the idea of a linear transition to capitalism, in which African American slaves became proletarian laborers. As Alex Lichtenstein noted in an essay provocatively entitled "Was the Emancipated Slave a Proletarian?" the answer to this question was definitely no: after emancipation, only a small minority of freedpeople were wage earners, and "prior to the New Deal, rural African Americans constituted an American peasantry" rather than a class of proletarians.[11]

The transition-to-capitalism thesis is further complicated by disagreements among historians over the nature of capitalism itself—disagreements that in some ways have been quite different among historians of the South from those among historians of Russia but that in both cases raise similar questions about the relationship of emancipation to other historical developments. Historians of Southern slavery have increasingly rejected the idea that the "peculiar institution" was a backward socioeconomic system impeding Southern development and fundamentally at odds with "free labor," maintaining instead that slavery—at least in the version that emerged in the antebellum South—was modern, efficient, and in many ways a quintessentially capitalist formation. If some scholars have viewed Southern slavery itself as a major case of capitalist economics, others have located the origins of Russian capitalism less in the post-emancipation exploitation of peasants by nobles than in that of peasants by other—richer—peasants. This thesis drew its first detailed exposition in 1899 in a lengthy book entitled *The Development of Capitalism in Russia*, in which Vladimir Lenin stressed the increasing post-emancipation stratification of the peasantry, with a peasant bourgeoisie—"the masters of the contemporary countryside"—exploiting the labor of the larger peasant proletariat of "allotment-holding wage workers." Describing this intra-peasant exploitation as a "progressive" if brutal development, Lenin argued that "agricultural capitalism has for the first time undermined the age-old stagnation of our agriculture."[12]

Underlying these debates are fundamental disagreements about the nature of "capitalism." As suggested above, in the Introduction, if the term is taken to mean the desire to pursue profit or make money on the basis of commercial endeavor—the buying and selling of commodities—then capitalism was by definition pervasive, not only after emancipation but also under slavery and serfdom (and throughout most of recorded history). This was true both among the masters, who strove to make money from the labor of their slaves and serfs as well as sometimes from treating those slaves and serfs as commodities themselves, and among the bondspeople, who took advantage wherever possible of commercial opportunities that were increasingly available to them. When slaves relied on the labor of family members to profit from the garden plots they were allotted, they can be said to have acted like little capitalists; as historian Larry Hudson argued, "The stronger the families, the better able they were" to engage in "property accumulation." The same was true of serf families, whose economic well-being was widely recognized as dependent on their size. After emancipation, former masters sought when possible to continue profiting from the labor of peasants and African Americans and, in Russia, to maximize the redemption income they received from their former serfs, while freedpeople endeavored to take advantage of new opportunities to maximize their income.[13]

If, however, capitalism is defined as a system of labor based on the separation of compensated workers from ownership of the means of production—that is, on some form of wages—it becomes less universal, and the "transition to capitalism" becomes more meaningful; under this understanding, slavery and serfdom were *by definition* noncapitalist forms of labor. Of course, historians (and others) are free to define things as they choose, but I would suggest that for at least three reasons this definition of "capitalism" is more useful than the income-accumulation model. First, whereas the latter describes a condition that is so universal across time and space as to render it almost meaningless, the labor-system definition is historically specific, describing a relationship that developed in particular places, at particular times, for particular reasons. Second, the labor-system definition is not simply imposed by historians on the past but is consistent with the understanding of nineteenth-century contemporaries. Although Karl Marx developed an elaborate theory of capitalism in *Das Kapital* and other works, most non-Marxists (who were often unaware of Marx's writings) referred to capitalism as the "free-labor system," which they understood in basically Marxist terms as a system based on compensated, voluntary labor in contrast to the forced labor that prevailed under slavery and serfdom. Third and most important, understanding capitalism as a particular labor system that emerged under particular conditions is consistent with the kind of broad social transformation that actually occurred. Although most free peasants and African Americans did not immediately become wage earners, the post-emancipation social order in both Russia and the Southern United States increasingly showed the earmarks of a system based on "free-labor" or capitalist principles, from the new centrality of contracts in relations between freedpeople and landowners to the decline of planter and pomeshchik paternalism and the growing salience of class rather than of legally defined status in social and economic relations. Although legal equality progressed substantially further in the United States than in Russia, the abolition of serfdom and subsequent reforms put Russia as well on the road to a basic transformation, in the words of historian Seymour Becker, from an "estate society . . . into some variant of a modern class society," with an accompanying governmental transformation into what historian Petr Zaionchkovskii termed a "bourgeois monarchy."[14]

As was evident in chapter 5, after emancipation both Russia and the Southern United States saw the proliferation of multiple, diverse forms of agricultural labor that ranged from wages to various forms of sharecropping to farming on owned or rented land. Despite the prevalence of peasantization, or family farming rather than wage labor, the social order in both countries can be described as increasingly "capitalistic" in several important respects. To begin, the reformers who drafted and implemented the new order—from government officials at the top to those who served at the local level as missionaries, teachers, Freedmen's Bureau agents, and peace mediators—consciously thought of themselves as promoting free labor, which they distinguished from coerced labor both by being compensated and voluntary and by providing the laborers with a variety of basic rights that often were grouped together as providing "personal freedom." Many of the proponents of the free-labor system, especially but not exclusively in the United States, were also committed to inculcating among the laborers a set of "bourgeois" values that varied in its precise composition but could include honesty, cleanliness, punctuality, orderliness, religion, self-improvement, civic virtue, and a desire to advance one's material condition through hard work. Free labor could come in different versions, ranging from draconian understandings of the obligation to be well behaved and work hard to democratic notions of full citizenship and equal rights, but in all of these versions free labor was distinct from labor that was forced and uncompensated.

Because free labor was voluntary rather than compelled, a central feature of the new system was the contract—presumably reached voluntarily between the contracting parties. Contracts or mutual agreements were ubiquitous after emancipation. As historian Amy Dru Stanley argued in describing them as the "dominant metaphor for social relations and the very symbol of freedom" in the post-emancipation era, contracts represented "relation[s] of voluntary exchange, ... premised on self ownership"; they helped Americans and Russians navigate the tricky question of what could and could not be bought and sold—and by whom—in an era that saw a dramatic expansion of market relations. As former slaves and serfs became freedpeople, contracts helped define the central features of their new lives. In the South, the Freedmen's Bureau supervised the introduction of labor contracts—and sometimes marriage contracts as well—while in Russia peace mediators and other government officials oversaw negotiations between peasants and landowners over statutory charters and redemption agreements, even as migrant laborers bargained with pomeshchiki or their representatives over the terms of their temporary employment. Negotiations between freedpeople and their former owners, which had sometimes existed informally under slavery and serfdom, were one-sided in the sense that planters and pomeshchiki had significantly more power than African Americans and peasants—as historian Caitlin Rosenthal observed, "The former slaves gained some control over work patterns and personal mobility, but they did not gain significant economic power"—but they were far from meaningless and represented a dramatically changed political dynamic. Inherent in these negotiations, which were now formally sanctioned by the government, were important new rights for the freedpeople—including the right *not* to come to terms—and important new limitations on the authority of former owners, who typically found the necessity of bargaining with their former property deeply humiliating. The power of contracts and other legal documents also indicated the fetishism of the written word in capitalist social relations: oral promises could be easily broken and were often worthless, but written agreements acquired a surprising sanctity that endured even under the most adverse conditions.[15]

The abolition of slavery and serfdom accentuated the freedpeople's access to commercial products and to commerce itself. Of course, that access had never been entirely lacking: slaves and serfs had engaged in numerous small-scale commercial ventures, and occasional more substantial operations as well. Being free, however, significantly expanded the ability of Blacks and peasants to engage in their own economic activities and also expanded their exposure to outside influences. Family farming was the most immediate and pervasive of these economic activities, as freedpeople raised agricultural goods for market as well as for home consumption; such farming represented a modest expansion of what had already existed for many Russian peasants (those whose principal obligation to their owners consisted of *obrok* payments) and a more substantial novelty for most African Americans, as well as for those peasants who as serfs had owed their owners labor services (*barshchina*) amounting to three or in some cases more than three days per week. The geographic mobility that followed in the wake of emancipation both facilitated the development of this family-oriented agricultural production and made possible other kinds of commercial activities, as Blacks and peasants increasingly left home to work in nearby cities and factories as well as to take advantage of other opportunities that ranged from engaging in trade to migrant agricultural labor, barge hauling, and dock work. In short, emancipation made possible a sharp increase in the already diverse economic activities of previously unfree African Americans and peasants.[16]

Increased exposure to outside influences reshaped the values and customs of these freedpeople in a variety of ways. The presence of outsiders, such as teachers, could have a significant impact, especially in the American South, where teachers and missionaries consciously promoted bourgeois behavioral traits in their interactions with freedpeople. Even more significant were the consequences of Black and peasant outmigration—whether temporary or long-term—as freedpeople observed and absorbed new ways and returned home with new values, products, and often money. Geographic mobility inevitably exposed freedpeople to experiences, ideas, and ways of behaving different from those with which they were familiar, and reduced the kind of parochialism that was often present in peasant and Black communities. Freedpeople learned about reading, voting, and signing contracts, but also about consumer products, ready-made clothing, and interacting with one another—and with members of other classes—as free men and women.

In both countries, this process went hand in hand with growing regional diversity, and often with the growing influence of urban culture as well. In Russia, the gap widened substantially between the southern provinces, where most peasants continued to work the land, and the less fertile northern provinces, where increasing numbers of peasant otkhodniki sought outside employment. As Carol S. Leonard noted, the north, where by 1913 only about 14 percent of the arable land was cultivated, was a "consumer" region, in contrast to the "producer" region in the south, where some two-thirds of the land was cultivated. Concurrently, "commercialization broadened the knowledge and skills of peasants and increased income inequality." In the Southern United States, there was similarly increasing regional variation, with family farming prevailing in the Deep South's cotton kingdom and the Upper South's tobacco lands while wage labor came to dominate the workforce on the sugar estates of southern Louisiana. Meanwhile, emancipation—and foreign competition—administered a crushing blow to the rice production of Lowcountry Georgia and South Carolina. In both Russia and the South, regional differentiation increased significantly in the late nineteenth and early twentieth centuries, accompanied by a surge in industrialization and overall economic development that overcame the temporary dislocations caused by emancipation and (especially in the American South) war.[17]

These developments had a growing impact on the freedpeople, who were exposed to—and increasingly adopted—"modern" ways. In Russia, if traditional peasant thinking and values—from suspicion of outsiders to widespread illiteracy to belief in magic and witchcraft—often survived emancipation relatively unchanged, new patterns of thought and behavior were increasingly evident from the 1880s, especially but by no means exclusively in areas where otkhod flourished. A host of new contacts interacted with increased literacy (especially among young men) to reshape the peasant world and worldview: outworkers returned either permanently or on temporary visits from cities to their native villages, teachers and priests interacted with curious villagers, and peasants became familiar with a variety of proto-democratic institutions, from peasant courts to district and provincial zemstvo assemblies. Meanwhile, in the words of historian Jeffrey Burds, "a mass consumer consciousness emerged among the peasants in the Central Industrial Region," with the spread of a restless "desire to succeed," conspicuous consumption, and new luxuries from white bread and sugar to cosmetics, newspapers, kerosene lamps, and comfortable furniture. In Viriatino (Morshansk district, Tambov Province), the pace of change accelerated markedly in the 1880s and 1890s, as peasants who could afford to do so began to replace traditional wooden huts with brick houses containing separate kitchens, use of purchased fabric increasingly replaced homespun clothing, and family life was revolutionized by divisions, resulting smaller size, marriages that gave new attention to "mutual personal inclination," and relaxation of strict patriarchal relations under which "it was customary for the head of the family to hold a switch in one hand throughout the meal" so as to "swat those who laughed too loud or talked too much." According to historian Boris Mironov, the growth of more "humane" family relations among peasants in the late nineteenth century—"due to the impact of urban culture, the expansion of migrant labor, the commercialization of agriculture, and the growing role of women in the peasant economy"—went hand in hand with a major change in peasant mentality, as "rationalism, pragmatism, economic calculation, and individualism gradually became the main determinants of conduct."[18]

The picture painted by these historians is one of accelerating change in the freedpeople's consciousness, worldview, and to some extent standard of living. Indeed, Mironov's suggestion that in the immediate post-emancipation years "humane" family relations reached only about 15 percent of the peasant population, with the "authoritarian family" undergoing "a slow decline among the remaining 85 percent," is broadly consistent with the accelerating rate of economic growth, industrialization, and urbanization that Russia experienced during the last quarter of the nineteenth century as well as with the testimony of various contemporaries. If most peasants remained unaware of and unconcerned with the "outside" world, according to correspondents of the Tenishev survey in Vladimir Province, in the 1890s peasant officials such as starosti and starshiny routinely read the easily accessible *Sel'skii Vestnik* (Rural Herald), and an increasing number of peasants also read other papers that used simple language, such as *Svet* (Light), *Birzhevye vedomosti* (Merchants' Gazette), and *Syn otechestva* (Son of the Fatherland), where they could learn about "wars, famines, harvests, and especially terrible events occurring in various places." When nobleman Aleksandr Engelgardt returned to his ancestral estate in Smolensk Province in 1872, after an absence of many years, he was struck by peasant poverty—"There is no grain, there is no work," and begging was ubiquitous—but within a few years he was emphasizing "how much has changed since Emancipation." The improvements included manners—"The peasants began to lose the habit of being flogged, of being punched in the mouth," and in court everyone "began to address the muzhik in the formal you form"—but also economic well-being. "Formerly," Engelgardt wrote in 1881, "peasants worked on the gentry estates and lived in poverty, they were constantly looking for work, money, and grain. Now they work on their own farms, they rent land from the landowners and prosper." With declining gentry cultivation, peasants paid more attention to their own land and embraced technological improvements such as "planting closer" and "acquiring ploughs." By the turn of the century, "peasant values expressed at township courts could well be described as bourgeois . . . ," wrote historian Jane Burbank. "As taxpayers, as participants in the market economy, as producers and sellers of commodities, peasants expected their courts to enforce contractual agreement and to protect property."[19]

Although in some ways the impact of freedom on freedpeople was more immediate in the Southern United States than in Russia—most obvious was the political revolution and full citizenship brought by Reconstruction—African Americans also experienced accelerated change during the half century after emancipation. As in Russia, the pace of industrialization and urbanization in the South picked up substantially in the 1880s and 1890s, and increasing numbers of former slaves came into contact with diverse features of "modern" life. The "amazing rise in African American literacy" and the surge in farm owners from 17,785 (2.2 percent of Black "farmers") in 1870 to 207,815 (24 percent) in 1910 were two features of this accelerating change. As historian Loren Schweninger noted, in criticizing "facile arguments about the re-emergence of slavery" after the end of Reconstruction, "It is difficult to view this period without being struck by the remarkable expansion of black property owning." A similar point could be made about the growing "economic opportunities of the black business community," which according to historian Robert Kenzer "were not severely hindered either by the end of Reconstruction during the 1870s or by disfranchisement" that followed.[20]

Of course, most former slaves were not landowners or businessmen, but many historians have placed the emergence of sharecropping and other forms of family farming within the context of a "profound" transformation toward "a more capitalist and market-driven society." Some scholars have seen sharecropping as essentially a primitive form of wage labor, while others, like Barbara Fields, have portrayed sharecropping as "a transitional form on the way to capitalist wage labor." (Significantly, Lenin made the same argument about Russia's version of sharecropping, *otrabotka*, which he saw as a remnant of serfdom that would increasingly yield to more progressive wage labor.) In any case, with the transformation of the slave South into the free-labor South, former slaves increasingly enjoyed the fruits of this capitalist revolution and were able to participate more actively than before in market relations. Purchasing ready-made products—from plantation stores, general (country) stores, and mail-order houses—was one of these fruits; as a freedwoman from Mississippi put it, "[My] greatest pleasure was independence—make my money, go and spend it as I see fit." Rural freedpeople "turned to stores for everything they needed," while in cities "blacks steadily accumulated property," including "considerable amounts of clothes, furniture, musical instruments, bicycles, and buggies."[21]

The transition to capitalism that followed emancipation in Russia and the Southern United States was a halting, uneven, and contested process; as historian Martin Ruef noted, "*Enduring uncertainty* was a defining feature of this transition between precapitalist and capitalist institutions."[22] Certainly, as many historians have emphasized, traditional values proved resilient, and there was much that did not change in the world and worldview of the former slaves and the serfs. At the same time, the end of bondage and the creation of diverse forms of free labor created the preconditions for an ongoing—indeed, accelerating—transition to a new social order, one predicated on (technically) voluntary labor relationships based on unequal power but not on legal coercion and legal distinctions in status. Nowhere was this change more evident than in the checkered fate of the former master class—the slaveholders and serfholders who lost most (in the United States, all) of their hereditary privileges and now struggled to establish themselves as businessmen (and occasionally women), capitalists in a new world of predatory capitalism.

In both countries, a sense of pervasive decline gripped the former masters. In part this sense reflected the fulfillment of oft-repeated prophesies: slaveholders and serfholders had been so vociferous in warning that emancipation would herald the destruction of an entire civilization that once slavery and serfdom were in fact overthrown, insisting that this destruction was well under way became an almost automatic refrain. In part, too, the sense of decline reflected a profound feeling of loss, a loss that in the South was doubly profound because, for most slaveholders, the loss of their slaves was compounded by the loss of their war. In the words of Sir Donald Mackenzie Wallace, whose travelogue of Russia went through numerous editions beginning in 1877, emancipation precipitated "a severe economic crisis" for noble landholders, a statement that could be applied with equal validity to former slaveholders in the Southern United States. Southern planters and Russian pomeshchiki found it deeply humiliating to have to bargain with people they considered inferior and were used to directing, and they acted in a variety of ways to reduce their contact with the freedpeople whom they had often claimed to love as members of their own families. This distancing ranged from fleeing the country (as with white Southerners who moved to Brazil or Cuba) to the more common option of moving from a home plantation or estate to a nearby city. More generally, however, it involved washing one's hands of direct supervision of agricultural operations—and of the human beings who made those operations possible—a move inherent in the widespread peasantization that occurred in both the South and Russia. Pomeshchik absenteeism, which was already common in Russia, became even more prevalent, while planter absenteeism, which had been less typical, became increasingly evident as well. In the well-chosen words of historian Gavin Wright, "laborlords" turned into "landlords."[23]

If planters and pomeshchiki nurtured an impressive array of grievances centering on their loss of status, power, and economic well-being, many historians have agreed that former slave owners and serfholders faced an existential crisis in the post-emancipation years. Roberta Thompson Manning, for example, echoed Wallace's observations, suggesting that emancipation—"an enormous blow to the landed gentry"—initiated "a prolonged period of economic crisis for the Russian Empire's leading estate" and concluding that "none of the palliatives available to the gentry after Emancipation could stem their inexorable economic decline." Diverse other historians have agreed with Manning that "economically, the nobles were losing their grip" and "both as owners and as cultivators of the soil they had gone into a precipitate decline," and indeed, despite the establishment of a Noble Land Bank in 1885 to prop up their economic position, "the erosion of the nobility's economic position seemed to be accelerating." According to Terence Emmons, the gentry—suffering from growing indebtedness, falling grain prices, and a disinclination to engage in capitalistic agriculture—underwent a pervasive economic decline during the last third of the nineteenth century, while historian Boris Mironov saw the nobility as not only losing most of its estate privileges but also experiencing widespread "impoverishment" after 1861.[24]

Historians of the post-emancipation South have described a similar crisis among former slave owners. In *Masters without Slaves*, James L. Roark provided a sensitive treatment of the planters' struggle to cope with the real and imagined loss of their world. Emphasizing both their "profound alienation" from the New South—"from the planters' perspective, the postbellum plantation was almost unrecognizable"—and the reality of their "gradual decline and relative poverty" in which "few escaped hardship," Roark also described the new challenges that planters faced "from small farmers, middle-class professionals, and the new urban, industrial class," which had been a central theme in C. Vann Woodward's influential earlier volume, *Origins of the New South, 1877–1913*. According to Woodward, the post-emancipation South saw the "downfall of the old planter class," and its replacement by a new, business-oriented class of merchants and industrial capitalists. Under the new order, "it was necessary that the acquisitive instincts not only become respectable, but that they be regarded as ambition," he explained. "Speculation should be awarded the prizes of courage and valor, and the profit motive mile-posted as the road to the good life."[25]

The thesis of the decline of the former owners is persuasive—within a carefully defined context. Certainly, compared to their previous status, former slaveholders and serfholders lost many of their legal privileges and found their new condition degrading and deplorable. When compared with what might have been or contrasted with the status of other people, however, their "decline" appears less than overwhelming. Most Southern slaveholders were supporters of an armed insurrection against the government of the United States, but rather than being tried for treason they were with very few exceptions welcomed back into the fold, as citizens of the United States. Although today many people favor compensating the descendants of slaves for their suffering, there was little serious discussion of such a policy in the 1860s, and it was Russian serfholders, not Russian serfs, who received compensation—in the form of redemption payments from the former serfs themselves. (Such compensation for the loss of human property was common in the nineteenth century: American emancipation was unusual in the international context in lacking any payment to the former owners.)

As for economic decline, here too context inevitably shapes conclusions. It is true that many planters suffered materially—along with other Southerners—in the post-emancipation years, but this was primarily as a result of the devastation caused by four years of unusually bloody warfare rather than the ending of slavery itself; between 1860 and 1880, Southern per capita income decreased 15 percent (from $103 to $88) even as the national average in the United States as a whole increased 35 percent (from $128 to $173); in 1860, Southern per capita income had been 80.5 percent of the national average, but by 1880 the South's income amounted to only 50.9 percent of the nation's. Needless to say, Russia did not experience anything remotely similar. It is also true that pomeshchiki lost much of the land they had owned under serfdom, but they were well compensated for this "loss," through redemption payments from peasants and additional land purchases (at significantly higher prices stemming from rising land value) by peasants and merchants; pomeshchiki owned substantially less land after than before emancipation, and their holdings continued to decrease, but they were hardly poorer as a result. As historian Seymour Becker put it, "The landed nobility was ... not so much undergoing a process of decline or impoverishment ... as it was experiencing a radical transformation—one, in large part, of its own choosing." A. P. Korelin, the leading Soviet expert on the post-emancipation nobility, estimated that from 1861 to 1897 Russian noblemen earned between 35.4 and 44.8 million rubles annually from redemption payments and sale of additional land, while rising land prices meant that the land that remained in noble hands at the end of the nineteenth century was worth more than twice what it had been at the time of emancipation.[26]

Indeed, most former slaveholders and serfholders remained vastly richer (as well as more privileged and powerful) than other Southerners and Russians. In Saratov Province, for example, 335 nobles owned 308,703 desiatiny of land in 1867, for an average holding of 921.5 desiatiny; by 1883, their numbers had decreased to 254, but their average holding had increased in size to 1,052 desiatiny (for a total noble landholding of 267,207.2 desiatiny). Of course, there was enormous variation in wealth among these nobles—some owned multiple estates with tens of thousands of desiatiny, while others were "impoverished," and an increasing number moved to cities and gave up landholding entirely; according to Boris Mironov, nobles who owned fewer than one hundred desiatiny of land were considered poor, and between 1861 and 1895 the proportion of these "poor" nobles increased from 41 percent to 64.4 percent. It is worth noting however, that, as Seymour Becker observed, nobles who sold their land received enormous profits, while the sharp rise in the price of land—from about thirteen rubles per desiatina on the eve of emancipation to ninety-three rubles at the beginning of the twentieth century—meant that "noble land increased in value faster than it decreased in extent." By contrast, peasant holdings were puny, and they contracted over time as the peasant population grew: in 1860, the average size of peasant allotment holdings (among serfs and state peasants) was 4.8 desiatiny per male soul, a figure that decreased to 2.6 desiatiny per soul by 1900 and was only modestly supplemented by peasant purchases of private land. Noble "impoverishment" must be considered within this context: "poor" nobles were poorer than rich nobles, and poorer than they wanted to be, but they were vastly richer than most Russians.[27]

Former slaveholders also remained economically dominant in the post-emancipation South. As historian Gavin Wright and others have shown, before emancipation, despite enormous variations in the wealth of slaveholders, the largest and most significant gap among free people was between slave owners and non–slave owners: in years immediately preceding the Civil War, "slaveholders controlled between 90 and 95 percent of [the South's] agricultural wealth," and in 1860 the "average" slave owner in the cotton South was 13.9 times as rich as the "average" non-slaveholding white. As a number of historians have demonstrated, despite the loss of wealth that slaveholders suffered from the uncompensated freeing of their slaves, there was considerable "planter persistence" after emancipation, and "landholdings remained extremely concentrated." Landed wealth was relatively unaffected by either emancipation or concomitant changes in the economic system, and—because slaveholders were also by far the largest landholders—the distribution of wealth in the post-emancipation South remained not only unequal but also largely unchanged. The South as a whole was substantially poorer than it had been—primarily as a result of wartime devastation—but those who had been wealthiest in 1860 usually remained wealthiest in 1870 and 1880 as well, while those who had been enslaved in 1860 remained the poorest. As Jonathan M. Wiener observed, in Alabama's Black Belt there was little difference between planter persistence rates from 1860 to 1870 and those from 1850 to 1860: "Almost all of the wealthiest planters of 1870 had been members of the antebellum planter elite." Even when increasing numbers of Southern African Americans began acquiring land, their holdings—unlike those of Russian peasants—did not represent a significant share of the South's landed wealth. A recent study of probate inventories in middle Georgia by Louis A. Ferliger and John D. Metz confirms the "marginal position [of Blacks] as property holders in the Georgia Piedmont" in the late nineteenth century: although African Americans constituted a majority of the population in two of the three counties studied and a substantial minority in the third, they "accounted for only seven percent of the combined total of probated estates captured in the sample." Southern peasantization took the form of freedpeople practicing family farming (often through sharecropping) on land owned by planters—and increasingly on small plots of land that they themselves owned—but there was no American equivalent to the massive transfer of land from nobles to peasants that occurred in post-emancipation Russia.[28]

In short, in both the Southern United States and Russia, former masters remained members of an economic elite, even as their wealth took new forms that accompanied changed social relations. This transformation was not always easy, and learning to emphasize efficiency and profitability could be especially difficult for Russian lords used to scorning bourgeois values as crass and degrading. Consider the post-emancipation behavior of two substantial landowners, William Storrow Lovell, owner of the Palmyra estate on Mississippi's Davis Bend, and Vasilii Yazykov, owner of the Yazykovo Selo estate in Simbirsk Province. Both men faced new problems as they learned to deal with free laborers, but as Sally Stocksdale has shown in her comparative study, whereas Lovell was "an entrepreneurial planter" and " 'new master' prototype," Yazykov (who, among his many distinctions, served as marshal of nobility for the Simbirsk district of Simbirsk Province from 1862 to 1873) proved unable or unwilling to adjust to changed conditions. Gradually, he divorced himself from virtually everything connected to his commercial interests, first renting his woolen factory to a series of merchants and eventually selling off the factory, his Yazykovo Selo estate (including the estate mansion), and his urban residence—which he first tried to protect by "selling" it to his wife—also to merchants. (Yazykov's wife chose a different way to distance herself from her former life: she "voluntarily entered the women's monastery located directly across the street from their city mansion.") Lovell, by contrast, proved "far more effective than his Russian counterpart" and continually made "adjustments and calibrations" in his management of Palmyra, which flourished until the 1890s, when—prompted by a fire that burned down the big house in 1894 and by a disastrous flood in 1897—the family moved to Birmingham, Alabama, to go into the coal business.[29]

Neither Yazykov nor Lovell was entirely typical of large landowners. The former was unusual in selling his entire home estate to a merchant rather than following the more common pattern of selling and/or renting parts of it to the resident peasants, and Yazykov's abandonment of his urban mansion was also unusual. Lovell's entrepreneurial energy may in part have reflected his Northern background, although Northerners who moved south before the abolition of slavery had usually assimilated quickly to the region's values. In any case, Lovell's neighbor on the Davis Bend, Joseph E. Davis, who had long exhibited paternalistic tendencies, took a very different route from Lovell's in distancing himself from his ex-slaves, by selling Brierfield and Hurricane plantations to their ambitious Black manager, Benjamin T. Montgomery. Planters and pomeshchiki reacted in a variety of ways to the changed conditions they faced, but they almost always felt humiliated by having to associate with free African Americans and peasants, and they adopted diverse strategies to limit such relationships, the most common of which was to abandon or sharply reduce their physical presence on estates and plantations. Accompanying this physical absenteeism was the widespread practice of what might be termed "mental absenteeism," that is, disengagement from dealing with African Americans and peasants and a rejection of the paternalism that—however accurate or inaccurate a reflection of their actual feelings—many masters had expressed for their human property. Such expression, which had been especially widespread in the South, now appeared obsolete and economically irrational, as former owners wasted little time in asserting—occasionally in words but more often in practice—as they waged relentless class warfare against free laborers, whom they rarely treated as members of their proverbial extended families. As historian James Roark put it, "The behavior of considerable numbers of planters demonstrated that they believed that the law which freed the slaves also freed the masters." Indeed, the rapidity with which they were able to internalize the values that accompanied mental absenteeism indicates the extent to which, rather than being replaced—and displaced—by a class of merchants, businessmen, and professionals, planters and pomeshchiki largely *became* merchants, businessmen, and professionals.[30]

Although the South and Russia experienced modest industrial and urban growth in the immediate post-emancipation years, the process accelerated markedly a generation later. Beginning in the 1880s, both societies embarked upon an economic transformation that was characterized by rapid industrialization and urbanization, accompanied by the trappings of capitalist behavior that a previous generation of slaveholders and serfholders would have rejected as crass and materialistic. Some simple statistics reveal the context. Between 1869 and 1899, the real value added by manufacturing in the eleven ex-Confederate states increased at an annual rate of 7.8 percent, versus 5.8 percent in the United States as a whole, while between 1880 and 1900 agricultural income decreased from 76 percent to 61 percent of all income produced in those states. Between 1870 and 1900, the industrial labor force (in manufacturing, mining, and forest work) almost quadrupled, from 227,000 to 820,000 workers, while during those years the number of workers employed in cotton textile factories (almost all of whom, unlike many other industrial laborers, were white) swelled from ten thousand to ninety-eight thousand. Alabama's pig iron production, centered in the New South city of Birmingham, grew at an especially impressive rate, from twelve thousand tons in 1872 to 817,000 in 1890 and 1,184,000 in 1900. Meanwhile, Southern railroad mileage surged from 24,866 miles to 61,761 miles, and "the number of stores in the South mounted with each passing year, even through the depressions of the 1870s and 1890s," reaching 150,653 (or 144 stores per county) in 1900. As historian Edward Ayers generalized, "Every measure of industrial growth raced ahead in the New South, the rates of change consistently outstripping national averages."[31]

Russia's industrial development was less obvious, because of the country's vast rural expanse and low population density, but equally significant. Although statistics are suggestive rather than precise, during the last three decades of the nineteenth century, factory production in the fifty provinces of European Russia increased by some 488 percent, in contrast to agricultural production, which grew by 85 percent. (In per capita terms the respective growth rates were 313 percent versus 54 percent.) Between the 1880s and the 1910s, agriculture's share of total economic output decreased from 57 percent to 51 percent, and during the half century from 1860 to 1913, the nonagricultural labor force quadrupled from 3.26 million persons to 13.08 million. Although Russia, like the American South, was still an "overwhelmingly rural [and] agricultural" society at the end of the nineteenth century, "the Russian economy had begun the process of overcoming its backwardness."[32]

Also striking was the pace of urbanization in Russia and the Southern United States. On the eve of emancipation, Russia had only two cities with more than a hundred thousand persons—Moscow and St. Petersburg; four decades later, according to the census of 1897, there were fourteen such cities, and both Moscow and St. Petersburg were home to more than a million inhabitants. Also notable was the growth in the number of small and mid-sized cities, with twenty thousand to a hundred thousand residents, from thirty-nine to 106, and an increase in the proportion of the overall urban population from 2.5 percent of all peasants and 14 percent of all non-peasants to 6.7 percent of peasants and 49 percent of non-peasants. By 1897, almost half the urban population—and more than two-thirds of the inhabitants of Moscow and St. Petersburg—were peasants. Urbanization progressed further in the American South than in Russia, but it was limited primarily to smaller cities, most of which were commercial centers linked by the expanding railroad network and "centering on trade with the countryside." A few, by contrast—like the new city of Birmingham, Alabama, which surged from a population of three thousand in 1880 to 133,000 in 1910 as a regional base of iron and steel production—emerged as manufacturing centers. In the ex-Confederate South, however, only New Orleans—whose population stood at 287,104 in 1900—rivaled the size of mid-level Northern cities; there was no Southern equivalent of Russia's metropolises of Moscow and St. Petersburg, and aside from New Orleans, Memphis, Tennessee, was the only Southern city whose population cracked a hundred thousand by 1900—barely, at 102,320. Southern urbanization was characterized by the growth of numerous small towns and cities, not major metropolitan centers. Still, the South's urban population, which had inched up from 6.9 percent to 8.7 percent of the total population between 1860 and 1880, surged to 15.1 percent by 1900. One other characteristic of note was that in contrast to pre-emancipation Southern cities, which were increasingly off-limits to enslaved African Americans, cities in the New South boasted large and growing Black populations. Increasing numbers of free Blacks took advantage of their new geographic mobility to move to cities, because of both the security and the employment opportunities they offered. In all five cities studied by historian Howard N. Rabinowitz (Nashville, Atlanta, Richmond, Montgomery, and Raleigh), African Americans made up a higher percentage of the population in 1890 than they had in 1860, and by the latter date between 39 percent (Nashville) and 59 percent (Montgomery) of the five cities' residents were Black.[33]

In both regions, this economic transformation seemed to support the free-labor argument of those who had seen bondage as fundamentally at odds with modernity, and in both former masters embraced the new order with sanguinity and often enthusiasm. The shift was especially remarkable in the South, where attacks on "Yankee" civilization as crudely moneygrubbing had once been integral to the defense of slavery but where after Reconstruction a New South creed celebrated the kind of commercial values that had formerly been reviled. Planters opened stores where they catered—at a hefty profit—to the needs of freedpeople, moved eagerly to exploit the region's coal and other natural resources, served with alacrity on the boards of expanding railroad companies, and directed the introduction and growth of cotton textile manufacturing (which had once been seen as the ultimate "Yankee" industry). The trend was evident even at the very top, among men who had led the Confederate Rebellion against Yankee ways; as historian Edward Ayers pointed out, "Of the 585 top leaders of the Confederacy, 292 became lawyers, 73 railroad officials, 39 merchants, 34 industrialists, 25 insurance men, and 23 bankers," while "only 193 assumed positions as planters or farmers after Appomattox." But it was not just among political leaders that this retreat from a civilization "gone with the wind" was evident: many sons of planters were eager to "carve out a niche for themselves in the postwar economy" far removed from the plantation world. "By the 1880s," Ayers noted, "the planters, and especially their children, were leaving the plantations."[34]

Russian noblemen were not far behind in deserting their estates, and in welcoming the kind of mercantile ventures that many had once scorned and that had for the most part until January 1863 been legally defined as open only to members of the merchant estate. On top of the massive redemption-produced transfer of land from pomeshchiki to peasants, nobles continued to sell their land and abandon their estates. Between 1862 and 1905, noble landholdings decreased from more than 87 million to about 51 million desiatiny, and from 1877 to 1905 the proportion of land in noble hands contracted from 18.7 percent to 13.7 percent of all land. This contraction was especially marked in the central industrial region, where infertile soil reduced the attractiveness of directing agricultural operations (and where peasant otkhodniki were most numerous as well): noble landholding there in 1897 was about half what it had been in 1862, whereas in the country as a whole it was about two-thirds and in all black-earth regions it was 71 percent. Absenteeism, which had long been widespread among Russia's wealthiest nobles, became much more common after emancipation: in 1858, about one-third of the country's nobles resided in urban areas, but by 1897 well over half (56.9 percent) did, and excluding the western provinces and left-bank Ukraine, where Polish nobles had unusually strong ties to the land, more than two-thirds of nobles were urban based. Under serfdom, the great majority of nobles had owned land (and serfs), but by 1895 almost half of all nobles were landless, and a decade later that figure had reached more than 60 percent. Despite a small back-to-the-land movement of conservative noble "soslovniki," self-styled gentlemen-farmers who deplored the abandonment of agriculture and held moneygrubbing capitalists in contempt, it was clear, in the words of historian Seymour Becker, that these men "were quite out of touch" with the views of most nobles, who continued to sell land and abandon their estates. Instead, nobles increasingly sought to make money where they could, as businessmen, investors, professionals, and government officials. At the turn of the twentieth century, 1,894 nobles owned 2,092 businesses employing at least fifteen workers and earning at least two thousand rubles per year, and another 1,426 held management positions in railroad companies. Historians have written of the transformation of the nobility into a variegated group with diverse occupations rather than "a unified social class," or, more simply, their "legal fiction" and "embourgeoisement."[35]

Some historians have also flirted with the idea that the South and Russia followed the so-called Prussian road or Prussian path to capitalism. First developed by Lenin in order to distinguish the kind of repressive agricultural relations evident in nineteenth-century Prussia, which were based on an alliance of large landowners (Junkers) and industrialists, from the democratic-capitalist model characteristic of farming in the Northern United States, the Prussian path idea has been applied to Russia and the Southern United States in a variety of forms, by a variety of (mostly Marxist) historians. One of the most powerful assertions of applicability of the Prussian path thesis to the post-emancipation South was by Jonathan Wiener, who argued, with particular attention to Alabama, that "the South's characteristic poverty and political oppression arose out of . . . the Prussian Road, with its dominant planter class and its labor-repressive system of agricultural production." Emphasizing planter persistence, Wiener argued that in the last third of the nineteenth century planters rejected full-throated New South industrialization in favor of more "limited industrial development in the context of a planter-dominated cotton-producing South." In Wiener's interpretation, it was crucial that planter-merchants represented primarily planters who became merchants (and therefore still had a planter's mentality) rather than merchants or industrialists who became planters. By contrast, Eugene D. Genovese, who agreed that Germany (and Japan) took the Prussian path—the Junkers were "an aristocracy [that] effectively crossed over into the ranks of the capitalist class"—

suggested that the Prussian path was not really applicable to the post-emancipation South, because its slaveholders did not, in fact, become true capitalists; rather, "when the planters went down, their way of life and its attendant ideology went down also." Harold D. Woodman painted still a different picture: arguing that planters were transformed into "capitalist landlords," albeit often with non-landed investments as well, he stressed the triumph of "capitalist agriculture," whose "orientation was urban, toward market and trade centers." And Barbara Fields, who conceded the existence of "growing bourgeois capitalist social relations" in the post-emancipation South, maintained that the South took neither the Prussian nor the American path; instead, Southern planters were closer to "a decadent colonial ruling class" than to "proud Junkers or boyars."[36]

Although most Soviet scholars agreed that post-emancipation Russia followed the Prussian path to capitalism, they differed significantly in their interpretations of this thesis. After citing Lenin approvingly and noting that both Germany and Russia experienced emancipation from above, as well as continued domination of the countryside by landholders and consequently continued serfdom-like exploitation of the peasantry, A. M. Anfimov stressed important differences between Germany's agrarian capitalism and Russia's: both countries could be said to have followed the Prussian path, but Germany's rural capitalism was far more developed than Russia's, and Germany's peasants enjoyed greater independence. A. P. Korelin emphasized the transitional nature of post-emancipation agricultural relations—"the old barshchina system was undermined but far from abolished"—and argued that regional variations in the development of capitalist agriculture remained important, variations that rendered the Prussian path thesis more persuasive in describing some regions than others. N. M. Druzhinin agreed that Russia followed the Prussian path, but he stressed that Russia's peasants were worse off than Germany's. Despite their emphasis on the Prussian path, however, these Soviet historians tended to pay relatively little attention to a central element in the Prussian path thesis—the nature and durability of the landowner-capitalist alliance—and largely ignored the apparent contradiction between the thesis and Lenin's conviction that Russian capitalism emerged primarily as a result of class divisions within the peasantry itself.[37]

The Prussian path model does not fit perfectly for either Russia or the South. It does not take account of the vibrant democracy that existed in much of the South during the Reconstruction years (and continued to exist in shrinking areas even thereafter), democracy that received support—albeit in decreasing measure over time—from the federal government in Washington. Nor does the model reflect the kind of family farming that fostered considerable independence in both the South and Russia (and was reinforced in much of Russia by communal authority). The model also fails to capture the considerable variation in agricultural relations that existed within the two societies, according both to regional differences and to individual proclivities.

The Prussian path works best for the South and Russia if understood loosely as a model of continued oppressive agricultural relations in a largely rural society under conditions of emerging capitalism. Both the South and Russia saw the abolition of bondage and the transition to free-labor relations during the 1860s. Both remained largely rural and agricultural but experienced accelerating industrialization and urbanization, especially from the 1880s. In both, the former slaveholders and serfholders remained in favored positions—although without most elements of the legally privileged status they had previously enjoyed—and were able to wield regional political power (if tempered for a while in the South). In both Russia and the South, as well, those former owners increasingly abandoned their previous roles as directors of agricultural enterprises in favor of engaging in diverse activities, including business-oriented ventures that defenders of the old order had typically scorned. And finally, in both societies the ongoing class struggle between ex-masters and ex-bondspeople tipped increasingly—and sometimes violently—in favor of the former, aided by local governments that themselves were more and more oppressive. The Prussian path model may not have precisely described what was going on in all of the South or Russia, but it encapsulated a general truth and came a lot closer to accuracy than did its theoretical opposite—the so-called American or democratic model that was widespread (although not ubiquitous) in the Northern United States.

With respect to the former owners, the essential development was the abolition of most of their legal privileges, and their gradual, halting, but persistent transformation into a diverse class of businessmen, professionals, landowners, and rentiers. The central element in this transformation was the loss of their right to own slaves and serfs, which in Russia was accompanied by other reforms that reduced or did away with the advantages of nobility and went far toward substituting class privileges for those stemming from legally defined status. (Among the most important changes were the judicial reform of 1864, which placed nobles "under the jurisdiction of the all-estate courts," and the military reform of 1874, which for the first time made nobles subject to military conscription.) As Seymour Becker put it, the process was one of "Russia's transition from a society based on estate privilege to one based on the legal equality of individuals," which rendered the nobility "no longer a meaningful social entity." As this happened, "Russian nobles showed little hesitation about treating land as simply a form of capital, once emancipation had created a free market in agricultural land," and many "moved to cities," where they became "career bureaucrats" or entered "occupations unknown to or shunned by their forebears." In both Russia and the South, this represented a transformation more than a decline—both Russian nobles and Southern planters remained wealthy and powerful, and the latter also had the advantage of whiteness in an increasingly race-conscious society—but former masters were now often "capitalist landlords," urban businessmen, professionals, and government bureaucrats. In the Southern United States, they had the same rights as everyone else, but even in Russia, as Becker stressed, "deprived of its privileged legal status and no longer identified with distinctive social roles or a distinctive style of life, the nobility was no longer a social reality."[38]

In both countries diversity flourished among the freedpeople, who entered occupations unavailable to slaves and serfs, partook of increasing economic stratification, and in a variety of ways pursued individual and family interests, even as they also identified increasingly with other former slaves and serfs as members of specific communities and in collective ventures that could exhibit religious, political, or economic characteristics. At the same time, however, freedpeople identified as African Americans and peasants in general. The growing salience of Blackness and peasantness was reflected not only in group self-identification but also in the perception of outsiders, as differences in status—most basically of free Blacks versus slaves and state peasants versus serfs—disappeared or were greatly diminished, and Americans and Russians became obsessed with the racial characteristics that supposedly defined Black and peasant behavior. Historians have debated the extent to which African Americans and peasants saw themselves as a "people" or "nation," a form of general identification that cut across and to some extent conflicted with their identification as individuals, family members, and members of specific communities, as well as with even more general identification as Americans and Russians. Meanwhile, white Americans and non-peasant Russians looked upon Blacks and peasants in ways that differed significantly from the self-perception of those Blacks and peasants, and white Americans came to hold strikingly different images of Blacks from those of peasants held by Russian nobles, merchants, and intellectuals. There was no Russian equivalent to the kind of virulent white racism that swept much of the United States in the late nineteenth century, and the various negative images of Black beasts who threatened law-abiding Americans stood in sharp contrast to the generally positive (if vaguely insulting) view of peasants as sturdy but simple folk who meant well and represented the essence of Russia itself. In short, complicating—and in some ways in opposition to—both the centripetal and centrifugal tendencies evident in the attachments of the freedpeople were both their racial self-identification as Blacks and peasants and the conflicting images of those Blacks and peasants held by other Americans and Russians.[39]

The sudden introduction of African American political participation provides a useful opening wedge in approaching the question of race as an important ingredient in Black self-identification. By asking whether elected Black officials thought of themselves as representing all their constituents or primarily their *Black* constituents one can begin to address the tricky issue of the extent to which African Americans identified in racial terms, and the ways such self-identification interacted with other characteristics—whether ideological, political, economic, or idiosyncratic. To some extent, this question of representation inhered in the peculiarities of the American democratic system itself: throughout American history politicians have put forth ambiguous positions with respect to whether they were morally bound to act in accordance with the views of their constituents in general, those who elected them, or their own consciences. If almost everyone has agreed that blindly following the wishes of the majority—or taking instruction from "the people"—constitutes an inappropriate exercise that approaches rule by plebiscite, ignoring the views of one's constituents entirely has seemed equally inappropriate. But given the sudden political participation of Black men who had previously been not only unenfranchised but unfree, and given the sharply divided electorate that existed in the wake of rebellion, war, and emancipation, the question assumed still greater salience when applied to the attachments of Black politicians and voters. Historians, too, have been divided on the matter.

When Abraham Lincoln spoke about Blacks deserving the quintessential American right to "self-government," he had in mind the right of a "man" to govern himself—that is, to run his own affairs rather than being bossed about. Most historians, by contrast, have meant something more than this. The two most comprehensive modern histories of Reconstruction have put forth different— although overlapping—interpretations of what Black self-government was all about. In what quickly became recognized as the most authoritative history of Reconstruction upon its publication in 1988, Eric Foner emphasized "the transformation of slaves into free laborers and equal citizens" and described "a massive experiment in interracial democracy without precedent in this or any other country that abolished slavery in the nineteenth century." Writing fifteen years later, Steven Hahn put forth a different view of what he termed Black "self-governance." Suggesting that "African Americans in the rural South contributed to the making of a new political nation," he argued that Blacks "made themselves into a new people—a veritable nation as many of them came to understand it." *His* understanding of "self-governance," which found expression in the book's title *A Nation under Our Feet,* was grounded in an assertion of Black nationalism, as expressed by two local leaders in Mississippi defending the idea of "colonization"—that is, emigration to somewhere (usually in Africa) where Blacks could in fact practice self-determination. "We wants to be a People," the leaders declared, but "we cant be it heare and find that we ar compel to leve this Cuntry." Indeed, Hahn paid a great deal of attention to the rise among African Americans of emigrationist sentiment, which he saw as "one of several strategies designed to create or reconstitute freed communities on a stable foundation—and at arm's length from whites." Foner, by contrast, saw interest in emigration as "moribund during Reconstruction" and of limited impact even later, because "most blacks were not prepared to surrender their claim to citizenship and equal rights." The comment of a correspondent of Blanche K. Bruce, one of two African Americans from Mississippi who served in the U.S. Senate in the late nineteenth century, was telling: "We are not Africans now, but colored Americans," he wrote, "and are entitled to American citizenship."[40]

The two positions were not entirely contradictory so much as reflecting a basic dualism inherent in the self-image of African Americans, who—depending on circumstances—could accentuate either their Americanness or their Blackness without totally rejecting the other. The relative appeal of these two identifications also varied over time: typically, when conditions seemed favorable to Black advancement, as during Reconstruction, it was easier for African Americans to stress their basic Americanness, whereas in times of greater white racism and oppression—as during the period leading up to the Civil War or that following the collapse of Reconstruction—Black nationalism seemed more appealing, and interest in emigration picked up. This interplay is clearly evident in the shifting priorities of Martin Delany, who for most of his life was an ardent Black nationalist and proponent of emigration to Africa, but during the Civil War and Reconstruction years tempered his Black nationalism by strongly backing the Union cause, serving as a major in the Union Army and then as a Freedmen's Bureau official at Hilton Head, South Carolina. Delany was hardly typical of most Black Southerners. He grew up free, in the North, was active in the abolitionist movement in the 1840s, embraced Black emigration to Africa in the 1850s, and—in part because of his familiarity with Northern white racism—was hostile to Yankee do-gooders who sought to work with the freedpeople during Reconstruction: "Believe not in these school teachers, emissaries, ministers and agents, because they never tell you the truth," he warned. Eccentric and elitist, by 1876 he had turned against the Republican Party—he blamed Yankee carpetbaggers for turning Southern Blacks from "polite, pleasant, agreeable, kindly common people" into "ill-mannerly, sullen, disagreeable" folk who were "filled with hatred and ready for resentment"—and was supporting Democrats Samuel J. Tilden for president and Wade Hampton for governor of South Carolina. But Delany's career illustrates how even the most committed Black nationalist could be attracted by the allure of equal American citizenship during the heady days of the 1860s. If "before the Civil War his allegiance was to a nation of race," for a brief period "after the war," in the words of historian Nell Irvin Painter, "his field broadened and his elitism and patriotism enfolded all the people of South Carolina, black and white."[41]

In fact, despite evidence of widespread interest among rural Black Americans in the *possibility* of emigrating to Africa—especially from the South's cotton-producing regions, where decentralized family farming left freedpeople, in Hahn's words, "far more vulnerable" than those in the South Carolina and Georgia Lowcountry or the sugar parishes of southern Louisiana—very few African Americans actually made the move. According to Hahn, from 1877 to 1880, only "388 blacks voyaged to West Africa, . . . for an annual average of just under one hundred," and even considering "the entire post-Civil War period . . . the total is less than 4,000 (3,812), or 238 annually." The small number of emigrants to Africa does not necessarily refute the self-identification of rural freedpeople as "Africans" or as members of a Black "nation" so much as indicate that this was not the *only* (or *primary*) way they thought of themselves. Like everyone else, rural freedpeople had multiple overlapping (and sometimes partially conflicting) identifications, and, especially in the post-Reconstruction years, anti-Black terrorism created a real interest among some African Americans in the opportunities for self-improvement via Africa touted by the American Colonization Society and its mouthpiece the *African Repository*. Given the difficulty and expense of moving to Africa, however—as well as news that filtered back of hardship, suffering, and frequent regret among African American migrants to Liberia—it is not surprising that this interest in emigrating was rarely consummated. By contrast, perhaps twenty thousand to twenty-five thousand disgruntled Black Southerners trekked to Kansas in one year (1879–80), and during the first half of the twentieth century millions more would travel north. Unlike migration to Africa, which had long been promoted by *white* nationalists who pushed for the involuntary removal of Blacks from America, movement to Kansas and to the North allowed those who uprooted themselves to maintain their sense of Americanness, even as they saw themselves as part of a Black exodus and even as their movement sometimes had distinctly communal overtones.[42]

The Russian contrast helps clarify this basic dualism of racial and democratic identity among post-emancipation African Americans. Peasant officials in Russia *never* represented anyone but other peasants. This was true of the starosty and starshiny who headed communes and volosti, as well as of members of communal and volost' assemblies and of judges in peasant courts, all of whom confined their attention to the world of the peasants. It was also true of peasant-elected members of district and provincial zemstvo assemblies, which included non-peasants and supposedly were multi-estate bodies that dealt with issues of broad general interest. Under the complicated electoral system that chose the members of these assemblies, peasants voted separately from members of other estates, and voted exclusively for peasant delegates, who even before the reduced representation resulting from the counterreform of 1889 constituted a far smaller proportion of the assembly members than peasants did of the district or provincial population. Russia was a monarchy, of course, rather than a democracy, and emancipated peasants were no more citizens than they had been as serfs. Although emancipation was part of a process that nudged the country away from a society divided into separate castes or estates, the idea of elections in which everyone took part as equal citizens remained unimaginable except to radicals and revolutionaries. As historian Corinne Gaudin observed, in a comment that was perhaps unduly generous in suggesting that the drafters of the emancipation provisions in theory favored an "all-estate" society and continued to hope for the "gradual evolution of former serfs into full citizens," the "system of rural administration" that they in fact established "largely segregated Russia's peasantry from the empire's general administrative and judicial systems."[43]

But coexisting with peasant consciousness was an even stronger communal consciousness under which peasants distinguished between insiders and outsiders. As we have seen, the emancipation legislation actually left the commune in a strengthened position, because it inherited many of the functions that had previously belonged to serf owners and their administrative hierarchy, such as deciding who could leave a village—either permanently or temporarily, as otkhodniki—and when families could divide. The commune also continued to exercise local governmental control in a way that was largely absent in the American South, with a host of peasant officials—from starosta and starshina at the top to *desiatskie* and *sotskie* ("tenths" and "hundredths")— responsible for maintaining rural order. In much of Russia, these local governments decided when to reapportion peasant landed allotments and who should receive how much land. Unlike American slaves, who were often sold and were accustomed to neighbors with different backgrounds, Russian serfs had been far more rooted in specific local communities and had developed a strong suspicion of outsiders—whether government officials, teachers, and other do-gooders with their strange ways, and even "outside" peasants—and strong attachments to inhabitants of their own villages. As historian Boris Mironov and others have stressed, "The peasant deemed it 'immoral' to deceive a neighbor or relative, but to deceive a government official or landlord was quite a different matter—indeed that was a moral deed worthy of encouragement." The distrust of outsiders extended to *peasant* outsiders as well, observed historian Stephen P. Frank, and those "outsiders whose offenses threatened the community," such as thieves and suspected witches, could face gruesome torture and death. In noting that the "centralized bureaucracy" was largely unable to extend its sway to Russia's "rural Communes," British observer Sir Donald Mackenzie Wallace generalized with some exaggeration that these peasant communes were "capital specimens of representative constitutional government of the extreme democratic type!"[44]

In short, even as Black Americans and Russian peasants identified themselves in racial terms—*as* Blacks and peasants—they differed in that Blacks also held a more general view of themselves as American citizens while peasants' attachments were more narrowly confined to specific local bodies (villages and communes). At the same time, cutting across their common racial loyalties were differences among Blacks and among peasants that partially counteracted shared, all-Black and all-peasant identification. One important fault line was between those who had previously been held in bondage and those who had been "free" (or in the Russian case, "state" peasants). Other significant distinctions among African Americans involved color and among both Blacks and peasants reflected increasing economic stratification, as well as differences relating to age, gender, education, and personal idiosyncrasy. If there was much that united the freedpeople after emancipation, this unity could sometimes appear elusive and superficial.

Historians have been reluctant to dwell on divisions and conflicts among peasants and African Americans—especially but not exclusively before emancipation—in part because doing so could seem to undermine an emphasis on unity among the oppressed. This reluctance characterized most Soviet historians, who typically celebrated the peasants' class struggle against their noble exploiters, and also most members of a recent generation of American scholars who have stressed Black resistance and solidarity in the face of white racism. Most, but not all. Recently, historians of Russian serfdom and those of American slavery have begun to pay attention to disagreements among serfs and slaves based on age and gender. In a study focusing on the Petrovskoe estate in Tambov Province, Steven Hoch found that "intergenerational antagonism was structurally endemic" and that "serf patriarchs," who typically ruled their families with an iron hand, constituted "a ruling stratum of peasants" who profited from the labor of their younger relatives. Dylan C. Penningroth made a similar argument about exploitative relationships among American slaves, noting that "few slaves could earn much by working alone. When enslaved people accumulated property, they usually did it by finding someone else to work for them." The "someone else" was often (although not always) a family member, including especially wives and children. And Jeff Forret has broadened the study of divisions among antebellum slaves by focusing on violent confrontations among the enslaved population, confrontations in which gender, age, and honor loomed large. Placing slave-on-slave violence in the broader context of the violence that was endemic to "the entire slaveholding South," he concluded that "violence was very much part of slaves' lives, but all that meant was that they were southern."[45]

As noted in chapters 5 and 6, recent historical attention to gender—and to a lesser extent age—has also underscored divisions among *post*-emancipation African Americans and peasants, and the renegotiations among members of peasant and Black families that were occasioned by emancipation. Other kinds of differences and divisions have generated considerable historical disagreement, especially among historians of the Russian peasantry. In part, these disagreements have been a function of the difference between establishing status distinctions among peasants and arguing for actual conflicts among them: the former did not necessarily lead to the latter. But even the process of establishing those status distinctions has been controversial. Historians have disagreed significantly, for example, over the extent of socioeconomic stratification that existed among post-emancipation peasants, and whether or not this stratification was growing more pronounced over time. In his early study *The Development of Capitalism in Russia,* Lenin argued that Russian capitalism owed more to growing socioeconomic differentiation among the peasantry, and the exploitation of poor peasants by their richer neighbors, than to entrepreneurial activity by nobles and merchants: "The old peasantry is not only 'differentiating,' it is being completely dissolved," he wrote in 1899, replaced by "the rural bourgeoisie (chiefly petty bourgeoisie) and the rural proletariat"; the former, who formed "not more than one-fifth of the total number of [peasant] households," constituted "the masters of the contemporary countryside." This thesis generated considerable tension among subsequent Soviet scholars, who were torn between stressing the peasants' communal solidarity in the face of oppression by those who represented holdovers from the "feudal" past and following Lenin's lead in emphasizing intra-peasant socioeconomic differentiation—or trying to do both at the same time.[46]

Although historians have continued to disagree on the subject, most Western and post-Soviet Russian scholars have concluded that Lenin exaggerated the extent of peasant differentiation during the last third of the nineteenth century. If emancipation made it easier for peasants to engage in activities that would enable them to accumulate property, such accumulation was usually relatively modest, and the practice of re-allocating peasant allotment land that most communes continued to follow during the 1860s and 1870s acted to retard the growth of extreme inequality among peasants. (For this reason, as Daniel Field noted, peasant stratification measured by possession of allotment land was typically less pronounced than that measured by other criteria, such as ownership of horses.) As Christine Worobec pointed out, general communal land repartitions occurred throughout Russia "immediately after emancipation" and remained common in much of the country thereafter, although in some areas—especially those in the south, with the most fertile land, where the most prosperous peasants tended to oppose repartition's equalizing impact—the process became rare or nonexistent. Boris Mironov concluded that in most areas "the Russian peasantry remained quite homogeneous in terms of property and social relations and exhibited only incipient traces of so-called bourgeois stratification before the 1917 Revolution," and other historians have agreed that the prevalence of family farming was not conducive to stratification within the peasantry. "We hardly find developments towards a two-sided, capitalist differentiation," concluded Heinz-Dietrich Löwe; indeed, except in the sparsely populated south, "wage labour became rarer instead of more frequent."[47]

Despite the existence of a tiny number of rich peasants—who had existed even under serfdom—socioeconomic stratification among peasants remained modest by most measurements. In Voronezh Province, peasant income between 1887 and 1896 varied from an average of 33.6 rubles per capita for poor households to 86.4 rubles for wealthy households. According to zemstvo censuses in sixty-nine districts of fourteen provinces, the number of horses per household ranged from an average of 0.5 in the Vladimir district of Vladimir Province to 2.3 in the Irbst district of Perm Province between 1893 and 1895. In four districts of Voronezh Province, the proportion of peasant "farms" employing hired workers decreased from 4.1 percent to 3.3 percent between 1887 and 1900, and "even on the largest farms . . ., family labour by far surpassed hired help." Because "wealthy" peasant families were almost always larger than average, when measured in per capita terms peasant income was even less stratified than when measured by household: in Tver Province, in the 1880s, the per capita income of peasants on farms with more than twenty-one desiatiny of land exceeded that of landless peasants by only 22 percent. In the village of Viriatino (in the Morshansk district of Tambov Province) in 1881, data from 245 of 252 peasant households revealed ownership of horses that Soviet authors regarded as demonstrating "extreme inequality": a substantial majority had one or two horses, while twenty-eight (11.4 percent) had none, thirty-six (14.7 percent) had three, and twenty-two (9 percent) had four or more. As this pattern suggested, whatever differences existed among peasants paled into insignificance compared to the gap between nobles and peasants: at the end of the 1870s, the average Russian peasant owned 5.2 desiatiny per soul, whereas the average noble pomeshchik (including those who were considered "impoverished") owned 637 desiatiny. Economic stratification was far more extreme among noble landowners than among peasants. In 1877, although the average noble landholding was 613 desiatiny and the median noble landholding was one hundred desiatiny, 1.6 percent of the holdings embraced more than five thousand desiatiny each and averaged 16,437 desiatiny; collectively, these richest 1.6 percent of noble landholders owned almost half (43.5 percent) of the noble land.[48]

Despite the limited nature of socioeconomic stratification among Russia's peasants, one kind of pervasive if relatively modest gap in wealth—that between former serfs and peasants who had managed to escape being owned by noble pomeshchiki—persisted during the post-reform era. These included peasants owned by the royal family, known before 1797 as court peasants and after then as appanage (*udel'nye*) peasants, but by far the largest number consisted of state peasants, who were in some ways the equivalent of free African Americans in the slave South: not quite free, but "slaves without masters." Originally composed of those who had managed to escape enserfment, state peasants swelled in numbers in the eighteenth century with the partial secularization of church lands by Peter I early in the century and their complete secularization by Catherine II in 1764, and continued to increase in the first half of the nineteenth century as a result of both natural population growth and fugitive serfs entering their ranks. Whereas in 1678 about one-fifth of Russia's peasants were state peasants, on the eve of emancipation they slightly outnumbered privately held serfs.[49]

State peasants before the 1860s were hardly "free." Like serfs, they had small allotments of land, owed dues (*obrok*, to the state, rather than *obrok* or *barshchina* or a combination of the two, to a private owner), and faced numerous legal restrictions. The biggest advantage that state peasants had over serfs was that not having noble owners, they faced less immediate interference in their lives. In addition, their material condition was slightly better than that of serfs, because their allotments were usually larger and their dues less onerous. This was especially true after the reforms initiated between 1837 and 1841 by P. D. Kiselev, head of the newly established Ministry of State Domains. Designed primarily to rationalize administration and reduce corruption, these reforms were part of the government's halting and erratic effort to grapple with the "peasant question," and they ultimately had relatively little impact on the lives of their supposed beneficiaries. Indeed, the reforms actually increased government supervision of state peasants (thereby supposedly improving their condition) and aroused protests from some who, leery of outside control, suspected an effort to turn them into serfs.[50]

Not covered by the emancipation decree and legislation of 1861, appanage and state peasants were "freed" in separate measures soon thereafter, in 1863 and 1866, respectively. The terms varied somewhat in detail—in theory, state peasants had already received personal freedom as part of the Kiselev reforms, and unlike former serfs, neither appanage nor state peasants had to deal with noble owners or their representatives—but in both cases the peasants, like former serfs, had to pay to receive allotments of land that they had previously been using and had considered their own. In both cases, as well, the appanage and especially the state peasants received somewhat better terms than the former serfs, with larger plots of land for which they owed smaller payments. At the time of emancipation, former serfs received an average of 3.38 desiatiny per male soul, while the corresponding figures for appanage and state peasants were 4.81 and 6.23 desiatiny per soul; by 1877, population growth had reduced the size of these average allotments to 2.91, 4.07, and 5.15 desiatiny, respectively. Most communes with average allotments of less than two desiatiny per soul (80.7 percent) were composed of former serfs; by contrast, most with average allotments of more than five desiatiny per soul (79.46 percent) were made up of former state peasants. It is worth noting, however, that the advantage of their more substantial allotments was partially offset by the tendency of state peasants to be concentrated in less fertile regions, including Siberia and the far north, where larger holdings were required for sustenance.[51]

As this concentration suggests, interaction between former serfs and former state peasants was limited, because they usually lived apart from each other. Because state peasants consisted principally of the descendants of those peasants who had escaped enserfment, they were most numerous in areas where serfdom was least widespread, and were especially prevalent in the border regions of the expanding Russian Empire. But even where state peasants and serfs lived close to one another, they typically were members of separate communities and interacted minimally. The same was true after emancipation as well. In the village of Viriatino, in Tambov Province, for example, "the lands of the state peasants were surrounded on all sides by the lands of the former serfs," but they constituted separate communes and volosti, with their own officials. "The two peasant communities lived side by side in the same village, not merging under a unified administration until the October Revolution."[52]

Although they shared a common peasant culture—including a collective mentality, a central ingredient of which was belief in the desirability of "relative equality of resources and burdens," and an intense suspicion of outsiders—both former serfs and former state peasants could be more struck by differences between them than by what they had in common. A central difference was the superior condition of state peasants, who not only had larger allotments and were burdened with lighter financial obligations but also never had to face the intrusive intervention in their lives by private owners or their agents. Before emancipation, fugitive serfs sometimes were able to join (and more often hoped to join) the ranks of state peasants, and when state peasants were given by the tsar to noble landowners and thereby effectively turned into serfs—a common occurrence until the end of the eighteenth century—they typically engaged in vigorous resistance. After emancipation, former state peasants continued to look down upon and hold themselves apart from former serfs; according to historian S. S. Kriukova, former state peasants in Riazan and Tambov Provinces held former serfs "in contempt," and it was considered shameful to allow one's daughter to marry a former serf. In short, peasants continued to be conscious of differences between former serfs and former state peasants even as those differences became increasingly remote with "the progressive abrogation of the differences existing between the classes or castes." To most other observers, however, the differences seemed insignificant: they were all "peasants."[53]

If economic stratification among peasants was relatively limited, this was even more the case among African Americans in the post-emancipation South. Whereas in much of Russia a central cause of equality of property holding was periodic redistribution of peasant allotments, freedpeople in the American South experienced a poverty-based equality: the vast majority of former slaves, who with emancipation received "nothing but freedom," owned no land at all during and immediately after the Reconstruction years—they typically lost the "gardens and provision grounds" that as slaves they had considered theirs but "did not own"—and precious little personal property too. Exceptions existed, including Blacks who were wealthy not just compared to the mass of freedpeople but by the standards of middle-class whites as well, though such wealth was highly unusual—it was most notable in cities—and did not indicate significant stratification among the African American population as a whole. Indeed, those who did accumulate small plots of land and assorted other possessions were rarely far removed in wealth or interest from their less fortunate neighbors. In 1870, only about 2 percent of Blacks engaged in agriculture owned their own land in the Deep South, and 2.2 percent in the Upper South. Perhaps more important, most of these landowning African Americans possessed only tiny plots of land, which they and their families worked themselves; these landholdings were valued on average at $544 in the Deep South and $625 in the Upper South. After 1870, as family farming became the backbone of the Southern economy, more African Americans purchased small landholdings of their own; by 1890, 18 percent of Blacks engaged in farming were landholders in the Deep South, and fully 33 percent owned land in the Upper South. Still, most of these farmers were very small landholders, living on the margin and not far removed from the sharecroppers and wage laborers with whom they rubbed shoulders. Indeed, many of them had themselves been sharecroppers and wage laborers, and some would be again, as falling prices of agricultural commodities forced widespread foreclosures among Black (and white) smallholders. As manuscript census returns indicated, their personal property holdings typically ranged from nonexistent to $500. In short, even more than Russian peasants, post-emancipation African

Americans were united by their class interests, and shared a common condition of owning little or no property.⁵⁴

As in Russia with state peasants, a partial exception to uniform Black poverty was provided by those African Americans who had escaped being slaves—Southern free Blacks. Although most antebellum Black Southerners were enslaved, a small minority were considered "free" (although certainly not equal). Even during the colonial period, a few African Americans enjoyed "free" status, but the first spurt in the South's free Black population occurred during and immediately following the American Revolution, when, spurred by the contradiction between slavery and the Revolutionary struggle for freedom from Britain, a significant number of planters—especially in the Upper South, where the demand for labor was less intense than farther south—freed some or all of their slaves. (Other slaves took advantage of chaotic conditions caused by war to escape.) During those years, the number of free African Americans more than tripled, and as a proportion of the Black population they almost doubled. After 1810, however, there were relatively few manumissions of enslaved Blacks, and although their numbers continued to increase, primarily from natural population growth, most free African Americans in the antebellum period were descended from those who had been freed following the American War for Independence. By 1860, there were more than a quarter of a million free people of color in the South, but they constituted a smaller proportion of the Black population than they had in 1810 or 1840 (see table 7.1).⁵⁵

Like state peasants in Russia, free Blacks were not evenly dispersed throughout the South. Relatively few lived in the Deep South, but those who did included a significant minority who were unusually prosperous. Concentrated in southern Louisiana and neighboring Gulf Coast urban areas such as Mobile and Pensacola, they were the beneficiaries of the Louisiana Purchase Treaty (1804) that gave them rights to U.S. citizenship and allowed them to maintain their unusual privileged status until, in the wake of the Civil War, the mass of

Table 7.1. Free African Americans in the Southern States

	1790	1810	1840	1860
Number	32,357	108,265	215,575	261,918
Percentage	4.7%	8.5%	8.0%	6.2%

Source: Ira Berlin, *Slaves without Masters: The Free Negro in the Antebellum South* (New York: Pantheon Books, 1974), 46–47, 136–37.

enslaved African Americans—now freed—caught up with them. A smaller number of elite African Americans lived in other Deep South cities, such as Charleston and Savannah. "Lower South free Negroes were not only more urban and light-skinned," generalized Ira Berlin, "but better educated, more skilled, and more closely connected with whites than those of the Upper South." Some of these privileged African Americans—especially "Creole" descendants of French and Spanish colonial settlers—owned slaves, and even more owned land. In 1830, 1,556 Black slave owners in the Deep South owned 7,188 slaves, and in 1860, 1,066 rural Black landowners in the Deep South (most in southern Louisiana), had average holdings worth $2,970. A few were much wealthier. In the Cane River region of Louisiana's Natchitoches Parish (County), a group of "gens de couleur libre" who prided themselves on their distinction from the mass of common Blacks established a flourishing "colony" or "society within a society" based on slave-worked cotton plantations. Originally representing one family (with the surname Metoyer), the Cane River colony grew through intermarriage by 1830 to encompass 183 people, with 287 slaves. In the Sumter District of South Carolina, William Ellison, himself freed from slavery as a young man in 1816, became a wealthy planter, whose "family probably owned about eighty slaves at the moment of emancipation, valued at perhaps $100,000."[56]

These rich African Americans were highly unusual. The great mass of Southern free Blacks—more than 85 percent in the late antebellum period—were located in the Upper South, where, as Ira Berlin pointed out, they "lived on the periphery of the South" and "worked on the margins of the Southern economy." In 1860, about 12.8 percent of African Americans in the Upper South were free, compared to 1.5 percent of those in the Deep South, and in general the farther north one went, the higher the proportion of Blacks who were free: in North Carolina 8.4 percent, Virginia 10.6 percent, Maryland 49.1 percent, and Delaware 91.7 percent. Although some of these free Blacks lived in cities, more than two-thirds were rural, and unlike in the Deep South, where three-quarters of the free people of color were what the Census Bureau termed "mulattoes," only 35 percent of those in the Upper South were of mixed racial origin. Clearly better off than slaves—although most worked in subordinate positions as farmhands, domestic servants, and laborers, in 1860 some 15 percent were small landowners, with average holdings worth $612— Upper South free Blacks rarely showed the kind of elitist disdain for the mass of African American slaves that was common in Louisiana. Indeed, free and enslaved Blacks interacted far more readily in the Upper South than in the

Deep South, fraternizing, befriending, and sometimes marrying one another. One reason this was possible is that they were more likely to come into contact with each other in the Upper than the Deep South, where far fewer African Americans were free and where the free and enslaved lived in separate worlds. (In 1860, 53.2 percent of free people of color in the Deep South lived in cities, but only 4.3 percent of slaves did.) Harriet Jacobs, a young enslaved woman who eventually ran away from her abusive master in Edenton, North Carolina, regularly paid visits to her free grandmother, who was widely respected by whites as well as Blacks and had "powerful white friends"; eventually, when Jacobs became a fugitive in the late 1830s, she spent more than six years hiding in her grandmother's small attic before making her way to freedom in the North. And the era's most famous African American, Frederick Douglass, received crucial financial help in his 1838 flight from slavery to freedom from a free Black woman, Anna Murray, who married him shortly thereafter.[57]

After emancipation, the main difference between those who had previously been enslaved and those who had been free disappeared, and—in most cases—so did consciousness of these differences. Where free Blacks had fraternized with, had sex with, befriended, protected, and sometimes married those who were enslaved, past differences in status quickly faded from view. One sign of this shared identification was the almost universal support of African Americans for the Republican Party, which was widely perceived to be the party of freedom. The situation was more complicated, however, for the small number of elite people of color in the Lower South, who now faced competing pressures. On the one hand it was hard not to be caught up in the stirring spread of freedom that was transforming the lives of African Americans, but on the other hand that very spread of freedom was accompanied by the reduction (if not quite the elimination) of elite privileges. In Mobile, Alabama, for example, at the same time that some "Creoles" were delighting in the political career of freeborn and bilingual Ovid Gregory, who earned a reputation as a "fiery Radical" at the Constitutional Convention of 1867 and then as a state legislator, others continued to celebrate their distinction from the mass of African Americans by meeting in elitist organizations like the Creole Fire Company Number 1 and even by supporting Democratic candidates for office. Receiving praise from the conservative white press, the Creole Firemen were ridiculed by the city's leading Republican paper for being "inflated with pride at their supposed superiority to 'common niggers' "; noting that "sensible people are heartily disgusted at them," the paper suggested that these Creoles "easily become the tools of the enemies of their whole race."[58]

These conflicting pressures are perhaps most strikingly evident in the brief history of a newspaper that started out as a mouthpiece of New Orleans's free, light-skinned, French-descended people of color but soon morphed into a radical exponent of rights for the mass of freedpeople. A successor to the bilingual newspaper *L'Union,* which appeared twice and then three times a week from September 1862 to July 1864, the New Orleans *Tribune* was also bilingual—with two editions, one in French and the other in English—but appeared daily. Directed mostly at "French-speaking free coloreds," the paper had a largely free black staff and ownership, and originally it "displayed some of the same caste pretensions that had plagued *L'Union,*" but under the editorship of the white Belgian socialist Jean-Charles Houzeau, who often *passed* for Black—as he put it, "I never sought to deny the rumor that I had African blood in my veins, because this belief helped to increase the confidence that the colored man had in me"—the paper acquired an increasingly radical character and advocated the right of freedpeople to vote and own the land they worked. "The cause that the 'Negro newspaper' was defending was after all only one chapter in the great universal fight of the oppressed of all colors and nations," Houzeau later explained. "Whether the victim is called serf in Russia, peasant in Austria, Jew in Prussia, proletarian in France, pariah in India, Negro in the United States, at heart it is the same denial of justice." Eventually, however, this position caused increasing strains between Houzeau and the paper's "proprietors," who favored a less flamboyantly radical policy, and although they tried to keep him on as editor he resigned in January 1868.[59]

The *Tribune*'s brief history provides a useful illustration of the conflicting tensions that accompanied efforts to overcome what Houzeau termed "the alienation of the black slave from the free man of color." These tensions continued to be evident, not so much in the relationship of those who had been free people of color and the new freedpeople—after all, all Blacks were now "free"—as in the relationship of those of dark and lighter color. Indeed, as historian Loren Schweninger pointed out, in noting the "rapid decline in affluent free persons of color" in the post-emancipation Lower South—especially in the countryside—"by the 1870s and 1880s, the families of the once prosperous free Negro farmers and planters had virtually disappeared from the landholding class." (The declining salience of previously free status was also evident in the Upper South: in Montgomery County, in the hill country of southwestern Virginia, previously free Blacks in the late 1860s were still more likely than former slaves to own property, but before long there was "no discernible economic advantage to having been free before 1865.") Within a few years of emancipation, "the vast majority" of Louisiana's free people of color "had lost not only their slaves, farm machinery, livestock, buildings, and personal possessions, but their land as well." To the extent that there was "a new economic elite," it was largely in the cities, where small businessmen, including barbers, retailers, restaurateurs, and undertakers—often but not always former slaves—served a largely Black clientele. The old urban free-Black elite did not suddenly disappear, and certainly some African Americans continued to demonstrate a good deal of snobbery toward the mass of Black freedpeople; as historian John Blassingame noted, "Many of the mulattoes were aristocrats and were somewhat paternalistic toward freedmen." But this attitude was no longer driven by the contempt of the free toward the enslaved. Color and what Blassingame referred to as "cultural differences" (including those based on differences between the French-speaking minority and the English-speaking majority) were now "the most important cause of social divisions in the Negro community."[60]

Color consciousness remained a notable feature of African American self-identification. This consciousness reflected not so much actual differences in economic status as subjective values driven by a social order in which "whiteness" was prized—and less often berated. Many light-skinned African Americans continued to take pride in their "respectable" appearance, which could carry a variety of meanings, from being close to white to dressing "nicely" to engaging in efforts to avoid looking like Africans by, for example, straightening their "kinky" hair. A major focus of this effort to achieve respectability, especially among women, was hair straightening, promoted by—among other entrepreneurs—Madam C. J. Walker, whose system relying on the hot comb "became the foundation of the Black beautician industry." "By the early 1900s," observed Ayana D. Byrd and Lori L. Tharps in *Hair Story*, "straight hair had become the preferred look to signal middle-class status." At the extreme version of this attraction to whiteness were the small number of African American Americans—one scholar has estimated 2,500 to 2,750 per year—who "passed for" (or, some would say, "became") white. At the same time, some dark-skinned African Americans took the opposite approach, dismissing those who strove to appear white as traitors to their race. Such pride in Blackness was especially common among some of the most fervent supporters of emigration to Africa. As Matthew J. Hetrick put it in his study of African Americans who moved (at least for a while) to Africa, "Those who identified as being African and had first-hand experience of Africa were increasingly concerned about racial purity and sensitive to tensions within the African American communities." Attitudes toward Africa continued to be a noteworthy component of conflicting racial views: if some African Americans looked upon Africa as a dark and savage continent, others were convinced that only by fully embracing their Africanness could Black Americans rise above their slavery-induced subservience. Seeking to wrest control of Liberia College from "the hands of mongrels," Edward Wilmot Blyden, who was born free in the Danish West Indies and lived in the United States before moving to Liberia in 1850, expressed this race pride with particular vehemence. Noting in 1874 "the bitterness which prevails in America between the *colored* and *black*," he suggested that those of mixed race were not *real* "Negroes": although the "colored" American might call himself a "Negro . . . and pretends to be proud of the name," Blyden continued, in fact "his contempt for the Negro is supreme."[61]

There were limits, however, to this color consciousness among African Americans, who came in many shades, from light (or as some Blacks called those with light skin, "yellow") to dark. Although the Census Bureau classified 20.9 percent of African Americans as "mulattoes" in 1910 (up from 11.2 percent in 1850), "officials of the census estimated that actually some three-quarters of the Negro population in America was mixed in some degree." As the example of the New Orleans *Tribune* indicates, those who were privileged and light skinned were stirred by the movement to grant equal rights to the mass of freedpeople. With emancipation, a major element of the gap separating the free people of color from the slaves disappeared; at the same time, many Southern whites who had previously tolerated (and even prized) them now "attacked the free mulatto population . . . with unprecedented virulence." As historian Joel Williamson put it, based in part on a narrowing of the "economic distance" between Blacks and mulattoes and in part on "a union of mulattoes and blacks in politics," there occurred "a melding of mulatto and black worlds." If to whites "all Negroes came to look alike," to African Americans differences in color seemed less significant than they formerly had.[62]

In short, post-emancipation African Americans' consciousness of differences in color—like differences based on age and sex—was real but limited, and did not vitiate their strong identification based on race and on shared American citizenship. Equally important in underlining this broad, general identification was the relatively minor degree of Black socioeconomic differentiation: although freedpeople were able to take advantage of new opportunities and to pursue new occupations, the vast majority of African Americans—including most of those who had previously been free—remained engaged in hard physical labor— as farmhands, sharecroppers, small landowners, domestic workers, and day laborers. They shared common class interests, and even the successful exceptions—teachers and ministers in the countryside, supplemented in cities by independent entrepreneurs such as hairdressers and restaurateurs—were rarely capitalists with numerous employees. Indeed, as late as the middle of the twentieth century, sociologist E. Franklin Frazier was able to argue that the so-called black bourgeoisie was something of a misnomer—especially in the Southern states—and was "comprised essentially of white collar workers."[63]

There was no necessary conflict among the various forms of identification evident in the Southern United States and in Russia in the post-emancipation period: African Americans and peasants felt diverse loyalties according to a combination of sex, age, occupation, wealth, place of residence, religion, language, nationality, heritage, and—among African Americans—color. Nevertheless, despite these variations, two broad generalizations—one encompassing similarity and the other difference—characterized their most basic identification. On the one hand, they shared a basic "racial" sense of being peasants, in Russia, and what most recent historians term "Blacks" or "African Americans" but in the nineteenth century were commonly termed "negroes" or "colored," in the Southern United States. On the other, they differed in that peasants displayed a strong local (communal) consciousness and were intensely suspicious of outsiders, whereas African Americans manifested an equally strong sense of being American citizens, with the same rights as those of other Americans. Both the similarity and the difference played major roles in shaping their post-emancipation behavior.

To outsiders—Russians who were not peasants and Southerners who were not African Americans—the multiple identifications that sometimes divided peasants and sometimes African Americans were largely invisible. When these outsiders looked at peasants and African Americans, they tended to see ... monolithic peasants and African Americans. This was true, with some exceptions, whether those outsiders were sympathetic or hostile. If to white Southerners "all Negroes came to look alike," to Russian government officials and intellectuals the question "Who is the Russian peasant?"—a slightly different version of the so-called peasant question that had been at the center of the debate over emancipation—implied the same homogenized understanding. Although the peasant image was usually more complex and less threatening than that of the African American, both Russians and Southerners created varying versions of the archetypal peasant and "negro." In both cases, however, the end result was the same: pervasive disillusionment.[64]

In both the South and Russia, outsiders—even while disagreeing on their precise characteristics—tended to hold homogenized views of Blacks and peasants, generalizing about their monolithic features rather than recognizing the increasing diversity that in fact existed. In a view that was widespread among planters, many white Southerners believed that without the protection afforded by caring slave owners, the Black race was slated for imminent extinction. "What Has Become of the Freedmen?" one Alabama newspaper headlined in 1867, adding that it was "quite certain" that there was "nothing like the number of negroes in this section, that there were two years ago." Another paper was more specific, estimating that there had been a "depreciation of [Black] laborers, by death alone, of nearly or quite one-half." Such views—born of self-deception based upon a combination of proslavery assumptions and an emancipation-generated shortage of labor that was particularly severe in the Deep South—became increasingly untenable when it became clear that Blacks were not in fact facing extinction; indeed, as historian George M. Fredrickson noted, "the census of 1880 appeared to demonstrate that the rate of increase of Southern Negroes was substantially greater than that of the whites." Less subject to statistical refutation was a related generalization that received widespread currency among Southern whites: "Freedom has worked great changes in the negro," opined the same newspaper that had suggested the dying off of half the Black population, "bringing out all his inherent savage qualities, and changing him from a docile and obedient servant into a worthless, thieving, troublesome vagrant, and a pest to society." Over and over, white Southerners reiterated the refrain that free "negroes" were at best troublesome and worthless and more likely savage. As former Alabama governor Robert Patton testified in 1883 before a U.S. Senate committee that was investigating labor relations, "In slavery times, the young negroes were raised under discipline and government," whereas "now they are running about night and day"; a small-town carriage manufacturer echoed the sentiment: under freedom, he said, "The young negroes here are growing up very worthless."[65]

Virtually no one in post-emancipation Russia saw the "peasant" as facing extinction (although some Soviet historians argued that privately held serfs lived in such abysmal conditions that they—as opposed to state peasants—were in fact "dying off"). Unlike Blacks in America, peasants did not seem like aliens; they constituted the great majority of the population and represented the face of the Russian people or nation (*narod*). But observers, who put forth differing versions of peasant character, usually tried to generalize about the typical peasant rather than coming to grips with the peasantry's diversity. For example, Olga Tian-Shanskaia, a young noblewoman who spent a number of years on her family's estate in Riazan Province at the turn of the twentieth century, presented an unflattering generalization of "Ivan" as (in the words of her translator and editor David Ransel) "brutal, selfish, and unfriendly." By contrast, Aleksandr Nikolaevich Engelgardt, a chemist and nobleman who returned to his family estate in Smolensk Province and wrote a series of "letters" describing peasant life in the 1870s and 1880s, was more sympathetic, rejecting the stereotype of the lazy, drunk, and dishonest peasant and arguing that peasants were typically hardworking (although they worked in spurts rather than consistently, "like the Germans"). Both Tian-Shanskaia and Engelgardt, however, like other observers, sought to capture the essence of the elusive homogenized "peasant," who remained a mystery to those unfamiliar with village life.[66]

The difference between the evolving images of Russian peasants and Black Americans in post-emancipation years is especially evident in advertisements, as indicated in Amanda Brickell Bellows's study *American Slavery and Russian Serfdom in the Post-Emancipation Imagination*. In both countries, advertising was an important feature of economies that were increasingly commercial, but the depiction of Blacks in advertisements was far more demeaning than that of peasants, who often appeared as "romanticized vision[s] of the Russian folk" and, indeed, as a "national symbol." "Saccharine images of young peasants were particularly common in confectionary ephemera," noted Bellows. "Packaging for George Borman's candies and chocolates feature[d] sentimental portraits of peasant children building snowmen in villages, playing the accordion, or holding dolls." Meanwhile, in poster advertisements, "manufacturers of non-durable goods like beer and cigarettes sought to transcend traditional economic and estate boundaries ... through depictions of the urban peasantry as socially integrated, knowledgeable consumers." African Americans, by contrast, never appeared as romanticized representatives of Americans or Southerners in white-owned company advertisements: rather, they were ridiculed as servile, lazy, ludicrous, or pretentious, derided as threatening or—if celebrated—praised as "faithful servants [and] loyal mammies." In short, "most white Americans continued to view the formerly enslaved through the lens of race."[67]

Although prevailing images of Russian peasants were more complex than those of Black Southerners, who were the objects of increasingly harsh racial vitriol, the overall trajectory was similar in the two countries, both in reflecting a growing disillusionment—among non-peasants and non–African Americans—with the consequences of emancipation and in reflecting a growing determination of propertied interests to salvage as much of the old order as possible. This disillusionment was more obvious in the South, both because of its racial expression and because of the far-reaching nature of the Reconstruction experiment, but perceptive analysts noted its presence in Russia as well. As Sir Donald Mackenzie Wallace explained after noting the negative evaluation of emancipation that he found pervasive in the 1870s, "I came to perceive that my authorities were far from being impartial observers. Most of them were evidently suffering from shattered illusions. They had expected that the Emancipation would produce instantaneously a wonderful improvement in the life and character of the rural population and that the peasant would become at once a sober, industrious model agriculturist." Wallace concluded archly: "These expectations were not realized."[68]

Historians have not agreed on the precise mix of Southern white sentiment with respect to post-emancipation African Americans or on the best terminology to describe this sentiment. Consider, for example, three of the most prominent historians of American race relations. In his influential book *The Strange Career of Jim Crow*, C. Vann Woodward described "three alternative philosophies of race relations" in addition to the "extreme racism" that eventually triumphed. "Liberals," who believed in racial equality, had the least support among post-Reconstruction whites. "Conservatives," who saw Blacks as "inferior" but favored a paternalistic policy rather than one of exclusion or outright hostility, were more numerous, as were "Southern radicals," populists who were willing—at least under the right circumstances, for a while—to support a class alliance with African Americans. In *The Crucible of Race,* Joel Williamson also saw Southern whites divided into "Liberals," "Conservatives," and "Radicals," but *his* Liberals were racial agnostics who "did not yet know the potential of the Negro," while Conservatives took for granted "Negro inferiority," and Radicals were racist extremists who "insisted that there was *no place* for the Negro in the future American society." Meanwhile, George M. Fredrickson presented still a different tripartite categorization of white racial thought, with paternalistic "Moderates" "attacked during the 1880s from two sides": by "die-hard racists" and a small group of "lonely spokesmen" who favored "a policy of genuine public equality."[69]

Despite these differences in terminology and to some extent in categorization, the overall trend was clear, as was the periodization underlying it. Not only were the three authors in substantial agreement on the growing prevalence among white Southerners of support for virulently racist policies, they also put forth similar tripartite stages of post-emancipation Southern history. First, although a small but significant number of white Southerners briefly joined Republican Reconstruction coalitions, most of these "scalawags" soon found such alliances untenable and came to support what conservatives termed "Redemption," thereby—in conjunction with declining Northern interest in pursuing a comprehensive restructuring of Southern society—dooming most states' Reconstruction regimes. Second, the immediate post-Reconstruction years witnessed what Woodward dubbed "forgotten alternatives," most of which allowed for some degree of racial tolerance, as white Southerners—cautious in the face of potential federal intervention—hesitated before turning to more extreme measures. Finally, beginning in the 1890s—Williamson set the start of "Radicalism's" sway in 1889—Southern whites embraced virulently racist programs that included massive disfranchisement of Black voters (in blatant violation of the Fourteenth and Fifteenth Amendments to the Constitution), a more thorough institutionalization of "Jim Crow" racial segregation, and acceptance of gruesome violence against African Americans in the form of lynching. Accompanying "efforts to ... justify lynching," explained Fredrickson, there emerged a new "stereotype of the 'Negro as beast.' "[70]

In recent years there has been a great deal of historical work detailing this three-stage progression. Although it is impossible to provide a detailed summary here of that large body of work, an essential point is that most Southern whites never voluntarily accepted Black equality—or for that matter the Confederacy's defeat—and refrained from immediately imposing the racist order they eventually promoted only because of the threat (and in some cases the reality) of federal force. As historian Gregory Downs observed, ex-Confederates "returned home from fighting still fighting" and were dissuaded only by the presence of the U.S. military, which was soon "overstretched and undermanned." Indeed, as this presence evaporated, so too did Southern white docility: of the one million federal troops in the South at the war's conclusion in April 1865, fewer than ninety thousand remained by the end of January 1866 (sixty-one thousand excluding those in Texas) and fewer than twenty-five thousand by the end of 1866. The result was a "false peace," during which "ex-Confederates launched campaigns of terror" and the army "created pockets of peace and stability" in a South that "was in a state of near anarchy." In short, Reconstruction governments—and Black freedom—were heavily dependent on military occupation, and as "the army's role was reduced to that of a bystander" these governments fell in one state after another.[71]

There were many twists and turns in the South during the post-emancipation decades: some states had longer, stronger Reconstruction programs than others, and in some—for example, Virginia during the early 1880s, when the "Readjuster" movement "redrew the lines of interracial cooperation"—Redemption at least briefly yielded to a second Reconstruction. Within individual states, there were also significant differences and anomalies. In Louisiana, where intense violence and terror between 1874 and 1876 brought an end to Republican rule, peace—and Black power—prevailed in the sugar parishes until the brutal suppression of a strike by sugar laborers in 1887, after which, in the words of historian John Rodrigue, "Redemption finally descended upon the sugar region." And in Wilmington, North Carolina, where "somehow the African American residents . . . managed to hold ex-slaveholders and employers at bay for a generation" and a Populist-Republican coalition governed in the mid-1890s, Redemption came only in November 1898, with an explosion of racial violence that left "more than ten African Americans . . . dead in the streets." Two years later, North Carolina enacted a constitutional amendment that effectively disfranchised most African American voters.[72]

But overall, despite this uneven pattern, the trajectory was clear: throughout the South, most whites refused to accept the political equality of African Americans and struggled to restore what was sometimes termed "home rule," which meant "white rule." As historian Anne Sarah Rubin explained, to former Confederates, who, even as they claimed the rights and privileges of American citizenship "continued to think of themselves as a separate people" and saw themselves as the "true victims of Reconstruction," white supremacy was of paramount importance—indeed, was central to their very identity. Humiliated by the loss of their war and their slaves, as well as by the presence of Black soldiers, Black voters, and Black officeholders, "[white] Southerners had no intention of giving up their politically, socially, and economically privileged position." It is not surprising, then, that Southern whites, including some who had never supported the Confederacy, increasingly adhered to an image of African Americans as a savage—or "unnerving"—people who fully justified white supremacy and the kind of violence necessary to achieve it. Noting the "blind, baffled, revengeful hatred" whites throughout the Deep South expressed toward African Americans, Northern journalist Whitelaw Reid concluded shortly after the war that "however kind they may have been to negro property, they were virulently vindictive against a property that escaped from their control."[73]

Recent historians have paid increased attention to the centrality of violence, intimidation, and terror in both the overthrow of Reconstruction and the subsequent strengthening of white supremacy through disfranchisement and the establishment of rigid racial segregation. This centrality was especially evident where the races were relatively even in numbers. By contrast, where African Americans constituted substantial majorities Republican power and Black political participation were more persistent, and in overwhelmingly white areas proponents of white racial domination could rely more on electoral politics and less on violence. (Even in such predominantly white areas, however, violence was hardly absent: as Michael Fitzgerald noted, for example, in the overwhelmingly white hill country of Alabama, conservatives engaged in what amounted to "upcountry ethnic cleansing.") The violence came in waves, ebbing and flowing but continuing until it had achieved the goal of overthrowing any remnants of Reconstruction regimes and establishing white supremacy through a combination of disfranchisement, racial segregation and subordination, and sporadic acts of torture designed to show what awaited those who challenged the new order. The first Ku Klux Klan, whose members killed, raped, and generally terrorized African Americans and white Republicans "on a massive scale" in the late 1860s and early 1870s, was the object of congressional hearings in 1871–72 that resulted in extensive testimony and led to the organization's effective suppression by 1872, but it was succeeded by a series of other groups (sometimes subsumed under the general category of "the Klan") such as the Red Shirts and Knights of the White Camelia that were instrumental in overthrowing Deep South Reconstruction regimes in the mid-1870s, through the kind of violence that historian Justin Behrend termed "not all that different from irregular warfare during the Civil War."[74]

During the so-called era of forgotten alternatives in the 1880s, despite the generally cautious stance of many Redeemers, who in Michael Fitzgerald's felicitous phrasing "proceeded with muffled oars," force was used when "necessary," as in the crushing of the sugar workers' strike in Louisiana through "a frenzy of violence against the strikers"; as one white observer predicted, the violence would, in her words, "settle the question of who is to rule[,] the nigger or the white man? for the next 50 years." (After the strike was crushed, she reported with pleasure: "The negroes are as humble as pie today, very different from last week.") In 1889, in an event that "crystallize[d] in one dramatic moment what happened throughout the South with the creation of Jim Crow law," Arkansas's recently defeated Republican congressional candidate John Clayton was murdered by Democrats who "feared they would end up in a federal penitentiary" for having stolen a ballot box filled "with the majority of [Conway] county's black Republican votes." As historian Kenneth C. Barnes observed, "Because the most prominent and socially respectable citizens of the county provided alibis for one another, no assassin was ever found." Beginning the following year with Mississippi's revised constitution, one Southern state after another effectively disfranchised its Black citizens (and some white citizens as well), through a combination of provisions that included such measures as poll taxes, literacy tests, and "grandfather clauses" (allowing men to vote whose grandfather had enjoyed the privilege in 1860). New segregation laws followed, as did an orgy of lynching directed primarily at young Black men accused of raping (or sometimes wanting to rape) white women, acting disrespectfully, or just being "uppity." "Lynchings tended to flourish where whites were surrounded by what they called 'strange niggers,' blacks with no white to vouch for them," wrote historian Edward Ayers. "For generations, young black men learned early in their lives that they could at any time be grabbed by a white mob . . . and dragged into the woods or a public street to be tortured, burned, mutilated."[75]

As the conservative reaction gained strength, most white Southerners held increasingly negative stereotypical views of African Americans. There *were* exceptions, including distinguished authors such as George W. Cable and Mark Twain (Samuel Clemens)—significantly, both Twain and Cable left the South and spent most of their adult lives in New England, as residents, respectively, of Hartford, Connecticut, and Northampton, Massachusetts. But the exceptions were increasingly unrepresentative of majority Southern white sentiment. Over and over, whites subscribed to recognizable Black stereotypes: African Americans were lazy, ignorant, comical, noisy, pretentious, annoying, and increasingly—if one believed the developing imagery—savage, threatening, and beast-like. Thomas Dixon Jr.'s best-selling novels *The Leopard's Spots* (1902) and *The Clansman* (1905), the latter of which provided the basis for D. W. Griffith's popular movie *The Birth of a Nation* (1915), graphically expressed the alarming and alarmist ideology that Joel Williamson dubbed "Radicalism"; the movie, like both novels, centered on the Reconstruction-era rape of virginal white girls by "bestial" Black men (played by *white* actors in blackface). As historian Grace Elizabeth Hale argued, these "extremely popular portrayals of Reconstruction" managed to appeal to Northern as well as Southern whites, by casting Black men—represented by the stereotypical "black beast rapist"—as "virtually alone responsible for the 'hell' of Reconstruction" and thus making possible a "national reconciliation" based on "the birth of the new Anglo Saxon nation." "Dixon's freedpeople confirmed early twentieth-century white Americans' worst prejudices and fears," explained Amanda Bellows: "They behaved brutishly after emancipation by 'terrorising the country, stealing, burning and murdering' "—as well as "by raping white women." Popular in the North as well as the South, *The Birth of a Nation* received high praise from President Woodrow Wilson, who observed that "it is all terribly true."[76]

Non-peasant Russians typically held more complex, less universally negative, images of the peasantry. In her book *Peasant Icons*, historian Cathy A. Frierson sketched eight different versions or "images of the Russian peasant," as educated Russians debated the peasant's characteristics during the decades immediately following emancipation. Some of these versions were particularly persistent. Perhaps the most favorable (and earliest to receive widespread currency) was the image of the peasant as representative of the *narod*, which connoted both the common people (as opposed to "society") and the Russian nation itself. Embodying peasant simplicity, passivity, and communality, this image inspired a generation of *narodniki*—in English usually called "populists," a confusing term, because these Russian populists were so different from Americans who went by that name—to work among the people and bring them enlightenment. A very different image was that of "the peasant as rational agriculturist," as depicted in *Aleksandr Nikolaevich Engelgardt's Letters from the Country* and the writings of journalist Gleb Ivanovich Uspenskii; this version of peasant life was shaped by "land, labor, and the struggle for existence." A new and increasingly widespread image by the late 1870s was that of the "gray peasant," "a weak human being who lacked either the moral or intellectual strength to survive with integrity in his changing world." The gray peasant was "a dreary and discouraging figure" who was prone to bouts of drunkenness. Less attractive still was the peasant as exploiter of kulaks (wealthy peasant farmers), a greedy village bully who was the opposite of the peasant as representative of the *narod*. Reflecting Russia's patriarchal culture, the female peasant—or *baba*—was an offshoot of the gray peasant, with implications of being a "hag" or "fishwife," although in other versions she could be "a seductive manipulating creature" or even an innocent victim of a misogynistic society.[77]

Most outsiders—including nobles, government officials, and educated Russians in general—certainly did not have especially positive images of peasants. Although these images varied considerably, they inclined in sum toward those that were negative: peasants tended to be simple, hardworking folk who were also lazy, greedy, ignorant, often duplicitous, and (among men) prone to drunkenness. What is more, the images became more negative over time. As the increasing prevalence of "gray peasant" imagery suggested, the hopes and excitement that emancipation had generated among at least some observers gradually yielded to discouragement and disillusionment, themes that were pervasive by the 1880s. As one might expect, this was especially true among noble landowners (who were hardly disinterested observers). As historian Stephen P. Frank noted, nobles typically saw post-emancipation peasants as "less deferential and more threatening" than they had been under serfdom and worried about a surge in criminality among peasants who lacked the proper supervision they had once received. Quoting a typical noble complaint that "this generation of peasants has grown up without character, wild, lazy, thievish, obstinate, . . . impudent and frenzied," Frank observed that educated Russians in general "looked upon former serfs and state peasants as culturally underdeveloped, backward, ignorant, immoral, and even degenerate." But although these views were in some ways reminiscent of white Southern perceptions of Black freedpeople who were out of control, except perhaps for some of the most extreme images of the conniving *baba*, no version of Russian peasants contained the sheer vitriol of the Southern white view of Blacks as alien savages and beast-like rapists. Peasants were, after all, quintessential Russians; no one could imagine all the peasants "dying off," or expelling them from Russia.[78]

And yet, one might ask how this different representation mattered, for the end result of emancipation in Russia was remarkably similar to that in the Southern United States. Just as the Southern Reconstruction effort inspired enormous expectations that were soon dashed, so too in Russia emancipation was part of a broader effort to restructure society—the so-called Great Reforms—that soon yielded to more conservative impulses, and Russia's reconstruction can be said to have ended in the 1870s. Indeed, well before then the reform initiative was already on the wane. The wave of peasant unrest that frightened authorities and that some Soviet historians saw as constituting a "revolutionary situation" quickly subsided: the partial figures compiled by the editors of the *Krest'ianskoe dvizhenie* series indicated that the 1,859 volneniia of 1861 (most in the spring and summer of that year) were followed by less than half as many in 1862, with sharply decreasing numbers throughout the decade of the 1860s, reaching a low of sixty in 1868 before rebounding slightly to sixty-five in 1869. Meanwhile, almost immediately after promulgating the emancipation edict, Tsar Alexander II, alarmed by the violent peasant reaction, began replacing reform-minded officials with more conservative appointments: one of the most notable of these changes was his firing in April 1861 of the liberal minister of internal affairs S. S. Lanskoi and his replacement by Petr Valuev, a move that indicated—in the words of historian David

Saunders—that "the government's main concern now seemed to be stifling dissent before it became intractable." In 1868, Valuev was himself replaced as minister of internal affairs by the even more conservative A. E. Timashev, who quickly made clear his desire "to abolish the [peace] mediators and replace them with appointees of his ministry." As historian Roxanne Easley noted, even before then, "by 1864, interest in the long and painstaking process of implementing the peasant reform had simply faded." By 1874, when the government in fact did away with the peace mediators and gave added power to noble officials, including the district marshal of nobility and *ispravnik*, it was clear that there had been a sharp shift from the heady days of 1861 to a renewed governmental emphasis on law and order.[79]

The conservative reaction grew stronger during the last quarter of the nineteenth century. As early as the 1870s, historian Corinne Gaudin noted, there was a "growing consensus" among politically aware Russians "that peasants were unable to rule themselves for their own common good": not only were they ignorant and immature, their communal and *volost'* meetings were dysfunctional, plagued by a combination of illiteracy, drunkenness, corruption, bribery, and bullying by a small number of rich and powerful *kulaki* or *miroedy* (literally, "mir eaters"). As nobleman S. A. Mordvinov, one of four senators serving on a committee investigating the "disintegration of local authority in rural Russia," put it in 1880, "Peasant self-government . . . has virtually ceased to exist. The village and volost' assemblies . . . have lost all credit in the eyes of the people. Decent peasants do not show up at the assembly, or are brought there against their will." Meanwhile, rather than "the village and *volost'* elders, who almost without exception are illiterate," it was the scribes who actually ran the meetings. Quoting a peasant proverb—"Before we were subordinate to the landlord; now it's the scribe"—Mordvinov concluded: "Peasants are indifferent toward elections, believing that even if a good person were to be elected, he would be corrupted by the office." The growing conviction that the behavior of the freed peasants was problematical led to the reemergence of an issue that had supposedly been resolved forever—the "peasant question"— with which (as in the generation before emancipation) one governmental commission after another grappled, for the most part unsuccessfully.[80]

The assassination of Alexander II in 1881 and the accession to the throne of his son Alexander III accentuated the conservative reaction. By nature far more authoritarian than his father, the new tsar, whose "political creed may be reduced to the tripartite formula . . . orthodoxy, autocracy, and nationality (*narodnost*), with special emphasis on autocracy," surrounded himself with influential reactionary advisers, including his tutor K. P. Pobedonostsev, who as chief procurator of the Holy Synod "encouraged the new tsar to embark upon a program of unremitting reaction," and Count D. A. Tolstoi, who served as minister of internal affairs from 1882 until his death in 1889 and was responsible for much of the specific legislation relating to supervision and control of the peasantry. There were countless manifestations of the increasingly conservative governmental thrust, which was founded on Pobedonostsev's conviction that democracy represented the "Great Falsehood of Our Time"—or as he put it succinctly, "The principle of the sovereignty of the people" was "among the falsest of political principles"—but when it came to government treatment of the peasants, two acts were of paramount importance. The first of these established a new position—the "land captain," or *zemskii nachal'nik*—to supervise and rein in the peasantry, and the second dramatically reduced the peasants' electoral clout in selecting delegates for district and provincial zemstvo assemblies, thereby also reducing their participation in those assemblies.[81]

Land captains represented a long-sought governmental effort to establish order among the peasants, whom officials increasingly saw as "an unruly lot." Termed by historian Thomas S. Pearson the "legislative benchmark of Alexander III's reign and the cornerstone in Tolstoi's centralization policy," the land captain reform of 1889 divided provinces into sixty to seventy precincts, each headed by a noble land captain who would supervise the peasants and overcome, in the words of historian Corinne Gaudin, "the bad behavior of volost and village elders." With some of the same functions as the peace mediators of a generation earlier, the land captains, like their predecessors, varied considerably in character and intent; unlike the peace mediators, however, they had the right to fire and arrest village officials, and they were generally welcomed by the local nobility, who saw them as their representatives in the effort to reestablish a noble presence in the countryside. Pushing the idea of "guardianship" over peasants—in the words of historian P. N. Zyrianov—"to a logical absurdity," and "quickly coming to see themselves as "surrounded by [peasant] enemies," they considered countermanding chaotic and corrupt peasant institutions, including *volost'* courts and village assemblies, to be at the heart of their role. In this goal they had some success; as Gaudin put it, the land captains gradually managed to erode peasant autonomy, as a result of which, "on the eve of World War I, the Russian village had lost much of the administrative self-sufficiency it might once have enjoyed." In short, "state officials had penetrated the village."[82]

Reforming zemstvo electoral procedures, effected in 1890, in some ways constituted the equivalent of African American disfranchisement in the Southern United States. Of course, the zemstva had never been shining examples of popular democracy: unlike noble landowners and urban dwellers, peasants chose their deputies in volost' assemblies, under a highly skewed electoral system guaranteed to reduce peasant representation. Although they formed the great majority of the population, in the first round of zemstvo elections, in the mid-1860s, peasants secured 38 percent of the seats in district zemstvo assemblies, and 11 percent of those in the provincial assemblies. (By contrast, nobles—who in most of Russia constituted less than 1 percent of the population—occupied 42 percent of the seats at the district level and 74 percent at the provincial level.) But the 1890 law, drafted by D. A. Tolstoi, provided for even more skewed elections. Under the new electoral procedure, which disfranchised a variety of previous voters (including Jews, priests, and peasants who were private proprietors rather than owners of communal allotments), voting was entirely by estate, with only three broad categories—noble property owners, non-noble property owners, and peasant members of village communes. (Increased property qualifications further limited the number participating from the first two categories.) More important, peasants could no longer elect their deputies in volost' assemblies; rather, they would now essentially nominate candidates there, submitting a list of potential deputies to the provincial governor, who would appoint whom he chose from the list. The result was a further contraction of peasant representation to 31 percent of district and less than 2 percent of provincial deputies. By 1903, nobles constituted 71.9 percent of district delegates and 94.1 percent of those at the provincial level. Even as the zemstva were increasingly active in undertaking ventures affecting education, public health, and the collection of statistics, peasants, whom reformers accused of "apathy" and "indifference" to zemstvo service, played a significantly diminished role in local governance.[83]

Underlying the conservative reactions in both the American South and Russia were two fundamental features that interacted to bring an end to the reformist waves represented by Reconstruction and the Great Reforms. Most obvious, in the continuing struggle between landed elites and the freedpeople, the balance gradually tipped in favor of the former—the planters and the pomeshchiki who, despite their apparent defeat in emancipation, retained the considerable advantage provided by wealth, privilege, and organization. That this was so is hardly surprising: similar results ensued virtually everywhere that bound labor yielded to free labor, and despite intense struggles over the nature of the new order, former masters were almost always able to protect their interests and salvage much—although not all—of their power and status as well. In Brazil and Jamaica, as in Prussia, slaves and serfs found that the new freedom was not quite so free as they had hoped, while landed elites found that being forced to give up their ownership of human property was not quite so catastrophic as they had feared. If anything, this triumph of old elites—who usually managed to turn themselves into new elites—was more easily engineered in most countries than in Russia and the South, where the Great Reforms and especially Reconstruction provided the context for more protracted class struggles that seemed for a while as if they might yield a substantial shift in the balance of power.[84]

Indeed, a second feature of developments in Russia and the Southern United States differentiated their history from that of other societies undergoing emancipation. Reconstruction and the Great Reforms, two atypical movements that in turn produced powerful conservative counterreform movements, provided an unusual dynamic that ultimately led to increasingly widespread disappointment and disillusionment that different segments of society felt for different reasons. This was especially true in the South, where the countermovement was particularly pronounced because of the sweeping nature of Reconstruction, but in Russia, too, emancipation was at the heart of what for a while seemed to herald a revolutionary transformation of the social order, which in turn generated a powerful conservative reaction. In short, radical reform proved disappointing in different ways to many Russians and Southerners—including the former slaves and serfs, who had hoped for even more sweeping measures, and their former owners, who clung to as many of their old prerogatives as possible. I return, briefly, to this theme of dashed expectations in the Epilogue, from a comparative perspective, but it is worth noting here, in conjunction with the effort of the former masters to roll back the gains that the freedpeople had secured.

Epilogue

A generation after emancipation, pervasive disillusionment characterized Russia and the Southern United States. Although details differed, the overall pattern was very much the same: in both countries, hopes generated by emancipation, Reconstruction, and the Great Reforms were dashed and replaced by widespread disillusionment, cynicism, and despair. Emancipation was at the center of societal experiments that were unusually far-reaching—especially in the South but to a lesser extent in Russia as well—and the unraveling of those experiments proved traumatic to almost all the actors in the ensuing drama.[1]

It is worth noting that most other nineteenth-century emancipations seemed even more unsuccessful, especially from the point of view of the freedpeople. Not only did these emancipations leave the freedpeople poor, exploited, and denied basic rights, but most lacked any equivalent of Reconstruction or Great Reforms. As historians such as David Baronov and Steven Mintz observed, the abolition of slavery in the Americas and serfdom in Eastern Europe was typically gradual, the former masters usually received generous compensation, and the freedpeople remained mired in poverty.[2]

In the British West Indies, where the British initiated a gradual emancipation in 1834, slave owners not only received monetary compensation but also benefited from "apprenticed" labor that was supposed to last—without pay—for six years (but was abruptly ended after four, in 1838). Meanwhile, in some British colonies, including Trinidad and British Guiana, freedpeople faced competition from newly imported indentured Indian and Chinese laborers, while in others, such as Jamaica, former slaves who appropriated unused land rejected commercial production for self-sufficient agriculture, and "sugar output fell dramatically," not returning to pre-emancipation levels for about a century.[3]

Cuban emancipation was even more gradual. The 1870 Moret Law began the process, by freeing slaves over sixty as well as those who were newborn. This measure, together with the elimination of new slave imports from Africa, reduced the number of slaves from 368,550 in 1862 to 199,094 in 1877. Then, in 1880, Spain introduced an eight-year *patronado* (patronage) period, with the full end of slavery ensuing over four years, in 1884–87; by 1883 there were only 99,566 *patrocicados,* and by 1885 their numbers had decreased to 53,381. Ironically, all this occurred with little abolitionist sentiment, and as historian Rebecca Scott noted, once slavery was abolished "the government made no effort to influence and moderate the integration of former slaves into the new society comparable to the efforts of the Freedmen's Bureau or the legislation that accompanied Reconstruction in the United States."[4] In Brazil, the last country in the Americas to abolish slavery, in 1888, emancipation was also a "drawn-out, patently calculated" occurrence, with slavery set on the road to eventual extinction (as in Cuba) by the abolition of imports of slaves from Africa in 1851, a process that was greatly accelerated in 1871 with the "free birth" law that freed newborn slaves. As historian Seymour Drescher has noted, after emancipation "there was no concerted effort to aid the freed slaves," who suffered from widespread neglect. Meanwhile, in southern Brazil (São Paulo), the freedpeople, who "had bargained too hard, and demanded too much," faced new competition when employers "flood[ed] the market with European immigrants"; between 1890 and 1914, some 1.5 million European laborers—the largest number of whom were Italians—arrived, depressing compensation for the ex-slaves.[5]

The end of serfdom in Eastern and Central Europe was equally problematic for those who were freed. In most cases, peasants lost their previous access to land, and often their ability to move was severely restricted as well. As noted above, in the Introduction, it became a stock argument of those planning the emancipation of Russia's serfs that the landless emancipation of the three Baltic provinces—Estland, Lifland, and Kurland—be avoided at all cost, but the terms of freedom for peasants in Prussia, Austria, and most of Poland were similarly harsh. In Prussia, where "emancipation . . . stretched out over decades" despite the initial emancipation edict of 1807, "the large noble estate owners gained the most from the agrarian reforms," and peasants lost most of the land (to which they lacked legal hereditary claims). In Austria, emancipation began in 1740 but was not completed until 1848; until that revolutionary year, efforts to ban compulsory labor obligations were unsuccessful, although a decree of 1798 allowed "voluntary" agreements between landowners and peasants. Even in 1848 "the emancipation law . . . enacted the program of agrarian reform that had been advocated by noble landowners." Since Poland was divided among Prussia, Austria, and Russia, those countries dictated the terms whereby the Polish peasantry was freed. Emancipation came first in Prussia-controlled Poland—gradually, beginning in 1807 (as in Prussia) and ending in 1860—"at the peasant's expense." The Austrian-controlled section was next, in 1848 (as in Austria), with landlords receiving compensation for the removal of peasant obligations in bonds, paid for by the peasants. Only in "Congress" (Russian-controlled) Poland, where the emancipation decree of 1861 did not apply, did the condition of the peasantry improve at least marginally, as the Russian government moved to undercut peasant support for a noble-led rebellion by awarding peasants the right to land in 1864 and paying the nobles sixty-four million rubles in compensation. Nowhere in Eastern Europe, however, did ex-serfs gain equal rights or republican citizenship.[6]

Considering all these cases of emancipation from slavery and serfdom suggests that they can be divided into three broad categories. At one extreme was the ending of slavery in the Southern United States, which was sudden, uncompensated, and resulted in a highly unusual effort to turn former slaves immediately into republican citizens, with equal civil and political rights. At the other extreme were most other cases of emancipation, which to varying extents were gradual and compensated and lacked any equivalent of the Reconstruction-inspired effort to improve the status of the freedpeople; indeed, most of these emancipations took greater care of the interests of the former landowners than those of the former bondspeople. In between was the ending of Russian serfdom, which lacked the suddenness and sweeping character of the American version but was far less drawn out than most other emancipations, provided compensation to the former masters but did not impose a landless settlement on the former serfs, and—most important—was part of an ongoing effort to remake the social order (the Great Reforms) that served as a less extreme but still significant equivalent of American Reconstruction.[7] Haiti, of course, was a case unto itself: like the United States, it abolished slavery violently, through civil war, but unlike the United States (and Russia), it lacked any real equivalent of Reconstruction (or the Great Reforms) and before long had descended from a wealthy (if brutal) colony to an impoverished (and brutalized) nation.[8]

Ultimately, the most important feature distinguishing these other emancipations from those in the Southern United States and Russia is that they occurred without any real equivalent of Reconstruction or Great Reforms. This absence meant that these other emancipations typically lacked the experimental character—and the accompanying hope and excitement—of those in Russia and the South, but also that they did not end with the same kind of dashed expectations. Indeed, it was the sequential upside and then downside of their "reconstructions" that made disillusionment especially pervasive in Russia and the Southern United States. After noting "the lack of organized programs to aid the [Brazilian] freedpeople," Rebecca Scott pointed out: "Equally significant, surely, is the relative absence [in Brazil] of the violence and vengeance so characteristic of white southern responses." Precisely because of the hopes that Reconstruction and the Great Reforms inspired, the conservative reactions that soon gripped the South and Russia were especially pronounced.[9]

These conservative reactions reflected the profound disillusionment— dashed expectations—that typified diverse groups of Southerners and Russians. Although disillusionment and disappointment were widespread, different categories of people expressed these sentiments differently, and for different reasons. Former slaveholders and serfholders lamented the loss of their privileges and strove to preserve them to the extent possible. Government officials—including many of the reformers who had once enthusiastically embraced emancipation—grew increasingly disappointed in the freedpeople's behavior, and they frequently concluded that former slaves and serfs were incapable of acting as responsible free people. Radicals also became unhappy with the course of events, with some blaming the freedpeople for not living up to expectations and others bemoaning the triumph of conservative policies designed to minimize the extent of change and prevent the emergence of egalitarian societies. Meanwhile, former slaves and serfs were unhappy with their continued poverty and oppression, expressing alarm at the triumph of reactionary forces that denied them the "true" freedom they thought they would enjoy.[10]

Because these perceptions of dashed expectations were so pervasive in Russia and the Southern United States, it is important to emphasize—as I have in much of this volume—the elements of social transformation that were widespread as well. The abolition of American slavery and Russian serfdom were both part of the multifaceted reorientation of the South and Russia from hierarchical societies based on forced labor to increasingly market-based societies in which distinctions were based less on rank and hereditary privilege than on ability, determination, education—and access to capital. The social transformations were by no means total or complete: both were hurtling, partial, and negated by contrary tendencies, some of which were remnants of the old order, and others of which were new manifestations of resistance to change. In the United States, the theoretical "republican" equality of rights that replaced slavery was undermined by the surge of racist thought and behavior that became increasingly routine—and increasingly entrenched—especially in the South. In Russia, the destruction of the estate-based social order was very partial: the nobility lost its principal defining characteristic—the right to own serfs—but maintained some legal privileges as well as its huge economic power. What is more, estates continued to have real although diminished legal distinctions, and Russia remained an autocracy (Russians were subjects, not citizens) in which political power continued to be distributed unevenly to different categories of people (principally nobles, merchants, townsmen, and peasants). In short, although emancipation in the two countries marked major shifts, accompanied by manifold changes introduced by Reconstruction and the Great Reforms, the shifts were bitterly contested, and remained partial in nature. Post-emancipation African Americans and peasants continued to struggle to overcome the legacy of the bondage under which they had labored, and the aftereffects of that bondage continued to be evident in multiple ways.

Still, despite these new disappointments, it is important to emphasize that emancipation in the United States and Russia did not presage a return to slavery, serfdom, or some other version of hereditary bondage, and the emancipation of the 1860s did indeed initiate a basic transformation of the social order. It is worth summarizing some of what this transformation meant to the freedpeople. "Personal" freedom—immediate in both countries—meant that freedpeople, unlike slaves and serfs, could marry at will and move geographically (in the South at will, in Russia at least in theory with communal rather than an owner's approval). Over time, despite the bitter, and at times violent, conservative resistance to these changes, freed status brought more extensive gains, including strengthening of family ties, employment in a growing number of previously restricted occupations, increased remuneration, landownership that was usually communal (and widespread) in Russia and more often individual (and less widespread but increasingly common) in the South, educational opportunities, the strengthening of communal associations in Russia and the establishment of independent organizations (including, especially, churches) in the South, and political organization that varied from communal and volost'-level "self-government" in Russia to—at least for a while—full citizenship and significant governmental positions in the United States, especially at the local and state levels in the Deep South. By virtually any standard, these changes were substantial, as indicated by the significant resistance to them among defenders of the old order.[11]

At the same time, by virtually any standard emancipation left most freedpeople mired in poverty, their gains under increasing assault from those who aimed to make the ensuing changes largely cosmetic. Throughout the South—and even in the North, where proponents of equal rights were in full retreat by the end of the nineteenth century—African Americans faced disfranchisement and "Jim Crow" segregation, and those who challenged or seemed to challenge the status quo were at growing risk of physical violence. In Russia, peasants (who constituted the vast majority of the population) were under similar pressure, as land captains sought to establish "order," the zemstva increasingly came under noble control, non-peasant observers became convinced that most peasants were indifferent to good governance, and the "peasant question" once again became a hot topic of conversation. In both countries, many former reformers became convinced that Blacks and peasants were incapable of living up to expectations. More and more, the hopes inspired by emancipation, Reconstruction, and the Great Reforms morphed into the "Great Disappointment" that beset Russia and the South in the post-emancipation era.[12]

The dashed expectations were, ironically, greatest precisely where the post-emancipation settlement had seemed the most sweeping and change had seemed most promising. There is, of course, a certain logic to this connection—great expectations are notoriously difficult to fulfill—and where the results of emancipation were most consequential and far-reaching was precisely where those results also generated the most intense opposition. This is one reason that historians have had such a difficult time deciding whether or not emancipation led to significant societal changes: the coexistence of new opportunities and new forms of exploitation and oppression has rendered even more difficult than usual the historian's task of distinguishing change from continuity. It is worth observing, however, that change is entirely compatible with continued (and even accentuated) racism, violence, and oppression: exploitation and cruelty may be constants in human relations, but not all forms of exploitation and cruelty are the same.

The poverty that most freedpeople experienced persisted for decades—and, indeed, remains evident among their descendants to this day. Of course, there *were* exceptional Blacks and peasants who defied the averages and managed to accumulate significant wealth, but these were atypical cases that had existed (albeit to a lesser extent) even in the days of slavery and serfdom: the great majority of freedpeople—and their children, grandchildren, and great grandchildren—remained on the margins even as the societies in which they lived lurched erratically toward capitalist (and in Russia, for a while, socialist) transformations. Statistics on the relative poverty of African Americans, the vast majority of whom had themselves been slaves or were the descendants of slaves, are the easiest to document. Because most ex-slaves started with "nothing but freedom," landholding among freedpeople in 1870 was minuscule: as noted in chapter 5, about 2 percent of Blacks who worked the land in the Deep South and 2.2 percent of those in the Upper South were landowners. Even when larger numbers of African Americans acquired farms over the following decades—by 1890, 18 percent of Black farmers owned their own land in the Lower South, as did 33 percent in the Upper South—most holdings were tiny: in 1890, the average farm was worth only $544, and many Black (and white) smallholders eventually lost their land through foreclosures during the depression of the 1890s. More than one hundred and fifty years after emancipation, the relative poverty of African Americans remains striking. There are many ways of measuring this inequality, but perhaps most telling is the following statistic: "Data from the 2016 Survey of Consumer Finances indicates that median black household net worth ($17,600) is only one-tenth of white net worth ($171,000)."[13]

Russian peasant landholding was far more widespread, as ex-serfs—and for that matter state peasants as well—"redeemed" the allotments, or what were typically slightly smaller versions of the allotments, that they had cultivated before the reforms. *Their* poverty was not based on lack of landownership so much as on ownership of insufficient (and, with population growth, increasingly insufficient) landholdings. What is more, they paid dearly for this land, with interest, over decades, in payments that were increasingly in arrears. Historians have debated whether Russian peasants were *really* as impoverished as their defenders maintained, but there can be little doubt that they were *relatively* poor, both compared to non-peasants (especially nobles) and also compared to before, with population growth producing substantial diminution of their average holdings over time. There can also be little doubt that most peasants were increasingly unable to support themselves on their diminished landholdings, leading to a massive growth of otkhodnichestvo in the late nineteenth century.[14]

Equally significant, to a considerable extent the impoverishment affected not just the freedpeople and their descendants but also the Southern United States and Russia in general, as societies that decades after emancipation still felt the effects of having been based on unfree labor. Although the idea of societies based on slavery and serfdom as being premodern has recently come under challenge, the antebellum South and pre-reform Russia had in a variety of ways been underdeveloped (as was evident not only in their overwhelmingly rural, agricultural character but more particularly in their relative poverty), and their underdeveloped characteristics were not easily overcome. As historian Gavin Wright has suggested, "The roots of [Southern] postbellum regional backwardness" rested "firmly in the antebellum era," and "the postwar North-South disparity of roughly two-to-one in per capita income, a persistent feature of the U.S. economy between the Civil War and World War II, was basically consistent with prewar patterns." In fact, during the seventy-five years since World War II as well, although the Southern economy grew more rapidly than the Northern, and the South's separate regional labor market finally was overcome, the Southern states continued to be the poorest in the country. Measured by per capita annual income, *all* the ex-Confederate states ranked below the national average of $28,899 in 2018, with Mississippi the poorest state (at $21,036) and Texas the ex-Confederate state that was closest to the national average (at $27,446). Analyzing Russia's continuing poverty is complicated by the Soviet interlude, which lasted for three-quarters of a century and provided what seemed like a decisive break with the past. Nevertheless, the 2019 statistic of per capita income ($11,585) compiled by the World Bank suggests that even today Russia's economy suffers from its earlier unfree status, and is at best on a level with those of many developing countries, such as Romania, Costa Rica, St. Lucia, Malaysia, Mauritius, and Mexico. (By contrast, the advanced countries of Western Europe have, like the United States, per capita incomes that are at least three times as great as Russia's.) Even more than the South's, Russia's economy—despite the presence of some individuals of enormous wealth—has continued to provide highly unequal incomes and to be fairly modest in overall scope.[15]

The "labor question"—who works for whom, and under what conditions—remained central to the freedpeople and their descendants. The terms of emancipation provided a first-stage answer to this question, but the freedpeople's struggle for a *true* freedom continually redefined this answer. What is more, their struggle, and that of other people throughout the world, continued through the twentieth century and into the twenty-first. Despite the widespread aspiration of those working for richer, more powerful people to work for themselves—either (for example) by owning their own land or by one of several variants of socialism—for the first time in centuries such hopes appear to have largely receded, as economic inequality intensifies and efforts of workers to better their condition through collective action (such as labor unions) become less and less likely. Indeed, combating a form of societal oppression sometimes known as "modern slavery" has recently "become a cause célèbre."[16]

The precise meaning of "modern slavery" is a subject of considerable dispute. Possible meanings include "sex trafficking, the sexual exploitation of people under the age of eighteen, bonded labor (debt bondage), forced labor, domestic servitude, child soldiering, forced child labor, hereditary or descent-based bondage, state-imposed forced labor, forced prison labor, and forced marriage." Clearly, "modern slavery" is something very different from the version that existed in the Southern United States or Russia (under the term "serfdom") in the eighteenth and first half of the nineteenth centuries: the "modern" variety is clearly highly exploitative, but it does not involve the hereditary ownership of human beings—which is everywhere illegal today—and it includes a significant component of forced sex. Indeed, some new "abolitionists" see any form of prostitution, whether legal or not, as an indication of "women's enslaved status." "In this view," pointed out Genevieve LeBaron and Jessica R. Pliley, "all prostitution is slavery." According to the Global Slavery Index (GSI) "compiled annually by the Walk Free Foundation," the number of modern slaves "ballooned from 29.8 million people . . . in 2013 to 40.3 million in 2018." Not to be outdone, "in late April 2020, the International Labour Organization announced that an estimated 1.6 billion workers in the world were newly vulnerable to exploitation and potential enslavement," and "a week later, on May 1, 2020, the *New York Times* reported in a front-page story that such a number may be closer to 2 billion workers."[17]

Therefore, it is useful to reiterate that the emancipation of the 1860s was indeed a turning point, which in some ways initiated and in others accentuated the social transformations already under way, in both Russia and the Southern United States. As this volume has demonstrated, there were significant differences in the context of these social transformations. Nevertheless, despite these different contexts, and despite the massive oppression that freedpeople faced in the two countries, their condition as "free" laborers was very different from what they had endured under bondage. It is no contradiction to suggest that this new freedom went hand in hand with the oppression that it generated, or that remnants of the old order survived the consolidation of the new. Human history is replete with diverse forms of violence, exploitation, and cruelty, but not all versions of this mistreatment are the same. The struggles of unfree laborers for human dignity continued after emancipation, even as the contexts in which they unfolded were radically new.

GLOSSARY

Russian and Russian-Language Terms (Russia),

English-Language Terms (U.S. South)

Russian-Language Terms (Plural in Parentheses)

baba (baby): informal (often derogatory) term for peasant woman

barshchina: corvée, dues paid in labor

bol'shak (bol'shaki): (here) head of traditional, patriarchal family (also *khoziain,* or "boss")

desiatina (desiatiny): land measure = 2.7 acres

desiatskii (desiatskie): tenth, tenner (peasant designated to keep order on a large estate)

dvorovyi, dvorovaia (dvorovye): house servant, house serf

ispravnik (ispravniki): noble police chief in each provincial district

kulak (kulaki): informal (often derogatory) term for rich peasant (literally: "fist")

mir: informal term for peasant communal organization (also "world" and "peace")

muzhik (muzhiki): informal term for peasant man

narod: nation, (common) people

obrok: quitrent, dues paid in money or in kind

obshchina (obshchiny): peasant commune

otkhod, otkhodnichestvo: (here) temporary peasant labor migration

otkhodnik (otkhodniki): migrant laborer, peasant temporarily working away from home estate

otrabotka: Russian version of sharecropping (literally: "working off")

polozhenie (polozheniia): (here) statute(s), regulation(s) of 1861, defining status of former serfs

pomeshchik (pomeshchiki): noble landowner

razdel: (here) the process of division or separation of large, patriarchal families into smaller, often nuclear, units

samosud: informal (often violent) peasant-administered justice

sazhen' (sazheni): land measure = 1/2,400 *desiatiny* (2,400 *sazheni* = 1 *desiatina*) *sel'skoe obshchestvo (sel'skie obshchestva):* village community (official name for the newly legalized *obshchina* or *mir*)

skhod: (here) assembly of peasants, at *sel'skoe obshchestvo* and *volost'* levels

sotskii (sotskie): hundredth (peasant designated to keep order on large estate)

starosta (starosty): chief peasant official (elder) in peasant commune

starshina (starshiny): chief peasant official (elder) in each *volost'*

uezd (uezdy): district, basic subdivision of each province; equivalent to county in United States

versta (versty): measure of distance = 1.067 kilometer

volia: (here) liberty, peasant ideal of *true* freedom, promised by the tsar

volnenie (volneniia): minor peasant rebellion; disturbance, outbreak, agitation, strike

volost' (volosti): township, new peasant administrative unit, usually consisting of several adjacent *sel'skie obshchestva*, created in 1861

zemstvo (zemstva): elected, all-estate council, at provincial and district levels, beginning in 1864

English-Language Terms on Russia (Russian-Language Terms in Parentheses)

allotment (*nadel'*), allotment lands (*nadel'nye zemli*): land allotted to—and to be redeemed (usually communally) by—peasants.

appanage peasants (*udel'nye krest'iane*): peasants owned by the imperial family (called "court peasants"—*dvortsovye krest'iane*—until 1797)

clerk, scribe (*pisar'*): peasant official at communal and *volost'* levels

commune (*obshchina, sel'skoe obshchestvo, mir*): organ of peasant village administration

district (*uezd*): basic subdivision of each province, equivalent to county in United States

farmstead (*usad'ba*): small plot of land attached to peasant hut

land captain (*zemskii nachal'nik*): noble official created in 1889 to supervise peasantry

marshal of nobility (*predvoditel' dvorianstva*): leader elected by noble assembly at both district and provincial levels

peace mediator (sometimes translated as peace arbiter) (*mirovoi posrednik*): new noble official created by emancipation legislation in 1861, to supervise peasant-pomeshchik relations (rough equivalent of Freedmen's Bureau official in Southern United States); abolished in 1874

precinct (*uchastok*): subdivision of district (*uezd*), each having one peace mediator and (later) one land captain

province (*guberniia*)

redemption (*vykup*): peasant payment for (redemption of) allotment lands

"revolutionary situation" (*revoliutsionnaia situatsiia*): belief of some (mostly) Soviet historians that conditions in 1859–61 created the basis for a true revolutionary situation in Russia

state peasants (*gosudarstvennye krest'iane*): peasants who, having escaped enserfment to private noble landowners, were owned by—and paid obligations to—the state

statutory charter (*ustavnaia gramota*): drawn up by a pomeshchik (or his representative), each charter defined the holdings and obligations of temporarily obligated peasants on an estate

temporarily obligated peasants (*vremenno-obiazannye krest'iane*): former serfs, before they began making redemption payments to acquire allotment lands

Third Department or Third Section (*Tret'e otdelenie*): political police

English-Language Terms on Southern United States

Carpetbagger: (often derogatory term for) Northerner (usually Republican) in Southern politics

Freedmen's Bureau: informal term for Bureau of Refugees, Freedmen, and Abandoned Lands, a temporary agency designed to supervise introduction of free labor; in each state, the bureau was headed by an assistant commissioner, usually a general in the Union Army

Redemption: commonly used term for end of Reconstruction (and Republican rule) and establishment of conservative (Democratic) government in a Southern state

Scalawag: (often derogatory term for) white Southerner who supported Republicans

Union League (also Loyal League): originally Civil War organization promoting Union cause in North, in South mobilized support for Republican Party and Reconstruction

NOTES

Introduction

1. See David Brion Davis, *Slavery and Human Progress* (New York: Oxford University Press, 1984); and Steven Mintz, "Models of Emancipation during the Age of Revolution," *Slavery and Abolition*, 17 (August 1996), 1–21. For overviews of the abolition of bondage in the Americas and Eastern Europe, see David Brion Davis, *Inhuman Bondage: The Rise and Fall of Slavery in the New World* (New York: Oxford University Press, 2006); Robert William Fogel and Stanley L. Engerman, *Time on the Cross: The Economics of American Negro Slavery* (Boston: Little, Brown, 1974), 29–38; Robin Blackburn, *The Overthrow of Colonial Slavery, 1776–1848* (London: Verso, 1988), and *The American Crucible: Slavery, Emancipation, and Human Rights* (London: Verso, 2011); Seymour Drescher, *From Slavery to Freedom: Comparative Studies in the Rise and Fall of Atlantic Slavery* (New York: New York University Press, 1999), and *Abolition: A History of Slavery and Antislavery* (Cambridge: Cambridge University Press, 2009); Jerome Blum, *The End of the Old Order in Rural Europe* (Princeton: Princeton University Press, 1978), pts. 2 and 3; and David Moon, *The Abolition of Serfdom in Russia, 1762–1907* (Harlow, England: Longman, 2001).

2. On Haiti, see, inter alia, Carolyn E. Fick, *The Making of Haiti: The Saint Domingue Revolution from Below* (Knoxville: University of Tennessee Press, 1990); Laurent Dubois, *Avengers of the New World: The Story of the Haitian Revolution* (Cambridge, MA: Harvard University Press, 2005); and Laurent Dubois and John D. Garrigue, *Slave Revolution in the Caribbean, 1789–1804: A Brief History with Documents* (New York: Bedford/St. Martin's, 2006).

3. On the eve of emancipation, there were approximately twenty-three million Russian serfs and four million Southern slaves. For statistics, see Peter Kolchin, *Unfree Labor: American Slavery and Russian Serfdom* (Cambridge, MA: Harvard University Press, 1987), 52–53, 364, 366. Most Russian censuses counted only males ("souls" or

"male souls"); doubling the number of male souls yields a rough approximation of the total population.

4. Unless otherwise noted, this section is based on Kolchin, *Unfree Labor.*

5. On the wide variety of different "slaveries," see Orlando Patterson, *Slavery and Social Death: A Comparative Study* (Cambridge, MA: Harvard University Press, 1982).

6. Russians sometimes used the same terms (*raby* and *rabstvo*) to refer to their serfs and serfdom that they used when referring to American slaves and slavery, and numerous scholars of Russian serfdom have stressed its slave-like characteristics. See Kolchin, *Unfree Labor,* 41–43. But for a largely contrary view, in which Russian serfdom appears closer to free labor than to slavery, see Alessandro Stanziani, *Bondage: Labor and Rights in Eurasia from the Sixteenth to the Early Twentieth Centuries* (New York: Berghahn, 2014).

7. For the statistical contrast, see Kolchin, *Unfree Labor,* 51–57. Although statistics on slaveholders are usually given as a proportion of the Southern white population, a more accurate figure for comparative purposes is slaveholders as a proportion of the *total* Southern population (white and Black, free and enslaved); between 1830 and 1860, this figure decreased from about 22 percent to about 17 percent.

8. According to a 2005 analysis, in 1830 "a southern white was just three times more likely to own slaves than was a southern free black." See David L. Lightner and Alexander M. Ragan, "Were African American Slaveholders Benevolent or Exploitative? A Quantitative Approach," *Journal of Southern History,* 71 (August 2005), 535–58 (quotation and statistic: 549).

9. Patterson, *Slavery and Social Death,* 179, 176.

10. For a pioneering historical essay on this question, see Barbara J. Fields, "Ideology and Race in American History," in *Region, Race, and Reconstruction: Essays in Honor of C. Vann Woodward,* ed. J. Morgan Kousser and James M. McPherson (New York: Oxford University Press, 1982), 142–77. The most recent manifestation of arguments for the constructed nature of race is evident in the burgeoning field of "whiteness studies"; see Peter Kolchin, "Whiteness Studies: The New History of Race in America," *Journal of American History,* 89 (June 2002), 154–73, and "Whiteness Studies II: An Update on the New History of Race in America," *Journal de la Societé des Américanistes,* 95, no. 1 (2009), 144–63.

11. For diverse perspectives on the internal economy, see Philip D. Morgan, "Work and Culture: The Task System and the World of Lowcountry Blacks, 1770 to 1880," *William and Mary Quarterly,* 39 (October 1982), 563–99; Lawrence T. McDonnell, "Money Knows No Master: Market Relations and the American Slave Community," in *Developing Dixie: Modernization in a Traditional Society,* ed. Winfred B. Moore Jr. et al. (Westport, CT: Greenwood Press, 1988), 31–44; Roderick A. McDonald, *The Economy and Material Culture of Slaves: Goods and Chattels on the Sugar Plantations of Jamaica and Louisiana* (Baton Rouge: Louisiana State University Press, 1993); Larry E. Hudson Jr., *To Have and to Hold: Slave Work and Family Life in Antebellum South Carolina*

(Athens: University of Georgia Press, 1997); Dylan Penningroth, "Slavery, Freedom, and Social Claims to Property among African Americans in Liberty County, Georgia, 1850–1880," *Journal of American History*, 84 (September 1997), 405–35; Dylan C. Penningroth, *The Claims of Kinfolk: African American Property and Community in the Nineteenth-Century South* (Chapel Hill: University of North Carolina Press, 2003); Anthony E. Kaye, *Joining Places: Slave Neighborhoods in the Old South* (Chapel Hill: University of North Carolina Press, 2007); Kathleen M. Hilliard, *Masters, Slaves, and Exchange: Power's Purchase in the Old South* (New York: Cambridge University Press, 2014); and several of the essays in *Cultivation and Culture: Labor and the Shaping of Slave Life in the Americas*, ed. Ira Berlin and Philip D. Morgan (Charlottesville: University Press of Virginia, 1993).

12. For the revealing story of a privileged serf and his constant struggle against arbitrary power, see Aleksandr Nikitenko, *Up from Serfdom: My Childhood and Youth in Russia, 1802–1824*, trans. Helen Saltz Jacobson (New Haven: Yale University Press, 2001).

13. For the Jamaican contrast, see Kolchin, *Unfree Labor*, 57, 237–38. Students of New World slavery have typically seen slavery as a system of labor exploitation predicated on the ownership of human beings; as Ira Berlin and Philip D. Morgan wrote, "Slaves worked. When, where, and especially how they worked determined, in large measure, the course of their lives." Some (but not all) experts on Africa, however, have depicted slavery as a system of "marginality" predicated on lack of belonging, and sociologist Orlando Patterson, describing slaves as "socially dead," denied the centrality to slavery of human ownership and defined slavery as *"the permanent, violent domination of natally alienated and generally dishonored persons."* Quotations are from Ira Berlin and Philip D. Morgan, "Labor and the Shaping of Slave Life in the Americas," in Berlin and Morgan, *Cultivation and Culture*, 1; and Patterson, *Slavery and Social Death*, 5 and 13. For additional perspectives on this question, see, inter alia, Davis, *Inhuman Bondage*, esp. 29–35; Igor Kopytoff and Suzanne Miers, "African 'Slavery' as an Institution of Marginality," in *Slavery in Africa: Historical and Anthropological Perspectives*, ed. Suzanne Miers and Igor Kopytoff (Madison: University of Wisconsin Press, 1977), 3–81; Paul E. Lovejoy, *Transformations in Slavery: A History of Slavery in Africa* (Cambridge: Cambridge University Press, 1983), 1–8; and Christine E. Sears, *American Slaves and African Masters: Algiers and the Western Sahara, 1776–1820* (New York: Palgrave Macmillan, 2012).

14. This section incorporates and builds on my argument in Peter Kolchin, "Some Controversial Questions Concerning Nineteenth-Century Emancipation from Slavery and Serfdom," in *Serfdom and Slavery: Studies in Legal Bondage*, ed. M. L. Bush (London: Longman, 1996), 43–51. For recent efforts to provide *general* explanations of emancipation, see Davis, *Inhuman Bondage*; Drescher, *Abolition*; and Blackburn, *The American Crucible*. For my evaluation of these three important books, see Peter Kolchin, "Putting New World Slavery in Perspective," *Slavery and Abolition*, 28 (August

2007), 277–88, and "Complicating the Big Picture: Robin Blackburn's *The American Crucible*," *Slavery and Abolition*, 33 (December 2012), 611–18.

15. Eric Williams, *Capitalism and Slavery* (1944; New York: Capricorn Books, 1966), 210.

16. Charles W. Ramsdell, "The Natural Limits of Slavery Expansion," *Mississippi Valley Historical Review*, 16 (September 1929), 151–71; Ulrich B. Phillips, *American Negro Slavery* (1918; Baton Rouge: Louisiana State University Press, 1966), esp. 359–401; Ulrich Bonnell Phillips, *The Slave Economy of the Old South: Selected Essays in Economic and Social History*, ed. Eugene D. Genovese (Baton Rouge: Louisiana State University Press, 1968); Eugene D. Genovese, *The Political Economy of Slavery: Studies in the Economy and Society of the Slave South* (New York: Vintage Books, 1965). The general economic interpretation of the United States is most closely associated with the name of Charles A. Beard, who argued that the Civil War, by transferring power from Southern slaveholders to Northern capitalists, constituted a "second American Revolution"; see Charles A. Beard and Mary R. Beard, *The Rise of American Civilization*, 2 vols. (New York: Macmillan, 1927), esp. chaps. 17 and 18.

17. V. I. Lenin, *The Development of Capitalism in Russia: The Process of the Formation of a Home Market for Large-Scale Industry* (1899, 1908; Moscow: Foreign Languages Publishing House, 1956). For the argument that the abolition of serfdom was in the objective interest of progressive Russian pomeshchiki, whether or not they recognized that interest, see P. A. Zaionchkovskii, *Otmena krepostnogo prava v Rossii*, 3rd ed. (Moscow: Prosveshchenie, 1968), 3, 87–88, 118. See, also, Peter I. Lyashchenko, *History of the National Economy of Russia to the 1917 Revolution*, trans. L. M. Herman (1939; New York: Macmillan, 1949), 276–78; and I. D. Koval'chenko, *Russkoe krepostnoe krest'ianstvo v pervoi polovine XIX v.* (Moscow: Izdatel'stvo Moskovskogo universiteta, 1967), 378–80. For the "dying out" thesis, see N. M. Shepukova, "Izmenenie udel'nogo vesa chastnovladel'cheskogo krest'ianstva v sostave naseleniia Evropeiskoi Rossii (XVII–pervaia polovina XIX v.)," *Voprosy istorii*, 1959, no. 12, 123–36.

18. Stanley L. Engerman, "Slavery and Emancipation in Comparative Perspective: A Look at Some Recent Debates," *Journal of Economic History*, 46 (June 1986), 330. For early assaults on the thesis that antebellum Southern slavery was economically backward and unprofitable, see Robert William Fogel and Stanley L. Engerman, *Time on the Cross: The Economics of American Negro Slavery* (Boston: Little, Brown, 1974); and Robert W. Fogel, *Without Consent or Contract: The Rise and Fall of American Slavery* (New York: Norton, 1989), esp. 60–113. Recent works that stress the modernity and capitalist nature of antebellum Southern slavery include *The Old South's Modern Worlds: Slavery, Region, and Nation in the Age of Progress*, ed. Diane Barnes et al. (New York: Oxford University Press, 2011); *Slavery's Capitalism: A New History of American Economic Development*, ed. Sven Beckert and Seth Rockman (Philadelphia: University of Pennsylvania Press, 2016); Edward Baptist, *The Half Has Never Been Told: Slavery and the Making of American Capitalism* (New York: Basic Books, 2014); Calvin

Schermerhorn, *The Business of Slavery and the Rise of American Capitalism, 1815–1860* (New Haven: Yale University Press, 2015), and *Unrequited Toil: A History of United States Slavery* (Cambridge: Cambridge University Press, 2018).

Recently, historians have begun applying terms such as "racial capitalism" and "the second slavery" to refer to the capitalist nature of nineteenth-century slavery in Brazil, Cuba, and the Southern United States. See Anthony E. Kaye, "The Second Slavery: Modernity in the Nineteenth-Century South and the Atlantic World," *Journal of Southern History*, 75 (August 2009), 627–50; Caitlin Rosenthal, "Capitalism When Labor Was Capital: Slavery, Power, and Price in Antebellum America," *Capitalism: A Journal of History and Economics*, 1 (Spring 2020), 296–337; Dale W. Tomich and Michael Zeuske, *The Second Slavery: Mass Slavery, World-Economy, and Comparative Microhistories* (Binghamton, NY: Fernand Braudel Center, Binghamton University, 2008); Diana Paton, "Gender History, Global History, and Atlantic Slavery: Racial Capitalism and Social Reproduction," *American Historical Review*, 127 (June 2022), 726–54; and *Slavery and Historical Capitalism during the Nineteenth Century*, ed. Dale W. Tomich (Lanham, MD: Lexington Books, 2017). For an analysis of some of these works, see Peter Kolchin, "Slavery, Commodification, and Capitalism," *Reviews in American History*, 44 (June 2016), 217–26. For a rejection of the idea that slavery was compatible with modernity, and for the argument that in Brazil and the United States "modern capitalism emerged not from the remaking of slavery in the nineteenth century but from its unmaking," see Roberto Saba, *American Mirror: The United States and Brazil in the Age of Emancipation* (Princeton: Princeton University Press, 2021), 2. For the recent historiography of American slavery, see works discussed in *Reinterpreting Southern Histories: Essays in Historiography*, ed. Craig Thompson Friend and Lorri Glover (Baton Rouge: Louisiana State University Press, 2020), 99–196. See, also, the treatment of slavery and capitalism in chapter 7, and sources listed in that chapter's notes 12–22.

For two very different transnational overviews, see Matthew Pratt Guterl, *American Mediterranean: Southern Slaveholders in the Age of Emancipation* (Cambridge, MA: Harvard University Press, 2008); and Sven Beckert, *Empire of Cotton: A Global History* (New York: Alfred A. Knopf, 2014). On the Caribbean, see, inter alia, Trevor G. Burnard, *Planters, Merchants, and Slaves: Plantation Societies in British America, 1650–1820* (Chicago: University of Chicago Press, 2015); and Trevor Burnard and John D. Garrigue, *The Plantation Machine: Atlantic Capitalism in French Saint-Domingue and British Jamaica* (Philadelphia: University of Pennsylvania Press, 2016).

19. Alfred A. Skerpan, "The Russian National Economy and Emancipation," in *Essays in Russian History: A Collection Dedicated to George Vernadsky*, ed. Alan D. Ferguson and Alfred Levin (Hamden, CT: Archon Books, 1964), 163–229; Richard L. Rudolph, "Agricultural Structure and Proto-Industrialization in Russia: Economic Development with Unfree Labor," *Journal of Economic History*, 45 (March 1985), 47–69; Evsey D. Domar and Mark J. Machina, "On the Profitability of Russian Serfdom," *Journal of Economic History*, 44 (December 1984), 919–56; Boris N. Mironov, "When and Why Was

the Russian Peasant Emancipated?" in *Serfdom and Slavery*, ed. Bush, esp. 325–35; Moon, *The Abolition of Serfdom in Russia*, 19–22; and Stanziani, *Bondage*, esp. 127–44. Although Zaionchkovskii contended that serf labor was less productive than free, he rejected the assertion that serf-based agricultural productivity was declining in the middle of the nineteenth century; see Zaionchkovskii, *Otmena krepostnogo prava*, 15. On repudiation of the "dying out" thesis, see Kolchin, *Unfree Labor*, 365–68.

20. The quotation is from Blum, *The End of the Old Order in Rural Europe*, 372. On hostility between New England's textile manufacturers and abolitionists, see Thomas H. O'Connor, *Lords of the Loom: The Cotton Whigs and the Coming of the Civil War* (New York: Charles Scribner's Sons, 1968). For four informative—and very different—accounts of American abolitionism, all of which repudiate the notion that its dominant motivation was economic, see Aileen S. Kraditor, *Means and Ends in American Abolitionism: Garrison and His Critics on Strategy and Tactics, 1834–1850* (New York: Pantheon, 1969); James Brewer Stewart, *Holy Warriors: The Abolitionists and American Slavery*, rev. ed. (New York: Hill and Wang, 1997); Richard S. Newman, *The Transformation of American Abolitionism: Fighting Slavery in the Early Republic* (Chapel Hill: University of North Carolina Press, 2002); and Manisha Sinha, *The Slave's Cause: A History of Abolitionism* (New Haven: Yale University Press, 2016). On British abolitionism, see, inter alia, Seymour Drescher, *Capitalism and Antislavery: British Mobilization in Comparative Perspective* (New York: Oxford University Press, 1987), and *The Mighty Experiment: Free Labor Versus Slavery in British Emancipation* (New York: Oxford University Press, 2002); David Eltis, *Economic Growth and the Ending of the Transatlantic Slave Trade* (New York: Oxford University Press, 1987); and Christopher Leslie Brown, *Moral Capital: Foundations of British Abolitionism* (Chapel Hill: University of North Carolina Press, 2006). See, also, Seymour Drescher, "The Long Goodbye: Dutch Capitalism and Antislavery in Comparative Perspective," *American Historical Review*, 99 (February 1994), 44–69.

21. Russia's per capita income at the time of emancipation was less than half that of France, Italy, and Germany and less than one-quarter that of Great Britain; see Peter Gatrell, *The Tsarist Economy, 1850–1917* (London: B. T. Batsford, 1986), 32. On Southern economic development, see especially Gavin Wright, *The Political Economy of the Cotton South: Households, Markets, and Wealth in the Nineteenth Century* (New York: Norton, 1978); Gavin Wright, *Slavery and American Economic Development* (Baton Rouge: Louisiana State University Press, 2006); and—more recently—Harry L. Watson and John D. Majewski, "On the Banks of the James or the Congaree: Antebellum Political Economy," in Friend and Glover, *Reinterpreting Southern Histories*, 166–96. "Something about the slave South held it back," observed Watson and Majewski (195–96), "and scholars who insist that the South was fully modern long before the Civil War . . . are surely exaggerating or seeing a partial picture." For a brief overview of slavery and the antebellum Southern economy, see Kolchin, *American Slavery*,

170–79. For examples of travel reports on Southern and Russian backwardness, see notes 27, 31, and 39 in this chapter.

22. James Oakes, *Slavery and Freedom: An Interpretation of the Old South* (New York: Alfred A. Knopf, 1990), 40–79 (quotation: 54). For clarification of this issue, see Elizabeth Fox-Genovese and Eugene D. Genovese, *Fruits of Merchant Capital: Slavery and Bourgeois Property in the Rise and Expansion of Capitalism* (Oxford: Oxford University Press, 1983), esp. 3–60; and Douglas R. Egerton, "Markets Without a Market Revolution: Southern Planters and Capitalism," *Journal of the Early Republic*, 16 (Summer 1996), 207–21. For more on capitalism's relationship with bondage and "free labor," see my chapter 7 (and references in that chapter's notes 12–22).

23. David Brion Davis, "Reflections on Abolitionism and Ideological Hegemony," in *The Antislavery Debate: Capitalism and Abolitionism as a Problem in Historical Interpretation*, ed. Thomas Bender (Berkeley: University of California Press, 1992), 176. In a highly charged debate published in that volume, historians David Brion Davis, John Ashworth, and Thomas L. Haskell agreed (albeit from diverse perspectives), that there was indeed some sort of connection between "capitalism and the origins of humanitarian sensibility," at least in Britain and the Northern United States. For a fine study emphasizing the pivotal relationship between emancipation and capitalism, see Amy Dru Stanley, *From Bondage to Contract: Wage Labor, Marriage, and the Market in the Age of Slave Emancipation* (Cambridge: Cambridge University Press, 1998). Soviet historians, following Marx and Lenin, typically described emancipation as an essential part of the transition to a capitalist order.

24. See the next section of this chapter.

25. This section and the one that follows build in part on arguments put forth in Kolchin, *Unfree Labor*, passim and esp. 359–73.

26. The quotation is from Lincoln's "Address to the Wisconsin State Agricultural Society, Milwaukee, Wisconsin" (30 September 1859), in *The Portable Abraham Lincoln*, ed. Andrew Delbanco (New York: Penguin Books, 1992), 158. For a perceptive analysis of Lincoln's opposition to slavery as rooted principally in hatred of labor exploitation rather than racial oppression, see James Oakes, *The Radical and the Republican: Frederick Douglass, Abraham Lincoln, and the Triumph of Antislavery Politics* (New York: W. W. Norton, 2007), esp. 57–61, 131–32. On the longtime assumption of the compatibility of slavery and human progress, followed by an unprecedented challenge to this assumption beginning in the last third of the eighteenth century, see Davis, *Slavery and Human Progress*. The best work on free-labor ideology in the United States is Eric Foner, *Free Soil, Free Labor, Free Men: The Ideology of the Republican Party before the Civil War* (New York: Oxford University Press, 1970). See, also, Eric Foner, *The Fiery Trial: Abraham Lincoln and American Slavery* (New York: W. W. Norton, 2010); and Howard Temperley, "Capitalism, Slavery and Ideology," *Past and Present*, 75 (May 1977), 94–118. On Russian versions of free-labor thought, see V. I. Semevskii, *Krest'ianskii vopros v Rossii v XVIII i pervoi polovine XIX veka*, 2 vols.

(St. Petersburg, 1888), I, 382–92; and Skerpan, "The Russian National Economy and Emancipation," 169–77.

27. Frederick Law Olmsted, *The Cotton Kingdom: A Traveller's Observations on Cotton and Slavery in the American Slave States*, 2 vols. (New York, 1861), I, 21 (quotation) and passim; A. P. Zablotskii-Desiatovskii, "O krepostnom sostoianii v Rossii. Zapiska A. Z-go D-go 1841 goda," in *Graf P. D. Kiselev i ego vremia. Materialy dlia istorii Imperatorov Aleksandra I, Nikolaia II i Aleksandra II*, 4 vols., ed. A. P. Zablotskii-Desiatovskii (St. Petersburg, 1882), IV, 271–344 (quotations: 327). On Zablotskii-Desiatovskii, see W. Bruce Lincoln, *In the Vanguard of Reform: Russia's Enlightened Bureaucrats, 1825–1861* (DeKalb: Northern Illinois University Press, 1982), 44–51.

28. C. Vann Woodward, "The Price of Freedom," in *What Was Freedom's Price?* ed. David G. Sansing (Jackson: University Press of Mississippi, 1978), 97; Daniel Field, *The End of Serfdom: Nobility and Bureaucracy in Russia, 1855–1861* (Cambridge, MA: Harvard University Press, 1976), 134. For elaboration of this contrast, see Kolchin, *Unfree Labor*, esp. 178–84, 360–63. For a different view of Russian serfholders, as true paternalists with a "loyalty to rural life" and a strong "commitment to family, estate, and locality," see Mary W. Cavender, *Nests of Gentry: Family, Estate, and Local Loyalties in Provincial Russia* (Newark: University of Delaware Press, 2007), 107, 191, 194–201 (quotation: 201).

29. On the intensifying debate over serfdom, see Semevskii, *Krest'ianskii vopros v Rossii*, II. On "enlightened" bureaucrats, see Lincoln, *In the Vanguard of Reform;* but for a caution on the limited nature of this enlightenment, see Daniel T. Orlovsky, *The Limits of Reform: The Ministry of Internal Affairs in Imperial Russia, 1812–1881* (Cambridge, MA: Harvard University Press, 1981), esp. 104–22. On lack of free speech hindering the development of pro-serfdom arguments, see Field, *The End of Serfdom*, 35–41. On the growth of a Russian public, see Abbott Gleason, *Young Russia: The Genesis of Russian Radicalism in the 1860s* (New York: Viking Press, 1980), 77–79; Gleason estimated that by 1855 there were some four thousand university students and perhaps twenty-five thousand to thirty thousand members of the "periodical-reading public" (78).

30. Quotations are from Field, *The End of Serfdom*, 98; Nicholas A. Riasanovsky, *A Parting of Ways: Government and the Educated Public in Russia, 1801–1855* (Oxford: Oxford University Press, 1976), 262; and Aleksandr Nikolaevich Radishchev, *A Journey from St. Petersburg to Moscow*, trans. Leo Wiener (1790; Cambridge, MA: Harvard University Press, 1958), 239 (quotation).

31. N. Tourgueneff, *La Russie et les russes*, 3 vols. (Brussels, 1847), II, 117, 111 (quotations). For examples of many travel accounts critical of serfdom, see Laurence Oliphant, *The Russian Shores of the Black Sea* (1852; New York: Arno Press, 1970), 63; and A. D. White, "The Development and Overthrow of the Russian Serf-System," *Atlantic Monthly*, 10 (November 1862), 549. For an early free-labor volley by a Frenchman who spent his youth in Russia, see M. P. D. de Passenans, *La Russie et l'esclavage, dans leurs*

rapports avec la civilisation européenne (Paris: Pierre Blanchard, 1822). On Alexander Herzen and other radicals in exile during the years preceding emancipation, see Edward Hallett Carr, *The Romantic Exiles: A Nineteenth Century Portrait Gallery* (1933; Boston: Beacon Press, 1956). From 1857 to 1867 Herzen edited a dissident journal, *Kolokol* [*The Bell*], 11 vols. (Moscow: Izdatel'stvo Akademii nauk SSSR, 1962–64); see Walter S. Hanchett Jr., "A Study of Hertsen's *Kolokol* Writings on the Peasant Problem, July 1, 1857–July 1, 1861" (M.A. thesis, University of Chicago, 1951). The novelist who best skewered serfholder pretensions was Ivan Turgenev; see especially *A Sportsman's Notebook*, trans. Charles and Natasha Hepburn (1852; London: Cresset Press, 1950). See Hannah Stern Goldman, "American Slavery and Russian Serfdom; A Study in Fictional Parallels" (Ph.D. diss., Columbia University, 1955).

32. *Trudy Volnago ekonomicheskago obshchestva k pooshchreniiu v Rossii zemledeliia i domostroitel'stva*, LXVI (1814), 109 (quotation). For the first-prize essay of Liudvig Iakob, a professor at the University of Kharkov and formerly at the University of Halle, see ibid., 1–105. On the Free Economic Society and the peasant question during the reign of Alexander I, see Semevskii, *Krest'ianskii vopros v Rossii*, I, 309–39. For the earlier activities of the Free Economic Society, under Catherine II, see M. T. Beliavskii, *Krest'ianskii vopros v Rossii nakanune vosstaniia E. I. Pugacheva (Formirovanie antikrepostnicheskoi mysli)* (Moscow: Izdatel'stvo Moskovskogo universiteta, 1965), 281–310.

33. Quotations are from Prince I. M. Dolgoruki, "Zhurnal puteshestviia iz Moskvy v Nizhnii" (1813), in *Chteniia v Imperatorskom obshchestve istorii i drevnostei Rossiiskikh pri Moskovskom universitete*, 72, no. 1, pt. 2 (1870), 17–18; Vorontsov to Kiselev, 17 February 1837, *Arkhiv kniazia Vorontsova*, 40 vols. (Moscow, 1870–97), XXXVIII, 15–17; Vorontsov to Kiselev, 20 October 1847, ibid., 149–50; and Zablotskii-Desiatovskii, *Graf P. D. Kiselev i ego vremia*, IV, 197. On Koshelev and Chicherin, see R. M. Davison, "Koshelyov and the Emancipation of the Serfs," *European Studies Review*, 33 (January 1973), 13–37; and Gary M. Hamburg, "Peasant Emancipation and Russian Social Thought: The Case of Boris N. Chicherin," *Slavic Review*, 50 (Winter 1991), 890–914. On free-labor arguments during the first quarter of the nineteenth century, see Semevskii, *Krest'ianskii vopros v Rossii*, I, 382–89; on free-labor arguments on the eve of emancipation, see Terence Emmons, *The Russian Landed Gentry and the Peasant Emancipation of 1861* (Cambridge: Cambridge University Press, 1968), 35, 41.

34. Quotations are from Catherine II, "The Instructions to the Commissioners for Composing a New Code of Laws," in *Documents of Catherine the Great: The Correspondence with Voltaire and the "Instruction" of 1767 in the English Text of 1768*, ed. W. F. Reddaway (Cambridge: Cambridge University Press, 1931), 262; *Krest'ianskoe dvizhenie v Rossii v 1826–1849 gg.: Sbornik dokumentov*, ed. A. V. Predtechenskii (Moscow: Izdatel'stvo sotsial'no-ekonomicheskoi literatury, 1961), 344–45; Semevskii, *Krest'ianskii vopros v Rossii*, II, 60–61.

35. See Kolchin, *Unfree Labor*, 369. Statistics are drawn from A. Troinitskii, *Krepostnoe naselenie v Rossii, po 10-i narodnoi perepisi* (St. Petersburg, 1861), 57–61. For the

suggestion that most provincial nobles remained quietly content with serfdom, see M. V. Dovnar-Zapol'skii, "Krepostniki v pervoi chetverti XIX v.," in *Velikaia reforma: Russkoe obshchestvo i krest'ianskii vopros v proshlom i nastoiashchem. Iubileinoe izdanie*, 6 vols. (Moscow, 1911), II, 128. See, also, Cavender, *Nests of Gentry*, for the argument that "the gentry [in Tver Province] saw the peasantry as in need of direction and control and saw the maintenance of order in the countryside as an important contribution by serfowners" (107). But for a contrasting view, emphasizing growing "abolitionist sentiment" among nobles, see Emmons, *The Russian Landed Gentry and the Peasant Emancipation of 1861*, 29–39 (quotation: 29).

36. William W. Freehling, *The Road to Disunion, Volume I: Secessionists at Bay, 1776–1854* (New York: Oxford University Press, 1990), esp. 121–210; Alison Goodyear Freehling, *Drift Toward Dissolution: The Virginia Slavery Debate of 1831–1832* (Baton Rouge: Louisiana State University Press, 1982); Hinton Rowan Helper, *The Impending Crisis of the South: How to Meet It* (1857), in *Ante-Bellum: Writings of George Fitzhugh and Hinton Rowan Helper on Slavery*, ed. Harvey Wish (New York: G. P. Putnam's Sons, 1960), 157–256 (quotations: 171, 195); J. D. B. De Bow, *The Interest in Slavery of the Southern Non-Slaveholder* (Charleston, 1860). On non-slaveholder resentments of "haughty" planters, see Olmsted, *The Cotton Kingdom*, passim.

37. There is an extensive historical literature on—and debate over—the growing sectional distinctiveness of the antebellum South; for a historiographical survey, see Peter Kolchin, *A Sphinx on the American Land: The Nineteenth-Century South in Comparative Perspective* (Baton Rouge: Louisiana State University Press, 2003), 15–29. On the centrality of the defense of slavery to antebellum Southern politics, see William J. Cooper Jr., *The South and the Politics of Slavery, 1828–1856* (Baton Rouge: Louisiana State University Press, 1978). For the increasing prevalence of racial defenses of slavery in the 1820s and 1830s, see Lacy K. Ford, *Deliver Us from Evil: The Slavery Question in the Old South* (New York: Oxford University Press, 2006). On the closing of Southern intellectual ranks, see Clement Eaton, *The Freedom-of-Thought Struggle in the Old South*, rev. and enlarged ed. (New York: Harper and Row, 1964); and John McCardell, *The Idea of a Southern Nation: Southern Nationalists and Southern Nationalism, 1830–1860* (New York: W. W. Norton, 1979).

38. For one of the most sensible of many recent efforts to come to grips with Southern economic growth in comparative perspective, see Wright, *Slavery and American Economic Development*. Anguished arguments over why the South lagged behind the North, and how it could (or whether it should) catch up, can be followed in the pages of *De Bow's Review*, beginning in 1846. For a probing examination of white Southern intellectuals' ambivalence toward material "progress," see Eugene D. Genovese, *The Slaveholder's Dilemma: Freedom and Progress in Southern Conservative Thought, 1820–1860* (Columbia: University of South Carolina Press, 1992). See, also, Peter Kolchin, *American Slavery, 1619–1877*, rev. ed. (New York: Hill and Wang, 2003), 169–189 (statistics: 175–77).

39. Quotations are from Harriet Martineau, *Society in America* (1837), ed. and abridged by Seymour Martin Lipset (Garden City, NY: Doubleday, 1962), 172; James Henry Hammond, "Letter to an English Abolitionist" (1845), in *The Ideology of Slavery: Proslavery Thought in the Antebellum South, 1830–1860*, ed. Drew Gilpin Faust (Baton Rouge: Louisiana State University Press, 1981), 193; Drew Gilpin Faust, *James Henry Hammond and the Old South: A Design for Mastery* (Baton Rouge: Louisiana State University Press, 1982), 190; ibid., 199. For emphasis on and analysis of "slavery in the abstract" as the dominant intellectual defense of Southern slavery, see Elizabeth Fox-Genovese and Eugene D. Genovese, *Slavery in White and Black: Class and Race in the Southern Slaveholders' New World Order* (New York: Cambridge University Press, 2008).

40. "To the Public," *Liberator* (1 January 1831), in *William Lloyd Garrison and the Fight against Slavery: Selections from The Liberator*, ed. William E. Cain (Boston: Bedford Books, 1995), 71, 72. For the suggestion that many Southern whites saw the abolitionist assault on slavery as the equivalent of "a terrorist attack . . . that justified almost any countermeasure, including summary justice and restrictions on civil liberties," see Ford, *Deliver Us from Evil*, esp. 481–504 (quotation: 482). There is an extensive historical literature on American abolitionism. For a good short survey, see Stewart, *Holy Warriors*; for a more thorough treatment, see Sinha, *The Slave's Cause*. For the shift from gradualist to immediatist abolitionism, and the role of Black agitators in propelling this shift, see Newman, *The Transformation of American Abolitionism*. For an insightful if at times quirky analysis of Garrisonian abolitionism, see Kraditor, *Means and Ends in American Abolitionism*. On American (and Russian) defenses of bondage, see Kolchin, *Unfree Labor*, esp. 170–77.

41. The Seward quotation is from Foner, *Free Soil, Free Labor, Free Men*, 41; Lincoln's is from *This Fiery Trial: The Speeches and Writings of Abraham Lincoln*, ed. William E. Gienapp (New York: Oxford University Press, 2002), 43–44, 51. For a survey of political antislavery, see Richard H. Sewell, *Ballots for Freedom: Antislavery Politics in the United States, 1837–1860* (New York: W. W. Norton, 1976). For a new study of "America's first civil rights movement," see Kate Masur, *Until Justice Be Done: America's First Civil Rights Movement, from the Revolution to Reconstruction* (New York: W. W. Norton, 2021). There is an enormous historical literature on Lincoln; for two recent biographies—one long and the other short—see David Herbert Donald, *Lincoln* (New York: Simon and Schuster, 1995); and Richard J. Carwardine, *Lincoln* (Harlow, England: Longman, 2003); on Lincoln and slavery, see Foner, *The Fiery Trial*. On violence against abolitionists, see Leonard L. Richards, *"Gentlemen of Property and Standing": Anti-Abolition Mobs in Jacksonian America* (Oxford: Oxford University Press, 1970); and David Grimsted, *American Mobbing: 1828–1861* (New York: Oxford University Press, 1998), esp. 3–82.

42. For brief surveys, see Kolchin, *Unfree Labor*, 140–46; and David Moon, *The Abolition of Serfdom in Russia* (Harlow, England: Longman, 2001), 37–48. For more detailed treatment, see Semevskii, *Krest'ianskii vopros v Rossii*, I and II, passim.

43. Vorontsov to Kiselev, 17 February 1837, *Arkhiv kniazia Vorontsova*, XXXVIII, 17; Zablotskii-Desiatovskii, *Graf P. D. Kiselev i ego vremia*, IV, 148–49; Semevskii, *Krest'ianskii vopros v Rossii*, II, 135–42 (quotation: 136).

44. S. V. Volkonskii, "Nekotoryia zamechaniia otnositel'no ulushcheniia byta pomeshchich'ikh krest'ian," *Trudy vysochaishe uchrezhdennoi Riazanskoi Uchenoi Arkhivnoi Komissii*, 6 (1891), 34. On emancipation in the Baltic provinces, see Blum, *Lord and Peasant in Russia*, 542–44; Edward C. Thaden with Marianna Foster Thaden, *Russia's Western Borderlands, 1710–1870* (Princeton: Princeton University Press, 1984); David Kirby, *The Baltic World, 1772–1993: Europe's Northern Periphery in an Age of Change* (London: Longman, 1995), 62–65; Iu. Iu. Kakhk, *"Ostzeiskii put' " perekhoda ot feodalizma k kapitalizmu: Krest'iane i pomeshchiki Estliandii i Lifliandii v XVIII-pervoi polovine XIX veka* (Tallinn: Eesti raamat, 1998); and Susan P. McCaffray, "Confronting Serfdom in the Age of Revolution: Projects for Serf Reform in the Time of Alexander I," *Russian Review*, 64 (January 2005), 1–21. On Prussia and Austria, as well as Prussian- and Austrian-controlled Poland, see Blum, *The End of the Old Order in Rural Europe*, passim; Robert M. Berdahl, "Paternalism, Serfdom, and Emancipation in Prussia," in *Oceans Apart? Comparing Germany and the United States*, ed. Erich Angermann and Marie-Luise Frings (Stuttgart: Klett-Cotta, 1981), esp. 40–44; Shearer Davis Bowman, *Masters and Lords: Mid-19th Century U.S. Planters and Prussian Junkers* (New York: Oxford University Press, 1993); Jerome Blum, *Noble Landowners and Agriculture in Austria, 1815–1848: A Study in the Origins of the Peasant Emancipation of 1848* (Baltimore: Johns Hopkins University Press, 1948); and Stefan Kieniewicz, *The Emancipation of the Polish Peasantry* (Chicago: University of Chicago Press, 1969).

45. Quotations are from Larissa Zakharova, "Autocracy and the Reforms of 1861–1874 in Russia: Choosing Paths of Development," in *Russia's Great Reforms, 1855–1881*, ed. Ben Eklof, John Bushnell, and Larissa Zakharova (Bloomington: Indiana University Press, 1994), 10; and Penza Province nobleman Nikolai Charykov, "Ob ulushchenii byta pomeshchich'ikh krest'ian v Penzenskoi gubernii," in *Zhurnal zemlevladel'tsev*, no. 7 (July 1858), 123. See, also, W. Bruce Lincoln, *Nicholas I: Emperor and Autocrat of All the Russias* (Bloomington: Indiana University Press, 1978), 187–95; and Moon, *Abolition of Serfdom in Russia*, 47.

46. Historian M. A. Rakhmatullin identified thirty-six volneniia in thirteen provinces between 1847 and 1850 that were specifically related to the ukaz of 1847; see his article "Zakonodatel'naia praktika tsarskogo samoderzhaviia: Ukaz ot noiabria 1847 goda i popytki ego primeneniia," *Istoriia SSSR*, 1982, no. 2, 35–52. On serf unrest, see Kolchin, *Unfree Labor*, 241–357 passim (on disorders in general), 321–26 (on rumors and outside events), and 284–85 (on rumors and migration during the Crimean War).

47. Nikitenko, *The Diary of a Russian Censor*, 15 (5 April 1827). For emphasis on the fear of violence from below as a major consideration in persuading Russian policy makers to undertake emancipation, see, inter alia, N. M. Druzhinin and V. A. Fedorov, "Krest'ianskoe dvizhenie v Rossii v XIX veke," *Istoriia SSSR*, 1977, no. 4, 107; and

Terence Emmons, "The Peasant and Emancipation," in *The Peasant in Nineteenth-Century Russia*, ed. Wayne S. Vucinich (Stanford: Stanford University Press, 1968), 44–45.

48. Semevskii, *Krest'ianskii vopros v Rossii*, II, 60–61 (quotation).

49. The quotation is from Faust, *James Henry Hammond and the Old South*, 346. On the politics of slavery and growing sectional consciousness in the South, see, inter alia, Cooper, *The South and the Politics of Slavery*; McCardell, *The Idea of a Southern Nation*; and William W. Freehling, *The Road to Disunion, Volume II: Sectionalists Triumphant, 1854–1861* (New York: Oxford University Press, 2007). On the movement to legalize the importation of slaves, see Ronald T. Takaki, *A Proslavery Crusade: The Agitation to Re-Open the African Slave Trade* (New York: Free Press, 1971). On the growing enforcement of conformity on slavery and sectional issues, see Eaton, *The Freedom-of-Thought Struggle in the Old South*.

50. For two very different perspectives on the flourishing economy of the late antebellum South, see Fogel, *Without Consent or Contract*, pt. I; and Wright, *Slavery and American Economic Development*.

51. Delbanco, *The Portable Abraham Lincoln*, 115, 195. The problem was one of means. For a recent emphasis on the Republicans' *desire* to abolish slavery, see James Oakes, *Freedom National: The Destruction of Slavery in the United States, 1861–1865* (New York: W. W. Norton, 2013), Oakes, "When Everybody Knew," in *Beyond Freedom: Disrupting the History of Emancipation*, ed. David W. Blight and Jim Downs (Athens: University of Georgia Press, 2017), 104–17, and Oakes, *The Crooked Path to Abolition: Abraham Lincoln, and the Antislavery Constitution* (New York: W. W. Norton, 2021). "Opposition to slavery was the Republican Party's sole *raison d'être*," Oakes noted ("When Everybody Knew," 105), "and it was widely assumed that Republicans fully intended to use all the power available to them under the Constitution to undermine slavery in the states, even without a civil war." Some Northerners went substantially further, favoring a variety of rights for free African Americans; see Masur, *Until Justice Be Done*.

Chapter 1. Emancipation Launched

1. See, inter alia, Philip D. Morgan, "Black Society in the Lowcountry, 1760–1810," in *Slavery and Freedom in the Age of the American Revolution*, ed. Ira Berlin and Ronald Hoffman (Charlottesville: University Press of Virginia, 1983), 83–141; Allan Kulikoff, "Uprooted Peoples: Black Migrants in the Age of the American Revolution," ibid., 143–71; Sylvia R. Frey, *Water from the Rock: Black Resistance in a Revolutionary Age* (Princeton: Princeton University Press, 1991); Cassandra Pybus, *Epic Journey of Freedom: Runaway Slaves of the American Revolution and Their Global Quest for Liberty* (Boston: Beacon Press, 2006); Simon Schama, *Rough Crossings: Britain, the Slaves and the American Revolution* (London: BBC, 2005); Alan Taylor, *The*

Internal Enemy: Slavery and War in Virginia, 1772–1832 (New York: W. W. Norton, 2013); Rebecca J. Scott, *Slave Emancipation in Cuba: The Transition to Free Labor, 1860–1899* (Princeton: Princeton University Press, 1985), 45–62, 111–23; Robin Blackburn, *The Overthrow of Colonial Slavery, 1776–1848* (London: Verso, 1988); David Baronov, *The Abolition of Slavery in Brazil: The "Liberation" of Africans through the Emancipation of Capital* (Westport, CT: Greenwood Press, 2000); Alejandro de la Fuente and Ariela Gross, *Becoming Free, Becoming Black: Race, Freedom, and Law in Cuba, Virginia, and Louisiana* (Cambridge: Cambridge University Press, 2020), esp. 79–131; Jerome Blum, *The End of the Old Order in Rural Europe* (Princeton: Princeton University Press, 1978); Jerome Blum, *Noble Landowners and Agriculture in Austria, 1815–1848: A Study in the Origins of the Peasant Emancipation of 1848* (Baltimore: Johns Hopkins University Press, 1948); Laurent Dubois, *Avengers of the New World: The Story of the Haitian Revolution* (Cambridge, MA: Harvard University Press, 2005); Laurent Dubois, *A Colony of Citizens: Revolution and Slave Emancipation in the French Caribbean, 1787–1804* (Chapel Hill: University of North Carolina Press, 2004); Laurent Dubois, *Haiti: The Aftershock of History* (New York: Picador, 2012); and David P. Geggus, *Slavery, War, and Revolution: The British Occupation of Saint Domingue, 1793–1798* (London: Oxford University Press, 1982). In 1770, there were an estimated 459,822 African Americans (the vast majority of whom were enslaved) in the future United States; the census of 1800 counted 893,602 slaves. *The Historical Statistics of the United States from Colonial Times to the Present* (New York: Basic Books, 1976), 1168, 14.

2. Andrew Johnson speech, 9 June 1864, in *Documentary History of Reconstruction: Political, Military, Social, Religious, Educational and Industrial, 1865 to 1906*, 2 vols., ed. Walter L. Fleming (1906; New York: McGraw Hill, 1966), I, 116. As early as the mid-1850s, leading Republicans had warned of a "slave power conspiracy" that, in direct opposition to the will of the founders, aimed to spread slavery throughout the United States; during the war it became a common argument that a minority of wealthy planters had tricked the majority of virtuous Southern whites into rebellion. For one of Lincoln's many prewar denunciations of the conspiracy to extend slavery (abetted, he believed, by unprincipled Northern Democrats), see his 1854 speech at Peoria, Illinois, on the Kansas-Nebraska Act, in *The Portable Abraham Lincoln*, ed. Andrew Delbanco (New York: Penguin Books, 1992), 41–83. On the prewar Republican belief in both a "slave power conspiracy" and the latent loyalty of non-slaveholding whites, see Eric Foner, *Free Soil, Free Labor, Free Men: The Ideology of the Republican Party before the Civil War* (New York: Oxford University Press, 1970), esp. 97–102, 119–23. On exaggerated Republican belief in Southern Unionism during the secession crisis, see David M. Potter, *Lincoln and His Party during the Secession Crisis* (New Haven: Yale University Press, 1942). For two different interpretations, see David Brion Davis, *The Slave Power Conspiracy and the Paranoid Style* (Baton Rouge: Louisiana State University Press, 1969); and Leonard L. Richards, *The Slave Power: The Free North and Southern Dominion, 1780–1860* (Baton Rouge: Louisiana State University Press, 2000).

For Northern war aims as rooted in "deliverance"—the desire to "deliver the South from the clutches of a conspiracy and to deliver to it the blessings of free society and of modern civilization"—see Elizabeth R. Varon, *Armies of Deliverance: A New History of the Civil War* (New York: Oxford University Press, 2019), 4 (quotation). On the Republicans' consensus that war would provide the opportunity to bring about what they all favored—the abolition of slavery—see James Oakes, *Freedom National: The Destruction of Slavery in the United States, 1861–1865* (New York: W. W. Norton, 2013), Oakes, "When Everybody Knew," in *Beyond Freedom: Disrupting the History of Emancipation,* ed. David W. Blight and Jim Downs (Athens: Georgia University Press, 2017), 104–17, and Oakes, *The Crooked Path to Abolition: Abraham Lincoln and the Antislavery Constitution* (New York: W. W. Norton, 2021). On Andrew Johnson's class-based view of Southern loyalty and treason, see W. E. B. Du Bois, *Black Reconstruction in America, 1860–1880* (New York: Harcourt, Brace, 1935), esp. 241–54; and Eric L. McKitrick, *Andrew Johnson and Reconstruction* (Chicago: University of Chicago Press, 1959), 85–92, 139–40. As president, Johnson quickly abandoned his support for land confiscation, but in offering amnesty to all Rebels except those worth $20,000 or more, his plan to "restore" (as opposed to reconstruct) the ex-Confederate states continued to rely on the assumption that rich planters were to blame for the Rebellion.

3. For detailed accounts of the deliberations that led to emancipation, see Daniel Field, *The End of Serfdom: Nobility and Bureaucracy in Russia, 1855–1861* (Cambridge, MA: Harvard University Press, 1976); P. A. Zaionchkovskii, *Otmena krepostnogo prava v Rossii,* 3rd ed. (1954, Moscow: Prosveshchenie, 1968), esp. 66–123, available in an English-language translation as *The Abolition of Serfdom in Russia,* ed. and trans. Susan Wobst (Gulf Breeze, FL: Academic International Press, 1978); and L. G. Zahkarova, *Samoderzhavie i otmena krepostnogo prava v Rossii, 1856–1861* (Moscow: Izdatel'stvo Moskovskogo universiteta, 1984), available in English in a condensed version as "Autocracy and the Abolition of Serfdom in Russia, 1856–1861," trans. Gary M. Hamburg, *Soviet Studies in History,* 26, no. 2 (Fall 1987), entire issue. For shorter surveys, see Jerome Blum, *Lord and Peasant in Russia from the Ninth to the Nineteenth Century* (New York: Princeton University Press, 1961), 575–92; Larissa Zakharova, "Autocracy and the Reforms of 1861–1874 in Russia: Choosing Paths of Development," trans. Daniel Field, in *Russia's Great Reforms, 1855–1881,* ed. Ben Eklof, John Bushnell, and Larissa Zakharova (Bloomington: Indiana University Press, 1994), 19–39; and David Moon, *The Abolition of Serfdom in Russia, 1762–1907* (Harlow, England: Longman, 2001), 56–69, which also contains (147–60) a useful collection of documents. For a short (forty-page) pamphlet surveying the English-language historical literature on Russian emancipation, see Maureen Perrie, *Alexander II: Emancipation and Reform in Russia, 1855–1881* (London: Historical Association, 1989). See, also, primary documents in *Padenie krepostnogo prava v Rossii: Dokumenty i materialy,* ed. V. A. Fedorov, 2 vols. (Moscow: Izdatel'stvo Moskovskogo universiteta, 1966–67), I, 59–92.

For a thoughtful essay on what Soviet historians termed the peasants' "naïve monarchism," see Daniel Field, "The Myth of the Tsar," in *Rebels in the Name of the Tsar*, ed. Daniel Field (Boston: Houghton Mifflin, 1976), 1–29. For the argument that by taking a circuitous path to emancipation Alexander II skillfully managed to disarm opponents of reform, see N. G. O. Pereira, "Alexander II and the Decision to Emancipate the Russian Serfs, 1855–1861," *Canadian Slavonic Papers*, 22 (March 1980), 99–115 (esp. 113–15), and Pereira, *Tsar Liberator: Alexander II of Russia, 1818–1881* (Newtonville, MA: Oriental Research Partners, 1983), 66. For a very different portrait of Alexander, as an indecisive conservative, see David Saunders, *Russia in the Age of Reaction and Reform, 1801–1881* (London: Longman, 1992), 204–38.

4. "Alexander II's Speech to the Marshals of the Nobility of Moscow Province, 30 March 1856," in Moon, *The Abolition of Serfdom*, 147–48.

5. Field, *The End of Serfdom* (quotations: 74–75, 76).

6. Quotations are from "Rescript of Alexander II to Vilno, Grodno, and Kovno General-Governor B. I. Nazimov, 20 November 1857," in Fedorov, *Padenie krepostnogo prava v Rossii*, I, 59–61. The tsar's rescript was in response to a request by a group of Lithuanian nobles who hoped to forestall a planned introduction of "inventories" regulating relations between noble landowners and their serfs by instituting a landless emancipation similar to one that had occurred in the three Baltic provinces in the early nineteenth century. Given the widespread perception that this emancipation had been problematical, the request was a tactical mistake. For an essay insisting that the tsar had said nothing of "freeing [the seigneurial peasants] or abolishing the serf condition" and intended only to promote the "gradual improvement of their way of life," see the editor's introduction to the first issue of the *Zhurnal zemlevladel'tsev* (*Landowners' Journal*), no. 1 (April 1858), 2.

7. "Petition from the First Group of Deputies of the Nobles' Provincial Committees to the Tsar, 26 August 1859," in Moon, *The Abolition of Serfdom in Russia*, 151–52.

8. "Rostovstev's Proposed Programme for Reform, 5 March 1859," in Moon, *The Abolition of Serfdom in Russia*, 150. On the "enlightened bureaucrats," see W. Bruce Lincoln, *In the Vanguard of Reform: Russia's Enlightened Bureaucrats, 1825–1861* (DeKalb: Northern Illinois University Press, 1982); on the "aristocratic opposition," see Ia. A. Khristoforov, " 'Aristokraticheskaia' oppositsiia reformam i problema organizatsii mestnogo upravleniia v Rossii v 50–70-e gody XIX veka," *Otechestvennaia istoriia*, 1 (January–February 2000), 3–18. For the suggestion that Tsar Alexander's aunt, Grand Duchess Elena Pavlovna, played an important behind-the-scenes role in lobbying on behalf of the enlightened bureaucrats and "provid[ing] the political protection necessary within the royal court for the reformers to see their work through to the end," see Shane O'Rourke, "Monarchy, Gender and Emancipation: Grand Duchess Elena Pavlovna of Russia and Princess Isabel of Brazil and the Ending of Servile Labour," *Slavery and Abolition*, 35 (March, 2014), 47–65 (quotation: 55).

9. "Speech of Alexander II to the State Council, 28 January 1861," in Fedorov, *Padenie krepostnogo prava v Rossii*, I, 66–67.

10. "Alexander II's Proclamation Announcing the Abolition of Serfdom, 19 February 1861," in Moon, *The Abolition of Serfdom in Russia*, 155–160 (quotations: 156, 159). On the provisions of the new legislation, see later in this chapter.

11. Alfred J. Rieber, "The Politics of Emancipation," in *The Politics of Autocracy: Letters of Alexander II to Prince A. I. Bariatinskii, 1857–1864*, ed. Alfred J. Rieber (Paris: Mouton, 1966), 15–58 (quotation 22); and Zakharova, "Autocracy and the Reforms of 1861–1874 in Russia" (quotation: 20). See, also, W. E. Mosse, *Alexander II and the Modernization of Russia* (1958; New York: Collier Books, 1962); Pereira, "Alexander II and the Decision to Emancipate the Russian Serfs"; and Saunders, *Russia in the Age of Reaction and Reform*, 204–38. On the evaporation of support for serfdom, see my Introduction above. For the Crimean War and its impact, see John Shelton Curtiss, *Russia's Crimean War* (Durham, NC: Duke University Press, 1979); and Orlando Figes, *The Crimean War: The Last Crusade* (London: Allen Lane, 2011). Military reform designed to bolster the army by making military service less burdensome in fact followed emancipation as one of the Great Reforms, culminating in 1874 in reduction of the term of active military service required of recruits to six years, followed by nine more in the reserves. See John S. Curtiss, "The Peasant and the Army," in *The Peasant in Nineteenth-Century Russia*, ed. Wayne S. Vucinich (Stanford: Stanford University Press, 1968), 115–16.

12. *Kolokol* (1857–67; reprinted in 11 vols., Moscow: Izdatel'stvo Akademii nauk SSSR, 1962–64): no. 1 (1 July 1857), 3; no. 7 (1 January 1858), 51–52; no. 9 (15 February 1858), 67; no. 15 (15 May 1858), 117. See Walter S. Hanchett Jr., "A Study of Alexander Hertsen's *Kolokol* Writings on the Peasant Problem, July 1, 1857–July 1, 1861" (M.A. thesis, University of Chicago, 1951).

13. Quotations are from Charles Henry Pearson, *Russia, by a Recent Traveller: A Series of Letters* (1859; London: Frank Cass, 1970), 11; and Aleksandr Nikitenko, *The Diary of a Russian Censor,* abridged, ed., and trans. Helen Saltz Jacobson (Amherst: University of Massachusetts Press, 1975), 13 January 1858, 166. On the new spirit of openness in the late 1850s, see Abbott Gleason, *Young Russia: The Genesis of Russian Radicalism in the 1860s* (New York: Viking, 1980), 79–113; and Zakharova, "Autocracy and the Reforms of 1861–1874 in Russia," 21–23.

14. For the Third Department's report, see its "Moral Political Review of 1859," in *Krest'ianskoe dvizhenie 1827–1869 godov*, 2 vols., ed. E. A. Morokhovets (Moscow: Gosudarstvennoe sotsial'no-ekonomicheskoe izdatel'stvo, 1931), I, 134–36 (quotation: 134). See, also, Zaionchkovskii, *Otmena krepostnogo prava v Rossii*, 100–101; David Christian, "A Neglected Great Reform: The Abolition of Tax Farming in Russia," in *Russia's Great Reforms*, 102–14, and David Christian, "The Black and Gold Seals: Popular Protests against the Liquor Trade on the Eve of Emancipation," in *Peasant Economy, Culture, and Politics of European Russia, 1800–1921*, ed. Esther Kingston-Mann and Timothy Mixter (Princeton: Princeton University Press, 1991), 261–93. According to Christian ("The Black and Gold Seals," 262), "of the 938 separate reports of peasant insubordi-

nation listed" for 1859, "as many as 636 (68 percent) involved either boycotts of vodka sales or attacks on taverns." For a more general study, see David Christian, *"Living Water": Vodka in Russian Society on the Eve of Emancipation* (New York: Oxford University Press, 1990). For more on peasant volneniia, see my chapter 2 (on the responses to emancipation), and Peter Kolchin, *Unfree Labor: American Slavery and Russian Serfdom* (Cambridge, MA: Harvard University Press, 1987), 241–357, passim (on previous volneniia, under serfdom). For documents on the collective flight generated by the Crimean War, see *Krest'ianskoe dvizhenie v Rossii v 1850–1856 gg.: Sbornik dokumentov*, ed. S. B. Okun' (Moscow: Izdatel'stvo sotsial'no-ekonomicheskoi literatury, 1963), 431–516, 593–95 (hereafter cited as *KD-4*). See also Kolchin, *Unfree Labor*, 283–84; and V. A. Fedorov, *Krest'ianskoe dvizhenie v tsentral'noi Rossii 1800–1860 (Po materialam tsentral'no-promyshlennykh gubernii)* (Moscow: Izdatel'stvo Moskovskogo universiteta, 1980), 126–32.

15. S. T. Slovutinskii, *General Izmailov i ego dvornia: Otryvki iz vospominanii* (Moscow: Academia, 1937), 256, 423–24; Fedorov, *Krest'ianskoe dvizhenie v tsentral'noi Rossii*, 47; B. G. Litvak, *Russkaia derevenia v reforme 1861 goda: Chernozemnyi tsentr, 1861–1895 gg.* (Moscow: Izdatel'stvo "Nauka," 1972), 17–18; and the Third Department's report for 1857, in Morokhovets, *Krest'ianskoe dvizhenie 1827–1869 godov*, I, 112–13.

16. Report for 1858, in Morokhovets, *Krest'ianskkoe dvizhenie 1827–1869 godov*, I, 123–25 (quotation: 124); report of Col. Zagorskii, staff officer of the Corps of Gendarmes for Voronezh Province, 5 December 1860, in *Krest'ianskoe dvizhenie v Voronezhskoi gubernii (1861–1863 gg.): Dokumenty i materialy* (Voronezh: Izdatel'stvo Voronezhskogo universiteta, 1961), 27.

17. Quotations are from *Zhurnal zemlevaldel'tsev*, no. 3 (May 1858), 30–31; no. 7 (July 1858), 121, 123; and no. 7 (July 1858), 36. On the lack of political independence among the Russian nobility, see Kolchin, *Unfree Labor*, 49–191, passim; and Field, *The End of Serfdom*, 137–41.

18. Michael Confino, "Les projets de réforme de la Noblesse (1855–1858)," in *Le Statut des paysans libérés du servage, 1861–1961*, ed. R. Portal (Paris: Mouton, 1963), 64–89 (quotation: 64); Terence Emmons, *The Russian Landed Gentry and the Peasant Emancipation of 1861* (Cambridge: Cambridge University Press, 1968), passim (quotation: 150; Unkovskii's removal and exile: 269–79); "Excerpts from the Memorandum of A. M. Unkovskii and A. A. Golovachev, Presented to Alexander II in December, 1857, in Response to the Imperial Rescript," in Emmons, *The Russian Landed Gentry and the Peasant Emancipation*, appendix II, 427–43. For other noble proposals, see Fedorov, *Padenie krepostnogo prava v Rossii*, I, 75–91. See also, inter alia, Zaionchkovskii, *Otmena krepostnogo prava v Rossii*, 95–97, 112–19; Field, *The End of Serfdom*, 173–232; Tatiana Bakounine, *Les domaines des Princes Kourakine dans le gouvernement de Saratov* (Paris: Les Presses modernes, 1929), 102; Zakharova, *Samoderzhavie i otmena krepostnogo prava v Rossii*; Khristoforov, " 'Aristokraticheskaia' oppozitsiia reformam," 4–9. It should be noted that while seeing the "liberal" position primarily as a

function of education and exposure to Western ideas, Emmons also recognized (193–205) the existence of regional patterns based on material conditions.

19. "Excerpts from the Memorandum of A. M. Unkovskii and A. A. Golovachev," 436 (quotation). For the observation that "the decision to emancipate the Russian serfs, though radical in its ramifications, was as conservative as possible in content and intent," see Pereira, "Alexander II and the Decision to Emancipate the Russian Serfs," 115.

20. Field, *The End of Serfdom*, 357–58. On the lack of independence and corporate consciousness of the serf-owning nobility, see S. A. Korf, *Dvorianstvo i ego soslovnoe upravelnie za stoletie 1762–1855 godov* (St. Petersburg, 1906), passim; A. Romanovich-Slavatinskii, *Dvorianstvo v Rossii ot nachala XVIII veka do otmeny krepostnago prava* (St. Petersburg, 1870), esp. 402–10, 490–500; and Kolchin, *Unfree Labor*, 49–191 passim (esp. 169). For the argument that the deliberations over the terms of emancipation produced a "transformation of the previously lifeless formal class organization of the gentry into a vehicle for the expression of the independent interests of an important segment of Russian society," see Emmons, *The Russian Landed Gentry and the Peasant Emancipation*, 309.

21. The quotation is from Wayne K. Durrill, *War of Another Kind: A Southern Community in the Great Rebellion* (New York: Oxford University Press, 1990), 6. For two fine studies emphasizing slave rebelliousness during the Civil War—the first in the form of a "general strike" and the second of a "rebellion . . . against the authority of their masters"—see Du Bois, *Black Reconstruction in America*, 55–83 (quotation: 55), and Steven Hahn, *A Nation under Our Feet: Black Political Struggles in the Rural South from Slavery to the Great Migration* (Cambridge, MA: Harvard University Press, 2003), 62–155 (quotation: 64). See, also, Stephanie McCurry, *Confederate Reckoning: Power and Politics in the Civil War South* (Cambridge, MA: Harvard University Press, 2010), for emphasis on the increasing resistance shown by slaves (and poor white women); and David Williams, *I Freed Myself: African American Self-Emancipation in the Civil War Era* (New York: Cambridge University Press, 2014). "That the Civil War was, among other things, a massive slave rebellion," McCurry concluded (259), "seems clear in hindsight." By contrast, in *Been in the Storm So Long: The Aftermath of Slavery* (New York: Alfred A. Knopf, 1979), 3–103, Leon F. Litwack emphasized the wide diversity of slaves' wartime responses.

For a succinct summary based on analysis of the *Freedom* documentary collection, see Ira Berlin et al., *Slaves No More: Three Essays on Emancipation and the Civil War* (Cambridge: Cambridge University Press, 1992), 1–76. For a short survey, with documents, emphasizing the extent to which "African Americans took the initiative to transform America's internal conflict into a war for freedom," see Paul D. Escott, *Paying Freedom's Price: A History of African Americans in the Civil War* (Lanham, MD: Rowman and Littlefield, 2017), 2 (quotation). For a historiographical survey, see Peter Kolchin, "Slavery and Freedom in the Civil War South," in *Writing the Civil War: The*

Quest to Understand, ed. James M. McPherson and William J. Cooper Jr. (Columbia: University of South Carolina Press, 1998), 241–60, 335–47. For the "persistent myth" of Black support for the Confederate Rebellion, see Kevin M. Lewis, *Searching for Black Confederates: The Civil War's Most Persistent Myth* (Chapel Hill: University of North Carolina Press, 2019).

22. Quotations are from Commander of the Department of North Carolina to the Secretary of War, Newbern, NC, 21 March 1862, and Proclamation by the Commander at Baltimore, Baltimore, 13 November 1861, in *Freedom: A Documentary History of Emancipation, 1861–1867*, ser. I, vol. I: *The Destruction of Slavery*, ed. Ira Berlin et al. (Cambridge: Cambridge University Press, 1985), 81, 79 (hereafter cited as *Freedom*, I-I). This volume contains numerous documents illustrating wartime flight, and the evolution of federal policy toward it. See, also, inter alia, Berlin et al., *Slaves No More*, passim; and Louis S. Gerteis, *From Contraband to Freedman: Federal Policy Toward Southern Blacks, 1861–1865* (Westport, CT: Greenwood Press, 1973). On fugitive slaves, see Yael A. Sternhell, *Routes of War: The World of Movement in the Confederate South* (Cambridge, MA: Harvard University Press, 2012), esp. 95–107. On contraband camps, see Chandra Manning, *Troubled Refuge: Struggling for Freedom in the Civil War* (New York: Alfred A. Knopf, 2016), esp. pts. I and II; Amy Murrell Taylor, *Embattled Freedom: Journeys through the Civil War's Slave Refugee Camps* (Chapel Hill: University of North Carolina Press, 2018); and Thavolia Glymph, *The Women's Fight: The Civil War's Battles for Home, Freedom, and Nation* (Chapel Hill: University of North Carolina Press, 2020), esp. 221–50. On the Second Confiscation Act, which authorized the confiscation of Rebel-owned slaves, see Oakes, *Freedom National*, 224–55.

23. The quotations are from Litwack, *Been in the Storm So Long* (Manigault), 106; and Mrs. W. D. Chadick Diary, typed copy, Alabama State Department of Archives and History, 27 March 1864. For examples of collective wartime flight, see *Freedom*, I-I, passim. For three of many observations on the increasingly collective nature of this flight, see Victor B. Howard, *Black Liberation in Kentucky: Emancipation and Freedom, 1862–1864* (Lexington: University Press of Kentucky, 1983), 108–21; Clarence L. Mohr, *On the Threshold of Freedom: Masters and Slaves in Civil War Georgia* (Athens: University of Georgia Press, 1986), 72–73; and Hahn, *A Nation under Our Feet*, 72–73. On the largely individual nature of *antebellum* slave resistance, in contrast to the more collective pattern prevalent among Russian serfs, see Kolchin, *Unfree Labor*, 241–301 (288–91 on antebellum slave flight). On slave defections' puncturing planters' paternalistic pretensions, see Eugene D. Genovese, *Roll, Jordan, Roll: The World the Slaves Made* (New York: Pantheon, 1974), 98–99.

24. Quotations are from James L. Roark, *Masters without Slaves: Southern Planters in the Civil War and Reconstruction* (New York: W. W. Norton, 1978), 77; Susanna Clay to her son Clement Clayborne Clay, 5 September 1863, in *The Civil War and Reconstruction: A Documentary Collection*, ed. William E. Gienapp (New York: W. W. Norton, 2001), 224; and Drew Gilpin Faust, *Mothers of Invention: Women of the Slaveholding South in the*

American Civil War (Chapel Hill: University of North Carolina, Press, 1996), 57, 62, 65. On the general erosion of slavery behind Confederate lines, see, inter alia, Roark, *Masters without Slaves*, 35–108; Berlin et al., *Slaves No More*, 1–76; Hahn, *A Nation under Our Feet*, 62–115; McCurry, *Confederate Reckoning;* 218–357; and Bruce Levine, *The Fall of the House of Dixie: The Civil War and the Social Revolution That Transformed the South* (New York: Random House, 2014). For the partial exception of Texas, where slavery was "less disturbed . . . than in any other Confederate state," see Randolph B. Campbell, *An Empire for Slavery: The Peculiar Institution in Texas, 1821–1865* (Baton Rouge: Louisiana State University Press, 1989), 231. On slaveholding women's difficulty controlling slaves, see especially Faust, *Mothers of Invention*, 53–79. For additional sources, see Kolchin, "Slavery and Freedom in the Civil War South," 245–47, 338–41.

25. Roark, *Masters without Slaves*, 45. On Confederate proposals to reform slavery, see Drew Gilpin Faust, *The Creation of Confederate Nationalism: Ideology and Identity in the Civil War South* (Baton Rouge: Louisiana State University Press, 1988), 72–81; for the link to antebellum reform, see Genovese, *Roll, Jordan, Roll*, 69–70. The best book on the Confederate debate over using Black soldiers is Bruce Levine, *Confederate Emancipation: Southern Plans to Free and Arm Slaves During the Civil War* (New York: Oxford University Press, 2006); see, also, Levine, *The Fall of the House of Dixie*, 243–68; Robert F. Durden, *The Gray and the Black: The Confederate Debate on Emancipation* (Baton Rouge: Louisiana State University Press, 1972); and McCurry, *Confederate Reckoning*, 310–57.

26. Mohr, *On the Threshold of Freedom*, 118, 119; Durrill, *War of Another Kind*, 142–43; Mary Jones Journal, 6 January 1865, 21 January 1865, in *The Children of Pride: A True Story of Georgia and the Civil War*, ed. Robert Manson Myers (New Haven: Yale University Press, 1972), 1241, 1247. On "refugeeing"—and movement of slaves in general—in the Confederate South, see Sternhell, *Routes of War,* esp. 94–107 and 167–79; and Glymph, *The Women's Fight*, passim.

27. Berlin et al., *Slaves No More*, 5–6; Barbara J. Fields, "Who Freed the Slaves?" in *The Civil War: An Illustrated History,* ed. Geoffrey C. Ward (New York: Knopf, 1990), 181; Hahn, *A Nation under Our Feet*, 83; James M. McPherson, "Who Freed the Slaves?" (1994), reprinted in his *Drawn with the Sword: Reflections on the American Civil War* (New York: Oxford University Press, 1996), 206, 196, 207. See, also, Ira Berlin, "Emancipation and Its Meaning in American Life," *Reconstruction*, 2, no. 3 (1994), 41–44; and Laura F. Edwards, *A Legal History of the Civil War and Reconstruction: A Nation of Rights* (New York: Cambridge University Press, 2015): "Slaves were not freed," Edwards wrote; "they freed themselves" (65–66). Earlier, McPherson had pioneered in exploring Black agency during the Civil War; see his book *The Negro's Civil War: How American Negroes Felt and Acted during the War for the Union* (New York: Pantheon Books, 1965).

28. For the two quotations, see Vincent Harding, *There Is a River: The Black Struggle for Freedom in America* (New York: Harcourt Brace Jovanovich, 1981), 225; and

McCurry, *Confederate Reckoning*, 361. See, also, Litwack, *Been in the Storm So Long*, 162; and Genovese, *Roll, Jordan, Roll*, 149–58. For depictions of the wartime destruction of slavery as a consequence of the interaction of decisions taken by both slaves and federal officials, see Roark, *Masters without Slaves*, 68–120; Durrill, *War of a Different Kind*, 68–90; and Steven V. Ash, *When the Yankees Came: Conflict and Chaos in the Occupied South, 1861–1865* (Chapel Hill: University of North Carolina Press, 1995), 149–56.

29. Alexander H. Stephens, 1861, in Gienapp, *The Civil War and Reconstruction*, 71–72; Abraham Lincoln to Horace Greeley, 22 August 1862, in Delbanco, *The Portable Abraham Lincoln*, 240. For evidence that both slave owners and Confederate leaders saw the war as one for slavery, see Roark, *Masters without Slaves*, 1–32, 68–108; Faust, *The Creation of Confederate Nationalism*, esp. 59–60; and Charles R. Dew, *Apostles of Disunion: Southern Secession Commissioners and the Causes of the Civil War* (Charlottesville: University Press of Virginia, 2001). For demonstration that most Confederate soldiers—whether slaveholders or not—strongly identified with slavery, see Chandra Manning, *What This Cruel War Was Over: Soldiers, Slavery, and the Civil War* (New York: Alfred A. Knopf, 2007), passim, esp. 11–12, 32–39, 106–10, 138–41. On Northern war aims, see notes 30 and 31 in this chapter.

30. Oakes, "When Everybody Knew," 116. But for the argument that Lincoln and most Republicans "turned their guns on slavery . . . only once they concluded that doing so offered the sole means of winning the war," see Levine, *The Fall of the House of Dixie*, 108. "Whatever Lincoln intended, his early speeches signaled limited interference" with slavery, asserted Laura F. Edwards in *A Legal History of the Civil War and Reconstruction*, 64.

31. Quotations are from V. Jacques Voegeli, *Free but Not Equal: The Midwest and the Negro during the Civil War* (Chicago: University of Chicago Press, 1967), 102; and *The Radical Republicans and Reconstruction, 1861–1870*, ed. Harold M. Hyman (Indianapolis: Bobbs-Merrill, 1967), 160–61. On the Republicans' shared antislavery convictions and their determination to make the war one for freedom, see Oakes, *Freedom National*, passim, Oakes, "When Everybody Knew," Oakes, *The Scorpion's Sting: Antislavery and the Coming of the Civil War* (New York: W. W. Norton, 2014), and Oakes, *The Crooked Path to Abolition*. On the radicalization of Union troops, see Manning, *What This Cruel War Was Over*, esp. 114–125; and James M. McPherson, *For Cause and Comrades: Why Men Fought in the Civil War* (New York: Oxford University Press, 1997), 117–30. On the growing role of "Radicals" within the Republican Party, see LeeAnna Keith, *When It Was Grand: The Radical Republican History of the Civil War* (New York: Hill and Wang, 2020). On the "logic of events" leading the Lincoln administration to adopt increasingly radical measures, see Levine, *The Fall of the House of Dixie*, esp. 137–40 (quotation: 139). For the argument that the Republicans' commitment to "limited government" limited the effectiveness of their opposition to slavery, see Patrick Rael, *Eighty-Eight Years: The Long Death of Slavery in the United States, 1777–1865* (Athens: University of Georgia Press, 2015) (quotation: 305).

32. Historians no longer credit the idea of a bitter struggle between vindictive radicals and a magnanimous Lincoln. For an early revisionist demonstration of the cooperation that often existed between Lincoln and radical Republicans, see David Donald, "The Radicals and Lincoln," in Donald, *Lincoln Reconsidered* (New York: Alfred A. Knopf, 1956), 103–27. The literature on Lincoln is vast, but for three recent (and very different) books that offer illuminating insights into Lincoln's antislavery thought and action, see Allen C. Guelzo, *Lincoln's Emancipation Proclamation: The End of Slavery in America* (New York: Simon and Schuster, 2004); James Oakes, *The Radical and the Republican: Frederick Douglass, Abraham Lincoln, and the Triumph of Antislavery Politics* (New York: W. W. Norton, 2007); and Foner, *The Fiery Trial*. For an example of the once widely held view that Lincoln and the radicals were bitter enemies, see T. Harry Williams, *Lincoln and the Radicals* (Madison: University of Wisconsin Press, 1941).

33. Richard Hofstadter, *The American Political Tradition* (New York: Alfred A. Knopf, 1948), 132; Final Emancipation Proclamation, 1 January 1863, in Delbanco, *The Portable Abraham Lincoln*, 271–72; Edwards, *A Legal History of the Civil War and Reconstruction*, 81–82 (quotation: 81).

34. The Constitution of the United States of America, Amendment XIII. On the significance of the Emancipation Proclamation as a "turning point in national policy as well as in the character of the war," see Foner, *Reconstruction*, 1–11 (quotation: 7). See also John Hope Franklin, *The Emancipation Proclamation* (Garden City, NY: Doubleday, 1963); Hans L. Trefousse, *Lincoln's Decision for Emancipation* (Philadelphia: J. B. Lippincott, 1975); and Guelzo, *Lincoln's Emancipation Proclamation*. On Black soldiers in the Civil War, see Dudley Taylor Cornish, *The Sable Arm: Negro Troops in the Union Army, 1861–1865* (1956; New York: W. W. Norton, 1966); Joseph T. Glatthaar, *Forged in Battle: The Civil War Alliance of Black Soldiers and White Officers* (New York: Free Press, 1990); *Freedom's Soldiers: The Black Military Experience in the Civil War*, ed. Ira Berlin, Joseph P. Reidy, and Leslie S. Rowland (Cambridge: Cambridge University Press, 1998); Douglas R. Egerton, *Thunder at the Gates: The Black Civil War Regiments That Redeemed America* (New York: Basic Books, 2016); Thomas Wentworth Higginson, *Army Life in a Black Regiment* (1869; New York: Collier Books, 1962); and McPherson, *The Negro's Civil War*, esp. 143–240. For wartime experiments with free labor, see my chapter 3.

35. The formation of Reconstruction policy, once a subject of hot historical debate, has fallen into general neglect. In addition to works cited, in notes 36–39 in this chapter, the following books have informed my treatment of the subject: Du Bois, *Black Reconstruction in America*, 128–380; McKitrick, *Andrew Johnson and Reconstruction*; W. R. Brock, *An American Crisis: Congress and Reconstruction, 1865–1867* (New York: Harper and Row, 1963); David Donald, *The Politics of Reconstruction, 1863–1867* (Baton Rouge: Louisiana State University Press, 1965); David Montgomery, *Beyond Equality: Labor and the Radical Republicans, 1862–1872* (New York: Alfred A. Knopf, 1967); Hans L. Trefousse, *The Radical Republicans: Lincoln's Vanguard for Racial Justice* (New York:

Alfred A. Knopf, 1969); Michael Perman, *Reunion without Compromise: The South and Reconstruction, 1865–1868* (Cambridge: Cambridge University Press, 1973); Michael Les Benedict, *A Compromise of Principle: Congressional Republicans and Reconstruction, 1863–1869* (New York: W. W. Norton, 1974); Ellen Du Bois, *Feminism and Suffrage: The Emergence of an Independent Women's Movement in America, 1848–1869* (Ithaca, NY: Cornell University Press, 1978); Eric Foner, *Reconstruction*, 176–345, and *The Second Founding: How the Civil War and Reconstruction Remade the Constitution* (New York: W. W. Norton, 2019); Xi Wang, *The Trial of Democracy: Black Suffrage and Northern Republicans, 1860–1910* (Athens: University of Georgia Press, 1997); Heather Cox Richardson, *The Death of Reconstruction: Race, Labor, and Politics in the Post-Civil War North, 1865–1901* (Cambridge, MA: Harvard University Press, 2001), 6–82; Gregory P. Downs, *After Appomattox: Military Occupation and the Ends of War* (Cambridge, MA: Harvard University Press, 2015); and Bruce Levine, *Thaddeus Stevens: Civil War Revolutionary, Fighter for Racial Justice* (New York: Simon and Schuster, 2021). For three recent surveys, see Fitzgerald, *Splendid Failure*, esp. 22–46; Allen C. Guelzo, *Reconstruction: A Concise History* (New York: Oxford University Press, 2018); and Summers, *The Ordeal of the Reunion*.

36. The quotation is from George W. Julian's speech of 17 November 1865 to the Indiana state legislature, in Michael Les Benedict, *The Fruits of Victory: Alternatives in Restoring the Union, 1865–1867* (Philadelphia: J. B. Lippincott, 1975), 93. The composition of the Thirty-Ninth Congress is from "Composition of Congress by Political Party, 1855–2008," Infoplease (http://www.infoplease.com/ipa/A0774721.html). A full complement of Congressmen consisted of seventy-four senators and 243 representatives, but, except for Tennessee, the former Confederate states did not return to representation until the Forty-First Congress (1869–71). On the Democratic Party, see Joel H. Silbey, *A Respectable Minority: The Democratic Party in the Civil War Era* (New York: W. W. Norton, 1977); and Jean H. Baker, *Affairs of Party: The Political Culture of Northern Democrats in the Mid-Nineteenth Century* (Ithaca, NY: Cornell University Press, 1983).

37. The quotation is from Carl Schurz, *Report on the Condition of the South* (1865; New York: Arno Press, 1969), 45, 39, 42. See, also, Whitelaw Reid, *After the War: A Tour of the Southern States, 1865–1866*, ed. C. Vann Woodward (1866; New York: Harper and Row, 1965), 439–47, 574–80, and passim; and Sidney Andrews, *The South Since the War*, intro. David Donald (1866; Boston: Houghton Mifflin, 1971), esp. 383–400. On actual conditions in the South—including the educational efforts of and atrocities against African Americans—see my chapters 3–6. For an influential description of growing Republican resentment of Southern white recalcitrance during the second half of 1865, see McKitrick, *Andrew Johnson and Reconstruction*, esp. 153–213.

38. On Thaddeus Stevens and confiscation, see esp. Eric Foner, "Thaddeus Stevens, Confiscation, and Reconstruction" (1974), reprinted in Foner, *Politics and Ideology in the Age of the Civil War* (New York: Oxford University Press, 1980), 128–49; and Levine, *Thaddeus Stevens*, 223–31. On the Southern Homestead Act, see my chapter 2.

For essays dealing with the new, Civil War–generated, emphasis on American citizenship, see *The Civil War and the Transformation of American Citizenship*, ed. Paul Quigley (Baton Rouge: Louisiana State University Press, 2018).

39. Quotations are from "Thaddeus Stevens on Territorialization and Confiscation," 18 December 1865, in Benedict, *Fruits of Victory*, 93; and Frederick Douglass, "What Should Be Done with Emancipated Slaves," *Douglass' Monthly*, January 1862, reprinted in *Frederick Douglass: The Narrative and Selected Writings*, ed. Michael Meyer (New York: Modern Library, 1984), 374. For the role in the overthrow of Reconstruction played by opposition to special privileges, see esp. Richardson, *The Death of Reconstruction*.

40. A streamlined outline of the basic terms of emancipation in first Russia and then the United States reveals the significant contrast between the two emancipations. The Russian terms, which were especially complicated, consist mostly of the provisions set forth in the lengthy statutory Regulations (*Polozheniia*) of 1861, with slight modification in subsequent legislation. For the full text of the Russian emancipation legislation, see *Polnoe sobranie zakonov Rossiiskoi Imperii*, 2nd ser., 55 vols. (1825–81), vol. 36 (1861), nos. 36,657–36,675 plus appendixes; a more convenient collection of the most important provisions is available in *Padenie krepostnogo prava v Rossii: Dokumenty i materialy*, vol. 2: *"Polozheniia 19 fevralia 1861 goda" i russkoe obshchestvo*, ed V. A. Fedorov (Moscow: Izdatel'stvo Moskovskogo universiteta, 1967), 7–63. For a recent English-language edition of these Regulations (which I have not used), see *The Laws of February 18–19, 1861 on the Emancipation of the Russian Peasants*, ed. and trans. Alan P. Pollard (Idyllwild, CA: Charles Schlacks, 2008). The principal sources of the American terms are the Thirteenth, Fourteenth, and Fifteenth Amendments to the Constitution, the Reconstruction Acts of 1867, and a variety of other legislative acts that helped to redefine the rights and opportunities of former slaves—and in some cases of citizens in general—in post-emancipation America. The various pieces of American legislation can be found in the *United States Statutes at Large*, vols. 13–16; and *The Political History of the United States during the Period of Reconstruction*, 2nd ed., ed. Edward McPherson (Washington, DC, 1875). They are more conveniently accessed in numerous collections, some of which are cited below. My focus in this section is on the emancipation settlements as set forth in this Russian and American legislation, not on how they eventually played out; the actual implementation of—and struggle over—the emancipation legislation is covered in subsequent chapters.

41. Letter of P. P. Abramov, 21 March 1861, in *KD-4*, 408; Geroid Tanquary Robinson, *Rural Russia under the Old Regime: A History of the Landlord-Peasant World and a Prologue to the Peasant Revolution of 1917* (New York: Macmillan, 1949), 65.

42. Fedorov, *Padenie krepostnogo prava*, II, passim. For brief surveys, see Kolchin, "After Serfdom," 91–94; and Moon, *Abolition of Serfdom in Russia*, 70–83. For more detail, see Zaionchkovskii, *Otmena krepostnogo prava*, and other sources cited below.

43. Fedorov, *Padenie krepostnogo prava*, II, 30–34 (quotation: 31). Peace mediators were supposed to be local hereditary noblemen owning at least five hundred desiatiny

of land, but elevated rank or educational attainment could substitute for up to 350 desiatiny of land and in the absence of qualified hereditary nobles, "personal" nobles (of lower, nonhereditary, rank) could serve if they owned a thousand desiatiny of land. (Since one desiatina = 2.7 acres, five hundred desiatiny was the equivalent of 1,350 acres, and a thousand desiatiny was the equivalent of 2,700 acres.) On the new rural administration of post-emancipation Russia, see, inter alia, A. P. Korelin, "Institut predvoditelei dvorianstva: O sotsial'nom i politicheskom polozhenii dvorian," *Istoriia SSSR*, 1978, no. 3 (May–June), 31–48; P. N. Zyrianov, "Sotsial'naia struktura mestnogo upravleniia kapitalisticheskoi Rossii (1861–1914 gg.)," *Istoricheskie zapiski*, 107 (Moscow: Izdatel'stvo "Nauka," 1982), 273–95; Natalia F. Ust'iantseva, "Accountable Only to God and the Senate: Peace Mediators and the Great Reform" (trans. Ben Eklof), in *Russia's Great Reforms*, 161–80; James I. Mandel, "Paternalistic Authority in the Russian Countryside, 1856–1906" (Ph.D. diss., Columbia University, 1978), 73–123; Jerman W. Rose, "The Russian Peasant Emancipation and the Problem of Rural Administration: The Institute of the *Mirovoi Posrednik*" (Ph.D. diss., University of Kansas, 1976); and other sources cited below.

44. Fedorov, *Padenie krepostnogo prava*, II, 16–27; Alfred J. Rieber, "The Sedimentary Society," in *Between Tsar and People: Educated Society and the Quest for Public Identity in Late Imperial Russia*, ed. Edith W. Clowes, Samuel D. Kassow, and James L. West (Princeton: Princeton University Press, 1991), 343–65 (quotation: 345). See, inter alia, in addition to sources cited in note 43 in this chapter, L. I. Kuchumova, "Sel'skaia pozemel'naia obshchina evropeiskoi Rossii v 60-70-e gody XIX v.," *Istoricheskie zapiski*, 106 (Moscow: Izdatel'stvo "Nauka," 1981), 323–47; A. N. Anfimov and P. N. Zyrianov, "Nekotorye cherty evoliutsii russkoi krest'ianskoi obshchiny v poreformennyi period (1861–1914 gg.)," *Istoriia SSSR*, 1980, no. 4, 24–41; and Boris Mironov, "The Russian Peasant Commune after the Reform of the 1860s," *Slavic Review*, 44 (Fall 1985), 438–67. On the pre-emancipation commune, and serfs' communal life, see V. A. Aleksandrov, *Sel'skaia obshchina v Rossii (XVII–nachalo XIX v.)* (Moscow: Izdatel'stvo "Nauka," 1976); and Kolchin, *Unfree Labor*, 200–206, 214–17, and 195–357 passim. Beginning in 1864, a third (and intermediate) level of government—district and provincial *zemstvo* assemblies—introduced the novel principle of local bodies representing all classes, including peasants; rigged from the start to make sure that nobles dominated these relatively powerless assemblies, the electoral system was reformed in 1890 to reduce peasant representation still further. See my chapters 4 and 7.

45. Fedorov, *Padenie krepostnogo prava*, II, 13–16, 27–28, 34–39 (quotations: 14, 35).

46. Fedorov, *Padenie krepostnogo prava*, II, 44–55. The size of landholdings and obrok payments was calculated collectively, as an average figure for all peasants on an estate, not separately for individual peasants.

47. Fedorov, *Padenie krepostnogo prava*, II, 37–38. For Ministry of Internal Affairs statistics on charters verified by 3 January 1863, see *Otmena krepostnogo prava: Doklady Ministrov vnutrennikh del o provedenii krest'ianskoi reformy 1861–1862* (Moscow:

Izdatel'stvo Akademii Nauk SSSR, 1950), 282. On the struggle over statutory charters, see my chapter 2.

48. Fedorov, *Padenie krepostnogo prava*, II, 39–44.

49. Fedorov, *Padenie krepostnogo prava*, 55–63, II. The Belorussian and Ukrainian provinces covered in the 1863 decrees were Vil'no, Grodno, Kovno, Minsk, Vitebsk, Kiev, Podolia, and Mogilev. On the pace, process, and terms of redemption, see Zaionchkovskii, *Otmena krepostnogo prava*, 233–59, 293; B. G. Litvak, *Russkaia derevnia v reforme 1861 goda: Chernozemnyi tsentr, 1861–1895 gg.* (Moscow: Izdatel'stvo "Nauka," 1972), 326–99; and N. M. Druzhinin, *Russkaia derevnia na perelome: 1861–1880 gg.* (Moscow: Izdatel'stvo "Nauka," 1978), 63–74, 260–63.

50. There is an extensive literature on the congressional debate over and enactment of Reconstruction legislation, much of it dating from the 1960s and 1970s. See, inter alia, McKitrick, *Andrew Johnson and Reconstruction;* Brock, *An American Crisis;* Benedict, *A Compromise of Principle;* and Foner, *Reconstruction*, 176–280. On republican citizenship, see Foner, *The Second Founding;* and Gregory P. Downs, *The Second American Revolution: The Civil War–Era Struggle over Cuba and the Rebirth of the American Republic* (Chapel Hill: University of North Carolina Press, 2019), 1–54, 132–42. For an analysis of the political imperative for compromise among radical and moderate Republican factions, see Donald, *The Politics of Reconstruction*, 53–82.

51. The quotations from the Civil Rights Act and the Fourteenth Amendment are from Benedict, *Fruits of Victory*, 101, 108. On Republican passage of (and unity on) the Civil Rights Act, see Benedict, *A Compromise of Principle*, 162–65. For how President Johnson's vetoes of this act and other Reconstruction legislation contributed to growing Republican consensus, see McKitrick, *Andrew Johnson and Reconstruction*, 274–325; and Foner, *Reconstruction*, 243–325.

52. Benedict, *Fruits of Victory*, 108, 114.

53. Benedict, *Fruits of Victory*, 110–111. For a cogent emphasis on the limited nature of the Reconstruction challenge to the federal system of government, see Michael Les Benedict, "Preserving the Constitution: The Conservative Basis of Radical Reconstruction," *Journal of American History*, 61 (June 1974), 65–90. The Fourteenth Amendment temporarily disqualified from holding elective office—and the Reconstruction Acts disfranchised—former government officials who after swearing to support the Constitution rebelled against the United States, but a series of amnesty acts (the most important of which was passed in 1872) restored their political rights; in the 1870s former Confederate leaders (including Vice President Alexander Stephens) once again served in Congress. See Jonathan T. Dorris, "Pardoning the Leaders of the Confederacy," *Mississippi Valley Historical Review*, 15 (1928), 3–21; William A. Russ, "Registration and Disfranchisement under Radical Reconstruction," ibid., 21 (1934), 163–80; and James A. Rawley, "The General Amnesty Act of 1872," ibid., 47 (1960), 480–84.

54. For general studies of the Freedmen's Bureau, see George R. Bentley, *A History of the Freedmen's Bureau* (Philadelphia: University of Pennsylvania Press, 1955); Wil-

liam S. McFeely, *Yankee Stepfather: General O. O. Howard and the Freedmen* (New Haven: Yale University Press, 1968); and Mary Farmer-Kaiser, *Freedwomen and the Freedmen's Bureau: Race, Gender, and Public Policy in the Age of Emancipation* (New York: Fordham University Press, 2010). Statewide studies include Paul A. Cimbala, *Under the Guardianship of the Nation: The Freedmen's Bureau and the Reconstruction of Georgia, 1865–1870* (Athens: University of Georgia Press, 1997); Barry A. Crouch, *The Freedmen's Bureau and Black Texans* (Austin: University of Texas Press, 1992); Howard A. White, *The Freedmen's Bureau in Louisiana* (Baton Rouge: Louisiana State University Press, 1970); and essays in *The Freedmen's Bureau and Reconstruction: Reconsiderations*, ed. Paul A. Cimbala and Randall M. Miller (New York: Fordham University Press, 1999). On the Southern Homestead Act, see Michael L. Lanza, *Agrarianism and Reconstruction Politics: The Southern Homestead Act* (Baton Rouge: Louisiana State University Press, 1990). For the actual operation of the Freedmen's Bureau and the Southern Homestead Act, see my chapters 2 and 3.

55. The Civil Rights Act of 1875 can also be considered a deviation from prevailing laissez-faire principles. Passed in the waning days of Reconstruction as a tribute to its sponsor, Charles Sumner, who had died the year before, the measure went well beyond previous legislation in stipulating the integration of "inns, public conveyances on land or water, theatres, and other places of public amusement" (although not public schools, which Sumner's original bill had included). Fleming, *Documentary History of Reconstruction*, II, 295–97 (quotation: 295). The bill lacked effective provisions for enforcement, however, and eight years later the Supreme Court declared it unconstitutional because the Fourteenth Amendment barred discriminatory action by states, not individuals.

56. Steven L. Hoch, "Did Russia's Emancipated Serfs Really Pay Too Much for Too Little Land? Statistical Anomalies and Long-Tailed Distributions," *Slavic Review*, 63 (Summer 2004), 247–74 (quotations: 248, 274). For suggestions that the economic condition of the post-emancipation peasantry was less than desperate, see my chapter 7, note 4. On the actual condition of the peasantry, see my chapters 2–7; my interest here is on the assumptions behind judgments on the nature of the emancipation settlement.

57. Hoch, "Did Russia's Emancipated Serfs Really Pay Too Much for Too Little Land?" 274; report of Orenburg Province Governor G. S. Aksakov to Minister of Internal Affairs P. A. Valuev, 13 March 1862, in *Krest'ianskoe dvizhenie v Rossii v 1861–1869 gg.: Sbornik dokumentov*, ed. L. M. Ivanov (Moscow: Izdatel'stvo sotsial'no-ekonomicheskoi literatury, 1964), 204 (hereafter cited as *KD-5*). See my chapter 2 for more on peasant understandings of emancipation.

58. For the Stevens quotation, see Eric Foner, *Nothing but Freedom: Emancipation and Its Legacy* (Baton Rouge: Louisiana State University Press, 1983), 8. Stevens's misconception was evidently widely shared by other radicals. For quotations reflecting the belief of Ida B. Wells and Frederick Douglass that ex-serfs in Russia were *given* land, see William A. Darity Jr. and A. Kirsten Mullen, *From Here to Equality: Repara-*

tions for Black Americans in the Twenty-First Century (Chapel Hill: University of North Carolina Press, 2020), 9 and 10. In arguing that the American slaves received "nothing but freedom," Foner was, of course, referring to the *economic* terms of emancipation; *politically*, the freedpeople received a good deal more than nothing.

59. For elaboration on this theme, see Peter Kolchin, "The Tragic Era? Interpreting Southern Reconstruction in Comparative Perspective," in *The Meaning of Freedom: Economics, Politics, and Culture after Slavery*, ed. Frank McGlynn and Seymour Drescher (Pittsburgh: University of Pittsburgh Press, 1992), 291–94. The quotations are from Crandall A. Shifflett, *Patronage and Poverty in the Tobacco South: Louisa County, Virginia, 1860–1900* (Knoxville: University of Tennessee Press, 1982), 64 and 103. Even Eric Foner, who stressed the revolutionary nature of emancipation and Reconstruction, termed Reconstruction a "failure"; Foner *Reconstruction*, 143. (Note, however, the more ambiguous implication of the book's subtitle, *America's Unfinished Revolution*.)

60. Howard N. Rabinowitz, "From Exclusion to Segregation: Southern Race Relations, 1865–1890," *Journal of American History*, 63 (1976), 325–50; Kolchin, "The Tragic Era?" esp. 297–302.

61. Kolchin, "The Tragic Era?" 294–97. In its gradual implementation, its concern for financial remuneration of the owners, and its lack of support for the rights of the freedpeople, the Russian settlement resembled both earlier serf emancipations, such as those in Prussia (1807) and Austria (1848), and other slave emancipations, such as those in the British West Indies (1833) and Brazil (1888). See Robert M. Berdahl, "Paternalism, Serfdom, and Emancipation in Prussia," in *Oceans Apart? Comparing Germany and the United States*, ed. Erich Angermann and Marie-Luise Frings (Stuttgart: Klett-Cotta, 1981), esp. 40–44; Blum, *Noble Landowners and Agriculture in Austria*, esp. 237–46; Stefan Kieniewicz, *The Emancipation of the Polish Peasantry* (Chicago: University of Chicago Press, 1969), 58–71, 133–39; and Steven Mintz, "Models of Emancipation During the Age of Revolution," *Slavery and Abolition*, 17 (August 1996), esp. 7–8. For emphasis on the unusual nature of post-emancipation Reconstruction in the Southern United States, see Foner, *Nothing But Freedom*, esp. Chapter 1; Thomas J. Pressly, "Reconstruction in the Southern United States: A Comparative Perspective," *OAH Magazine of History*, 4 (Winter 1989), 14–35; and Steven Hahn, "Class and State in Postemancipation Societies: Southern Planters in Comparative Perspective," *American Historical Review*, 95 (February 1990), 75–98. For the Jamaican and Brazilian contrasts, see Thomas C. Holt, *The Problem of Freedom: Race, Labor, and Politics in Jamaica and Britain, 1832–1938* (Baltimore: Johns Hopkins University Press, 1992); Robert Brent Toplin, *The Abolition of Slavery in Brazil* (New York: Atheneum, 1972), 247–66; and George Reid Andrews, "Black and White Workers: Sao Paulo, Brazil, 1888–1928," *Hispanic American Historical Review*, 68 (1988), 491–524. Even Haiti paid compensation to the former slave owners.

62. *Kolokol*, no. 95 (1 April 1861), 797; *Kolokol*, no. 97 (1 May 1861), 813; *Kolokol*, no. 96 (15 April 1861), 806; J. Lang, *Results of the Serf Emancipation in Russia* (New York,

1864), 4; A. D. White, "The Development and Overthrow of the Russian Serf System," *Atlantic Monthly*, 10 (November 1862), 538–52; Foner, *Nothing but Freedom*, 8.

63. *The Liberator*, 29 December 1865, in *William Lloyd Garrison and the Fight against Slavery*, 179–83 (quotation: 182); Clemenceau quoted in Brock, *An American Crisis*, 82; Julian speech, 17 November 1865, in Benedict, *The Fruits of Victory*, 93–94.

Chapter 2. What Kind of Freedom?

1. Eric Foner, *The Story of American Freedom* (New York: W. W. Norton, 1998); Ivan Boltin, *Primechaniia na Istoriiu drevniia i nyneshniia Rossii g. Leklerka*, 2 vols. (Pechatano v tipografii gornago uchilishcha, 1788), II, 235–36.

2. Thomas Jefferson to William Stephens Smith, 13 November 1787, in *The Papers of Thomas Jefferson*, 44 vols., ed. Julian P. Boyd, XII (Princeton: Princeton University Press, 1955), 355–57, accessed at https://founders.archives.gov/documents/Jefferson/01-12-02-0348. Later, Jefferson termed the effort to prevent the spread of slavery to Missouri "a fire-bell in the night [that] awakened and filled me with terror"; Jefferson to John Holmes, 22 April 1820, in *The Portable Thomas Jefferson*, ed. Merrill D. Peterson (New York: Viking Press, 1975), 568. On proslavery and pro-serfdom arguments, see Peter Kolchin, *Unfree Labor: American Slavery and Russian Serfdom* (Cambridge, MA: Harvard University Press, 1987), 170–77.

3. Prince I. M. Dolgoruki, "Zhurnal puteshestviia iz Moskvy v Nizhnii" (1813), in *Chteniia v Imperatorskom obshchestve istorii i drevnostei Rossiiskikh pri Moskovskom universitete*, LXXII (1870), no. 1, pt. 2, 17–18; William Lloyd Garrison, "Declaration of the National Anti-Slavery Convention" (14 December 1833), in *William Lloyd Garrison and the Fight against Slavery: Selections from The Liberator*, ed. William E. Cain (Boston: Bedford Books, 1995), 92, 91.

4. The most famous white advocate of racial equality was William Lloyd Garrison, who for many years edited the *Liberator*; for a convenient collection of his writings, see Cain, *William Lloyd Garrison and the Fight against Slavery*. Among Black abolitionists, Frederick Douglass was preeminent. See his three (progressively longer and more detailed) autobiographies, the first of which was especially influential: *Narrative of the Life of Frederick Douglass: An American Slave, Written by Himself* (1845; New York: New American Library, 1968); and *Frederick Douglass: The Narrative and Selected Writings*, ed. Michael Meyer (New York: Random House, 1984). On Douglass, Garrison, and radical abolitionism in general, see, inter alia, Aileen S. Kraditor, *Means and Ends in American Abolitionism* (New York: Pantheon Books, 1967); David W. Blight, *Frederick Douglass: Prophet of Freedom* (New York: Simon and Schuster, 2018); and Manisha Sinha, *The Slave's Cause: A History of Abolition* (New Haven: Yale University Press, 2016). The most famous radical exile from Russia was Alexander Herzen, who for many years edited *Kolokol [The Bell]*; see the eleven-volume reprint (Moscow: Izdatel'stvo Akademii nauk SSSR, 1962–64). On Herzen, exiles, and radical egalitarians in general, see, inter alia,

Walter S. Hanchett Jr., "A Study of Alexander Hertsen's *Kolokol* Writings on the Peasant Problem, July 1, 1857–July 1, 1861" (M.A. thesis, University of Chicago, 1951); Edward Hallett Carr, *The Romantic Exiles: A Nineteenth Century Portrait Gallery* (1933; Boston: Beacon Press, 1961); and Franco Venturi, *Roots of Revolution: A History of the Populist and Socialist Movements in Nineteenth-Century Russia* (New York: Alfred A. Knopf, 1964), esp. 1–203. On free Blacks and state peasants, see, inter alia, Ira Berlin, *Slaves without Masters: The Free Negro in the Antebellum South* (New York: Pantheon Books, 1974); N. M. Druzhinin, *Gosudarstvennye krest'iane i reforma P. D. Kiseleva*, 2 vols. (Moscow: Izdatel'stvo Akademii nauk SSSR, 1946, 1958); Olga Crisp, "The State Peasants under Nicholas I," *Slavonic and East European Review*, 37 (June 1959), 387–412; and Jerome Blum, *Lord and Peasant in Russia from the Ninth to the Nineteenth Century* (1961; New York: Atheneum, 1966), esp. 475–503.

5. Abraham Lincoln, Address to the State Agricultural Society, Milwaukee, Wisconsin (1859), *The Portable Abraham Lincoln*, ed. Andrew Delbanco (New York: Penguin Books, 1992), 157, and Speech on the Kansas-Nebraska Bill at Peoria, Illinois (1854), ibid., 63. On Lincoln and slavery, see Eric Foner, *The Fiery Trial: Abraham Lincoln and American Slavery* (New York: W. W. Norton, 2010). For general free-labor arguments against slavery and serfdom, see my chapter 1, above. For an insightful analysis of the way free-labor advocates visualized the post-emancipation South, and the centrality of the idea of "contract" in their thinking, see Amy Dru Stanley, *From Bondage to Contract: Wage Labor, Marriage, and the Market in the Age of Slave Emancipation* (Cambridge: Cambridge University Press, 1998).

6. Kolchin, *Unfree Labor*, passim, esp. 108–10, 242; Frederick Law Olmsted, *The Cotton Kingdom: A Traveller's Observations on Cotton and Slavery in the American Slave States* (New York, 1861), I, 106 (quotation). On claims of former slaves filed with the Southern Claims Commission—which included personal possessions but not, significantly, landed property—see especially Dylan C. Penningroth, *The Claims of Kinfolk: African American Property and Community in the Nineteenth-Century South* (Chapel Hill: University of North Carolina Press, 2003), 1–12, 45–130.

7. Kolchin, *Unfree Labor*. For emphasis on "self-governance" as central to the slaves' aspirations, see Steven Hahn, *A Nation under Our Feet: Black Political Struggles in the Rural South from Slavery to the Great Migration* (Cambridge, MA: Harvard University Press, 2003), 1–115. On Russia, see V. A. Aleksandrov, *Sel'skaia obshchina v Rossii (XVII–nachalo XIX v.)* (Moscow: Izdatel'stvo "Nauka," 1976); and G. A. Kavtaradze, "Zhaloby krest'ian pervoi poloviny XIX veka kak istochnik dlia izucheniia ikh sotsial'nikh trebovanii," *Vestnik Leningradskogo universiteta*, 1968, no. 28, 54–61. The quotation is from Frederick Douglass, "What Should Be Done with the Emancipated Slaves" (1862), in Meyer, *Frederick Douglass: The Narrative and Selected Writings*, 374. See also my chapter 1, above.

8. For the argument that many peasants envisioned emancipation as producing a return to an earlier idealized version of communal proto-democracy, see G. A.

Kavtaradze, "K istorii krest'ianskogo samosoznaniia perioda reform 1861 g.," *Vestnik Leningradskogo universiteta,* 1969, no. 14, 54–64. For the suggestion of a similar communal mentality among antebellum Southern slaves, see Anthony E. Kaye, *Joining Places: Slave Neighborhoods in the Old South* (Chapel Hill: University of North Carolina Press, 2007). For the evolution—and contrast—of political consciousness among freed African Americans and peasants, see my chapter 4.

9. Peace mediator quoted in Roxanne Easley, *The Emancipation of the Serfs in Russia: Peace Arbitrators and the Development of Civil Society* (London: Routledge, 2009), 76; letter from "R," *Huntsville Advocate,* 9 November 1865; Baptist minister Basil Manly to his sister Jane, 8 June 1865, Tuscaloosa, Basil Manly Papers, University of Alabama Library; J. B. Moore diary, 24 November 1865, typed copy, Alabama State Department of Archives and History, Montgomery, AL.

10. James Roark, *Masters without Slaves: Southern Planters in the Civil War and Reconstruction* (New York: W.W. Norton, 1977), 86, 157; "Petition of the Tula Gentry Assembly to Alexander II, December 1861," and "Resolution of the Voronezh Gentry Assembly, 4 February 1862," in Terence Emmons, *The Russian Landed Gentry and the Peasant Emancipation of 1861* (Cambridge: Cambridge University Press, 1968), 454, 460.

11. Minister of Justice Count V. N. Panin to Oberprokuror of the Church Synod Count A. P. Tolstoi, 24 November 1860, in "Tserkov' i reforma 1861 g.," ed. Z. Gurskaia, *Krasnyi arkhiv,* 72, no. 5 (1935), 183 (quotations); "Iz obzor deistvii Ministerstva vnutrennikh del po zemskomu otdelu s 1 ianvaria 1861 po 19 fevralia 1863 g.," in "Reforma 1861 g. i krest'ianskoe dvizhenie," ed. M. Lur'e, *Krasnyi arkhiv,* 75, no. 2 (1936), 64–65; editor's introduction to *Krest'ianskoe dvizhenie v 1861 godu posle otmeny krepostnogo prava,* ed. E.A. Morokhovets (Moscow: Izdatel'stvo Akademii nauk SSSR, 1949), 3–14. See, also, A. Z. Popel'nitskii, "Pervye shagi krest'ianskoi reformy (Po doneseniiam svitskikh general-maiorov i fligel'-adiutantov, s marta po iiul' 1861 g.)," in *Velikaia reforma: Russkaia obshchestvo i krest'ianskii vopros v proshlom i nastoiashchem: Iubileinoe izdanie,* 6 vols. (Moscow, 1911), V, 179–211; *Otmena krepostnogo prava: Doklady Ministrov vnutrennikh del o provedenii krest'ianskoi reformy 1861–1862* (Moscow: Izdatel'stvo Akademii nauk SSSR, 1950), 152–61; and Daniel Field, "The Year of Jubilee," in *Russia's Great Reforms, 1855–1881,* ed. Ben Eklof, John Bushnell, and Larissa Zakharova (Bloomington: Indiana University Press, 1994), 40–43.

12. Lur'e, ed., "Reforma 1861 g.," 64–65; Morokhovets, *Krest'ianskoe dvizhenie v 1861 godu,* passim (quotation: 4); Jerman W. Rose, "The Russian Peasant Emancipation and the Problem of Rural Administration: The Institution of the *Mirovoi Posrednik*" (Ph.D. diss, University of Kansas, 1976), 79.

13. Natalia F. Ust'iantseva, "Accountable Only to God and the Senate: Peace Mediators and the Great Reforms," in Eklof et al., *Russia's Great Reforms,* 162–65; N. M. Druzhinin, *Russkaia derevnia na perelome: 1861–1880 gg.* (Moscow: Izdatel'stvo "Nauka," 1978), 38–41; A. P. Korelin, *Dvorianstvo v poreformennoi Rossii 1861–1904 gg.: Sostav, chislennost,' korporativnaia organizatsiia* (Moscow: Izdatel'stvo "Nauka," 1979),

191–96; Rose, "The Russian Peasant Emancipation," 71–77, 90; Easley, *Emancipation of the Serfs in Russia*, 52–92. For typical lists of the initial members of these bodies for one province (Kaluga), see *Pomiatnaia knizhka Kaluzhskoi gubernii na 1862 i 1863 gody, izdannaia Kaluzhskim Gubernskim Statisticheskim Komitetom* (Kaluga, 1863), 2 (for the provincial committee) and 19–54 (for each district's administration).

14. As Edward L. Ayers has pointed out, "Nearly 2.8 million enslaved people"—out of some 3.5 million in the Confederate states—"lived in such places where the absence of a consistent Federal military presence allowed slaveholders to buy, sell, rent, and punish enslaved people even after Lee's surrender"; see Ayers, *The Thin Light of Freedom: The Civil War and Emancipation in the Heart of America* (New York: W. W. Norton, 2017), 344. On the diverse wartime experiences of Southern slaves, and their struggle to be "free," see my chapter 1, above; and, for a historiographical essay, Peter Kolchin, "Slavery and Freedom in the Civil War South," in *Writing the Civil War: The Quest to Understand*, ed. James M. McPherson and William J. Cooper Jr. (Columbia: University of South Carolina Press, 1998), 241–60, 335–47. For a classic study of this process in the sea islands of South Carolina, see Willie Lee Rose, *Rehearsal for Reconstruction: The Port Royal Experiment* (Indianapolis: Bobbs-Merrill, 1964).

15. Journal Letter Kept by Miss Charlotte St. J. Ravenel of Pooshee Plantation for Miss Meta Heyward, 1 April 1865, Thomas Porcher Ravenel Papers, in "Records of Ante-Bellum Plantations from the Revolution through the Civil War," ed. Kenneth M. Stampp, microfilm Series B, reel 4 (original in South Carolina Historical Society). The tenuous nature of freedom applied even to areas of the North that temporarily came under Confederate control. As Edward L. Ayers noted (in *The Thin Light of Freedom*, 46–47), when Confederate soldiers invaded Franklin County, Pennsylvania, in the summer of 1863, they captured some fifty African Americans—some former slaves, some freeborn—and sent them south to be sold into slavery.

16. Interview with Jimmie Green, in *Weevils in the Wheat: Interviews with Virginia Ex-Slaves*, ed. Charles L. Perdue Jr., Thomas E. Barden, and Robert K. Phillips (Charlottesville: University Press of Virginia, 1976), 127. Juneteenth, also known as Emancipation Day, became an official holiday in Texas in 1979 and—according to a bill passed with unanimous support in the U.S. Senate and only fourteen negative votes in the House of Representatives—a federal holiday in 2021. See http://www.juneteenth.com; "The Handbook of Texas Online" (http://www.tsonline.org/handbook/online/articles/JJ/lkj1.html); and William H. Wiggins Jr., *O Freedom! Afro-American Emancipation Celebrations* (Knoxville: University of Tennessee Press, 1987), passim. For engaging combinations of personal musings and historical analysis, see Annette Gordon-Reed, *On Juneteenth* (New York: Liveright, 2021); and Clint Smith, *How the Word Is Passed: A Reckoning with the History of Slavery across America* (New York: Little, Brown, 2021), 173–208. According to Smith, no evidence supports the "long-held myth"—which was "embedded . . . into local folklore"—that "General Gordon Granger stood on the balcony of Ashton Villa in Galveston, Texas, and read the order

that announced the end of slavery." Still, Juneteenth became "a day to solemnly remember what the country has done to Black Americans and a day to celebrate all that Black Americans have overcome" (quotations: 173, 205).

17. Eric Foner, *Reconstruction: America's Unfinished Revolution, 1863–1877* (New York: Harper and Row, 1988), 68–70, 142–53; William S. McFeely, *Yankee Stepfather: General O. O. Howard and the Freedmen* (1968; New York: W. W. Norton, 1970); *The Freedmen's Bureau and Reconstruction: Reconsiderations*, ed. Paul A. Cimbala and Randall M. Miller (New York: Fordham University Press, 1999); and Mary Farmer-Kaiser, *Freedwomen and the Freedmen's Bureau: Race, Gender, and Public Policy in the Age of Emancipation* (New York: Fordham University Press, 2010).

18. Thomas W. Conway to Lieutenant Colonel C. T. Christensen, Assistant Adjutant General, New Orleans, 3 June 1865, *The War of the Rebellion: A Compilation of the Official Records of the Union and Confederate Armies* (Washington, DC: Government Printing Office, 1897), ser. I, vol. XLIX, pt. II, 954; Paul A. Cimbala, *Under the Guardianship of the Nation: The Freedmen's Bureau and the Reconstruction of Georgia, 1865–1870* (Athens: University of Georgia Press, 1997), 22–25. On selection of the original assistant commissioners, see McFeely, *Yankee Stepfather*, 65–68.

19. Quotations are from Randall M. Miller, "The Freedmen's Bureau and Reconstruction: An Overview," in Cimbala and Miller, *The Freedmen's Bureau and Reconstruction*, xv; and Captain D. W. Whittle to O. O. Howard, 8 June 1865, Union Springs, AL, Freedmen's Bureau Papers (hereafter FBP) Assistant Adjutant General's Office, Letters Received. On the restoration governments, see, inter alia, Michael Perman *Reunion without Compromise: The South and Reconstruction, 1865–1868* (New York: Cambridge University Press, 1973). For the importance—and inadequacy—of the occupying Union Army, see Gregory P. Downs, *After Appomattox: Military Occupation and the Ends of War* (Cambridge, MA: Harvard University Press, 2015), and "Anarchy at the Circumference: Statelessness and the Reconstruction of Authority in Emancipation North Carolina," in *After Slavery: Race, Labor, and Citizenship in the Reconstruction South*, ed. Bruce E. Baker and Brian Kelly (Gainesville: University Press of Florida, 2013), 98–121. On problems posed by the constitutional dichotomy between federal and state authority, see Laura F. Edwards, *A Legal History of the Civil War and Reconstruction: A Nation of Rights* (New York: Cambridge University Press, 2015), passim.

20. C. C. Andrews, "To the Freedmen of Selma and Vicinity," 9 May 1865, *The War of the Rebellion*, ser. I, vol. XLIX, pt. II, 729; Captain Charles Soule, Chairman of the Commission on Contracts, to the Freedmen of Orangeburg District, 12 June 1865, FBP, Assistant Adjutant General's Office, Letters Received; Circular of Major General A. P. Veimarn to Peasants of Inflianskie districts, April, 1861, in *Krest'ianskoe dvizhenie v 1861 godu*, doc. 11, 29–30; Speech by Alexander II to Township and Village Peasant Elders of Moscow Province, 25 November 1862, in Moon, *The Abolition of Serfdom in Russia*, doc. 26, 167; Brigadier-General J. McArthur, General Orders No. 26, Selma, 26 May 1865, *The War of the Rebellion*, ser. I, vol. XLIX, pt. II, 916.

21. See, inter alia, reports to Alexander II from the following aides-de-camp, all in Morokhovets, *Krest'ianskoe dvizhenie v 1861 godu:* K. L. Dadiani (Vologda Province), 17 March and 31 March 1861, 38 and 39; A. G. Reitern (Ekaterinoslavl Province), 3 April 1861, 59; G. A. Krieger (Orenburg Province), 21 March 1861, 129; L. A. Iankovskii (Saratov Province), 14 March, 204; I. V. Gurko (Samara Province), 19 March 1861, 194; F. F. Vintsegerode (Tambov Province), 15 June 1861, 230–31. For Lanskoi's comments, in the first of a series of weekly reports from the Ministry of Internal Affairs on conditions surrounding emancipation, see *Otmena krepostnogo prava,* 31 March 1861, 7–8. On the joyful response to emancipation and grateful references to the tsar-liberator in Russian folklore, see N. L. Brodskii, "Krepostnoe pravo v narodnoi poezii," in *Velikaia reforma,* IV, 31–33.

22. Report of steward P. P. Abramov to pomeshchik Zubin, 21 March 1861, *Krest'ianskoe dvizhenie v 1857-mae 1861 gg.: Sbornik dokumentov,* ed. S. B. Okun' (Moscow: Izdatel'stvo sotsial'no-ekonomicheskoi literatury, 1963), 408–9 (hereafter cited as *KD-4*); A. A. Essen to Alexander II (Simbirsk Province), 19 April 1861, Morokhovets, *Krest'ianskoe dvizhenie v 1861 godu,* 214; N. I. Arapov to Alexander II (Kostroma Province), 23 July 1861, ibid., 104; M. K. Naryshkin to Alexander II (Grodno Province), 31 March 1861, ibid., 52–54; Field, "The Year of Jubilee," 41.

23. Report of Major Laks, staff officer of Corps of Gendarmes (Penza Province) to Chief of Gendarmes Dolgorukov, 18 March 1861, in "Kandeevskoe vosstanie v 1861 g.," ed. E. Sedovaia, *Krasnyi arkhiv,* 92, no. 1 (1939), 92; M. Butskovskii (Kiev Province) to Vladimir Nilovich Lavrov, 9 March 1861, in "Semdesiat piat' let nazad (19 fevralia 1861 g.)," ed. I. Kuznetsov, *Krasnyi arkhiv,* 74, no. 1 (1936), 8; Uzhumetskii-Gritsevich (Nizhnii Novgorod Province) to A. I. Uzhumetskii-Gritsevich, 14 March 1861, ibid., 9; Major General F. F. Vintsengerode (Tambov Province) to Alexander II, 15 June 1861, in Morokhovets, *Krest'ianskoe dvizhenie v 1861 godu,* 230. For other examples of calm and impassive peasant responses, see Kuznetsov, "Semdesiat piat' let nazad," 8–25; Morokhovets, *Krest'ianskoe dvizhenie v 1861 godu,* passim; *Otmena krepostnogo prava,* 7–27, passim.

24. Major General V. I. Bariatinskii (Moscow Province) to Alexander II, 6 March 1861, in Morokhovets, *Krest'ianskoe divizhenie v 1861 godu,* 123, 124; Baron A. N. Korf (Podolia Province) to Alexander II, 1 April 1861, ibid., 168. See, also, Kuznetsov, "Semdesiat piat' let nazad," 1–13 passim.

25. Aleksandr Nikitenko, *The Diary of a Russian Censor,* abridged, ed., and trans. Helen Saltz Jacobson (Amherst: University of Massachusetts Press, 1975), 18 August and 30 August 1861, 228, 229.

26. See my chapter 1, above. The quotation is from J. B. Moore Diary, 30 April 1862. On Black caution in dealing with Union soldiers, see Paul D. Escott, *Slavery Remembered: A Record of Twentieth-Century Slave Narratives* (Chapel Hill: University of North Carolina Press, 1979), 122–27. In *Been in the Storm So Long: The Aftermath of Slavery* (New York: Knopf, 1979), 3–166, Leon F. Litwack emphasized the varied wartime be-

havior of Southern African Americans. For depiction of more unwavering Black assertions of freedom, see Ira Berlin et al., *Slaves No More: Three Essays on Emancipation and the Civil War* (Cambridge: Cambridge University Press, 1992). On African Americans' "vengeful rage" and destruction of property after the flight of white slave owners from Port Royal, South Carolina, see Julie Saville, *The Work of Reconstruction: From Slave to Wage Laborer in South Carolina, 1860–1880* (New York: Cambridge University Press, 1994), 34. For the suggestion that in Lowcountry Georgia "for a few weeks [in early 1865] the scene bore a certain resemblance to an outburst of the peasantry during the Russian Revolution," see William Dusinberre, *Them Dark Days: Slavery in the American Rice Swamps* (New York: Oxford University Press, 1996), 377.

27. Charlotte Brown, in Perdue et al., *Weevils in the Wheat*, 58–59; Sidney Andrews, *The South Since the War: As Shown by Fourteen Weeks of Travel and Observation in Georgia and the Carolinas* (Boston: Ticknor and Fields, 1866), 353.

28. Thavolia Glymph, *Out of the House of Bondage: The Transformation of the Plantation Household* (New York: Cambridge University Press, 2008), 137–66 (quotation: 143).

29. J. W. Osborne, Assistant Commissioner for Florida, to Commissioner Howard, Tallahassee, 1 November 1865, FBP, Assistant Adjutant General's Office, Letters Received; letter from "Proxter," *Montgomery Daily Advertiser*, 5 August 1865; Daily Selma Times, 5 August 1865. See, also, Sternhell, *Routes of War*, 167–79.

30. James Mallory Diary, 4 July 1865, Southern Historical Collection, University of North Carolina.

31. Davis Tillson to Commissioner Howard, Savannah, 11 December 1865, FBP, Assistant Adjutant General's Office, Letters Received; Charles Stearns, *The Black Man of the South, and the Rebels; or, the Characteristics of the Former and the Recent Outrages of the Latter* (New York: American News Co., 1872), 31, 113, 45; Thomas Conway, General Superintendent, Bureau of Free Labor, Department of the Gulf, to Lieutenant C. T. Christensen, Assistant Adjutant General, New Orleans, 3 June 1865, *War of the Rebellion*, ser. I, vol. XLIX, pt. II, 954; Colonel L. F. Hubbard to Captain W. H. F. Randall, Assistant Adjutant General, Demopolis, AL, 20 May 1865, ibid., 855; General Edward Hatch, Eastport, MS to W. D. Whipple, Assistant Adjutant General, 22 June 1865, FBP, Assistant Adjutant General's Office, Letters Received.

32. Assistant Commissioner Samuel Thomas to Commissioner Howard, Vicksburg, MS, 7 August and 15 August 1865, FBP, Assistant Adjutant General's Office, Letters Received; Brigadier General J. McArthur to Lieutenant Colonel J. Hough, Assistant Adjutant General, Selma, 9 June 1865, *War of the Rebellion*, ser. I, vol. XLIX, pt. II, 975–76; Brigadier General C. C. Andrews to Lieutenant Colonel C. T. Christensen, Assistant Adjutant General, Selma, 11 May 1865, ibid., 728; Basil Manly to his sister Jane, Tuscaloosa, 8 June 1865, Manly Family Papers; Josiah Gorgas Diary, 2 June 1865, typed copy in Southern Historical Collection, University of North Carolina.

33. Whitelaw Reid, *After the War: A Tour of the Southern States, 1865–1866* (1866), ed. C. Vann Woodward (New York: Harper and Row, 1965), 389. Carl Schurz, *Report*

on the Condition of the South (1866; New York: Arno Press and the New York Times, 1969, originally published as Senate Exec. Doc. No. 2, 39th Congress, 1st Session, 1865), 15. Schurz conceded (27) that there were "a good many constitutionally lazy individuals" among the freedpeople, but he suggested that such laziness was a general Southern trait rather than one peculiar to African Americans.

34. Foner, *Reconstruction*, 112–18 (quotation: 115); New York *Daily Tribune*, 12 December 1865; *Daily Selma Times*, 28 November 1865. For more on the freedpeople's evolving political behavior, see my chapter 4; on the colored conventions, see sources listed in chapter 4, note 12.

35. Major General N. G. Kaznakov to Alexander II, 18 March and 13 April 1861, in Morokhovets, *Krest'ianskoe dvizhenie v 1861 godu*, 77, 79. For all nine reports, see 76–95.

36. Kaznakov to Alexander II, 16 April, 26 April, 24 May, in Morokhovets, *Krest'ianskoe dvizhenie v 1861 godu*, 80, 86, 94–95.

37. Quotations are from Valuev's reports of 3 June 1861 and 12 May 1861, in *Otmena krepostnogo prava*, 37, 31. See ibid., 7–27 for Lanskoi's reports and 27–51 for Valuev's reports through 21 July. Other sources indicate the same pattern. See, e.g., the reports in Morokhovets, *Krest'ianskoe dvizhenie v 1861 godu;* and in Lur'e, "Reforma 1861 g. i krest'ianskoe dvizhenie."

38. For a fuller characterization of volneniia, together with descriptions and analyses of them under serfdom, see Kolchin, *Unfree Labor*, 257–313.

39. Report of peace mediator Nikolai Sabaneev to Vice-Governor N. P. Mezentsov, Rybinskii district, Iaroslavl Province, 10 June 1861, in *Krest'ianskoe dvizhenie v 1861–1869 gg.: Sbornik dokumentov*, ed. L. M. Ivanov (Moscow: Izdatel'stvo sotsial'no-ekonomicheskoi literatury, 1964), 116–18 (quotations: 117, 118) (hereafter cited as *KD-5*).

40. Report of A. Nagurskii, ispravnik of Korotoganskii district, to the governor of Voronezh Province, 1 May 1861, in *Krest'ianskoe dvizheniev Voronezhskoi gubernii (1861–1863 gg.): Dokumenty i materialy* (Voronezh: Izdatel'stvo Voronezhskogo universiteta, 1961), 41–42 (quotation: 41) (hereafter cited as *KD-Vor-1*); report of Staff Officer of the Corps of Gendarmes Gur'ev to the head of the Third Department, Voronezh, 5 June 1861, *KD-Vor-1*, 44.

41. Report of Tula Province Governor P. M. Daragan to Minister of Internal Affairs Valuev, Tula, 30 September 1861, *KD-5*, 108–09.

42. Petition of peasants of Rostovtsy village, Kashirskii district, Tula Province to Tsar Alexander II, May 1862, *KD-5*, 110–11.

43. Report of staff officer Gur'ev of Corps of Gendarmes in Voronezh Province to the head of the Third Department, 7 April 1861, *KD-Vor-1*, 37; report of Voronezh Governor Chertkov to Minister of Internal Affairs Lanskoi, no later than 10 April 1861, *KD-Vor-1*, 37–41.

44. The best source on the Bezdna volnenie is Daniel Field, *Rebels in the Name of the Tsar* (Boston: Houghton Mifflin, 1976), 31–111, which contains both abundant documentary source material and Field's own analysis. Quotations are from Adjutant

General A. S. Apraksin's Second Report to the Tsar, 19 April 1861, in Field, *Rebels in the Name of the Tsar*, 59 (quotation 1); telegram of Governor P. F. Kozlialinov to the Minister of Internal Affairs, 13 April 1861, ibid., 37 (quotation 2); report by Governor Kozlialinov to the Minister of Internal Affairs, 14 April 1861, ibid., 40 (quotation 3); report of Apraksin to Tsar Alexander, 15 April 1861, ibid., 48 (quotation 4); Field's analysis, 34 (quotations 5 and 6). There was dispute about the number of casualties: according to various officials, 51, "up to 60," and "up to 70" peasants were killed (ibid., 47, 39, and 40). For other reports on the Spassk volnenie, see Morokhovets, *Krest'ianskoe dvizhenie v 1861 godu*, 72–75; and (for Minister of Internal Affairs Lanskoi's brief summary account), *Otmena krepostnogo prava*, 21–22.

45. Report of Lieutenant Colonel Khodkevich, staff officer of Corps of Gendarmes in Pskov Province, to V. A. Dolgorukov, 12 July 1861, *KD-5*, 94.

46. Ibid., 94–95.

47. See Kolchin, *Unfree Labor*, 257–313.

48. A. M. Anfimov, "Krest'ianskoe dvizhenie v Rossii vo vtoroi polovine XIX veka," *Voprosy istorii*, 1973, no. 5, 18–19; *KD-5*, 18; Zaionchkovskii, *Otmena krepostnogo prava v Rossii*, 175; Terence Emmons, "The Peasant and Emancipation," in *The Peasant in Nineteenth-Century Russia*, ed. Wayne S. Vucinich (Stanford: Stanford University Press, 1968), 54. For the pre-emancipation-era comparison, see Kolchin, *Unfree Labor*, 322. For smaller figures, based on incomplete Ministry of Internal Affairs statistics, see Lur'e, "Reforma 1861 g. i krest'ianskoe dvizhenie," 71.

49. See *Revoliutsionnaia situatsiia v Rossii v 1859–1861 gg.*, 8 vols., ed. M. V. Nechkina et al. (Moscow: Izdatel'stvo Akademii nauk SSSR, 1960–74); and, for a skeptical analysis, Charles C. Adler Jr., "The 'Revolutionary Situation, 1859–1861': The Uses of an Historical Conception," *Canadian Slavic Studies*, 3 (1969), 383–99; Adler concluded (390) that the "Revolutionary Situation" volumes "do not bear out the thesis of revolutionary causality." (He conceded, however, that they do "provide a vivid and illuminating picture of mid-century Russia" [390]). See, also, Abbott Gleason, "The Great Reforms and Historians Since Stalin," in Eklof et al., *Russia's Great Reforms*, 7–9, 11. For a dissenting suggestion by an American scholar that "the Soviet versions" of events—complete with the "revolutionary situation"—"appear to have more substance than do most Western ones," see the pamphlet by Allan K. Wildman, *The Defining Moment: Land Charters and the Post-Emancipation Agrarian Settlement in Russia, 1861–1863*, Carl Beck Papers in Russian and East European Studies, Number 1205 (Pittsburgh: Center for Russian and East European Studies, University of Pittsburgh, 1996), 2 (quotation).

50. As usual, precise figures vary, but on the basis of the *Krest'ianskoe dvizhenie* compilations, Anfimov concluded that military force was used in 937 of the 1,889 volneniia that occurred in 1861; Anfimov, "Krest'ianskoe dvizhenie v Rossii," 18–19. The less complete Ministry of Internal Affairs figures, which did not cover many of the smaller outbreaks, indicate a much higher proportion of volneniia in 1861 put

down by force: 499 of 784 (63.6 percent); Lur'e, "Reforma 1861 g. i krest'ianskoe dvizhenie," 76. During the period 1801–60, soldiers were used to put down 162 of 1,119 volneniia in seven central industrial provinces, and even during the five-year period 1844–49, which includes the unusually widespread disturbances of 1848, soldiers were needed to restore order on only 125 of 349 estates. See V. A. Fedorov, *Krest'ianskoe dvizhenie v Tsentral'noi Rossii 1800–1860 (Po materialam tsentral'no-promyshlennykh gubernii)* (Moscow: Izdatel'stvo Moskovskogo universiteta, 1980), 46, 48; and Iu. I. Gerasimov, "Krest'ianskoe dvizhenie v Rossii v 1844–1849 gg.," *Istoricheskie zapiski*, 50 (1955), 266. The quotation on whipping is from Dm. Gavrilov to Iakov Aleksandrovich Solov'ev, Vladimir Province, 19 May 1861, in Kuznetsov, ed., "Semdesiat piat' let nazad," 21–22.

51. On limitations of the federal military occupation, see Downs, *After Appomattox*. On the combination of humiliation, despair, and anger felt by former Confederates after the war, see Anne Sarah Rubin, *A Shattered Nation: The Rise and Fall of the Confederacy* (Chapel Hill: University of North Carolina Press, 2005), esp. 145–63. For a sensitive account of the efforts of planters to cope with the loss of their slaves, see Roark, *Masters without Slaves*, 68–155.

52. C. W. Clarke, Lieutenant and Provost Marshal, District of East Mississippi, to Alabama Assistant Commissioner Wager Swayne, 14 July 1865, FBP, Alabama Letters Received; A. E. Kirnn, Superintendent of Freedmen, to O. O. Howard, 13 June 1865, FBP, Assistant Adjutant General's Office, Letters Received; Huntsville *Advocate*, 19 October 1865; C. S. Brown, Lieutenant Colonel Commanding, 3rd Subdistrict of South Carolina, to Brigadier General C. H. Howard, Chief of Staff, Anderson, SC, 23 October 1865, FBP, South Carolina Letters Received; Schurz, *Report on the Condition of the South*, 45–46.

53. Report of the Joint Committee on Reconstruction, H. R. No. 30, 39 Cong., 1 Sess., 1866; *Testimony Taken by the Joint Select Committee to Enquire into the Condition of Affairs in the Late Insurrectionary States*, 10 vols. (Washington, DC: Government Printing Office, 1872). There is an extensive secondary literature on violence in the postemancipation South. See, inter alia, Allen W. Trelease, *White Terror: The Ku Klux Klan Conspiracy and Southern Reconstruction* (New York: Harper and Row, 1971); George C. Rable, *But There Was No Peace: The Role of Violence in the Politics of Reconstruction* (Athens: University of Georgia Press, 1984); Hannah Rosen, *Terror in the Heart of Freedom: Citizenship, Sexual Violence, and the Meaning of Race in the Postemancipation South* (Chapel Hill: University of North Carolina Press, 2009); Douglas R. Egerton, *The Wars of Reconstruction: The Brief, Violent History of America's Most Progressive Era* (New York: Bloomsbury Press, 2014); and, more generally, Foner, *Reconstruction*, passim.

54. Davis Tillson, Special Order 130 (5 September 1865), in report of 22 September 1866, Augusta, Georgia, FBP, Assistant Adjutant General's Office, Letters Received. See, also, Tillson's annual report to Commissioner Howard, Augusta, 1 November 1866, FBP, Assistant Adjutant General's Office, Annual Reports. On Campbell, see

Russell Duncan, *Freedom's Shore: Tunis Campbell and the Georgia Freedmen* (Athens: University of Georgia Press, 1986), 24 (quotation). For the career of Aaron A. Bradley, a similarly militant Black leader in Lowcountry Georgia, see Joseph P. Reidy, "Aaron A. Bradley: Voice of Black Labor in the Georgia Lowcountry," in *Southern Black Leaders of the Reconstruction Era*, ed. Howard N. Rabinowitz (Urbana: University of Illinois Press, 1982), 281–308. On the freedpeople's collective struggle for land in Lowcountry South Carolina immediately following the war, see Saville, *The Work of Reconstruction*, 72–101. On the growth of Black political militance, see my chapter 4.

55. See Peter Kolchin, *First Freedom: The Responses of Alabama's Blacks to Emancipation and Reconstruction* (Westport, CT: Greenwood Press, 1972), 32–33. For similar examples of "insurgency" against overseers, among freedpeople formerly owned by Paul Cameron, both on Cameron's home plantation (Fairntosh) in North Carolina and on his absentee-owned plantation in Alabama, see Sydney Nathans, *A Mind to Stay: White Plantation, Black Homeland* (Cambridge, MA: Harvard University Press, 2017), 93–126.

56. On the largely unchanged worldview of Southern planters in the immediate post-emancipation months, see Roark, *Masters without Slaves*, 94–155.

57. John Floyd King to Lin Caperton, 31 January 1867, quoted in Roark, *Masters without Slaves*, 153–54.

58. On the development of postwar labor relations, see my chapter 5. For the centrality of contract to the thinking of free-labor spokesmen, see especially Stanley, *From Bondage to Contract*. On the struggle over control of Black women's labor in the post-emancipation South, see Thavolia Glymph, *Out of the House of Bondage: The Transformation of the Plantation Household* (New York: Cambridge University Press, 2008), esp. 137–67.

59. For general treatments, see, especially, Hahn, *A Nation under Our Feet*, 128–54, and Hahn, " 'Extravagant Expectations' of Freedom: Rumour, Political Struggle, and the Christmas Insurrection Scare of 1865 in the American South," *Past and Present*, 157 (November 1997), 122–58; Dan T. Carter, "The Anatomy of Fear: The Christmas Day Insurrection Scare of 1865," *Journal of Southern History*, 42 (August 1976), 345–64; and Foner, *Reconstruction*, 153–70, passim.

60. Josiah Gorgas Diary, 30 August 1865; Circular from North Carolina Assistant Commissioner E. Whittlesey, 15 August 1865, U.S. House of Representatives, 39 Cong., 1 Sess., Executive Doc. 70, Serial 1256, 4–5.

61. Sharkey to Howard, 10 October 1865, FBP, Assistant Adjutant General's Office, Letters Received; Ann to Charles E. Bridges, Lumpkin, AL, 7 September 1865, Charles Bridges Papers, Duke University Library; report of Assistant Superintendent Spencer Smith, Tuskegee, AL, 2 December 1865, FBP Alabama Operations Reports; M. D. Sterrett to Governor Parsons, Columbiana, Shelby County, AL, 11 December 1865, Lewis E. Parsons Papers, Alabama State Department of Archives and History; Tillson to Howard, Savannah, GA, 11 December 1865, FBP, Assistant Adjutant General's Office, Letters Received.

62. Saxton to Howard, Charleston, 6 December 1865, FBP, Assistant Adjutant General's Office, Letters Received; Osborn to Howard, Tallahassee, 1 November 1865, FBP, Assistant Adjutant General's Office, Letters Received; Wager Swayne, Freedmen's Bureau Circular No. 1, Montgomery, AL, 7 September 1865, in *Montgomery Daily Advertiser*, 9 September 1865; Gardner, "Facts for Freedmen," *Alabama Beacon*, 24 November 1865.

63. Osborn to Howard, Tallahassee, 1 November 1865, FBP, Assistant Adjutant General's Office, Letters Received; Thomas to Howard, Vicksburg, 14 October 1865, FBP, Assistant Adjutant General's Office, Letters Received; Thomas to Howard, Vicksburg, 1 November 1865, FBP, Assistant Adjutant General's Office, Letters Received; Assistant Inspector General F. Sergent Free to Thomas, Vicksburg, 1 November 1865, FBP, Assistant Adjutant General's Office, Letters Received. But for a report from northern Mississippi that took at face value both African Americans' expectations of land division and the threat of a year-end uprising, see Chaplain Thomas Smith to Captain J. H. Weber, Jackson, MS, 3 November 1865, FBP, Assistant Adjutant General's Office, Letters Received.

64. Schurz to President Johnson, New Orleans, 15 September 1865, Andrew Johnson Papers, Library of Congress; *Clarke County* [Alabama] *Journal*, 9 November 1865; Soule to Howard, Charleston, 8 September 1865, FBP, Assistant Adjutant General's Office, Letters Received.

65. In his quantitative analysis of the FWP narratives, Paul Escott found that 56.8 percent of the 701 interviewees who spoke of their experiences with Union soldiers complained of theft or destruction, and an additional 6.8 percent reported "other mistreatment." Although there is no doubt that Union soldiers engaged in such depredations, given the conditions under which the interviews were conducted Escott's figures must be approached with considerable caution: indeed, it would have taken unusual courage for an elderly Black person to challenge the conventional picture of Yankee villainy that prevailed in the South during the 1930s. See Escott, *Slavery Remembered*, 122–27 (quotation: 124; statistics: 126).

66. Field, *Rebels in the Name of the Tsar*, 1–29, 208–15 (quotations: 214, 209, 211, 209).

67. Hahn, *A Nation under Our Feet*, 57–60, 127–54 (quotations: 137–38, 135, 146, 128, 152). Hahn specifically applied the term "naïve monarchism" (60) to set the slaves' use of rumor in historical context. See also Hahn, " 'Extravagant Expectations' of Freedom."

68. Report of aide-de-camp M. L. Dubel't to Alexander II on Iaroslavl Province, 20 June 1861, Morokhovets, *Kresti'anskoe dvizhenie v 1861 godu*, 258; report of Minister of Internal Affairs Valuev, *Otmena krepostnogo prava*, 1 September 1861, 67; report of aide-de-camp A. A. Essen to Alexander II on Simbirsk Province, 3 June 1861, in Morokhovets, *Krest'ianskoe dvizhenie v 1861 godu*, 220.

69. Brevet Lieutenant Colonel B. F. Smith to H. W. Smith, Georgetown, S.C., 21 January 1866, FBP, South Carolina Letters Received; C. W. Dudley to Chaplain B. F.

Whittemore, Bennettsville, S.C., 22 January 1866, FBP, Assistant Adjutant General's Office, Letters Received; Assistant Commissioner Samuel Thomas to Commissioner Howard, Vicksburg, Mississippi, 31 January 1866, FBP, Assistant Adjutant General's Office, Letters Received; J. B. Moore Diary, 11 March 1866. See also, Kolchin, *First Freedom*, 38.

Chapter 3. The Struggle Continues

1. See Eric Foner, "Thaddeus Stevens, Confiscation, and Reconstruction," in Foner, *Politics and Ideology in the Age of the Civil War* (New York: Oxford University Press, 1980), 128–49. On the Southern Homestead Act, see Michael L. Lanza, *Agrarianism and Reconstruction Politics: The Southern Homestead Act* (Baton Rouge: Louisiana State University Press, 1990), and "'One of the Most Appreciated Labors of the Bureau': The Freedmen's Bureau and the Southern Homestead Act," in *The Freedmen's Bureau and Reconstruction: Reconsiderations*, ed. Paul A. Cimbala and Randall M. Miller (New York: Fordham University Press, 1999), 67–92; and Claude F. Oubre, *Forty Acres and a Mule: The Freedmen's Bureau and Black Landownership* (Baton Rouge: Louisiana State University Press, 1978).

2. See my chapters 1 and 2, above, and sources cited in chapter 1, notes 43 and 54, and in chapter 2, notes 12, 13, 17, 18, and 19. Although the term "mirovoi posrednik" is usually translated as "peace mediator" or "peace arbitrator," it also carried the connotation of "*community* mediator" (since the village commune was informally known as the "mir"). For recognition of the dual meaning of "mirovoi posrednik," see Roxanne Easley, *The Emancipation of the Serfs in Russia: Peace Arbitrators and the Development of Civil Society* (London: Routledge, 2009), 45.

3. For overviews, see N. F. Ust'iantseva, "Institut mirovykh posrednikov v otsentke sovremennikov (Po materialam gazety 'Mirovoi posrednik')," *Vestnik Moskovskogo universiteta*, ser. 8, Istoria (1984, no. 1), 64–75, and "Accountable Only to God and the Senate: Peace Mediators and the Great Reforms," in *Russia's Great Reforms, 1855–1881*, ed. Ben Eklof, John Bushnell, and Larissa Zakharava (Bloomington: Indiana University Press, 1994), 161–80; Jerman W. Rose, "The Russian Peasant Emancipation and the Problem of Rural Administration: The Institution of the *Mirovoi Posrednik*" (Ph.D. diss., University of Kansas, 1976); Easley, *Emancipation of the Serfs in Russia*, revised from her Ph.D. dissertation, "'The Friends of Our Enemies': The Institution of *Mirovoi Posrednik* in the Russian Emancipation of 1861" (Ph.D. diss., University of Oregon, 1997); William S. McFeely, *Yankee Stepfather: General O. O. Howard and the Freedmen* (New Haven: Yale University Press, 1968); and Cimbala and Miller, *The Freedmen's Bureau and Reconstruction*. For the general argument that the Union military was spread too thin throughout the Reconstruction South, see Gregory P. Downs, *After Appomattox: Military Occupation and the Ends of War* (Cambridge, MA: Harvard University Press, 2015).

4. The quotation is from Rose, "The Russian Peasant Emancipation and the Problem of Rural Administration," 111.

5. Quotations are from Ust'iantseva, "Accountable Only to God and the Senate," 172–73; and Barry A. Crouch, *The Freedmen's Bureau and Black Texans* (Austin: University of Texas Press, 1992), 128, ix. On the evolving historiography of the Freedmen's Bureau, see Peter Kolchin, "Slavery and Freedom in the Civil War South," in *Writing the Civil War: The Quest to Understand*, ed. James McPherson and William J. Cooper (Columbia: University of South Carolina Press, 1998), 251–53. The Freedmen's Bureau was succeeded by an agency known as the Freedmen's Branch (1872–79) that historians have largely ignored. Indeed, historian Dale Kretz has observed that "there currently exists no scholarly treatment of the Freedmen's Branch," a watered-down federal agency focused on "as-yet-unpaid claims for bounties owed to Black veterans and their heirs." See Dale Kretz, *Administering Freedom: The State of Emancipation after the Freedmen's Bureau* (Chapel Hill: University of North Carolina Press, 2022), 58–99 and 321–29 (Freedmen's Branch), quotations: 321 and 58.

For an important (and I think largely persuasive) exception to the prevalent trend toward taking the disinterested character of the peace mediators at face value, see Allan K. Wildman, *The Defining Moment: Land Charters and the Post-Emancipation Agrarian Settlement in Russia, 1861–1863*, Carl Beck Papers in Russian and East European Studies Number 1205 (Pittsburgh: Center for Russian and East European Studies, University of Pittsburgh, 1996), esp. 34–36, 56.

6. Report of Jno. C. Moore, Fayette Co., Alabama, 25 August 1867, FBP, Alabama Monthly Operations Reports; A. Geddis to Alabama Commissioner Wager Swayne, Tuskegee, Alabama, 7 September 1865, FBP, Alabama Operations Reports; Captain C. B. Wilder to Lieutenant J. W. Hayes, Fort Monroe, Virginia, 15 September 1865, FBP, Assistant Adjutant General's Office, Letters Received; Circular from Davis Tillson, 3 October 1865, U.S. House of Representatives, 39 Cong., 1 Sess., Exec. Doc. 70, Ser. 1256, 59. On Langston, see William Francis Cheek and Aimee Lee, *John Mercer Langston and the Fight for Black Freedom, 1829–65* (Urbana: University of Illinois Press, 1989).

7. Quotations are from Easley, *Emancipation of the Serfs in Russia*, 83; N. M. Druzhinin, *Russkaia derevnia na perelome: 1861–1880 gg.* (Moscow: Izdatel'stvo "Nauka," 1978), 33–34; and the report of Nikolai Obolenskii, peace mediator of Luzhskii district, St. Petersburg Province, to Vice-Governor E. K. Chopskii, in *Krest'ianskoe dvizhenie v Rossii v 1861–1869 gg.: Sbornik dokumentov*, ed. L. M. Ivanov (Moscow: Izdatel'stvo sotsial'no-ekonomicheskoi literatury, 1964), 433–34 (hereafter cited as *KD-5*). See, also, Ust'iantseva, "Accountable Only to God and the Senate," 170–77; Rose, "The Russian Peasant Emancipation and the Problem of Rural Administration," 2, 96–97, 135–77; A. P. Korelin, *Dvorianstvo v poreformennoi Rossii 1861–1904 gg.: Sostav, chislennost,' korporativnaia organizatsia* (Moscow: Izdatel'stvo "Nauka," 1979), 180–91; James I. Mandel, "Paternalistic Authority in the Russian Countryside, 1856–1906" (Ph. D. diss., Columbia University, 1978), 75–86. For the argument that the "rancorous

criticism" by pomeshchiki of mediators is "indirect but telling evidence of their probity and efficiency," see Daniel Field, "The Year of Jubilee," in Eklof et al., *Russia's Great Reforms, 1855–1861*, 43–44; but for the opposite conclusion, that "the presence of mediators well-disposed toward peasants is not at all registered in the materials I examined, but I did find many examples of the opposite kind," see Wildman, *The Defining Moment*, 56 (note 28).

8. Fullerton to Howard, telegram, New Orleans, 2 November 1865, FBP, Assistant Adjutant General's Office, Letters Received; U.S. Bureau of Refugees, Freedmen, and Abandoned Lands, *Report of the Administration of Freedmen's Affairs in Louisiana by J. S. Fullerton*, 2 December 1865, 1–2, 13; "Report of James B. Steedman and J. S. Fullerton on Freedmen's Bureau Affairs in Virginia and North Carolina," 8 May 1866, U.S. House of Representatives, 39 Cong., 1 Sess., Ser. 1263, Exec. Doc. 120, 63–72. On a similar power struggle in Georgia, see Cimbala, *Under the Guardianship of the Nation*, 28–42.

9. Easley, *Emancipation of the Serfs in Russia*, 137, 137–38, 133–37 (quotation: 136); Terence Emmons, *The Russia Landed Gentry and the Peasant Emancipation of 1861* (Cambridge: Cambridge University Press, 1968), 344–46; report of Minister of Internal Affairs Petr Valuev, 1 Sepember 1861, *Otmena krepostnogo prava: Doklady Ministrov vnutrennikh del o provedenii krest'ianskoi reformy 1861–1862* (Moscow: Izdatel'stvo Akademii nauk SSSR, 1950), 67. On reports of mediators abusing peasants by "striking them in the face, pulling their beards . . ., and personally flogging them," see Easley, *Emancipation of the Serfs in Russia*, 99.

10. Howard to Charles Nordhoff, Assistant Editor of the New York *Evening Post*, Washington, DC, 19 March 1866, FBP, Assistant Adjutant General's Office, Letters Sent.

11. On Yazykov's cousin, I am indebted to my former graduate student Sally Stocksdale, who wrote a Ph.D. dissertation comparing emancipation on a Russian estate (Yazykovo Selo, in Simbirsk Province) and an American plantation (Palmyra, in Mississippi), recently published as a book; see Sally Stocksdale, *When Emancipation Came: The End of Enslavement on a Southern Plantation and a Russian Estate* (Jefferson, NC: McFarland, 2022). On the Tula Province pomeshchik/peace mediator, see the report of Tula Province Governor P. M. Daragan to Minister of Internal Affairs Valuev, 30 September 1861, *KD-5*, 108–09. It is hard to avoid the conclusion that the current emphasis among Russian historians on the fair-mindedness of the peace mediators is at least in part a reaction against prevalent earlier—Soviet—depictions of them as conscious agents of class oppression; see, for example, Ust'iantseva, "Accountable Only to God and the Senate," 172–73. For emphasis on the mediators' close ties to the local nobility in Saratov and Orel Provinces, see Wildman, *The Defining Moment*. On the Freedmen's Bureau as an "in between" force "representing the northern free labor ideology itself," see Eric Foner, "Reconstruction and the Crisis of Free Labor," in his *Politics and Ideology in the Age of the Civil War*, 97–127 (quotation: 101).

12. Wildman, *The Defining Moment*.

13. On the legislative provisions surrounding the charters, see my chapter 1, above. If peasants refused to accept a charter, the peace mediator would hear and record their objections, in some cases also consulting with the provincial committee on peasant affairs and/or the other mediators in the district, before proceeding to affirm the charter; see L. P. Gorlanov, "Akty i protokoly mirovykh posrednikov kak istochnik po istorii realizatsii reformy 1861 g. (Po materialam Kostromskoi gubernii)," *Istoriia SSSR*, 1972, no. 2, 118–19.

14. See *Padenie krepostnogo prava v Rossii: Dokumenty i materialy*, vol. 2: *"Polozheniia 19 fevralia 1861 goda" i Russkoe obshchestvo*, ed. V. A. Fedorov (Moscow: Izdatel'stvo Moskovskogo universiteta, 1967), 44–55. For examples of charters, see *Agrarnoi vopros v Rossii (ot reformy do revoliutsii) (1861–1917): Materialy i kommentarii*, ed I. V. Chernyshev (Kursk: Izdatel'stvo "Sovetskaia derevnia," 1927), 51–76; *Le Statut des paysans libérés du servage, 1861–1961*, ed. R. Portal (Paris: Mouton, 1963), 251; and *Krest'ianskoe dvizhenie v Voronezhskom gubernii (1861–1863 gg.): Dokumenty i materialy* (Voronezh: Izdatel'stvo Voronezhskogo universiteta, 1961) (hereafter cited as *KD-Voronezh-1*), 117–19.

15. Statutory charter dated 25 October 1862, *KD-Voronezh-1*, 117–19. One desiatina is equal to 2.7 acres; it is also the equivalent of 2,400 square sazheni. There appears to be a small error in this charter—or in its recording—since in fact 5,229 rubles amounts to nine rubles (not ten) per soul (5,299 ÷ 581 = 9).

16. Doc. # 3, 10 July 1862, Chernyshev, *Agrarnoi vopros v Rossii*, 58–62.

17. For more on how the charters affected the actual condition of peasants, see my chapter 5. The statutory charters did not cover all peasants: exceptions included house servants (dvorovye), who were covered by a separate provision of the emancipation legislation and did not receive allotment land, and peasants living on very small estates, with fewer than twenty souls, whose status was defined by special "inventories."

18. See, inter alia, P. A. Zaionchkovskii, *Otmena krepostnogo prava v Rossii*, 3rd ed. (Moscow: Proshveshchenie, 1968), 193–213; Gorlanov, "Akty i protokoly mirovykh posrednikov," 118–25; Field, "The Year of Jubilee," 45–49; and Wildman, *The Defining Moment*, passim. For a summary statement of the peasants' stubborn expectation of a new *volia*, see the report on activities of the Third Department (political police) for 1862, in E. A. Morokhovets, ed., *Kres'tianskoe dvizhenie 1827–1869 godov*, 2 vols. (Moscow: Gosudarstvennoe sotsial'no-ekonomicheskoe izdatel'stvo, 1931), II, 25.

19. Reports of 19 October 1861, 21 December 1861, 3 January 1862, 1 February 1862, 7 March 1862, and 4 July 1862, in *Otmena krepostnogo prava: Doklady ministrov vnutrennikh del*, 76, 91, 96, 105, 119, 189–90, 193. For Alexander's speech, see Fedorov, *Padenia krepostnogo prava v Rossii*, II, 83–84.

20. *National Freedman*, I (1 April 1865), 99 (Frazier quotation); A. J. Willard, Lieutenant Colonel Commanding 4th Sub-District, Georgetown, SC, 7 November 1865, to Captain George W. Hooker, Assistant Adjutant General, FBP, South Carolina Letters Received.

21. Assistant Commissioner Davis Tillson to Howard, Augusta, Georgia, 1 November 1866, FBP, Assistant Adjutant General's Office, Letters Received.

22. F. D. Sewell, Assistant Inspector General, to S. C. Armstrong, 5th District Virginia Superintendent, Washington DC, 15 February 1867, FBP, Assistant Adjutant General's Office, Letters Sent; Sewell to Howard, Washington DC, 20 February 1867, FBP, Assistant Adjutant General's Office, Letters Received; Howard to "Colored People on Taylor Farm," Washington DC, 10 August 1869, FBP, Assistant Adjutant General's Office, Letters Sent; Howard to Major General Canby, Commander, 1st Military District, Washington DC, 10 August 1869, FBP, Assistant Adjutant General's Office, Letters Sent.

23. "Autauga Citizen," in *Montgomery Advertiser*, 6 January 1867; *Greensboro* [Alabama] *Beacon*, 24 August 1867; *Elmore* [Alabama] *Standard*, 16 August 1867; report of Assistant Superintendent E. W. Busby, Northumberland County, Virginia, 28 March 1866, FBP, Assistant Adjutant General's Office, Letters Received.

24. For an overview of the Southern Homestead Act and its limitations, see especially Lanza, *Agrarianism and Reconstruction Politics;* on Black landownership in general, see Oubre, *Forty Acres and a Mule;* and Loren Schweninger, *Black Property Owners in the South, 1790–1915* (Urbana: University of Illinois Press, 1990), 146–226.

25. M. G. Stearns, Sub-Assistant Commissioner, to Charles Mundee, Assistant Adjutant General, Quincy, Florida, 31 August 1866, FBP, Assistant Adjutant General's Office, Letters Received; Assistant Commissioner J. G. Foster to Howard, Tallahassee, October 1866, FBP, Assistant Adjutant General's Office, Annual Reports; Assistant Commissioner John A. Sprague to Howard, Tallahassee, 31 December 1866, FBP, Assistant Adjutant General's Office, Letters Received; General Ralph Ely, Civil Agent for Emigration, to Brevet Major General E. E. Woodruff, Charleston, 3 January 1867, Assistant Adjutant General's Office, Letters Received. Statistics are from Joe M. Richardson, "An Evaluation of the Freedmen's Bureau in Florida," *Florida Historical Quarterly*, 41 (1963), 231. The estimate of homesteaders constituting roughly one-fifth of Florida's Black families is based on a Black population for the state of 77,183 (the average of census figures for 1860 and 1870) and an assumption of five persons per family.

26. Report of Assistant Superintendent William H. H. Peck, Tuscaloosa, 20 October 1866, FBP, Alabama Monthly Operations Reports; Alabama *State Sentinel*, 10 June 1867 (statistic on claims in northern Alabama); reports of Sub-Assistant Commissioner James Gillette, Mobile, 21 May 1868, FBP, Alabama Operations Reports, and 29 May 1868, FBP, Assistant Adjutant General's Office, Letters Received. See Peter Kolchin, *First Freedom: The Responses of Alabama's Blacks to Emancipation and Reconstruction* (Westport, CT: Greenwood Press, 1972), esp. 134–35.

27. J. H. Bull, Special Clerk to Assistant Commissioner Foster, "Preliminary Report of Public Lands," Tallahassee, 27 October 1866, FBP, Assistant Adjutant General's Office, Annual Reports; W. J. Purman, Special Agent, to Acting Assistant Adjutant General Woodruff, New Smyrna, Florida, 20 March 1867, FBP, Assistant Adjutant General's Office, Letters Received; F. D. Sewell to Howard, Washington

D.C., 11 May 1868, FBP, Assistant Adjutant General's Office, Letters Received; F. D. Sewell to Ely, Washington D.C., 20 March 1867, FBP, Assistant Adjutant General's Office, Letters Sent; J. E. Quentin to Congressman Robert C. Schenck, Madison, Florida, 23 July 1867, FBP, Assistant Adjutant General's Office, Letters Received.

28. Assistant Commissioner John Sprague to Howard, Jacksonville, 30 July 1868, FBP, Assistant Adjutant General's Office, Letters Received; Richardson, "An Evaluation of the Freedmen's Bureau in Florida," 231. In 1870, 16,161 out of a total of 503,595 rural Black families (3.2 percent) in the Deep South and 14,937 out of 308,900 (4.8 percent) in the Upper South owned land; see Schweninger, *Black Property Owners in the South*, 146, 153.

29. Amy Dru Stanley, *From Bondage to Contract: Wage Labor, Marriage, and the Market in the Age of Slave Emancipation* (Cambridge: Cambridge University Press, 1998), ix–x.

30. Osborn Circular, 15 November 1865, U.S. Congress, 39. Cong., 1 Sess., House Exec. Doc. 70 (Serial 1256), 86–87; Register of Contracts, vol. 101, FBP, Arkansas Book Records; Davis Tillson Circular, 3 October 1865, U.S. House of Representatives, 39 Cong., 1 Sess., Exec. Doc. 70, Ser. 1256, 59; Captain J. W. Cogswell to Alabama Assistant Commissioner Wager Swayne, Columbia, 25 September 1865, FBP, Alabama Letters Received; Wager Swayne to Howard, 4 September 1865, FBP, Alabama Weekly Reports; Sub-Assistant Commissioner J. E. Quentin to Assistant Commissioner Osborne, Madison, Florida, 1 May 1866, FBP, Assistant Adjutant General's Office, Letters Received; report of Assistant Superintendent William H. H. Peck, Tuscaloosa, 20 October 1866, FBP, Alabama Monthly Operations Reports.

31. Lieutenant Colonel A. J. Willard to Captain George W. Hooker, Assistant Adjutant General, Georgetown, South Carolina, 7 November 1865, FBP, South Carolina Letters Received; Sub-Assistant Commissioner J. E. Quentin to Brigadier General Charles Monden [sp.?], Assistant Adjutant General, Madison, Florida, 1 August 1866, FBP, Assistant Adjutant General's Office, Letters Received; Assistant Commissioner J. G. Foster to Howard, Tallahassee, 8 October 1866, FBP, Assistant Adjutant General's Office, Letters Received.

32. Report of Orenburg Province Governor G. S. Aksakov to Valuev, 13 March 1862, *KD-5*, 204–5. (See my chapter 1, above.) On *volia* as a peasant ideal and expectation, which to many non-peasants implied "complete anarchy and idleness," see Daniel Field, *Rebels in the Name of the Tsar* (Boston: Houghton Mifflin, 1976) esp. 31–32 (quotation: 32).

33. According to figures compiled by the Ministry of Internal Affairs, peasants presented at least 1,622 collective petitions from July 1861 through 1863: see statistics in *KD-5*, editor's introduction, 21.

34. Petition from peasant representative Stepan Ivanov Malyshev, Poliany village, Varnavinskii district, Kostroma Province, to Tsar Alexander II, no later than July 1862, *KD-5*, 178–81 and 559 (note 109). The petition was eventually forwarded to the governor, who in a report upheld the actions of the pomeshchik and authorities.

35. Report of Kostroma Province Governor N. A. Rudzevich to Valuev, 13 September 1862, *KD-5*, 187. Malyshev and Zametaev had in fact presented a second petition to the tsar complaining of mistreatment by various officials as well as the seventy-five soldiers stationed in Poliany. Noting that "we have come to complete ruin and have no one from whom to receive help and defense" except the emperor himself, they begged him to abolish their burdensome obrok, protect them from abuse at the hands of local officials, and "allot us land according to the legal Polozhenie and prohibit any further torture of us." Petition by S. I. Malyshev and P. A. Zametov to Alexander II, 21 August 1862, *KD-5*, 185–86.

36. Rudzevich to Valuev, 13 September 1862, *KD-5*, 188–89.

37. Petition of peasants of Podosinovka village, Novokhoperskii district, Voronezh Province (signed by Andrei Devakov and Vasilii Dereviankin) to Alexander II, May 1863, *KD-Voronezh-1*, 110–11.

38. Report of Voronezh Governor M. I. Chertkov to Valuev, 6 August 1862, *KD-5*, 134–37.

39. Report of Podolia Province Governor R. I. Braunshveig to Valuev, 16 April 1863, *KD-5*, 314; *KD-Voronezh-1*, 111. On the mixed relations of peasants and priests under serfdom, see Kolchin, *Unfree Labor*, 223–27.

40. Report of Tula Province Governor P. M. Daragan to Valuev, 30 September 1861, *KD-5*, 108–09; petition of peasant representative S. I. Ziukin to Alexander II on behalf of peasants of Begoshcha, Putivl'skii district, Kursk Province, no later than 31 August 1864, *KD-5*, 351–54. The Ministry of Internal Affairs noted that Ziukin's complaint was "totally inappropriate." On the lengthy volnenie of the Begoshcha peasants, see also the report of Kursk Province Governor P. A. Izvol'skii to Valuev, 7 May 1864, *KD-5*, 349–51.

41. Wildman, *The Defining Moment*, 18, 20, 27–32, 47. Partial statistics on volneniia indicate 1,889 in 1861 (with greatest intensity April–June), 844 in 1862, and 509 in 1863; by contrast, the average number of outbreaks per year between 1796 and 1855 was 37.7. Especially noteworthy is the surge in the number of peasant petitions reported by the Ministry of Internal Affairs, from 118 in the second half of 1861 to 1,247 in 1862. See statistics in the editor's introduction to *KD-5*, 18, 21, and in my chapter 2, above.

42. See Minister of Internal Affairs Valuev's reports of 11 August 1861, 1 September 1861, 2 May 1862, 4 July 1862, 1 November 1862, and 3 January 1863, *Otmena krepostnogo prava*, 58–59, 67 (quotation), 145, 186, 251, 282. On the peace mediators in Voronezh Province, see the report of Ivan Lasanevich, chairman of the Bogucharskii district conference of peace mediators, to the governor of Voronezh Province, 11 May 1862, *KD-Voronezh-1*, 63 (quotation).

43. Report of 3 January 1863, *Otmena krepostnogo prava*, 282–87. The rate of charter implementation was especially low in the western provinces, where revolutionary unrest in Poland loomed large, and to a lesser extent in the remote southeastern bor-

der region, where policies enunciated in St. Petersburg could be hard to enforce: in Minsk Province, for example, only 15.72 percent of peasants were covered by charters that had been implemented, and in Stavropol' Province the figure was 40.46 percent. The proportion of peasants signing charters also was typically low in these provinces.

44. See my chapter 2, above, and that chapter's note 48. Ministry of Internal Affairs statistics also showed a dramatic plunge of the number of peasant petitions, which had flooded government offices in reaction to the statutory charters, from 1,247 in 1862 to 257 in 1863. Statistics are from *KD-5*, 18 and 21; see also N. M. Druzhinin and V. A. Fedorov, "Krest'ianskoe dvizhenie v Rossii v XIX veke," *Istoriia SSSR*, 1977, no. 4, 118–21. For an indication of the very partial nature of the *Krest'ianskoe dvizhenie* statistics, consider that although those statistics count 3,817 volneniia for the years 1861–69 in all of Russia, local archives reveal almost as many—3,092—during those years in the nine Ukrainian provinces alone; see A. M. Anfimov, "Krest'ianskoe dvizhenie v Rossii vo vtoroi polovine XIX veka," *Voprosy istorii*, 1973, no. 5, 20.

45. Report of Poltava Province Governor A. P. Volkov to Valuev, 12 April 1863, *KD-5*, 323–25; report of Major Vill', head of the Mozyrskii district (Volhynia Province) gendarme administration to Manager of the Third Department N. V. Mezentsov, 9 October 1864, *KD-5*, 337–38; report of staff officer Colonel Zholobov, of Volhynia Province Corps of Gendarmes, 14 November 1864, *KD-5*, 338–39.

46. Contract, 26 June 1865, Henry Watson Papers; Huntsville *Advocate*, 19 October 1865; "Agreement between Bill Gourdin & the freed men and women on his Plantation," February 1867, Gourdin-Gaillard Family Papers, 1795–1886, Charleston and Georgetown Districts, South Carolina, in Stampp, "Records of Ante-Bellum Southern Plantations from the Revolution through the Civil War," microfilm Series B, reel 7.

47. Sub-Assistant Commissioner J. E. Quentin to Assistant Commissioner Foster, Madison, Florida, 1 October 1866, FBP, Assistant Adjutant General's Office, Letters Received.

48. South Carolina Sub-Assistant Commissioner G. P. M. Dougall to Acting Assistant Adjutant General E. R. Chase, Anderson, South Carolina, 31 October 1866, FBP, South Carolina Letters Received; Mississippi Assistant Commissioner Alvan C. Gillem to Howard, Vicksburg, 10 October 1867 (describing conditions in late 1866), FBP, Assistant Adjutant General's Office, Annual Reports; report of Assistant Superintendent William H. H. Peck, Tuscaloosa, Alabama, 10 October 1866, FBP, Alabama Monthly Operations Reports; Virginia Assistant Commissioner O. Brown to Howard, Richmond, 4 December 1867, FBP, Assistant Adjutant General's Office, Letters Received; Burnit [Bernard] Houston to George S. Houston, Athens, Alabama, 3 August 1867, George S. Houston Papers, Duke University Library; Mississippi Assistant Commissioner Gillem to Howard, Vicksburg, 5 August 1867, FBP, Assistant Adjutant General's Office, Letters Received. On the struggle between the two Houstons, see also Sub-Assistant Commissioner Jno. B. Callis to Agent J. Danforth, Huntsville, 31 July

1867, Houston Papers, and George S. Houston to Assistant Commissioner Wager Swayne, Athens, 16 September 1867, Houston Papers.

49. Frances Butler letter from late 1868, quoted in Frances Butler Leigh, *Ten Years on a Georgia Plantation Since the War* (London: Richard Bentley and Son, 1883), 128; Selma *Daily Messenger*, 18 December 1867; John Parrish to Henry Watson, Greensboro, Alabama, 19 December 1867, Watson Papers; South Carolina Assistant Commissioner R. K. Scott (quoting a sub-assistant commissioner) to Howard, Charleston, 23 January 1867, FBP, Assistant Adjutant General's Office, Letters Received; Assistant Superintendent J. W. Sharpe to Virginia Assistant Commissioner Brown, Lexington, Virginia, 31 December 1866, FBP, Assistant Adjutant General's Office, Letters Received; *Greensboro [Alabama] Beacon*, 12 January 1867; John Parrish to Henry Watson, Greensboro, Alabama, 19 December 1867, Watson Papers. On belief in the coming extinction of African Americans and on efforts to find replacements in European immigrants, see my chapters 5 and 7. For a fine study of Southern planters' evolving views of free Black labor, see James L. Roark, *Masters without Slaves: Southern Planters in the Civil War and Reconstruction* (New York: W. W. Norton, 1977), chaps. 4 and 5.

50. Assistant Commissioner Alvan C. Gillem to Howard, Vicksburg, 10 April 1867, FBP, Assistant Adjutant General's Office, Letters Received; Gillem to Howard, Vicksburg, 31 March 1868, FBP, Assistant Adjutant General's Office, Letters Received.

51. B. H. True to Howard, Madison (Morgan County), Georgia, 22 February 1868, FBP, Assistant Adjutant General's Office, Letters Received; James Mallory Diary, 5 June 1868.

52. Assistant Commissioner Sprague to Howard, Tallahassee, 31 March 1867, FBP, Assistant Adjutant General's Office, Letters Received; Sprague to Howard, Jacksonville, 31 March 1868 and 30 April 1868, FBP, Assistant Adjutant General's Office, Letters Received; Georgia Assistant Commissioner C. C. Sibley to Howard, Macon, 23 May 1867 and Atlanta, 11 June 1868, FBP, Assistant Adjutant General's Office, Letters Received; Assistant Commissioner O. Brown to Howard, Richmond, 28 May 1867, FBP, Assistant Adjutant General's Office, Letters Received; letter from "F.M.G.," *Daily Selma Messenger*, 9 May 1867, and *Montgomery Weekly Advertiser*, 14 May 1867; report of Sub-Assistant Commissioner C. W. Pierce, Demopolis (Greene County) Alabama, 11 June 1867, FBP, Alabama Operations Reports; (Alabama) *Independent Monitor*, 16 June 1868; George Hagin to Watson, Greene County, 5 June 1868, Watson Papers; (Alabama) *State Sentinel*, 8 April 1868.

53. Louisiana Assistant Commissioner J. A. Mower to Acting Assistant Adjutant General F. D. Sewell, New Orleans, 31 July 1867, FBP, Assistant Adjutant General's Office, Letters Received; Mower to Colonel E. Whittlesey, New Orleans, 30 September 1867, FBP, Assistant Adjutant General's Office, Annual Reports; South Carolina Assistant Commissioner R. K. Scott to Howard, Charleston, 1 October 1867, FBP, Assistant Adjutant General's Office, Annual Reports.

54. Florida Sub-Assistant Commissioner M. L. Stearns to Acting Assistant Adjutant General Woodruff, Quincy, Florida, 31 December 1866, FBP, Assistant Adjutant General's Office, Letters Received; Bernard Houston to George S. Houston, Athens, Alabama, 3 August 1867, George S. Houston papers. For a bureau agent who challenged the conventional wisdom and suggested that "those who have worked for a portion of the Crop will . . . realize more at the end of the year, than those who have worked for wages," see Florida Assistant Commissioner J. G. Foster to Howard, Tallahassee, October 1866, FBP, Annual Reports of Assistant Commissioners. On garden plots and the "internal economy" under slavery, see, inter alia, Dylan C. Penningroth, *The Claims of Kinfolk: African American Property and Community in the Nineteenth-Century South* (Chapel Hill: University of North Carolina Press, 2003), 45–109.

55. Mississippi Assistant Commissioner Alvan C. Gillem to Howard, Vicksburg, 20 January 1867, FBP, Assistant Adjutant General's Office, Letters Received, reporting on the observation of the sub-assistant commissioner in Jackson County; South Carolina Assistant Commissioner Scott to Howard, Charleston, 1 October 1867, FBP, Assistant Adjutant General's Office, Annual Reports; James Mallory Diary, 30 December 1867, Southern Historical Collection, University of North Carolina.

56. Mississippi Assistant Commissioner Alvan C. Gillem to Howard, Vicksburg, 15 June 1867, FBP, Assistant Adjutant General's Office, Letters Received; Virginia Assistant Commissioner O. Brown to Howard, Richmond, 28 May 1867, FBP, Assistant Adjutant General's Office, Letters Received.

57. Reports of Sub-Assistant Commissioners Jacob R. Remby, Ocala, Florida, 28 February 1867, and J. H. Durkee, Gainesville, 5 February 1867, FBP, Assistant Adjutant General's Office, Letters Received; Assistant Commissioner Gillem to Howard, Vicksburg, Mississippi, 31 March 1868, FBP, Assistant Adjutant General's Office, Letters Received; report of Sub-Assistant Commissioner William E. Connelly, Eufaula, Alabama, 1 August 1867, FBP, Alabama Operations Reports; *Montgomery Advertiser*, 14 May 1867. On the distinction between "share wages" and "share cropping," see Roger L. Ransom and Richard Sutch, *One Kind of Freedom: The Economic Consequences of Emancipation* (Cambridge: Cambridge University Press, 1977), esp. 66–105. See my chapter 5.

58. *West Alabamian*, 12 June 1867.

59. Captain Henry Seton, Officer of Board for Making Contracts, to Colonel B. F. Smith, Georgetown, South Carolina, 21 January 1866, FBP, South Carolina Letters Received; B. F. Smith to H. W. Smith, Georgetown, 21 January 1866, FBP, South Carolina Letters Received; Mobile *Advertiser and Register,* 22 June 1866 (quoting the *Montgomery Advertiser*). Unions and strikes were more common in cities than in the countryside; see, e.g., the *Montgomery Advertiser,* 12 March 1867, on the formation of "an association of Freedmen" in Selma, "whose principal object is to enforce the pay of $20 'and found' by employers."

60. *Montgomery Advertiser,* 31 October 1867; Leigh, *Ten Years on a Georgia Plantation,* 128 (quoting her 1868 letter), and 204–7. On her experiment with British laborers, see my chapter 5.

61. *Greensboro* [Alabama]] *Beacon,* 7 December 1867; letter of forty-one Blacks to Assistant Commissioner Wager Swayne, Tuscumbia, 17 June 1867, FBP, Alabama Letters Received. See also the petition to Howard of Edward Farrington and other African Americans, complaining: "Many of our sisters and brothers" in Holly Springs, Mississippi, "as well as children of our deceased sisters and brothers, are held in bondage by their former owners, who do not treat them well, are not giving them any education, [and] look upon them as born for Slavery"; Farrington and other to Howard, Holly Springs, 18 November 1867, FBP, Assistant Adjutant General's Office, Letters Received.

62. For elaboration on this contrast, see my Introduction, above, and Kolchin, *Unfree Labor.*

Chapter 4. The Politics of Freedom

1. See Peter Kolchin, *Unfree Labor: American Slavery and Russian Serfdom* (Cambridge, MA: Harvard University Press, 1987), esp. pt. II.

2. *Padenie krepostnogo prava v Rossii: Dokumenty i materialy,* vol. II: *"Polozheniia 19 fevralia 1861 goda" i Russkoe obshchestvo,* ed. V. A. Fedorov (Moscow: Izdatel'stvo Moskovskogo universiteta, 1967), 16–17 (quotation: 16). Since one versta = 1.067 kilometers, twelve versty was the equivalent of about 12.8 kilometers. For the full text of the new legislation on peasant self-government, see *Polnoe sobranie zakonov Rossiiskoi Imperii,* 2nd ser., 55 vols. (St. Petersburg: Gosudarstvennaia tipografiia, 1830–84), XXXVI (1861), # 36,657, pp. 141–69.

3. Fedorov, *Padenie krepostnogo prava v Rossii,* 17–20 (quotation: 20). Above the peasant police were non-peasant (noble) police officials: each provincial district had one *ispravnik* (police chief), aided by several *stanovye pristavy* (captains); see Stephen P. Frank, *Crime, Cultural Conflict, and Justice in Rural Russia, 1856–1914* (Berkeley: University of California Press, 1999), 30–36.

4. Fedorov, *Padenie krepostnogo prava v Rossii,* 21–25 (quotation: 23). On the new peasant courts, see Peter Czap Jr., "Peasant Class Courts and Peasant Customary Justice in Russia, 1861–1912," *Journal of Social History,* 1 (Winter 1967), 149–78; Frank, *Crime, Cultural Conflict, and Justice in Rural Russia,* 36–50; and P. N. Zyrianov, "Sotsial'naia struktura mestnogo upravleniia kapitalisticheskoi Rossii (1861–1914 gg.)," *Istoricheskie zapiski,* no. 107 (Moscow: Izdatel'stvo "Nauka," 1982), 256–61. For a study that focuses on a later period, see Jane Burbank, *Russian Peasants Go to Court: Legal Culture in the Countryside, 1905–1917* (Bloomington: Indiana University Press, 2004).

5. For emphasis on this element of continuity, see Boris Mironov, "The Russian Peasant Commune after the Reforms of the 1860s" (trans. from Russian by Gregory

L. Freeze), *Slavic Review,* 44 (Fall 1985), 438–67; L. V. Kuchumova, "Sel'skaia pozemel'naia obshchina evropeiskoi Rossii v 60-70-e gody XIX v.," *Istoricheskie zapiski,* no. 106 (Moscow: Izdatel'stvo "Nauka," 1981), 323–47; and Zyrianov, "Sotsial'naia struktura mestnogo upravleniia kapitalisticheskoi Rossii," esp. 236–46. According to Mironov, "The Russian Peasant Commune" (446–47), about 19 percent of starosty were literate in the 1880s. See, also, Boris Mironov with Ben Eklof, *A Social History of Imperial Russia, 1700–1917,* 2 vols. (Boulder, CO: Westview Press, 2000), I, 286–370 (quotation: 309). Mironov has calculated that in 1880, starosty served an average of 2.4 years; ibid., 332.

6. G. A. Kavtaradze, "K istorii krest'ianskogo samososnaniia perioda reformy 1861 g.," *Vestnik Leningradskogo universiteta,* 1969, no. 14, 54–64 (quotation: 63). On the peasants' goal of "the complete separation of their community from the landlord . . . and hence the *obshchina* closing in on itself," see, also, Franco Venturi, *Roots of Revolution: A History of the Populist and Socialist Movements in Nineteenth Century Russia* (New York: Alfred A. Knopf, 1964), 218. On the enormous gulf between "narod" and "obshchestvo"—the peasant masses and educated "society"—see Abbott Gleason, *Young Russia: The Genesis of Russian Radicalism in the 1860s* (New York: Viking Press, 1980), 1–17.

7. Mironov, "The Russian Peasant Commune," 447–56; G. A. Alekseichenko, "Prigovory sel'skikh skhodov kak istochnikov po istorii krest'ianskoi obshchiny v Rossii vtoroi poloviny XIX veka (Po materialam Tverskoi gubernii)," *Istoriia SSSR,* 1980, no. 6, 116–25; Mironov, *A Social History of Imperial Russia,* I, 313. For a typical Soviet argument that officials were agents of noble landowners, see N. M. Druzhinin, *Russkaia derevnia na perelome: 1861–1880 gg.* (Moscow: Izdatel'stvo "Nauka," 1978), 44.

8. Report of Tula Province Governor P. M. Daragan to Minister of Internal Affairs Valuev, 30 September 1861, in *Krest'ianskoe dvizhenie v Rossii v 1861–1869 gg.: Sbornik dokumentov,* ed. L. M. Ivanov (Moscow: Izdatel'stvo ekonomicheskoi literatury, 1964), 108–9 (hereafter cited as *KD-5*); petition of peasant representative Semen Ivanov Ziukin to Alexander II, Begoshcha village, Putivl'skii district, Kursk Province, no later than 31 August 1864, *KD-5,* 352–53.

9. Fedorov, *Padenie krepostnogo prava v Rossii,* 27.

10. Quotations are from Charles W. Buckley to Carl Schurz, Montgomery, 15 August 1865, Carl Schurz Papers, Library of Congress; and Dylan C. Penningroth, *The Claims of Kinfolk: African American Property and Community in the Nineteenth-Century South* (Chapel Hill: University of North Carolina Press, 2003), 80. For innovative— and sometimes divergent—interpretations of slave property ownership, individual interest, and communal values, see Penningroth, *Claims of Kinfolk,* 45–110; Anthony E. Kaye, *Joining Places: Slave Neighborhoods in the Old South* (Chapel Hill: University of North Carolina Press, 2007); and Larry E. Hudson Jr., *To Have and to Hold: Slave Work and Family Life in Antebellum South Carolina* (Athens: University of Georgia Press, 1997). On the "quasi-institutional expression" of the antebellum slaves'

"protopeasant consciousness," see especially Steven Hahn, *A Nation under Our Feet: Black Political Struggles in the Rural South from Slavery to the Great Migration* (Cambridge, MA: Harvard University Press, 2003), 13–61 (quotations: 43, 44).

11. On Montgomery and the Davis Bend "experiment," which was soon expanded to include neighboring plantations on the Bend, see Janet Sharp Hermann, *The Pursuit of a Dream* (New York: Oxford University Press, 1981) (quotation: 46). In 1865, the Davis Bend community was entirely self-governing, with its own elected court and five schools that employed eleven teachers and enrolled 743 pupils. See Freedmen's Bureau Assistant Commissioner Samuel Thomas to Commissioner Howard, Vicksburg, 14 October 1865, FBP, Assistant Adjutant General's Office, Letters Received; and *National Freedman*, 15 July 1865, 179. On the New Orleans *Tribune* (1864–68), see Jean Claude Houzeau, *My Passage at the New Orleans Tribune: A Memoir of the Civil War Era*, ed. David C. Rankin and trans. from French by Gerard F. Denault (Baton Rouge: Louisiana State University Press, 1984), with an informative essay by David C. Rankin.

12. Quotations are from August Meier, *Negro Thought in America, 1880–1915* (Ann Arbor: University of Michigan Press, 1963), 5; Hahn, *A Nation under Our Feet*, 120; and Peter Kolchin, *First Freedom: The Responses of Alabama's Blacks to Emancipation and Reconstruction* (Westport, CT: Greenwood Press, 1972), 153 and 158. For proceedings of both antebellum and postwar colored conventions, see *Proceedings of the Black State Conventions, 1840–1865*, 2 vols., ed. Philip S. Foner and George E. Walker (Philadelphia: Temple University Press, 1979–80); and *Proceedings of the Black National and State Conventions, 1865–1900*, I, ed. Philip S. Foner and George E. Walker (Philadelphia: Temple University Press, 1986). For the Colored Conventions Project, directed by P. Gabrielle Foreman and Jim Casey, see https://coloredconventions.org and (for the Colored Conventions Digital Records) https://omeka.coloredconventions.org; this ongoing project will eventually contain the records of more than two hundred conventions held between the 1830s and the 1890s. See, also, *The Colored Convention Movement: Black Organizing in the Nineteenth Century*, ed. P. Gabrielle Foreman, Jim Casey, and Sarah Patterson (Chapel Hill: University of North Carolina Press, 2021); and Eric Foner, *Reconstruction: America's Unfinished Revolution, 1863–1877* (New York: Harper and Row 1988), 110–19.

13. The quotations are from Michael W. Fitzgerald, *Reconstruction in Alabama: From the Civil War to Redemption in the Cotton South* (Baton Rouge: Louisiana State University Press, 2017), 125; and John C. Rodrigue, *Reconstruction in the Cane Fields: From Slavery to Free Labor in Louisiana's Sugar Parishes, 1862–1880* (Baton Rouge: Louisiana State University Press, 2001), 78. For developments discussed in this and the next three paragraphs, see—in addition to other sources cited—Foner, *Reconstruction*, 281–307, 316–33; Hahn, *A Nation under Our Feet*, 163–215; Adam Fairclough, *The Revolution That Failed: Reconstruction in Natchitoches* (Gainesville: University Press of Florida, 2018), 85–106; Sydney Nathans, *A Mind to Stay: White Plantation, Black*

Homeland (Cambridge, MA: Harvard University Press, 2017), 107–26; and Kolchin, *First Freedom*, 154–57. On the constitutional conventions, see Richard L. Hume and Jerry B. Gough, *Blacks, Carpetbaggers, and Scalawags: The Constitutional Conventions of Radical Reconstruction* (Baton Rouge: Louisiana State University Press, 2008).

14. A[rthur] Bingham to W. H. Smith, Talladega, Alabama, 14 April 1867, Wager Swayne Papers, Alabama State Department of Archives and History; Hahn, *A Nation under Our Feet*, 198. On the Union League, see Michael W. Fitzgerald, *The Union League Movement in the Deep South: Politics and Agricultural Change during Reconstruction* (Baton Rouge: Louisiana State University Press, 1989).

15. John Parrish to Henry Watson, 13 August and 6 August, 1867, Henry Watson Papers, Duke University Library; Hahn, *A Nation under Our Feet*, 176; *Montgomery Advertiser*, 19 June 1868; Elsa Barkley Brown, "To Catch the Vision of Freedom: Reconstructing Southern Black Women's Political History, 1865–1880," in *African American Women and the Vote, 1837–1965*, ed. Ann D. Gordon et al. (Amherst: University of Massachusetts Press, 1997), 66–99 (quotations: 73, 74). At the Colored Convention that met in Raleigh, North Carolina, in September 1865, "one half of the gallery was set apart for the use of the ladies"; see *Christian Recorder*, 28 October 1865. On Reconstruction efforts of women—including Southern Black women—to vote, see "Women Who Went to the Polls, 1868 to 1873," in *The Selected Papers of Elizabeth Cady Stanton and Susan B. Anthony*, vol. II, ed. Ann D. Gordon (New Brunswick, NJ: Rutgers University Press, 1997), 645–54.

16. *Daily Selma Messenger*, 16 April 1867; Montgomery *Weekly Advertiser*, 23 April 1867; *Montgomery Advertiser*, 23 May 1867, citing a letter to the Columbus *Sun;* Alabama *Beacon*, 22 June 1867; James Mallory Diary, 26 September 1867, Southern Historical Collection, University of North Carolina. On "cooperationists," see Foner, *Reconstruction*, 292–94.

17. Julie Saville, *The Work of Reconstruction: From Slave to Wage Labor in South Carolina, 1860–1870* (New York: Cambridge University Press, 1970), 143–95 (quotations: 144, 150, 161); *State Sentinel* (Alabama), 24 May 1867. A teacher immediately after the war, Turner began his political career in 1867 as a delegate to the Alabama Colored Convention and then as an election registrar for Elmore and Autauga Counties, before going on to serve in the state legislature; see Kolchin, *First Freedom*, 165; and Eric Foner, *Freedom's Lawmakers: A Directory of Black Officeholders during Reconstruction*, rev. ed. (Baton Rouge: Louisiana State University Press, 1996), 217.

18. Foner, *Freedom's Lawmakers*, ix; Foner, *Reconstruction*, 112–13; Hahn, *A Nation under Our Feet*, 121–25; Kolchin, *First Freedom*, 152, 157–58. On Thompson's career, see Howard N. Rabinowitz, "Holland Thompson and Black Political Participation in Montgomery, Alabama," in *Southern Black Leaders of the Reconstruction Era*, ed. Howard N. Rabinowitz (Urbana: University of Illinois Press, 1982), 249–80.

19. Richard Lowe, "The Freedmen's Bureau and Local Black Leadership," *Journal of American History*, 80 (December 1993), 990–91 (first quotation), 992–94 (statistics),

997 (second quotation); and Richard Lowe, "Local Black Leaders during Reconstruction in Virginia," *Virginia Magazine of History and Biography*, 103 (April 1995), 195–98 (statistics). Noting that "the bureau's official version of local Black leadership did not correspond perfectly with that of Black voters in the hinterlands," Lowe suggested that some bureau agents may have deliberately omitted the most outspoken and assertive African Americans from their lists; Lowe, "The Freedmen's Bureau," 996.

20. Foner, *Reconstruction*, 317–18 (convention delegate statistics); Hume and Gough, *Blacks, Carpetbaggers, and Scalawags*, 12–13; Kolchin, *First Freedom*, 160–62; Justin Behrend, *Reconstructing Democracy: Grassroots Black Politics in the Deep South after the Civil War* (Athens: University of Georgia Press, 2015), 6 (quotation).

21. Cox to John C. Keffer, Grand Secretary of Alabama's Union League, Tuscaloosa, 29 June 1867, Wager Swayne Papers; Daniel B. Thorp, *Facing Freedom: An African American Community in Virginia from Reconstruction to Jim Crow* (Charlottesville: University of Virginia Press, 2017), 194–98 (quotation: 198). On Webb's murder, see Kolchin, *First Freedom*, 162; Fitzgerald, *Reconstruction in Alabama*, 128; and Nathans, *A Mind to Stay*, 115. On white terrorist activity in general, and the Ku Klux Klan specifically, see, inter alia, Allen W. Trelease, *White Terror: The Ku Klux Klan Conspiracy and Southern Reconstruction* (New York: Harper and Row, 1971); Douglas R. Egerton, *The Wars of Reconstruction: The Brief, Violent History of America's Most Progressive Era* (New York: Bloomsbury, 2014); and additional works cited below in note 40 of this chapter.

22. Foner, *Reconstruction*, 318–19; Foner, *Freedom's Lawmakers*, passim; Hahn, *A Nation under Our Feet*, 207–8; Hume and Gough, *Blacks, Carpetbaggers, and Scalawags*, 14–19, 26–29; Kolchin, *First Freedom*, 163–67.

23. "African Americans in the rural South contributed to the making of a new political nation," Hahn wrote, "while they made themselves into a new people—a veritable nation as many of them came to understand it." See Hahn, *A Nation under Our Feet*, 9.

24. For the redemption legislation, see my chapter 1, above, and Fedorov, *Padenie krepostnogo prava v Rossii*, II, 39–44. For a short description, see Moon, *The Abolition of Serfdom in Russia*, 79–82. The state advanced pomeshchiki 80 percent of the redemption sum when the peasant allotments were the maximum size allowed in the statutory charter guidelines, and 75 percent otherwise.

25. The quotation is from Druzhinin, *Russkaia derevnia na perelome*, 74. Statistics are from Zaionchkovskii, *Otmena krepostnogo prava*, 250–52.

26. Redemption Agreement between agent Mikhail Mikhailovich Grevs and temporarily obligated peasants of Agrafena Ivanovna Korostovtsova, 20 November 1863, village of Lutovinaia, Lutovinovskaia volost', Biriuchenskii district, Voronezh Province, in *Krest'ianskoe dvizhenie v Vorononezhskoi gubernii (1861–1863 gg.): Dokumenty i materialy* (Voronezh: Izdatel'stvo Voronezhskogo universiteta, 1961), 120–22 (hereafter cited as *KD-Voronezh-1*).

27. Report of Olonets Province Governor Iu. K. Arsen'ev to Minister of Internal Affairs Valuev, 26 February 1866, in *KD-5*, 426–30 (quotations: 426, 429, 428, 426, 429).

28. Ibid., 430 and 582, note 355 (quotations: 582, 430, 430, 582).

29. Report of Nikolai Obolenskii, peace mediator of Luzhskii district, St. Petersburg Province, to Vice-Governor E. K. Chapskii, 9 September 1866, in *KD-5*, 443–47 (quotations: 443, 444, 447); report of Tula Province governor P. M. Daragan to Alexander II, 17 July 1864, in *KD-5*, 369–71 (quotations: 370, 371); report of Tambov Province governor N. M. Gorting to Minister of Internal Affairs Valuev, 21 May 1867, in *KD-5*, 483–85 (quotations: 483, 484).

30. Report of Kursk Province Governor P. A. Izvol'skii to Minister of Internal Affairs Valuev, 7 May 1864, *KD-5*, 349–51; petition of peasant representative Semen Ivanov Ziukin to Alexander II, no later than 31 August 1864, *KD-5*, 351–54 (quotation: 351); report of Voronezh Province Governor V. A. Trubetskoi to Valuev, 29 April 1865, *KD-5*, 374–76 (quotations: 375, 376).

31. Record of communal gathering of peasants of Tokmovo village, Insarskii district, Penza Province, 1 March 1864, *KD-5*, 355–66 (first, fourth, and fifth quotations: 356); report of Penza Province Governor V. P. Aleksandrovskii to Valuev, 27 June 1864, 357–59 (second and third quotations: 357).

32. Reports of Voronezh Province Governor V. A. Trubetskoi to Minister of Internal Affairs A E. Timashev, 8 August 1868, 494–95, and 7 October 1868, *KD-5*, 495–97 (quotations: 496, 494, 497); report of Lieutenant Colonel Turtsevich, staff officer of the Corps of Gendarmes in Vitebsk Province, to Chief of the Corps P. A. Shuvalov, 16 September 1866, *KD-5*, 414.

33. Moon, *The Abolition of Serfdom in Russia*, 76, 101; Druzhinin, *Russkaia derevenia na perelome*, 55; Wildman, *The Defining Moment*, 47.

34. Zaionchkovskii, *Otmena krepostnogo prava*, 255–59; Druzhinin, *Russkaia derevnia na perelome*, 54–55. Quotations are from two petitions from representatives of peasant-*darstvenniki* in Bobrovskii district of Voronezh Province to the governor, the first from Tal'skoe and Nikol'skoe villages, no later than 18 September 1883, and the second from Novaia Chigla and Aleksandrovskoe villages, 15 November 1875, both in *Krest'ianskoe dvizhenie v Voronezhskoi gubernii (1864–1904 gg.): Sbornik dokumentov* (Voronezh: Izdatelstvo Voronezhskogo universiteta, 1964), 39–40, 33–34 (hereafter cited as *KD-Voronezh-2*). The first petition was signed by peasants Ivan Kondrat'ev and Vasilii Shishliannikov for themselves and two illiterate peasants, Semen Pokataev and Fedor Shirokov; the second was signed for the illiterate peasants by merchant Andrei Koz'min Polibin.

35. Of 41,627 redemptions initiated by January 1, 1870, 19,644 resulted from mutual agreements between peasants and pomeshchiki and 21,983 from unilateral actions taken by pomeshchiki. Statistics in this paragraph are from Zaionchkovksii,

Otmena krepostnogo prava, 251–53; see, also, Druzhinin, *Russkaia derevnia na perelome*, 63–73; and Moon, *Abolition of Serfdom in Russia*, 103–4.

36. Report of Samara Province Governor G. S. Aksakov to Minister of Internal Affairs A. E. Timashev, 25 August 1869, *KD-5*, 543; and report of Captain Pekarskii, assistant to Saratov Province's gendarme administration in Khvalunskii district, Saratov Province, to the Third Department, 1 April 1969, *KD-5*, 544–45 (quotation: 544). On the slowing of redemptions in the 1870s, see Zaionchkovskii, *Otmena krepostnogo prava*, 293; Druzhinin, *Russkaia derevnia na perelome*, 63–73; and Moon, *Abolition of Serfdom in Russia*, 103–4.

37. Report of N. S. Birin, head of Nizhnii Novgorod Province gendarme administration, to N. K. Shmit, manager of the Third Department, 11 August, 1879, in *Krest'ianskoe dvizhenie v Rossii v 1870–1880 gg.: Sbornik dokumentov*, ed. P. A. Zionchkovskii (Moscow: Izdatel'stvo "Nauka," 1968), 342 (hereafter cited as *KD-6*); letter from a pomeshchik with illegible signature to Shmit, Tambov Province, 7 May 1879, *KD-6*, 367; gendarme officer G. S. to A. I. Muratov, head of the Tula Province gendarme administration, 2 January 1880, *KD-6*, 371; L. S. Makov, Minister of Internal Affairs, in excerpt from journal of Committee of Ministers, 5–13 June 1879, *KD-6*, 380–81. For reports of similar rumors elsewhere, see *KD-6*, 330–31, 372–74, 378–80, 402.

38. For the two decrees, see Fedorov, *Padenie krepostnogo prava v Rossii*, II, 58–61 (quotation: 60). According to Druzhinin, *Russkaia derevnia na perelome*, 260–63, the 1881 measure resulted in a reduction of total redemption payments in the thirty provinces from 35,518,948 to 25,823,006 rubles per year; the average reduction per household was from sixteen rubles, twenty-nine kopecks to eleven rubles, eighty-four kopecks. On the growing crisis of the late 1870s, see Thomas S. Pearson, *Russian Officialdom in Crisis: Autocracy and Local Self-Government, 1861–1900* (Cambridge: Cambridge University Press, 1989), 60–118. On *Narodnaia Volia* and Alexander II's assassination, see Franco Venturi, *Roots of Revolution: A History of the Populist and Socialist Movements in Nineteenth-Century Russia* (New York: Alfred A. Knopf, 1964), esp. 633–720.

39. For Ministry of Internal Affairs reports on disorders during the 1880s and early 1890s, see documents in "Krest'ianskoe dvizhenie v kontse XIX v. (1881–1894 gg.)," ed. P. Sofinev, *Krasnyi arkhiv* LXXXIX–XC, nos. 4–5 (1938), 208–57; quotations are from "Zapiska o krest'ianskikh besporiadkakh, byvshikh v razlichnykh mestnostiakh imperii v techenie 1881–1888 gg.," ibid., 215–22 (quotations: 219, 219, 222). On the increase in peasant arrears during the 1860s and 1870s, see, e.g., Druzhinin, *Russkaia derevnia na perelome*, 75–83; but for a challenge to this widely shared historical perception, see Steven L. Hoch, "On Good Numbers and Bad: Malthus, Population Trends and Peasant Standard of Living in Late Imperial Russia," *Slavic Review*, 53 (Spring 1994), 41–75 (esp. 42–48). For continued peasant unrest in the 1880s and 1890s, see A. M. Anfimov, "Krest'ianskoe dvizhenie v Rossii vo vtoroi polovine XIX veka," *Voprosy istorii*, 1973, no. 5, 13–31 (esp. 25–29).

40. For overviews of Reconstruction, see especially Foner, *Reconstruction*, 346–459; Hahn, *A Nation under Our Feet*, 216–313 (quotation: 219); and—for a volume accompanying a PBS television series—Henry Louis Gates, *Stony the Road: Reconstruction, White Supremacy, and the Rise of Jim Crow* (New York: Penguin Books, 2019); other sources are cited below. On the violent reaction, see, inter alia, Foner, *Reconstruction*, 425–59; Hahn, *A Nation under Our Feet*, 265–313; George C. Rable, *But There Was No Peace: The Role of Violence in the Politics of Reconstruction* (Athens: University of Georgia Press, 1984); Hannah Rosen, *Terror in the Heart of Freedom: Citizenship, Sexual Violence, and the Meaning of Race in the Postemancipation South* (Chapel Hill: University of North Carolina, Press, 2009); Trelease, *White Terror;* Egerton, *The Wars of Reconstruction;* and Kenneth C. Barnes, *Who Killed John Clayton? Political Violence and the Emergence of the New South, 1861–1893* (Durham, NC: Duke University Press, 1998). For extensive testimony on the Ku Klux Klan and other terrorist organizations, see *Testimony Taken by the Joint Select Committee to Inquire into the Condition of Affairs in the Late Insurrectionary States*, 13 vols. (Washington, DC: Government Printing Office, 1872).

41. On delegate composition, see Hume and Gough, *Blacks, Carpetbaggers, and Scalawags*, 12–13; 12 white delegates were of undetermined geographic origin. See, also, Foner, *Reconstruction*, 316–33; and Hahn, *A Nation under Our Feet*, 206–15.

42. On the wealth of delegates (usually drawn from the 1870 census), see Hume and Gough, *Blacks, Carpetbaggers, and Scalawags*, 18; the median and average wealth was $3,180 and $9,016 for Southern white delegates, and $4,000 and $8,448 for Northern white delegates. On Smalls, see Foner, *Freedom's Lawmakers*, 978; and Okon E. Uya, *From Slavery to Public Service: Robert Smalls, 1839–1915* (New York: Oxford University Press, 1971); on Smalls and Bonnefoi, see Hume and Gough, *Blacks, Carpetbaggers, and Scalawags*, appendix C.

43. Hume and Gough, *Blacks, Carpetbaggers, and Scalawags*, 20–22. Hume and Gough (ibid., 271–72) categorized 88.5 percent of the Black delegates and 87.5 percent of the Northern white delegates as "radicals," with most of the remainders "moderates." The more numerous Southern white delegates, by contrast, were evenly divided across the political spectrum, with 39.5 percent "radicals," 39.5 percent "conservatives," and 21.1 percent "moderates." As Foner noted, heavy white abstention in the election of delegates significantly reduced the number of conservative delegates: *Reconstruction*, 316–17. The quotations on interracial marriage are from the *Official Journal of the Constitutional Convention of the State of Alabama, Held in the City of Montgomery, Commencing on Tuesday, November 5th, A.D. 1867* (Montgomery: Barrett and Brown, 1868), 188–89. For information on Carraway, who had fought in the war with the 54th Massachusetts Volunteer Infantry Regiment, represented Mobile in Alabama's constitutional convention, and would soon serve a term as Speaker of the Alabama House of Representatives before his untimely death in 1870, see Kolchin, *First Freedom*, 164; Foner, *Freedom's Lawmakers*, 41; and Michael W. Fitzgerald, *Urban*

Emancipation: Popular Politics in Reconstruction Mobile, 1860–1895 (Baton Rouge: Louisiana State University Press, 2002), 16–17 and passim. For the argument that "the uneducated Negroes followed the Radical Carpetbag leaders," see Malcolm Cook McMillan, *Constitutional Developments in Alabama, 1798–1901: A Study in Politics, the Negro, and Sectionalism* (Chapel Hill: University of North Carolina Press, 1955), 118. As used in the 1860s, the term "social equality" connoted something close to the current understanding of "integration."

44. Hahn, *A Nation under Our Feet*, 211 (quotation). For the suggestion that "black delegates, who were hardly a cross section of the constituents who elected them, were generally much more interested in issues of legal equality or the franchise than in land reform, which remained a major concern of the black electorate," see Hume and Gough, *Blacks, Carpetbaggers, and Scalawags*, 267. Even Eric Foner, who stressed the revolutionary nature of changes sweeping the South, agreed that "the new constitutions, taken together, failed to satisfy the economic aspirations that had animated much of the grass-roots organizing of 1867"; Foner, *Reconstruction*, 329. For emphasis on the radicalism of Black Republican politicians, who "invariably endorsed numerous radical policies that accurately reflected their constituents' views," see Behrend, *Reconstructing Democracy*, 119–46 (quotation: 120). For an extreme version of the now-discredited argument that the new Black politicians were woefully unprepared for leadership, see Claude G. Bowers, *The Tragic Era: The Revolution after Lincoln* (1929; Boston: Houghton Mifflin, 1962), passim. Describing the "astonishing conventions," Bowers lamented (216) that "Negroes and carpetbaggers dominated," while "property and intelligence [were] excluded." For a more moderate version of this interpretation, see William A. Dunning, *Reconstruction, Political and Economic: 1865–1877* (New York: Harper and Brothers, 1907), who also concluded (112) that "the mass of the delegates consisted of whites and blacks whose ignorance and inexperience in respect to political methods were equaled only by the crudeness and distortion of their ideas as to political and social ends."

45. Quotations are from Hahn, *A Nation under Our Feet* (quotations 1 and 4), 211 and 213; and *Official Journal of the Constitutional Convention of the State of Alabama* (quotations 2 and 3), 22–23 and 61. For biographical information on Strother, Bayne, and Whipper, see Hume and Gough, *Blacks, Carpetbaggers, and Scalawags*, appendix C (following 308); and Foner, *Freedom's Lawmakers*, 206–7, 13–14, and 226–27.

46. The first quotation is from the Mobile *Advertiser and Register*, 27 November 1867; the second is from *Documentary History of Reconstruction: Political, Military, Social, Religious, Educational and Industrial, 1865 to 1906*, ed. Walter L. Fleming, 2 vols. (1906; New York: McGraw Hill, 1966), I, 455–56.

47. Hume and Gough, *Blacks, Carpetbaggers, and Scalawags*, passim, esp. 13, 24, 93, 256, 271, 344; and Foner, *Reconstruction*, passim. On Alabama's four-day election of February 4–7, 1868, which both ratified the state constitution and chose officials of the new state government, see Kolchin, *First Freedom*, 171–75; and Fitzgerald, *Reconstruction in Alabama*, 63–71.

48. Hume and Gough, *Blacks, Carpetbaggers, and Scalawags,* 250 (first and second quotations); and Foner, *Reconstruction,* 319 (third quotation). On Reconstruction as a revolutionary movement to "build an egalitarian society" based on the assumption of "equal citizenship for all," see Eric Foner, *The Second Founding: How the Civil War and Reconstruction Remade the Constitution* (New York: W. W. Norton, 2019), xix and xxix (quotations); and Gregory P. Downs, *The Second American Revolution: The Civil War–Era Struggle over Cuba and the Rebirth of the American Republic* (Chapel Hill: University of North Carolina Press, 2019), 11–54. For an admiring new biography of Thaddeus Stevens as a fiery proponent of the "Second American Revolution," see Bruce Levine, *Thaddeus Stevens: Civil War Revolutionary, Fighter for Racial Justice* (New York: Simon and Schuster, 2021) (quotation: 10). On the transformation of citizenship into a basic right, see Paul Quigley, "Introduction," and Laura F. Edwards, "Afterword," both in *The Civil War and the Transformation of American Citizenship,* ed. Paul Quigley (Baton Rouge: Louisiana State University Press 2018), 1–17 and 217–36. But see, also, *The Revolution that Failed,* in which historian Adam Fairclough first observed (105) that "the Louisiana 1868 Constitution . . . gave blacks virtually all that they desired, at least on paper," but then concluded (127) that "the Republican Party . . . was not a revolutionary party" but a party "of property, middle-class respectability, and, increasingly, big business."

49. The most notable exception to the pattern described in this paragraph was Georgia, a Deep South state in which—despite a large Black population (46 percent)—unusually intense squabbling among Republican factions led to the temporary expulsion of African American representatives from the state legislature in 1868 and the overthrow of the Reconstruction government as early as 1871. On the strange history of Georgia's Reconstruction, see C. Mildred Thompson, *Reconstruction in Georgia: Economic, Social, Political, 1865–1872* (New York: Columbia University Press, 1915); Elizabeth S. Nathans, *Losing the Peace: Georgia Republicans and Reconstruction, 1865–1871* (Baton Rouge: Louisiana State University Press, 1968); Edmund L. Drago, *Black Politicians and Reconstruction in Georgia: A Splendid Failure* (Athens: University of Georgia Press, 1992); Russell Duncan, *Freedom's Shore: Tunis Campbell and Georgia Freedmen* (Athens: University of Georgia Press, 1986), 42–110, passim; and—at the local level, in southwest Georgia—Susan Eva O'Donovan, *Becoming Free in the Cotton South* (Cambridge, MA: Harvard University Press, 2007). Virginia, an Upper South state with an unusually large Black population (46 percent), represented a different kind of anomaly, in that the state's early Redemption (1870) proved less than definitive, and what amounted to a second Reconstruction occurred a decade later (1879–83) under the Readjusters, reformers who forged a radical coalition of African Americans and lower-class whites. See Hahn, *A Nation under Our Feet,* 367–84; James Tice Moore, "Black Militancy in Readjuster Virginia, 1879–1883," *Journal of Southern History,* 41 (May 1975), 167–86; and Jane Dailey, *Before Jim Crow: The Politics of Race in Postemancipation Virginia* (Chapel Hill: University of North Carolina Press,

2000). At least 291 African Americans held elective office *after* Reconstruction governments fell; Foner, *Freedom's Lawmakers*, xxix. See table 4.1 for the number of Black officeholders by state. For emphasis on the wide diversity of African Americans' Reconstruction experiences, see the editors' introduction to *After Slavery: Race, Labor, and Citizenship in the Reconstruction South*, ed. Bruce E. Baker and Brian Kelly (Gainesville: University Press of Florida, 2013), esp. 9–13.

50. The quotation is from the Fifteenth Amendment (Section 1) to the U.S. Constitution. On the wartime Republican determination to seize the moment to begin a radical transformation of the social order, see my chapter 1, above; and especially James Oakes, *Freedom National: The Destruction of Slavery in the United States, 1861–1865* (New York: W. W. Norton, 2013). On the scope and radicalism of the Reconstruction venture, see W. E. B. Du Bois, "Reconstruction and Its Benefits," *American Historical Review*, 15 (July 1910), 781–99; and, for a comparative perspective, Peter Kolchin, "Reexamining Southern Emancipation in Comparative Perspective," *Journal of Southern History*, 81 (February 2015), 7–40.

Recently, scholars have placed new emphasis on the extent to which American Civil War–era radicals were participants in—and saw themselves as part of—an international movement to promote progressive change. See Don H. Doyle, *Nations Divided: America, Italy, and the Southern Question* (Athens: University of Georgia Press, 2002), *The Cause of All Nations: An International History of the American Civil War* (New York: Basic Books, 2013), and "The Republic on Trial or Slavery under Fire? International Perspectives on the Nature of America's Civil War," in *The Civil War and Slavery Reconsidered: Negotiating the Peripheries*, ed. Laura R. Sandy and Marie S. Molloy (New York: Routledge, 2019), 21–36; Enrico Dal Lago, "Lincoln, Cavour, and National Unification: American Republicanism and Italian Liberal Nationalism in Comparative Perspective," *Journal of the Civil War Era*, 2 (2013), 85–113, *The Age of Lincoln and Cavour: Comparative Perspectives on Nineteenth-Century American and Italian Nation-Building* (New York: Palgrave Macmillan, 2015), and *William Lloyd Garrison and Giuseppe Mazzini: Abolition, Democracy, and Radical Reform* (Baton Rouge: Louisiana State University Press, 2013); and W. Caleb McDaniel, *The Problem of Democracy in the Age of Slavery: Garrisonian Abolitionists and Transatlantic Reform* (Baton Rouge: Louisiana State University Press, 2013).

For two recent books that put the Confederate Rebellion in the context of European nationalist and secessionist movements, see Niels Eichhorn, *Liberty and Slavery: European Separatists, Southern Secession, and the American Civil War* (Baton Rouge: Louisiana State University Press, 2019); and Ann L. Tucker, *Newest Born of Nations: European Nationalist Movements and the Making of the Confederacy* (Charlottesville: University of Virginia Press, 2020). For struggles over Reconstruction as a continuation of the Civil War, see Gregory P. Downs, *After Appomattox: Military Occupation and the Ends of War* (Cambridge, MA: Harvard University Press, 2015); and Caroline E. Janney, *Ends of War: The Unfinished Fight of Lee's Army after Appomattox* (Chapel

Hill: University of North Carolina Press, 2021). Despite Lee's surrender to Grant at Appomattox, Janney observed (6), "a deep and abiding commitment to the Confederacy had not ended with the surrender. In some ways, it had only begun."

51. Quotations are from Assistant Commissioner Edwin Beecher to Commissioner Howard, Montgomery, AL, 10 November 1868, FBP, Assistant Adjutant General's Office, Letters Received; and Hume and Gough, *Blacks, Carpetbaggers, and Scalawags*, 254. See Carol K. Rothrock Bleser, *The Promised Land: The History of the South Carolina Land Commission, 1869–1890* (Columbia: University of South Carolina Press, 1969); and Louis R. Harlan, "Desegregation in New Orleans Public Schools during Reconstruction," *American Historical Review,* 67 (April 1962), 663–75. On the state constitutions' guarantee of "political and civil rights of all citizens," see Hume and Gough, *Blacks, Carpetbaggers, and Scalawags,* passim (quotation: 250). For an early assertion of Reconstruction's accomplishments, see Du Bois, "Reconstruction and Its Benefits."

52. Noting that "the political transformation" of Reconstruction was "profound, but ephemeral," historian Laura F. Edwards pointed to the continued divided authority between federal and state governments, as well as to an excessive focus on individual rights that was inadequate when dealing with basic "structural inequalities" requiring "collective solutions," as major factors limiting Reconstruction's endurance; Edwards, *A Legal History of the Civil War and Reconstruction,* 110, 173 (quotations). On the insufficiency of Federal occupation forces, see especially Downs, *After Appomattox,* and Gregory P. Downs, "Anarchy at the Circumference: Statelessness and the Reconstruction of Authority in Emancipation North Carolina," in Baker and Kelly, *After Slavery,* 98–121 (second quotation: 106). As a result of "the federal government's massive and nearly immediate demobilization," by late 1866 only 1,226 federal troops remained in all of North Carolina; Downs, "Anarchy at the Circumference," 108. For a graphic illustration of the insufficiency of federal occupation forces, see Gregory P. Downs and Scott Nesbit, "Mapping Occupation: Force, Freedom, and the Army in Reconstruction," http://mappingoccupation.org/ (March 2015). For a perceptive treatment of the humiliation and anger of ex-Confederates, and their determination to resist what they saw as a punitive Reconstruction imposed by hated Yankees, see Anne Sarah Rubin, *A Shattered Nation: The Rise and Fall of the Confederacy* (Chapel Hill: University of North Carolina Press, 2005), 141–71, 240–48. But for a contrary interpretation, emphasizing political rivalries and infighting among Black Republicans as the principal cause of Reconstruction's overthrow—at least in Mobile—see Fitzgerald, *Urban Emancipation.* Mobile's "black Republican leaders seldom met violence at the hands of their Democratic opponents, but they did square off against their factional rivals time and time again," Fitzgerald wrote (5). "Here, then, is one answer to . . . whether Reconstruction could have turned out differently," he continued "—basically, no" (5–6). The defense of white supremacy (first quotation) is from Fleming, *Documentary History of Reconstruction,* I, 425–26.

53. Rubin, *A Shattered Nation*, 164. At least 158 of 1,510 African American officeholders during Reconstruction were "victimized by violence," including thirty-five who were murdered; Foner, *Freedom's Lawmakers*, xxviii. On Black perception of the Klan as "a later form of the ante-bellum patrols," see Gladys-Marie Fry, *Night Riders in Black Folk History* (Knoxville: University of Tennessee Press, 1975), 154; and Hahn, *A Nation under Our Feet*, 270. On the Klan as "a guerilla movement," see Hahn, *A Nation under Our Feet*, 269. But for the argument that "fighting during Reconstruction was not that different from irregular warfare during the Civil War," see Justin Behrend, "When Neighbors Turn against Neighbors: Irregular Warfare and the Crisis of Democracy in the Civil War Era," in *Beyond Freedom: Disrupting the History of Emancipation*, ed. David W. Blight and Jim Downs (Athens: University of Georgia Press, 2017), 90–103 (quotation: 97). For the recent suggestion that the Klan was disproportionately composed of "downwardly mobile sons of middling slaveholders" bitter at their losses of wealth, war, and slaves, see Michael W. Fitzgerald, "Ex-Slaveholders and the Ku Klux Klan: Exploring the Motivations of Terrorist Violence," in Baker and Kelly, *After Slavery*, 143–75 (quotation: 155). See, also, the sources listed above in note 40 of this chapter.

54. The quotations are from an address on 30 November 1868 by former Confederate Colonel Aleibiade de Blanc, in Fleming, *Documentary History of Reconstruction*, II, 345, 344, 346.

55. Foner, *Freedom's Lawmakers*, xiv–xv; see also Peter Kolchin, "Scalawags, Carpetbaggers, and Reconstruction: A Quantitative Look at Southern Congressional Politics, 1868–1872," *Journal of Southern History*, 45 (February 1979), 63–76. On Pinchback's interesting career, see Foner, *Freedom's Lawmakers*, 171–72; and James Haskins, *Pinckney Benton Stewart Pinchback* (New York: Macmillan, 1973).

56. Quotations are from Behrend, *Reconstructing Democracy*, 150 (on Black officeholders), and 201, 191, and 200 (on freedwomen pressuring their husbands to vote Republican). On freedpeople's collective political consciousness that encouraged political participation by women as well as men, see above in this chapter, note 15.

57. Per-capita figures are calculated from statistics in Foner, *Freedom's Lawmakers*, xiv; and *The Statistical History of the United States from Colonial Times to the Present* (New York: Basic Books, 1976), 24–36.

58. For a sophisticated elaboration of both the particularistic and general manifestations of Black political consciousness, see Hahn, *A Nation under Our Feet*. Hahn stressed both the overall desire of African Americans to constitute themselves "a new people—a veritable nation" (9) and the commitment of Black political leaders "to constructing a political and civil society in the South in which the lines of exclusion based on race or previous condition would be eliminated, in which popular control over government would be expanded, and in which the state would help promote the welfare and aspirations of its ordinary citizens" (209). For the argument that Black Reconstruction congressmen saw themselves as representing not only their constituents

but all African Americans, "thus explicitly positioning themselves as national spokesmen for their race," see Luis-Alejandro Dinnella-Borrego, *The Risen Phoenix: Black Politics in the Post-Civil War South* (Charlottesville: University of Virginia Press, 2016), 9 (quotation).

59. Kermit E. McKenzie, "Zemstvo Organization and Role Within the Administrative Structure," in *The Zemstvo in Russia: An Experiment in Local Self-Government*, ed. Terence Emmons and Wayne S. Vucinich (Cambridge: Cambridge University Press, 1982), 31–78; Dorothy Atkinson, "The Zemstvo and the Peasantry," in Emmons and Vucinich, *The Zemstvo in Russia*, 79–132; David Saunders, *Russia in the Age of Reaction and Reform, 1801–1881* (London: Longman, 1992), 253–66 (quotation: 266). For statistics on peasant and noble deputies, see Atkinson, "The Zemstvo and the Peasantry," 84–86; and Alexander Polunov, *Russia in the Nineteenth Century: Autocracy, Reform, and Social Change, 1814–1914*, ed. Thomas C. Owen and Larissa G. Zakharova, trans. Marshall S. Shatz (Armonk, NY: M. E. Sharpe, 2005), 110–15. W. Bruce Lincoln termed the zemstvo reform a "limited administrative deconcentration" in *The Great Reforms: Autocracy, Bureaucracy, and the Politics of Change in Imperial Russia* (DeKalb: Northern Illinois University Press, 1990), 105.

60. The first quotation is from Catherine Evtuhov, *Portrait of a Russian Province: Economy, Society, and Civilization in Nineteenth-Century Nizhnii Novgorod* (Pittsburgh: University of Pittsburgh Press, 2011), 148, who provided an unusually positive assessment of the zemstvo reform. The second is from Polunov, *Russia in the Nineteenth Century*, 114.

61. The quotation is from Atkinson, "The Zemstvo and the Peasantry," 111. For the growing disillusionment with peasant self-government—and indeed with the emancipation reform itself—see my chapter 7. For the view that the architects of emancipation "envision[ed] the gradual evolution of former serfs into full citizens" and "civilized adulthood," but that "little would come of these evolutionary hopes," see Corinne Gaudin, *Ruling Peasants: Village and State in Late Imperial Russia* (DeKalb: Northern Illinois University Press, 2007), 16, 19, 16.

Chapter 5. Free Labor

1. For Black migration during the Great Jubilee, see my chapter 2, notes 28–33, above; the quotation is from Colonel L. F. Hubbard to Captain W. H. F. Randall, Assistant Adjutant General, Demopolis, AL, 20 May 1865, *War of the Rebellion: A Compilation of the Official Records of the Union and Confederate Armies*, ser. 1, vol. XLIX, pt. II (Washington, DC: Government Printing Office, 1897), 855. For a description of the "tide of negro emigration . . . flowing westward, from the comparatively barren hills of northern Georgia to the rich cotton plantations of the Mississippi," see J. T. Trowbridge, *A Picture of the Desolated States; and the Work of Restoration* (Hartford, CT: L. Stebbins, 1868), 460. For Freedmen's Bureau-assisted moves, especially to engage in

agricultural work in the Deep South, see William G. Thomas, Richard G. Healey, and Ian Cottingham, "Reconstructing African American Mobility after Emancipation, 1865–1867," *Social Science History*, 41 (Winter 2017), 673–704. On interest in—and the reality of—Black emigration, see Steven Hahn, *A Nation under Our Feet: Black Political Struggles in the Rural South from Slavery to the Great Migration* (Cambridge, MA: Harvard University Press, 2003), esp. 317–63; on Kansas, see Nell Irwin Painter, *Exodusters: Black Migration to Kansas after Reconstruction* (1977; New York: Norton, 1992). On the Great Migration, see, inter alia, Carole Marks, *Farewell—We're Good and Gone: The Great Black Migration* (Bloomington: Indiana University Press, 1989); James Grossman, *Land of Hope: Chicago, Black Southerners, and the Great Migration* (Chicago: University of Chicago Press, 1989); Nicholas Lemann, *Promised Land: The Great Black Migration and How It Changed America* (New York: Alfred A. Knopf, 1991); Milton C. Sernett, *Bound for the Promised Land: African American Religion and the Great Migration* (Durham, NC: Duke University Press, 1997); and Isabel Wilkerson, *The Warmth of Other Suns: The Epic Story of the Great Migration* (New York: Random House, 2010).

2. William Cohen, *At Freedom's Edge: Black Mobility and the Southern White Quest for Racial Control, 1861–1915* (Baton Rouge: Louisiana State University Press, 1991), 4. For Cohen's earlier assertion of widespread debt peonage, see his "Negro Involuntary Servitude in the South: A Preliminary Analysis," *Journal of Southern History*, 62 (February 1976), 31–60. For Black flight during the Civil War, see Yael A. Sternhell, *Routes of War: The World of Movement in the Confederate South* (Cambridge, MA: Harvard University Press, 2012), esp. 93–107, 167–79; and Chandra Manning, *Troubled Refuge: Struggling for Freedom in the Civil War* (New York: Alfred A. Knopf, 2016), 45–149.

3. David Moon, "Peasant Migration, the Abolition of Serfdom, and the Internal Passport System in the Russian Empire c. 1800–1914," in *Coerced and Free Migration: Global Perspectives*, ed. David Eltis (Stanford: Stanford University Press, 2002), 324–57 (esp. 330–32). For the Emancipation Statute's provisions for leaving the commune, see Article 130 of the General Polozhenie, "Ob uvol'nenii krest'ian iz sel'skikh obshchestv," in *Padenie krepostnogo prava v Rossii: Dokumenty i materialy*, II: "*Polozhenie 19 fevralia 1861 goda*" *i Russkoe obshchestvo*, ed. V. V. Fedorov (Moscow: Izdatel'stvo Moskovoskogo universiteta, 1967), 26. For the essay on otkhodniki, see N. L.-V., "Markitanty," in *Pamiatnaia knizhka Kaluzhskim Gubernskim Statisticheskim Komitetom* (Kaluga, 1863), 193–203 (quotations: 201, 195).

4. See Moon, "Peasant Migration," 330–37 (quotation: 37); Donald W. Treadgold, *The Great Siberian Migration: Government and Peasant in Resettlement from Emancipation to the First World War* (Princeton: Princeton University Press, 1957), 32; N. A. Iakimenko, "Agrarnye migratsii v Rossii (1861–1917 gg.)," *Voprosy istorii*, 1983, no. 3, 17–31 (statistics: 20); and Boris Mironov with Ben Eklof, *The Social History of Imperial Russia, 1700–1917*, 2 vols. (Boulder, CO: Westview Press, 2000), I, 18 (statistics on rates of growth).

5. Stepniak, *The Russian Peasantry: Their Agrarian Condition, Social Life and Religion* (New York: Harper and Brothers, 1888), 7; *Byt Velikorusskikh krest'ian-zemlepashtsev: Opisanie materialov etnograficheskogo biuro Kniasia V. N. Tenisheva (na primere Vladimirskoi gubernii)*, ed. B. M. Firsov and I. G. Kieseleva (St. Petersburg: Izdatel'stvo Evropeiskogo Doma, 1993), 43.

6. Timothy Mixter, "The Hiring Market as Workers' Turf: Migrant Agricultural Laborers and the Mobilization of Collective Action in the Steppe Grainbelt of European Russia, 1853–1913," in *Peasant Economy, Culture, and Politics of European Russia, 1800–1921*, ed. Esther Kingston-Mann and Timothy Mixter (Princeton: Princeton University Press, 1991), 294–340; Jeffrey Burds, *Peasant Dreams and Market Politics: Labor Migration and the Russian Village, 1861–1905* (Pittsburgh: University of Pittsburgh Press, 1998), 21–17, 60–61 (statistics). On women otkhodniki, see especially Barbara Alpern Engel, *Between the Fields and the City: Women, Work, and the Family in Russia, 1861–1914* (Cambridge: Cambridge University Press, 1994).

7. See Peter Kolchin, *Unfree Labor: American Slavery and Russian Serfdom* (Cambridge, MA: Harvard University Press, 1987), 334–43 (on serfs) and 343–52 (on slaves); on the diversity of slave occupations, see also Peter Kolchin, *American Slavery: 1619–1877*, rev. ed. (New York: Hill and Wang, 2003), 105–11. For commercial activities among serfs, see, inter alia, N. S. Svidirov, "Torguiushchie krest'iane kontsa krepostnogo epokhi (Po materialam pervoi poloviny XIX stoletiia)," *Istoriia SSSR*, 1969, no. 5, 48–67; Henry Rosovsky, "The Serf Entrepreneur in Russia," *Explorations in Entrepreneurial History*, 6 (May 1954), 207–33; and (for a case study) the narrative of N. N. Shipov, "Istoriia moei zhizni: Razskaz byvshago krepostnago krest'ianina N. N. Shipova," *Russkaia starina*, 30 (1881), 133–48, 221–40, 437–78, 665–78. On Black property holders, see, inter alia, Ira Berlin, *Slaves Without Masters: The Free Negro in the Antebellum South* (New York: Pantheon Books, 1974), esp. 241–49, 271–83; and Loren Schweninger, *Black Property Owners in the South, 1790–1915* (Urbana; University of Illinois Press, 1990). African American slave owners have fascinated historians. For a few of many studies, see Carter G. Woodson, *Free Negro Owners of Slaves in the United States in 1830: Together with Absentee Ownership of Slaves in the United States in 1830* (Washington, DC: Association for the Study of Negro Life and History, 1924); Larry Koger, *Black Slave Owners: Free Black Slave Masters in South Carolina, 1790–1860* (Jefferson, NC: McFarland, 1985); Gary B. Mills, *The Forgotten People: Cane River's Creoles of Color* (Baton Rouge: Louisiana State University Press, 1977); and Michael P. Johnson and James L. Roark, *Black Masters: A Free Family of Color in the Old South* (New York: Norton, 1984). Sometimes free African Americans purchased their own relatives to render them effectively free; see David L. Lightner and Alexander M. Ragan, "Were African American Slaveholders Benevolent or Exploitative? A Quantitative Approach," *Journal of Southern History*, 71 (August 2005), 535–58.

8. Quotations are from Frederick Douglass, *Narrative of the Life of Frederick Douglass, an American Slave, Written by Himself* (1845; New York: New American Library,

1968), 50; and Charles C. Jones Jr. to Rev. C. C. Jones, 1 October 1856, in *The Children of Pride: A True Story of Georgia and the Civil War*, ed. Robert Manson Myers (New Haven: Yale University Press, 1972), 242. On the limited slave population of antebellum Southern cities, see Kolchin, *American Slavery*, 176–78, 257 (statistics). For two important studies of urban slavery, the first of which emphasized the greater freedom provided by urban life and the second the greater demand for agricultural labor in explaining the declining proportion in slaves in late antebellum Southern cities, see Richard C. Wade, *Slavery in the Cities: The South, 1820–1860* (New York: Oxford University Press, 1964); and Claudia Dale Goldin, *Urban Slavery in the American South, 1820–1860* (Chicago: University of Chicago Press, 1976).

9. Jerome Blum, *Lord and Peasant in Russia: From the Ninth to the Nineteenth Century* (Princeton: Princeton University Press, 1961), 281; Mironov, *A Social History of Imperial Russia*, I, 435 (size of cities), 473 (peasants a decreasing proportion of urban population), 475, 476 (proportion of peasants and non-peasants living in cities); I. Link, "Goroda Tul'skoi gubernii," in *Materialy dlia statistiki Rossiiskoi imperii* . . . (St. Petersburg, 1841), III, 81–205 (esp. 162–75), and E. Kaipesh, "Goroda Riazanskoi gubernii," ibid., III, 3–80 (esp. 26–39). On the origins of Russian serfdom, see Kolchin, *Unfree Labor*, 1–10.

10. The 1900 census statistics are from *The Statistical History of the United States from Colonial Times to the Present* (New York: Basic Books, 1976), 22. For the five major cities, see Howard N. Rabinowitz, *Race Relations in the Urban South, 1865–1890* (New York: Oxford University Press, 1978), 19. As Rabinowitz noted (19), because the 1890 census undercounted Blacks, "especially in Southern cities," the actual growth of the urban Black population was even larger than indicated by his statistics. For the influx of rural Blacks to Alabama's cities immediately following the end of slavery, see Peter Kolchin, *First Freedom: The Responses of Alabama's Blacks to Emancipation and Reconstruction* (1972; Tuscaloosa: University of Alabama Press, 2008), 4–11 (statistics: 11). Between 1860 and 1870, the Black population of Alabama's four largest cities (Mobile, Montgomery, Huntsville, and Selma) surged 57.8 percent, while the white population edged down 0.4 percent. Rabinowitz's and Kolchin's statistics for 1860 include free African Americans as well as slaves. On the reasons for Black migration to cities, see Rabinowitz, *Race Relations in the Urban South*, 22–24; and Kolchin, *First Freedom*, 10–11.

11. Mironov, *The Social History of Imperial Russia*, I, 425–480, passim (statistics: 432, 475, 474). See, also, Peter Gatrell, *The Tsarist Economy, 1850–1917* (London: B. T. Batsford, 1986), esp. 67–69; Robert E. Johnson, "Peasant and Proletariat: Migration, Family Patterns, and Regional Loyalties," in *The World of the Russian Peasant: Post-Emancipation Society and Culture*, ed. Ben Eklof and Stephen Frank (Boston: Unwin Hyman, 1990), 81–99; and (for statistics based on the 1897 census), *Obshchii svod po imperii rezul'tatov razrabotki dannykh pervoi vseobshchei perepisi naseleniia, proizvedennoi 28 ianvaria 1897 g.* (St. Petersburg, 1905), I, 12–13. On Russia's growing economic

regionalism, with a "producer" south and a "consumer" north (where by 1913 only 14 percent of the arable land was being cultivated), see Carol S. Leonard, *Agrarian Reform in Russia: The Road from Serfdom* (Cambridge: Cambridge University Press, 2011), 195–96.

12. Jeffrey Burds suggested that in the late nineteenth century "typically 50–65 percent of an otkhodnik's annual earnings were sent home" to families in Iaroslavl Province; Burds, *Peasant Dreams and Market Politics*, 135. In 1874, 142,819 male peasants and 64,188 female peasants resided in St. Petersburg, composing, respectively, 37.8 percent of the male and 22.1 percent of the female population; see *Pamiatnaia knizhka S.-Peterburgskoi gubernii: Izdanie S.-Peterburgskago stolichnago i gubernskago statisticheskago komiteta* (St. Petersburg, 1877), Pt. II, 4–5. Statistics on otkhodnichestvo in Tver Province are from Engel, *Between the Fields and the City*, 70–71.

13. Tera W. Hunter, *To 'Joy My Freedom: Southern Black Women's Lives and Labors after the Civil War* (Cambridge, MA: Harvard University Press, 1997), 241 (on male and female population of Atlanta). On residence and family status of African Americans in sample districts of Alabama in 1870, see Kolchin, *First Freedom*, 67–72.

14. Rabinowitz, *Race Relations in the Urban South*, 61–69 (quotation: 61–62). See, also, Kolchin, *First Freedom*, 129–31; and John W. Blassingame, *Black New Orleans, 1860–1880* (Chicago: University of Chicago Press, 1973), esp. 58–64. For a focus on laundresses and other domestic workers in Atlanta, see Hunter, *To 'Joy My Freedom*. On "skilled" workers in Mobile, see Michael W. Fitzgerald, *Urban Emancipation: Popular Politics in Reconstruction Mobile, 1860–1890* (Baton Rouge: Louisiana State University Press, 2002), passim.

15. Rabinowitz, *Race Relations in the Urban South*, 61, 64 (statistics), 89; U.S. Congress, Senate, *Report of the Committee of the Senate upon the Relations between Labor and Capital* (Washington, DC: Government Printing Office, 1885), IV, 451; Schweninger, *Black Property Owners in the South*, 180 (statistic on homeownership), 216–26. Before moving to Montgomery in 1876, Green had an earlier career as a Republican politician, representing rural Hale County, Alabama, first in the Constitutional Convention, then in the state house of representatives (1868–74), and finally in the state senate (1874–75); see Eric Foner, *Freedom's Lawmakers: A Directory of Black Officeholders during Reconstruction*, rev. ed. (Baton Rouge: Louisiana State University Press, 1996), 90–91. On Black businessmen, see also W. E. B. Du Bois, *The Negro in Business* (Atlanta: Atlanta University Publications, 1899); and Robert C. Kenzer, *Enterprising Southerners: Black Economic Success in North Carolina, 1865–1915* (Charlottesville: University Press of Virginia, 1997), esp. 35–66.

16. Mironov, *The Social History of Imperial Russia*, I, 476–80; Johnson, "Peasant and Proletariat," esp. 82–86; Engel, *Between the Fields and the City*, 126–206 (quotation: 201; prostitution: 166–82). According to Engel, about half the prostitutes in St. Petersburg were peasants, but since peasant women constituted far less than half of the city's female population—in 1874, 22.1 percent of St. Petersburg's women were

peasants—the incidence of prostitution among them was substantially higher than among other social groups; for 1874 population statistics, see *Pamiatnaia knizhka S.-Peterburgskoi gubernii*, II, 4–5.

17. Mironov, *The Social History of Imperial Russia*, I, 480–91 (quotations: 480, 487); Burds, *Peasant Dreams and Market Politics*, 145–62; Engel, *Between the Fields and the City*, 75–77.

18. Of more than twenty-two thousand claims filed before the Southern Claims Commission, 5,004 were "allowed," of which 498 were for claims from ex-slaves and an additional 335 from free Blacks. Penningroth suggested, however, that these "allowed claims . . . represent only a tiny fraction of the South's enslaved property owners": Dylan C. Penningroth, *The Claims of Kinfolk: African American Property and Community in the Nineteenth-Century South* (Chapel Hill: University of North Carolina Press, 2003), 70 (statistic), 76 and 138 (quotations), 45–78 on "informal" property-ownership among slaves. For an innovative recent study of the complex and contradictory property relations that existed under antebellum slavery, see Kathleen M. Hilliard, *Masters, Slaves, and Exchange: Power's Purchase in the Old South* (New York: Cambridge University Press, 2014).

19. Eric Foner, *Nothing but Freedom: Emancipation and Its Legacy* (Baton Rouge: Louisiana State University Press, 1983). On the "agrarian notion," see Frederick Law Olmsted, *The Cotton Kingdom: A Traveller's Observations on Cotton and Slavery in the American Slave States* (New York, 1861), I, 106; for the similar understanding that because labor produced wealth, what whites saw as "theft" represented what slaves saw as "taking" what was legitimately theirs, see Eugene D. Genovese, *Roll, Jordan, Roll: The World the Slaves Made* (New York: Pantheon Books, 1974), 599–609. On the renegotiation of property relations, see Penningroth, *Claims of Kinfolk*, esp. 131–61. For reversal of the limited land distribution policy of the army and the Freedmen's Bureau, see my chapter 3, above.

20. Charles W. Buckley to Carl Schurz, Montgomery, 19 August 1865, Carl Schurz Papers, Library of Congress; Testimony of Major General Clinton B. Fiske, 30 January 1866, U.S. Congress, *Report of the Joint Committee on Reconstruction* (Washington, DC: Government Printing Office, 1866), pt. III, 31; Schweninger, *Black Property Owners in the South*, 164, 174 (statistics). The eight Lower South states included Alabama, Arkansas, Florida, Georgia, Louisiana, Mississippi, South Carolina, and Texas; the Upper South included the seven states of Delaware, Kentucky, Maryland, Missouri, North Carolina, Tennessee, and Virginia, plus the District of Columbia. On Black landownership in Alabama in the immediate post-emancipation years, see Kolchin, *First Freedom*, esp. 134–37. On African American Creoles in New Orleans and Mobile, see the sources listed in my chapter 7, notes 58, 59, and 60.

21. Statistics are from Schweninger, *Black Property Owners in the South*, 164, 166, and 174; Claude F. Oubre, *Forty Acres and a Mule: The Freedmen's Bureau and Black Land Ownership* (Baton Rouge: Louisiana State University Press, 1978), 178–79 (for

1900); and Daniel B. Thorp, *Facing Freedom: An African American Community in Virginia from Reconstruction to Jim Crow* (Charlottesville: University of Virginia Press, 2017), 89–100 (quotation: 97–98). For the argument that "the economic opportunities of the black business community were not severely hindered by the end of Reconstruction during the 1870s or by disfranchisement . . . in the 1890s," see Kenzer, *Enterprising Southerners*, 6. For a recent study featuring the purchase in the mid-1870s of an absentee-owned plantation near Greensboro, Alabama, by a dozen former slaves, who were able to pay for what became family farms ranging from thirty to 240 acres over a period of several years, "in cotton rather than cash," with "no money down," see Sydney Nathans, *A Mind to Stay: White Plantation, Black Homeland* (Cambridge, MA: Harvard University Press, 2017), esp. 127–62 (quotations: 135).

22. N. M. Druzhinin, *Russkaia derevnia na perelome: 1861–1880 gg.* (Moscow: Izdatel'stvo "Nauka," 1978), 50; Peter I. Lyashchenko, *History of the National Economy of Russia to the 1917 Revolution*, trans. from Russian by L. M. Herman (1939; New York: Macmillan, 1949), 392; and Steven L. Hoch, "Did Russia's Emancipated Serfs Really Pay Too Much for Too Little Land? Statistical Anomalies and Long-Tailed Distributions," *Slavic Review*, 63 (Summer 2004), 247–74 (quotation: 248).

23. Report of Orenburg Province Governor G. S. Aksakov to Minister of Internal Affairs Petr Valuev, 13 March 1862, in *Krest'ianskoe dvizhenie v Rossii v 1861–1869 gg.: Sbornik dokumentov*, ed. L. M. Ivanov (Moscow: Izdatel'stvo sotsial'nogo-ekonomicheskogo literatury, 1961), 204–5 (hereafter cited as KD-5). For more on Hoch's argument, see my chapter 1, above.

24. Hoch, "Did Russia's Emancipated Serfs Really Pay Too Much for Too Little Land?" 273. For the statutory charters and redemption process, see my chapters 1–4, above.

25. Leonard, *Agrarian Reform in Russia*, 43–45 (quotation: 43); Moon, *The Abolition of Serfdom in Russia*, 98–99; Hoch, "Did Russia's Emancipated Serfs Really Pay Too Much for Too Little Land?" 274 (quotation); B. G. Litvak, *Russkaia dervenia v reforme 1861 goda: Chernozemnyi tsentr, 1861–1895 gg.* (Moscow: Izdatel'stvo "Nauka," 1972), 179–96; A. Ia. Degtiarev et al., *Novgorodskaia derevnia v reforme 1861 goda: Opyt izucheniia c ispol'zovaniem EVM* (Leningrad: Izdatel'stvo Leningradskogo universiteta, 1989), 134–39 (quotation: 135); S. G. Kashchenko, *Reforma 19 fevralia 1861 goda v Sankt-Peterburgskoi gubernii* (Leningrad: Izdatel'stvo Leningradskogo universiteta, 1990), 132–37. For suggestions of a smaller—4.1 percent—reduction in the average size of peasant allotments, see G. M. Hamburg, *Politics of the Russian Nobility, 1881–1905* (New Brunswick, NJ: Rutgers University Press, 1984), 23; note, however, that this average includes 24 percent and 18 percent *increases* in allotment sizes in Belorussian and western Ukrainian provinces, respectively. In *The Social History of Imperial Russia*, Boris Mironov also estimated an overall reduction in ex-serf landholding of "about 4 percent across European Russia" but "16 percent in the central black-earth region" (I, 333).

26. Leonard, *Agrarian Reform in Russia*, 43 (first quotation); A. M. Anfimov and P. N. Zyrianov, "Nekotorye cherty evoliutsii Russkoi krest'ianskoi obshchiny v poreformennyi period (1861–1914 gg.)," *Istoriia SSSR*, 1980, no. 4, 24–41 (statistic: 29); Druzhinin, *Russkaia derevnia na perelome*, 116–17; David Kerans, *Mind and Labor on the Farm in Black-Earth Russia, 1861–1914* (Budapest: Central European University Press, 2001), 29 (on Tambov Province); Mironov, *The Social History of Imperial Russia*, I, 41–42 (second quotation). Allotments (excluding additional purchased land) in 1877–78 ranged from a high of 4.71 desiatiny per soul in the north and 4.39 in the northwest to a low of 2.50 and 2.15 desiatiny per soul in the fertile Middle Volga and central agricultural regions; Druzhinin, *Russkaia derevnia na perelome*, 116–17.

27. Statistics are from Druzhinin, *Russkaia derevnia na perelome*, 141–46; and Teodor Shanin, *Russia as a "Developing Society": The Roots of Otherness: Russia's Turn of Century*, vol. 1 (1985; New Haven: Yale University Press, 1986), 137. See, also, Gatrell, *The Tsarist Economy*, 110–18; Leonard, *Agrarian Reform in Russia*, 47–49; Hamburg, *Politics of the Russian Nobility*, 31–38; and A. P. Korelin, *Dvorianstvo v poreformennoi Rossii 1861–1904 gg.: Sostav, chislennost,' korporativnaia organizatsiia* (Moscow: Izdatel'stvo "Nauka," 1979), 54–59. On the increasing predilection of pomeshchiki to abandon direct agricultural production, see later in this chapter.

28. In 1871 the arrears on redemption payments owed by former serfs totaled 12,862,198 rubles, a figure that swelled to 19,732,710 rubles by 1881; see P. A. Zaionchkovskii, *Otmena krepostnogo prava v Rossii*, 3rd ed. (Moscow: Prosveshchenie, 1968), 304–5. For emphasis on the growing land hunger of peasants in the overwhelmingly agricultural, black-earth Tambov Province, where the rural population almost doubled from 1.77 million in 1858 to 3.23 million in 1914, see Kerans, *Mind and Labor in the Farm in Black-Earth Russia*, 28–32 (statistics: 29).

29. Quotations are from report of William E. Connolly, Sub-Assistant Commissioner, Eufaula, AL, 1 August 1867, FBP, Alabama Operations Reports; Mobile *Daily Register*, 30 May 1869; Thorp, *Facing Freedom*, 75, 81, 79; Wallace Jones to George Noble Jones, El Destino, FL, 2 November 1871, in *Florida Plantation Records from the Papers of George Noble Jones*, ed. Ulrich B. Phillips and James David Glunt (St. Louis: Missouri Historical Society, 1927), 193; John A. Alvord to O. O. Howard, Macon, GA, 15 January 1870, FBP, Assistant Adjutant General's Office, Letters Received; Roger L. Ransom and Richard Sutch, *One Kind of Freedom: The Economic Consequences of Emancipation* (New York: Cambridge University Press, 1977), 68. See, inter alia, Gavin Wright, *Old South, New South: Revolutions in the Southern Economy Since the Civil War* (New York: Basic Books, 1986), 84–106; Ransom and Sutch, *One Kind of Freedom*, 56–105; Edward Royce, *The Origins of Southern Sharecropping* (Philadelphia: Temple University Press, 1983), passim; Thavolia Glymph, *Out of the House of Bondage: The Transformation of the Plantation Household* (New York: Cambridge University Press, 2008), 49–66; Lynda Morgan, *Emancipation in Virginia's Tobacco Belt, 1850–1870* (Athens: University of Georgia Press, 1992), 187–96; Kolchin, *First Freedom*, 30–55.

30. Sally Stocksdale, *When Emancipation Came: The End of Enslavement on a Southern Plantation and a Russian Estate* (Jefferson, NC: McFarland, 2022), 131–40 (quotation: 132–33). On "the sheer variety of local experiences during Reconstruction," see the essays in *After Slavery: Race, Labor, and Citizenship in the Reconstruction South*, ed. Bruce E. Baker and Brian Kelly (Gainesville: University Press of Florida, 2013), 9 (quotation: editors' introduction).

31. Janet Sharp Hermann, *The Pursuit of a Dream* (New York: Oxford University Press, 1981), 109–216 (quotations: 192–213). For a brief biographical sketch of Benjamin Montgomery, see Foner, *Freedom's Lawmakers*, 151–52. On the Mound Bayou colony, see Hermann, *The Pursuit of a Dream*, 219–45 (quotations: 223, 243).

32. Laura F. Edwards, *Gendered Strife and Confusion: The Political Culture of Reconstruction* (Urbana: University of Illinois Press, 1997), 82, 88–89. For freedpeople subletting land to other freedpeople, and hiring Black farmhands in Hale County, Alabama, see Nathans, *A Mind to Stay*, 152–53.

33. John C. Willis, *Forgotten Time: The Yazoo-Mississippi Delta after the Civil War* (Charlottesville: University Press of Virginia, 2000), 8, 31, 2, 41, 50, 114, 180 (quotations). Stressing the "heterogeneous mix" of the region's labor relations (16), Willis noted (4) that "the Delta's history seldom corresponded with the chronologies of the rest of the postbellum South."

34. Richard Follett, "Legacies of Enslavement: Plantation Identities and the Problem of Freedom," in Richard Follett, Eric Foner, and Walter Johnson, *Slavery's Ghost: The Problem of Freedom in the Age of Emancipation* (Baltimore: Johns Hopkins University Press, 2011), 50–84 (first quotation: 57); Richard Follett, *The Sugar Masters: Planters and Slaves in Louisiana's Cane World, 1820–1860* (Baton Rouge: Louisiana State University Press, 2005), 86–87, 139–41; Follett, "Legacies of Enslavement," 51 (second quotation); Richard Follett, "The Rise and Fall of American Sugar," in Richard Follett, Sven Beckert, Peter Coclanis, and Barbara Hahn, *Plantation Kingdom: The American South and Global Commodities* (Baltimore: Johns Hopkins University Press, 2016), 61–90 (third quotation: 88); Follett, "Rise and Fall of American Sugar," 84 (fourth quotation). See, also, Rebecca J. Scott, *Degrees of Freedom: Louisiana and Cuba after Slavery* (Cambridge, MA: Harvard University Press, 2005), 30–93 passim (esp. 37–38, 47, 83).

35. Peter Coclanis, "The Road to Commodity Hell: The Rise and Fall of the First American Rice Industry," in Follett et al., *Plantation Kingdom*, esp. 30–38 (first quotation: 37); Peter A. Coclanis, *The Shadow of a Dream: Economic Life and Death in the South Carolina Low Country, 1670–1920* (New York: Oxford University Press, 1989), 142 (on South Carolina's declining share of American rice production); Foner, *Nothing but Freedom*, 81–105 (second and third quotations: 86 and 108). See, also, Julie Saville, *The Work of Reconstruction: From Slave to Wage Labor in South Carolina, 1860–1870* (New York: Cambridge University Press, 1994), 72–142 passim. On the postemancipation transformation of plantation rice cultivation on one family's holdings

in Lowcountry Georgia, see Malcolm Bell Jr., *Major Butler's Legacy: Five Generations of a Slaveholder's Family* (Athens: University of Georgia Press, 1987), esp. 392–450; and Frances Butler Leigh, *Ten Years on a Georgia Plantation Since the War* (1883; New York: Negro Universities Press, 1969). For the development and evolution of the task system, see especially Philip D. Morgan, "Work and Culture: The Task System and the World of Lowcountry Blacks, 1770 to 1880," *William and Mary Quarterly*, 38 (July 1981), 418–41. For emphasis on African American "oppositional communities" in Georgia's Lowcountry, communities that "emanated from shared African traditions" and that "resisted neodependency and neopaternalism" after the Civil War, see Karen Cook Bell, *Claiming Freedom: Race, Kinship, and Land in Nineteenth-Century Georgia* (Columbia: University of South Carolina Press, 2018) (quotations: 2, 3, 4). On the harsh material conditions on antebellum rice plantations, see William Dusinberre, *Them Dark Days: Slavery in the American Rice Swamps* (New York: Oxford University Press, 1996).

36. For a very brief survey of these arrangements, see Moon, *The Abolition of Serfdom in Russia*, 111–13. See later in this chapter for elaboration.

37. Report of Lieutenant Colonel Khodkevich, staff officer of the Corps of Gendarmes in Pskov Province, to V. A. Dolgorukov, head of the Third Section (political police), 12 July 1861, in *KD-5*, 93; Firsov and Kiseleva, *Byt Velikorusskikh krest'ian-zemlepashtsev*, 43–45, 206–8 (quotations: 207, 44–45). For early assertions of poor work by freed peasants, as well as refusal to work for nobles and general reduction of acreage sown, see, e.g., Charles Adler Jr., "Domestic Russia in 1861: A Contemporary Perspective," *Canadian Slavic Studies*, 3 (1969), 326–46 (esp. 343); the weekly report of the Minister of Internal Affairs Petr Valuev, 27 June 1862, in *Otmena krepostnogo prava; Doklady Ministrov vnutrennikh del o provedenii krest'ianskoi reform 1861–1862* (Moscow: Izdaetel'stvo Akademii nauk SSSR, 1950), 183 (on Voronezh Province); and more generally, the reports of the tsar's aides-de-camp in *Krest'ianskoe dvizhenie v 1861 godu posle otmeny kreptnogo prava*, ed. E. A. Morokhovets (Moscow: Izdatel'stvo Akademii nauk SSSR, 1949), passim. On the sharp reduction in the scope of noble-directed agriculture, see Hamburg, *Politics of the Russian Nobility*, 27–32; Korelin, *Dvorianstvo v poreformennoi Rossii*, 54–59; and Shanin, *Russia as a "Developing Society,"* esp. 136–40.

38. For a succinct explanation of the *otrabotka* system, see the editor's introduction in *KD-5*, 15. The quotations are from Engelgardt's Letter III (1873), in *Aleksandr Nikolaevich Engelgardt's Letters from the Country, 1872–1887*, ed. and trans. Cathy A. Frierson (New York: Oxford University Press, 1993), 55; and Korelin, *Dvorianstvo v poreformennoi Rossii*, 70. For Lenin's contrast between progressive (capitalist) wage labor and backward (servile) *otrabotka*, see V. I. Lenin, *The Development of Capitalism in Russia: The Process of the Formation of a Home Market for Large-Scale Industry* (1899; Moscow: Foreign Languages Publishing House, 1956), 190–262.

39. Mixter, "The Hiring Market as Workers' Turf," 294–340 (quotations: 311, 335). Mixter emphasized the "endemic conflict . . . between migrant workers and employ-

ers" (299–300), but for the suggestion that on "the large nobles' estates in the black earth region . . . the *batrak,* or hired laborer, accepted terms very like servile arrangements," see Leonard, *Agrarian Reform in Russia,* 138. See, also, Gatrell, *The Tsarist Economy,* 89–90; and Iakimenko, "Agrarnye migratsii v Rossi," 17–26.

40. Frierson, *Aleksandr Nikolaevich Engelgardt's Letters from the Country,* Letter VII (1879), 157–63 (quotation: 159); Firsov and Kiseleva, *Byt Velikorusskikh krest'ian-zemlepashstev,* 43–45 (quotations: 44, 43). Peasants as well as pomeshchiki sometimes hired temporary workers, especially "in a period of the heaviest field work," such as harvest time, when short-term workers could earn from eighty kopecks to one ruble twenty-five kopecks per day, while those hired for the entire season received fifty to seventy rubles (Firsov and Kiseleva, *Byt Velikorusskikh krest'ian-zemlepashstev,* 208). On child laborers, who usually received "one-third the lowest rate of the typical adult male worker," see esp. Boris B. Gorshkov, *Russia's Factory Children: State, Society, and Law, 1800–1917* (Pittsburgh: University of Pittsburgh Press, 2009), 2 (quotations in the text and in this note). Despite a poorly enforced 1882 law under which "the state progressively restricted children's employment in industry and introduced compulsory schooling for working children" (10), as late as 1897 "it is likely that . . . children age fifteen and younger constituted some 9–12 percent of Russia's industrial labor" (56).

41. Stocksdale, *When Emancipation Came,* 101–2, 119–21 (quotation: 121).

42. On the division between the "consumer" north and the "producer" south, see Leonard, *Agrarian Reform in Russia,* 195. The statistics on passports issued to peasants are from Burds, *Peasant Dreams and Market Politics,* 22–23. On significant otkhodnichestvo in the overwhelmingly agricultural regions of Riazan and Tambov Provinces, mostly to work for local landowners but also to engage in seasonal migrant labor in the steppes, see S. S. Kriukova, *Russkaia krest'ianskaia sem'ia vo vtoroi polovine XIX v.* (Moscow: Rossiiskaia Akademiia nauk, 1994), 61–66.

43. Engel, *Between the Fields and the City,* 101 (first quotation); ibid., 103; Rose Glickman, "Peasant Women and Their Work," in Eklof and Frank, *The World of the Russian Peasant,* esp. 50–54 (second quotation: 54); Burds, *Peasant Dreams and Market Politics,* 25 (preponderance of *male* otkhodniki); Engel, *Between the Fields and the City,* 70–71 (statistics on Tver Province otkhodniki).

44. Burds, *Peasant Dreams and Market Politics,* 25–27 (sex ratio in Iaroslavl Province); Glickman, "Peasant Women and Their Work," 53 (first quotation); N. L.-V., "Markitanty," 195 (second quotation); Barbara Engel, "The Women's Side: Male Outmigration and the Family Economy in Kostroma Province," orig. in *Slavic Review,* 45 (Summer 1986), 257–71, reprinted in Eklof and Frank, *The World of the Russian Peasant,* 65–80 (third quotation: 74). Women were more central than men to antebellum slave communities, in part because men were far more often hired out, sold off, and given passes to visit spouses held by different owners; see Deborah G. White, "Female Slaves: Sex Roles and Status in the Antebellum Plantation South," *Journal of Family History,* 8 (Fall 1983), 248–61.

45. Quotations are from the letter of Laborers of the White Hall Agricultural Society (Edward L. Carey, President) to Howard, Frederick County, Virginia, 18 March 1871, FBP, Assistant Adjutant General's Office, Letters Received; the Mobile *Advertiser and Register*, 31 March 1867, quoting the Mobile *Evening News*; and Hunter, *To 'Joy My Freedom*, 91 and 95 (see, also, 74–97). On urban labor actions, see also Rabinowitz, *Race Relations in the Urban South*, 73–76; and Fitzgerald, *Urban Emancipation*, 88–93. On sugar workers of southern Louisiana, see Rebecca J. Scott, " 'Stubborn and Disposed to Stand Their Ground': Black Militia, Sugar Workers and the Dynamics of Collective Action in the Louisiana Sugar Bowl, 1863–87," *Slavery and Abolition*, 20 (April 1999), 103–26. For collective land purchases by freedpeople, see Edward Magdol, *A Right to the Land: Essays on the Freedmen's Community* (Westport, CT: Greenwood Press, 1977), passim, esp. 174–99. On the more communal lives of Russian serfs than American slaves, see Kolchin, *Unfree Labor*, 195–357, passim.

46. Quotations are from the *Montgomery Advertiser*, 31 October 1867; the *Selma Daily Messenger*, 19 December 1867; and the *Alabama Beacon* (Greensboro), 7 December 1867.

47. The quotation is from Gregory P. Downs, *After Appomattox: Military Occupation and the Ends of War* (Cambridge, MA: Harvard University Press, 2015), 215. On post-reform violence and reaction, see my chapter 7.

48. Frierson, *Aleksandr Nikolaevich Engelgardt's Letters from the Country*, 55; Georg Brandes, *Impressions of Russia*, trans. Samuel C. Eastman (1889; New York: Thomas Y. Crowell, 1966), 36–37; Penningroth, *The Claims of Kinfolk*, 157, 156, citing and quoting Laura M. Towne, *Letters and Diary of Laura M. Towne; Written from the Sea Islands of South Carolina, 1862–1884*, ed. Rupert Sargent Holland (1912; New York, 1969), 23.

49. Quotations are from Nathans, *A Mind to Stay*, 121; U.S. Congress, Senate, *Report of the Committee of the Senate upon the Relations between Labor and Capital* (Washington, DC: Government Printing Office, 1885), IV, 48–50, 656; and James I. Mandel, "Paternalistic Authority in the Russian Countryside, 1856–1906" (Ph. D. diss., Columbia University, 1978), 129, 123. For planters' evolving perception of African Americans in the post-emancipation South, see James L. Roark, *Masters without Slaves: Southern Planters in the Civil War and Reconstruction* (New York: W. W. Norton, 1977), 156–209. For educated Russians' diverse views of post-emancipation peasants, see Cathy A. Frierson, *Peasant Icons: Representations of Rural People in Late Nineteenth-Century Russia* (New York: Oxford University Press, 1993); and for a perceptive new comparative study, see Amanda Brickell Bellows, *American Slavery and Russian Serfdom in the Post-Emancipation Imagination* (Chapel Hill: University of North Carolina Press, 2020).

50. Leigh, *Ten Years on a Georgia Plantation*, quotations: 128, 128, 156, 207. On the recruitment of immigrant labor in the post-emancipation Caribbean and Brazil, see, inter alia, W. Kloosterboer, *Involuntary Labour Since the Abolition of Slavery: A Survey of Compulsory Labour Throughout the World* (London: E. J. Brill, 1960), esp. 8–16, 32–39; William A. Green, *British Slave Emancipation: The Sugar Colonies and the Great Experi-*

ment, 1830–1865 (London: Oxford University Press, 1976), 163–75, and "Plantation Society and Indentured Labour: The Jamaican Case, 1834–1865," in *Colonialism and Migration: Indentured Labour before and after Slavery*, ed. P. C. Emmer (Dordrecht: Martinus Nijhoff, 1986), 163–86; P. C. Emmer, "The Meek Hindu: The Recruitment of Indian Labourers for Service Overseas, 1870–1916," ibid., 187–207; and George Reid Andrews, "Black and White Workers: São Paulo, Brazil, 1888–1928," in Rebecca Scott et al., *The Abolition of Slavery and the Aftermath of Emancipation in Brazil* (Durham, NC: Duke University Press, 1988), 85–118.

51. Leigh, *Ten Years on a Georgia Plantation*, esp. 204–8 (quotations: 205, 206, 202, 227, 226, 237, 239–40). The daughter of Lowcountry planter Pierce Butler and the English actress Frances Anne Kemble (who divorced in 1849), Butler Leigh lived for much of the ten-year period 1866–1876 on Butler's Island, but she spent months at time—including virtually all of the sickly summer seasons—away, often at the family's home in Philadelphia or in England. After her father died in 1867, she inherited the Georgia holdings (including Butler's Island), and in 1871 she married Englishman James Wentworth Leigh. For a history of the Butler family, see Bell, *Major Butler's Legacy*.

52. On the experiment with Chinese laborers in southern Louisiana, see Moon-Ho Jung, *Coolies and Cane: Race, Labor, and Sugar in the Age of Emancipation* (Baltimore: Johns Hopkins University Press, 2006). Quotations are from Leigh, *Ten Years on a Georgia Plantation*, 269; Whitelaw Reid, *After the War: A Tour of the Southern States, 1865–1866*, ed. C. Vann Woodward (1866; New York: Harper and Row, 1965), 417; John C. Rodrigue, *Reconstruction in the Cane Fields: From Slavery to Free Labor in Louisiana's Sugar Parishes, 1862–1880* (Baton Rouge: Louisiana State University Press, 2001), 137; and Jung, *Coolies and Cane*, 77–78, and 122.

53. Bell, *Major Butler's Legacy*, 418 (first quotation); Jung, *Coolies and Cane*, 87 (second and third quotations), 184 (fourth quotation); Rodrigue, *Reconstruction in the Cane Fields*, 137–38 (fifth quotation: 137).

54. Roark, *Masters without Slaves*, 165–69 (quotations: 166, 167); Jung, *Coolies and Cane*, 197 (quotation on railroad workers); Roland Berthoff, "Southern Attitudes toward Immigration, 1865–1914," *Journal of Southern History*, 17 (August 1951), 328–60. For the continued, but futile, interest of Southern whites in attracting Asian and European laborers to replace slaves, see Royce, *The Origins of Southern Sharecropping*, 119–49; and Matthew Pratt Guterl, *American Mediterranean: Southern Slaveholders in the Age of Emancipation* (Cambridge, MA: Harvard University Press, 2008), 145–83. As Guterl pointed out (179), "By 1870, the South actually had fewer foreign-born residents than it did in 1860."

55. Roark, *Masters without Slaves*, 121–31 (quotation: Henry Graves to his brother, 2 September 1867, 123); Todd W. Wahlstrom, *The Southern Exodus to Mexico: Migration across the Borderlands after the American Civil War* (Lincoln: University of Nebraska Press, 2015). Wahlstrom suggested (28) that the total number of Southern emigrants to Mexico may have reached five thousand. Most of them were "small to middling

ex-slaveholders who had previously relocated from such states as South Carolina and Georgia to Texas" (xxii), but they also included small numbers of African Americans, the majority of whom moved "under duress" and "chose to leave their former masters behind at the nearest opportunity" (39). After Emperor Maximilian's overthrow and the establishment of a republican regime in 1867, Southern migration to Mexico "dropped dramatically" (28).

56. Roark, *Masters without Slaves*, 126–31; Cyrus B. Dawsey and James M. Dawsey, "Leaving: The Context of the Southern Emigration to Brazil," in *The Confederados: Old South Immigrants in Brazil*, ed. Cyrus B. Dawsey and James M. Dawsey (Tuscaloosa: University of Alabama Press, 1995), 11–23. Dawsey and Dawsey estimated that a total of two thousand to four thousand white Southerners moved to Brazil after the Civil War, although fewer were there at any one time. For an interesting narrative written in 1943 by a woman who had experienced the post–Civil War emigration to Brazil as a young child, more than three-quarters of a century earlier, see "The Journey: The Sarah Bellona Smith Turner Ferguson Narrative," in Dawsey and Dawsey, *The Confederados*, 27–49. Describing primitive conditions that the new arrivals faced—"No one wore shoes or socks when we came here" and "Ploughs were not in use until the Americans introduced them"—Ferguson praised Emperor Dom Pedro II "for his foresight in bringing foreigners in to develop Brazil, realizing as he did that the riches here lying dormant would never be developed by the natives" (i.e., the Brazilians). Quotations are from "The Journey," 27 (text), 49 and 33 (this note).

57. For an interesting case study of a failed effort to find a slaveholder's paradise in Cuba, where one Southern exile found herself bemoaning the unsavory choice of using "stupid negroes or dazed Chinese" as laborers, see Guterl, *American Mediterranean*, chap. 3: "The Promise of Exile," 80–113 (quotation: 97).

58. Myers, *The Children of Pride*, 1307, 1319, 1337–38, 1438 (quotations), 1568 (biographical sketch).

59. Leigh, *Ten Years on a Georgia Plantation*; Bell, *Major Butler's Legacy*, 392–450, passim; Watson to his daughter Julia, 16 December 1865, Watson Papers; agreement between George Hagin and freedman W. L. Camp, 1 February 1866, Watson Papers; Roark, *Masters without Slaves*, 203 (last quotation). See, also, Kolchin, *First Freedom*, 32–33.

60. Quotations are from the Mobile *Daily Register*, 30 May 1869; Leigh, *Ten Years on a Georgia Plantation*, 249–50; J. B. Moore Diary, 24 April 1865, Alabama State Department of Archives and History; Daniel McNeill to William McLaurin, 27 February 1871, quoted in Roark, *Masters without Slaves*, 201. See, also, Nathans, *A Mind to Stay*, 93–126. On the decline of planter paternalism, see, inter alia, Robert A. Gilmour, "The Other Emancipation: Studies in the Society and Economy of Alabama Whites during Reconstruction" (Ph.D. diss., Johns Hopkins University, 1972), esp. 229–57; Roark, *Masters without Slaves*, 143–47, 197–203; and Pierre L. Van den Berghe, *Race and Racism: A Comparative Perspective* (New York: John Wiley and Sons, 1967), 25–33, 85.

61. At the time of the tenth census, in 1858, the male population of Russia was 28,935,190, of whom 23,350,494 were peasants. Close to half these peasants were privately held serfs—earlier substantially more than half of all peasants had been serfs—while of the remainder most were state peasants and others were owned by the Crown. See Kolchin, *Unfree Labor*, 52, 366; and my chapter 7 here.

62. Daniel Field, *The End of Serfdom: Nobility and Bureaucracy in Russia, 1855–1861* (Cambridge, MA: Harvard University Press, 1976), 134 (quotation); see, also, the Introduction to this book. For more extensive elaboration on the absenteeism and absentee mentality of Russian serfholders, as well as the contrast with American slaveholders, see Kolchin, *Unfree Labor*, esp. 58–61, 98–102, 148–49, 178–84, and 360–63.

63. Major General N. G. Kaznakov to Alexander I, 24 May 1861, in Morokhovets, *Krest'ianskoe dvizhenie v 1861 godu*, 94; Lieutenant Colonel Khodkevich, staff officer of the Corps of Gendarmes, to V. A. Dolgorukov, 12 July 1861, in *KD-5*, 93; John Crampton to Russell, 9 February 1861, and Francis Napier to Russell, 8 May 1861, in Adler Jr., "Domestic Russia in 1861," 333, 343; reports of Minister of Internal Affairs Petr Valuev, in *Otmena krepostnogo prava*, 183, 182 (quotation), 147. For other reports, see Morokhovets, *Krest'ianskoe dvizhenie v 1861 godu*, passim.

64. *Trudy Iaroslavskago gubernskago statisticheskago komiteta*, no. 3 (Iaroslavl, 1866), 8–9; Korelin, *Dvorianstvo v poreformennoi Rossii 1861–1904 gg.*, 128–29. A disproportionate share of hereditary nobles in the fifty provinces of European Russia—62 percent in 1858, 46 percent in 1897—were located in the nine western provinces (Korelin, *Dvorianstvo v poreformennoi Rossii*, 40). "Personal" nobles, who unlike hereditary nobles did not pass on their noble status to their children and did not usually have hereditary landed estates, were far more likely to live in cities. In Iaroslavl Province in 1865, 90.3 percent of personal nobles lived in cities, as did 76.5 percent in Russia as a whole (including the nine western provinces) in 1897.

65. Hamburg, *Politics of the Russian Nobility, 1881–1905*, 27.

66. Stocksdale, *When Emancipation Came*, 96, 119–21, 141. Stocksdale described the hotel in her dissertation, "In the Midst of Liberation: A Comparison of a Russian Estate and a Southern Plantation at the Moment of Emancipation" (Ph.D. diss., University of Delaware, 2016), 190–98. Most of the merchants with whom Yazykov dealt were members of ethnic minorities—most Tatars but at least one a Chuvash.

67. Frierson, *Aleksandr Nikolaevich Engelgardt's Letters from the Country*, 100. For a somewhat different interpretation, see Priscilla Roosevelt, *Life on the Russian Country Estate: A Social and Cultural History* (New Haven: Yale University Press, 1995). "Most [noble] memoirists assure us that their families welcomed the changes [brought by emancipation] . . . but some never adjusted to the new world," Roosevelt explained (319). Emphasizing the varied responses of pomeshchiki, she noted (320) that "numerous historic estates were in shambles by the end of the [nineteenth] century, but a few were being rescued and restored."

68. Seymour Becker, *Nobility and Privilege in Late Imperial Russia* (DeKalb: Northern Illinois University Press, 1985), 31–39; Korelin, *Dvorianstvo v poreformennoi Rossii*, 54–59; Gatrell, *The Tsarist Economy*, 113–15; Druzhinin, *Russkaia derevnia na perelome*, 136–46. Even in Saratov Province in 1883, peasants owned almost as much land as nobles, and including land held by merchants nobles held less than half the land: nobles owned 267,207.2 desiatiny (49.6 percent), merchants owned 31,663 desiatiny (5.9 percent), peasants owned 228,218 desiatiny (42.3 percent) communally and 12,018.3 desiatiny (2.2 percent) privately; computed from statistics in *Sbornik statisticheskikh svedenii po Saratovskoi gubernii*, I (Saratov, 1883), section I, 12–16.

69. Gatrell, *The Tsarist Economy*, 112; Shanin, *Russia as a "Developing Society,"* 136 (statistic on landownership), 10 (quotation 1), 101–02 (quotation 2); Leonard, *Agrarian Reform in Russia*, 175. Shanin's view of pre-Revolutionary Russia as a society dominated by family farming and independent peasant producers challenged the very different interpretation by V. I. Lenin of an emerging capitalist economy in which the peasantry became increasingly divided between a small rural bourgeoisie and a larger mass of exploited laborers; Lenin, *The Development of Capitalism in Russia*, 174. For more on the nature of the Russian free-labor economy, see my chapter 7.

70. Ransom and Sutch, *One Kind of Freedom*, 56–80 (statistics: 69); Wright, *Old South, New South*, 17–50. For emphasis on family farming among the freedpeople, see Sharon Ann Holt, *Making Freedom Pay: North Carolina Freedpeople Working for Themselves, 1865–1900* (Athens: University of Georgia Press, 2000), and "Making Freedom Pay: Freedpeople Working for Themselves, North Carolina, 1865–1900," *Journal of Southern History*, 60 (May 1994), 229–62. On the "surprising revival of small farm ownership after the Civil War" in the Lower Cape Fear area of southeastern North Carolina, see Adrienne Monteith Petty, *Standing Their Ground: Small Farmers in North Carolina Since the Civil War* (New York: Oxford University Press, 2013). Petty wrote of a "massive shift" of both white and Black "small farm owners into family-oriented commercial agriculture" (quotations: 29 and 43). See, also, Jeffrey R. Kerr-Ritchie, *Freedom's Seekers: Essays on Comparative Emancipation* (Baton Rouge: Louisiana State University Press, 2013), on the freedpeople's "conscious decisions not to work in old ways" (126–50, quotation: 128). Although Kerr-Ritchie emphasized the New-World "withdrawal . . . away from the 'slave' crop toward alternative means of lives and labor" (131), in most of the South the emergence of family farming was not accompanied by a rejection of commercial production.

Chapter 6. Free Labor II

1. On interference in the family lives of American slaves and Russian serfs—and the more pervasive nature of the former than the latter—see Peter Kolchin, *Unfree Labor: American Slavery and Russian Serfdom* (Cambridge, MA: Harvard University Press, 1987), 111–20.

2. For a pioneering "revisionist" study that emphasized the strength and cohesiveness of Black families under slavery, see Herbert G. Gutman, *The Black Family in Slavery and Freedom, 1750–1925* (New York: Pantheon Books, 1976). More recent—"post-revisionist"—scholars, while agreeing with revisionists on the resilience of slave families, have been struck by their diverse structures, under highly varied conditions. See, e.g., Brenda E. Stevenson, *Life in Black and White: Family and Community in the Slave South* (New York: Oxford University Press, 1996), esp. 159–257. For a brief survey, see Peter Kolchin, *American Slavery, 1619–1877* (New York: Hill and Wang, 1993), esp. 96–99, 118–27, 133–43. For a recent book focusing on enslaved *men's* experiences of sexual abuse, see Thomas A. Foster, *Rethinking Rufus: Sexual Violation of Enslaved Men* (Athens: University of Georgia Press, 2019).

3. Stuart M. Taylor, Assistant Adjutant General for South Carolina and Florida, General Orders No. 8, 11 August 1865, U.S. House of Representatives, 39 Cong., 1 Sess., ser. 1256, Exec. Doc. 70 (19 March 1866), 109 (quotations 1 and 2); Act to Regulate Domestic Relations of Negroes, 21 December 1865, South Carolina State Laws, U.S. House of Representatives, 39 Cong., 1 Sess., ser. 1263, Exec. Doc. 118, 13–14; State Laws Regarding Freedmen, ibid., 30–32; *Official Journal of the Constitutional Convention of the State of Alabama* (Montgomery, 1868), 262–63; Wager Swayne's Circular, 7 September 1865, in *Montgomery Daily Advertiser,* 9 September 1865 (quotation 3).

4. Quotations are from Amy Dru Stanley, *From Bondage to Contract: Wage Labor, Marriage, and the Market in the Age of Slave Emancipation* (New York: Cambridge University Press, 1998), 2 and 46; C. W. Buckley to Alabama Assistant Commissioner Wager Swayne, 1 Sept. 1865, FBP, Alabama Operations Reports; Langston to Commissioner O. O. Howard, 20 November 1867, FBP, Assistant Adjutant General's Office, Letters Received; Gillem to Howard, Vicksburg, MS, 15 July 1867, FBP, Assistant Adjutant General's Office, Letters Received; Sub-Assistant Commissioner Captain George E. Pingus, Darlington, SC, quoted by Freedmen's Bureau Assistant Commissioner for South Carolina Robert K. Scott to Howard, Charleston, 23 May 1867, FBP, Assistant Adjutant General's Office, Letters Received. A month after his letter emphasizing the depravity of rural Black Mississippians, however, Gillem suggested that "the greatest immorality exists in the vicinity of the larger towns where the freedpeople congregated during or immediately at the conclusion of the war"; Gillem to Howard, Vicksburg, 25 August 1867, FBP, Assistant Adjutant General's Office, Letters Received. For efforts by bureau agents to promote marital fidelity (and other bourgeois values) among freedpeople, see especially Mary Farmer-Kaiser, *Freedwomen and the Freedmen's Bureau: Race, Gender, and Public Policy in the Age of Emancipation* (New York: Fordham University Press, 2010). For the similar *wartime* preoccupation with marital fidelity of "military men and politicians," who "turned again and again to the institution of marriage and the heterosexual patriarchal family to impose order on a massive, chaotic process" of emancipation, see Stephanie McCurry, *Women's War: Fighting and Surviving the American Civil War* (Cambridge, MA: Harvard University

Press, 2019), 63–123 (quotation: 64). On the abolitionists' emphasis on the sexual depravity bred by slavery, see Ronald Walters, "The Erotic South: Civilization and Sexuality in Abolitionism," *American Quarterly*, 25 (March 1973), 177–201.

5. Columbus *Sun*, quoted in *Montgomery Daily Advertiser*, 23 November 1865 (quotation 1); "Act to Regulate Domestic Relations of Negroes," 21 December 1865, State Laws Regarding Freedmen, South Carolina, U.S. House of Representatives, 39 Cong., 1 Sess., ser. 1263, Exec. Doc. 118, 13–14; M. French to Assistant Commissioner Scott, Charleston, 6 November 1866, FBP, Assistant Adjutant General's Office, Annual Reports (quotation 2); 11 January 1866, State Laws Regarding Freedmen, Florida, U.S. House of Representatives, 39 Cong., 1 Sess., ser. 1263, Exec. Doc. 118, 21; Sub-Assistant Commissioner F. E. Grossman to Brevet Major L. L. McHenry, Assistant Adjutant General, Lake City, FL, 1 September 1866, FBP, Assistant Adjutant General's Office, Letters Received (quotation 3); Assistant Commissioner John T. Sprague to Commissioner Howard, Jacksonville, 1 October 1867, FBP, Assistant Adjutant General's Office, Annual Reports. For emphasis on the importance that marriage assumed to freedpeople, as a way "to affirm their freedom," see Laura F. Edwards, *Gendered Strife and Confusion: The Political Culture of Reconstruction* (Urbana: University of Illinois Press, 1997), 47.

6. Certificates of Marriage, Arkadelphia, AR, September 1865, FBP, Arkansas Book Records; 23 November 1865, State Laws Regarding Freedmen, Mississippi, U.S. House of Representatives, 39 Cong., 1 Sess., ser. 1263, Exec. Doc. 118, 26; typical marriage form, Jackson, Mississippi, 28 September 1865, FBP, Certificates of Marriage (quotation 1); Mississippi Assistant Commissioner Samuel Thomas to Commissioner Howard, Vicksburg, 14 October 1865, FBP, Assistant Adjutant General's Office, Letters Received (quotation 2); Virginia Assistant Commissioner O. Brown to Commissioner Howard, Richmond, 17 October 1866, FBP, Assistant Adjutant General's Office, Annual Reports; Sub-Assistant Commissioner J. W. Remington to Brown, Norfolk, Virginia, 30 April 1867, FBP, Assistant Adjutant General's Office, Letters Received; Brown to Howard, Richmond, 8 October 1867, FBP, Assistant Adjutant General's Office, Annual Reports (quotation 3). On the Freedmen's Bureau's compilation of marriage registers in Virginia, see also Daniel B. Thorp, "Cohabitation Registers and the Study of Slave Families in Virginia," *Slavery and Abolition*, 37 (December 2016), 744–60; and Edward L. Ayers, *The Thin Light of Freedom: The Civil War and Emancipation in the Heart of America* (New York: W. W. Norton, 2017), 379–83.

7. On post-emancipation efforts to reunite African American families separated under slavery, see especially Heather Andrea Williams, *Help Me to Find My People: The African American Search for Family Lost in Slavery* (Chapel Hill: University of North Carolina Press, 2012), 139–200 (quotations: 166, 165); see, also, Catherine A. Jones, *Intimate Reconstructions: Children in Postemancipation Virginia* (Charlottesville: University of Virginia Press, 2015), 50–54. On chaotic wartime conditions that led to additional family separations, see Yael A. Sternhell, *Routes of War: The World of Movement in the Con-*

federate South (Cambridge, MA: Harvard University Press, 2012), 93–154; Chandra Manning, *Troubled Refuge: Struggling for Freedom in the Civil War* (New York: Alfred A. Knopf, 2016), esp. 45–160; and Jim Downs, *Sick from Freedom: African-American Illness and Suffering during the Civil War and Reconstruction* (New York: Oxford University Press, 2012). Sometimes, high-level Freedmen's Bureau officials intervened to help locate missing family members; see, e.g., a letter from Commissioner Howard to Mississippi Assistant Commissioner Brevet Major General Thomas J. Wood asking for help finding Lucy Ann Smith, "who, when last heard from, was in Vicksburg" after having been sold from her home in Washington "to traders, who took her to Mississippi." Noting that "her mother is anxious to have her join her at Washington," Howard suggested: "You could look her up by allowing this note to go to the Colored Churches." Washington, 1 December 1866, FBP, Assistant Adjutant General's Office, Letters Sent.

8. Quotations are from J. G. Dodge, Superintendent of Freedmen, Hilton Head, 6 April 1865, in *Freedmen's Record*, vol. 1, no. 5 (May 1865), 73; Williams, *Help Me to Find My People*, 172; H. R. Pease, Freedmen's Bureau Superintendent of Education for Mississippi, to John W. Alvord, Bureau General Superintendent of Education, Vicksburg, MS, 20 July 1869, FBP, Education Department, Letters Received; Mobile *Advertiser and Register*, 14 August 1866; Williams, *Help Me to Find My People*, 168, 187. For another case of a freedman returning from military service to find his wife " 'legally' married to another man," see A. P. Ketchum, Acting Assistant Adjutant General, to Lieutenant J. F. Allison, Assistant Superintendent in Rocky Mount, NC, 28 March 1867, FBP, Assistant Adjutant General's Office, Letters Sent. See, also, Edward L. Ayers, who pointed out (in *The Thin Line of Freedom*, 375) that although "in a few instances" the Freedmen's Bureau in Augusta County, Virginia, was able to locate missing family members, more often the effort ended in failure because "slavery had taken people unimaginably far from their families. . . . Without information about their whereabouts, they might as well be in Texas or Florida."

9. See, especially, Jeffrey Burds, *Peasant Dreams and Market Politics: Labor Migration and the Russian Village, 1861–1905* (Pittsburgh: University of Pittsburgh Press, 1998); Barbara Alpern Engel, *Between the Fields and the City: Women, Work, and the Family in Russia, 1861–1914* (Cambridge: Cambridge University Press, 1994), and "The Women's Side: Male Outmigration and the Family Economy in Kostroma Province," in *The World of the Russian Peasant: Post-Emancipation Society and Culture*, ed. Ben Eklof and Stephen Frank (Boston: Unwin Hyman, 1990), 65–80. Other sources are cited below.

10. N. L-V, "Markitanty," in *Pamiatnaia knizhka Kaluzhskoi gubernii na 1862 i 1863 gody, izdannaia Kaluzhskim gubernskim statisticheskim komitetam* (Kaluga, 1863), 193–203 (quotations: 193, 195); and *Trudy Iaroslavskago gubernskago statisticheskago komiteta*, no. 3, (Iaroslavl, 1866), 53.

11. For statistics on otkhodnichestvo, see my chapter 5, above, and Burds, *Peasant Dreams and Market Politics*, 21–25. On the prevalence and varied nature of otkhod in

Vladimir Province, see responses to the Tenishev ethnographic survey, reprinted in *Byt Velikorusskikh krest'ian-zemlepashtsev: Opisanie materialov Etnograficheskogo biuro Kniazia V. N. Tenisheva (na primere Vladimirskoi gubernii)*, ed. B. M. Firsov and I. G. Kiseleva (St. Petersburg: Izdatel'stvo Evropeiskogo doma, 1993), 206–8.

12. The quotation is from Stepniak, *The Russian Peasantry: Their Agrarian Condition, Social Life and Religion* (New York: Harper and Brothers, 1888), 74. On family divisions, see especially Cathy Frierson, "Razdel: The Peasant Family Divided," *Russian Review*, 46 (1987), 35–52, and "Peasant Family Divisions and the Commune," in *Land Commune and Peasant Community in Russia: Communal Forms in Imperial and Early Soviet Society*, ed. Roger Bartlett (New York: St. Martin's Press, 1999), 302–20; and Christine D. Worobec, *Peasant Russia: Family and Community in the Post-Emancipation Period* (Princeton: Princeton University Press, 1991), 78–103. For an emphasis on the continuity of peasant family structures in Riazan and Tambov Provinces, see S. S. Kriukova, *Russkaia krest'ianskaia sem'ia vo vtoroi polovine XIX v.* (Moscow: Rossiiskaia akademiia nauk, 1994); by contrast, for the argument that "private initiative and the opportunity to live independently, beyond the control of one's elders, were strong motivations for household divisions," see Boris Mironov with Ben Eklof, *A Social History of Imperial Russia, 1700–1917*, 2 vols. (Boulder, CO: Westview Press, 2000), I, 138.

13. Worobec, *Peasant Russia*, 78–103 (quotation: 80). Statistics are from Frierson, "Peasant Family Divisions," 309; and N., "O krest'ianskikh semeinykh razdelakh v Voronezhskoi gubernii," in *Voronezhskii iubileinyi sbornik v pamiat' trekhsotletiia g. Voronezha* (Voronezh, 1886), 333–34. For a liberal pomeshchik's emphasis on the harmful effects of *razdely*, for which *baby* were frequently responsible, see *Aleksandr Nikolaevich Engelgardt's Letters from the Country, 1872–1887*, ed. and trans. Cathy A. Frierson (New York: Oxford University Press, 1993), Letter VII (1879), 163–68; for the similar conclusion of a nobleman who served as a "land captain" in Tambov Province from 1889 to 1896, see Aleksandr Novikov, *Zapiski zemskago nachal'nika* (St. Petersburg, 1899), 20. For the argument that noneconomic causes—especially "the tension of personal relations" and sometimes dissatisfaction of young wives—predominated in breaking up families, see Frierson, "Razdel," 46 (quotation). For emphasis on "*baby's* squabbles" and "*baby's* quarrels" as underlying divisions, see the reports on Vladimir Province in the ethnographic survey headed by Prince V. N. Tenishev in the 1890s, in Firsov and Kiseleva, *Byt Velikorusskikh krest'ian-zemlepashtsev*, 195 (quotations).

14. Thavolia Glymph, *Out of the House of Bondage: The Transformation of the Plantation Household* (New York: Cambridge University Press, 2008). On the growth of small-scale family farming among freedpeople in North Carolina, see Sharon Ann Holt, "Making Freedom Pay: Freedpeople Working for Themselves, North Carolina, 1865–1900," *Journal of Southern History*, 60 (May 1994), 229–62, and *Making Freedom Pay: North Carolina Freedpeople Working for Themselves, 1865–1900* (Athens: University of Georgia Press, 2000). See, also, inter alia, Elizabeth Fox-Genovese, *Within the Plantation Household: Black and White Women of the Old South* (Chapel Hill: Uni-

versity of North Carolina Press, 1988); Dylan C. Penningroth, *The Claims of Kinfolk: African American Property and Community in the Nineteenth-Century South* (Chapel Hill: University of North Carolina Press, 2003), esp. 163–86; and Peter Kolchin, *First Freedom: The Responses of Alabama's Blacks to Emancipation and Reconstruction* (1972; Tuscaloosa: University of Alabama Press, 2008), 45–78. For a graphic depiction of the shift from the collective to individual family-oriented life as small-scale sharecropping replaced plantation agricultural in the Deep South, see two maps of the Barrow Plantation in central Georgia, the first from 1860 and the second from 1881, originally published in *Scribner's Monthly,* 21 (April 1881), 832–33, reproduced in Roger L. Ransom and Richard Sutch, *One Kind of Freedom: The Economic Consequences of Emancipation* (New York: Cambridge University Press, 1977), 72. For recent scholarship on Black women in slavery and freedom, and on changing gender relations, see Vanessa M. Holden and Edward E. Baptist, "Nineteenth-Century Enslavement of Africans and African Americans in the United States South," in *Reinterpreting Southern Histories: Essays in Historiography,* ed. Craig Thompson Friend and Lorri Glover (Baton Rouge: Louisiana State University Press, 2020), 99–138; Catherine Clinton and Emily West, "Gender and Sexuality in the Old South," ibid., 139–65; and Bruce E. Baker and Elaine S. Frantz, "Against Synthesis: Diverse Approaches to the History of Reconstruction," ibid., 218–44. As Clinton and West observed (142–43), "the greatest transformation in southern gender history . . . has been the dramatic expansion of work on women of color. . . . Enslaved and free black women became more visible between the 1980s and the 2010s."

Although "global historians have been slow to take gender history seriously," Diane Paton pointed out that in the Atlantic World "emancipation meant an increasingly sharp definition of gender"; see Diane Paton, "Gender History, Global History, and Atlantic Slavery: On Racial Capitalism and Social Reproduction," *American Historical Review,* 127 (June 2022), 726–54 (quotations: 727, 753).

15. William Bird to Wager Swayne, Chambers County, AL, 28 August 1867, FBP, Alabama Letters Received; Bill Wyrosdick to Swayne, Crenshaw County, AL, 22 May 1867, FBP, Alabama Letters Received. For the argument that emancipation led white Southerners to impose a more rigid prohibition on sexual relations between Black men and white women than had existed under slavery, see Martha Hodes, *White Women, Black Men: Illicit Sex in the Nineteenth-Century South* (New Haven: Yale University Press, 1997), esp. 147–75. "Black Freedom brought a marked shift away from uneasy white toleration for sex between black men and white women," Hodes wrote (147), "and a move toward increasingly violent intolerance." In what amounted to a "sexualization of politics" (167), whites came to conflate Black men's political activity with their "alleged sexual liaisons with white women" (148). This newly violent intolerance culminated in the 1880s and 1890s in a surge of lynchings of Black men, typically occasioned by "false accusations of rape" of white women (176–208; quotation 176). See my chapter 7.

16. Hiram Read to General Pope, Auburn, AL, 10 August 1867, FBP, Alabama Letters Received. For a discussion of white use of county courts "to maintain a hold over black labor," including that of children, see Erik Mathisen, "Emancipation in the Dock: The Problems of Freedom in the Reconstruction Courtroom," in *The Civil War and Slavery Reconsidered: Negotiating the Peripheries*, ed. Laura R. Sandy and Marie S. Molloy (New York: Routledge, 2019), 169–82 (quotation: 177).

17. *Montgomery Daily Advertiser*, 14 December 1865, supplement.

18. The two quotations are from FBP, Alabama Letters Sent: John Easley to President Johnson, Marietta, GA, 24 September 1866; and Probate Judge J. M. Henderson to Assistant Commissioner Wager Swayne, Sparta, Conecuh County, AL, 25 January 1866. Commissioner Howard sent transportation orders dated 6 November for Easley's children. See, also, Kolchin, *First Freedom*, 63–67; and Rebecca Scott, "The Battle over the Child: Child Apprenticeship and the Freedmen's Bureau in North Carolina," *Prologue*, 10 (Summer 1978), 101–13.

19. Governor North to Brevet Major General Robinson, Raleigh, 29 October 1866, FBP, Assistant Adjutant General's Office, Letters Received; North to Robinson, Raleigh, 1 November 1866, ibid. (quotation 1); Robinson to North, Raleigh, 30 October 1866, ibid. (quotation 2); Robinson to North, Raleigh, 3 November 1866, ibid.; Acting Assistant Adjutant General A. P. Ketchum to Assistant Commissioner J. Bomford, Washington, 1 February 1867, FBP, Assistant Adjutant General's Office, Letters Sent (quotation 3); Edwards, *Gendered Strife and Confusion*, 47–54 (quotations 4 and 5: 50 and 54). See, also, Karin L. Zipf, "Reconstructing 'Free Woman': African-American Women, Apprenticeship, and Custody Rights during Reconstruction," *Journal of Women's History*, 12 (Spring 2000), 8–30.

20. Assistant Superintendent Spencer Smith to Judge J. F. Waddell, Tuskegee, 27 December 1865, FBP, Alabama Letters Received (quotation 1); statement of Laura Taylor to Fred Mashibah, Sub-Assistant Commissioner, Columbus, GA, 31 July 1866, FBP, Alabama Letters Received (quotation 2); Fred Mashibah to Assistant Adjutant General O. D. Kinsman, Columbus, GA, 1 August 1866, FBP, Alabama Letters Received; Lucy Abney to Swayne, sworn to before Robert Anngton, Jr., Livingston, Sumter County, 9 April 1867, FBP, Alabama Letters Received (quotation 3); O. P. Slater to Swayne, Marengo County, 22 April 1867, FBP, Alabama Letters Received (quotation 4); Judge Jno M. Henderson to Swayne, Evergreen, AL, 26 November 1867, FBP, Alabama Letters Received (quotation 5).

21. Assistant Superintendent Spencer Smith to Cadle, Tuskegee, 1 January 1866, FBP, Alabama Letters Received (quotation 1); J. F. Waddell to Wager Swayne, Crawford, AL, 4 January 1866, FBP, Alabama Letters Received; Probate Judge J. Henderson to Swayne, Conecuh County, 25 January 1866, FBP, Alabama Letters Received; Swayne Circular No. 4, 19 December 1865, reprinted in Mobile *Advertiser and Register*, 4 January 1866 (quotation 2).

22. Probate Judge B. W. Starke to Swayne, Elba, AL, 15 January 1866, FBP, Alabama Letters Received; General Orders No. 3, Montgomery, 16 April 1867, reprinted

in the Montgomery *Weekly Advertiser*, 23 April 1867; Swayne to Howard, Montgomery, 1 October 1867, FBP, Alabama Annual Report.

23. Report of Sub-Assistant Commissioner Robert Smith, Opelika, AL, 29 June 1867, FBP, Alabama Operations Reports (quotation). See, also, Sub-Assistant Commissioner J. F. McGogy to Assistant Adjutant General O. D. Kinsman, Talladega, 5 June 1867, FBP, Alabama Letters Received; and Sub-Assistant Commissioner S. S. Gardner to Kinsman, Greenville, AL, 18 June 1867, FBP, Alabama Operations Reports. Focusing on Mississippi, historian Erik Mathisen has argued that the struggle to combat the apprenticing of their children was closely linked to the freedpeople's efforts to gain control of other "possessions they believed to be rightfully theirs"; see Mathisen, *The Loyal Republic: Traitors, Slaves, and the Remaking of Citizenship in Civil War America* (Chapel Hill: University of North Carolina Press, 2018), 156–59 (quotation: 158). On the importance of community support for African American families, see Edwards, *Gendered Strife and Confusion*, 58–59, 61. See, also, Wilma King, *Stolen Childhood: Slave Youth in Nineteenth-Century America* (Bloomington: Indiana University Press, 1995), 151–54.

24. See, especially, Stanley, *From Bondage to Contract*, 138–48, 157–74, 187–90; also, Edwards, *Gendered Strife and Confusion*, 147–61. According to historian Sharon Romeo, African American women in Missouri—and, one might add, in other states as well—had a "gendered conception of citizenship," with "political priorities" that "included protection from physical violence, family reunification, custody of children, and the freedom to choose marital, romantic, and sexual partners." See Sharon Romeo, *Gender and the Jubilee: Black Freedom and the Reconstruction of Citizenship in Civil War Missouri* (Athens: University of Georgia Press, 2016), 123 (quotation). On domesticity and separate spheres, see Linda K. Kerber, "Separate Spheres, Female Worlds, Woman's Place: The Rhetoric of Women's History," *Journal of American History*, 75 (June 1988), 9–39; and Jeanne Boydston, *Home and Work: Housework, Wages, and the Ideology of Labor in the Early Republic* (New York: Oxford University Press, 1990). For an earlier version of separate spheres, which stressed the need for "true" women to adhere to the "four cardinal virtues" of "piety, purity, submissiveness, and domesticity," see Barbara Welter, "The Cult of True Womanhood: 1820–1860," *American Quarterly*, 18 (Summer 1966), 151–74 (quotation: 151). The Fisk quotation is from Farmer-Kaiser, *Freedwomen and the Freedmen's Bureau*, 14.

25. Assistant Commissioner John Sprague to Howard, Tallahassee, 28 February 1867, FBP, Assistant Adjutant General's Office, Letters Received; Henry Watson to W. A. and G. Maxwell and Co., Northampton, MA, 11 July 1866 (quotation), and Watson to his daughter Julia, Greensboro, AL, 16 December 1865, Henry Watson Papers, Duke University Library; Selma *Daily Messenger*, 13 March 1866; Thomas J. Wolfe, Probate Judge, to Captain S. C. Green, Linden, Marengo County, AL, 10 January 1868, FBP, Alabama Letters Received; John William De Forest, *A Union Officer in the Reconstruction*, ed. James H. Croushore and David Morris Potter (New Haven: Yale University

Press, 1948), 94, quoted in Leslie A. Schwalm, *A Hard Fight for We: Women's Transition from Slavery to Freedom in South Carolina* (Urbana: University of Illinois Press, 1997), 205; Joseph De Lyon to Howard, Savannah, 17 February 1866, FBP, Assistant Adjutant General's Office, Letters Received.

26. Schwalm, *A Hard Fight for We*, 206 (statistic), 201 (first quotation); Kolchin, *First Freedom*, 68; Glymph, *Out of the House of Bondage*, 137–203; Ransom and Sutch, *One Kind of Freedom*, 44–47 (statistics computed from table 3.3, 45). See Holt, "Making Freedom Pay," and *Making Freedom Pay*, passim (second quotation: 2); and Adrienne Monteith Petty, *Standing Their Ground: Small Farmers in North Carolina Since the Civil War* (New York: Oxford University Press, 2013), 13–54.

For landownership by Black women in Georgia's Lowcountry, see Karen Cook Bell, *Claiming Freedom: Race, Kinship, and Land in Nineteenth-Century Georgia* (Columbia: University of South Carolina Press, 2018), table A13 (96–98), which lists 105 Black women landowners in Chatham County, Georgia in 1876; most of these women owned very small plots of land, valued at one hundred to five hundred dollars, but the wealthiest among them owned land valued at $5,800. The reduction in hours worked by Black children reflected the successful resistance to apprenticing and more generally the changed family dynamics under which effective power over young African Americans shifted from their former owners to their parents. An important component of this shift, to be treated more fully later in this chapter, was the widespread schooling of Black children. Going to school did not preclude engaging in work—whether in the fields or at odd jobs—and the short school season partially accommodated the work needs of rural families. Still, full-time students could not be full-time workers, and the rise of first privately run schools (with Freedmen's Bureau support) and then state-sponsored public schools inevitably acted to reinforce the impact of other developments that were already transforming African American families throughout the South.

27. On serf families, see Kolchin, *Unfree Labor*, esp. 211–17. For the serfholder instruction, see "Nakaz kn. A. M. Cherkasskogo prikazchiku sela Markova (Moskovskogo uezda)" (1719), in "Nakazy votchinnym prikazchikam pervoi chetverti XVIII v.," ed. I. F. Petrovkskaia, *Istoricheskii arkhiv*, 8 (1953), 254.

28. The quotation is from Wallace, *Russia on the Eve of War and Revolution*, ed. and intro. Cyril E. Black, from rev. 1912 ed. (1st ed. 1877; New York: Vintage Books, 1961), 264. For emphasis on continuity, see, inter alia, Worobec, *Peasant Russia*, arguing that, despite changes, "the normative extended family . . . remained predominant" (12) because "culture is the slowest of all human creations to adapt to change" (14). See, also, Kriukova, *Russkaia krest'ianskaia sem'ia*, 192–95. For greater emphasis on changed family relations, see Mironov, *A Social History of Imperial Russia*, I, esp. 125–57.

29. Statistics are from *Sbornik statisticheskikh svedenii po Saratovskoi gubernyi*, 4 vols., I (Saratov, 1883), section III, summary table at end, 2–3; and Mironov, *A Social History of Imperial Russia*, I, 125. For slightly different figures, see, e.g., Frierson,

"Razdel," 43–44. For household size by province in 1897, based on the census of that year, see Worobec, *Peasant Russia*, 104.

30. Kriukova, *Russkaia krest'ianskaia sem'ia*, 56–58; Firsov and Kiseleva, *Byt Velikorusskikh krest'ian-zemlepashtsev*, 181.

31. Mironov, *A Social History of Imperial Russia*, I, 131–33 (quotations: 131, 133). In 1897, 50.5 percent of European Russia's rural households were nuclear, 42 percent were complex/extended, and 2.9 percent were single occupant, but more peasants still lived in complex/extended households (56 percent) than in nuclear (34.2 percent) or single-occupant (0.5) dwellings; Mironov, *A Social History of Imperial Russia*, I, 132. Statistics on Voronezh Province are from *Voronezhskii iubileinyi sbornik*, 334–35.

32. Mironov, *A Social History of Imperial Russia*, I, quotations: 145, 150, 157, 157. For emphasis on continuity, see works by Worobec and Kriukova, cited in note 28 of this chapter.

33. King, *Stolen Childhood*, 149 (quotation). For work challenging the assumption of ubiquitous harmonious relations within slave families and slave communities, see, inter alia, Peter Kolchin, "Reevaluating the Antebellum Slave Community: A Comparative Perspective," *Journal of American History*, 70 (December 1983), 579–601; Ann Patton Malone, *Sweet Chariot: Slave Family and Household Structure in Nineteenth-Century Louisiana* (Chapel Hill: University of North Carolina Press, 1992); Stevenson, *Life in Black and White*, 159–257; Penningroth, *The Claims of Kinfolk;* and Jeff Forret, *Slave against Slave: Plantation Violence in the Old South* (Baton Rouge: Louisiana State University Press, 2015). As noted below, Penningroth has also pioneered in probing the changing nature of divisions among African Americans in the *post*-emancipation years.

34. Report of Sub-Assistant Commissioner George E. Pingus, Darlington, SC, quoted by Assistant Commissioner R. K. Scott to Commissioner Howard, Charleston, 23 May 1867, FBP, Assistant Adjutant General's Office, Letters Received; Watkins, quoted in Edwards, *Gendered Strife and Confusion*, 59; William Bird to Alabama Assistant Commissioner Wager Swayne, Chambers County, AL, 28 August 1867, FBP, Alabama Letters Received; Silas Clear quoted in Nancy Bercaw, *Gendered Freedoms: Race, Rights, and the Politics of Household in the Delta, 1861–1875* (Gainesville: University Press of Florida, 2003), 99. For similar assertions of spousal ownership, see Stanley, *From Bondage to Contract*, who quoted a Tennessee freedman as explaining that he married his wife "to wait on me" and a North Carolina freedman as announcing of his wife, "I consider her my property" (49).

35. Penningroth, *The Claims of Kinfolk*, 176–80 (quotation 176); Farmer-Kaiser, *Freedwomen and the Freedmen's Bureau* 141–57, 166–71 (quotations: 166, 11). Penningroth found that "fully 5 percent of all complaints that freedwomen brought to the Freedmen's Bureau court in Mississippi involved violence by their husbands" (180). Some Black women evidently accepted—at least publicly—their husbands' right to treat them violently. "Wife beating among the negroes has of late become so common that the negro women seem to labor under the impression that their husbands have a

perfect right to beat them on all and every occasion," observed the Mobile *Daily Register* (2 July 1868). "Numerous cases have been brought before the Mayor, where negroes have treated their wives in a most brutal manner, yet, in almost every instance, the women have begged the Mayor to let their husbands off."

36. Penningroth, *The Claims of Kinfolk*, 164–70 (quotations: 164, 170); Jones, *Intimate Reconstructions*, 63; Bercaw, *Gendered Freedoms*, 132. On slaves' use of children to cultivate garden plots, see Penningroth, *The Claims of Kinfolk*, 82–84. For the argument that large slave families were best able to accumulate property, see Larry E. Hudson Jr., *To Have and to Hold: Slave Work and Family Life in Antebellum South Carolina* (Athens: University of Georgia Press, 1997), esp. 32–78. (Note how this argument resembles the assumption in Russia that large peasant families were the most economically viable.) For a different approach to Black children after emancipation, stressing competing visions of freedom, see Mary Niall Mitchell, *Raising Freedom's Child: Black Children and Visions of the Future after Slavery* (New York: New York University Press, 2008).

37. Theodore Rosengarten, *All God's Dangers: The Life of Nate Shaw* (New York: Random House, 1974), 3–93, passim (quotations: 26, 26, 23, 17).

38. U.S. Congress, Senate, *Report of the Committee of the Senate upon the Relations between Labor and Capital* (Washington, DC: Government Printing Office, 1885), IV, 48–49, 656. See Kolchin, *First Freedom*, 184–86.

39. Kolchin, *First Freedom*, 67–72; Orville Vernon Burton, *In My Father's House Are Many Mansions: Family and Community in Edgefield, South Carolina* (Chapel Hill: University of North Carolina Press, 1985), 26–62, 318–19 (quotation: 318). Nancy Bercaw noted a similar contrast between rural and urban Black residents of the Mississippi Delta in 1870: "Nuclear families comprised 89 percent of all African-American households remaining on the land. In contrast, nuclear families comprised only 48 percent of [Black] households in the cities"; Bercaw, *Gendered Freedoms*, 120. Sharon Ann Holt found slightly larger households—averaging more than six persons—prevalent among rural African Americans in Granville County, North Carolina; see Holt, *Making Freedom Pay*, 96. For the argument that "the Negro community in New Orleans was remarkably successful in stabilizing families during Reconstruction," see John W. Blassingame, *Black New Orleans, 1860–1880* (Chicago: University of Chicago Press, 1973). "By 1880," Blassingame concluded, "the Negro family had evolved into a patriarchal institution almost as stable as the white family" (79). For a somewhat different emphasis, on freedpeople putting Black family beliefs into practice, see Gutman, *The Black Family in Slavery and Freedom*, 385–431. On the centrality of kinship ties to the post-emancipation black struggle, see Hahn, *A Nation under Our Feet*, 166–70. For the now-dated debate of the 1960s over the dysfunction of Black families in twentieth-century urban ghettos, dysfunction that many social scientists linked to the supposed matriarchal structure, disruption, and consequent weakness of enslaved African American families, see, inter alia, Daniel Patrick Moynihan, *The Negro Family:*

The Case for National Action (Washington, DC: Government Printing Office, 1965); Thomas F. Pettigrew, *A Profile of the Negro American* (Princeton: D. Van Nostrand, 1964); Kenneth B. Clark, *Dark Ghetto: Dilemmas of Social Power* (New York: Harper and Row, 1965); and Lee Rainwater and William L. Yancey, eds., *The Moynihan Report and the Politics of Controversy* (Cambridge, MA: MIT Press, 1967).

40. Bercaw, *Gendered Freedoms*, 106–16 (quotation: 110); Noralee Frankel, *Freedom's Women: Black Women and Families in Civil War Era Mississippi* (Bloomington: Indiana University Press, 1999), 124–25. For "taking up" and "sweethearting" under slavery, see Anthony E. Kaye, *Joining Places: Slave Neighborhoods in the Old South* (Chapel Hill: University of North Carolina Press, 2007), esp. 51–82. On the diversity of African American families under slavery, see, inter alia, Malone, *Sweet Chariot*; and Stevenson, *Life in Black and White*, 159–257. But see, also, Daniel B. Thorp, *Facing Freedom: An African American Community in Virginia from Reconstruction to Jim Crow* (Charlottesville: University of Virginia Press, 2017), 43–69, on Blacks in Montgomery County, Virginia. Thorp concluded (69) that "for most members of Montgomery County's African American community after the Civil War family meant nuclear, patriarchal, two-parent families."

41. Firsov and Kiseleva, *Byt Velikorusskikh krest'ian-zemlepashtsev*, 185 (on "complete authority" and arranged marriages in Shuiskii district), and 266 (on harsh treatment in Melenkovskii and Shuiskii districts); *The Village of Viriatino; An Ethnographic Study of a Russian Village from before the Revolution to the Present*, ed. and trans. Sula Benet (Garden City, NY: Doubleday, 1970; originally Moscow, 1958), 120–22 (quotation: 121) (on Morshansk district of Tambov Province); Stephen P. Frank, *Crime, Cultural Conflict, and Justice in Rural Russia, 1856–1914* (Berkeley: University of California Press, 1999), 8–10, 19–30 (quotation: 9); Olga Semyonova Tian-Shanskaia, *Village Life in Late Tsarist Russia*, ed. David L. Ransel, trans. Ransel with Michael Levine (Bloomington: Indiana University Press, 1993), 24–61 (quotations: 51, 52). On health and life expectancy of Russian peasants, see my chapter 7.

42. Firsov and Kiseleva, *Byt Velokorusskikh krest'ian-zemlepashtsev*, 264; Rose Glickman, "Peasant Women and Their Work," in *The World of the Russian Peasant: Post-Emancipation Society and Culture*, ed. Ben Eklof and Stephan Frank (Boston: Unwin Hyman, 1990), 45–63 (quotation: 46). Another respondent to the Tenishev survey, also from the Melenkovskii district, explained (264) that the birth of a boy was "always a joy" because it would typically lead to an increase in the family's land allotment and therefore to an improvement in "the family's well-being." By contrast, a third respondent, from Vladimir Province's Shuiskii district, suggested (264) that especially "where members of the family work in a factory," a girl was more welcome because she was more likely to become a "helper" and because she would be "more modest and obedient" than a boy. For a brief summary of the roles and hardships of women in serf families, see Kolchin, *Unfree Labor*, 215–16. On the continued preference for boys over girls, see Tian-Shanskaia, *Village Life in Late Tsarist Russia*, 9–10; and Novikov,

Zapiski zemskago nachal'nika, who noted (14) that "from the moment of birth the fate of the baba is worse than that of the muzhik." On the normality of wifebeating, see, inter alia, Engel, *Between the Fields and the City*, 16–32; and Christine D. Worobec, "Victims or Actors? Russian Peasant Women and Patriarchy," in *Peasant Economy, Culture, and Politics of European Russia, 1800–1921*, ed. Esther Kingston-Mann and Timothy Mixter (Princeton: Princeton University Press, 1991), esp. 199–205.

43. Engel, "The Woman's Side," 74 (quotation 1); Engel, *Between the Fields and the City*, 34–63 (quotation 2: 51); Worobec, "Victims or Actors?" 184–87; Engel, "The Woman's Side," 71 (quotation 3). In *A Social History of Imperial Russia*, Boris Mironov described a similar increased authority for *widows* within households, but not in assemblies, where they "lacked official recognition" (I, 345).

44. Engel, *Between the Fields and the City*, 73–74, 126–27, 166–97 (quotation 1: 73); Brenda Meehan-Waters, "To Save Oneself: Russian Peasant Women and the Development of Women's Religious Communities in Prerevolutionary Russia," in *Russian Peasant Women*, ed. Beatrice Farnsworth and Lynn Viola (New York: Oxford University Press, 1992), 121–33 (quotations 2 and 3: 122, 123). According to Engel (*Between the Fields and the City*, 181–82), St. Petersburg's prostitutes typically had intercourse for the first time between the ages of fifteen and nineteen, 14 percent of the time through rape.

45. Frierson, "Peasant Family Divisions and the Commune," 303–20 (quotation: 317); Engel, *Between the Fields and the City*, 16–33 (quotation: 32); Beatrice Farnsworth, "The Litigious Daughter-in-Law: Family Relations in Rural Russia in the Second Half of the Nineteenth Century," in Farnsworth and Viola, *Russian Peasant Women*, 89–106 (quotations: 102, 103). Divorce among peasants was exceedingly rare, but the rate increased from 1.3 per thousand in the 1860s to 4.2 per thousand in 1914 (Engel, *Between the Fields and the City*, 26–27). For the suggestion by a government official in Tambov Province in the 1890s that old men played a patriarchal role only in large, prosperous peasant families and had little influence in most families, see Novikov, *Zapiksi zemskago nachal'nika*, 18–20. Although the *bol'shukha* was usually the *bol'shak*'s wife, she could also be his widow, or even his "eldest daughter-in-law, if the bol'shak [was] a widower"; Firsov and Kiseleva, *Byt Velikorusskikh zemlepashtsev*, 182 (Vladimir Province, Shuiskii district). See, also, Firsov and Kiseleva, *Byt Velikorusskikh zemlepashtsev*, 188, for several reports from Vladimir Province that peasants typically treated the elderly "indifferently, without respect" (quotation from Susdal'skii district).

46. Engel, *Between the Fields and the City*, 75–77, 125 (quotation 1); Burds, *Peasant Dreams and Market Politics*, 19 (quotation 2), 30–34, 70–75, 143–83, 186–218; Benet, *The Village of Viriatino*, 62–66 (on changes in peasant housing); Worobec, *Peasant Russia*, 119–216 (151–74 on marriage patterns); Laura Engelstein, *The Keys to Happiness: Sex and the Search for Modernity in Fin-de-Siècle Russia* (Ithaca, NY: Cornell University Press, 1992), 4 (quotation 3); Mironov, *A Social History of Imperial Russia*, I, 157 (quotation 4). For emphasis on the continued post-emancipation patriarchal character of the peasant family, see also Kriukova, *Russkaia krest'ianskaia sem'ia*; and Benet, *The

Village of Viriatino, whose authors argued that fundamental changes in family relations came only with the spread of capitalist relations to the countryside in the 1880s and 1890s. For a very brief description of traditional courting and marriage rituals under serfdom, see Kolchin, *Unfree Labor*, 214–17.

47. Tian-Shanskaia, *Village Life in Late Tsarist Russia*, 67 (quotation 1), 21 (quotation 2); Novikov, *Zapiski zemskago nachal'nika*, 9–14 (quotation 3: 10); Frierson, *Aleksandr Nikolaevich Engelgardt's Letters from the Countryside*, Letter I (1872), 34 (quotation 4); Worobec, "Victims or Actors?" 199–205 (quotation 5: 204); Sally West, *I Shop in Moscow: Advertising and the Creation of Consumer Culture in Late Tsarist Russia* (DeKalb: Northern Illinois University Press, 2011), 159–73 (quotations 6 and 7: 159, 164); Engelstein, *The Keys to Happiness*, 97 (quotation 8). See, also, Glickman, "Women and the Peasant Commune"; and Glickman, "Peasant Women and Their Work," 45–63. Belief in witchcraft and accusation of women as "witches" remained common among Russian peasants in the second half of the nineteenth century, long after such views had largely disappeared in Western Europe and the United States; the witch, or klikusha, explained Christine Worobec, "symbolized the out-of-control woman." See Worobec, *Possessed*, xii (quotation).

48. Harriet A. Jacobs, *Incidents in the Life of a Slave Girl, Written by Herself*, ed. Jean Fagan Yellin (1861; Cambridge, MA: Harvard University Press, 1987), 8; Frederick Douglass, *Narrative of the Life of Frederick Douglass, An American Slave: Written by Himself* (1845; New York: New American Library, 1968), 53 (quotation). For the administrative roles of peasant clerks and stewards, see Kolchin, *Unfree Labor*, 62. On slave and serf literacy and illiteracy, see Janet Duitsman Cornelius, *"When I Can Read My Title Clear": Literacy, Slavery, and Religion in the Antebellum South* (Columbia: University of South Carolina Press, 1991); Heather Andrea Williams, *Self-Taught: African American Education in Slavery and Freedom* (Chapel Hill: University of North Carolina Press, 2005), 7–29; B. N. Mironov, "Literacy in Russia, 1797–1917: New Historical Information through the Application of Retrospective Predictive Methods," *Soviet Studies in History*, 25 (Winter 1986–87), 89–117 (originally published as "Gramotnost' v Rossii 1797–1917: Poluchenie novoi istoricheskoi informatsii s pomoshch'iu metodov retrospektivnogo prognozirovaniia," *Istoriia SSSR*, 1985, no. 4, 137–53); and Ben Eklof, *Russian Peasant Schools: Officialdom, Village Culture, and Popular Pedagogy, 1861–1914* (Berkeley: University of California Press, 1986), 19–49. According to Eklof (35), in 1857 the chances of any Russian child (including a noble child) attending a government-sponsored school was one in 138; a peasant's chance would have been statistically close to nonexistent. For memoirs written by elite, literate peasants, see N. N. Shipov, "Istoriia moei zhizni: Razskaz byvshago krepostnago krest'ianina N. N. Shipova," *Russkaia starina*, 30 (1881), 133–48, 221–40, 437–78, 665–78; and Aleksandr Nikitenko, *Up from Serfdom: My Childhood and Youth in Russia, 1804–1824*, trans. Helen Saltz Jacobson (New Haven: Yale University Press, 2001). Nikitenko's father, Nikolai Petrovich Nikitenko, who as a boy was chosen to sing in Count N. P. Sheremetev's choir, attended a

special school for the choirboys, where he learned to read and write before becoming the count's chief clerk. See, also, John MacKay, "Introduction: Serfs as Writers," in *Four Russian Serf Narratives*, ed. and trans. John MacKay (Madison: University of Wisconsin Press, 2009), 3–22.

49. J. Lang, *Results of the Serf Emancipation in Russia* (eight-page pamphlet, New York: Loyal Publication Society, 1864), 5–6, 4 (quotations); *Pamiatnaia knizhka Kaluzhskoi gubernii na 1862 i 1863 gody*, 145–46. On the American Missionary Association, see Joe M. Richardson, *Christian Reconstruction: The American Missionary Association and Southern Blacks, 1861–1890* (Athens: University of Georgia Press, 1986). For two pioneering studies of missionary educational efforts, one during and the other following the Civil War, see Willie Lee Rose, *Rehearsal for Reconstruction: The Port Royal Experiment* (New York: Random House, 1964); and Jacqueline Jones, *Soldiers of Light and Love: Northern Teachers and Southern Blacks, 1865–1873* (Chapel Hill: University of North Carolina Press, 1980). For leading freedmen's aid society journals, see *American Missionary* (American Missionary Association), *National Freedman* (National Freedman's Relief Association), and *Freedmen's Record* (New-England Freedmen's Aid Society).

50. The quotation is from an abstract of a report by Miss A. C. Peckham in the *National Freedman*, vol. I, no. 6 (15 July 1865), 192. For some basic secondary works on freedpeople's education in the South, see, inter alia, Williams, *Self-Taught*; Ronald E. Butchart, *Schooling the Freedpeople: Teaching, Learning, and the Struggle for Black Freedom, 1861–1876* (Chapel Hill: University of North Carolina Press, 2010); Christopher Span, *From Cotton Field to Schoolhouse: African American Education in Mississippi, 1862–1875* (Chapel Hill: University of North Carolina Press, 2009); Kolchin, *First Freedom*, 79–106; Robert Francis Engs, *Educating the Disfranchised and Disinherited: Samuel Chapman Armstrong and Hampton Institute, 1839–1893* (Knoxville: University of Tennessee Press, 1999); and Adam Fairclough, *A Class of Their Own: Black Teachers in the Segregated South* (Cambridge, MA: Harvard University Press, 2007). For two very different early studies, see Henry Lee Swint, *The Northern Teacher in the South, 1862–1870* (Nashville: Vanderbilt University Press, 1941), and Horace Mann Bond, *Negro Education in Alabama: A Study in Cotton and Steel* (1939; New York: Atheneum, 1969), 73–119. On peasant education in Russia, see Eklof, *Russian Peasant Schools*; Ben Eklof, "Face to the Village: The Russian Teacher and the Peasant Community, 1880–1914," in *Land Commune and Peasant Community in Russia: Communal Forms in Imperial and Early Soviet Society*, ed. Roger Bartlett (New York: St. Martin's Press, 1990), 339–62; Jeffrey Brooks, *When Russia Learned to Read: Literacy and Popular Literature, 1861–1917* (Princeton: Princeton University Press, 1985); and Mironov, "Literacy in Russia."

51. The two quotations are from "American Freedmen's Inquiry Commission, Preliminary Report" (30 June 1863), in *The Radical Republicans and Reconstruction, 1861–1870*, ed. Harold Hyman (Indianapolis: Bobbs-Merrill, 1967), 120; and Rev. Thomas Callahan, in the *Liberator*, 8 January 1864, quoted in *The Negro's Civil War: How American Negroes Felt and Acted during the War for the Union*, ed. James M.

McPherson (New York: Random House, 1965), 212. For diverse facets of wartime education of African Americans, in the occupied South and in the Union Army, see Rose, *Rehearsal for Reconstruction*, esp. 85–88 and 229–35; Williams, *Self-Taught*, 30–66; Manning, *Troubled Refuge*, esp. 53–54, 85–87, 108–09; John W. Blassingame, "The Union Army as an Education Institution for Negroes," *Journal of Negro Education*, 34 (Spring 1965), 152–59; and Chandra Manning, *What This Cruel War Was Over: Soldiers, Slavery, and the Civil War* (New York: Random House, 2007), 192–93.

52. Quotations are from Second Annual Report of New England Freedmen's Aid Society, *Freedmen's Record*, vol. I, no. 4 (April 1865), 53; Foner, *Reconstruction*, 96; Annual Report of William T. Briggs, Superintendent of Colored Schools in North Carolina, *National Freedman*, vol. I, no. 7 (15 August 1865), 217–18; and Elliott Whipple to Rev. E. P. Smith, LaFayette, AL, 17 June 1867, American Missionary Association Papers, Fisk University. See sources listed on the South in notes 48, 49, 50, and 51 of this chapter.

53. John W. Alvord, Consolidated Monthly School Report, April 1867, FBP, Assistant Adjutant General's Office, Letters Received; Report of Wager Swayne, 31 October 1866, U.S. Congress, Senate, Ex. Doc. No. 6, 39th Congress, 2nd Sess., p. 12. These figures, which varied substantially by state, should be regarded as approximate and indicative of trends, rather than precise, because the Freedmen's Bureau did not receive reports from all schools. In February 1867, of 5,325 Black students in "regularly reporting" schools in Alabama, 1,075 paid tuition, while 4,250 were admitted free; FBP, Alabama Educational Division, Consolidated School Reports. (A substantial number of additional students attended schools that were not "regularly reporting.")

54. Quotations are from John W. Alvord to Howard, Washington, D.C., 18 December 1866, Abstract of School Reports, FBP, Assistant Adjutant General's Office, Letters Received; and Letter from W. C. Gannett, Savannah, 28 April 1865, *Freedmen's Record*, vol. I, no. 6 (June 1865), 92. For the argument that "a commitment to the emancipation of their people made the black teachers by far the most important of the teachers in the first generation of postbellum black education," see Butchart, *Schooling for the Freedpeople*, 44.

55. Quotations are from Bella Gibbons to Mrs. Cowing, Charlottesville, VA, 3 February 1868, in *Freedmen's Record*, vol. IV, no. 3 (March 1868), 42; B. F. Whitlemore, Superintendent of Education for the Military District of Eastern South Carolina, to Acting Assistant Commissioner Brevet Brigadier General Gile, Darlington, SC, 25 May 1866, FBP, South Carolina Letters Received; Philena Carking, Charlottesville, VA, 14 February 1868, in *Freedmen's Record*, vol. IV, no. 3 (March 1868), 36; and Williams, *Self-Taught*, 171. On Black teachers as officeholders, see Foner, *Freedom's Lawmakers*, xxi; and Fairclough, *A Class of Their Own*, 48–49.

56. Report of J. W. Alvord, 1 January 1866, U.S. Congress, House Exec. Doc. No. 70, 39th Congress, 1st Sess., 342 (quotation 1); Edwin Beecher to John W. Alvord, Montgomery, AL, 5 January 1870, FBP, Alabama Educational Division, Semi-Annual Report of the Superintendent of Education (quotation 2); R. M. Manly, Virginia Superintendent

of Education, to Howard, Richmond, 22 May 1867, FBP, Assistant Adjutant General's Office, Letters Received (quotation 3); Span, *From Cotton Field to Schoolhouse*, 33, 42 (quotations 4 and 5).

57. Butchart, *Schooling the Freedpeople*, appendix A, 79–83 (general statistics); 57, 67 (quotations); 52–77 (Southern white teachers); 17–51 (Southern Black teachers). See, also, Freedmen's Bureau statistics in FBP, Educational Division, Consolidated Statistical Reports. For a good description of the diversity of teachers in Montgomery County, Virginia's freedpeople's schools—all of which were "owned by the freedpeople themselves"—see Thorp, *Facing Freedom*, 133, 134. Of nine known teachers who taught there from February 1867 to June 1870, there were "three white northern women, one black northern man, one foreign-born black man, one white southern man, one black southern man, and two black men of unknown origin." Thorp noted (134) that "five of the nine were black, [and] six of the nine were men."

58. D. Burt, Tennessee Superintendent of Education, to Assistant Commissioner J. R. Lewis, Nashville, 31 October 1866, FBP, Assistant Adjutant General's Office, Annual Reports (quotations 1 and 4); letter of Philena Carkin, Charlottesville, VA, 14 February 1868, in *Freedmen's Record*, vol. IV, no. 3 (March 1868), 36 (quotation 2); Butchart, *Schooling the Freedpeople*, 43 (quotation 3).

59. J. E. Greenfield to G. M. Edmunds, Columbus, MS, 30 July 1867, FBP, Education Division, Letters Received (quotation 1); Fairclough, *A Class of Their Own*, 138 (quotation 2), 149 (statistic and quotation 3), 13–14 (statistic), and 61 (quotation 4).

60. FBP, Education Division, Consolidated Statistical Reports (statistics); Butchart, *Schooling the Freedpeople*, 27, 28 (quotations 1 and 2); Kolchin, *First Freedom*, 90–91 (on Talladega Normal School; quotation 3: 91); J. G. Chandron, Superintendent of Education, Talladega County, to Rev. H. E. Brown, Talladega, AL, 30 October 1869, American Missionary Association Papers (quotation 4). For a study of a Black normal school established in Hampton, Virginia, in 1868, see Engs, *Educating the Disfranchised and Disinherited*, esp. 70–143.

61. Kolchin, *First Freedom*, 97 (on establishment of public schools in Alabama and on teachers' salaries); Foner, *Reconstruction*, 365–68; Howard N. Rabinowitz, "From Exclusion to Segregation: Southern Race Relations, 1865–1890," *Journal of American History*, 63 (September 1976), 325–50. See, also, Rabinowitz, "Half a Loaf: The Shift from White to Black Teachers in the Negro Schools of the Urban South, 1865–1890," *Journal of Southern History*, 40 (November 1974), 565–94. On the experiment with integrated schools in southern Louisiana, see Louis R. Harlan, "Desegregation in New Orleans Public Schools during Reconstruction," *American Historical Review*, 67 (April 1962), 663–75.

62. *Otmena krepostnogo prava: Doklady Ministrov vnutrennikh del o provedenii krest'ianskoi reform 1861–1862* (Moscow: Izdatel'stvo Akademii nauk SSSR, 1950), 114 (Podolia Province, 22 February 1862), 109 (Smolensk Province, 8 February 1862), 188 (Vologda Province 4 July 1862), 169 (Perm Province, 6 June 1862); Eklof, *Russian Peasant Schools*, 70–214, 254–55 (quotation: 84).

63. Frierson, *Aleksandr Nikolaevich Engelgardt's Letters from the Country*, 90 (quotations 1 and 2); Novikov, *Zapiski zemskago nachal'nika*, 11–14; Tian-Shanskaia, *Village Life in Late Tsarist Russia*, 45 (quotation 3); Eklof, *Russian Peasant Schools*, 481 (quotation 4). For an account similar to Engelgardt's of peasants' reluctance to send their children to school in "the south of Russia" shortly after emancipation, see Brooks, *When Russia Learned to Read*, 3. When the parents of some thirty children who were being taught by a priest discovered that "the schooling was not compulsory, they ordered their children home, and the experiment in primary education came to an end." The priest, noting that the parents considered sending their children to school "as a loss of needed work time" and therefore "request[ed] that I assign their children a salary for attending school," reported that the peasants had, in his words, "decisively crushed every inclination and love I had for the matter." The priest's account originally appeared in the clerical magazine *Pravoslavnoe obozrenie* [*Orthodox Review*] (November 1863), 157–59.

64. Frierson, *Aleksandr Nikolaevich Engelgardt's Letters from the Country*, 90 (quotation 1); Brooks, *When Russia Learned to Read*, 36–38 (quotation 2: 37). Commune schools, although similar to literacy schools, were officially considered to constitute a distinct category.

65. Brooks, *When Russia Learned to Read*, 41 (quotation). On the Russian parish clergy, which represented a hereditary caste, see especially Gregory L. Freeze, *The Parish Clergy in Nineteenth-Century Russia* (Princeton: Princeton University Press, 1983); and, for background, Gregory L. Freeze, *The Russian Levites: Parish Clergy in the Eighteenth Century* (Cambridge, MA: Harvard University Press, 1977). See, also, later in this chapter. On the complex relationship between priests and serfs, see Kolchin, *Unfree Labor*, 222–27. On the zemstva, see my chapters 4 and 7. Zemstvo spending on education, which was greatest at the district level, expanded significantly during the last two decades of the nineteenth century. In Nizhnii Novgorod Province, for example, zemstvo spending on education was at first funneled largely "to existing parish schools . . . with clerical teachers," but "by 1900 . . . zemstvo schools dotted the countryside"; see Catherine Evtuhov, *Portrait of a Russian Province: Economy, Society, and Civilization in Nineteenth-Century Nizhnii Novgorod* (Pittsburgh: University of Pittsburgh Press, 2011), 154–58 (quotation: 154).

66. Brooks, *When Russia Learned to Read*, 36–54 (statistics calculated from table I, p. 38); Eklof, *Russian Peasant Schools*, passim (119 on the shift from peasant-led schools to zemstvo- and state-run schools; 315–51 on schools' adjustment to schedule of village life); Mironov, *A Social History of Imperial Russia*, I, 264 (statistic on peasants in higher education). According to Eklof, *Russian Peasant Schools* (453), as late as 1911, when about half of all children in the Russian empire attended primary school at least for a brief time, only one in three or four of those pupils graduated (by completing four years), and of those who graduated, one in twelve—or about 1.0–1.4 percent of all children—continued on to higher education in a gymnasium. Since these

figures included non-peasants (including nobles), the chances of a peasant child going to a gymnasium or university would have been lower still and, in Eklof's words, "if 'he' were a she, the chances of passing each stage were much slimmer" (453). Earlier, in the 1870s and 1880s, the chances of a peasant gaining access to higher education would have been even slimmer.

The few girls who attended gymnasia—who were overwhelmingly from the ranks of the nobility and townspeople—attended all-female schools that were essentially finishing schools, "terminal institutions that prepared women for the traditional female vocation of teachers of small children, not public service or professional careers." Women were not admitted to Russian universities as regular students until after the Bolshevik Revolution of 1917. A small number of women—almost none of them peasants—attended special "public lectures for women" offered as substitutes for university attendance, beginning in 1869, but these lectures faced increasing government restrictions after the assassination of Tsar Alexander II in 1881; new "auditors" to these courses were barred in 1886, and most of the programs were canceled in 1889. Thereafter, "the ancient capital and provincial university towns would remain without women's higher courses until Nicholas II approved their re-establishment in the early twentieth century." See Sophie Satina, *Education of Women in Pre-Revolutionary Russia,* trans. from Russian by Alexandra F. Poustchine (New York: self-published, 1966), 63–138; and Christine Johanson, *Women's Struggle for Higher Education in Russia* (Kingston: McGill-Queen's University Press, 1987), 29–32, 39–50, 64–76, 95–101 (quotations: 32 and 100).

67. Quotations are from Eklof, *Russian Peasant Schools,* 278; and Eklof, "Face to the Village," 358. On the number and composition of teachers, see Eklof, *Russian Peasant Schools,* 181–214; on the resentment of outsiders, see ibid., 215–48. Aside from the great majority of teachers in zemstvo and church schools, the 126,501 rural teachers in 1911 included nine thousand in Jewish schools and 12,600 in Muslim schools: Eklof, *Russian Peasant Schools,* 183. In the immediate post-emancipation period, teachers were overwhelmingly male: in Iaroslavl Province in 1865, for example, there were 427 male and thirty-one female teachers (not all of whom taught in schools for peasants); see *Trudy Iaroslavskago gubernskago statisticheskago komiteta,* no. 3 (Iaroslavl, 1866), 60–61.

68. African American school statistics are from the Consolidated General Superintendent's Monthly School Report, June 1867, FBP, Assistant Adjutant General's Office, Letters Received; these figures do not include non-reporting schools, with an estimated 14,027 pupils, or Sabbath Schools, with an additional 78,451 attendees; and *The Statistical History of the United States from Colonial Times to the Present* (based on *Historical Statistics of the United States, Colonial Times to 1970, Prepared by the United States Bureau of the Census*) (New York: Basic Books, 1976), 370.

69. School statistics from Russia are from *Pamiatnaia knizhka Kaluzhskoi gubernii na 1862 i 1863 gody,* 145; *Trudy Iaroslavskago gubernskago statisticheskago komiteta,* 60–61; *Sbornik statisticheskikh svedenii po Saratovskoi gubernii,* I (Saratov, 1883), section III,

3, II (Saratov, 1884), section III, 33, and IV (Saratov, 1884), section II, 105; Benet, *The Village of Viriatino*, 149–50 (quotation: 150); and Eklof, *Russian Peasant Schools*, 287. Figures for Saratov Province include non-peasants as well as peasants. For the Tenishev survey response, see Firsov and Kiseleva, *Byt Velikoruskkikh krest'ian-zemlepashtsev*, 267–68; the recollection of the landowner's daughter is from Satina, *Education of Women in Pre-Revolutionary Russia*, 24.

70. *Sbornik statisticheskikh svedenii po Saratovskoi gubernii*, same volumes and pages as in note 69, above; *Sbornik statisticheskikh svedenii po Moskovskoi gubernii. Tom pervyi. Izdanie Moskovskago gubernskago zemstva: Moskovskii uezd* . . . (Moscow, 1877), 80–81; Benet, *The Village of Viriatino*, 150 (quotation); Mironov, "Literacy in Russia, 1797–1917," 89–177 (statistics by gender: 106–7, and by age: 100). Most but not all rural residents were peasants; the literacy rate for peasants alone would have been slightly lower than these overall figures. Mironov's estimates of literacy rates for rural Russia were slightly higher than those that appeared in zemstvo-sponsored studies, in part because the zemstvo figures—unlike Mironov's—are for peasants only, and in part because peasants sometimes concealed their literacy, "fearing they would incur new obligations" (Mironov, "Literacy in Russia," 108). Censuses of peasant literacy in eight provinces between 1863 and 1873 indicated literacy rates of 12.2 percent for males and 1.5 percent for females (Mironov, "Literacy in Russia," 111.)

71. Fairclough, *A Class of Their Own*, 101 (on the contrast between attendance at public schools and the earlier freedpeople's schools, which "had reached, at most, 10 percent of the black school-age population"). For a somewhat higher estimate of the proportion of Black children attending the freedpeople's schools in Alabama, see Kolchin, *First Freedom*, 98–99. School attendance rates for children aged five to nineteen of "Negro and other races" in the United States—most of whom were African Americans in the South—was about one-third in any given year in the late nineteenth century (according to the censuses of 1880 and 1890, 33.8 percent and 32.9 percent, respectively), but those statistics reflect both a static analysis and an unreasonably expansive understanding of "school-age" population: *over time* the majority of five- to nineteen-year olds attended school for at least a couple of years, and because very few sixteen- to nineteen-year olds attended school, it is likely that at any given time a majority of children between the ages of (say) eight and twelve were in school; see *Statistical History of the United States*, 370. For atypical recognition by an early historian of the schools' extraordinary impact on African Americans, see W. E. B. Du Bois, *Black Reconstruction in America, 1860–1880* (1935; Cleveland: World Publishing, 1964), 637–69. "Had it not been for the Negro school and college," Du Bois concluded (667), "the Negro would, to all intents and purposes, have been driven back to slavery." For literacy rates of African Americans, the great majority of whom lived in the South in the late nineteenth century, see *Statistical History of the United States*, 382.

72. Literacy statistics for Russia are from, and in some cases based on, Mironov, "Literacy in Russia," 106–11 (quotation: 111). As evidence of the rapid spread of

education in Russia, Mironov observed that "by 1911, 28.3 percent of the children between the ages of 8 and 11 were enrolled" in school, a figure that—depending on one's interpretation—could equally well justify an assertion of *slow* educational progress in Russia; see Mironov, *A Social History of Imperial Russia*, I, 340. Similarly, Eklof saw peasant schools as largely successful at the most basic level, noting that "peasant children were learning how to read, write, and count, often with surprising success"; Eklof, *Russian Peasant Schools*, 390.

73. UNESCO, *Progress of Literacy in Various Countries: A Preliminary Statistical Study of Available Census Data Since 1900* (Paris, 1953), 41; Du Bois, *Black Reconstruction in America*, 637; Edward J. Blum, *Reforging the White Republic: Race, Religion, and American Nationalism, 1865–1898* (Baton Rouge: Louisiana State University Press, 2005), 83.

74. Fairclough, *A Class of Their Own*, 16–19, 267–306 passim, 135–74 passim (quotations: 17, 17, 272, 152, 174).

75. For treatment of many of these contradictory trends, see (in addition to this chapter) my chapters 4 and 5, above.

76. Quotations are from "Report of the Committee on the Religious Instruction of the Colored People," *Minutes of the Forty-Sixth Annual Session of the Alabama Baptist State Convention* (Atlanta, 1869), 11; *Minutes of the Seventeenth Annual Session of the Bigbee [Alabama] Baptist Association* (October, 1869), 6–7; W. G. Kephart, Chaplain, 10th Iowa Veterans, to Tappan, Decatur, AL, 9 May 1865, American Missionary Association Papers, Fisk University, Nashville; and Joe M. Richardson, *Christian Reconstruction: The American Missionary Association and Southern Blacks, 1861–1890* (Athens: University of Georgia Press, 1986), 154. For the missionary efforts of Northern Methodists, who struggled with Southern Methodists for influence among the freedpeople, see letters and reports to James F. Chalfant, Superintendent of the West Georgia and Alabama District of the Methodist Episcopal Church (North), in the Freedmen's Aid Society Papers for Western Georgia and Alabama of the Methodist Episcopal Church, Interdenominational Theological Seminary, Atlanta. For an overview of Black and white religion in Georgia and Tennessee during Reconstruction, see Daniel W. Stowell, *Rebuilding Zion: The Religious Reconstruction of the South, 1863–1877* (New York: Oxford University Press, 1998). Stowell noted (85–89, quotation: 85) that Southern white Christians went through "five stages of accommodation" to the Black withdrawal from white churches, from initially insisting that no changes were needed to finally accepting Black denominational independence. On Black religion under slavery, see, inter alia, *Masters and Slaves in the House of the Lord: Race and Religion in the American South, 1740–1870*, ed. John B. Boles (Lexington: University Press of Kentucky, 1988); Albert J. Raboteau, *Slave Religion: The "Invisible Institution" in the Antebellum South* (New York: Oxford University Press, 1978); and Eugene D. Genovese, *Roll, Jordan, Roll: The World the Slaves Made* (New York: Pantheon Books, 1974), esp. 161–284.

77. Charles S. Smith, *A History of the African Methodist Episcopal Church* (Philadelphia: Book Concern of the A.M.E. Church. 1922), 92 (statistic); and Mobile *Nationalist,* 12 July 1866 (quotation). See Owen Hunter Draper, "Southern Religious Adjustments to Freedom, 1865–1867" (M.A. thesis, University of Alabama, 1966); Charles Hays Rankin, "The Rise of Negro Baptist Churches in the South through the Reconstruction Period" (Master of Theology Essay, New Orleans Baptist Theological Seminar, 1955); and Stowell, *Rebuilding Zion,* 65–99. To counter the A.M.E. and A.M.E.Z. Churches, the white Southern Methodists sponsored a subservient Colored Methodist Episcopal Church in America, but its appeal among African Americans was limited, and in 1874 its membership throughout the South was only 74,799; see Charles T. Thrift, "Rebuilding the Southern Church," in *The History of American Methodism,* 3 vols., ed. Emory Stevens Bucke (New York: Abingdon Press, 1964), II, 284–88.

78. Justin Behrend, *Reconstructing Democracy: Grassroots Black Politics in the Deep South after the Civil War* (Athens: University of Georgia Press, 2015), 45–59; Foner, *Freedom's Lawmakers,* xxi; Edmund L. Drago, *Black Politicians and Reconstruction in Georgia: A Splendid Failure* (Baton Rouge: Louisiana State University Press, 1982). For a brief biographical sketch of Jacobs, see Foner, *Freedom's Lawmakers,* 166. For Drago's statement about Black politicians in Georgia, see his *Black Politicians and Reconstruction in Georgia,* 20. For emphasis on the "intersection between religion and politics" in post-emancipation Virginia, and the extent to which "black church conventions became the tools for pushing the political levers of change," see Nicole Myers Turner, *Soul Liberty: The Evolution of Black Religious Politics in Postemancipation Virginia* (Chapel Hill: University of North Carolina Press, 2020), passim (quotations: 1 and 146).

On Black "collective efforts toward enterprise," including mutual aid and fraternal societies, see especially Robert C. Kenzer, *Enterprising Southerners: Black Economic Success in North Carolina, 1865–1915* (Charlottesville: University Press of Virginia, 1989), 67–106 (quotation: 67); Edward Magdol, *A Right to the Land: Essays on the Freedmen's Community* (Westport, CT: Greenwood Press, 1977), 76–81, especially on the proclivity of Baptists for mutuality; and—for a later period, at the turn of the twentieth century—Walter B. Weare, *Black Business in the New South: A Social History of the North Carolina Mutual Life Insurance Company* (Urbana: University of Illinois Press, 1973). See my chapter 5, above, on communal land purchases by African Americans.

On religion among the freedpeople, see, inter alia, Stowell, *Rebuilding Zion,* esp. 65–99; William E. Montgomery, *Under Their Own Vine and Fig Tree: The African-American Church in the American South, 1865–1900* (Baton Rouge: Louisiana State University Press, 1993); Paul Harvey, *Redeeming the South: Religious Cultures and Racial Identities among Southern Baptists, 1865–1925* (Chapel Hill: University of North Carolina Press, 1997), 45–74, 107–35, 167–94; Matthew Harper, *The End of Days: African American Religion and Politics in the Age of Emancipation* (Chapel Hill: University of North Carolina Press, 2016); and Kolchin, *First Freedom,* 107–27. For an older classic, see Carter G. Woodson, *The History of the Negro Church* (Washington, DC: Associated Publishers, 1921).

79. Quotations are from Wallace, *Russia on the Eve of War and Revolution*, 379; and Firsov and Kiseleva, *Byt Velikorusskikh krest'ian-zemlepashtsev*, 151–52 (from Melenkovskii, Viazemskii, Shuiskii, and Muromskii districts of Vladimir Province). On the unpredictable relationship between priests and post-emancipation peasants, see also my chapter 3, above. On the Russian clergy in the post-emancipation period, see esp. Freeze, *The Parish Clergy in Nineteenth-Century Russia*; and Freeze, "Caste and Emancipation: The Changing Status of Clerical Families in the Great Reforms," in *The Family in Imperial Russia: New Lines of Historical Research*, ed. David L. Ransel (Urbana: University of Illinois Press, 1978), 124–50. On the pre-emancipation parish clergy, see Freeze, *The Russian Levites*; and on relations between serfs and priests, see Kolchin, *Unfree Labor*, 223–27.

80. Quotations are from Freeze, *The Parish Clergy*, 397 (Pobedonostsev); and Firsov and Kiseleva, *Byt Velikorusskikh krest'ian-zemlepashtsev*, 148 (from Melenkovskii district) and 149 (from Kovrovskii district).

81. Quotations are from Worobec, "Victims or Actors?" 183; and (on Voronezh Province) Chris J. Chulos, *Converging Worlds: Religion and Community in Peasant Russia, 1861–1917* (DeKalb: Northern Illinois University Press, 2003), 17. On "the resilience of peasant customs and institutions," see, also, Worobec, *Peasant Russia*; for the persistence of traditional beliefs in Viriatino (Tambov Province), see Benet, *The Village of Viriatino*, 127–48.

82. See Firsov and Kiseleva, *Byt Velikorusskikh krest'ian-zemlepashtsev*, 118–77; Chulos, *Converging Worlds*, 17–20; Benet, *The Village of Viriatino*, 127–48; and—on witches and witchcraft—Worobec, *Possessed*. Quotations are from Firsov and Kiseleva, *Byt Velikorusskikh krest'ian-zemlepashtsev*, 128. On the "peasant spiritual world" as "a busy, crowded, and eventful place, where God, saints, and angels jostled unclean spirits, all of whom intervened in human affairs," see Rose L. Glickman, "The Peasant Woman as Healer," in *Russia's Women: Accommodation, Resistance, Transformation*, ed. Barbara Evans Clements et al. (Berkeley: University of California Press, 1991), 148–162 (quotation: 151–52). See, also, Kolchin, *Unfree Labor*, 228–29.

83. Firsov and Kiseleva, *Byt Velikorusskikh krest'ian-zemlepashtsev*, 123–24 (confronting werewolves, Melenkovskii district); 131 (violence against sorcerers and witches, Melenkovskii district); 131 (running through fire, Muromskii district); 131 (merrymaking and weddings, Shuiskii district); 131 (court complaints, Muromskii district).

84. Stepniak, *The Russian Peasantry*, 218; Firsov and Kiseleva, *Byt Velikorusskikh krest'ian-zemlepashtsev*, 133–35 (on superstitions), 129–32 (healers versus ill-intentioned magicians). Intellectuals and professional doctors looked down on healers, but their folk medicine, which was heavily based on ritual charms and magic, appealed to peasants suspicious of outsiders and professed experts. See Samuel C. Ramer, "Traditional Healers and Peasant Culture in Russia, 1861–1917," in *Peasant Economy, Culture, and Politics of European Russia, 1800–1921*, ed. Esther Kingston-Mann and Timothy Mixter (Princeton: Princeton University Press, 1991), 207–32.

85. Firsov and Kiseleva, *Byt Velikorusskikh krest'ian-zemlepashtsev,* 136–37.

86. Quotations are from Frank, *Crime, Cultural Conflict, and Justice in Rural Russia,* 176; Chulos, *Converging Worlds,* 27 and 96; and Firsov and Kiseleva, *Byt Velikorusskikh krest'ian-zemlepashtsev* (Shuiskii district), 151.

87. For quotations, see George White in *Weevils in the Wheat: Interviews with Virginia Ex-Slaves,* ed. Charles L. Perdue, Thomas E. Barden, and Robert Phillips (Charlottesville: University Press of Virginia, 1976), 310; and H. C. Bruce, *The New Man. Twenty-Nine Years a Slave. Twenty-Nine Years a Free Man* (York, PA, 1895), 57. Bruce was the older brother of Blanche K. Bruce, one of two Black senators from Mississippi (the only two African American senators during Reconstruction). See, also, Kolchin, *Unfree Labor,* 227–28. On the efforts of African Americans to secure (and practice) *professional* medical care, see Gretchen Long, *Doctoring Freedom: The Politics of African American Medical Care in Slavery and Emancipation* (Chapel Hill: University of North Carolina Press, 2012).

88. There is a lengthy historiography centered on disagreement about the extent of "African survivals" among Southern slaves (and, subsequently, freedpeople). For two early studies that staked out opposing positions on this question, see Melville J. Herskovits, *The Myth of the Negro Past* (New York: Harper and Brothers, 1941), which emphasized the persistence of "Africanisms" among Black Americans, and E. Franklin Frazier, *The Negro Family in the United States,* rev. and abridged ed. (1939; Chicago: University of Chicago Press, 1966), which argued for the quintessential Americanness of African Americans. For contrast between the rootedness of Russian peasants and the historical discontinuity experienced by African Americans, see Kolchin, *Unfree Labor,* 196–98.

Chapter 7. Interpreting Emancipation

1. Quotations are from Thavolia Glymph, "Black Women and Children in the Civil War: Archive Notes," in *Beyond Freedom: Disrupting the History of Emancipation,* ed. David W. Blight and Jim Downs (Athens: University of Georgia Press, 2017), 122; Jim Downs, *Sick from Freedom: African-American Illness and Suffering during the Civil War and Reconstruction* (Oxford: Oxford University Press, 2012), 7 and 168; Diane Miller Sommerville, *Aberration of Mind: Suicide and Suffering in the Civil War-Era South* (Chapel Hill: University of North Carolina Press, 2018), 122 and 123; and Carole Emberton, "Unwriting the Freedom Narrative: A Review Essay," *Journal of Southern History,* 82 (May 2016), 378, 378, and 394. For important work on the contraband camps, see Thavolia Glymph, " 'This Species of Property': Female Slave Contrabands in the Civil War," in *A Woman's War: Southern Women, Civil War, and the Confederate Legacy,* ed. Edward D. C. Campbell Jr. and Kym S. Rice (Richmond, VA: Museum of the Confederacy, 1996), 55–71 and 202–6 (notes), "Black Woman and Children in the Civil War," 121–35, and *The Women's Fight: The Civil War's Battles for Home, Freedom,*

and Nation (Chapel Hill: University of North Carolina Press, 2020), esp. 221–50; Chandra Manning, *Troubled Refuge: Struggling for Freedom in the Civil War* (New York: Alfred A. Knopf, 2016), esp. 31–238; and Amy Murrell Taylor, *Embattled Freedom: Journeys through the Civil War's Slave Refugee Camps* (Chapel Hill: University of North Carolina Press, 2019). For mistreatment of refugees by Union troops—including the widespread rape of "girls and women"—see Glymph, *The Women's Fight*, 106–17 (quotation: 109). See, also, Carole Emberton, " 'Cleaning Up the Mess': Some Thoughts on Freedom, Violence, and Grief," in Blight and Downs, *Beyond Freedom*, 136–44.

For a discussion of the new "historiographical emphasis on death and disease, or on the many and varied shortcomings of both the Lincoln administration and the Union Army in regard to black refugees," see Susan Mary Grant, " 'The Contraband's Death Is More Miserable Than Her Life': Violence, Visibility and the Medicalization of Freedom in the American Civil War," in *The Civil War and Slavery Reconsidered: Negotiating the Peripheries*, ed. Laura R. Sandy and Marie S. Molloy (New York: Routledge, 2019), 145–68 (quotation: 147). Terming Reconstruction "a disastrous failure" based on the "delusion" that Black suffrage would guarantee Black equality, historian Adam Fairclough criticized the Republican Party for its defense of "property, middle-class respectability, and, increasingly, big business," and asserted that "the Civil War abolished slavery only to condemn former slaves to another century of systematic oppression"; see his book *The Revolution that Failed: Reconstruction in Natchitoches* (Gainesville: University Press of Florida, 2018), quotations: 15, 107, 127, 18. Stressing that although the Civil War ended slavery, "it didn't end antiblack racism," Henry Louis Gates Jr. noted that the result was "quasi-freedom or quasi-slavery," or even "neo-slavery"; Gates, *Stony the Road: Reconstruction, White Supremacy, and the Rise of Jim Crow* (New York: Penguin Press, 2019), 14, 15, 17 (quotations). For an earlier argument that "the limited improvement in the status of the Negro in this country was not worth the expenditure in the lives required to make that improvement possible," see John S. Rosenberg, "Toward a New Civil War Revisionism," *American Scholar*, 38 (Spring 1969), 261.

2. Quotations are from Peter I. Lyashchenko, *History of the National Economy of Russia to the 1917 Revolution*, trans. L. M. Herman (1939; New York: Macmillan, 1949), 392; editor M. Shevchenko's introduction to *Krest'ianskoe dvizhenie v Voronezhskoi gubernii (1864–1904 gg.): Sbornik dokumentov* (Voronezh: Izdatel'stvo Voronezhskogo universiteta, 1964), v, iv, ix; and Boris Mironov with Ben Eklof, *A Social History of Imperial Russia, 1700–1917*, 2 vols. (Boulder, CO: Westview Press, 2000), I, 333.

3. Quotations are from Thavolia Glymph's introduction to *Essays on the Postbellum Southern Economy*, ed. Thavolia Glymph and John J. Kushma (College Station: Texas A&M University Press, 1985), 3, 8; Eric Foner, *Reconstruction: America's Unfinished Revolution, 1863–1877* (New York: Harper and Row, 1988), 603; Edward L. Ayers, *The Thin Light of Freedom: The Civil War and Emancipation in the Heart of America* (New York: W. W. Norton, 2017), 459, 460, and 461; LeeAnna Keith, *When It Was*

Grand: The Radical Republican History of the Civil War (New York: Hill and Wang, 2020), 4, 291; James L. Roark, *Masters without Slaves: Southern Planters in the Civil War and Reconstruction* (New York: W. W. Norton, 1977), 156, 203; and Robert C. Kenzer, *Enterprising Southerners: Black Economic Success in North Carolina, 1865–1915* (Charlottesville: University Press of Virginia, 1989), 6.

Lynda J. Morgan, who saw the Civil War as a war "for industrial capital," reconciled the revolutionary nature of emancipation in Virginia with the inadequacy of the Reconstruction effort on behalf of the freedpeople by arguing that the positive changes emanating from emancipation were almost all the result of action by the freedpeople themselves, "who exerted significant influence on the contours of postwar society"; see her *Emancipation in Virginia's Tobacco Belt, 1850–1870* (Athens: University of Georgia Press, 1992), 11, 226. Although Brian P. Luskey wrote about "the frauds of free labor in Civil War America," he did not argue that "free labor" was worse than—let alone similar to—slavery. Rather, his focus was on Northerners who took advantage of the war to exploit those less fortunate than themselves or, as he put it, "the speculations of those who tried to turn wage labor transactions to their benefit in the Civil War era." Labor brokers and those termed "intelligence officers" were "brazen thieves," and "if the coercion of slavery was eroding, the subtle coercions of free labor were taking hold." In short, capitalism was exploitative, and "Northerners fought for speculation as much as liberal democracy." See Luskey, *Men Is Cheap: Exposing the Frauds of Free Labor in Civil War America* (Chapel Hill: University of North Carolina Press, 2020), passim (quotations: 2, 4, 50, 111).

4. Quotations are from P. A. Zaionchkovskii, *Otmena krepostnogo prava v Rossii*, 3rd ed. (1954; Moscow: Prosveshchenie, 1968), 306; Carol S. Leonard, *Agrarian Reform in Russia: The Road from Serfdom* (Cambridge: Cambridge University Press, 2011), 50; David Moon, *The Abolition of Serfdom in Russia, 1762–1907* (Harlow, England: Longman, 2001), 114; David Saunders, *Russia in the Age of Reaction and Reform, 1801–1881* (London: Longman, 1992), 272; and Boris Mironov and Brian A'Hearn, "Russian Living Standards under the Tsars: Anthropometric Evidence from the Volga," *Journal of Economic History,* 68 (September 2008), 901. For the argument that major changes in the peasants' standard of living, resulting from capitalist transformation, became widespread only in the last two decades of the nineteenth century, see the collective work by Soviet historians on the village of Viriatino (in the Morshansk district of Tambov Province) *The Village of Viriatino: An Ethnographic Study of a Russian Village from before the Revolution to the Present,* ed. and trans. Sula Benet (1958; Garden City, NY: Doubleday, 1970), passim.

For examples of many English-language works challenging the concept of peasant post-emancipation immiseration, see James Y. Simms Jr., "The Crisis in Russian Agriculture at the End of the Nineteenth Century: A Different View," *Slavic Review,* 36 (September 1977), 377–98; Elvira M. Wilbur, "Was Russian Peasant Agriculture Really That Impoverished? New Evidence from a Case Study from the 'Impoverished

Center' at the End of the Nineteenth Century," *Journal of Economic History*, 43 (March 1983), 137–44; Robert Bidelux, "Agricultural Advance under the Russian Village Commune System," in Land Commune and Peasant Community in Russia: Communal Forms in Imperial and Early Soviet Society, ed. Roger Bartlett (New York: St. Martin's Press, 1990), 196–218; Stephen G. Wheatcroft, "Crisis and the Condition of the Peasantry in Late Imperial Russia," in Peasant Economy, Culture, and Politics of European Russia, 1800–1921, ed. Esther Kingston-Mann and Timothy Mixter (Princeton: Princeton University Press, 1991), 128–72; Steven L. Hoch, "On Good Numbers and Bad: Malthus, Population Trends and Peasant Standard of Living in Late Imperial Russia," *Slavic Review*, 53 (Spring 1994), 41–75; and Hoch, "Did Russia's Emancipated Serfs Really Pay Too Much for Too Little Land? Statistical Anomalies and Long-Tailed Distributions," *Slavic Review*, 63 (Summer 2004), 247–74. The implication in many of these pieces, explicit in Hoch's most recent article, is that the peasants got a pretty good deal in the emancipation settlement of 1861.

5. Manning, *Troubled Refuge*, 153; Downs, *Sick from Freedom*, 41; Gretchen Long, Doctoring Freedom: The Politics of African American Medical Care in Slavery and Emancipation (Chapel Hill: University of North Carolina Press, 2012), 44–69 (quotation: 46); and Edward Meeker, "Mortality Trends of Southern Blacks, 1850–1910: Some Preliminary Findings," *Explorations in Economic History*, 13 (January 1976), 13–42 (statistics: 24 and 26, quotation: 25). On wartime movement of Blacks, see Yael A. Sternhell, Routes of War: The World of Movement in the Confederate South (Cambridge, MA: Harvard University Press, 2012), esp. 7, 93–107, 167–69, and 196–99. On continued Black movement after the Civil War, see William Cohen, At Freedom's Edge: Black Mobility and the Quest for Racial Control, 1861–1915 (Baton Rouge: Louisiana State University Press, 1991); and William G. Thomas III, Richard G. Healey, and Ian Cottingham, "Reconstructing African American Mobility after Emancipation, 1865–1867," *Social Science History*, 41 (Winter 2017), 673–704.

It is important to recognize that among white Americans as well much of the nineteenth century saw declining life expectancy quite apart from the Civil War years, especially in the rapidly growing cities, which were increasingly overcrowded, unsanitary, polluted, and disease ridden. "Nineteenth-century Americans were a sickly people," observed historian Richard White, who also noted the prevalence in cities of "dark, dank, and filthy" tenements that were increasingly breeding grounds for "tuberculosis, typhoid, dysentery, and other waterborne diseases"; see Richard White, The Republic for Which It Stands: The United States during Reconstruction and the Gilded Age, 1865–1896 (New York: Oxford University Press, 2017), 477–517 (quotations: 477 and 517).

6. Quotations are from Mironov, A Social History of Imperial Russia, I, 42, and Boris N. Mironov, "New Approaches to Old Problems: The Well-Being of the Population of Russia from 1821 to 1910 as Measured by Physical Stature," *Slavic Review*, 58 (Spring 1999), 30. Stephen G. Wheatcroft offered slightly different figures but agreed with Mironov on the reduced height of recruits born in the years 1860–64, with a

sharp increase for those born after 1868; see his "The Great Leap Upwards: Anthropometric Data and Indicators of Crisis and Secular Change in Soviet Welfare Levels, 1880–1960," ibid., 42. On disruptions of manufacturing and "grain sowings between 1861 and 1863," see Peter Gatrell, "The Meaning of the Great Reform in Russian Economic History," in *Russia's Great Reforms, 1855–1881*, ed. Ben Eklof, John Bushnell, and Larissa Zakharova (Bloomington: Indiana University Press, 1994), 90. For the temporary decline in peasant living standards in the Morshansk district of Tambov Province following emancipation, see Benet, *The Village of Viriatino*, chap. 1 (esp. 28). On exceptionally high mortality rates among peasant children, see David L. Ransel, "Infant Care Culture in the Russian Empire," in *Russia's Women: Accommodation, Resistance, Transformation*, ed. Barbara Evans Clements, Barbara Alpern Engel, and Christine D. Worobec (Berkeley: University of California Press, 1991), 114–15. In Iaroslavl Province in 1865, 30.2 percent of babies died before the age of one, and 41.7 percent died before the age of five; computed from statistics in *Trudy Iaroslavskago gubernskago statisticheskago komiteta*, III (Iaroslavl, 1866), 14–15, 18–19. As late as 1897, life expectancy at birth in the Russian Empire was 31.3 for men and 33.4 for women, but it was lowest of all for ethnic Russians—27.5 for men and 29.8 for women; see Mironov, *A Social History of Imperial Russia*, I, 109. (These figures include all classes, not just peasants.) For more on the short-term disruption experienced by African Americans and peasants as a result of war and emancipation, see my chapters 1 and 2, above.

7. Daniel B. Thorp, *Facing Freedom: An African American Community in Virginia from Reconstruction to Jim Crow* (Charlottesville: University of Virginia Press, 2017), 5–6; Manning, *Troubled Refuge*, 285–86. Similarly, in *Embattled Freedom*, Amy Murrell Taylor explained that despite the "illness and death that plagued these [refugee] camps," her emphasis was on the "survivors," who "were, after all the majority." Their story was that of "the basic urgency of building a new life" (18).

8. For more detailed treatment of material in this recapitulation, see the text and notes from appropriate parts of my previous chapters, above.

9. Eric Foner, *Nothing but Freedom: Emancipation and Its Legacy* (Baton Rouge: Louisiana State University Press, 1983). Between 1860 and 1900, the peasants' average land allotment per soul decreased from 4.8 to 2.6 desiatiny, a reduction that was only partially countered by additional land purchases and rentals; see Leonard, *Agrarian Reform in Russia*, 174. Noble landholdings were typically vastly greater: in Saratov Province, for example, 335 nobles owned 308,703 desiatiny of land in 1867, and 254 nobles owned 267,207.2 desiatiny in 1883. During this period, the average size of a noble holding increased from 921.5 to 1,052 desiatiny. See *Sbornik statisticheskikh svedenyi po Saratovskoi gubernyi*, I (Saratov, 1883), section I, 12, 16.

10. Joseph P. Reidy, *Illusions of Emancipation: The Pursuit of Freedom and Equality in the Twilight of Slavery* (Chapel Hill: University of North Carolina Press, 2019), 21.

11. Teodor Shanin, *Russia as a "Developing Society": The Roots of Otherness: Russia's Turn of Century*, vol. I (1985; New Haven: Yale University Press, 1986), 93–102, 110–24, 135–95 (quotation: 186); Leonard, *Agrarian Reform in Russia*, 175; Robert Bidelux, "Agricultural Advance under the Russian Village Commune System," in *Land Commune and Peasant Community in Russia: Communal Forms in Imperial and Early Soviet Society*, ed. Roger Bartlett (New York: St. Martin's Press, 1990), 196–218 (quotation: 200); Alex Lichtenstein, "Was the Emancipated Slave a Proletarian?" *Reviews in American History*, 26 (March 1998), 124–45 (quotation: 131). See, also, inter alia, Peter Gatrell, *The Tsarist Economy, 1850–1917* (London: B. T. Batsford, 1986), 110–15; and Sharon Ann Holt, "Making Freedom Pay: Freedpeople Working for Themselves, North Carolina, 1865–1900," *Journal of Southern History*, 60 (May 1994), 229–62, and *Making Freedom Pay: North Carolina Freedpeople Working for Themselves, 1865–1900* (Athens: University of Georgia Press, 2000). As historian Stephanie McCurry has suggested, viewing the antebellum South as capitalist "effectively dispenses with the historical divide of Civil War and emancipation. . . . Rejecting forty years of Marxist scholarship on the relationship between slavery and capitalism," she pointed out, "this new scholarship unsettles the idea of Reconstruction as a fundamental divide or revolutionary juncture in American history"; see Stephanie McCurry, *Women's War: Fighting and Surviving the American Civil War* (Cambridge, MA: Harvard University Press, 2019), 127–30 (quotation: 128).

12. On "modernity" and the capitalist nature of antebellum Southern slavery, see, inter alia, *The Old South's Modern Worlds: Slavery, Region, and Nation in the Age of Progress*, ed. L. Diane Barnes, Brian Schoen, and Frank Towers (New York: Oxford University Press, 2011); Edward E. Baptist, *The Half Has Never Been Told: Slavery and the Making of American Capitalism* (New York: Basic Books, 2014); Calvin Schermerhorn, *The Business of Slavery and the Rise of American Capitalism, 1815–1860* (New Haven: Yale University Press, 2015), and *Unrequited Toil: A History of United States Slavery* (Cambridge: Cambridge University Press, 2018); Caitlin Rosenthal, *Accounting for Slavery: Masters and Management* (Cambridge, MA: Harvard University Press, 2018), and "Capitalism When Labor was Capital: Slavery, Power, and Price in Antebellum America," *Capitalism: A Journal of History and Economics*, 1 (Spring 2020), 296–337; and the scholarship discussed in Harry L. Watson and John D. Majewski, "On the Banks of the James or the Congaree: Antebellum Political Economy," in *Reinterpreting Southern Histories: Essays in Historiography*, ed. Craig Thompson Friend and Lorri Glover (Baton Rouge: Louisiana State University Press, 2020), 166–96. For an analysis of some of the recent literature on the subject, see Peter Kolchin, "Slavery, Commodification, and Capitalism," *Reviews in American History*, 44 (June 2016), 217–26; and Watson and Majewski, "On the Banks of the James or the Congaree." As Watson and Majewski observed (195–96), "Something about the slave South held it back, and scholars who insist that the South was fully modern long before the Civil War . . . are surely exaggerating or seeing a partial picture." Roberto Saba concurs with this argu-

ment; see *American Mirror: The United States and Brazil in the Age of Emancipation* (Princeton: Princeton University Press, 2021).

For an early controversial assertion of antebellum slavery's efficiency and capitalist nature, see Robert William Fogel and Stanley L. Engerman, *Time on the Cross: The Economics of American Negro Slavery* (Boston: Little, Brown, 1974), and *Time on the Cross: Evidence and Methods—A Supplement* (Boston: Little, Brown, 1974); this work was followed by Robert William Fogel, *Without Consent or Contract: The Rise and Fall of American Slavery* (New York: W. W. Norton, 1989), accompanied three years later by three supplementary volumes (one of "Evidence and Methods" and two of "Technical Papers"). For Lenin's argument, see V. I. Lenin, *The Development of Capitalism in Russia: The Process of the Formation of a Home Market for Large-Scale Industry* (1899; Moscow: Foreign Language Publishing House, 1956), quotations: 178, 655, 325. For Shanin's critique of this argument, see his *Russia as a "Developing Society,"* esp. 150–73; Shanin suggested (150–56) that after 1906 Lenin recognized that he had exaggerated the extent of peasant stratification and therefore of peasant capitalism.

13. Larry E. Hudson Jr., *To Have and to Hold: Slave Work and Life in Antebellum South Carolina* (Athens: University of Georgia Press, 1997), xxi, xx. For a more recent version of slaves as capitalists—also focusing on South Carolina—see Justene Hill Edwards, *Unfree Markets: The Slaves' Economy and the Rise of Capitalism in South Carolina* (New York: Columbia University Press, 2021). For slaves' exploiting the labor of other slaves—often their family members—see Dylan C. Penningroth, *The Claims of Kinfolk: African American Property and Community in the Nineteenth-Century South* (Chapel Hill: University of North Carolina Press, 2003), 80–86. Historian Caitlin Rosenthal has noted that "scholars connected with the revival in interest in capitalism within history departments have generally preferred not to define the term," fearing that such a definition "could artificially constrain their analysis." Significantly, however, although Rosenthal stressed "capitalist" features of slavery—such as careful recordkeeping—she also noted key differences between slavery and free-labor capitalism. "Factory owners had to negotiate," she wrote, "but planters simply purchased men and women and compelled them to work." After emancipation, "the freedpeople could quit—and did." In short, "masters' extensive power and access to violence increased their ability to implement all kinds of management experiments." (Rosenthal, *Accounting for Slavery*, quotations: 209 [note 4], 158, 7.) For the widespread recognition—by contemporaries and historians—that the well-being of serf families depended in part on their size, see Peter Kolchin, *Unfree Labor: American Slavery and Russian Serfdom* (Cambridge, MA: Harvard University Press, 1987), 214 and 341.

14. Quotations are from Seymour Becker, *Nobility and Privilege in Late Imperial Russia* (DeKalb: Northern Illinois University Press, 1985), 6; and Zaionchkovskii, *Otmena krepostnogo prava v Rossii*, 4. For Marx's magnum opus on capitalism, see Karl

Marx, *Capital*, 3 vols., ed. Frederick Engels (1867–94; New York: International, 1967). For a potent assertion of the overall noncapitalist nature of the slave South, despite the presence of some capitalist features, see Elizabeth Fox-Genovese and Eugene D. Genovese, *Fruits of Merchant Capital: Slavery and Bourgeois Property in the Rise and Expansion of Capitalism* (New York: Oxford University Press, 1983), esp. 3–60. See, also, Douglas R. Egerton, "Markets without a Market Revolution: Southern Planters and Capitalism," *Journal of the Early Republic*, 16 (Summer 1996), 207–21; Steven Hahn, "Emancipation and the Development of Capitalist Agriculture: The South in Comparative Perspective," in *What Made the South Different?* ed. Kees Gispen (Jackson: University Press of Mississippi, 1990), 71–88 and 166–71 (notes), with a "Commentary" by Peter Kolchin, ibid., 88–96 and 171–72 (notes); and Kolchin, "Slavery, Commodification, and Capitalism." For *contract* as a central metaphor of capitalism, see esp. Amy Dru Stanley, *From Bondage to Contract: Wage Labor, Marriage, and the Market in the Age of Slave Emancipation* (New York: Cambridge University Press, 1998). For a recent suggestion that "a consensus seems to be emerging on the idea that capitalist and precapitalist elements coexisted in the minds and behaviors of most American slaveholders in the antebellum era," see Cathal Smith, *American Planters and Irish Landlords in Comparative and Transnational Perspective: Lords of Land and Labor* (New York: Routledge, 2021), 10.

15. Stanley, *From Bondage to Contract*, x, 3 (quotations); Rosenthal, *Accounting for Slavery*, 183. On contracts and negotiations, see my chapters 3–5, above. For an example of the enduring power of written documents—and the commensurate power that inhered in refusing to sign such documents—see the autobiography of Ned Cobb, an illiterate African American in Alabama who even when in jail on trumped-up charges in the early twentieth century was able to outwit a white planter who sought to cheat him out of his property by securing his signature to a "mortgage paper" that he claimed was "just a paper"; Cobb responded "No, sir. I aint signin no paper no way, shape, form, or fashion"—and he kept his land. Theodore Rosengarten, *All God's Dangers: The Life of Nate Shaw* (New York: Alfred A. Knopf, 1974), 327–30 (quotation: 328).

16. See my chapter 5, above. On conditions and terms of labor under slavery and serfdom, see Kolchin, *Unfree Labor*, passim.

17. Leonard, *Agrarian Reform in Russia*, 195; Peter Coclanis, "The Road to Commodity Hell: The Rise and Fall of the First American Rice Industry," in Richard Follett, Sven Beckert, Peter Coclanis, and Barbara Hahn, *Plantation Kingdom: The American South and Global Commodities* (Baltimore: Johns Hopkins University Press, 2016), 12–38. For a good overview of this post-emancipation regionalization, see Richard Follett's introduction to Follett et al., *Plantation Kingdom*, 3–11. On the acceleration of economic growth and industrialization from the 1880s, see (inter alia) Gavin Wright, *Old South, New South: Revolutions in the Southern Economy Since the Civil War* (New York: Basic Books, 1986); Roger L. Ransom and Richard Sutch, *One Kind of Free-*

dom: The Economic Consequences of Emancipation (Cambridge: Cambridge University Press, 1977); Gatrell, *The Tsarist Economy;* Paul R. Gregory, *Before Command: An Economic History of Russia from Emancipation to the First Five-Year Plan* (Princeton: Princeton University Press, 1994); and Leonard, *Agrarian Reform in Russia*.

18. Jeffrey Burds, *Peasant Dreams and Market Politics: Labor Migration and the Russian Village, 1861–1905* (Pittsburgh: University of Pittsburgh Press, 1998), 143–85 (quotations: 145, 153); Benet, *The Village of Viriatino*, 62–64, 82–90, 91–93, 107 (quotation), 97 (quotation); Mironov, *A Social History of Imperial Russia*, I, 157, and I, 487 (quotations). On the role of advertising—made possible by "industrialization, urbanization, growing literacy, improved printing technologies, and rising consumerism"—in the growth of "modern" attitudes among Russian peasants, see Sally West, *I Shop in Moscow: Advertising and the Creation of Consumer Culture in Late Tsarist Russia* (DeKalb: Northern Illinois University Press, 2011), 30 (quotation). As West pointed out (180–81), peasants (many of whom were otkhodniki) constituted a majority of the population in late nineteenth-century Moscow and St. Petersburg.

19. Quotations are from Mironov, *A Social History of Imperial Russia*, I, 157; *Byt Velikorusskikh krest'ian-zemlepashtsev: Opisanie materialov Etnograficheskogo biuro Kniazia V. N. Tenisheva (na primere Vladimirskoi gubernii)*, ed. B. M. Firsov and I. G. Kiseleva (St. Petersburg: Izdatel'stvo Evropeiskogo doma, 1993), 171; *Aleksandr Nikolaevich Engelgardt's Letters from the Countryside, 1872–1887*, ed. Cathy A. Frierson (New York: Oxford University Press, 1993), Letter I (1872), 30, Letter VIII (1880), 186, Letter VIII (1880), 186, Letter X (1881), 215, Letter X (1881), 221; and Jane Burbank, *Russian Peasants Go to Court: Legal Culture in the Countryside, 1905–1917* (Bloomington: Indiana University Press, 2004), 266. "The end of serfdom opened the way for the development of capitalism in [Russian] agriculture," concluded historian Boris B. Gorshkov in *Peasants in Russia from Serfdom to Stalin: Accommodation, Survival, Resistance* (London: Bloomsbury, 2018), 125. On peasant adaptation of technological improvements, including the shift in plowing from the traditional wooden sokha to the more efficient plug, see Leonard, *Agrarian Reform in Russia*, 198–200. But for emphasis on continued peasant backwardness in Tambov Province—from resistance to the plug and indifference to the teachings of agronomists to cruel child-rearing practices and persistent religious superstition—see David Kerans, *Mind and Labor on the Farm in Black-Earth Russia, 1861–1914* (Budapest: Central European University, 2001). Kerans described a peasant "mind-set that could easily produce a stubborn, intransigent indifference to technological innovation" (149), as well as "underdevelopment of... empirical learning and the experimental ethos" (149), "economic fatalism" (166), and "a minimalist work ethic" (169).

20. Quotations are from Edward J. Blum, *Reforging the White Republic: Race, Religion, and American Nationalism, 1865–1898* (Baton Rouge: Louisiana State University Press, 2005), 83; Loren Schweninger, *Black Property Owners in the South, 1790–1915* (Urbana: University of Illinois Press, 1990), 183–84 (statistic: 164); Kenzer, *Enterprising Southerners*, 6.

21. Martin Ruef, *Between Slavery and Capitalism: The Legacy of Emancipation in the American South* (Princeton: Princeton University Press, 2014), 2; Barbara Jeanne Fields, "The Advent of Capitalist Agriculture: The New South in a Bourgeois World," in Glymph and Kushma, *Essays on the Postbellum Southern Economy*, 84; Lenin, *Development of Capitalism in Russia*, 190–95; Ted Ownby, *American Dreams in Mississippi: Consumers, Poverty, and Culture, 1830–1898* (Chapel Hill: University of North Carolina Press, 1999), 67; Edward L. Ayers, *The Promise of the New South: Life after Reconstruction* (New York: Oxford University Press, 1992), 13, and 69–70. On the revolutionary transformation of the post-emancipation South, see, also, Harold D. Woodman, "The Reconstruction of the Cotton Plantation in the New South," in Glymph and Kushma, *Essays on the Postbellum Southern Economy*, 95–119. On the spread of Southern consumer culture, and its role in simultaneously promoting and undermining racial segregation, see Grace Elizabeth Hale, *Making Whiteness: The Culture of Segregation in the South, 1890–1940* (New York: Random House, 1998), 121–97.

22. Ruef, *Between Slavery and Capitalism*, 3.

23. Sir Donald Mackenzie Wallace, *Russia on the Eve of War and Revolution*, ed. and intro. Cyril E. Black, from revised 1912 edition (New York: Vintage Books, 1961), 162; Gavin Wright, "From Laborlords to Landlords: The 'Liberation' of the Southern Economy," chapter 2 of *Old South, New South*, 17–50. As with the previous section of the present chapter, the argument here is based on—and to some extent recapitulates—material cited above in earlier chapters; see especially chapter 2 and (on peasantization and the growth of owner absenteeism) chapter 5.

24. Roberta Thompson Manning, *The Crisis of the Old Order in Russia: Gentry and Government* (Princeton: Princeton University Press, 1982), 8, 4, 10; Geroid Tanquary Robinson, *Rural Russia under the Old Regime: A History of the Landlord-Peasant World and a Prologue to the Peasant Revolution of 1917* (New York: Macmillan, 1949), 131; G. M. Hamburg, *Politics of the Russian Nobility, 1881–1905* (New Brunswick: Rutgers University Press, 1984), 118; Terence Emmons, *The Russian Landed Gentry and the Peasant Emancipation of 1861* (London: Cambridge University Press, 1968), 420–22; Mironov, *A Social History of Imperial Russia*, I, 219. On the contraction of noble landholding in the post-emancipation decades, see A. P. Korelin, *Dvorianstvo v poreformennoi Rossii 1861–1904 gg.: Sostav, chislennost', korporativnaia organizatsiia* (Moscow: Izdatel'stvo "Nauka," 1979), 54–68. "Almost half" of all marshals of nobility in the post-emancipation period "had mortgaged estates," noted historian G. M. Hamburg in "Portrait of an Elite: Russian Marshals of Nobility, 1861–1917," *Slavic Review*, 40 (Winter 1981), 585–602 (quotation: 593); this was especially true of those in the black-earth region.

25. James L. Roark, *Masters without Slaves: Southern Planters in the Civil War and Reconstruction* (New York: W. W. Norton, 1977), 181, 196, 176, 195; C. Vann Woodward, *Origins of the New South, 1877–1913* (Baton Rouge: Louisiana State University Press, 1951), passim (quotation: 20–21); C. Vann Woodward, *Tom Watson, Agrarian Rebel* (New York: Macmillan, 1938), 89.

26. Fogel, *Without Consent or Contract*, 89; Seymour Becker, *Nobility and Privilege in Late Imperial Russia* (DeKalb: Northern Illinois University Press, 1985), 54; Korelin, *Dvorianstvo v poreformennoi Rossii*, 59. Borrowing money from the Noble Land Bank was not necessarily a sign of economic distress among noble landowners: throughout modern history, wealthy investors—from agricultural elites to large corporations—have used debt to finance economic projects and have been borrowers as well as lenders. By contrast, the 1874 collapse of the Freedman's Savings Bank during the depression of the 1870s caused real economic hardship to tens of thousands of African American depositors, although some of them eventually received partial reimbursement for the value of their usually tiny accounts. On the Freedman's Savings Bank, and its failure, see Carl R. Osthaus, *Freedmen, Philanthropy, and Fraud: A History of the Freedman's Savings Bank* (Urbana: University of Illinois Press, 1976).

27. *Sbornik statisticheskago gubernskago svedenii po Saratovskoi gubernii*, I (Saratov, 1883), part I, 12, 16; Mironov, *A Social History of Imperial Russia*, I, 218; Becker, *Nobility and Privilege in Late Imperial Russia*, 43–44; Leonard, *Agrarian Reform in Russia*, 43, 174. As Becker pointed out (46, 44), between 1863 and 1914 nobles received some 3.011 billion rubles from land sales, and between 1862 and 1905 the value of rural land owned by hereditary nobles increased from 1.278 billion rubles to 4.879 billion rubles—an increase of 282 percent. On the size of peasant landholdings, see above, chapter 5, notes 25–28.

28. Wright, *The Political Economy of the Cotton South*, 34–42 (quotation: 35); Kolchin, *Unfree Labor*, 166; Ransom and Sutch, *One Kind of Freedom*, 78 (quotation), and 40–55 on "The Myth of the Prostrate South"; Louis P. Ferliger and John D. Metz, *Cultivating Success in the South: Farm Households in the Postbellum Era* (New York: Cambridge University Press, 2014), 48. On planter persistence, see Jonathan M. Wiener, *Social Origins of the New South: Alabama, 1860–1885* (Baton Rouge: Louisiana State University Press, 1978), 3–34 (quotation: 11); and Kenneth S. Greenberg, "The Civil War and the Redistribution of Land: Adams County, Mississippi, 1860–1879," *Agricultural History*, 52 (April 1978), 292–307. On Black landholding, see my chapter 5, above, and sources in that chapter's notes 20 and 21.

29. Sally Stocksdale, *When Emancipation Came: The End of Enslavement on a Southern Plantation and a Russian Estate* (Jefferson, NC: McFarland & Company, 2022), passim (quotations: 127, 128, 120, 125, 128, 133). See above, Chapter 5. Marshals of Nobility, elected by noble assemblies for three-year terms, were typically wealthy and influential landowners; see Hamburg, "Portrait of an Elite."

30. Roark, *Masters without Slaves*, 145. See above, Chapter 5 (on Benjamin Montgomery, and on disaffection with free Black and peasant labor), and sources in that chapter's notes 59 and 60 (on hostile comments about African Americans). Even more contradictory to planters' regarding Blacks as inferior (childlike) members of their extended families, who needed constant support (and occasional correction), was the racist violence that engulfed much of the South during and especially after Reconstruction; see below, in this chapter.

31. Wright, *Old South, New South*, 59, 61, 159, 165 (statistics on manufacturing, agricultural income, industrial labor force, pig iron production); Ayers, *The Promise of the New South*, 111 (number of cotton textile workers), 81 (number of stores), 22 (quotation); *The South's Development* (Baltimore: published by *Manufacturers' Record*, 1924), 125 (railroad mileage).

32. Gregory, *Before Command*, 44, 28–29 (on agricultural versus industrial production); Gatrell, *The Tsarist Economy*, 85 (on non-agricultural labor force). Quotations are from David Moon, "Estimating the Peasant Population of Late Imperial Russia from the 1897 Census: A Research Note," *Europe-Asia Studies*, 48 (1996), 151; and Gregory, *Before Command*, 36.

33. For Russia: Mironov, *A Social History of Imperial Russia*, I, 432 (on the number of cities), and I, 475–76 (on the proportion of peasants and non-peasants in cities); David Moon, "Peasant Migration, the Abolition of Serfdom, and the Internal Passport System in the Russian Empire c. 1800–1914," in *Coerced and Free Migration: Global Perspectives*, ed. David Eltis (Stanford, CA: Stanford University Press, 2002), 345–46 (on peasants as proportion of population in Moscow and St. Petersburg). Mironov's figures exclude the Caucasus, Poland, Finland, and central Asia. For the South: James C. Cobb, *Industrialization and Southern Society, 1877–1984* (Chicago: The Dorsey Press, 1984), 22 (quotation); Ayers, *Promise of the New South*, 55–80 (on commercial versus manufacturing centers); Donald B. Dodd and Wynelle S. Dodd, comp., *Historical Statistics of the South, 1790–1970* (Tuscaloosa: University of Alabama Press, 1973), passim (for statistics on the urban population of Southern states, by state). Based on these state figures, the urban population of the eleven ex-Confederates states as a whole increased from 601,680 in 1860 to 1,128,659 in 1880 and to 2,813,294 in 1900. Statistics on the growing number and percentage of African Americans in five Southern cities are from Howard N. Rabinowitz, *Race Relations in the Urban South, 1865–1890* (New York: Oxford University Press, 1978), 19. For restrictions on—and the declining numbers of—enslaved Blacks in Southern cities, see Richard C. Wade, *Slavery in the Cities: The South, 1820–1860* (New York: Oxford University Press, 1964), 16–27, 243–46, 326–27; and Kolchin, *Unfree Labor*, 349–50. The U.S. Census Bureau defined "urban" settlements as those with at least 2,500 persons.

34. Ayers, *Promise of the New South*, 81–131 (quotations 1, on top Confederates: 458, note 51, and quotation 3, on leaving plantations: 240); Roark, *Masters without Slaves*, quotation 2: 151. For a somewhat different interpretation, in which planters appropriated some bourgeois characteristics—"planters became planter-merchants and continued their domination of the black belt" (107)—but successfully resisted the challenge posed by New South capitalists, see Wiener, *Social Origins of the New South*. Despite this emigration from the plantations, Southern whites increasingly celebrated the Old South's supposedly chivalric plantation values; for emphasis on how the militarily defeated South "won" the propaganda war, see Heather Cox Richardson, *How the South Won the Civil War: Oligarchy, Democracy, and the Continuing Fight for the Soul*

of America (New York: Oxford University Press, 2020). On paternalistic defenses of slavery and attacks on bourgeois values, see especially Eugene D. Genovese, *The World the Slaveholders Made: Two Essays in Interpretation* (New York: Pantheon Books, 1969); Elizabeth Fox-Genovese and Eugene D. Genovese, *Slavery in White and Black: Class and Race in the Southern Slaveholders' New World Order* (New York: Cambridge University Press, 2008); and Elizabeth Fox-Genovese and Eugene D. Genovese, *Fatal Self-Deception: Slaveholding Paternalism in the Old South* (New York: Cambridge University Press, 2011).

35. Quotations are from Becker, *Nobility and Privilege in Late Imperial Russia*, 89 and 171 (quotation 1, on *soslovniki*, and quotation 3, on "legal fiction"); Hamburg, *Politics of the Russian Nobility*, 15 (quotation 2); and Manning, *Crisis of the Old Order in Russia*, 43 (quotation 4). On the law of 8 January 1863, which allowed people of all ranks to engage in commercial enterprise, see Korelin, *Dvorianstvo v poreformennoi Rossii*, 107. Statistics on noble landholding are from Korelin, *Dvorianstvo v poreformennoi Rossii*, 54–59 and 127–28; and Becker, *Nobility and Privilege in Late Imperial Russia*, 28–29 and 36–43. For evidence that in 1865 about half of Iaroslavl Province's hereditary nobles and the great majority of its lower-ranking personal nobles (whose honorific status was not passed on to descendants) lived in cities rather than on landed estates, see *Trudy Iaroslavskago gubernskago statisticheskago komiteta*, 3rd issue (Iaroslavl, 1866), 8–9. For emphasis on nobles increasingly moving back to the countryside and "taking the management of their family estates into their own hands," see Manning, *Crisis of the Old Order in Russia*, 11–23 (quotation: 11). But for the contrary view that, in propounding the idea that nobles should return to their estates and resume their rightful role as country gentlemen, *soslovniki* were hardly typical of most nobles, who continued to sell their landed property and move to cities, see Becker, *Nobility and Privilege in Late Imperial Russia*, 67–89. Although she did not explicitly address the question of increasing landowner absenteeism, historian Catherine Evtuhov's argument that the Great Reforms produced a "flowering of the provinces" and created a new "emergence of a local consciousness" implicitly moved in a very different direction; see Catherine Evtuhov, *Portrait of a Russian Province: Economy, Society, and Civilization in Nineteenth-Century Nizhnii Novgorod* (Pittsburgh: University of Pittsburgh Press, 2011), 12, 5 (quotations). On business activities of nobles, see Korelin, *Dvorianstvo v poreformennoi Rossii*, 116–19.

36. Quotations are from Wiener, *Social Origins of the New South*, 72–73 and 201–2; Genovese, *The World the Slaveholders Made*, 229 and 230; Woodman, "The Reconstruction of the Cotton Plantation in the New South," 111, 113, and 111; and Fields, "The Advent of Capitalist Agriculture," 74 and 87. For a useful discussion of the variants of Prussian path theory, which he ultimately found not applicable to the South because he considered it already capitalist under slavery, see Shearer Davis Bowman, *Masters and Lords: Mid-19th-Century U.S. Planters and Prussian Junkers* (New York: Oxford University Press, 1993), 103–11. Although Wiener cited Barrington Moore Jr.,

Social Origins of Dictatorship and Democracy: Lord and Peasant in the Making of the Modern World (Boston: Beacon Press, 1966) as a major exponent of the Prussia path thesis, Moore never actually used the term. For Lenin's development of the concept, see his "Two Types of Bourgeois Agrarian Evolution" (1907), in V. I. Lenin, *The Agrarian Programme of Social-Democracy in the First Russian Revolution, 1905–1907*, in V. I. Lenin, *Collected Works* (Moscow: Progress, 1972), vol. XIII, 238–42.

37. A. M. Anfimov, "Prusskii put' razvitiia kapitalizma v sel'skom khoziaistve i ego osobennosti v Rossii (Sravnitel'no-istoricheskii ocherk)," *Voprosy istorii*, 1965, no. 7, 62–76; Korelin, *Dvorianstvo v poreformennoi Rossii*, 70–76 (quotation: 70); N. M. Druzhinin, "Osobennosti genezisa kapitalizma v Rossii v sravnenii so stranami Zapadnoi Evropy i SShA," *Novaia i noveishaia istoriia*, 1972, no. 5, 59–65; Lenin, *The Development of Capitalism in Russia*, esp. 174–78. See, also, Lyashchenko, *History of the National Economy of Russia to the 1917 Revolution*, 392–93.

38. Quotations are from Mironov, *A Social History of Imperial Russia*, I, 216 (quotation 1); Becker, *Nobility and Privilege in Late Imperial Russia*, 154 (quotation 2), 172 (quotation 3), 171 (quotation 4), and 171 (quotation 6); Woodman, "The Reconstruction of the Cotton Plantation in the New South," 111 (quotation 5). See, also, Manning, *The Crisis of the Old Order in Russia*, 43, and Mironov, *A Social History of Imperial Russia*, I, 216–21 and 266–67.

39. On centrifugal and centripetal forces unleashed by emancipation, see chapters 2–6 of this book. The following pages of this section address the self-identification of Black Americans and Russian peasants; the next section deals with their conflicting images among other Americans and Russians.

40. Quotations are from Foner, *Reconstruction*, xxv (quotation 1), 598 (quotation 6), 599 (quotation 7), and 599–600 (quotation 8); and Steven Hahn, *A Nation under Our Feet: Black Political Struggles in the Rural South from Slavery to the Great Migration* (Cambridge, MA: Harvard University Press, 2003), 5 (quotation 2), 9 (quotation 3), 333 (quotation 4), and 322 (quotation 5). On Reconstruction as an effort "to build an egalitarian society on the ashes of slavery," a society based on the key concept of "equal citizenship for all," see also Eric Foner, *The Second Founding: How the Civil War and Reconstruction Remade the Constitution* (New York: W. W. Norton, 2019), quotations: xix, xxix. Similarly, Nicole Myers Turner, arguing that in their religious associations Blacks "made the case for their inclusion in the American democratic polity," noted that in 1866 a Baptist association in Virginia passed "a resolution to remove the word 'African' from the churches on the grounds that they . . . were American, not African." See Turner, *Soul Liberty: The Evolution of Black Religious Politics in Postemancipation Virginia* (Chapel Hill: University of North Carolina Press, 2020), 39, 37 (quotations).

For Hahn's treatment of rural Black emigrationism, see *A Nation under Our Feet*, 317–63. For the suggestion that Hahn "may understate the extent to which the vast majority of African Americans embraced their role as American citizens," see Luis-

Alejandro Dinnella-Borrego, *The Risen Phoenix: Black Politics in the Post-Civil War South* (Charlottesville: University of Virginia Press, 2016), 7. For an earlier assertion of Black nationalism during Reconstruction, see Lerone Bennett Jr., *Black Power, U.S.A.: The Human Side of Reconstruction, 1867–1877* (Chicago: Johnson, 1967); and for a still earlier depiction of radical interracial democracy, see W. E. B. Du Bois, *Black Reconstruction in America, 1860–1880* (1935; Cleveland: World Publishing, 1964). For Abraham Lincoln's understanding of "self-government," see my chapter 2, above.

41. Quotations are from Eric Foner, *Freedom's Lawmakers: A Directory of Black Officeholders during Reconstruction*, rev. ed. (Baton Rouge: Louisiana State University Press, 1996), 60; and Nell Irvin Painter, "Martin R. Delany: Elitism and Black Nationalism," in *Black Leaders of the Nineteenth Century*, ed. Leon Litwack and August Meier (Urbana: University of Illinois Press, 1988), 165 and 171. On Delany, see also Robert S. Levine, *Martin Delany, Frederick Douglass, and the Politics of Representative Identity* (Chapel Hill: University of North Carolina Press, 1997); and Matthew J. Hetrick, "African American Colonization and Identity: 1780–1925" (Ph.D. diss., University of Delaware, 2013), 135–53, 169–79, 214–19, 222–34, and 238–44. Hetrick suggested a "spectrum" of approaches to Africa among Black intellectuals in the United States, ranging from those who identified *"with* Africa" to those who identified *"as* African" to those who identified as *"being* African" (5, italics added). For two thoughtful studies of Black racial identification under slavery, see Michael A. Gomez, *Exchanging Our Country Marks: The Transformation of African Identities in the Colonial and Antebellum South* (Chapel Hill: University of North Carolina Press, 1998); and James Sidbury, *Becoming African in America: Race and Nation in the Early Black Atlantic* (New York: Oxford University Press, 2007).

42. Quotations are from Hahn, *A Nation under Our Feet*, 353 and 355. On the number of Black Southern migrants to Kansas in 1879–80, see Cohen, *At Freedom's Edge*, 168–97 and 302–11; see, also, Nell Irwin Painter, *Exodusters: Black Migration to Kansas after Reconstruction* (1977; New York: Norton, 1992), 147. On the movement of African Americans to "return" to Africa, and the difficulties faced by Blacks who actually emigrated there, see, inter alia, *New Directions in the Study of African American Recolonization*, ed. Beverly C. Tomek and Matthew J. Hetrick (Gainesville: University Press of Florida, 2017); *Classical Black Nationalism: From the American Revolution to Marcus Garvey*, ed. Wilson Jeremiah Moses (New York: New York University Press, 1996); Tom W. Shick, *Behold the Promised Land: A History of Afro-American Settler Society in Nineteenth-Century Liberia* (Baltimore: Johns Hopkins University Press, 1980); and Edwin Redkey, *Black Exodus: Black Nationalist and Back-to-Africa Movements, 1890–1910* (New Haven: Yale University Press, 1969). On the movement to whiten America through the largely involuntary "colonization" of Blacks in Africa (and occasionally elsewhere), a movement that led to the founding in 1816 of the American Colonization Society, see Philip J. Staudenraus, *The African Colonization Movement, 1816–1865* (New York: Columbia University Press, 1961); and Eric Burin, *Slavery and the Peculiar*

Solution: A History of the American Colonization Society (Gainesville: University Press of Florida, 2005).

For the argument that the freedpeople's post-Reconstruction migration to Oklahoma and Africa were part of the same story—"part of a continuum of flight from the late-nineteenth-century South" (quotation: 5)—see Kendra Taira Field, *Growing Up with the Country: Family, Race, and Nation after the Civil War* (New Haven: Yale University Press, 2018).

43. Corinne Gaudin, *Ruling Peasants: Village and State in Late Imperial Russia* (DeKalb: Northern Illinois University Press, 2007), 16. "The reform legislation elevated the status of ex-serfs but did not eliminate status differences," noted Daniel Field, who blamed their persistence on "deliberate choices made by the regime and embodied in the reform legislation"; "The Year of Jubilee," in *Russia's Great Reforms, 1855–1861*, ed. Ben Eklof, John Bushnell, and Larissa Zakharova (Bloomington: Indiana University Press, 1994), 51, 52. See, also, Gregory L. Freeze, "The *Soslovie* (Estate) Paradigm and Russian Social History," *American Historical Review*, 91 (February 1986), esp. 25–35.

44. Quotations are from Boris Mironov, "The Russian Peasant Commune after the Reforms of the 1860s," trans. Gregory L. Freeze, *Slavic Review*, 44 (Fall 1985), 444; Stephen P. Frank, *Crime, Cultural Conflict, and Justice in Rural Russia, 1856–1914* (Berkeley: University of California Press, 1999), 246; and Wallace, *Russia on the Eve of War and Revolution*, 275. See, inter alia, L. V. Kuchumova, "Sel'skaia pozemel'naia obshchina Evropeiskoi Rossii v 60-70-e gody XIX v.," *Istoricheskie zapiski*, 106 (Moscow: Izdatel'stvo "Nauka," 1981), 323–47; Peter Czap Jr., "Peasant-Class Courts and Peasant Customary Justice in Russia, 1861–1912," *Journal of Social History*, 1 (Winter 1967), 149–78; Stephen P. Frank, "Popular Justice, Community and Culture among the Russian Peasantry, 1870–1900," *Russian Review*, 46 (1987), 239–65; and Cathy Frierson, "Crime and Punishment in the Russian Village: Rural Concepts of Criminality at the End of the Nineteenth Century," *Slavic Review*, 46 (Spring 1987), 55–69. See, also, earlier chapters of this book, and Kolchin, *Unfree Labor*, part II, passim, esp. 200–206, and 331–34.

45. Quotations are from Steven L. Hoch, *Serfdom and Social Control in Russia: Petrovskoe, a Village in Tambov* (Chicago: University of Chicago Press, 1986), 132 and 128; Dylan C. Penningroth, *The Claims of Kinfolk: African American Property and Community in the Nineteenth-Century South* (Chapel Hill: University of North Carolina Press, 2003), 80; and Jeff Forret, *Slave against Slave: Plantation Violence in the Old South* (Baton Rouge: Louisiana State University Press, 2015), 395. On violence and militarism in the antebellum South, see John Hope Franklin, *The Militant South, 1800–1861* (Cambridge, MA: Harvard University Press, 1956).

46. Lenin, *The Development of Capitalism in Russia*, quotations: 174, 177, 178. For emphasis by Soviet historians on increasing peasant stratification among post-emancipation peasants, see, inter alia, Zaionchkovskii, *Otmena krepostnogo prava v Rossii*, 293–94; I. D. Koval'chenko, *Russkoe krepostnoe krest'ianstvo v pervoi polovine XIX v.*

(Moscow: Izdatel'stvo Moskovskogo universiteta, 1967), 352–56; and N. M. Druzhinin, "Vliianie agrarnykh reform 1860-kh godov na ekonomiku Russkoi derevni," *Istoriia SSSR*, 1975, no. 5, 30–33. Although there is no intrinsic contradiction between the existence of socioeconomic stratification and communal solidarity, emphasizing both at the same time has been difficult because they seemed to go in opposite directions, and open disagreement with Lenin could be risky. For an account of a "scathing attack on Leninist-style kulak theories by [historian] A. M. Anfimov," an attack that led three years later to his being "stripped of much of his authority and forced to relocate to a minor post in the Siberian Section of the Soviet Academy of Sciences," see Burds, *Peasant Dreams and Market Politics*, 250 (note 47); Anfimov's "attack" appeared in 1961 in *Voprosy istorii sel'skogo khoziaistva, krest'ianstva i revoliutsionnogo dvizheniia v Rossii*, 218–35. For Anfimov's own (posthumous) account of the controversy, see his "Neokonchennye spory," in *Voprosy istorii*, no. 5 (1997), 49–72. For gender-based divisions and conflicts among post-emancipation peasants, see especially my chapter 6, above. For a critique of the assumption of peasant solidarity, see Corinne Gaudin's *Ruling Peasants*, in which she argued (12) that "village solidarity was fragile at best and at most times absent."

47. Quotations are from Christine D. Worobec, *Peasant Russia: Family and Community in the Post-Emancipation Period* (Princeton: Princeton University Press, 1991), 25 (see, also, 25–29); Mironov, *A Social History of Imperial Russia*, I, 252–53; and Heinz-Dietrich Löwe, "Differentiation in Russian Peasant Society: Causes and Trends, 1880–1905," in *Land Commune and Peasant Community in Russia: Communal Forms in Imperial and Early Soviet Society*, ed. Roger Bartlett (New York: St. Martin's Press, 1990), 190–91. See, also, Daniel Field, "Stratification and the Russian Peasant Commune: A Statistical Enquiry," in Bartlett, *Land Commune and Peasant Community in Russia*, esp. 145–49; Robert Bidelux, "Agricultural Advance under the Russian Village Commune System," ibid., esp. 200–201; Gatrell, *The Tsarist Economy*, 76; and Elvira M. Wilbur, "Peasant Poverty in Theory and Practice: A View from Russia's 'Impoverished Center' at the End of the Nineteenth Century," in *Peasant Economy, Culture, and Politics of European Russia, 1800–1921*, ed. Esther Kingston-Mann and Timothy Mixter (Princeton: Princeton University Press, 1991), 105, 117–23. On the continued practice of communal repartition in the non-black-earth zone but its gradual cessation in the central black-earth region, see A. M. Anfimov and P. N. Zyrianov, "Nekotorye cherty evoliutsii Russkoi krest'ianskoi obshchiny v poreformennyi period (1861–1914 gg.)," *Istoriia SSSR*, 1980, no. 4, 30–31. Aside from varying according to geography, repartition could also vary according to the category of peasant. In Tambov Province's village of Viriatino, which included both former state peasants and former serfs, the last communal reapportionment of land among those who had been state peasants occurred in 1872, but among former serfs such redivisions continued to occur on an annual basis until 1881, and then occurred again a final time in 1894; Benet, *The Village of Viriatino*, 7, 9–12. For refutation of the widespread belief—among both con-

temporaries and historians—that communal repartition sapped peasant initiative and innovation, see Esther Kingston-Mann, "Peasant Communes and Economic Innovation: A Preliminary Inquiry," in Kingston-Mann and Mixter, *Peasant Economy, Culture, and Politics of European Russia*, 23–51. She countered (51) that "the commune's clear advantage . . . was that it permitted a sharing of the numerous risks and dangers involved in a grassroots rural development."

48. Gatrell, *The Tsarist Economy*, 76; Field, "Stratification and the Russian Peasant Commune," 145–46; Löwe, "Differentiation in Russian Peasant Society," 183, 186; Benet, *The Village of Viriatino*, 22; Zaionchkovskii, *Otmena krepostnogo prava v Rossii*, 295 (on noble versus peasant landownership). The statistic on stratification among noble landholders is from Korelin, *Dvoriantstvo v poreformennoi Rossii*, 62. According to Mironov (*A Social History of Imperial Russia*, I, 252), a peasant household was considered poor if it owned one horse (or no horses at all), midrange if it owned two horses, and wealthy if it owned three horses or more.

49. See Kolchin, *Unfree Labor*, 26–31, 38–39, 52, 367–68. For the changing numbers of different categories of peasants, see V. M. Kabuzan, *Izmeneniia v razmeshchenii naseleniia Rossii v XVIII-pervoi polovine XIX v.* (Moscow: Izdatel'stvo "Nauka," 1971), appendix 2; and N. M. Shepukova, "Izmenenie udel'nogo vesa chastnovladel'cheskogo krest'ianstva v sostave naseleniia Evropeiskoi Rossii (XVIII-pervaia polovina XIX v.)," *Voprosy istorii*, 1959, no. 12, 123–36. On state peasants in the first half of the nineteenth century, see Olga Crisp, "The State Peasants under Nicholas I," *Slavonic and East European Review*, 37 (June 1959), 387–412; Jerome Blum, *Lord and Peasant in Russia from the Ninth to the Nineteenth Century* (1961; New York: Atheneum, 1966), 475–503; and N. M. Druzhinin, *Gosudarstvennye krest'iane i reforma P. D. Kiseleva*, 2 vols. (Moscow: Izdatel'stvo Akademii nauk SSSR, 1946, 1958). "Slaves without masters" is drawn from the title of a book by Ira Berlin: *Slaves without Masters: The Free Negro in the Antebellum South* (New York: Pantheon Books, 1974).

50. On the Kiselev reforms, see, especially, Druzhinin, *Gosudarstvennye krest'iane i reforma P. D. Kiseleva*, I, 476–611. For a Third Department report for 1835 complaining that state peasants lacked "supervision" and therefore "year after year become poor and depraved," see *Krest'ianskoe dvizhenie 1827–1869 godov*, 2 vols., ed. E. A. Morokhovets (Moscow: Gosudarstvennoe sotsial'no-ekonomicheskoe izdatel'stvo, 1931), I, 18. For examples of resistance to these reforms—including the so-called potato riots of 1841–43, in which state peasants in several provinces resisted government orders to grow potatoes, a new crop with which they were unfamiliar—see *Materialy dlia istorii krepostnago prava v Rossii, Izvlecheniia iz sekretnykh otchetov Ministerstva vnutrennikh del za 1836–1856 g.* (Berlin, 1872), 71–76, 93–99; *Krest'ianskoe dvizhenie v Rossii v 1826–1849 gg.: Sbornik dokumentov*, ed. A. V. Predtechenskii (Moscow: Izdatel'stvo sotsial'no-ekonomicheskoi literatury, 1961), 407–35 (hereafter cited as *KD-2*); M. S. Valevskii, "Volneniia krest'ian v Zaural'skoi chasti Permskago kraia v 1842–1843 gg.," *Russkaia starina*, XXVI (1879), 411–32 and 627–46; and P. G. Ryndziunskii, "Dvizhe-

nie gosudarstvennykh krest'ian v Tambovskoi gubernii v 1842–1844 gg.," *Istoricheskie zapiski*, 54 (1955), 315–26. See, also, Druzhinin, *Gosudarstvennye krest'iane i reforma P. D. Kiseleva*, II, 456–524.

51. N. M. Druzhinin, "Vliianie agrarnykh reform 1860-kh godov na ekonomiku russkoi derevni," *Istoriia SSSR*, 1975, no. 5, 28–29; N. M. Druzhinin, *Russkaia derevnia na perelome: 1861–1880 gg.* (Moscow: Izdatel'stvo "Nauka," 1978), 121. For regional variations in peasant landholdings, by peasant category, see Druzhinin, *Russkaia derevnia na perelome*, 116–17.

52. The quotation is from Benet, *The Village of Viriatino*, 7. On state peasants living primarily where there were few serfs, see Druzhinin, *Gosudarstvennye krest'iane i reforma P. D. Kiseleva*, 311–17; Blum, *Lord and Peasant in Russia*, 475–503; and Crisp, "The State Peasants under Nicholas I," 390. For a table showing the evolving regional distribution of peasants, by category, see David Moon, *The Russian Peasantry, 1600–1930: The World the Peasants Made* (London: Longman, 1999), 105. For the seventeenth- and eighteenth-century origins, and population statistics, see Kolchin, *Unfree Labor*, 27–30; Ia. E. Vodarskii, *Naselenie Rossii v kontse XVII-nachale XVIII veka Chislennost' sotsial'no-klassovyi sostav, razmeshcheniia* (Moscow: Izdatel'stvo "Nauka," 1977); and Kabuzan, *Izmeneniia v razmeshchenii naseleniia Rossii v XVII-pervoi polovine XIX v.*

53. Quotations are from Worobec, *Peasant Russia*, 40; Kriukova, *Russkaia krest'ianskaia sem'ia*, 70; and Anatole Leroy-Beaulieu, *The Empire of the Tsars and the Russians*, 3 vols., trans. Z. A. Ragozin (1893; New York: AMS Press, 1969), I, 306. Empress Catherine II (1762–96) transferred more than eight hundred thousand state peasants to private ownership by noble landowners, and her son Emperor Paul (1796–1801) added some six hundred thousand more during his brief reign; see Druzhinin, *Gosudarstvennye krest'iane i reforma P. D. Kiseleva*, I, 84–89. On volneniia and petitions by peasants protesting their "illegal" transfer to serfdom, see Kolchin, *Unfree Labor*, 308–10; and Druzhinin, *Gosudarstvennye krest'iane i reforma P. D. Kiseleva*, I, 23–34, 102–20.

54. On Black landowning, see my chapter 5, above. Statistics are from Loren Schweninger, *Black Property Owners in the South, 1790–1915* (Urbana: University of Illinois Press, 1990), 164, 174. The quotation is from Penningroth, *The Claims of Kinfolk*, 77. Most claims from former slaves to the Southern Claims Commission for property lost during the Civil War were for amounts ranging from $100 to $499; the median successful claim was for $300, and the median award was $140. See Penningroth, *The Claims of Kinfolk*, 73.

55. The most comprehensive study of free people of color in the antebellum South remains Berlin, *Slaves without Masters*: statistics, 46–47, 136–37. For similar (but slightly different) figures, see Kolchin, *Unfree Labor*, 53. See, also, Julie Winch, *Between Slavery and Freedom: Free People of Color from Settlement to the Civil War* (Lanham: Rowman and Littlefield, 2014); and Warren Eugene Milteer Jr., *Beyond Slavery's*

Shadow: Free People of Color in the South (Chapel Hill: University of North Carolina Press, 2021).

56. Berlin, *Slaves without Masters*, 181; Schweninger, *Black Property Owners in the South*, 104, and 81; Gary B. Mills, *The Forgotten People: Cane River's Creoles of Color* (Baton Rouge: Louisiana State University Press, 1977), 79 and 108; Michael P. Johnson, *Black Masters: A Free Family of Color in the Old South* (New York: W. W. Norton, 1984), 312. See, also, Larry Koger, *Black Slaveowners: Free Black Slave Masters in South Carolina, 1790–1860* (Jefferson, NC: McFarland, 1985). On free Creoles of color in Louisiana, see, also, Caryn Cossé Bell, *Revolution, Romanticism, and the Afro-Creole Protest Tradition in Louisiana, 1718–1868* (Baton Rouge: Louisiana State University Press, 1997); and Emily Clark, *The Strange History of the American Quadroon: Free Women of Color in the Revolutionary Atlantic World* (Chapel Hill: University of North Carolina Press, 2013). Even in Louisiana, however, as Alejandro de la Fuente and Ariela T. Gross pointed out, "an enslaved person could live his entire life without ever meeting a free person of color." In this respect, Louisiana and Virginia differed considerably from Cuba, where "the link between whiteness and citizenship . . . did not crystallize in the same way" (219). See *Becoming Free, Becoming Black: Race, Freedom, and Law in Cuba, Virginia, and Louisiana* (Cambridge: Cambridge University Press, 2020). Not all Black slaveholders held slaves exclusively for their *labor;* some owned—and protected—members of their own families; see David L. Lightner and Alexander M. Ragan, "Were African American Slaveholders Benevolent or Exploitative? A Quantitative Approach," *Journal of Southern History*, 71 (August 2005), 535–58.

57. Berlin, *Slaves without Masters*, 217 (quotation), and 137, 177–78 (statistics); Schweninger, *Black Property Owners in the South*, 75 (on free Black landowners); Kolchin, *Unfree Labor*, 490 (note 43), on urban proportion of free and enslaved African Americans in Deep South; Harriet A. Jacobs, *Incidents in the Life of a Slave Girl: Written by Herself*, ed. and intro. Jean Fagan Yellin (1861; Cambridge, MA: Harvard University Press, 1987), passim, xxvii (editor's introduction: quotation); and David W. Blight, *Frederick Douglass: Prophet of Freedom* (New York: Simon and Schuster, 2018), 81–82. On free Blacks in the antebellum Upper South, see, also, John Hope Franklin, *The Free Negro in North Carolina, 1790–1860* (Chapel Hill: University of North Carolina Press, 1943); Luther Porter Jackson, *Free Negro Labor and Property Holding in Virginia, 1830–1860* (1942; New York: Atheneum, 1969); Tommy L. Bogger, *Free Blacks in Norfolk Virginia, 1790–1860: The Darker Side of Freedom* (Charlottesville: University Press of Virginia, 1997); and Christopher Phillips, *Freedom's Port: The African American Community of Baltimore, 1790–1860* (Urbana: University of Illinois Press, 1997).

58. On Ovid Gregory, see Peter Kolchin, *First Freedom: The Responses of Alabama's Blacks to Emancipation and Reconstruction* (Westport, CT: Greenwood Press, 1972), 142, 162 (quotation); Michael W. Fitzgerald, *Urban Emancipation: Popular Politics in Reconstruction Mobile, 1860–1890* (Baton Rouge: Louisiana State University Press, 2002), esp. 12–13 and 112–13; and Foner, *Freedom's Lawmakers*, 91. On Mobile's Cre-

oles, and Creole Fire Company Number 1, see Kolchin, *First Freedom*, 140–43; and Fitzgerald, *Urban Emancipation*, 12–13 and 73–74. The quotation is from the *Mobile Nationalist*, 26 April 1866. Conservative white Alabamians ridiculed Gregory both as a "deserter and renegade from his own (creole) class" and as "no black man, nor the prototype or friend of the blacks"; see *Mobile Advertiser and Register*, 30 November 1867.

59. For a perceptive analysis of the New Orleans *Tribune*, and Houzeau's role as its editor, see David C. Rankin's "Introduction" to Jean-Charles Houzeau, *My Passage at the New Orleans* Tribune: *A Memoir of the Civil War Era*, ed. and intro. David C. Rankin, trans. Gerard F. Denault (1870; Baton Rouge: Louisiana State University Press, 1984), 1–67 (quotations 1 and 2: 33 and 35). For Houzeau's account, see *My Passage at the New Orleans* Tribune (quotations 3 and 4: 83–84 and 75). See, also, Rebecca J. Scott, "Asserting Citizenship and Refusing Stigma: New Orleans Equal-Rights Activists Interpret 1803 and 1848," in *New Orleans, Louisiana and Saint-Louis, Senegal: Mirror Cities in the Atlantic World, 1659–2000s*, ed. Emily Clark, Ibrahima Thioub, and Cécile Vidal (Baton Rouge: Louisiana State University Press, 2019), 146–67 (159–60 on Houzeau, *L'Union*, and the New Orleans *Tribune*). After Houzeau's departure, the paper suffered an immediate decline, cut back to a weekly publication schedule, and went out of existence in 1871; Rankin, "Introduction," 56. On some of the limitations faced by Black-run newspapers in the post-emancipation era, see David Prior, "Our Papers," chapter 4 of his book *Between Freedom and Progress: The Lost World of Reconstruction Politics* (Baton Rouge: Louisiana State University Press, 2019), 107–30.

60. Quotations are from Houzeau, *My Passage at the New Orleans* Tribune, 81 (quotation 1); Schweninger, *Black Property Owners in the South*, 208 (quotation 2), 191–92 (quotation 4), 195 (quotation 5); Thorp, *Facing Freedom*, 114 (quotation 3); John W. Blassingame, *Black New Orleans, 1860–1880* (Chicago: University of Chicago Press, 1973), 153 (quotation 6), 155 (quotation 7). On urban Black businessmen in the Lower South, see Schweninger, *Black Property Owners in the South*, 216–26. For emphasis on continued post-emancipation friction between elite African Americans—including political leaders—and the mass of rural Black freedpeople, see, e.g., Leon F. Litwack, *Been in the Storm So Long: The Aftermath of Slavery* (New York: Alfred A. Knopf, 1979), 521–22; Thomas C. Holt, *Black over White: Negro Political Leadership in South Carolina during Reconstruction* (Urbana: University of Illinois Press, 1977), 43–71; and Brian Kelly, "Class, Factionalism, and the Radical Retreat: Black Laborers and the Republican Party in South Carolina, 1865–1900," in *After Slavery: Race, Labor, and Citizenship in the Reconstruction South*, ed. Bruce E. Baker and Brian Kelly (Gainesville: University Press of Florida, 2013), 199–220. Luis-Alejandro Dinnella-Borrego, by contrast, has challenged the notion that Black leaders were "out of touch with the fundamental concerns of their constituents"; he suggested that "far from being out of touch or unrepresentative of their constituents, African American politicians were fundamentally committed to defending and securing the rights and aspirations of all their

constituents, especially the newly freed slaves." Dinnella-Borrego, *The Risen Phoenix*, 6, 14 (quotations).

61. Quotations are from Ayana D. Byrd and Lori L. Tharps, *Hair Story: Untangling the Roots of Black Hair in America*, rev. ed. (New York: St. Martin's Griffin, 2014), 30 and 32; and Hetrick, "African American Colonization and Identity," 235 and (on Blyden) 203–5. Although interest in cosmetic products such as hair straighteners and skin whiteners was controversial—and appeared to some as an effort to look white—historians Shane White and Graham White have argued that in fact they represented a generational desire of young African Americans "not to be limited to the ways of their parents and grandparents." To many young Blacks, "these products represented modernity"; Shane White and Graham White, *Stylin': African American Expressive Culture from Its Beginnings to the Zoot Suit* (Ithaca, NY: Cornell University Press, 1998), 190. Blyden taught Greek and Latin at Liberia College and eventually served as its president from 1880 to 1884, before moving to Freetown, in British-controlled Sierra Leone, where he became a Muslim and died in 1912. See, also, Hollis R. Lynch, *Edward Wilmot Blyden: Pan-Negro Patriot, 1832–1912* (New York: Oxford University Press, 1968).

The estimate on the number of African Americans who "passed" for white is from sociologist John H. Burma; on this estimate—and passing in general—see Joel Williamson, *New People: Miscegenation and Mulattoes in the United States* (New York: Free Press, 1980), 100–103; Williamson suggested (103) that "the great age of passing began around 1880 and was over, practically, by 1925" because by then "those who could pass and wanted to had done so." For a more recent study of passing, see Allyson Vanessa Hobbs, *A Chosen Exile: A History of Racial Passing in American Life* (Cambridge, MA: Harvard University Press, 2014). As Hobbs argued, passing increased markedly in the late nineteenth and early twentieth centuries: whereas during Reconstruction "the prospect of being both black and a citizen existed" and therefore "this period offered compelling reasons . . . not to pass as white" (74), during the repressive Jim Crow era "light-skinned blacks had plenty of reasons to pass" (125).

62. Quotations are from Williamson, *New People*, 63, 65, 81, 87, 78, and 62. For negative views of "yellow" African Americans among rural Black youth in the early twentieth century, see Charles S. Johnson, *Growing Up in the Black Belt: Negro Youth in the Rural South* (1941; New York: Schocken Books, 1967), 262–63. For the argument that "ordinary African-Americans did not share the white world's preoccupation with color," see Mia Bay, *The White Image in the Black Mind: African-American Ideas about White People, 1830–1925* (New York: Oxford University Press, 2000), 162–71 (quotation: 162).

63. E. Franklin Frazier, *Black Bourgeoisie: The Rise of the New Middle Class* (New York: Free Press, 1957), 52 (quotation). Most Black businesses had few if any employees and were "operated by their owners" (54). Frazier also cited (51) census material indicating that in 1949 the vast majority (87.6 percent) of Southern "Negroes with

Incomes" earned less than $2,000 per year (equivalent to $21,325.64 in 2020) and only 0.7 percent earned $4,000 or more (equivalent to $42,651.28 in 2020); for changing values of the dollar, see www.dollartimes.com. For an earlier suggestion that African Americans should be led by a highly educated "Talented Tenth," see W. E. B. Du Bois, *The Souls of Black Folk,* ed. and intro. David W. Blight and Robert Gooding-Williams (1903; Boston: Bedford Books, 1997), 100. The term "Talented Tenth" clearly represented a metaphorical exaggeration, since as Du Bois pointed out (100), the number of graduates from "Southern Negro colleges" in the late nineteenth century was tiny: 143 between 1875 and 1880, 413 between 1885 and 1890, and "over 500" between 1895 and 1900.

64. Quotations are from Williamson, *New People,* 62; and Cathy A. Frierson, *Peasant Icons: Representations of Rural People in Late Nineteenth-Century Russia* (New York: Oxford University Press, 1993), 3.

65. On the widespread belief that Black Americans were fated for extinction, see, e.g., George M. Fredrickson, *The Black Image in the White Mind: The Debate on Afro-American Character and Destiny, 1817–1914* (New York: Harper and Row, 1971), 236–40; and Kolchin, *First Freedom,* 8–9. Quotations are from *Alabama Beacon,* 12 January 1867 (quotation 1); Mobile *Advertiser and Register,* 7 April 1866 (quotation 2); Fredrickson, *The Black Image in the White Mind,* 239 (quotation 3); Mobile *Daily Register,* 3 January 1869 (quotation 4); U.S. Congress, Senate, *Report of the Committee of the Senate upon the Relations between Labor and Capital,* 4 vols. (Washington, DC: Government Printing Office, 1885), IV, 48–49 (quotation 5), and 656 (quotation 6). For more on testimony before this Senate committee, see my chapter 5, above.

66. For the contrast between African Americans as "outsiders" and peasants as quintessential Russians, see Kolchin, *Unfree Labor,* 43–46. For a Soviet article arguing that serfs were "dying off," see Shepukova, "Izmenenie udel'nogo vesa chastnovladel'cheskogo krest'ianstva v sostave naseleniia Evropeiskoi Rossii," 123–36 (esp. 133–36); for a brief summary of this demographic controversy, see Kolchin, *Unfree Labor,* 363–69. Quotations are from Olga Semyonova Tian-Shanskaia, *Village Life in Late Tsarist Russia,* ed. David L. Ransel (Bloomington: Indiana University Press, 1993), xxv–xxvi; and Frierson, *Aleksandr Nikolaevich Engelgardt's Letters from the Country,* Letter IV (1874), 82–85 (quotation: 84). For differing versions—"images"—of the Russian peasant, see especially Frierson, *Peasant Icons;* and Amanda Brickell Bellows, *American Slavery and Russian Serfdom in the Post-Emancipation Imagination* (Chapel Hill: University of North Carolina Press, 2020).

67. Bellows, *American Slavery and Russian Serfdom,* 152–85 (quotations: 166, 166, 167, 173, 174, 184). Because African Americans represented a small share of the American population and a substantially smaller share of the country's buying power, except for companies making products that specifically targeted Black customers— such as certain kinds of beauty products—there was little reason to worry about whether advertisements would offend African Americans. "Firms owned by African

Americans," by contrast, "created respectful representations that differed significantly from the caricatures of white-owned businesses that dominated the broader marketplace" (183). Of course, peasants also had less money than non-peasants, but because they represented a large majority of Russia's population they were more important as potential customers. On the growth of advertising in Russia, see West, *I Shop in Moscow.*

68. Wallace, *Russia on the Eve of War and Revolution,* 338–39. See below, in the Epilogue, for further development of this theme of disillusionment.

69. C. Vann Woodward, *The Strange Career of Jim Crow,* 3rd rev. ed. (1955; New York: Oxford University Press, 1974), chap. 2 ("Forgotten Alternatives"), 31–66, and chap. 3 ("Capitulation to Racism"), 67–110 (quotations: 44, 45, 48, 60); Joel Williamson, *The Crucible of Race: Black-White Relations in the American South Since Emancipation* (New York: Oxford University Press, 1984), 1–8, 44–323 (quotations: 5, 6, 6); Fredrickson, *The Black Image in the White Mind,* 165–282 (quotations: 216, 216, 217). See, also, George M. Fredrickson, *The Arrogance of Race: Historical Perspectives on Slavery, Racism, and Social Inequality* (Middletown, CT: Wesleyan University Press, 1988), esp. 142–82.

70. Woodward's second chapter (31–66) in *Strange Career* is entitled "Forgotten Alternatives"; Williamson wrote (111) in *Crucible of Race* that "Radicalism appeared in strength in 1889 and spread rapidly through the South"; Fredrickson, *Arrogance of Race,* quotation: 275.

71. Quotations and statistics are from Gregory P. Downs, *After Appomattox: Military Occupation and the Ends of War* (Cambridge, MA: Harvard University Press, 2015), 9 (quotation 1), 90 (quotation 2), 89–90 and 262 (statistics on federal troops in the South), 138 (quotations 3 and 4), 215 (quotation 5), 180–81 (quotation 6), and 233 (quotation 7); see, also, Gregory P. Downs, "Anarchy at the Circumference: Statelessness and the Reconstruction of Authority in Emancipation North Carolina," in Baker and Kelly, *After Slavery,* 98–121; Gregory P. Downs and Scott Nesbit, "Mapping Occupation: Force, Freedom, and the Army in Reconstruction," http://mappingoccupation.org/ (March 2015); and Caroline E. Janney, *Ends of War: The Unfinished Fight of Lee's Army after Appomattox* (Chapel Hill: University of North Carolina Press, 2021). For emphasis on weaknesses stemming from divided governmental authority and "the era's individualized definition of rights," see Laura F. Edwards, *A Legal History of the Civil War and Reconstruction: A Nation of Rights* (New York: Cambridge University Press, 2015). The three Reconstruction amendments to the Constitution "left the basic authority over individuals' legal status to the states . . . ," Edwards noted. "Congressional Republicans flatly refused to address the economic conditions of the former slaves" (quotations: 173, 110, 112). For the argument that those Southern whites who supported the Union cause in Alabama, and often became scalawags after the Civil War, were not especially sympathetic to African Americans or even opposed to slavery, see Michael W. Fitzgerald, *Reconstruction in Alabama: From Civil War to Redemp-*

tion in the Cotton South (Baton Rouge: Louisiana State University Press, 2017), 18. For the suggestion that scalawags were often the weak link in the Southern states' Republican coalition governments, see Peter Kolchin, "Scalawags, Carpetbaggers, and Reconstruction: A Quantitative Look at Southern Congressional Politics, 1868–1772," *Journal of Southern History,* 45 (February 1979), 63–76.

72. Turner, *Soul Liberty,* 106–43 (quotation: 110); John C. Rodrigue, *Reconstruction in the Cane Fields: From Slavery to Free Labor in Louisiana's Sugar Parishes, 1862–1880* (Baton Rouge: Louisiana State University Press, 2001), 15–91 (quotation: 90); Susan Eva O'Donovan, "Mapping Freedom's Terrain: The Political and Productive Landscapes of Wilmington, North Carolina," in Baker and Kelley, *After Slavery,* 176–98 (quotation: 179); and Glenda Elizabeth Gilmore, *Gender and Jim Crow: Women and the Politics of White Supremacy in North Carolina, 1896–1920* (Chapel Hill: University of North Carolina Press, 1996), 105–18 (quotation: 111). On the Readjusters, see esp. Jane Dailey, *Before Jim Crow: The Politics of Race in Postemancipation Virginia* (Chapel Hill: University of North Carolina Press, 2000); and Hahn, *A Nation under Our Feet,* 364–93. For an analysis of events in Wilmington, see also Margaret M. Mulrooney, *Race, Place, and Memory: Deep Currents in Wilmington, North Carolina* (Gainesville: University Press of Florida, 2018).

73. Anne Sarah Rubin, *A Shattered Nation: The Rise and Fall of the Confederacy* (Chapel Hill: University of North Carolina Press, 2005), 143–63 (on Southern white identity), 7, 143, 240 (quotations); Fairclough, *The Revolution that Failed,* 42 (quotation); Whitelaw Reid, *After the War: A Tour of the Southern States, 1865–1866,* ed. C. Vann Woodward (1866; New York: Harper and Row, 1965), 417, 418 (quotations). For overviews of the assault on Reconstruction, see Foner, *Reconstruction,* 412–59, 524–601; and Hahn, *A Nation under Our Feet,* 265–313. On planters' bitterness and humiliation, see, also, Roark, *Masters without Slaves,* passim.

74. Quotations are from Fitzgerald, *Reconstruction in Alabama,* 230 (quotation 1); Elaine Frantz Parsons, *Ku-Klux: The Birth of the Klan during Reconstruction* (Chapel Hill: University of North Carolina Press, 2015), 6 (quotation 2); and Justin Behrend, "When Neighbors Turn against Neighbors: Irregular Warfare and the Crisis of Democracy in the Civil War Era," in Blight and Downs, *Beyond Freedom,* 90–102 (quotation 3: 97). On white hostility to African Americans leading to a growing Black exodus from, and therefore a whitening of, hill-country Alabama immediately after the Civil War, see Kolchin, *First Freedom,* 14–19. For two major works on the Klan, with very different approaches, see Allen W. Trelease, *White Terror: The Ku Klux Klan Conspiracy and Southern Reconstruction* (New York: Harper and Row, 1971); and Parsons, *Ku-Klux.* See, also, George C. Rable, *But There Was No Peace: The Role of Violence in the Politics of Reconstruction* (Athens: University of Georgia Press, 1984); Hannah Rosen, *Terror in the Heart of Freedom: Citizenship, Sexual Violence, and the Meaning of Race in the Postemancipation South* (Chapel Hill: University of North Carolina Press, 2009); and, for the argument that the Klan was increasingly composed of

"downwardly mobile sons of middling slaveholders" who felt that "the war had wrecked their future," Michael W. Fitzgerald, "Ex-Slaveholders and the Ku Klux Klan: Exploring the Motivation of Terrorist Violence," in Baker and Kelly, *After Slavery* (quotation: 156). For the congressional hearings and testimony on the Ku Klux Klan, see *Testimony Taken by the Joint Select Committee to Inquire into the Condition of Affairs in the Late Insurrectionary States*, 10 vols. (Washington, DC.: Government Printing Office, 1872).

75. Quotations are from Fitzgerald, *Reconstruction in Alabama*, 317; Rodrigue, *Reconstruction in the Cane Fields*, 187 (three quotations); Kenneth C. Barnes, *Who Killed John Clayton? Political Violence and the Emergence of the New South, 1861–1893* (Durham, NC: Duke University Press, 1998), 2, 1; and Ayers, *The Promise of the New South*, 157, 158. On the Louisiana sugar workers' strike, see also Rebecca J. Scott, "Fault Lines, Color Lines, and Party Lines: Race, Labor, and Collective Action in Louisiana and Cuba," in Frederick Cooper, Thomas C. Holt, and Rebecca Scott, *Beyond Slavery: Explorations of Race, Labor, and Citizenship in Postemancipation Societies* (Chapel Hill: University of North Carolina Press, 2000), 61–106 (esp. 76–83). On disfranchisement, see J. Morgan Kousser, *The Shaping of Southern Politics: Suffrage Restriction and the Establishment of the One-Party South, 1880–1910* (New Haven: Yale University Press, 1974); and Michael Perman, *Struggle for Mastery: Disfranchisement in the South, 1888–1908* (Chapel Hill: University of North Carolina Press, 2001). As for segregation, despite lots of new legislation it is important to remember that separation, if not formal (legal) segregation, had long characterized life in the most important and pervasive Southern institutions: this was especially true of schools and churches, conforming in the former case to the wishes of most whites and in the latter to those of most Blacks.

76. Quotations are from Hale, *Making Whiteness*, 79; Bellows, *American Slavery and Russian Serfdom*, 211–12; and Williamson, *The Crucible of Race*, 176 (for Woodrow Wilson). For Cable's defense of civil rights for African Americans, see George W. Cable, *The Negro Question: A Selection of Writings on Civil Rights in the South*, ed. Arlin Turner (New York: W. W. Norton, 1958). For Dixon's novels, see Thomas Dixon Jr., *The Leopard's Spots: A Romance of the White Man's Burden—1875–1900* (New York: Doubleday, Page, 1902), and *The Clansman* (New York: Doubleday, Page, 1905); on these novels, and the film *The Birth of a Nation*, see Williamson, *The Crucible of Race*, 140–79. See, also, Lawrence J. Friedman, *The White Savage: Racial Fantasies in the Postbellum South* (Englewood Cliffs, NJ: Prentice-Hall, 1970), 168–72. For the broader context of the national reconciliation that Dixon's novels and Griffith's film facilitated, see Nina Silber, *The Romance of Reunion: Northerners and the South, 1865–1900* (Chapel Hill: University of North Carolina Press, 1997); and David W. Blight, *Race and Reunion: The Civil War in American Memory* (Cambridge, MA: Harvard University Press, 2001).

77. Frierson, *Peasant Icons*, 32–53 (on the peasant as *narod*), 76–100 (on the peasant as "rational agriculturist"), 116–38 (on the "gray peasant"), 139–60 (on the peas-

ant as kulak), 161–80 (on the *baba*), and quotations: 3, 77, 99–100, 118, 162, 180; 32–53. On Engelgardt's letters, see Frierson, *Aleksandr Nikolaevich Engelgardt's Letters from the Country*. On Russian *narodniki*, see Franco Venturi, *Roots of Revolution: A History of the Populist and Socialist Movements in Nineteenth-Century Russia* (New York: Alfred A. Knopf, 1964), passim.

78. Frank, *Crime, Cultural Conflict, and Justice in Rural Russia*, 8–10 and 19–30 (quotations: 9, 10, 10). See, also, my chapters 2–4, above.

79. Quotations are from Saunders, *Russia in the Age of Reaction and Reform*, 241–42; Roxanne Easley, *The Emancipation of the Serfs in Russia: Peace Arbitrators and the Development of Civil Society* (London: Routledge, 2009), 177; and James I. Mandel, "Paternalistic Authority in the Russian Countryside, 1856–1906" (Ph. D. diss., Columbia University, 1978), 93. On post-emancipation volneniia, see my chapters 2, 3, and 4, above, and, for annual statistics, *Krest'ianskoe dvizhenie v Rossii v 1861–1869 gg.: Sbornik dokumentov*, ed. L. V. Ivanov (Moscow: Izdatel'stvo sotsial'no-ekonomicheskoi literatury, 1964), 18 and 21 (hereafter cited as *KD-5*); see, also, other sources cited in my chapter 3, above, note 44. On historians' debate over the existence of a "revolutionary situation," see my chapter 2, above, and the sources listed in that chapter's note 49. On growing governmental conservatism—especially within the Ministry of Internal Affairs—see, also, Jerman W. Rose, "The Russian Peasant Emancipation and the Problem of Rural Administration: The Institution of the Mirovoi Posrednik" (Ph.D. diss, University of Kansas, 1976), 159–77; and Daniel T. Orlovsky, *The Limits of Reform: The Ministry of Internal Affairs in Imperial Russia, 1802–1881* (Cambridge, MA: Harvard University Press, 1981), 124–205.

80. Gaudin, *Ruling Peasants*, 9–26 (quotation: 19). For a very different interpretation of the village meeting (*skhod*) as an example of peasant democracy in action—in the author's words (244) "the first political school for the peasants"—see P. N. Zyrianov, "Sotsial'naia struktura mestnogo upravleniia kapitalisticheskoi Rossii (1861–1914 gg.)," *Istoricheskie zapiski*, 107 (Moscow: Izdatel'stvo "Nauka," 1982), 226–302, esp. 238–46. On the emerging perception of a crisis in rural administration, see Thomas S. Pearson, *Russian Officialdom in Crisis: Autocracy and Local Self-Government, 1861–1900* (Cambridge: Cambridge University Press, 1989), 60–118 (quotations: 79, and 84–85 on Mordvinov). See, also, George Yaney, *The Urge to Mobilize: Agrarian Reform in Russia, 1861–1930* (Urbana: University of Illinois Press, 1982), 12–48; Francis William Wcislo, *Reforming Rural Russia: State, Local Society, and National Politics, 1855–1914* (Princeton: Princeton University Press, 1990), 48–63; and David A. J. Macey, *Government and Peasant in Russia, 1861–1906: The Prehistory of the Stolypin Reforms* (DeKalb: Northern Illinois University Press, 1987), 5–40.

81. Quotations are from Michael T. Florinsky, *Russia: A History and an Interpretation, in Two Volumes* (New York: Macmillan, 1947), II, 1087; Konstantin P. Pobedonostsev, *Reflections of a Russian Statesman* (which originally appeared in Russian as *Moskovskii sbornik*), trans. in 1898 by Robert Crozier Long (1898; Ann Arbor:

University of Michigan Press, 1965), xviii (Murray Polnar's "Foreword"), and 32 ("The Great Falsehood of Our Time").

82. Gaudin, *Ruling Peasants*, 10 (quotation 1), 48 (quotation 3), 83 (quotation 4), 207 (quotations 6 and 7); Pearson, *Russian Officialdom in Crisis*, 164–209 (quotation 2: 164); Zyrianov, "Sotsial'naia struktura mestnoga upravleniia," 263–72 (quotation 5: 264). See, also, Corinne Gaudin, "LES ZEMSKIE NAČAL'NIKI AU VILLAGE: Coutumes administratives et culture paysanne en Russie, 1889–1914," *Cahiers du Monde Russe*, 36 (July–September 1995), 249–72; Yaney, *The Urge to Mobilize*, 49–143; Mandel, "Paternalistic Authority in the Russian Countryside," 178–228; and Korelin, *Dvorianstvo v poreformennoi Rossii*, 196–207. For an analysis of the social composition of land captains in 1903, see A. A. Liberman, "Sostav instituta zemskikh nachal'nikov," *Voprosy istorii*, 1976, no. 8 (August), 201–4. For a memoir of a liberal land captain in Tambov Province, see Aleksandr Novikov, *Zapiski zemskago nachal'nika* (St. Petersburg: Tipografiia M. M. Stasiulevicha, 1899); on Novikov, see Samuel C. Ramer, "Democracy versus the Rule of a Civic Elite: Aleksandr Ivanovič Novikov and the Fate of Self-Government in Russia," *Cahiers du Monde Russe et Soviétique*, 23, nos. 2–3 (April–September 1981), 167–85.

83. Dorothy Atkinson, "The Zemstvo and the Peasantry," in *The Zemstvo in Russia: An Experiment in Local Self-Government*, ed. Terrence Emmons and Wayne S. Vucinich (Cambridge, Eng.: Cambridge University Press, 1982), 79–132 (quotations on "apathy" and "indifference": 111); Korelin, *Dvorianstvo v poreformennoi Rossii*, 208–16; Kermit E. McKenzie, "Zemstvo Organization and Role within the Administrative Structure," in Emmons and Vucinich, *The Zemstvo in Russia*, 31–78 (esp. 31–44). See, also, Pearson, *Russian Officialdom in Crisis*, 210–44. In most of Russia, nobles constituted less than 1 percent of the population, and even counting Poland—where the proportion of nobles was unusually large—hereditary and personal nobles made up only about 1.5 percent of the Russian Empire's population in 1897; see statistics in Korelin, *Dvorianstvo v poreformennoi Rossii*, 40 and 44. Peasant participation on the district boards was never widespread: in the 1860s, peasants and Cossacks together constituted about 19 percent of the board membership, a number that fell substantially after 1890 (Atkinson, "The Zemstvo and the Peasantry," 84 and 89.) But for an atypical suggestion of a "flowering of the provinces [that] continued unabated until the Revolution of 1905 and beyond," see Evtuhov, *Portrait of a Russian Province*. "The crucial institution here was the zemstvo," she asserted (quotations: 12). Waxing particularly enthusiastic about zemstvo spending on education and medicine, she suggested (146) that "the zemstvos established what was virtually a socialized health care system, with the character of the rural physician becoming a major figure in the post-emancipation countryside."

84. See my Epilogue. The great exception here was Haiti (former Saint-Domingue), where emancipation was the product of a massive revolutionary war that precluded a restoration of the old slaveholding elite. On developments in Haiti, see,

inter alia Carolyn E. Fick, *The Making of Haiti: The Saint Domingue Revolution from Below* (Knoxville: University of Tennessee Press, 1990); Laurent Dubois, *Avengers of the New World: The Story of the Haitian Revolution* (Cambridge, MA: Harvard University Press, 2004); Laurent Dubois and John D. Garrigue, *Slave Revolution in the Caribbean, 1789–1804: A Brief History with Documents* (New York: Bedford/St. Martin's, 2006); Laurent Dubois, *Haiti: The Aftershocks of History* (New York: Picador, 2012); and "The Ransom: The Root of Haiti's Misery: Reparations to Enslavers," a Special Series of Articles in the *New York Times* (nytimes.com/haiti-debt).

Epilogue

1. See especially my chapters 4, 5, and 7, above. For an extreme assertion of Southern suffering and unhappiness, which embraced "all white Southerners, and many African Americans as well," see Diane Miller Sommerville, *Aberration of Mind: Suicide and Suffering in the Civil War-Era South* (Chapel Hill: University of North Carolina Press, 2018). Because "the Civil War psychologically and emotionally damaged Southerners," she wrote, some of them concluded that killing themselves "made sense" (quotations: 20).

2. David Baronov, "The Abolition of Servile Labor East and West," in his book *The Abolition of Slavery in Brazil: The "Liberation" of Africans through the Emancipation of Capital* (Westport, CT: Greenwood Press, 2000), 79–116; and Steven Mintz, "Models of Emancipation during the Age of Revolution," *Slavery and Abolition*, 17 (August 1996), 1–21. In the words of historian Robin Blackburn, "Post-emancipation societies remained racially stratified and oppressive"; Blackburn, *The American Crucible: Slavery, Emancipation, and Human Rights* (London: Verso Books, 2011), 455. See, also, Peter Kolchin, "The Tragic Era? Interpreting Southern Reconstruction in Comparative Perspective," in *The Meaning of Freedom: Economics, Politics, and Culture after Slavery*, ed. Frank McGlynn and Seymour Drescher (Pittsburgh: University of Pittsburgh Press, 1992), 291–311 (esp. 294–302). On the *causes* of emancipation—in general and elsewhere—see my Introduction, above, and sources in that chapter's notes 1, 2, 14, 15, 18, 20, and 23.

3. Stanley L. Engerman, "Economic Adjustments to Emancipation in the United States and British West Indies," *Journal of Interdisciplinary History*, 13 (Autumn 1982), 191–220 (quotation: 198). See, also, Stanley L. Engerman, "Slavery and Emancipation in Comparative Perspective: A Look at Some Recent Debates," *Journal of Economic History*, 46 (June 1986), 313–39; W. Kloosterboer, *Involuntary Labour Since the Abolition of Slavery: A Survey of Compulsory Labour Throughout the World* (Leiden: E. J. Brill, 1960), 3–16; William A. Green, *British Slave Emancipation: The Sugar Colonies and the Great Experiment, 1830–1865* (London: Oxford University Press, 1976); and Thomas C. Holt, *The Problem of Freedom: Race, Labor, and Politics in Jamaica and Britain, 1832–1938* (Baltimore: Johns Hopkins University Press, 1992).

4. Rebecca J. Scott, *Slave Emancipation in Cuba: The Transition to Free Labor, 1860–1899* (Princeton: Princeton University Press, 1985), 87 and 140 (statistics), 285 (quotation), and passim.

5. Baronov, *The Abolition of Slavery in Brazil*, 146 (quotation) and 187–96; Seymour Drescher, "Brazilian Emancipation in Comparative Perspective," in Rebecca Scott et al., *The Abolition of Slavery and the Aftermath of Emancipation in Brazil* (Durham, NC: Duke University Press, 1988), 23–54 (quotation: 53); George Reid Andrews, "Black and White Workers: São Paulo, Brazil, 1888–1928," in Scott et al., *The Abolition of Slavery and the Aftermath of Emancipation*, 85–118 (quotations: 112 and 117). For the contrast of antislavery in Cuba and Brazil with that in the United States, see, also, Laird W. Bergad, *The Comparative Histories of Slavery in Brazil, Cuba, and the United States* (Cambridge: Cambridge University Press, 2007), 271–89. "There were no democratic pretensions" and little moral opposition to slavery among the elites of Cuba and Brazil, asserted Bergad (272), and in neither country was slavery "a contentious regional issue that politically divided either nation or colony" (273). In Brazil, where abolitionism was "a top-down movement" (283), it was Emperor Dom Pedro II who was "most responsible for spreading the message that slavery could not be sustained indefinitely" (289).

6. Robert M. Berdahl, "Paternalism, Serfdom, and Emancipation in Prussia," in *Oceans Apart? Comparing Germany and the United States*, ed. Erich Angermann and Marie-Luise Frings (Stuttgart: Klett-Cotta, 1981), 29–44 (quotations: 44, 41); Edith Murr Link, *The Emancipation of the Austrian Peasant, 1740–1798* (New York: Columbia University Press, 1949), 89–184 (quotation: 168); Jerome Blum, *Noble Landowners and Agriculture in Austria, 1815–1848: A Study in the Origins of the Peasant Emancipation of 1848* (Baltimore: Johns Hopkins University Press, 1948), 239–46 (quotation: 239); Stefan Kieniewicz, *The Emancipation of the Polish Peasantry* (Chicago: University of Chicago Press, 1969), 66 (quotation), 133–39 and 154–89. On emancipation in the Baltic provinces, and the lessons Russian reformers drew from it, see sources cited above on that topic, in my Introduction, note 44.

7. For a very different interpretation, see Robin Blackburn, who, conflating Reconstruction and the subsequent racist violence of the Jim Crow era, maintained (*American Crucible*, 462) that "blacks of the U.S. South gained least from the ending of slavery." And for an argument against the idea that emancipation in the South was "exceptional," see Jeffrey R. Kerr-Ritchie, *Freedom's Seekers: Essays on Comparative Emancipation* (Baton Rouge: Louisiana State University Press, 2013), 2–13. Insisting that Black men in the United States "were enfranchised for the purpose of political expediency" (7–8), Kerr-Ritchie rejected the notion that "emancipated southern blacks enjoyed more political power than other newly freed peoples" (7).

8. For years, Haiti served as a shining example to many Black Americans; see Brandon R. Byrd, *The Black Republic: African Americans and the Fate of Haiti* (Philadelphia: University of Pennsylvania Press, 2020). But for a very different view, and the assertion that "the Haitian revolution suggested the unleashing of pure id," see David

Brion Davis, *Inhuman Bondage: The Rise and Fall of Slavery in the New World* (New York: Oxford University Press, 2006), 157–74 (quotation: 172). For a much more positive depiction of the Haitian Revolution, see Blackburn, *American Crucible*, 173–219, and for the suggestion that "an older view of U.S. uniqueness is being replaced by a newer argument for Haiti's uniqueness," see Kerr-Ritchie, *Freedom's Seekers*, 8 (quotation) and 62–79. On developments in Haiti, see sources cited above in my chapter 7, note 84.

9. The quotation is from Rebecca J. Scott, "Exploring the Meaning of Freedom: Postemancipation Societies in Comparative Perspective," in Scott, et al., *The Abolition of Slavery and the Aftermath of Emancipation*, 1–22 (quotation: 6). Earlier, Southern white recalcitrance had, ironically, *propelled* Black progress. As Edward L. Ayers suggested, from 1865 to 1868 "the intransigence of white Southerners drove Reconstruction further than many Republicans had foreseen or desired"; see Ayers, *The Thin Light of Freedom: The Civil War and Emancipation in the Heart of America* (New York: W. W. Norton, 2017), xxii–xxiii, 281, 370 (quotation). For an earlier development of this thesis, see Eric L. McKitrick, *Andrew Johnson and Reconstruction* (Chicago: University of Chicago Press, 1960), 15–41, and passim.

10. See my chapter 7, above, notes 69–76 (on the South) and notes 77–83 (on Russia).

11. See my chapters 1–7, above.

12. See sources listed in my chapter 7, above, notes 69–83. On ways in which the South "won" the Civil War, see Heather Cox Richardson, *How the South Won the Civil War: Oligarchy, Democracy, and the Continuing Fight for the Soul of America* (New York: Oxford University Press, 2020); of course, the victory was that of a particular version of the South—and of particular Southerners (who in most states were not in the majority). The term "The Great Disappointment" is the title of chapter 4 of John Maynard's book *The Russian Peasant and Other Studies* (1942; New York: Collier Books, 1962), 57–70.

13. On the figures of Black Southern landholding in 1870, see my chapter 5, above, and its note 20; for the situation in 1890, see chapter 5, and its note 21. The quotation on median household net worth is from William A. Darity Jr. and A. Kirsten Mullen, *From Here to Equality: Reparations for Black Americans in the Twenty-First Century* (Chapel Hill: University of North Carolina Press, 2020), 31. As the New York *Times* reported recently (Patricia Cohen, "Beyond Covid's Turmoil, Race Wealth Gap Lingers," *New York Times*, 12 April 2021, B1), "For every dollar a typical white household has, a Black one has 12 cents"; what is more, this "divide . . . has grown over the last half-century." Gaps in income are rarely as large as gaps in wealth, but for evidence that Blacks' per capita income "*has remained . . . at about 60 percent*" that of whites in recent years, see Darity and Mullen, *From Here to Equality*, 38.

14. On the redemption process and the increasing insufficiency of peasant allotments, see my chapter 5, above, and that chapter's notes 22–28. For the contrast between peasant and noble landholdings in Saratov Province in 1883, see my chapter 7, above, note 9.

15. See Gavin Wright, *Slavery and American Economic Development* (Baton Rouge: Louisiana State University Press, 2006), quotation (123–24); on the persistence of the South's separate regional labor market, see Gavin Wright, *Old South, New South: Revolutions in the Southern Economy Since the Civil War* (New York: Basic Books, 1986), passim, esp. 4–15, 64–70. Deeming this book "an extended essay on the economic consequences of slavery" (10), Wright argued that "the economic structure generated under slavery took many years to overcome" (11). For statistics on recent per capita income levels, by state, see https://en.wikipedia.org/wiki/List_of_U.S._states_and_territories_by_income. For the World Bank figures on Russia and other countries, see https://www.macrtrends.net/countries/RUS/russia/gdp-per-capita. Countries with per capita incomes similar to Russia's include Romania ($12,920), Costa Rica ($12,244), St. Lucia ($11,611), Malaysia ($11,414), Mauritius ($11,099), and Mexico ($9, 946). Some Western European figures include those of Germany ($46,259), Great Britain ($42,300), and France ($40,494). The average for all countries in the world is $11,429—not far from Russia's most recent figure. Comparing statistics from the Soviet period is complicated by the presence of many free or heavily subsidized items, including education, health care, rent, public transportation, and bread. The last World Bank figure on per capita gross domestic product from 1990, the year before the Soviet Union imploded, was $3,493. For challenges to the idea of a "premodern" South, see my chapter 7, above, and sources in that chapter's note 12.

16. Genevieve LeBaron and Jessica R. Pliley, "Introduction: Fighting Modern Slavery from Past to Present," in *Fighting Modern Slavery and Human Trafficking: History and Contemporary Policy*, ed. Genevieve LeBaron, Jessica R. Pliley, and David W. Blight (Cambridge: Cambridge University Press, 2021), 1–33 (quotation: 2).

17. Quotations are from LeBaron and Pliley, "Introduction," 13, 9, and 25; and David W. Blight, "Preface," in LeBaron, Pliley, and Blight, *Fighting Modern Slavery and Human Trafficking*, xv–xx (quotation: xviii). As Luis C. deBaca pointed out (232) in the volume's "Afterword" (225–50), "in a post-Emancipation world where slavery is illegal, enslavement is no longer a status, but a crime." At Yale University's Gilder-Lehrman Center for the Study of Slavery, Resistance, and Abolition, a Modern Slavery Working Group headed by LeBaron and Pliley has been spearheading the study of "modern slavery"; *Fighting Modern Slavery* is a product of a conference held there in 2018. For another organization grappling with "modern slavery," see the webpage of Historians Against Slavery (www.historiansagainstslavery.org). Founded in 2011 by James Brewer Stewart, this organization has sponsored a series of books under the rubric "Slaveries Since Emancipation," published by Cambridge University Press. See, also, Kevin Bales, *Disposable People: New Slavery in the Global Economy* (1999; Berkeley: University of California Press, 2012); and James Brewer Stewart, *Human Bondage and Abolition: New Histories of Past and Present Slaveries* (New York: Cambridge University Press, 2018).

BIBLIOGRAPHICAL NOTE

Primary sources in abundance—many of them published—provide documentary evidence on Russia and the Southern United States in the second half of the nineteenth century. Indeed, the historian is likely to have more trouble deciding which sources to use than finding appropriate evidence.

The emancipation provisions can be found in official government documents but are more conveniently accessed in numerous edited collections that have proliferated in both countries. For the complete version of Tsar Alexander II's Emancipation Proclamation, and the accompanying legislation (regulations or "polozheniia"), see *Polnoe sobranie zakonov Rossiiskoi Imperii*, 2nd ser., 55 vols. (1825–81), vol. 36 (1861), no. 36,650 (pp. 128–34) on the Proclamation, and nos. 36,657–36,675 (pp. 141–403) on the legislation. For more convenient versions of the most important provisions, see David Moon, *The Abolition of Serfdom in Russia, 1762–1907*, esp. "Document 19: Alexander II's Proclamation Announcing the Abolition of Serfdom, 19 February 1861" (Harlow, England: Pearson Education, 2001), 155–60; and V. A. Fedorov, ed., *Padenie krepostnogo prava v Rossii: Dokumenty i materialy*, vol. 2: "*Polozheniia 19 fevralia 1861 goda" i russkoe obshchestvo* (Moscow: Izdatel'stvo Moskovskogo universiteta, 1967), 7–63. For the main American acts abolishing slavery—President Lincoln's 1863 Emancipation Proclamation and the 1865 Thirteenth Amendment to the Constitution—and the accompanying legislation that included the Reconstruction Acts of 1867 as well as the Fourteenth and Fifteenth Amendments to the Constitution, see *The Constitution of the United States of America* and the *United States Statutes at Large*, vols. 13–16. These acts can be more conveniently accessed, however, in several collections of documents, including Andrew Delbanco, ed., *The Portable Abraham Lincoln* (New York: Penguin Books, 1992), and Michael Les Benedict, ed., *The Fruits of Victory: Alternatives in Restoring the Union, 1865–1867* (Philadelphia: J. B. Lippincott, 1975).

There are abundant collections of documentary materials detailing the various antecedents of and reactions to these emancipatory events. For Russia, see three major collections: for reports of the political police, see E. A. Morokhovets, ed., *Krest'ianskoe dvizhenie 1827–1869 godov*, 2 vols. (Moscow: Godsudarstvennoe sotsial'no-ekonomicheskoe izdatel'stvo, 1931); for reports of aides (one sent by the tsar to each province) on the immediate reactions to emancipation, see E. A. Morokhovets, ed., *Krest'ianskoe dvizhenie v 1861 godu posle otmeny krepostnogo prava* (Moscow: Izdatel'stvo Akademii nauk SSSR, 1949); and for weekly reports of the minister of internal affairs on conditions following the end of serfdom, see *Otmena krepostnogo prava: Doklady Ministrov vnutrennikh del o provedenii krest'ianskoi reform 1861–1862* (Moscow: Izdatel'stvo Akademii nauk SSSR, 1950). For the American South, see the ongoing series originally edited by Ira Berlin, *Freedom: A Documentary History of Emancipation, 1861–1867* (Cambridge: Cambridge University Press, 1985–); see esp. the first volume in the series, *The Destruction of Slavery* (ser. 1, vol. 1, 1985). Also important are the multivolume series *The War of The Rebellion: A Compilation of the Official Records of the Union and Confederate Armies* (Washington, DC: Government Printing Office, 1897); and the voluminous papers of the Bureau of Refugees, Freedmen, and Abandoned Lands (Freedmen's Bureau), which I accessed at the National Archives in Washington, DC. Many of the Freedmen's Bureau Papers are now available in digital form ("The Freedmen's Bureau Online") at www.freedmensbureau.com. On the Colored Conventions that met throughout the South after emancipation, see Philip S. Foner, *Proceedings of the Black National and State Conventions, 1865–1900, I* (Philadelphia: Temple University Press, 1986); P. Gabrielle Foreman, Jim Casey, and Sarah Patterson, eds., *The Colored Conventions Movement: Black Organizing in the Nineteenth Century* (Chapel Hill: University of North Carolina Press, 2021); and the digital records at the Colored Convention Project (directed by P. Gabrielle Foreman and Jim Casey): https://colored-conventions.org and https://omeka.coloredconventions.org.

Sources casting light on the preparations for emancipation include, for Russia, V. A. Fedorov, ed., *Padenia krepostnogo prava v Rossii: Dokumenty i materialy*, vol. I: *Sotsial'no-ekonomicheskie predposylki i podgotovka krest'ianskoi reformy* (Moscow: Izdatel'stvo Moskovskogo universiteta, 1966); S. B. Okun,' ed., *Krest'ianskoe dvizhenie v Rossii v 1857-mae 1861 gg.: Sbornik dokumentov* (Moscow: Izdatel'stvo sotsial'no-ekonomicheskoi literatury, 1963), cited as *KD-4*; *Zhurnal zemlevladel'tsev* (a monthly journal reflecting the views of noble landowners in 1858–59); and "Excerpts from the Memorandum of A. M. Unkovskii and A. A. Golovachev, presented to Alexander II in December, 1857," in "Response to the Imperial Rescript," in Terence Emmons, *The Russian Landed Gentry and the Peasant Emancipation of 1861* (Cambridge: At the University Press, 1968), 427–43 (appendix II). For the Southern United States, sources illustrating the coming of emancipation include James M. McPherson, ed., *The Negro's Civil War: How American Negroes Felt and Acted during the War for the Union* (New York: Random House, 1965); and Kenneth M. Stampp, ed., "Records of Ante-Bellum Plantations from the Revolution through the Civil War" (microfilm records). Some other sources are listed below.

Southern slave narratives and autobiographies provide unusually extensive information on African American responses to emancipation. See George P. Rawick, ed., *The American Slave: A Composite Autobiography*, 19 vols. (Westport, CT: Greenwood Press, 1972), and *Supplement, Series 1*, 12 vols. (Westport, CT: Greenwood Press, 1977); and Charles L. Perdue et al., eds., *Weevils in the Wheat: Interviews with Virginia Ex-Slaves* (Charlottesville: University Press of Virginia, 1976). Some autobiographies of ex-slaves contain extensive material on the post-emancipation period: see, e.g., Frederick Douglass's third autobiography, *Life and Times of Frederick Douglass Written by Himself* (rev. ed., 1892; London: Collier-Macmillan, 1962); H. C. Bruce, *The New Man: Twenty-Nine Years a Slave. Twenty-Nine Years a Free Man* (York, PA: P. Anstadt and Sons, 1895); and, for the perceptive recollections of an African American born *after* emancipation, Theodore Rosengarten, ed., *All God's Dangers: The Life of Nate Shaw* (New York: Random House, 1974). There are few Russian equivalents, but see N. N. Shipov, "Istoriia moei zhizni; razskaz byvshago krepostnago krest'ianina N. N. Shipova," *Russkaia starina*, 30 (1881), 133–48, 221–40, 437–78, 665–78; "Zapiska krepostnoi," *Russkaia starina*, 145 (1911), 140–51; and, for an account by an unusual serf who after winning his freedom became a government official, Aleksandr Nikitenko, *The Diary of a Russian Censor*, abridged, ed., and trans. Helen Saltz Jacobson (Amherst: University of Massachusetts Press, 1975). The first two of these autobiographical accounts are included in John Mackay, ed. and trans., *Four Russian Serf Narratives* (Madison: University of Wisconsin Press, 2009).

For investigations and hearings conducted by the congressional committees in the United States, see *Report of the Joint Committee on Reconstruction* (H.R. No. 30, 39 Cong., 1 Sess., 1866); *Testimony Taken by the Joint Select Committee to Inquire into the Condition of Affairs in the Late Insurrectionary States*, 10 vols. (Washington, DC: Government Printing Office, 1872); and U.S. Congress, Senate, *Report of the Committee of the Senate upon the Relations between Labor and Capital*, vol. 4 (Washington, DC: Government Printing Office, 1885). For decennial census material, see *The Historical Statistics of the United States from Colonial Times to the Present* (New York: Basic Books, 1976); and Donald B. Dodd and Wynelle S. Dodd, comps., *Historical Statistics of the South, 1790–1970* (Tuscaloosa: University of Alabama Press, 1973). For statistical information on Russia, see (on the national census of 1897) *Obshchii svod po imperii razrabotki dannykh pervoi vseobshchei perepisi naseleniia proizvedennoi 28 ianvaria 1897 g.* (St. Petersburg, 1905). There are also many governmental statistical reports at the provincial level; see, e.g., *Pamiatnaia knizhka S.-Peterburgskoi gubernii* (St. Petersburg: Izdanie S.-Peterburgskago stolichnago i gubernskago statisticheskago komiteta, 1877); *Saratovskii sbornik: Materialy dlia izucheniia Saratovskoi gubernii* (Saratov: Tipografiia Gubernskago Pravleniia, 1881); *Trudy Iaroslavskago gubernskago statisticheskago komiteta*, 3rd ed. (Iaroslavl': V gubernskoi tipografii, 1866); and *Sbornik statisticheskikh svedenii po Moskovskoi gubernii. Tom pervyi. Izdanie Moskovskago gubernskago zemstva* (Moscow: Tipografiia M. N. Lavrova i K°, 1877). For published collections of responses to ethnographic surveys, see L. I. Kuchimov, comp., *Dokumenty po istorii krest'ianskoi obshchiny 1860–1880 gg.*, vol. I (Moscow: Akademiia nauk SSSR, Institut istorii SSSR, 1983); and (for Vladimir Province), B. M. Firsov and I. G. Kiseleva, eds., *Byt Veliorusskikh krest'ian-zemlepashtsev: Opisanie materialov etnograficheskeskogo biuro Kniazia V. N. Tenisheva (na primera Vladimirskoi gubernii)* (St. Petersburg: Izdatel'stvo Evropeiskogo doma, 1993).

Travel accounts and descriptions of conditions reflected the widespread interest that events in Russia and the American South generated. For Russia, these accounts were often (although not always) by foreigners. Some were very short, designed to give those unfamiliar with Russian conditions an idea of what was going on; see J. Lang, *Results of the Serf Emancipation in Russia* (New York: Loyal Publication Society, 1864); and A. D. White, "The Development and Overthrow of the Russian Serf-System," *Atlantic Monthly*, 10 (November 1862), 538–52. Others (often published later) were longer, and assumed more familiarity with essential developments; see Sir Donald Mackenzie Wallace, *Russia on the Eve of War and Revolution*, ed. and intro. Cyril E. Black (New York: Vintage Books, 1961; from rev. ed. 1912; first ed. 1877); Anatole Leroy-Beaulieu, *The Empire of the Tsars and the Russians*, 3 vols., trans. from third French edition, 1902–5 (first edition: 1881–89) by Z. A. Ragosin (New York: AMS Press, 1969); and Stepniak (revolutionary Sergei Kravchinskii), *The Russian Peasantry: Their Agrarian Condition, Social Life and Religion* (New York: Harper and Brothers, 1888). Accounts of the South were often written by Northern visitors; examples include Whitelaw Reid, *After the War: A Tour of the Southern States*, ed. C. Vann Woodward (1866; New York: Harper and Row, 1965); Sidney Andrews, *The South Since the War*, intro. David Donald (1866; Boston: Houghton Mifflin, 1971); J. T. Trowbridge, *A Picture of the Desolated States: And the Work of Restoration, 1865–1868* (Hartford, CT: L. Stebbins, 1868); and—for the report of a radical Republican Union general—Carl Schurz, *Report on the Condition of the South* (1865; New York: Arno Press, 1969).

Other writings by radical abolitionists can be followed in William E. Cain, ed., *William Lloyd Garrison and the Fight against Slavery: Selections from the Liberator* (Boston: Bedford Books, 1995), as well as in Garrison's newspaper, the *Liberator* (beginning in January 1831). See, also, William E. Gienapp, ed., *This Fiery Trial: The Speeches and Writings of Abraham Lincoln* (New York: Oxford University Press, 2002); and Harold M. Hyman, ed., *The Radical Republicans and Reconstruction, 1861–1870* (Indianapolis: Bobbs-Merrill, 1967); Michael Meyer, ed., *Frederick Douglass: The Narrative and Selected Writings* (New York: Modern Library, 1984); and George W. Cable, *The Negro Question: A Selection of Writings on Civil Rights in the South*, ed. Arlin Turner (New York: W. W. Norton, 1958). Censorship precluded the publication of similar writings in Russia, but see Aleksandr Herzen's journal, *Kolokol* (1857–67), published from abroad with Herzen using the pseudonym "Iskander," reprinted in 11 volumes (Moscow: Izdatel'stvo Akademii nauk SSSR, 1962–64).

As I noted in the Preface, I have made use in this volume of earlier research I conducted on emancipation in Alabama. Aside from the Freedmen's Bureau Papers and the manuscript census returns of the Ninth (1870) Census (both at the National Archives), the records of greatest significance from this research are the J. B. Moore Diary (Alabama State Department of Archives and History); the James Mallory Diary (Southern Historical Collection, University of North Carolina); the Henry Watson Papers (Duke University Library); the Wager Swayne Papers (Alabama State Department of Archives and History); the American Missionary Association Papers (Fisk University); and the following Alabama newspapers: *Alabama Beacon* (Greensboro), *Clark County Journal*, Huntsville *Advocate*, Mobile *Advertiser and Register*, Montgomery *Daily Advertiser*, the *Nationalist* (Mobile), Selma *Daily Messenger*, and the *Daily State Sentinel* (Montgomery). Other especially informative newspapers include the New Orleans *Tribune*, and the *New-York Daily Tribune*. Also valuable are journal publications of various associations established in the North to aid the Southern freedpeople: see, especially, *American Missionary* (American Missionary Association), *National Freedman* (National Freedman's Relief Association), and *Freedmen's Record* (New England Freedmen's Association).

For published reactions of landholders and government officials who—unlike most pomeshchiki and officials—tried to adjust to new conditions, see (for Russia) Cathy A. Frierson, ed., *Aleksandr Nikolaevich Engelgardt's Letters from the Country, 1872–1887* (New York: Oxford University Press, 1993); Olga Semyonova Tian-Shanskaia, *Village Life in Late Tsarist Russia*, ed. David L. Ransel (Bloomington: Indiana University Press, 1993); and Aleksandr Novikov, *Zapiski zemskago nachal'nika* (St. Petersburg: Tipografiia M. M. Stasiulevicha, 1899). Southern landowners were more likely to display basic racism than understanding of changed conditions: see, e. g., Frances B. Leigh, *Ten Years on a Georgia Plantation Since the War* (1883; New York: Negro Universities Press, 1969); and Robert Manson Myers, ed., *The Children of Pride: A True Story of Georgia and the Civil War* (New Haven: Yale University Press, 1972). For the more vitriolic racism that became widely held by Southern whites in the late nineteenth and early twentieth centuries, see two novels by Thomas Dixon Jr.: *The Leopard's Spots: A Romance of the White Man's Burden, 1875–1900* (New York: Doubleday Page, 1902), and *The Clansman* (New York: Doubleday Page, 1905).

For material on volneniia and unrest among emancipated Russian peasants—often subsumed under the term the "peasant movement"—see documents in two major collections, cited as KD-5 and KD-6: L. M. Ivanov, ed., *Krest'ianskoe dvizhenie v Rossii v 1861–1869 gg.: Sbornik dokumentov* (Moscow: Izdatel'stvo sotsial'no-ekonomicheskoi literatury, 1964); and P. A. Zaionchkovskii, ed., *Krest'ianskoe dvizhenie v Rossii v 1870–1880 gg.: Sbornik dokumentov* (Moscow: Izdatel'stvo "Nauka," 1968). See, also, I. Kuznetsov, ed., "Semdesiat piat' let nazad (19 fevralia 1861 g.)," *Krasnyi arkhiv*, 74, no. 1 (1936), 5–36; E. Sedovaia, "Kandeevskoe vosstanie v 1861 g.," *Krasnyi arkhiv*, 92, no. 1 (1939), 91–132; P. Sovinov, ed., "Krest'ianskoe dvizhenie v kontse XIX v.

(1881–1894 gg.)," *Krasnyi arkhiv*, 89–90, nos. 4–5 (1938), 208–57; and Daniel Field, ed., *Rebels in the Name of the Tsar* (Boston: Houghton Mifflin, 1976), 31–111.

There is no precise American equivalent to these works on the Russian "peasant movement," but American historians have published many collections of documents on the post-emancipation years, collections in which the activities of freedpeople assume prime importance. See, in addition to collections already cited, Walter L. Fleming, ed., *Documentary History of Reconstruction: Political, Military, Social, Religious, Educational and Industrial, 1865 to 1906*, 2 vols. (1906; New York: McGraw Hill, 1966); and William E. Gienapp, ed., *The Civil War and Reconstruction: A Documentary Collection* (New York: W. W. Norton, 2001).

An extensive historical literature exists on emancipation and its aftereffects in Russia and the Southern United States. The following lists of secondary works mention only a few of the most important books; others appear in this volume's notes. These two lists are arranged alphabetically by author and are limited to twenty-six books each. (Two books, by Amanda Brickell Bellows and Sally Stocksdale, which compare developments in the two countries, appear on both lists.)

Major Secondary Sources on Russia

Becker, Seymour. *Nobility and Privilege in Late Imperial Russia*. DeKalb: Northern Illinois University Press, 1985.

Bellows, Amanda Brickell. *American Slavery and Russian Serfdom in the Post-Emancipation Imagination*. Chapel Hill: University of North Carolina Press, 2020.

Benet, Sula, ed. and trans. *The Village of Viriatino: An Ethnographic Study of a Russian Village from before the Revolution to the Present*. 1958; Garden City, NY: Doubleday, 1970.

Burds, Jeffrey. *Peasant Dreams and Market Politics: Labor Migration and the Russian Village, 1861–1905*. Pittsburgh: University of Pittsburgh Press, 1998.

Druzhinin, N. M. *Gosudarstvennye krest'iane i reforma P. D. Kiseleva*, 2 vols. Moscow: Izdatel'stvo Akademii nauk SSSR, 1946, 1958.

———. *Russkaia derevnia na perelome: 1861–1880 gg*. Moscow: Izdatel'stvo "Nauka," 1978.

Easley, Roxanne. *The Emancipation of the Serfs in Russia: Peace Arbitrators and the Development of Civil Society*. London: Routledge, 2009.

Eklof, Ben. *Russian Peasant Schools: Officialdom, Village Culture and Popular Pedagogy, 1861–1914*. Berkeley: University of California Press, 1986.

Eklof, Ben, John Bushnell, and Larissa Zakharova, eds. *Russia's Great Reforms, 1855–1881*. Bloomington: Indiana University Press, 1994.

Engel, Barbara Alpern. *Between the Fields and the City: Women, Work, and the Family in Russia, 1861–1914*. Cambridge: Cambridge University Press, 1994.

Field, Daniel. *The End of Serfdom: Nobility and Bureaucracy in Russia, 1855–1861.* Cambridge, MA: Harvard University Press, 1976.

Frank, Stephen P. *Crime, Cultural Conflict, and Justice in Rural Russia, 1856–1914.* Berkeley: University of California Press, 1999.

Frierson, Cathy. *Peasant Icons: Representations of Rural People in Late Nineteenth-Century Russia.* New York: Oxford University Press, 1993.

Gatrell, Peter. *The Tsarist Economy, 1850–1917.* London: B. T. Batsford, 1986.

Korelin, A. P. *Dvorianstvo v poreformennoi Rossii, 1861–1904 gg.: Sostav, chislennost', korporativnaia organizatsiia.* Moscow: Izdatel'stvo "Nauka," 1979.

Lenin, V. I. *The Development of Capitalism in Russia: The Process of the Formation of a Home Market for Large-Scale Industry.* 1899; trans. from 2nd ed., 1908. Moscow: Foreign Languages Publishing House, 1956.

Litvak, B. G. *Russkaia derevnia v reforme 1861 goda: Chernozemnyi tsentr 1861–1895 gg.* Moscow: Izdatel'stvo "Nauka," 1972.

Lyashchenko, Peter I. *History of the National Economy of Russia to the 1917 Revolution,* trans. L. M. Herman. 1939; New York: Macmillan, 1949.

Mironov, Boris, with Ben Eklof. *A Social History of Imperial Russia, 1700–1917,* 2 vols. Boulder, CO: Westview Press, 2000.

Moon, David. *The Abolition of Serfdom in Russia, 1762–1907.* Harlow, England: Longman, 2001.

Shanin, Teodor. *Russia as a "Developing Society": The Roots of Otherness: Russia's Turn of Century, Volume I.* 1985; New Haven, CT: Yale University Press, 1986.

Stocksdale, Sally. *When Emancipation Came: The End of Enslavement on a Southern Plantation and a Russian Estate.* Jefferson, NC: McFarland, 2022.

Velikaia reforma: Russkoe obshchestvo i krest'ianskii vopros v proshlom i nastoiashchem. Iubileinoe izdanie, 6 vols, ed. A. K. Dzhivelegov, S. P. Mel'gunov, and V. I. Pichet. Moscow: Izdanie T-va I. D. Sytina, 1911.

Worobec, Christine D. *Peasant Russia: Family and Community in the Post-Emancipation Period.* Princeton: Princeton University Press, 1991.

Zaionchkovskii, P. A. *Otmena krepostnogo prava v Rossii,* 3rd. ed. Moscow: Prosveshchenie, 1968. (Also published in English, without footnotes, ed. and trans. Susan Wobst, *The Abolition of Serfdom in Russia.* Gulf Breeze, FL: Academic International Press, 1978.)

Zakharova, L. G., L. P. Gorlanova, and A. T. Topchii, comps. *Otmena krepostnogo prava v Rossii: Ukazatel' literatury (1856–1989 gg.).* Tomsk: Izdatel'stvo Tomskogo universiteta, 1993 (listing 2,069 works, arranged topically).

Major Secondary Sources on the American South

Bellows, Amanda Brickell. *American Slavery and Russian Serfdom in the Post-Emancipation Imagination.* Chapel Hill: University of North Carolina Press, 2020.

Berlin, Ira, et al. *Slaves No More: Three Essays on Emancipation and the Civil War.* Cambridge: Cambridge University Press, 1992.

Blight, David W. *Frederick Douglass: Prophet of Freedom.* New York: Simon and Schuster, 2018.

Downs, Gregory P. *After Appomattox: Military Occupation and the Ends of War.* Cambridge, MA: Harvard University Press, 2015.

Du Bois, W. E. Burghardt. *Black Reconstruction in America, 1860–1880.* 1935; Cleveland: World Publishing, 1964.

Fairclough, Adam. *A Class of Their Own: Black Teachers in the Segregated South.* Cambridge, MA: Harvard University Press, 2007.

Farmer-Kaiser, Mary. *Freedwomen and the Freedmen's Bureau: Race, Gender, and Public Policy in the Age of Emancipation.* New York: Fordham University Press, 2010.

Foner, Eric. *Freedom's Lawmakers: A Directory of Black Officeholders during Reconstruction,* rev. ed. New York: Oxford University Press, 1996.

———. *Reconstruction: America's Unfinished Revolution, 1863–1877.* New York: Harper and Row, 1988.

Glymph, Thavolia. *The Women's Fight: The Civil War Battles for Home, Freedom, and Nation.* Chapel Hill: University of North Carolina Press, 2020.

Guterl, Matthew Pratt. *American Mediterranean: Southern Slaveholders in the Age of Emancipation.* Cambridge, MA: Harvard University Press, 2008.

Hahn, Steven. *A Nation under our Feet: Black Political Struggles in the Rural South from Slavery to the Great Migration.* Cambridge, MA: Harvard University Press, 2003.

Hume, Richard L., and Jerry B. Gough. *Blacks, Carpetbaggers, and Scalawags: The Constitutional Conventions of Radical Reconstruction.* Baton Rouge: Louisiana State University Press, 2008.

Litwack, Leon. *Been in the Storm So Long: The Aftermath of Slavery.* New York: Alfred A. Knopf, 1979.

McCurry, Stephanie. *Confederate Reckoning: Power and Politics in the Civil War South.* Cambridge, MA: Harvard University Press, 2010.

Manning, Chandra. *Troubled Refuge: Struggles for Freedom in the Civil War.* New York: Alfred A. Knopf, 2016.

———. *What This Cruel War Was Over: Soldiers, Slavery, and the Civil War.* New York: Random House, 2007.

Oakes, James. *Freedom National: The Destruction of Slavery in the United States, 1861–1865.* New York: W. W. Norton, 2013.

Oubre, Claude F. *Forty Acres and a Mule: The Freedmen's Bureau and Black Land Ownership.* Baton Rouge: Louisiana State University Press, 1978.

Penningroth, Dylan C. *The Claims of Kinfolk: African American Property and Community in the Nineteenth-Century South.* Chapel Hill: University of North Carolina Press, 2003.

Roark, James L. *Masters without Slaves: Southern Planters in the Civil War and Reconstruction*. New York: W. W. Norton, 1978.

Rodrigue, John C. *Reconstruction in the Cane Fields: From Slavery to Free Labor in Louisiana's Sugar Parishes, 1862–1880*. Baton Rouge: Louisiana State University Press, 2001.

Rose, Willie Lee. *Rehearsal for Reconstruction: The Port Royal Experiment*. 1964; New York: Vintage Books, 1967.

Stanley, Amy Dru. *From Bondage to Contract: Wage Labor, Marriage, and the Market in the Age of Slave Emancipation*. New York: Cambridge University Press, 1998.

Stocksdale, Sally. *When Emancipation Came: The End of Enslavement on a Southern Plantation and a Russian Estate*. Jefferson, NC: McFarland, 2022.

Wright, Gavin. *Old South, New South: Revolutions in the Southern Economy Since the Civil War*. New York: Basic Books, 1986.

Index

Abney, Lucy, 263
abolitionists: moral rejection of slavery, 13, 74; Radical Republicans and, 22, 28, 72, 75; Russian example, 71; transition to free labor, 9, 14
African Americans: advertisement depictions, 507n67; American citizenship, 338–39, 341, 353–54, 359, 498n40; anti-Black terrorism, 106, 192, 339; Black businesses, 354, 506n63; Black folklore of "the surrender," 82; Black nationalism, 338–40; Black politicians, 170, 174, 186–87, 337, 505n60; Black-run newspapers, 351, 505n59; census, 208, 353, 355, 396n1, 450n10; commercial products and, 319; communal identification of, 298; Creoles, 350, 505n58; economic stratification, 347, 354; emigration and, 338–39, 353; family farming and, 315, 335; folk religion, 304–5; "Jim Crow" laws and segregation, 203, 358, 360–61, 374, 510n75; Juneteenth, 82, 415n16; land holdings, 322, 328, 347–48, 375; laziness stereotype, 14, 91, 109–10, 122, 148, 150, 267, 356, 361; life expectancy, 311; literacy and, 171; lynchings of, 358, 361, 467n14; model colonies, 234; moment of freedom for, 81–82; movement locally and to Northern cities, 203–4, 208; "negro jobs" or skilled positions, 210; Northern goodwill, 67; nuclear families, 472n39; occupational diversity of, 165–66; political rights of, 63–64; poverty of, 375, 515n13; professionals and businessmen, 210–11; racial self-identification, 336–37, 339; radical movement, 446n58; skin color and, 166, 171, 185–86, 213, 349, 351–53, 506n61; slave-owning Blacks, 349, 504n56; suicides and, 309; "Talented Tenth," 506n63; Union soldiers and, 90, 114, 423n65; urban economic elite, 352; violence against, 172, 189, 445n52, 446n53, 467n15, 495n30; white racism and, 71, 337–38, 342, 357, 486n1. *See also* Ku Klux Klan
African Repository, 339
A'Hearn, Brian, 311
Alabama: anti-Black violence, 106; apprenticing law and apprenticing law, 261–64; "Black Patrols," 111; Black women's work, 267; census (1870),

Alabama: *(continued)*
273–74; Civil War experience, 48; constitutional convention of, 187–88; governmental authorities of, 83; interracial marriage stance, 186; labor contracts and, 137, 149–51; land purchases, 213–14; lien law, 190; literacy and education, 283–85, 288; marriage recognition, 251–52; planters and labor disputes, 235; response to Black organization, 156; Southern free Blacks, 350; Southern Homestead Act and, 134–35; "upcountry ethnic cleansing," 360; volnenie-like protest, 108–9; voting rights in, 83

Alabama and Chattanooga Railroad, 240

Alabama *Beacon*, 170

Alabama Colored Convention, 94, 167, 437n17

Aleksandr Nikolaevich Engelgardt's Letters from the Country, 362

Alexander I (emperor), 18, 39

Alexander II (emperor): accession of (1856), 26, 34–35; assassination of (1881), 183, 364; comparison to Lincoln, 53; Crimean War defeat, 39; deliberations on emancipation, 8, 37–41, 43–44, 363; literacy and education, 480n66; nobles and, 55, 78; petitions to, 37, 78, 139–41, 178–79; praise for, 71; praise for emancipation plan, 69; rescript move toward emancipation, 36, 398n6; rumors of real volia debunked, 131, 140; Spassk district volnenie, 101. *See also* Russian emancipation

Alexander III (emperor), 183–84, 364–65

Alvord, John W., 221, 284–85

American Colonization Society, 339

American Freedmen's Inquiry Commission, 82, 282

American Missionary Association (AMA), 281, 283, 288, 299

American Revolution, 1, 19, 33, 51, 348

American Slavery and Russian Serfdom in the Post-Emancipation Imagination (Bellows), 356

Andrews, C. C., 85, 93

Anfimov, A. M., 218, 334, 420n50

appanage (udel'nye) peasants or court peasants, 344–46

Apraksin, A. S., 101

Apraksina, S. V., 141

Arkansas, 134, 137, 172, 253, 360

Arsen'ev, Iu. K., 177

Ashworth, John, 389n23

Atkinson, Dorothy, 196

Atlantic Monthly, 71

Austria, 25, 33, 370–71, 411n61

Ayers, Edward L., 310, 330, 332, 361, 415nn14–15, 515n9

Bakunin, Nikolai, 123

Baltic provinces, 24–25, 370, 398n6

Banks, Nathaniel, 224

Barnes, Kenneth C., 360

Baronov, David, 369

barshchina (labor obligations): confusion after emancipation, 97–99; landowner view of, 78; otrabotka (sharecropping) and, 228; owed to master, 5; peasants and seigneurial labor, 102; post-emancipation, 60, 62, 320; redemptions and, 182; statutory charters and, 127–28, 130; undermining of, 334

Bayne, Thomas, 187

Beard, Charles A., 386n16

Becker, Seymour, 318, 326–27, 333, 335–36, 495n27

Bedin, Aleksandr, 141–42
Beecher, Edward, 190
Behrend, Justin, 172, 193, 360
Bellows, Amanda Brickell, 356, 361
Belykh, Ivan Aleksandrovich, 128
Bercaw, Nancy, 272, 274, 472n39
Berlin, Ira, 349, 385n13
Bidelux, Robert, 315
Bird, William, 259, 271
The Birth of a Nation (movie), 361–62
Birzhevye vedomosti (Merchants' Gazette), 322
Black children: apprenticing, 233, 261–65, 469n23, 470n26; literacy and education, 481n71; parents' control of, 272–73, 275
Black women: education and, 293; land ownership and, 470n26; violence against, 471n35; work and, 265–67, 469n24
Blassingame, John W., 352, 472n39
Blum, Edward J., 296
Blum, Jerome, 11
Blyden, Edward Wilmot, 353, 506n61
Bolshevik Revolution (1917), 215, 316, 480n66
Boltin, Ivan, 74
Bomford, J., 262
Bonnefoi, Emile, 185
Brandes, Georg, 236
Brant, Nadezhda Pavlovna, 128
Brazil: emancipation in, 1, 370, 372; emancipation settlements, 411n61; emigration to Brazil, 241; immigrant replacement labor, 237; literacy and education, 296; new freedom in, 367; racial capitalism, 387n18; slavery in, 21
British Guiana, 369
British West Indies, 369, 411n61
Brooks, Jeffrey, 291

Brown, C. S., 106
Brown, Elsa Barkley, 169
Brown, Orlando, 149, 151, 154, 171
Bruce, Blanche K., 338, 485n87
Bruce, H. C., 305, 485n87
Buckley, Charles W., 165
Burbank, Jane, 322
Burds, Jeffrey, 321, 451n12
Bureau of Refugees, Freedmen, and Abandoned Lands. *See* Freedmen's Bureau
Burnside, Ambrose E., 46
Burton, Vernon, 274
Butchart, Ronald E., 285–86, 288
Butler, Benjamin, 224
Butler Leigh, Frances, 150, 156, 237–38, 242–43, 459n51
Butlers and Butler Island, 150, 237–38, 242, 459n51
Byrd, Ayana D., 352

Cable, George W., 361
Cameron, Paul C., 236
Campbell, Tunis, 107, 122
Canby, Edward R. S., 133
capitalism, 12, 315–18, 323, 332, 343, 372, 374–75, 389n23, 491n13. *See also* Prussian path
carpetbaggers, 185–86, 339
Carraway, John, 186–87
Catherine II (empress), 16–18, 345, 503n53
Chadick, W. D., 47
Cherepanov (peace mediator), 128
Chernigov Province, 244
Chicherin, Boris, 18
Chinese workers, 238–40, 369
Christian Reconstruction (Richardson), 299
Christian Recorder, 254
Chulos, Chris J., 302, 304

churches and religion: African Methodist Episcopal Church, 299; African Methodist Episcopal Zion Church, 299; Alabama Baptists, 298; Baptists, 299; Black churches, 298–300, 305, 483n77; Colored Methodist Episcopal Church, 483n77; Methodists, 299; Northern Methodist Episcopal Church, 299; Orthodox Church, 281, 289, 291, 300–301, 304, 345; Pine Street Baptist, 300; Wall Street Baptist Church, 300

Civil Rights Act (1866), 63, 158, 410n55

Civil War: "back" to Africa, 3; Black agency, 46, 50, 403n27; goals of Union and Confederacy, 51; industrial capitalism and, 487n3; radical politics of, 34–35

Civil War (South): Confederate military exemption law, 48; disintegration of Southern slavery, 29, 78; foreign support politics, 52; living conditions, 311; massive slave rebellion, 46–47, 401n21, 403n27; slaveholders' favorites flight, 47; Yankee hatred, 78

Civil War (Union): Black Union troops, 54; "contrabands of war," 47; Second Confiscation Act (1862), 47

The Clansman (Dixon), 361

Clarke, C. W., 106

Clarkson, Thomas, 21

Clay, Henry, 20

Clay, Susanna, 48

Clayton, John, 360–61

Clemenceau, Georges, 72

Cobb, Ned, 272–73, 492n15

Cohen, William, 203

comparisons between Russia and United States: balance of power and, 66–67; common goals of self-ownership and self-government, 113–14; disappointment over emancipation, 369, 372, 374, 515n12; industrialization and urbanization, 330–31, 335; landowner behaviors, 328–29; lives of freedpeople, 232; obstacles for newly freed, 70–71; political rights and differences, 15–16, 160–61; processes after emancipation, 54–55; Reconstruction and Russian emancipation, 62–63; response to emancipation, 113; Russian peace mediators and American Freedman's Bureau, 59, 67; "self-liberation" and "revolutionary situation," 50–51; terms of emancipation settlements, 57–58; timing and participants in "free labor" deliberation, 34–35, 45. *See also* freedpeople

comparisons between slavery and serfdom: agricultural labor and, 3; bondholders' commitments, 8; census of slaves and serfs, 383n3; chattel slavery and, 3; estate size, 5; outsiders or natives, 3, 7–8; quasi-independence, 6–7; raby and rabstvo (slaves or serfs), 384n6; racial and nonracial systems, 5–6, 384n8; ratios of master and slave or serf, 4

comparisons of Russian and African American freedpersons: acquisition of land, 202; agriculture and, 211–12; autonomy and mobility of, 202–3, 206; general or local view of themselves, 341, 354; outsiders' views of, 354–57; regional diversity, 320–21; stratification and, 174, 197, 336, 341; urbanization and, 208–9; working for planters and pomeshchiki, 201–2

comparisons post-emancipation: agriculture and, 219, 313; churches and religion, 305; class struggle, 249; conservative power of, 367; disappointment over terms of emancipation, 307–8; families and, 276; flight from management, 249; former slave owners and nobles, 324; freedom and choice, 305–6; free labor and, 196–97, 248–49; government agencies for new order, 120–23; labor relations after emancipation, 120–21, 138, 219–20; land ownership and, 119, 248–49; leaders or former slave and peasant interests, 173–74; literacy and education, 280–82, 293–95, 321; modern ways, 320–21; non-servile conditions of labor, 174; outmigration from land, 320; personal freedom, 314–15; personal mobility, 319–20; poverty, 313–14; pushback from former slaveholders and nobles, 197; sharecropping and land rental, 218; struggles of age and gender, 342. *See also* Freedmen's Bureau; Office of Peace Mediators

Confederates and Confederacy: Black troops of, 49; careers after Civil War, 332; "false peace" of, 358; government intrusion and, 48; military exemption law, 48; post–Civil War treatment proposed, 55; preservation of slavery and, 51; Reconstruction threats, 85; slavery reformers and, 48–49

Confino, Michael, 44

Constantine, Grand Duke, 36, 38

constitutional conventions: Black and White delegates, 173, 186, 441n43; conservative opposition, 188; equal citizenship and, 168, 189; lien laws proposal, 187; Reconstruction Acts (1867) and, 185; variations from state to state, 188; voter registration and, 172; women's suffrage proposal, 187

contraband camps, 47, 254, 308, 311

Conway, Thomas W., 83, 123
Cox, George W., 172
Crampton, John, 244
Creole Fire Company Number 1, 350
Crimean War, 8, 26, 29, 34, 39, 41, 230, 311–12
Crouch, Barry A., 122
The Crucible of Race (Williamson), 357
Cuba: abolition in, 33; Chinese workers and, 238–39; emancipation in, 370; racial capitalism, 387n18; slavery in, 21, 514n5; whiteness and citizenship, 504n56; white Southerners to, 241

Dadiani, K. L., 86
Daily Selma Times, 94
Das Kapital (Marx), 317
Davis, David Brion, 12, 389n23
Davis, Jefferson, 82, 223
Davis, Joseph E., 166, 222, 329
Davis Bend community, 166, 221–23, 328–29, 436n11
De Bow, J. D. B., 20
De Forest, John W., 266
de la Fuente, Alejandro, 504n56
Delany, Martin, 338–39
Delaware, 27, 349, 452n20
The Development of Capitalism in Russia (Lenin), 316, 343
Dinnella-Borrego, Luis-Alejandro, 505n60
Dix, John A., 47
Dixon, Thomas, Jr., 361
Dolgoruki, I. M., 17, 74
Donaldsonville (Louisiana) *Chief*, 239
Douglas, Stephen, 28
Douglass, Frederick, 57, 66, 77, 207, 280, 350
Downs, Gregory P., 190, 235, 358
Downs, Jim, 308, 311
Drago, Edmund L., 300

Drescher, Seymour, 370
Druzhinin, N. M., 215, 334
Du Bois, W. E. B., 296, 481n71, 507n63

Edwards, Laura F., 53, 223, 262, 445n52, 508n71
Ekaterinoslavl Province, 86
Eklof, Ben, 290, 292, 295, 479n66, 482n72
Ellison, William, 349
Ely, Ralph, 134–35
emancipation: abolitionism and, 10, 12, 16, 22; capitalism and, 9–12; Eastern Europe and, 369–72; goals of freedpeople and former owners, 78–79; land ownership and, 76; Western hemisphere countries, 369–72
Emancipation Edict of 1861, 268
Emancipation Proclamation (1863), 49–51, 53–54, 81, 83
emancipation settlements, 25, 57–58, 411n61
Emberton, Carole, 309
Emmons, Terence, 44, 325, 401n18
Engel, Barbara Alpern, 232, 277–78, 451n16
Engelgardt, Aleksandr Nikolaevich, 228–29, 246–47, 279, 289–90, 322, 356
Engelstein, Laura, 278–79
Engerman, Stanley L., 10
Escott, Paul D., 423n65
Evtuhov, Catherine, 195, 497n35

Fairclough, Adam A., 287, 296–97, 443n48, 486n1
Farmer-Kaiser, Mary, 272
Farnsworth, Beatrice, 278
Federal Writers Project interviews, 114, 423n65
Fedorov, V. A., 42

female peasants: divorces and, 474n45; domestic violence and, 278–80; outwork of, 277; patriarchy and, 276–77, 279; prostitution and, 211, 277, 451n16, 474n44
Ferliger, Louis A., 328
Feshchenkov, Efim, 143, 165
Field, Daniel, 15, 36, 45, 115–16, 244, 343, 500n43
Fields, Barbara J., 50, 323, 334
Fifteenth Amendment (1869, 1870), 55–56, 64, 158, 190, 358, 407n40, 444n50
Fisk, Clinton B., 213, 265
Fitzgerald, Michael W., 360
Florida: Blacks in local government, 193; constitutional convention of, 188; homesteaders and census, 428n25; labor contracts and, 137–38, 149, 154, 221; Lower South, 452n20; marriage recognition, 253; redemption of Reconstruction government, 189; Southern Homestead Act and, 65, 112, 134–36, 212
Foner, Eric: Blacks and land ownership, 213, 226; "colored conventions" and, 94; economic emancipation, 411n58; on education, 282; on emigration, 338; interracial democracy, 337; understanding freedom, 73; an unfinished revolution, 310, 313, 411n59
former slave owners: absenteeism and distance from laborers, 241–42, 324, 329; amnesty and property, 222; anti-Black violence, 106; capitalist landlords, 336; compensation for, 70; complaints of, 91, 324; economic crisis, 325; economic status, 326–28; emigration from plantations, 240–41, 459n55, 460n56, 496n34; failure to impose dependent labor, 154;

fear that freed Blacks would not work, 109–10; flight from management, 248; freedpeople negotiations and, 109; immigrant replacement labor, 237–40; loss of privileges, 372; response to Black organization, 156, 234–35; restoration of land, 213; rumors of massive insurrection, 107, 110–12, 116–17, 170; sale of plantations, 222; sharecropping and, 221, 243; treason or forgiveness, 325–26. *See also* Black children

Forret, Jeff, 342

Foster, J. G., 134–35, 138

Fourteenth Amendment, 56, 63–64, 158, 190, 358, 407n40, 409n51, 409n53, 410n55

Frank, Stephen P., 341, 363

Frankel, Noralee, 274

Frazier, E. Franklin, 354

Frazier, Garrison, 131

Fredrickson, George M., 355, 357–58

Freedman's Savings Bank, 495n26

Freedmen's Bureau: bureaucracy of, 84; centrist policies of, 124–25; confusion over role, 233; diversity of, 122; divided government authority, 83–85; establishment and abolition of, 65, 82–83, 120; former Union Army officers and, 67, 82–83, 122; Freedmen's Branch successor, 425n5; free labor doctrine and, 57; General Orders No. 3 and apprenticeship, 262–64; General Orders No. 8 and marriage recognition, 251–54; internal disputes and criticism, 123; labor contracts and, 137, 148, 156–57, 318; literacy and education, 281, 283, 293; on marriage relationships, 271; policies of, 79; revisionist history of, 121–22; views of Blacks and Whites, 122;

volnenie-like protest, 108–9. *See also* Black children; Union League

Freedom (documentary), 50

freedpeople: balance of power and, 308; collective action among laborers, 155–56, 433n59; disappointments of, 372; diversity of, 336; fears of losing freedom, 114–15; poverty of, 369, 374–75; self-ownership and self-government, 85–86, 95, 107, 154–55, 373; temporary initial restraint, 95; worldwide literacy, 296. *See also* serfs and serfdom; slaves and slavery

freedpeople (Russia): bourgeois values and, 322; capitalism and, 315; conditions of, 309–10; conflicting goals with pomeshchiki, 232; independent actors, 297; literacy and education, 281, 289–92, 295–96, 321–22, 364, 475n48, 479nn63–64, 481n70, 482n72; local self-rule, 195; "naïve monarchism," 103, 114–16, 423n67; response to emancipation, 86–89, 95–97; suspicion of pomeshchiki, 114

freedpeople (United States): Black leaders and leadership, 161, 165–67, 170–73; Black or White teachers, 284–87; bourgeois values and, 320; caution in postwar months, 94, 108; citizenship and voter registration, 161, 168–69, 172–73, 371; colored conventions, 94, 167, 170–71, 173; conditions of, 308–9; conflicting goals with former slave owners, 232–33; conservative white "cooperationists" and, 170; higher education, 287–88; individualism of, 297–98; labor relations after emancipation, 93, 108–9, 112, 314; literacy and education, 281–89, 295–97, 477n53; living conditions, 310–11; "Long Reconstruction," 312–13;

freedpeople (United States): (*continued*) market relations and, 322; meaning of freedom, 92–93; movement of former slaves, 91; obstacles for newly freed, 226; proto-political activity, 165; radical Reconstruction policies, 169–71; Reconstruction and, 85; response to emancipation, 92–94; rumor of reestablishment of slavery, 134; segregated schools, 288–89; self-government participation, 185; self-ownership and self-government, 169; St. Catherine's Island all-Black enclave, 107; suspicion of Whites, 112

freedpeople families (Russia): effect of emancipation on, 255; family fragmentation, 255–56; razdel (division), 257–58

freedpeople families (United States): effect of emancipation on, 251; group marriage ceremonies, 253; independent Black households, 258–59; marriage recognition, 251–53; patriarchal values, 259, 467n14; relationships and rules of, 270–75; search for family members, 254–55, 465nn7–8. *See also* Black children; Black women

Free Economic Society for the Encouragement in Russia of Agriculture and Household Management, 17

Freehling, William W., 19

free labor and free labor doctrine: abolitionism and, 9, 13–14, 22; bourgeois values and, 318; capitalism and, 12; comparison to slavery, 487n3; crisis of the Union, 28; docile workforce, 235–36; effect of, 232; labor contracts and, 137–38, 318–19; Lincoln and, 53; meaning of, 201; productivity and profitability, 15, 17–18; radical version of, 76; Republican Party and, 20; timing of emancipation, 34; transition to free labor, 335

free-soil movement, 22, 28
French, M., 253
Frierson, Cathy A., 362
Fullerton, Joseph S., 123

Gagarin, Pavel, 180
Gardner, S. S., 111
Garibaldi, Giuseppe, 71
Garrison, William Lloyd, 22, 72, 74, 412n4
Gates, Henry Louis, Jr., 486n1
Gaudin, Corinne, 340, 364–65
Geddis, A., 122
Genovese, Eugene D., 10, 333
Georgia: absentee landlords, 6, 241–42; Blacks behind Union lines, 81; Blacks in elective office, 441n49; Civil War experience, 47, 49, 81; Civil War–liberated areas, 54; constitutional convention of, 188; Freedmen's Bureau in, 83, 92, 122; governmental authorities of, 83; labor contracts and, 150–51, 156; land holdings, 328; rice plantations, 225, 234, 321; Sea Isles all-Black enclave, 107; Sherman and clergymen meeting, 131–32
Gillem, Alvan C., 149–51, 154–55, 252, 463n4
Glickman, Rose L., 276
Global Slavery Index (GSI), 377
Glymph, Thavolia, 259, 267, 308, 310
Golovachev, A. A., 44
Gorgas, Josiah, 93, 110
Gough, Jerry B., 189
Gourdin, Bill, 147–48
Grant, Ulysses S., 82
Great Britain: abolitionism and, 10; capitalism and, 389n23; coercion of the marketplace, 12, 21

Great Reforms: disappointment over emancipation, 369, 373–74; ending of, 366–67; military reform after emancipation, 399n11; provinces and, 497n35; restructure of society, 308, 363; war-triggered transformation, 33–34
Greeley, Horace, 51, 53
Green, James K., 170, 210, 451n15
Green, Silas, 271
Gregory, Ovid, 350, 505n58
Grevs, Mikhail Mikhailovich, 176
Griffith, D. W., 361
Grimes, James W., 52
Grimké, Sarah and Angelina, 27
Grodno Province (Lithuania), 36, 87, 409n49
Gross, Ariela T., 504n56

Hagin, George, 242
Hahn, Steven: Black suffrage and, 169, 173, 185, 438n23, 446n58; emigrationist sentiment, 338–39; "naïve monarchism," 423n67; radical Congress, 167; Reconstruction and democracy, 187; rumors' effect on slaves and freedpeople, 115–16; self-liberation thesis and, 50; slave flight as rebellion, 46
Hair Story (Byrd and Tharps), 352
Haitian Revolution, 1, 8, 33, 46, 70, 371, 512n84
Hale, Grace Elizabeth, 361
Hamburg, G. M., 245
Hammond, James Henry, 21–22, 27
Hampton, Wade, 170, 339
Harding, Vincent, 51
Haskell, Thomas L., 389n23
Hatch, Edward, 92
Helper, Hinton Rowan, 19, 27
Herzen, Alexander (Iskander), 40–41, 71, 391n31, 412n4

Hetrick, Matthew J., 352, 499n41
Hobbs, Allyson Vanessa, 506n61
Hoch, Steven L., 68–69, 216–17, 342
Hodes, Martha, 467n14
Hofstadter, Richard, 53
Holt, Sharon Ann, 267, 472n39
Homestead Act (1862), 65
Houston, Bernard, 149, 153
Houston, George S., 149, 153
Houzeau, Jean-Charles, 351, 505n59
Howard, O. O.: African American support for, 125; contract system and, 138; education and, 284–85; family morality and, 252–53; Freedmen's Bureau head, 82; homesteading and, 135; labor rights and, 234, 264; letters to, 106, 110, 112; prostitution and, 266; reports to, 83, 92–93, 113, 117, 123, 134, 150; Taylor Farm and, 132–33; voting rights and, 149
Hudson, Larry E., Jr., 317
Hume, Richard L., 189
Huntsville (Alabama) *Advocate*, 78, 106

Iakimenko, N. A., 205
Iaroslavl Province: earnings sent home, 231, 451n12; females in, 277; literacy and education, 293, 480n67; mortality rates, 489n6; nobles of, 245, 497n35; personal nobles, 461n64; population statistics, 256–57; volneniia after emancipation, 98
The Impending Crisis of the South (Helper), 19, 27
indentured labor, 237, 262, 264, 369
Independent Monitor (Alabama), 151
The Interest in Slavery of the Southern Non-Slaveholder (De Bow), 20
International Labour Organization, 377
Iusupov, Nikolai Borisovich, 127–28

Jacobs, Harriet A., 280, 350
Jacobs, Henry P., 300
Jacobs Benevolent Society, 300
Jamaica, 367, 369
Jefferson, Thomas, 74, 412n2
Johnson, Andrew: amnesty for slaveholders, 222, 397n2; Black children and restoration governments, 261; citizenship act veto, 63–64; Freedmen's Bureau and, 123; impeachment of, 55; marriage recognition, 251; plantation owners as traitors, 35; Reconstruction policies and, 118; "restoration" plan, 56, 83, 132, 213; revocation of abandoned land order, 132; Schurz tour of Southern states, 93, 106, 112; Sherman's Field Order 15 and, 225
Jones, Catherine A., 272
Jones, Charles C., Jr., and Mary, 241–42
Jones, Mary, 49
Julian, George W., 55, 72

Kaluga Province, 87, 95, 124, 231, 244, 293
Kaluga Province Statistical Committee, 204, 256, 281
Kansas, 203, 223, 340
Kansas-Nebraska Act (1854), 27
Kavtaradze, G. A., 164
Kaye, Anthony E., 77
Kazan Province, 101–2, 131, 244
Kaznakov, N. G., 95–96
Keith, Lee-Anna, 310
Kentucky, 5, 20, 265, 452n20
Kenzer, Robert C., 310, 323
Kerans, David, 493n19
Ketchum, A. P., 262
Kiev Province, 88, 231, 409n49
King, Wilma, 271
Kiselev, P. D., 17–18, 24, 345

Knights of the White Camelia, 191–92, 360
Kolokol (The Bell), 40, 412n4
Kondrat'ev, Ivan, 439n34
Korelin, A. P., 245, 326, 334
Korobov, Demid, 143, 164
Korostovtsova, Agrafena Ivanovna, 176
Koshelev, Aleksandr, 18
Kostroma Province, 87, 139
Kovno Province (Lithuania), 36, 409n49
Kozlialinov, P. F., 101
Kravchinskii, Sergei Mikhailovich "Stepniak," 205, 257, 303
Kresti'anskoe dvizhenie series, 146
Kretz, Dale, 425n5
Kriukova, S. S., 346
Ku Klux Klan, 107, 172, 191, 360
Kurdiukov, Iakov, 176
Kursk Province, 142, 164, 178–79, 182, 257
Kusheleva, Ekaterina Dmitrievna, 179

labor and land (Russia): agricultural production and, 244; collective petitions, 139, 429nn33–34, 430n35, 430n40; exemptions from statutory charters, 427n17; factory and mine workers, 229–30; labor arrangements, 226–28; land allotment questions, 216–18; land allotments, 141, 143, 147, 205–6, 208, 217–19, 453n25, 454n26, 462n68; land purchases, 219, 227; land redemptions, 157, 174–85, 202, 212, 215–16, 439nn34–35, 439nn34–38; land redemptions and allotments, 58, 139; mandatory land transfers, 183–84; purchase and rental of land, 247–48; rumors of land distribution, 183, 217; statutory charter distrust, 130–31; statutory charter guidelines, 139–43, 164, 216;

statutory charter implementation statistics, 144, 145t, 430n43, 431n44; statutory charters and labor contracts, 126–31, 138, 235; statutory charters and parish priests, 141–42; temporary workers, 457n40; type and quality of soil, 216; wage labor, 228–29; women's role, 231–32, 451n16; working land and ownership, 234

labor and land (United States): abandoned land, 83, 111, 132; Black land ownership, 212–14, 214t, 224, 429n28, 452n18, 452n20; collective action among laborers, 234, 314; control of, 109–10; free labor doctrine, 136–37; labor contracts, 137, 147–54; labor shortages, 154–56, 224–25, 229, 233, 235, 238, 262; labor unions and strikes, 234; labor variations postemancipation, 202, 220–23; land redistribution, 65, 110–12, 116–19, 131–33, 136, 213; Republican Party and, 119; squatters, 132; Taylor Farm, 132–33; wage labor, 136, 224; working conditions, 155. *See also* sharecropping; Southern Homestead Act

Lang, J., 71, 281

Langston, John Mercer, 122, 252

Lanksoi, M. S., 123

Lanskoi, Sergei S., 87, 96, 105, 118, 363

LeBaron, Genevieve, 377

Lee, Robert E., 82

Lenin, Vladimir I., 10, 316, 333–34, 343, 389n23, 462n69, 491n12, 501n46

Leonard, Carol S., 217–18, 230, 247, 311, 316, 320

The Leopard's Spots (Dixon), 361

Le Temps (newspaper), 72

Letour, Erastus, 255

Liberator, 22, 72, 412n4

Lichtenstein, Alex, 316

Lincoln, Abraham: "anti-Southern" Republican, 27; free labor and, 13, 53, 76; Great Emancipator, 54; "House Divided" speech, 23; Kansas-Nebraska Act speech, 396n2; Lincoln-Douglas debate, 28; preservation of the Union, 50–52; Republican Party and, 8, 53, 405n32; self-government understanding, 77, 160, 163, 337–38. *See also* Emancipation Proclamation

Litvak, B. G., 42, 217

Louisiana: annual labor contracts, 152; Blacks behind Union lines, 81; Blacks in local government, 193; bondspeople census, 5; Caine River colony, 349; Chinese workers in, 238–40; constitutional convention in, 172–73, 185, 188; education and, 190–91, 282, 288, 293; Freedmen's Bureau in, 123; free persons of color in, 352, 504n56; labor shortages in, 224; land purchases, 213; plantation work in, 203; redemption of Reconstruction government, 189, 359; Southern free Blacks, 348, 351; Southern Homestead Act and, 134; sugar plantations in, 225, 234, 241, 293, 320, 360; sugar workers' strike, 359–60; violence and racism in, 192, 359

Louisiana Immigration Company, 240

Louisiana Purchase Treaty (1804), 348

Lovell, Joseph, 221–22

Lovell, William Storrow, 328–29

Lowcountry. *See* rice plantations

Löwe, Heinz-Dietrich, 343

Lowe, Richard, 171, 438n19

Loyal Association of Colored Ladies, 169

Luklianov, Nikopor, 128

L'Union (newspaper), 351

Luskey, Brian P., 487n3

Lyashchenko, Peter I., 216, 309

Majewski, John D., 388n21
Makov, L. S., 183
Malyshev, Stepan Ivanov, 139–40, 429n34, 430n35
Mandel, James I., 237
Manigault, Louis, 47
Manly, Basil, 93
Manning, Chandra, 311–12
Manning, Roberta Thompson, 325
Martineau, Harriet, 21
Marx, Karl, 12, 317, 389n23
Maryland, 27, 52, 349, 452n20
Masters without Slaves (Roark), 325
Mathisen, Erik, 469n23
McCurry, Stephanie, 401n21
McPherson, James M., 50, 403n27
Meekar, Edward, 311
Meier, August, 167
Merkel, Garlieb, 17
Metz, John D., 328
migrant labor (Russia): to cities, 211; countryside work, 228–29, 231; out-migration from land, 204–5, 256–57, 314, 320–21; outside work, 206, 276–78; outside world and, 301, 341; serfs and, 207; single men as, 209; support by otkhodnichestvo, 375
Miliutin, Nikolai, 37
Ministry of Education (Russia), 291–92, 294
Ministry of Internal Affairs (Russia), 80, 131, 296, 420n50, 429n33, 430n40, 431n44
Ministry of State Domains (Russia), 345
Ministry of War (Russia), 296
Minsk Province, 409n49, 431n43
Mintz, Steven, 369
Mironov, Boris N.: on effect of emancipation, 309, 311–12; on the family, 269–70, 279, 321–22; on land allotments, 218, 453n25; on literacy, 294–95; on literacy and education, 482n72; on nobility, 325, 327; on outsiders, 341; on peasantry, 343; on peasant self-government, 164; on starosty service, 435n5; widows and, 474n43
Mississippi: Black children and apprenticing, 469n23; Black enfranchisement and disenfranchisement, 168, 361; Blacks in government, 166, 172, 193, 338; capitalism and, 323; Chinese workers, 238; constitutional convention of, 188–89; Davis Bend community, 222–23; former slave owners and, 106, 328; freedpeople's response to emancipation, 92–93; labor contracts and, 117, 149–50, 153–56; land distribution expectation, 134; literacy and education, 285, 287; marriage recognition, 252–53; Mound Bayou, 223–24, 234; patriarchy and, 271, 274, 471n35; planned insurrection, 110, 112; plantation work in, 203; poorest state, 376; redemption of Reconstruction government, 189; religion in, 300; search for family members, 255
Missouri, 412n2, 452n20, 469n24
Mixter, Timothy, 229
Mobile *Daily Register*, 221
Mobile *Nationalist*, 299
"modern slavery," 11, 376–77, 516n17
Mogilev Province, 409n49
Mohr, Clarence, 49
Montgomery, Benjamin T., 166, 222–23, 329
Montgomery, Isaiah, 223–24
Montgomery, Thornton, 223
Montgomery Daily Advertiser, 91, 133, 155, 169–70
Moon, David, 217, 311
Moore, Barrington, Jr., 498n36

Moore, J. B., 243
Moore, Jno C., 122
Mordvinov, S. A., 364
Moret Law (Cuba 1870), 370
Morgan, Lynda J., 487n3
Moscow Province, 35, 85, 88, 182, 209, 230–31, 257, 294
Murray, Anna, 350

Napier, Francis, 244
National Freedman's Relief Association, 281
A Nation under Our Feet (Hahn), 338
Nazimov, V. A., 36
New England Freedmen's Aid Society, 282, 284
New Orleans *Times*, 239
New Orleans *Tribune*, 166, 351, 353
New York Times, 377, 515n13
Nicholas I (emperor), 18, 25–26, 34, 36, 39
Nicholas II (emperor), 184, 480n66
Nikitenko, Aleksandr, 26, 41, 89
Nikitenko, Nikolai Petrovich, 475n48
Nikitin, Fedor, 99, 164
Nizhnii Novgorod Province, 17, 58, 87–88, 183, 217, 479n65
Noble Land Bank, 247, 325, 495n26
North Carolina: Black children and, 261–62; Black progress in, 310, 349; constitutional convention of, 188–89; constitutional conventions in, 172; emancipation in, 49; family morality and, 252; former slave owners in, 91; fugitive slaves, 46; land promises, 110; literacy and education, 283, 322; marriage recognition, 252; marriage recognition in, 271; redemption of Reconstruction government, 189, 359; Southern free Blacks, 349
Novikov, Aleksandr, 279, 290

Oakes, James, 12, 52, 395n51
Oberry, Wilson, 236
Obolenskii, Nikolai, 123
obrok (quitrent): abolition of, 430n35; annual payments, 60–62, 69, 128, 345; calculation of, 408n46; cash or kind, 4–5; confusion after emancipation, 98; obligations continued, 78, 97, 100, 102, 130; redemptions and, 182–83; refusals to pay, 139, 142, 177; response of pomeschiki, 44; statutory charters and, 127, 176; variations in use, 6; village assembly post emancipation, 162
Office of Peace Mediators: abolition of, 120, 364–65; administrative discord, 123; confusion over role, 233; diversity of mediators, 122–23; favoring the peasants, 142; Freedmen's Bureau comparison, 67, 79, 84–85, 138, 158, 234, 318–19; government officials, 80, 117; history of, 121–22; land allotments, 177; land allotments and, 126, 128; land dispute, 102; local hereditary nobles, 407n43; "mirovoi posrednik" definition, 424n2; neutral government figures, 105; peasant disorder, 164–65, 178, 180; peasant-landlord relations, 58–59, 78–79; pomeshchiki and, 121, 124–25; selection of, 81, 83; Soviet depiction of, 426n11; statutory charters and, 61, 129–30, 139–41, 143–44, 176, 319; statutory charters and labor contracts, 141, 427n13; village schools and, 289
Ogarev, Nikolai, 40, 71
Olmsted, Frederick Law, 14–15, 76
Olonets Province, 5, 176
"On the Abolition of Serfdom in Russia" (Perovslii), 24

Orenburg Province, 69, 86, 123, 130, 139
Origins of the New South, 1877–1913 (Woodward), 325
Osborn, T. W., 111–12, 137
otkhod. *See* migrant labor
otkhodniki. *See* migrant labor
otrabotka (sharecropping), 227–28, 323, 451n12
Out of the House of Bondage (Glymph), 259

Painter, Nell Irvin, 339
Panin, Viktor N., 38
Parrish, John, 108
Parson, Lewis, 111
Paton, Diane, 467n14
Patterson, Orlando, 5, 385n13
Patton, Robert, 273, 355
Paul (emperor), 503n53
peace mediators. *See* Office of Peace Mediators
Pearson, Charles Henry, 41
Pearson, Thomas S., 365
Peasant Icons (Frierson), 362
peasantization, 315–16, 318, 324, 328
Peasant Land Bank, 181
"peasant movement," 42, 104
peasants, post-emancipation: capitalism and, 493nn18–19; census of population (1858), 461n61; class struggle, 342–43; commercial products and, 319–20; communal life, 314; communes and, 340–41; family farming and, 315, 335, 462n68; family transformation, 267–70, 277–79, 314, 321–22, 471n31; folk religion, 301–4, 484n84; intergenerational struggles, 275, 342; land acquisitions, 214–15, 218–19, 327, 341, 375; land redemptions, 489n6; living conditions, 311; migration to cities, 207, 211, 321; movement and migration, 204–5; narod (common people or Russian nation), 355, 362; officials and citizenship, 340–41, 500n43; outsiders or natives, 341; outsiders' views of, 355–56, 362–63; outwork, 256; peasantness, 336; peasant stratification, 206, 316, 342–44, 347, 491n12, 501n46, 501n47; rural labor, 226–27; supplementary work, 227–28; supplemented income of, 205–6; technological improvements, 493n19; temporary employment, 319; temporary migration (otkhodnichestvo), 205–6, 209, 211, 230–31, 256, 314, 375; urban work and living quarters, 211. *See also* female peasants
peasant self-government: communal consciousness and self-rule, 59, 164–65, 364–66, 512n83; communal plan, 37, 59; peasant police, 162, 434n3; pre-emancipation carryovers, 163–64; proto-political peasant institutions, 161, 163; sel'skoe obshchestvo (village society, community), 161–62, 165; volost' (canton, township), 161–63, 434n2; zemstva and, 165, 195–96, 314, 321, 340, 366, 408n44
Penningroth, Dylan C., 166, 212, 236, 271–72, 342, 452n18, 471n35
Penza Province, 88, 179
People's Will, 183
Perm Province, 180, 289, 344
Perovskii, I. A., 24
Peter I (emperor), 345
Petrov, Anton, 101–2
Phillips, Ulrich B., 10
Pliley, Jessica R., 377
Pobedonostsev, K. P., 301, 365
Podolia Province, 88, 131, 142, 289, 409n49

Pokataev, Semen, 439n34
Poland, 245, 370–71, 430n43, 512n83
Polibin, Andrei Koz'min, 439n34
Polish Revolution (1863), 62, 118, 158, 430n43
Poltava Province, 146
pomeshchiki (aristocratic landowners): absenteeism and distance from laborers, 244–45, 324, 329, 332–33; allotment disputes, 43–45; committee on relations with serfs, 36; decline in pomeshchik-directed agriculture, 227; economic crisis, 324–25; economic stratification, 344; excessive punishment, 23; free peasant labor and, 243–44; hereditary or personal nobles, 461n64; land redemptions, 175, 180–82, 216; loss of land, 44–45, 326–27, 333; loss of privileges, 372–73; mercantile careers, 332; move to cities, 245, 324; name changes for same results, 78; power over peasants, 24, 78, 165; privileges of, 335–36; redemption claims, 175, 326, 438n24; response to emancipation, 43–45, 96–97; response to free labor, 235; sale of estates, 245–47, 495n27; serfs' disputes and, 42–43; source of income and, 15; statutory charter difficulties, 130; supervision of peasant labor, 245; transferred to house servants, 19; view of peasants by, 237, 363; wealth variations, 327
prostitution, 211, 277, 377, 474n44
Provincial Office of Peasant Affairs, 102
Prussia: compensation for loss of human property, 70; emancipation in, 9, 33, 370–71; emancipation settlements, 25, 411n61; new freedom in, 367
Prussian path, 333–35

Pskov Province, 102, 227, 244
Pugachev Rebellion of 1773–74, 74

Quitman, John A., 221

Rabinowitz, Howard N., 70, 210, 289, 331, 450n10
Radishchev, Aleksandr, 16
Raevskaia, Anna Mikhailovna, 141
Rakhmatullin, M. A., 394n46
Ransom, Roger L., 221, 248, 267
Reconstruction: Black suffrage and, 64, 148; Civil War and emancipation, 190, 443n50; collapse of, 310, 358–59, 366–67, 486n1; Congressional and public deliberation, 54–55; Congressional makeup during, 55, 406n36; criticism of, 69–70; disappointment over emancipation, 369; federal state divide, 445n52; governmental structure during, 83–84; history of, 337–38; Joint Congressional Committee on, 56, 107; land confiscation proposal, 57, 397n2; laissez-faire attitude of government, 71; overthrow and terrorism of, 184–85, 360; radical policies of, 167; scalawags and, 358; slaves into republican citizens, 63; war-triggered transformation, 33–34; White Southerners and, 515n9
Reconstruction Acts (1867), 56, 64, 151, 158, 167–68, 185, 189, 407n40, 409n53. See also constitutional conventions
Reconstruction Amendments, 508n71
Reconstruction governments: Blacks in local government, 193–94, 194t; Black women's role, 193; constitutional conventions and, 168; in Georgia, 443n49; longevity and character of, 189–90; marriage recognition,

Reconstruction governments: *(continued)* 251; military occupation and, 358; opposition to, 184; overthrow of, 214; public schools and, 283, 288, 291; schools, 70; white majority legislatures, 192–93; White violence and, 191

"Redeemer" governments, 295, 360

Red Shirts, 191, 360

Reid, Whitelaw, 93, 238, 359

Reidy, Joseph P., 313

republicanism, definition of, 190

Republican Party: abolitionists and, 20, 395n50; Blacks in, 284, 339, 350; Civil War opportunity, 34, 52–53; defense of property, 443n48, 486n1; land distribution and, 119; Lincoln and, 8; Reconstruction and, 55, 63

Riasanovsky, Nicholas V., 16

Riazan Province: charter resistance, 130; children in, 275–76; former state peasants, 346–47; literacy and education, 290; nuclear families, 269, 279; pomeshchiki in disputes, 124; population of, 207; volneniia in, 42

rice plantations, 47, 225–26, 234, 266, 321

Richardson, Joe M., 299

Rieber, Alfred A., 39, 59

Roark, James L., 48, 78, 310, 325, 329

Robinson, Assistant Commissioner, 262

Robinson, G. T., 58

Romeo, Sharon, 469n24

Rosenthal, Caitlin, 319, 491n13

Rostovstev, Iakov Ivanovich, 38

Rozenberg (estate manager), 139

Rubin, Anne Sarah, 192, 359

Rudzevich, N. A., 139–40

Ruef, Martin, 323

Russia: children in, 275–76; conservatives and, 364–66; early days of emancipation, 117; freedom and equality, 73–75; "Great Falsehood of Our Time," 365; industrialization and urbanization, 330–31; land captains (zemskii nachal'nik), 365; life expectancy, 312, 488n6; military service, 8, 26, 34, 39, 41, 162, 258; peasant administrative organizations, 59; per capita income, 388n21; poverty in, 376; urban population and, 208–9. *See also* Office of Peace Mediators; Prussian path

Russia and the Russians (Turgenev), 16

Russia as a "Developing Society" (Shanin), 315

Russian emancipation: administrative agencies of, 80–81; Editing Commissions, 38; gradual transition to freedom, 60–61, 70, 79, 411n61; land allotments, 60–62, 66, 68–69, 126–30, 313, 489n9; liberal views and, 44–45; Main Committee on the Peasant Question, 37–38; Polozheniia (emancipation statutes), 39, 407n40; redemption period, 61–62, 126, 409n49; Secret Committee on the Peasant Question, 36–37; steps leading up to, 35–41; volia and volia (freedom) rumors, 130; volia andvolia (freedom) rumors, 131, 139–40, 143, 146–47, 217

Russian emancipation decree (19 February 1861), 58–60, 69, 80, 102, 183, 345, 371

Russian nobles: census of, 512n83; compensation for loss of serfs, 371; marshals of nobility, 35–36, 102, 495n29; role in emancipation, 35; social standing and dominant power, 67. *See also* pomeshchiki

The Russian Peasantry (Kravchinskii), 303
Russian women: folk religion and, 303–4, 475n47; image of, 363; literacy and education, 293–95, 480n66; widows and, 474n43

Sabaneev, Nikolai, 98
Samara Province, 87, 97, 183, 231
Saratov Province: literacy and education, 293–94; passports in, 257; peasant landholdings, 462n68; pomeshchiki landholdings, 247, 327, 489n9; population statistics, 268; redemption payments and, 180, 183; serfs in, 5; trade with Germans, 205, 230
Saunders, David, 311, 363–64
Saville, Julie, 170
Saxton, Rufus, 107, 111
Schurz, Carl, 56, 93, 106–7, 112, 419n33
Schweninger, Loren, 323, 351
Scott (South Carolina assistant commissioner), 152–53
Scott, Rebecca, 370, 372
Second Confiscation Act (1862), 47
self-government: basic American right, 28; doctrine of, 75–77; freedpeople and, 86, 126, 197; maximum degree of, 95, 107, 113; political struggle and, 160. *See also* peasant self-government
self-government (United States): post–Civil War states, 64; slaves and local consciousness in, 77
self-ownership, 74–76, 86, 107, 137
Selma *Daily Messenger*, 150, 266
Selma *Times*, 91
Sel'skii Vestnik (Rural Herald), 322
Semi-Weekly Natchitoches Times, 239
serfs and serfdom: allotments of, 4–5; anti-serfdom movement, 16–18; censorship and autocracy, 23; Crimean War and, 41; disappointment over terms of emancipation, 89; economic and military effect of, 39–40; fear of destabilizing society, 24, 26; fear of landless proletariat, 25; freeing or partial freeing, 23–24, 26; intelligentsia and, 17; land transfers and, 19; limits on control by serfholders, 4–5; noble serfholders and, 3–4, 7, 15, 18–19, 384n7; productivity of, 388n18; Pugachev Rebellion of 1773–74, 41, 74; response to emancipation, 86–87; seigneurial land and allotments, 76, 89; urban population and, 207–8. *See also* appanage (udel'nye) peasants or court peasants; freedpeople; Russian emancipation; state peasants; volneniia
Seward, William, 22
Sewell, F. D., 132, 135
Shanin, Teodor, 248, 315, 462n69, 491n12
sharecropping: capitalist wage labor and, 323; definition of, 136; family farming and, 248; former owners and employment, 196, 220–22; former slave owners and, 242–43; Russian peasants and otrabotka, 228; share wages or share renting, 154–55, 223–25, 227, 318; swindling and, 153
Sharkey, W. L., 110, 112
Shaw, Nate. *See* Cobb, Ned
Sheping, Maria Dmitrievna, 179
Shepukova, N. M., 10
Sherman, William T., 131–32, 225
Shidlovskii, V., 176
Shishliannikov, Vasilii, 439n34
Sibley, C. C., 151
Sick from Freedom (Downs), 308
Simbirsk Province, 87, 117, 125, 230, 246, 328

slaves and slavery: abolitionism and, 13, 19, 22; "black codes" post Civil War, 56; Civil War and Reconstruction flight, 46–47, 91; Civil War disintegration of, 49–50; Compromise of 1850, 27; definition of, 7, 385n13; demise of, 8, 10, 21; intergenerational struggles, 342; John Brown's raid on Harper's Ferry, 27; literacy laws, 280; marriages of, 251; Nat Turner insurrection, 19; "racial capitalism" or "second slavery," 387n18; reactions to emancipation, 89–91; "self-liberation thesis," 50–51; slave-on-slave violence, 342; tenuous circumstances of freedom, 415nn14–15. *See also* freedpeople

Slovutinskii, S. T., 42

Smalls, Robert, 185

Smith, Spencer, 263

Smolensk Province, 228–29, 247, 279, 289–90, 322, 356

Sommerville, Diane Miller, 308–9

Soule, Charles C., 85, 113

South Carolina: absentee landlords, 6, 241; Blacks behind Union lines, 81; Blacks in local government, 193; Black women's work, 266; census (1870 and 1880), 274; constitutional convention of, 185, 187–88; constitutional conventions in, 172–73, 188; convention of white South Carolinians, 191; "cooperationists," 170; emigration consideration, 339; family separation, 254; freedpeople of, 107, 111; integrated schools, 190–91; labor contracts and, 106, 138, 147, 149–50, 152, 155; land distribution and, 132, 134; land promises, 113, 117; literacy and education in, 285, 288; marriage recognition, 251–53, 271, 463n4; pro-slavery Whites from, 21, 27, 82, 85; redemption of Reconstruction government, 189; relations with plantation owners, 236; rice plantations, 321; rice plantations of, 225–26, 234; Southern free Blacks, 349; Southern Homestead Act supplement, 190; state and federal legislators, 192–93; voting rights in, 64; wealthy Blacks, 349

Southern Claims Commission, 76, 212–13, 452n18, 503n54

Southern free Blacks, 348–52

Southern Homestead Act (1866), 57, 65, 119, 134–36, 190, 212

Southern slavery and slaveholders: agriculture and, 21, 27, 207; Blacks as outsiders, 7; Civil War plantation disintegration, 48; commitment to slavery, 8; complaints by former slave owners, 91–92; concentration of wealth, 14; deadlock on abolition, 27; economics of, 386n16, 388n21; European descent of slaveholders, 3; geographical sections, 4; gradual emancipationism proposed, 19; laws "softening" bondage, 23; laziness of both, 419n33; name changes for same results, 78; Northern assault on, 22; plots of land to slaves, 6; post–Civil War traitors, 55; pro-slavery ideologues, 19–22; "refugeeing," 49; slave-master relations, 46; "slave power conspiracy," 396n2; unified antislavery action, 23; urban slave population, 207; way of life, 15

Southern states: census of population (1858), 496n33; commercialism, 332; education for Blacks, 280, 288; industrialization and urbanization, 330–32; lower Southern states, 452n20; Prussian path and, 333–35; racial capitalism, 387n18; "Radicalism," 358,

508n70; reconstruction of, 64, 133; regional backwardness, 376, 516n15; reshaping of, 189–90; urban population and, 208; white racism and, 372–73

Southern Whites: fear of revolutionary changes, 192; postwar unease, 94–95; view of Black race, 355, 357–58, 361–62; white supremacy and, 184, 191, 241, 359–60

Span, Christopher, 285

Sprague, John A., 134–35, 151

Stanley, Amy Dru, 136–37, 252, 318

Stanton, Edwin McMasters, 46, 131

state peasants, 18, 23, 75, 208, 218, 336, 345–47, 501n47, 503n53

State Sentinel (Alabama), 152

Stearns, Charles, 92

Steedman, James B., 123

Stephens, Alexander H., 51

Stevens, Thaddeus, 57, 69, 71–72, 410n58

Stocksdale, Sally, 328

St. Petersburg Province, 128, 177, 209, 217, 230–31, 257

The Strange Career of Jim Crow (Woodward), 357

Strother, Alfred, 187

sugar estates and workers, 203, 224–25, 238, 241, 320–21, 339, 359–60, 369

Sumner, Charles, 22, 410n55

Sutch, Richard, 221, 248, 267

Svet (Light), 322

Swayne, Wager, 111, 137, 156, 252, 259, 261, 263–64, 271, 283–84

Syn otechestva (Son of the Fatherland), 322

Tambov Province: charter resistance, 130; emancipation manifesto response, 87–88; former state peasants, 346–47; land allotments, 218, 454n28; landowner complaints, 183; literacy and education, 290, 293–94; nuclear families, 269; passports in, 231; Petrovskoe estate study, 342; resettlement on free lands, 178; state peasants in, 346

Tauride Province, 229

Taylor, Laura, 263

Tenishev, V. N., 227, 269

Tenishev Ethnographic Bureau survey, 227, 229, 269, 275–76, 293, 300–304, 322, 473n42

Tennessee, 81, 189, 265, 286–87, 331

Texas, 47, 82–83, 122, 172, 185, 188, 376, 452n20

Tharps, Lori L., 352

Third Department (political police), 18, 41–43

Thirteenth Amendment (1865): Johnson's restoration plan, 56; landownership question, 131; Northern missionary teachers and, 281; preservation of the Union and, 51; ratification of, 90; response to emancipation, 72; restoration governments and, 261; self-liberation thesis and, 50; slavery's legal end, 54, 81

Thomas, Samuel, 92–93, 112, 117

Thompson, Holland, 171

Thorp, Daniel B., 214, 312, 473n40

Tian-Shanskaia, Olga, 275, 279, 290, 356

Tilden, Samuel J., 339

Tillson, Davis, 92, 107, 111, 122, 132, 137

Timashev, A. E., 364

Tolstoi, Dmitrii A., 178, 184, 365–66

Tolstoy, Leo, 123

Toussaint L'Ouverture, François-Dominique, 8

Towne, Laura, 236

Treadgold, Donald, 205
Trinidad, 237, 369
Troubled Refuge (Manning), 312
Trubetskoi, Petr Nikitich, 139–40
Tsilorovskii, Nikolai, 124
Tula Province, 78, 99–100, 125, 142, 164, 178, 183, 207, 217
Turgenev, Ivan, 391n31
Turgenev, Nicholas, 16–17
Turner, Nat, 19
Turner, Nicole Myers, 498n40
Turner, William V., 170, 437n17
Tver Province, 44–45, 124, 209, 231, 344
Twain, Mark (Samuel Clemens), 361

ukaz, 26, 101, 147, 180, 184, 394n46
Union League (Loyal League), 168–69, 284, 287
United States: early days of emancipation, 117; freedom and equality, 73–75; life expectancy, 488n5; slavery and crisis of union, 27–28; transition to emancipation, 81
universal manhood suffrage, 64, 168, 170, 173, 186, 189–90
Unkovskii, A. M., 44
Uspenskii, Gleb Ivanovich, 362
U.S. Senate hearings on labor relations (1883), 273
Ust'iantseva, N. F., 121

Valuev, Petr: land allotments and, 177, 179; law-and-order bureaucrat, 105, 118; liberal views and, 124; on literacy and education, 289; peasant disorder, 96–97, 100, 139, 143, 363–64; on peasant leaders, 117; on Polish uprising (1863), 158; statutory charters and, 130, 144
Vil'no Province, 409n49

Virginia: Blacks behind Union lines, 81; Blacks in local government, 171, 438n19; freedpeople's actions, 487n3; free persons of color, 504n56; labor contracts and, 150, 234; land ownership and, 214; marriage recognition, 253; "Readjuster" movement, 359; Southern free Blacks, 349
Vitebsk Province, 85, 180, 409n49
Vladimir Province: children in, 275, 473n42; economic conditions, 344; extrajudicial punishments, 105; females in, 276; folk religion, 302; landowners and, 124; literacy and education, 293; nuclear families, 269; Orthodox Church and, 301; outside world and, 322; supplementary work, 205; survey responses in, 227, 229
Volhynia Province, 146
Volkonskii, S. V., 25
volneniia (collective disorders or uprisings): examples of, 41, 394n46; incidence by year, 146t, 430n41; Krest'ianskoe dvizhenie series, 104, 363, 420n50, 431n44; negotiations or military force, 97; numbers of, 42; peasant disorder, 113; Pskov district of Pskov Province, 102; redemption of inferior land, 177–78; similarity in Southern collective action, 155; Spassk district of Kazan Province, 101–2; statutory charter grievances rejections and, 143, 146; stifling dissent, 364; use after emancipation, 98–99, 103–5; vodka sales or taverns, 399n14; Voronezh Province revolt, 100–101
Vologda Province, 86, 289
Volozhkin, Vasilii, 176
Voronezh Province: allotment complaints, 141, 181, 217; economic conditions, 344; on emancipation, 43;

family divisions in, 258; land under cultivation, 244; nobles' complaints, 78; nuclear families, 270; obligatory redemptions, 179; peasants' conditions, 309; peasants' revolts in, 100; seigneurial labor, 99; statutory charters and, 127, 144, 176
Vorontsov, M. S., 17, 24

Waddell, J. F., 263
Wade, Benjamin F., 53
Walker, C. J., 352
Wallace, Donald Mackenzie, 268, 300, 324–25, 341, 357
wars and end to slavery: Austria, 25, 33, 370–71; Cuba's Ten Years' War, 33; Napoleonic invasion, 33. *See also* American Revolution; Haitian Revolution
Washing Society, 234
"Was the Emancipated Slave a Proletarian?" (Lichtenstein), 316
Watkins, Dink, 271
Watson, Harry L., 388n21, 490n12
Watson, Henry, 108–9, 113, 147, 151, 242
Webb, Alex, 172
Wemyss, J. A., 108
West, Sally, 279, 493n18
West Indies, 296
Wheatcroft, Steven G., 488n6
Whipper, William J., 187
White, A. D., 71
White, George, 305
White, Graham, 506n61
White, Richard, 488n5
White, Shane, 506n61
"whiteness studies," 384n10
Whittle, D. W., 83
Whittlesey, E., 110–11
Wiener, Jonathan M., 328, 333
Wilder, C. B., 122

Wildman, Allan K., 126, 143, 181
Willard, A. J., 132
Williams, Eric, 9
Williams, Heather Andrea, 255, 285
Williamson, Joel, 353, 357–58, 361, 506n61, 508n70
Willis, John C., 224, 455n33
Wilson, Woodrow, 362
Winn, E. S., 171
Woodman, Harold D., 334
Woodward, C. Vann, 15, 325, 357–58
World Bank, 376, 516n15
Worobec, Christine D., 258, 279, 301, 343, 475n47
Wright, Gavin, 248, 324, 327, 376, 516n15
Wyrosdick, Bill, 259–60

Yazykov, Vasilii, 125, 230, 246, 328–29, 461n66
Yazykov woolen factory, 230, 246, 328

Zablotskii-Desiatovskii, Andrei P., 14–15, 37
Zaionchkovskii, Petr A., 310, 318, 388n19
Zakharova, Larissa, 40
Zametaev, P. A., 140, 430n35
zemstva: literacy and education, 291–92, 295–96, 479nn65–66, 480n67, 481n70; noble control, 374; socialized health care, 512n83. *See also* peasant self-government
zemstvo assemblies: peasants and nobles' roles, 195; provincial and district assembles, 165, 195; schools and health care role, 195
Zhurnal zemlevladel'tsev (Landowners' Journal), 43
Ziukin, Semen Ivanov, 142, 430n40
Zyrianov, P. N., 218, 365